Handbook of Evidence-Based Interventions for Children and Adolescents

Lea A. Theodore, PhD is a Psychologist Licensed by the Board of Psychology in New York and Virginia. She is a Full Professor in the Graduate Program in School Psychology Program at the College of William and Mary. She has worked in private practice and consults in public and private schools, hospital, and behavioral health centers. Since receiving her doctorate from the University of Connecticut in 2002, she has published or has in press approximately 70 refereed articles and chapters, and has conducted numerous invited and peer-reviewed presentations at national conferences. Dr. Theodore received the *Early Career Alumni Award* from the University of Connecticut in 2009, in part because of her national ranking as one of the top 20 most productive authors in school psychology. She was Associate Editor for *School Psychology Quarterly* (2007–2012), one of the top-tier journals in the field, and currently sits on the editorial boards of several national and international educational and psychological journals where she provides professional reviews of manuscripts. Her scholarship and her practice focus on promoting science, practice, and policy relevant to psychology and education. Dr. Theodore's research, in particular, focuses on the development of effective and efficient intervention strategies to improve students' academic and behavioral functioning, which is critically important to the field.

Dr. Theodore is active in Division 16 (School Psychology) of the American Psychological Association (APA), for which she has served as Division co-chair and chair of the APA Annual Conference Hospitality Suite, co-chair and chair of the Division's Annual Convention program, and as a member of the Conversation/Videotape Series committee. Dr. Theodore extended her contributions to APA in nationally elected positions, including Vice-President of Division 16 Membership (2006–2008), Vice President of Professional Affairs (2009–2011), and is currently the President of the Division of School Psychology, additionally serving on the Division's Executive Committee. Further, Dr. Theodore served as the APA Representative to the Public Interest (PI) Directorate Network and was invited to serve as the Division's representative to co-write the 2012 *School Psychology Petition to the Commission for the Recognition of Specialties in Professional Psychology* (CRSPP) within the APA. As an advocate for mental health services, Dr. Theodore lobbied legislators on Capitol Hill for the passage of the *Mental Health Parity Act* in 2008, and most recently, the *Mental Health Reform Act* (S. 1945) and *Helping Families in Crisis Act (H.R. 2646)* in November, 2015. She has received several *Outstanding Service* awards and recognitions from the American Psychological Association for her vast contributions.

Handbook of Evidence-Based Interventions for Children and Adolescents

Lea A. Theodore, PhD

Editor

SPRINGER PUBLISHING COMPANY
NEW YORK

Springer Publishing Company, LLC
11 West 42nd Street
New York, NY 10036
www.springerpub.com

Acquisitions Editor: Nancy S. Hale
Compositor: Newgen KnowledgeWorks

ISBN: 978-0-8261-2794-5
e-book ISBN: 978-0-8261-2795-2

16 17 18 19 20 / 5 4 3 2 1

The author and the publisher of this Work have made every effort to use sources believed to be reliable to provide information that is accurate and compatible with the standards generally accepted at the time of publication. The author and publisher shall not be liable for any special, consequential, or exemplary damages resulting, in whole or in part, from the readers' use of, or reliance on, the information contained in this book. The publisher has no responsibility for the persistence or accuracy of URLs for external or third-party Internet websites referred to in this publication and does not guarantee that any content on such websites is, or will remain, accurate or appropriate.

Library of Congress Cataloging-in-Publication Data
Names: Theodore, Lea A., editor.
Title: Handbook of evidence-based interventions for children and adolescents / Lea A. Theodore, PhD, editor.
Description: New York: Springer Publishing Company, 2017. | Includes index.
Identifiers: LCCN 2016009581 | ISBN 9780826127945
Subjects: LCSH: Child psychopathology. | Adolescent psychopathology. | Evidence-based psychiatry.
Classification: LCC RJ499 .H3319 2016 | DDC 618.92/89—dc23
LC record available at https://lccn.loc.gov/2016009581

Special discounts on bulk quantities of our books are available to corporations, professional associations, pharmaceutical companies, health care organizations, and other qualifying groups. If you are interested in a custom book, including chapters from more than one of our titles, we can provide that service as well.

For details, please contact:
Special Sales Department, Springer Publishing Company, LLC
11 West 42nd Street, 15th Floor, New York, NY 10036–8002
Phone: 877–687-7476 or 212–431-4370; Fax: 212–941-7842
E-mail: sales@springerpub.com

Printed in the United States of America by McNaughton & Gunn.

For my mother, Maria P. Theodore, a simply extraordinary woman whose grace, intellect, gentle kindness, humility, integrity, and giving spirit have made me the woman I am today.

Contents

Contributors

Kelly N. Banneyer, MA
Graduate Student
University of Texas, Austin
Austin, Texas

Georgia D. Belk, MEd
Graduate Student
Lehigh University
Bethlehem, Pennsylvania

Bruce A. Bracken, PhD
Professor
The College of William and Mary
Williamsburg, Virginia

Melissa A. Bray, PhD
Professor and Director of School
    Psychology
The University of Connecticut
Storrs, Connecticut

Jacqueline A. Brown, PhD, NCSP
Assistant Professor of School
    Psychology
University of Montana
Missoula, Montana

Jeffrey D. Burke, PhD
Associate Professor
Department of Psychology
University of Connecticut
Storrs, Connecticut

Marisa A. del Campo
Doctoral Student
University of Connecticut
Storrs, Connecticut

Sandy Capaldi, PsyD
Clinical Faculty; Practicum &
    Workshop Coordinator
Department of Psychiatry
Penn Behavioral Health
Perelman School of Medicine
Center for the Treatment and Study of Anxiety
    and Department of Psychiatry
University of Pennsylvania
Philadelphia, Pennsylvania

John S. Carlson, PhD
Professor of School Psychology
Michigan State University
East Lansing, Michigan

Ralph E. Cash, PhD, ABPP
Professor of School Psychology
Nova Southeastern University
College of Psychology
Fort Lauderdale, Florida

Danielle Centeno, MA
Violence Prevention Clinical Research
    Coordinator
The Children's Hospital of Philadelphia
Philadelphia, Pennsylvania

Trisha Chase, MS
Graduate Student
Utah State University
Logan, Utah

Melissa A. Collier-Meek, PhD
Assistant Professor
University of Massachusetts, Boston
Boston, Massachusetts

Catherine Cook-Cottone, PhD
Associate Professor
University at Buffalo, SUNY
Buffalo, New York

Erika A. Crawford, MA
Graduate Student
Temple University
Philadelphia, Pennsylvania

Laura M. Crothers, PhD
Professor of School Psychology
Duquesne University
Pittsburgh, Pennsylvania

Andrew S. Davis
Professor of Psychology
Ball State University
Muncie, Indiana

John E. Desrochers, PhD, ABPP
School Psychologist
New Canaan Public Schools
New Canaan, Connecticut

Mary Lynn Doolan, MEd
Graduate Student
College of Education, Health, and Human Services
Kent State University
Kent, Ohio

George J. DuPaul, PhD
Professor of School Psychology
Lehigh University
Bethlehem, Pennsylvania

Corrine Fallon, MS, EdS
Doctoral Intern
Duquesne University
Pittsburgh, Pennsylvania

Benjamin S. Fernandez, MS Ed
School Psychologist
Loudoun County Public Schools
Loudoun, Virginia

Scott M. Fluke, MA
Graduate Student
Department of Educational Psychology
University of Nebraska, Lincoln
Lincoln, Nebraska

Edna B. Foa, PhD
Professor of Clinical Psychology in Psychiatry
Department of Psychiatry
Penn Behavioral Health
Perelman School of Medicine
Center for the Treatment and Study of Anxiety
    and Department of Psychiatry
University of Pennsylvania
Philadelphia, Pennsylvania

Maria G. Fraire, PhD
Postdoctoral Fellow
Child and Adolescent OCD Unit
McLean Hospital/Harvard Medical School
Boston, Massachusetts

Mary A. Fristad, PhD, ABPP
Professor of Psychiatry, Psychology and Human
    Nutrition
Director of Research and Psychological Services
    in the OSU Division of Child and Adolescent
    Psychiatry
The Ohio State University
Columbus, Ohio

Douglas Fuchs, PhD
Professor, Department of Special Education
Vanderbilt University
Nashville, Tennessee

Aileen Fullchange
Graduate Student
Department of Counseling, Clinical, and School
    Psychology
University of California, Santa Barbara
Santa Barbara, California

Michael James Furlong, PhD
Professor
Department of Counseling, Clinical, and School
    Psychology
University of California, Santa Barbara
Santa Barbara, California

Rich Gilman, PhD
Psychologist
Division of Child and Adolescent Psychiatry
Professor
UC Department of Pediatrics
Cincinnati Children's Hospital Medical Center
Cincinnati, Ohio

Ronald P. Glazier, PhD, NCSP
School Psychologist
Denver Public Schools
Denver, Colorado

Sara E. Gonzalez, MA
Graduate Student
Department of Educational Psychology
University of Nebraska, Lincoln
Lincoln, Nebraska

Frank M. Gresham, PhD
Professor of School Psychology
Department of Psychology
Louisiana State University
Baton Rouge, Louisiana

Amy C. Gross, PhD, LP, BCAB-D
Assistant Professor
University of Minnesota
Minneapolis, Minnesota

Melissa J. Hagan, PhD, MPH
Assistant Professor
San Francisco State University
San Francisco, California

Thorhildur Halldorsdottir, PhD
Max Planck Institute of Psychiatry
Munich, Germany

Robyn S. Hess, PhD, ABPP
Professor of School Psychology
University of Northern Colorado
Greeley, Colorado

Jill Holtz, MA
Graduate Student
University of Nebraska, Lincoln
Lincoln, Nebraska

E. Scott Huebner, PhD
Professor of Psychology
University of South Carolina
Columbia, South Carolina

Tammy L. Hughes, PhD
Professor of School Psychology
Duquesne University
Pittsburgh, Pennsylvania

Debra Hyatt-Burkhart, PhD
Assistant Professor of Counselor Education
Duquesne University
Pittsburgh, Pennsylvania

Alexandra M. Ingram, BA
Graduate Student
Arizona State University
Tempe, Arizona

Kathryn E. Jaspers, PhD
Assistant Professor of School Psychology
University of Houston-Clear Lake
Houston, Texas

Elissa Jelalian, PhD
Associate Professor
Psychiatry and Human Behavior
Alpert Medical School of Brown University
Weight Control and Diabetes Research Center
Brown University
Providence, Rhode Island

Shane R. Jimerson, PhD
Professor and Chair
Department of Clinical, Counseling, and School
    Psychology
University of California, Santa Barbara
Santa Barbara, California

Elana R. Kagan, MA
Graduate Student
Temple University
Philadelphia, Pennsylvania

Devin M. Kearns, PhD
Assistant Professor of Special Education
The University of Connecticut
Storrs, Connecticut

Christopher A. Kearney, PhD
Distinguished Professor and Chair of Psychology
University of Nevada, Las Vegas
Las Vegas, Nevada

Thomas J. Kehle, PhD
Professor of School Psychology
The University of Connecticut
Storrs, Connecticut

Phillip C. Kendall, PhD, ABPP
Professor
Board Certified in Child and Adolescent Clinical
    Psychology
Board Certified in Cognitive and Behavioral
    Therapy
Distinguished University Professor
Laura H. Carnell Professor of Psychology
Director
Child and Adolescent Anxiety
    Disorders Clinic
Temple University
Philadelphia, Pennsylvania

Jered B. Kolbert, PhD
Professor of Counselor Education
Duquesne University
Pittsburgh, Pennsylvania

Theresa L. Lafavor, PhD
Assistant Professor
Assessment Coordinator
Pacific University
Hillsboro, Oregon

Adele A. Larsson, MA
Associate Director
Neuropsychology Laboratory
Student Supervisor
Psychoeducational Diagnostic and Intervention
    Clinic
Doctoral Student in School Psychology
Ball State University
Muncie, Indiana

Stephen S. Leff, PhD
Professor of Clinical Psychology
Codirector: Violence Prevention Initiative
The Children's Hospital of Philadelphia
University of Pennsylvania
Philadelphia, Pennsylvania

Rolf Loeber, PhD
Distinguished Professor of Psychiatry
Professor of Psychology and Epidemiology
University of Pittsburgh
Pittsburgh, Pennsylvania

James J. Mazza, PhD
Professor of School Psychology
College of Education at the University
    of Washington
Seattle, Washington

Daniel F. McCleary, PhD, NCSP, LSSA, LP
Assistant Professor of School Psychology
Stephen E. Austin State University
Nacogdoches, Texas

Lisa N. McCleary, NCSP, BCBA-D
Assistant Professor of School
    Psychology
Stephen E. Austin State University
Nacogdoches, Texas

Mary Beth McCullough, PhD
Pediatric Psychologist
Cincinnati Children's Hospital Medical Center
Cincinnati, Ohio

Merilee McCurdy, PhD
Director and Associate Professor of School
    Psychology
University of Tennessee
Knoxville, Tennessee

Kristen L. McMaster, PhD
Department of Special Education
University of Minnesota
Minneapolis, Minnesota

Molly R. Meers, PhD
Clinical Psychologist
Nationwide Children's Behavioral Health Services
Westerville Close to Home
Columbus, Ohio

David N. Miller, PhD
Associate Professor of School Psychology
University at Albany, SUNY
Albany, New York

W. John Monopoli, MA
Research Affiliate
Ohio University
Athens, Ohio

Zachary R. Myers, MA
Graduate Student
Department of Education Psychology
University of Nebraska, Lincoln
Lincoln, Nebraska

Alyssa Newman, MS
Graduate Student
Nova Southeastern University
College of Psychology
Fort Lauderdale, Florida

Lindsey M. O'Brennan, PhD
Professor of School Psychology
University of South Florida
Tampa, Florida

Elisabeth C. O'Bryon, PhD
Research Affiliate
Yale University
New Haven, Connecticut

Thomas H. Ollendick, PhD
University Distinguished Professor
Director
Child Study Center
Department of Psychology
Virginia Polytechnic Institute and
    State University
Blacksburg, Virginia

Gretchen Gimpel Peacock
Professor of Psychology
Utah State University
Logan, Utah

Jeremy S. Peterman, MA
Graduate Student
Temple University
Philadelphia, Pennsylvania

Kerry K. Prout, MS
Graduate Student
Utah State University
Logan, Utah

Kristina Puzino, MS
Graduate Student
Lehigh University
Bethlehem, Pennsylvania

Lisa Ranzenhofer, PhD
Postdoctoral Research Fellow
Weight Control and Diabetes
    Research Center
The Miriam Hospital/Brown University Warren
    Alpert Medical School
Brown University
Providence, Rhode Island

Kendra L. Read, PhD
Clinical Psychology
Stanford University
Stanford, California

Melissa A. Louvar Reeves, PhD, NCSP
Professor
Winthrop University
Rock Hill, South Carolina

Tyler L. Renshaw, PhD
Assistant Professor of Psychology
Louisiana State University
Baton Rouge, Louisiana

Julia V. Roehling, MA
Graduate Student
University of Nebraska, Lincoln
Lincoln, Nebraska

Margaret R. Rogers, PhD
Professor of School Psychology
University of Rhode Island
Kingston, Rhode Island

Melissa M. Root, PhD
Assistant Professor in Residence
Department of Educational Psychology
University of Connecticut
Storrs, Connecticut

Brittany M. Rudy, PhD
Clinical Psychologist
University of South Florida
Tampa, Florida

Lisa M. Hagermoser Sanetti, PhD
Associate Professor
University of Connecticut
Storrs, Connecticut

Frank J. Sansosti, PhD, NCSP
Associate Professor of School Psychology
College of Education, Health, and Human
   Services
Kent State University
Kent, Ohio

Kari A. Sassu, PhD, NCSP
Associate Professor
Counseling and School Psychology
Southern Connecticut State University
New Haven, Connecticut

Margaret Semrud-Clikeman, PhD, LP, ABPdN
Professor of Pediatrics
Division Director
Clinical Behavioral Neuroscience
University of Minnesota
Minneapolis, Minnesota

Casey R. Shannon, PhD
Assistant Professor of Psychology
Ferkauf Graduate School of Psychology
Yeshiva University
Bronx, New York

Kyleigh K. Sheldon, BA
Graduate Student
University of Nevada, Las Vegas
Las Vegas, Nevada

Nina D. Shiffrin, PhD
Psychologist
Private Practice
Rockville, Maryland

Allison Siroky, MA
Graduate Student
Michigan State University
East Lansing, Michigan

Christopher H. Skinner, PhD
Professor of School Psychology
University of Tennessee
Knoxville, Tennessee

Audrey Smerbeck, PhD
Assistant Professor
Department of Psychology
Rochester Institute of Technology
Rochester, New York

Kevin D. Stark, PhD
Professor of School Psychology
Clinical Director
Dell Children's Medical Center
Director
Psychological Service Center
Director
Texas Child Study Center
Director
Psychology Services at Dell Children's Medical
   Center
University of Texas, Austin
Austin, Texas

Eric A. Storch, PhD
Professor
Departments of Pediatrics (primary), Health
   Policy & Management, Psychiatry &
   Neurosciences, and Psychology
Director of Research for Developmental
   Pediatrics
All Children's Hospital—Johns Hopkins Medicine
Clinical Director
Rogers Behavioral Health—Tampa Bay
University of South Florida
Tampa, Florida

Susan M. Swearer, PhD
Professor of School Psychology
Department of Educational Psychology
University of Nebraska, Lincoln
Lincoln, Nebraska

Michael E. Tansy, PhD, ABPP
Psychologist
Private Practice
Mesa, Arizona

Lea A. Theodore, PhD
Professor of School Psychology
The College of William and Mary
Williamsburg, Virginia

Sarah Valley-Gray, PsyD, ABPP
Professor and Director of Training
School Psychology Doctoral Program
Nova Southeastern University
College of Psychology
Fort Lauderdale, Florida

Rebecca K. Vujnovic, PhD, NCSP
Psychologist
Private Practice
Buffalo, New York

Tracy Evian Waasdorp, PhD, MEd
The Children's Hospital of Philadelphia
Department of Psychology
Johns Hopkins School of Public Health
Department of Mental Health
Philadelphia, Pennsylvania

Leah A. Wang, MA, BS
Graduate Student
University of Texas, Austin
Austin, Texas

Sharlene A. Wolchik, PhD
Professor
Arizona State University
Tempe, Arizona

Shannon Worton, PsyD
Assistant Professor
Carlos Albizu University
Pembroke Pines, Florida

Laurie J. Zandberg, PsyD
Instructor
Department of Psychiatry
Penn Behavioral Health
Perelman School of Medicine
Center for the Treatment and Study of Anxiety
    and Department of Psychiatry
University of Pennsylvania
Philadelphia, Pennsylvania

Sophia Zavrou, PsyD
Postdoctoral Fellow
Rothman Center for Pediatric Neuropsychiatry
University of South Florida
Tampa, Florida

Foreword

Tremendous progress has been made over the past three decades in the area of evidence-based interventions and practices. As a long-time champion of the evidence-based practices movement in psychology (American Psychological Association Task Force on Evidence-Based Practice for Children and Adolescents, 2008) and school of psychology in particular (e.g., Kratochwill & Stoiber, 2000; Kratochwill & Shernoff, 2004), I was delighted to be invited by Lea Theodore to write a foreword for this major and significant contribution to the scientific literature. The *Handbook of Evidence-Based Interventions for Children and Adolescents* (hereafter called the *Handbook*) represents another milestone in progress in the social sciences and education in evidence-based practice. This work is not a handbook of best practices; it is a handbook of empirical practices and there is a very major difference. In this regard, evidence-based interventions are not designated only through expert opinion or consensus. Evidence-based practices, as the term implies, are based on scientific evidence, usually quantitative experimentation that has allowed the testing of the intervention or procedure under conditions that invoke strong causal inference for their effectiveness.

On review of this work and reflection on the significance of the contribution, I believe that this *Handbook* will impact at least three major areas of professional work in psychology, mental health, and education. First and foremost, the impact will be in the area of professional *practice*. The contributing chapter authors present major updates on the interventions for a wide range of childhood disorders and problems. And these are interventions that advance our options for making a very significant difference in the lives of children and families. This *Handbook* is also comprehensive, with coverage of childhood problems that occur across most clinical and applied settings, such as schools, clinics, medical centers, and community settings. In this regard, this *Handbook* will be of tremendous relevance and application for psychologists in practice in multiple specialty areas as well as for other mental health professionals who wish to provide the best mental health and educational services that we have available.

Second, this *Handbook* will impact *research* on evidence-based interventions. With the empirical focus of the contributions to this work, it is clear that we have intervention benchmarks that can be used with a high probability of positive outcomes. But contributors have been able to identify areas where research is needed to either expand the effectiveness of procedures and/or where critical research work must be done to advance knowledge in the range of applications. In many cases, the contributing authors have also identified issues that impact implementation of evidence-based interventions in their areas of focus. In implementation work we are learning not only of options for customizing and accommodating evidence-based interventions but also factors that must be addressed when these interventions are adopted, scaled up, and sustained in practice settings (Forman, 2015). And we are now seeing numerous options for research methodology on implementation science, including our traditional randomized clinical trial studies and single-case research designs. Moreover, in future work, we must invoke replication studies and new methodologies for understanding our intervention protocols; moving forward will require the use of mixed methods to more fully understand how best to implement these interventions in clinical and applied settings.

Third, this *Handbook* provides a rich curriculum for *training* the next generation of graduate students in evidence-based practice. The focus on quality graduate training in evidence-based practices must be a major agenda for psychology and related fields (Kratochwill, 2007). Graduate training is a key leverage point for making a significant impact on the wide range of mental health and educational problems of our youth; but, graduate training programs in psychology and related fields have significant challenges in this work. For psychology graduate training programs, the challenges include how evidence-based interventions are packaged and structured, researchers' understanding of how culture affects efficacy, and continual shifts in evidence-based practice designations. To address the challenges ahead, we (Shernoff, Bearman, & Kratochwill, in press) made some "policy recommendations" that are relevant to the theme and focus of this *Handbook*:

- We suggested that developing graduate students' technical skills in delivering evidence-based practices is as equally critical as developing proficiency in functioning as evidence-based providers, and professional training and practice standards should reflect both domains of training as well.
- We recommended that professional training standards reflect the urgent need to ensure that practicum students and interns continue to have exposure to and experience with evidence-based practices during these formative training experiences.
- Prioritizing common elements (i.e., those elements that are common to many evidence-based interventions) over entire training curricula can streamline how mental health programs are organized and may avert clinical and applied setting organizations from investing scarce resources in purchasing all manualized interventions with overlapping content.
- Although dissemination and implementation models do not have a strong presence in our professional practice guidelines, training in such models can enhance the way in which information about mental health practices spreads in applied and clinical settings and can facilitate the development of shared norms and values regarding mental health interventions that are delivered.

Lea Theodore and the contributors to this *Handbook* have done a great service to the mental health and education fields. Their work will have far-reaching positive impact on practice, research, and training and, ultimately, on serving the mental health needs of children and adolescents.

Thomas R. Kratochwill, PhD
Sears Bascom Professor and Director
School of Psychology Program
University of Wisconsin-Madison

REFERENCES

American Psychological Association Task Force on Evidence-Based Practice for Children and Adolescents (2008). *Disseminating evidence-based practice for children and adolescents: A systems approach to enhancing care.* Washington, DC: American Psychological Association.

Forman, S. G. (2015). *Implementation of mental health programs in schools: A change agent's guide.* Washington, DC: American Psychological Association.

Kratochwill, T. R. (2007). Preparing psychologists for evidence-based practice: Lessons learned and challenges ahead. *American Psychologist, 62,* 826–843.

Kratochwill, T. R., & Shernoff, E. S. (2004). Evidence-based practice: Promoting evidence-based intervention in school psychology. *School Psychology Quarterly, 18,* 389–408.

Kratochwill, T. R., & Stoiber, K. C. (2000). Empirically supported interventions in school psychology: Conceptual and practice issues: Part II. *School Psychology Quarterly, 15,* 233–253.

Shernoff, E. S., Bearman, S. K., & Kratochwill, T. R. (in press). Training the next generation of school psychologists to deliver evidence-based mental health practices: Current challenges and future directions. *School of Psychology Review.*

Preface

THE EVOLUTION OF EVIDENCE-BASED INTERVENTIONS: BRIDGING RESEARCH AND PRACTICE

According to the eminent scholar W. Edwards Deming (http://www.goodreads.com) "It is not enough to do your best; you first have to know what to do and then do your best." This quote underscores the significance of evidence-based practice or interventions that have been documented to be effective through empirical support. The application of evidence-based practice leads to consistent and efficacious service provision within the helping professions by guiding well-informed decision making. Empirical, replicated, research-based evidence is the foundation of science; for scientist-practitioners, providing evidence-based interventions is the sine qua non. For schools, children, and families, evidence-based interventions are the basis of augmenting children's and adolescents' intellectual and emotional functioning, and a healthy lifelong development. Investigating the evolving base of scientific knowledge in effective practices is a movement that has been implemented in medicine; education; and clinical, counseling, and school psychology. Mental health professionals are at the forefront of providing ameliorative services to children, adolescents, and families; it is important to note that it is the use of evidence-based interventions that is the hallmark of sound, effective professional practice.

A southern anecdote succinctly captures the importance of meaningful interventions. The saying goes, "You can weigh a pig ten times a day, but if you don't feed it, it ain't gonna grow any bigger." Mental health professionals have long been experts at providing diagnostic and prognostic assessments in diverse areas such as information processing, intellectual functioning, academic achievement and skill development, personality development, and so on. These assessments contribute immensely to our understanding of the individual differences and psychosocial development of children and adolescents. However, it is only the subsequent application of effective interventions designed to ameliorate diagnosed deficits and overcome deleterious prognostications that ultimately contribute to children's overall healthy development. Hence, although diagnostic and evaluative information sheds essential light on the overall functioning of the child, including personal strengths and weaknesses, it is ultimately effective treatments that are most needed—it is not only feeding the pig, but also feeding it a "proven diet" that helps it grow bigger and stronger!

Although many graduate programs in the helping professions teach students which interventions are known to be effective, programs very rarely train their students how to implement those very same practices. That is, students seldom implement the specific treatments they learn *about* because they seldom learn *how* to do so. Failure to select and implement appropriate evidence-based interventions is dangerous because instructional practices, academic accommodations, medication recommendations, and restrictive behavioral procedures and behavioral placements are often based on the premise that programs or interventions will resolve the presenting problems. Failing to "feed the pig," or failing to intervene effectively after assessing and diagnosing deficits, also results in compounded adjustment difficulties or psychosocial problems in children and adolescents. For instance, in addition to failing to resolve the referral issue, ineffective treatments may contribute to a wide range of progressive and compounding intrapersonal problems (e.g., depression, substance abuse), interpersonal social-psychological difficulties (e.g., interpersonal relationships, peer rejection), or negative academic outcomes (e.g., poor academic achievement, increased absenteeism, school dropout). These adverse factors impede children's and adolescents' healthy development. The culmination of these unresolved and exacerbated psychosocial issues can result in a life of seriously diminished quality. Simply said, the personal and societal costs of not intervening or intervening ineffectively cannot be underestimated.

The *Handbook of Evidence-Based Interventions for Children and Adolescents* focuses on applied, empirically supported interventions proven to make significant contributions to the practice and preparation of professionals in school, counseling, clinical and child clinical psychology, social work, special education, school counseling, and speech and language pathology—that is, helping professionals working in school and clinical settings. The need for such a book is based on three significant limitations of extant intervention-oriented books and handbooks:

1. Other books tell the reader which interventions to employ, but fail to explain specifically how to implement them.
2. They focus on single contexts or settings (i.e., either school-based interventions or those that may be implemented in a clinical setting).
3. They focus on a too specific, narrowly defined list of topics.

The *Handbook of Evidence-Based Interventions for Children and Adolescents* counters these three cited limitations. First, the book is a comprehensive treatment of the most salient issues that mental health professionals face in educational and clinical settings (e.g., school crisis and response, educational issues and disorders, childhood psychopathology, social and emotional functioning, physical- and health-related disorders, neuropsychological disorders). Second, it provides practitioners with empirically supported interventions,

as well as step-by-step methods that illustrate how to implement these interventions with children and adolescents. Third, the interventions addressed in the book may be employed by a diverse collection of professionals in the schools, as well as those working in private practice and community and mental health settings. The book provides readers with a clear, empirically supported connection between intervention research and practice throughout the helping professions.

With the most salient intervention-related topics and issues facing mental health professionals written by undisputed leaders in their respective fields, this compilation of chapters is dedicated to empirically supported interventions in school, counseling, clinical and child clinical psychology, social work, special education, and school counseling. The *Handbook of Evidence-Based Interventions for Children and Adolescents* has been organized into six broad sections: School Crisis and Response, Educational Issues and Disorders, Childhood Psychopathology, Social and Emotional Functioning, Physical- and Health-Related Disorders, and Neuropsychological Disorders, with each chapter focusing on immediate and relevant issues that individuals working with children encounter. Each chapter begins with an overview and a summary of the base of evidence for interventions vis-à-vis each topic. Serving as a theoretically derived, yet practical resource for school- and clinic-based professionals, the final part of each chapter provides evidence-based interventions with practical step-by-step guidance in intervention implementation and examples of application. By providing mental health professionals with sound, evidence-based interventions in a cogent, step-by-step manner, the gap between research and practice is bridged, thereby leading to improved academic, social, and emotional adjustment and/or functioning of children and adolescents, ultimately resulting in sound intervention science and practice by not only describing which interventions are best suited for specific disorders, but also by providing guidelines for how best to implement those procedures. Hence, the focus is on the practical aspects of helping children and adolescents by providing interventions for practitioners to implement, ultimately giving them the option of employing what also works with their unique and individual strengths as helping professionals as well as a "best fit" for children.

Although evidence-based practice is critical in helping children, we also need continued research efforts, researchers with innovative ideas that may be tested and retested to promulgate evidence-based interventions so that the field does not grow stagnant. Continued research regarding the most effective and research-based methods are integral to not only supporting children, but cultivating and developing healthy adults as well. By enhancing the lives of children, we may teach children the capacity to overcome, endure, and transform into resilient, prosperous individuals. These are the efforts and attributes that this Handbook seeks to espouse.

Lea A. Theodore

Acknowledgments

Special thanks to Nancy Hale, Editorial Director, who believed in my concept for this book and the practical utility that it holds for all mental health professionals. Her excitement about this project paralleled my own. I am most grateful for her positive encouragement and expert editorial guidance, which facilitated the coordination of this endeavor.

For Dr. Bruce A. Bracken: When I shared my idea of developing this book, which I had since 2004, I never imagined how much you would encourage me to bring this dream to fruition. From its inception to completion, you have been my biggest supporter, mentor, and sounding board. This work would not have been possible without your expert guidance and thoughtful edits. Your active support is a gift for which I will always be grateful.

Introduction

P A R T

Treatment Integrity: Evidence-Based Interventions in Applied Settings

Lisa M. Hagermoser Sanetti and Melissa A. Collier-Meek

OVERVIEW[1]

Today's community and educational contexts require the selection, adoption, implementation, and evaluation of evidence-based interventions, treatments that have been proven to be effective in multiple outcome evaluations. Various initiatives for reform in mental health settings and education-related laws (e.g., 2001 reauthorization of the Elementary and Secondary Education Act), movements (e.g., multitiered systems of support), government agencies (e.g., Institute of Education Science's Doing What Works and What Works Clearinghouse resources), and professional organizations (e.g., National Association of School Psychologists, Council for Exceptional Children) advocate evidence-based interventions as the foundation of service delivery for children and adolescents with academic, behavioral, and social-emotional problems. For these evidence-based interventions to benefit youth, they must be implemented in practice as they were during their validation. The extent to which interventions are implemented as planned is referred to as treatment integrity (also referred to as "treatment fidelity," "procedural reliability," "procedural fidelity," or "treatment implementation"; Sanetti & Kratochwill, 2009a). Collecting, analyzing, and evaluating treatment integrity data, along with child outcome data, are critical to ensuring

the validity of decisions made about intervention effectiveness.

Attention to the role of treatment integrity for data-based decision making has increased significantly over the past 5 years (McInerney & Elledge, 2013). A child's response to evidence-based interventions that are *implemented as planned* is evaluated to determine whether the current intervention should be continued, discontinued, or replaced by a more or less intensive intervention. Currently, most decisions regarding the effectiveness of child interventions are made with only progress-monitoring data (Cochrane & Laux, 2008). These decisions assume that the intervention has been consistently and completely implemented as intended. However, most intervention research indicates that interventions are not employed with adequate treatment integrity (Noell et al., 2005; Noell, Witt, Gilbertson, Ranier, & Freeland, 1997). Unfortunately, if a treatment is not implemented with fidelity, inaccurate decisions regarding the child are often made. Invalid and incorrect intervention decisions cause high costs for children (e.g., inappropriately restrictive or intensive interventions and placements) and systems (e.g., time of personnel selecting intervention, resource costs of high-intensity interventions). To make accurate decisions about a child's response to an intervention, it is essential to evaluate both progress-monitoring data and treatment integrity data, and to promote higher levels of treatment integrity when needed (Kilgus, Collier-Meek, Johnson, & Jaffery, 2014; Sanetti & Kratochwill, 2009a).

There are myriad interventions being implemented within multitiered systems of support and across various service contexts (e.g., community and clinical settings, juvenile justice) with limited resources available for intervention evaluation. It is essential for those who are implementing or evaluating interventions to systematically decide how best to assess, analyze, and promote treatment integrity (Barnett, Hawkins, & Lentz, 2011). This chapter provides an overview of treatment integrity assessment foundations, guidelines for developing a treatment integrity assessment plan, analyzing treatment integrity and child outcomes together, and promoting treatment integrity. Together, this information may facilitate the development of high-quality, feasible, and defensible intervention evaluation in applied contexts.

TREATMENT INTEGRITY ASSESSMENT FOUNDATIONS

In the following subsections, an overview of the current conceptualization of treatment integrity as a multidimensional construct, as well as commonly used assessment methods and possible response formats, is discussed.

Dimensions

Over the past decade, scholars have proposed that treatment integrity is multidimensional (Sanetti & Kratochwill, 2009a), and emerging evidence suggests that these dimensions have evaluation utility (Sanetti & Fallon, 2011). The primary dimension is *adherence*, or the extent to which intervention steps are implemented as planned. Adherence is a prerequisite for other relevant dimensions (e.g., quality, frequency, and duration), which cannot be assessed unless an intervention is implemented. When an intervention is implemented, it may be relevant to evaluate *quality*, or the competence with which intervention steps are implemented. Moreover, it may be useful to evaluate the frequency and duration of intervention sessions. To highlight the relationship among adherence, duration, and

frequency, consider an intervention that is implemented once a week for 30 minutes. A review of progress-monitoring data suggests that the child is not going to make his or her goal. Adherence, frequency, and duration data are collected and indicate that adherence was high and the intervention was competently delivered as intended (every Tuesday for 30 minutes). However, the child attended the group only 6 of the past 10 weeks (i.e., frequency), and left 10 minutes early on 2 days (i.e., duration). Adherence data would indicate whether the intervention sessions were implemented as planned. Frequency and duration data would identify that the child was exposed to only 53% of the intervention (160 minutes of instruction). Analyzing adherence, frequency, and duration data together would result in different conclusions about the implementation of the intervention and the child's response than if only adherence data were collected (i.e., the intervention was implemented with fidelity, but the child had not *received* the intervention with sufficient frequency and duration to benefit). Although it may be simpler to collect only adherence data, this brief case example highlights the importance of gathering treatment data on frequency and duration. A comprehensive treatment integrity evaluation process will likely result in more accurate decision making when multiple dimensions of treatment integrity are considered rather than a single dimension.

Assessment Methods

Given the nascent nature of the treatment integrity literature base, there are few formally validated measures of implementation. Some packaged interventions include a treatment integrity measure (e.g., Good Behavior Game; Embry, 2003); however, the vast majority of interventions do not, and practitioners are left to create their own treatment integrity measures. The most commonly used methods include direct observation of implementation, evaluation of permanent products that result from implementation, and self-report of implementation (Sanetti & Kratochwill, 2009a). These methods vary considerably with regard to several characteristics, including the (a) frequency with which the method can be completed; (b) ability of the method to include all intervention steps (e.g., there might not be a permanent product for every intervention step); (c) defensibility of the method (e.g., directness, empirical support, reliability data); (d) time, training, and personnel necessary to complete the assessment; and (e) intrusiveness of data collection. The basic procedures and advantages and disadvantages of each are briefly discussed here followed by a general description of response formats, or the rating options commonly used for each (see Sanetti et al., 2014 for more detailed discussion of treatment integrity assessment).

Direct Observation. One of the most commonly used methods for measuring treatment integrity is direct observation (Lane, Bocian, MacMillan, & Gresham, 2004). This method requires the intervention to be divided into a comprehensive list of discrete, observable, and measurable intervention steps. Next, it is important to determine how and when implementation will be rated during an observation (e.g., partial interval recording throughout, global ratings at conclusion of observation period), who will complete the observations, whether observer training is needed, if inter-rater reliability observations will be completed, and how and when to schedule observations (e.g., when is the intervention being implemented, how frequently will implementation be observed). There are no empirically supported guidelines for making these decisions; rather, considerations related to feasibility, reliability, and evaluation utility should drive decision making (see "Developing a Treatment Integrity Assessment Plan" section of this chapter).

Direct observation is a highly flexible assessment method. That is, it is relatively simple to create treatment integrity instrumentation and observation procedures that meet the needs of a variety of interventions (e.g., academic, behavioral, social-emotional). Furthermore, depending on the intervention, adherence, quality, frequency, and duration may all be able to be measured using this method (Sanetti & Collier-Meek, 2015). Direct observation is the most direct form of treatment integrity assessment, and is the most defensible when high-stake decisions (e.g., movement to a more intensive intervention, referrals for special education) need to be made. Unfortunately, direct observation is also highly resource intensive with respect to the time required for conducting observations and training observers. Furthermore, having

someone physically in the intervention setting may alter the behavior(s) of those being observed and may not be acceptable to the individual implementing the intervention. Finally, depending on the scope of the intervention, it may not be possible to observe all aspects of intervention implementation (e.g., behavioral support plans implemented throughout the day; interventions implemented across home and school).

Permanent Product Review. Permanent product review is another method that has been frequently used to assess treatment integrity in school-based research (e.g., Noell et al., 2005). This method requires the collection of products that naturally result from intervention implementation. First, as with direct observation, the intervention is divided into a comprehensive list of discrete, observable, and measurable intervention steps. Next, the products that result from implementation are considered and mapped onto intervention steps, and decision rules for how products will be rated are determined. For instance, completed ratings on a child's daily self-monitoring form may indicate that a child was given prompts and adequate time to rate his or her behavior throughout the day.

Permanent product review can be a relatively time-efficient and comprehensive treatment integrity assessment method, as it does not require additional time on the part of the implementer and all instances of implementation can be sampled with minimal intrusiveness and reactivity (Lane et al., 2004). Interventions with forms (e.g., self-monitoring, Check-in Check-out) or worksheets (e.g., academic math problems) are well suited for permanent product review. The collection and analysis of the products may require some training, but could be completed by a variety of individuals in an applied setting. That said, many interventions simply do not result in products that could be used, or result only in products for a small subset of intervention steps. Even for those interventions that are well suited to permanent product review, the collection and analysis of the products may be time intensive, and often quality of implementation cannot be measured based on products.

Self-Report. Self-report is the most commonly used method of treatment integrity assessment by school professionals (Cochrane & Laux, 2008).

Similar to direct observation, this method requires the intervention be divided into a comprehensive list of discrete and measurable intervention steps. Next, how the individual implementing the treatment rates each step as well as when and how often observations will be completed need to be determined.

As with direct observation, self-report instrumentation may be designed for almost any intervention. Further, it offers considerable flexibility in format (e.g., checklists, narrative notes) and delivery (e.g., paper and pencil, e-mail, electronic fill-in forms), is highly resource efficient, can target multiple dimensions of treatment integrity, may be completed frequently, and requires minimal training. Despite these benefits, much of the available research suggests that most individuals implementing an intervention (herein after called "implementers") will overestimate their level of adherence, resulting in data that are not accurate (e.g., Noell et al., 2005). There is some more recent evidence, however, to suggest that daily self-report (Sanetti & Kratochwill, 2011) and intervention training (Fallon, personal communication, 2014) can result in more accurate self-report data. These results are consistent with the self-report literature in medicine (Riekert, 2006); thus, it may be that accurate self-report data can be obtained, but that additional research is needed to identify the variables related to self-report that increase accurate responding. For example, medical researchers have found increased self-report accuracy when there is a shorter rating period (e.g., daily vs. weekly rating), implementers are informed that inconsistency in treatment integrity data may occur, and that these data are not being used to judge the implementer (Riekert, 2006). Self-report of treatment integrity should be used only when low-stake decisions (e.g., ensuring Tier 1 implementation: Response to Intervention) will be made with the data or in combination with other treatment integrity assessment tools.

Response Formats

Once a format of the treatment integrity assessment method has been chosen and the intervention steps have been operationally defined (and, for permanent product review, products have been mapped to intervention steps), response formats must be determined. Just as there are different options for the treatment integrity assessment method, there are different options for the response format for each intervention step. The response format selected depends on the treatment integrity dimension (e.g., adherence, quality) and specificity of information to be collected (Table 1.1).

For adherence, across all methods, a simple occurrence/nonoccurrence or present/absent rating could be used. Alternatively, across all methods, adherence could be rated more globally using a Likert-type scale, such as (a) implemented according to plan, (b) implemented with deviation, (c) not implemented despite an opportunity for implementation, or (d) no opportunity/not applicable (Sanetti & Collier-Meek, 2015). Quality data are typically available only from direct observation and self-report methods, and are often collected using a Likert-type scale such as (a) 4 = *excellent*, "step implemented skillfully as indicated by: appropriate interaction, smooth/natural looking, appropriate timing, and competent implementation"; (b) 3 = *good*, "step implemented adequately, but in a less skillful manner; step somewhat flawed in at least one of the indicators under 'excellent'"; (c) 2 = *fair*, "step implemented poorly in a manner that is inadequate or seriously flawed in at least one of the indicators under 'excellent'"; (d) 1 = *poor*, "step implemented poorly, with none of the indicators under 'excellent'" (Sanetti, Kratochwill, & Long, 2013, p. 61). For frequency and duration, an observer or implementer may provide a narrative response regarding the duration of the intervention (e.g., start and end times) or rate that the intervention occurred within a specific duration (e.g., greater than or equal to 20 minutes, less than 20 minutes; between 16–20 minutes, 21–25 minutes, and 26–30 minutes). When permanent product review is used, the number of products can provide an estimate of frequency and duration for an individual intervention. For group or class-wide interventions, the target child's attendance may provide information about frequency and duration. Regardless of assessment method, it may be informative to provide an area for the observer or implementer to make notes about any implementation deviations, barriers, or facilitators that may inform adjustments to the intervention or treatment integrity support.

TABLE 1.1

RESPONSE FORMATS BY TREATMENT INTEGRITY DIMENSION AND ASSESSMENT METHOD			
Treatment Integrity Assessment Methods	Dimensions of Treatment Integrity		
	Adherence	Quality	Dosage/Exposure
Direct observation	• Occurrence/nonoccurrence • Likert scale with behavioral anchors	• Likert scale with behavioral anchors	• Start and end time of observation minus time child was not present (e.g., went to bathroom) • Greater than, equal to, or less than a predetermined amount of time • Multiple-choice time frames • Narrative response re: number of minutes/sessions
Permanent product review	• Present/absent • Likert scale with behavioral anchors	• Typically not able to rate quality from permanent product	• If a classwide or group intervention: number of products from all sessions (dosage) compared with attendance records (exposure) • If an individual intervention: products from all sessions
Self-report	• Occurrence/nonoccurrence • Likert scale with behavioral anchors • Narrative response	• Likert scale with behavioral anchors • Narrative response	• Multiple-choice time frames • Narrative response re: number of minutes/sessions • Greater than, equal to, or less than a predetermined amount of time

DEVELOPING A TREATMENT INTEGRITY ASSESSMENT PLAN

The following is a multistep process for: (a) identifying the purpose for collecting treatment integrity data, (b) determining the intervention level and type of treatment integrity data needed, and (c) considering the level of risk for implementation failure and erroneous decisions.

Purpose of Assessment

The first step when considering treatment integrity assessment is to identify the purpose for the implementation data. Although treatment integrity is often discussed with respect to data-based decision making, there are other purposes for collecting treatment integrity data, such as evaluation, diagnostic decision making, progress monitoring, and screening (Chafouleas, Riley-Tillman, & Sugai, 2007). When *evaluation* is the purpose, the goal is to obtain a global, summative snapshot of implementation, meaning that the overall implementation of a curriculum may be assessed to determine whether a policy is being carried out appropriately. When *diagnosis* is the purpose, the goal is to assess treatment integrity to ensure that high-stakes decisions about a child's classification based on intervention response are valid (e.g., team evaluating a child's response to intensive intervention to determine if the child should be considered for special education classification). When *progress monitoring* is the purpose, the goal is to assess treatment integrity for a specific intervention to ensure valid, data-based decisions can be made regarding child support services (e.g., school team monitoring ongoing interventions that are lower stakes to make data-based decisions regarding appropriate level of intervention). When *screening* is the purpose, the goal is to identify those implementers who are at risk of or are demonstrating poor intervention implementation so that decisions can be made regarding professional development needs (e.g., collect data on teachers' classroom management strengths and weaknesses so that targeted support can be provided).

Type of Data Needed

The second step is to consider, given the purpose of the assessment, what type of treatment integrity data need to be collected. For example, if an individual is developing a treatment integrity assessment plan for a child or adolescent with a history of not responding to Tier 2 or small group interventions, who is transitioning to a more intensive Tier 3 intervention, professionals may want to collect adherence, quality, duration, and frequency data given the importance of fully understanding all possible reasons for the child's response or nonresponse (e.g., poor adherence, inadequate exposure, and highly variable quality of intervention delivery). Alternatively, mental health professionals may screen all teachers' use of behavior-specific praise to evaluate their implementation of this important classroom management practice. Following this evaluation, professionals may collect more specific treatment integrity data (e.g., adherence, quality, frequency) to determine which teachers need differential support to improve their classroom management.

Intervention Level

The third step is to consider what intervention level is being assessed. For example, a mental health professional may assess the implementation of a curriculum or delivery of a particular intervention. It is important to consider the level of intervention (i.e., Tiers 1, 2, 3), the level of risk of not implementing an intervention, as well as the scope of assessment. The implementation of a Tier 1 school-wide curriculum, for example, will require all teachers to be evaluated, address all children's needs simultaneously, and have appropriate resources. In comparison, an intensive, individualized intervention (Tier 3) will require fewer resources as only one teacher will be involved, may have variable intervention complexity, and has the situational risk of being evaluated for special education.

Level of Risk

The fourth step is considering both (a) the risk for implementation failure and (b) the risk of harm resulting from implementation failure (Barnett et al., 2011). Risk of implementation failure is often assessed relative to intervention complexity (e.g., Sanetti, Gritter, & Dobey, 2011). That is, the more complex the intervention, the higher the risk that the intervention will not be implemented as planned. An intervention may be made more complex due to: (a) the number of intervention steps, (b) whether the intervention is implemented in the same manner each time, (c) the number of individuals who need to implement the intervention, or (d) the environment of intervention delivery.

Another type of risk that varies across interventions is situational risk. As defined by Barnett and colleagues (2014), "Situational risk is an estimate of harm or cost to a child or others if the intervention is not carried out adequately" (p. 101). Mental health professionals regularly design and implement interventions with high situational risk, such as those related to child academic failure, possible special education classification, behavioral or social-emotional diagnosis, self-harm, and harm to others. Furthermore, interventions that are large in scope, such as those that involve entire communities or school populations, may be considered to be of high situational risk due to the large scale of the potential harm if they are not implemented well. When situational risk is considered to be high, a treatment integrity assessment plan should be multimethod (e.g., direct observation and self-report) with immediate, high-frequency data collection and evaluation (Barnett et al., 2011). Situational risk may be considered to be moderate during the initial implementation of an intervention, especially if the implementer is not familiar with the intervention. When situational risk is moderate, a treatment integrity assessment plan may be multimethod with immediate, high-frequency data collection and evaluation during the initial implementation phase, which is faded to less frequent, single-method (e.g., direct observation) treatment integrity assessment once adequate implementation and positive child outcomes are demonstrated. Finally, situational risk may be considered to be low when an intervention has been in place for a while, child outcome data have been consistently positive, and treatment integrity data have been consistently adequate. When situational risk is low, a treatment integrity assessment plan may include less frequent, single-method assessment.

ANALYZING ASSESSMENT OUTCOMES

Once a treatment integrity assessment plan is developed and treatment integrity and child outcome assessment data are being collected as planned, it is necessary to evaluate these data to make valid, data-based decisions about intervention effectiveness. Evaluation of these data (e.g., treatment integrity and child outcome data) allows for four possible data profiles, each of which is associated with different next steps (see Table 1.2).

The first two data profiles are associated with positive child outcomes that indicate the child is improving sufficiently to meet his or her intervention goal. In the first data profile, the data could indicate positive child outcomes and adequate[2] levels of treatment integrity. In this case, it would be appropriate to continue the intervention as the child is responding to the intervention as it is currently being implemented. Periodic review of progress-monitoring data and treatment integrity data are nevertheless warranted to ensure sufficient child progress continues and high levels of intervention implementation are sustained. In the second profile, the data indicate sufficiently positive child outcomes and low treatment integrity. In this case, there may be other factors influencing outcomes, the expected rate of child progress may need to be updated, or there may be issues with treatment integrity assessment. Further investigations of these potential issues could result in a team continuing the intervention at its current level of implementation, bolstering levels of implementation and the rate of child progress, or adjusting the treatment integrity forms or assessment plan.

The last two data profiles involve poor child outcomes that suggest that improvement is insufficient to meet the child's intervention goal(s). In the third profile, the data may indicate poor child outcomes and adequate treatment integrity. In this case, after reviewing for potential treatment integrity assessment issues, it would be appropriate to increase the intensity of the intervention or change the intervention. Alignment of the intervention with the problem should be considered, and, if possible, the intervention intensity should be increased (e.g., more frequent intervention sessions). If the intensity of the intervention is deemed appropriate or it is not possible to change, a different or more intensive intervention may be warranted. In the fourth data profile, the data may demonstrate poor child outcomes and low treatment integrity. In this case, it is necessary to promote treatment integrity levels; it is not possible to evaluate intervention effectiveness until a child is exposed to the intervention as planned (Kilgus et al., 2014; Sanetti & Kratochwill, 2009a).

PROMOTING TREATMENT INTEGRITY

To deliver interventions as designed, most implementers will require some support. In response to this need and the critical importance of maintaining

TABLE 1.2

HOW TO ANALYZE ASSESSMENT OUTCOMES TO IDENTIFY DATA-DRIVEN ACTION STEPS			
		Child Outcomes	
		Positive/Sufficient to Meet Goal	**Poor/Insufficient to Meet Goal**
Treatment Integrity	**Adequate**	Continue intervention	Increase intensity of the intervention or change intervention
	Inadequate	Review (a) factors that may have influenced intervention outcomes, (b) the expected rate of progress, and (c) treatment integrity assessment	Promote treatment integrity

high levels of treatment integrity, a series of implementation support strategies, such as performance feedback and prompting have been identified (Fallon, Collier-Meek, Maggin, Sanetti, & Johnson, 2015; Simonsen, MacSuga, Fallon, & Sugai, 2012). These strategies vary in their intensity (e.g., onetime meeting, ongoing meetings), areas to target (e.g., knowledge of intervention, motivation to implement), and extent of research support (e.g., emerging support, identified as an evidence-based practice). Delivering research-based implementation support strategies can facilitate high initial levels of implementation and/or bolster low levels of treatment integrity and, in turn, support child outcomes.

For practitioners to provide the implementation supports in an efficient and effective manner, these strategies may be organized within a conceptual framework, Multi-Tiered Implementation Supports (MTIS; Sanetti, Kratochwill, Collier-Meek, & Long, 2014; Sanetti & Collier-Meek, 2015). Just as children receiving support through the multitiered systems of support described earlier in the chapter (e.g., response to intervention through Tiers 1, 2, and 3), implementers can benefit from foundational research-based training (i.e., Tier 1) and ongoing assessment used to target increased levels of support as needed (i.e., Tiers 2 and 3). Organizing implementation supports within a multitiered framework is aligned with best practice in professional development, which indicates that implementers require ongoing levels of support to be successful (Joyce & Showers, 2002; Sanetti & Collier-Meek, 2015). In addition, organizing intervention strategies from brief and informal to intense and continuous is resource efficient. Research-based treatment integrity promotion strategies for mental health professionals are discussed in the following text.

With respect to treatment integrity provided in schools, implementation support delivered at the Tier 1 level should be easy to implement and amenable to use during consultation (Sanetti & Collier-Meek, 2015). Notably, these strategies may be employed by mental health professionals in clinical and community settings as well. Tier 1 implementation support may include how consultation is approached, the manner in which an intervention is selected, or how the implementer is trained. High levels of treatment integrity have been associated with collaborative

consultation, in which the implementer and consultant together identify the intervention, plan implementation, and intervention monitoring (Kelleher, Riley-Tillman, & Power, 2008); expert-driven consultation, in which the consultant determines the intervention and plans for implementation and monitoring (Schoenwald, Sheidow, & Letourneau, 2004); instructional coaching, in which intensive and differentiated support is provided by a skilled coach (Knight, 2007); and the Classroom Check-Up, a classroom management support model that incorporates motivational interviewing techniques (Reinke, Lewis-Palmer, & Merrell, 2008). Utilizing one of these consultation approaches may increase the likelihood that the intervention is systematically identified and supported, and, through these processes, may impact the treatment integrity with which the intervention is delivered.

More broadly, Tier 1 implementation supports may also include how an intervention is identified. When selecting an intervention, it is critical that the intervention addresses the child concern and is appropriate for the context (Kratochwill, 2008). Once baseline data are collected, an appropriate evidence-based intervention that is practical for the implementer and suitable for the context is identified. Allowing the implementer the opportunity to practice implementing the interventions before the treatment is employed can result in higher levels of implementation (Dart, Cook, Collins, Gresham, & Chenier, 2012). Collaboratively discussing an intervention with an implementer is suggested (Kratochwill, 2008; Reinke et al., 2008). To support preparation for delivering an intervention, implementation planning that involves (a) detailed logistical preparation for each of the intervention steps, and (b) the proactive identification of potential implementation barriers, may be used (Sanetti et al., 2014).

Once an intervention is selected, it is critical to ensure that an implementer has the skills to deliver and follow through with the intervention. In most cases, training is needed so that the intervention is implemented as intended, with high treatment integrity, and ultimately resulting in positive changes for the child. Direct training includes teaching the implementer each intervention step; having a consultant model the intervention; practicing the intervention with the implementer, and providing him or her with positive, yet corrective, feedback

(Sterling-Turner, Watson, & Moore, 2002). In addition, providing reference materials, such as intervention scripts (Ehrhardt, Barnett, Lentz, Stollar, & Reifin, 1996) or intervention manuals that detail intervention implementation (Randall & Biggs, 2008), can increase treatment integrity by supporting the implementer's skills.

In schools, Tier 2 strategies are warranted when Tier 1 strategies are provided and low levels of treatment integrity persist (Sanetti et al., 2014). However, these same strategies may be employed by all mental health professionals. Tier 2 strategies involve more intensive implementation support and are designed to target a particular issue that is challenging for the implementer, such as intervention delivery skill, lack of appropriate fit, or need for reminders. To support the implementer's ability to deliver the intervention with skill, role-play (Trevisan, 2004) or participant modeling (Tschannen-Moran & McMaster, 2009), which involves systematic training, modeling, demonstration, and feedback that are targeted to the implementation scenarios and context, respectively, may be provided. Other strategies focus on defining intervention implementation and treatment integrity assessment (i.e., treatment integrity planning protocol; Sanetti & Kratochwill, 2009b), or planning implementation and remediating barriers (i.e., implementation planning; Sanetti et al., 2013, 2014). For implementers who have difficulty remembering to employ an intervention, prompts and self-monitoring may be used (Petscher & Bailey, 2006; Simonsen et al., 2012).

Treatment integrity data can be used to guide the appropriate Tier 2 implementation support. For instance, if an implementer delivers an intervention with low treatment integrity or provides the intervention throughout the day but with low levels of quality, role-play or participant modeling may be appropriate. If the implementer regularly omits particular intervention steps, it may be appropriate to reteach just these specific steps. If the implementer delivers the intervention with high adherence, but does not do so regularly, then prompts or self-monitoring may be useful.

Finally, Tier 3 strategies are the most intensive implementation support and are delivered individually on an ongoing (e.g., weekly, response-dependent) basis, in school systems as well as clinical settings. Tier 3 strategies are to be provided to implementers with persistently low treatment integrity. In other cases, Tier 3 implementation supports may be appropriate when the intervention is intensive and implementation is low, as it may not be appropriate to wait to deliver Tier 2 and then Tier 3 implementation supports. Performance feedback that involves verbal and/or graphic displays of implementation and child outcome data is effective (Fallon et al., 2015).

CONCLUSION

Ensuring evidence-based interventions are implemented with adequate treatment integrity is critical to evaluating and supporting child outcomes (Kilgus et al., 2014; Sanetti & Kratochwill, 2009a). Treatment integrity, a multidimensional construct, may be assessed by direct observation, permanent product review, or self-report through varied response formats. To determine the appropriate assessment method requires consideration of the purpose of assessment, type of data needed, intervention level, and type of implementation or situational risk. Together with child outcome data, treatment integrity data can be analyzed to determine data-driven next steps related to the intervention and implementation. If support is needed, it can be delivered to implementers within MTIS to efficiently and effectively provide research-based treatment integrity promotion strategies. Such ongoing and systematic attention to treatment integrity will maximize the benefit of the evidence-based interventions.

NOTES

1. Writing of this chapter was partially supported by the Institute of Education Sciences, U.S. Department of Education, through Grant R324A10005 to the University of Connecticut. The opinions expressed are those of the authors and do not represent views of the Institute or the U.S. Department of Education.
2. There is no agreed-upon level of "adequate" treatment integrity that is applicable across interventions (Sanetti & Kratochwill, 2009a). Rather, at this time, intervention-specific research and a review of treatment integrity data along with progress-monitoring data can be used to determine the level of implementation necessary to reach the child outcome goal.

SELECT BIBLIOGRAPHY

IRIS Center Modules on Implementing a Program or Practice with Fidelity. Retrieved from http://iris .peabody.vanderbilt.edu/module/ebp_02/#content *Two modules provide content related to implementation of evidence-based interventions in multiple formats (text, video demonstrations, audio interviews with experts and practicing educators, and interactive activities).*

National Implementation Research Network. Retrieved from http://nirn.fpg.unc.edu *The website provides free online modules, lessons, tools, and resources about implementation relevant across human services professions.*

PRIME: Multi-tiered Implementation Support Framework. Retrieved from http:// implementationscience.uconn.edu/prime/ resources *This is a manual developed for school-based practitioners that includes sections on a multitiered implementation support model, Tier 1 supports (direct training, implementation planning), collection of data (treatment integrity, student outcomes), analyzing treatment integrity and student outcome data together, using data to identify next steps and Tier 2 (participant modeling, role-play, raising awareness, motivational consulting) and Tier 3 (performance feedback) supports. Research-supported assessments and implementation support protocols provided.*

REFERENCES

Barnett, D., Hawkins, R., & Lentz, E. (2011). Intervention adherence for research and practice: Necessity or triage outcome? *Journal of Educational and Psychological Consultation, 21*, 175–190. doi:1 0.1080/10474412.2011.595162

Barnett, D., Hawkins, R., McCoy, D., Wahl, E., Shier, A., Denune, H., & Kimener, L. (2014). Methods used to document procedural fidelity in school-based intervention research. *Journal of Behavioral Education, 23*, 89–107. doi:10.1007/s10864–013–9188-y

Chafouleas, S. M., Riley-Tillman, T. C., & Sugai, G. (2007). *School-based behavioral assessment: Informing intervention and instruction.* New York, NY: Guilford Press.

Cochrane, W. S., & Laux, J. M. (2008). A survey investigating school psychologists' measurement of treatment integrity in school-based interventions and their beliefs about its importance. *Psychology in the Schools, 45*, 499–507. doi:10.1002/pits.20319

Dart, E. H., Cook, C. R., Collins, T. A., Gresham, F. M, & Chenier, J. S. (2012). Test driving interventions to increase treatment integrity and student outcomes. *School Psychology Review, 41*, 467–481. Retrieved from http://www.nasponline .org/publications/spr/index.aspx?vol=41&issue=4

Ehrhardt, K. E., Barnett, D. W., Lentz, F. E. Jr, Stollar, S. A., & Reifin, L. H. (1996). Innovative methodology in ecological consultation: Use of scripts to promote treatment acceptability and integrity. *School Psychology Quarterly, 11*, 149–168. doi:10.1037/h0088926

Embry, D. D. (2003). *The PAX good behavior game.* Center City, MN: Hazelden Publishing and Educational Services.

Fallon, L. M., Collier-Meek, M. A., Maggin, D. M., Sanetti, L. M. H., & Johnson, A. H. (2015). Is performance feedback an evidence-based intervention? A systematic review and evaluation of single-case research. *Exceptional Children, 8*, 227–246. doi:10.1177/0014402914551738

Joyce, B., & Showers, B. (2002). *Student achievement through staff development* (3rd ed.). Alexandria, VA: Association for Supervision and Curriculum Development.

Kelleher, C., Riley-Tillman, T. C., & Power, T. J. (2008). An initial comparison of collaborative and expert-driven consultation on treatment integrity. *Journal of Educational and Psychological Consultation, 18*, 294–324. doi:10.1080/10474410802491040.

Kilgus, S. P., Collier-Meek, M. A., Johnson, A. H., & Jaffery, R. (2014). Applied empiricism: Ensuring the validity of response-to-intervention decisions. *Contemporary School Psychology, 18*, 1–12. doi:10.1007/s40688–013-0009-z

Knight, J. (2007). *Instructional coaching: A partnership approach to improving instruction.* Thousand Oaks, CA: Corwin Press.

Kratochwill, T. R. (2008). Best practices in school-based problem-solving consultation: Applications in prevention and intervention systems. In A. Thomas & J. Grimes (Eds.), *Best practice in school psychology V* (pp. 1673–1688). Bethesda, MA: National Association of School Psychologists.

Lane, K. L., Bocian, K. M., MacMillan, D. L., & Gresham, F. M. (2004). Treatment integrity:

An essential—but often forgotten—component of school-based interventions. *Preventing School Failure, 48*, 36–43. doi:10.3200/PSFL.48.3.36–43

McInerney, M., & Elledge, A. (2013). *Using a response to intervention framework to improve student learning: A pocket guide for state and district leaders*. American Institutes for Research. Retrieved from www.rti4success.org/sites/default/files/Response_to_Intervention_Pocket_Guide_2.pdf

Noell, G. H., Witt, J. C., Gilbertson, D. N., Ranier, D. D., & Freeland, J. T. (1997). Increasing teacher intervention implementation in general education settings through consultation and performance feedback. *School Psychology Quarterly, 12*, 77–88. doi:10.1037/h0088949

Noell, G. H., Witt, J. C., Slider, N. J., Connell, J. E., Gatti, S. L., Williams, K. L.,.... Duhon, G. J. (2005). Treatment implementation following behavioral consultation in schools: A comparison of three follow-up strategies. *School Psychology Review, 34*, 87–106. Retrieved from http://www.nasponline.org/publications/spr/abstract.aspx?ID=1782

Petscher, E. S., & Bailey, J. S. (2006). Effects of training, prompting, and self-monitoring on staff behavior in a classroom for students with disabilities. *Journal of Applied Behavior Analysis, 39*, 215–226. doi:10.1901/jaba.2006.02–05

Randall, C. M., & Biggs, B. K. (2008). Enhancing therapeutic gains: Examination of fidelity to the model for the intensive mental health program. *Journal of Child and Family Studies, 17*, 191–205. doi:10.1007/s10826–007-9159–9

Reinke, W. M., Lewis-Palmer, T., & Merrell, K. (2008). The Classroom Check-Up: A classwide teacher consultation model for increasing praise and decreasing disruptive behavior. *School Psychology Review, 37*, 315–332. Retrieved from http://www.ncbi.nlm.nih.gov/pmc/articles/PMC2603055

Riekert, K. A. (2006). Integrating regimen adherence assessment into clinical practice. In W. T. O'Donohue & E. R. Levensky (Eds.), *Promoting treatment adherence: A practical handbook for health care providers* (pp. 17–34). Thousand Oaks, CA: Sage.

Sanetti, L. M. H., & Collier-Meek, M. A. (2015). A multi-tiered system of support for educators' implementation: A pilot study. *Psychology in the Schools, 52*, 815–828.

Sanetti, L. M. H., & Fallon, L. M. (2011). Treatment integrity assessment: How estimates of adherence, quality, and exposure influence interpretation of implementation. *Journal of Educational and Psychological Consultation, 21*, 209–232.

Sanetti, L. M. H., Gritter, K. L., & Dobey, L. (2011). Treatment integrity of interventions with children in the school psychology literature from 1995 to 2008. *School Psychology Review, 40*, 72–84.

Sanetti, L. M. H., & Kratochwill, T. R. (2009a). Toward developing a science of treatment integrity: Introduction to the special series. *School Psychology Review, 38*, 445–459.

Sanetti, L. M. H., & Kratochwill, T. R. (2009b). Treatment integrity assessment in the schools: An evaluation of the *Treatment Integrity Planning Protocol* (TIPP). *School Psychology Quarterly, 24*, 24–35.

Sanetti, L. M. H., & Kratochwill, T. R. (2011). An evaluation of the treatment integrity planning protocol and two schedules of treatment integrity self-report: Impact on implementation and report accuracy. *Journal of Educational and Psychological Consultation, 21*, 284–308.

Sanetti, L. M. H., Kratochwill, T. R., Collier-Meek, M. A., & Long, A. C. J. (2014). *PRIME manual*. Storrs, CT: University of Connecticut.

Sanetti, L. M., Kratochwill, T. R., & Long, A. C. (2013). Applying adult behavior change theory to support mediator-based intervention implementation. *School Psychology Quarterly: The Official Journal of the Division of School Psychology, American Psychological Association, 28*(1), 47–62.

Schoenwald, S. K., Sheidow, A. J., & Letourneau, E. J. (2004). Toward effective quality assurance in evidence-based practice: Links between expert consultation, therapist fidelity, and child outcomes. *Journal of Clinical Child and Adolescent Psychology: The Official Journal for the Society of Clinical Child and Adolescent Psychology, American Psychological Association, Division 53, 33*(1), 94–104.

Simonsen, B., MacSuga, A. S., Fallon, L. M., & Sugai, G. (2012). Teacher self-monitoring to increase specific praise rates. *Journal of Positive Behavior Interventions, 15*, 3–13. doi:1098300712440453

Sterling-Turner, H. E., Watson, T. S., & Moore, J. W. (2002). The effects of direct training and treatment integrity on treatment outcomes in school consultation. *School Psychology Quarterly, 17,* 47–77. doi:10.1521/scpq.17.1.47.19906

Trevisan, M. S. (2004). Practical training in evaluation: A review of the literature. *American Journal of Evaluation, 25,* 255–272. doi:10.1016/j.ameval.2004.03.002

Tschannen-Moran, M., & McMaster, P. (2009). Sources of self-efficacy: Four professional development formats and their relationship to self-efficacy and implementation of a new teaching strategy. *Elementary School Journal, 110,* 228–245. doi:10.1086/605771

Crisis and Response

Evidence-Based Interventions for Comprehensive School Crises

Melissa A. Louvar Reeves and Benjamin S. Fernandez

OVERVIEW

It is not a matter of *if*, but *when* a school will experience a crisis. School mental health professionals need to know how to assist staff and students in their emotional recovery and facilitate the reestablishment of coping and problem-solving abilities. Comprehensive school crisis interventions focus on more than just crisis response; the foundation of healing in the aftermath of a crisis begins with prevention initiatives that build student resiliency to help students cope. The purpose of this chapter is to discuss comprehensive school crisis interventions, identify the characteristics that define a crisis, find ways to assess for the level of traumatic impact, and determine what interventions can be provided to help with response and recovery. The PREPaRE Model of crisis prevention and intervention will be highlighted.

THE IMPORTANCE OF CRISIS INTERVENTION

Crises can occur suddenly, are often viewed as extremely negative, and can generate feelings of helplessness and powerlessness (Brock et al., 2009). These events have the potential to impact students and staff psychologically as well as disrupt the learning environment. There are six general categories of crises: (a) acts of war and/or terrorism; (b) violent and/or unexpected death(s); (c) threatened death and/or injury; (d) human-caused disasters; (e) natural disasters; and (f) severe illness or injury (Brock et al., 2009). Children are a vulnerable population and in the absence of quality crisis interventions, there can be negative short- and long-term implications on learning, cognitive development, and mental health. For most students and staff, recovery is the norm, but some may require more direct support from school-employed mental health professionals to mitigate traumatic impact, help in recovery, and bring the children back to a level of healthy academic, social, and emotional functioning.

ETIOLOGY AND FACTORS CONTRIBUTING TO SCHOOL CRISES

Crisis Characteristics

Brock et al. (2009) identified three crisis event characteristics: (a) the incident is perceived as extremely negative, (b) it is uncontrollable and causes feelings of helplessness and/or powerlessness, and (c) the crisis is a sudden and unexpected event that happens with little to no warning. Although some events can be predicted (e.g., death from a long-term illness), events that are perceived as more negative (human-caused violent acts) have a greater sense of uncontrollability, generate a greater sense of helplessness or powerlessness, tend to have higher traumatic impact, and have a significant effect on how the event is perceived (Brock et al., 2009; Foa, Zinbarg, & Rothbaum, 1992). In contrast, if an individual has time to prepare for an event, the resulting impact from the trauma may be significantly lower (Saylor, Belter, & Stokes, 1997).

Crisis Event Variables

There are four crisis event variables that interact and contribute to the level of potential traumatization: (1) event predictability, (2) consequences of the event, (3) duration, and (4) intensity (Brock et al., 2009). In general, human-caused violent events (assaults, threats, acts of terror) tend to be more traumatizing than natural disasters.

Predictability. This involves the extent to which an event is anticipated. The less predictable an incident, the less likely the individual(s) are able to prepare for the consequences of the crisis.

Consequences. Consequences are the positive and negative results of a crisis. Some crises lead to positive changes (e.g., prevention programs, additional staff development, changes in crisis plans), whereas others lead to devastation (e.g., severe injuries, death, destruction of homes and communities). Events with fatalities result in greater levels of trauma than incidents with only injuries (Charuvastra & Cloitre, 2008). Generally, the more significant and severe the consequences (e.g., death), the greater the potential that a person will be psychologically harmed by the crisis.

Duration. Duration is the length of time a crisis occurs. The longer a child and/or an adolescent is exposed to a crisis, the greater the likelihood that he or she will experience trauma. In a study of school-aged children who were victims of Hurricane Katrina in New Orleans, the long duration of the devastating effects of the hurricane and subsequent challenges, such as being displaced, experiencing loss of loved ones, resulted in more intense trauma exposures (Kronenberg et al., 2010).

Intensity. This includes sensorial experiences such as experiencing or witnessing gruesome aspects of death, dying, and overall devastation. Figure 2.1 illustrates the interactions between crisis variables that determine the level of traumatic impact.

Crisis Event Consequences

In general, the majority of people will recover from a crisis. However, if initial crisis reactions endure, individuals can develop a mental illness and negative social-emotional and academic consequences. The disorders most commonly associated with crisis exposure are posttraumatic stress disorder (PTSD), anxiety disorders, substance-related disorders, dissociative disorders, depression, and sleep disorders (Brock et al., 2009). PTSD can develop if traumatic reactions persist longer than 4 weeks (American Psychological Association [APA], 2013). Schools and students may experience decline in academic performance, increase in behavioral problems, and increase in absenteeism and tardiness. These issues may add to already existing academic, behavioral, and social and emotional functioning difficulties as well as preexisting mental illness.

EVIDENCE-BASED INTERVENTIONS AND EMPIRICAL SUPPORT FOR SCHOOL CRISES

Evidence-based interventions focusing on physical and psychological safety may be implemented to prevent a crisis from occurring or mitigate the traumatic impact of a crisis event by building resiliency in students. This requires schools to create and maintain emergency management plans that take into account not only the school, students, and staff, but also the community and resources available to assist in times of crisis.

Crisis Models: M-PHAT and U.S. Department of Education

The U.S. Department of Education (DOE, 2013) advocates that schools develop high-quality emergency responses using the five mission areas of preparedness: (a) prevention, (b) mitigation, (c) protection, (d) response, and (e) recovery. *Prevention* is described as the actions taken by schools to decrease the possibility that an incident will occur (e.g., prevention program, positive

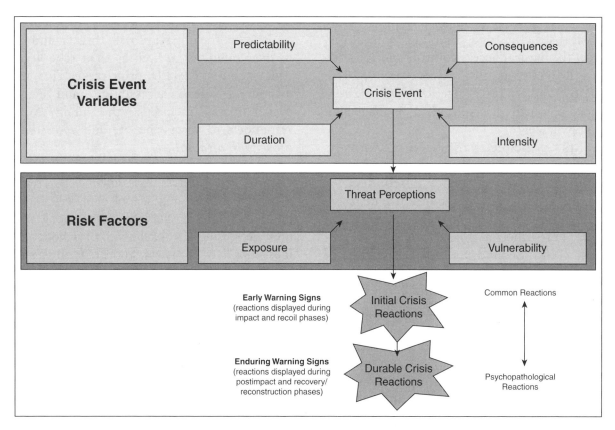

FIGURE 2.1 The relationship among the crisis event, threat perceptions, and crisis reactions.

Source: Brock (2011). Copyright 2011 by the National Association of School Psychologists, Bethesda, MD. Reprinted with permission of the publisher: www.nasponline.org.

behavior supports). *Mitigation* may be characterized by what is done to eliminate or reduce the loss of life and property damage by lessening the impact of a threat or a hazard (e.g., having one point of entry with good visitor-screening procedures; U.S. DOE 2009). *Protection* is the ongoing action that protects students, staff, property, and visitors from hazards or potential threats (e.g., school resource officers). *Response* includes activating emergency response protocols (e.g., lockdowns, crisis interventions). *Recovery* includes providing longer-term crisis interventions and restoring the learning environment. In addition to guidance provided by the U.S. DOE, schools can use the M-PHAT model: Multi-*Phase*, Multi-*Hazard*, Multi-*Agency*, and Multi-*Tiered* approach (Reeves, Kanan, & Plog, 2010). This model ensures that the actions taken by the school and district safety and crisis teams account for all potential hazards (weather related, suicides, student threats, etc.), are able to

work collaboratively with various agencies (fire and rescue, law enforcement, etc.), and allows for the delivery of multitiered crisis supports and interventions based on demonstrated need.

Physical Safety

Physical safety includes initiatives that involve keeping schools safe and secure via addressing the physical structures of a building (Brock et al., 2009; Reeves, Conolly-Wilson, Pesce, Lazzaro, & Brock, 2012; Reeves et al., 2011; Sprague & Walker, 2005). Although not the focus of this chapter, physical safety initiatives are crucial to comprehensive school safety and help to prevent and mitigate crises events. One of the most widely accepted concepts utilized to address physical safety is the concept of Crime Prevention Through Environmental Design (CPTED). CPTED originally included three principles important for securing the physical structure of a school: (a) natural surveillance, (b) natural access control, and (c) territoriality (Reeves et al., 2011; Reeves et al., 2012; Sprague & Walker, 2005). The U.S. DOE (2013) references a fourth principle, titled management and maintenance.

The first principle, *natural surveillance*, is designed to increase observation, detection, and reporting of trespassers or misconduct, as individuals are less likely to commit a negative act if they know they will be identified and held accountable for their actions (Sorenson, Hayes, & Atlas, 2008). Second, *natural access control* focuses on monitoring the individuals who enter and exit schools. Schools should have clearly marked signs and entrances, have one point of entry that is consistently monitored with all other doors to the building locked, strategically placed surveillance cameras, and established and consistently implemented protocol for visitor-screening and sign-in policy, and mandatory identification badges (Sprague & Walker, 2005; U.S. DOE, 2013). Although metal detectors may help in some settings, without the implementation of other safety measures, they are meaningless. *Territoriality*, the third aspect of keeping a school safe, may be defined as a sense of shared ownership and pride that empowers students and staff members to challenge inappropriate behavior and protect their "turf" (Schneider, Walker, & Sprague, 2000; Sorenson et al., 2008). It includes establishing a confidential reporting process and creates a welcoming environment and sense of community (e.g., students paint a mural to communicate a sense of community and pride). Finally, the newest concept, *management and maintenance*, emphasizes the importance of caring for school properties. Maintaining manicured grounds minimizes the possibility and opportunity for schools to be used as breeding grounds for criminal activity (Sorenson et al., 2008; U.S. DOE, 2013).

Vulnerability Assessments

The U.S. DOE (2013) advocates that schools conduct multiple types of risk and vulnerability assessments. These include the following.

Site Assessment. Schools need to identify and understand the impact of risk, threats, and hazards in their buildings as well as their school grounds (this includes CPTED principles). This involves examining safety, accessibility, and emergency preparedness, including the ability of first responders to access the site and *accessibility for those with disabilities.*

Culture and Climate Assessment. The creation of a positive culture and school climate is integral to the promotion of connectedness among students, thus decreasing the likelihood of school violence. It is important to assess student, faculty, and staff perceptions of safety as well as the identification of problem behaviors to improve school climate. The National Association of School Psychologists (NASP) PREPaRE Workshop 1 curriculum addresses how to assess these factors for the enhancement of the overall physical and psychological safety of everyone in schools (Reeves et al., 2011).

School Threat Assessment. A threat assessment team should be developed with key personnel, including the principal, counselor, school psychologist, and nurse, to identify individual(s) who may pose a threat before it may be carried out. The assessment team may refer the identified child or children for support and services, if appropriate. It is important to note that just because a child makes a threat does not mean he or she poses a threat; thus, appropriate training of threat assessment teams is critical to ensure appropriate actions are taken. Moreover, each member of the crisis team has specific responsibilities that he or she carries out with respect to assessment and triage following a school violence incident.

Capacity Assessment. This type of evaluation examines the resources available to mitigate and respond to a crisis event. The identification of staff capabilities to include clearly assigned roles and responsibilities; staff training to carry out their assigned duties; and the equipment, supplies, and personnel resources available to ensure a quality execution of response and recovery protocols is warranted. The U.S. Department of Homeland Security (2013) has published a document titled *K–12 School Security Checklist*, which helps schools assess many of the areas listed

earlier and includes psychological safety (www
.illinois.gov/ready/SiteCollectionDocuments/
K–12SchoolSecurityPracticesChecklist.pdf).

Psychological Safety

Psychological safety includes initiatives that focus on
the emotional and behavioral well-being of students,
faculty, and staff (Brock et al., 2009; Reeves et al.,
2011; Reeves et al., 2012). School-based prevention
programs are successful in reducing a wide range of
problems and increasing positive outcomes (Durlak
et al., 2011); thus, they are critical to school safety
initiatives.

Universal Interventions. Universal, school-wide
initiatives that promote a positive and safe school
climate build personal resiliency and ensure that
the emotional needs of students are met. Such plans
are critical to addressing psychological safety and
building protective factors that mitigate traumatic
impact (Reeves et al., 2010). First, it is important
to train all individuals implementing prevention-
related activities such as social skills training,
bullying interventions, and problem-solving
strategies. Furthermore, practicing training parents
whose children are the recipients of such activities
serves to enhance these curricula. Second, the crisis
team should have a step-by-step plan for crisis
responding that includes implementation activities,
timelines, which individuals are responsible for
certain activities, resources available, and training.
Finally, universal interventions include frameworks
such as a multitiered system of supports (MTSS;
Cowan, Vaillancourt, Rossen, & Pollitt, 2013),
positive behavioral supports (Cohen, Kincaid, &
Childs, 2007; OSEP Technical Assistance Center
on PBIS, 2014; Sprague & Horner, 2012), response
to intervention (National Center on Response to
Intervention, 2010; www.rtinetwork.org/learn/
what/whatisrti; www.rti4success.org), safe and civil
schools (www.safeandcivilschools.com), social-
emotional learning (www.safeandcivilschools.
com), and can also include school-wide bullying
and violence prevention programs. The document
titled *A Framework for Safe and Successful Schools*
(Cowan et al., 2013) provides a great overview of
MTSS and how to address comprehensive school
safety.

Targeted Interventions. Targeted interventions
should be provided for students who require
additional supports and are paired with universal
interventions. Such interventions should address
both academic and social-emotional needs of
children and adolescents (Reeves et al., 2010).
These interventions often include small group
work in addressing emotional regulation, anger
management, social skills, grief and loss, coping
strategies, substance abuse, bullying and violence
prevention, suicide prevention, and problem
solving, with the goal being increase of resiliency
and skills to improve functioning.

Intensive Interventions. In addition to universal
and targeted interventions, intensive interventions
are warranted for further support and treatment
of students with more serious difficulties, such as
suicidal behaviors, threats to others, and/or more
serious mental health issues that require services
beyond what a school district can provide. This
often includes systems of care and wraparound
services that are tailored to the child's specific
needs and often involve working with medical
and/or community agencies (Center for Effective
Collaboration and Practice, 2014).

Evaluation of Psychological Trauma

When a crisis occurs, it is critical to assess the
level of traumatic impact experienced by students
to determine the appropriate level of interventions. Not every child/adolescent will need direct
crisis intervention supports as those with strong
resiliency and support systems will utilize their
natural support systems to help with recovery.
Therefore, interventions should be delivered to
students based only on demonstrated need by the
psychological triage team (Brock et al., 2009), or
based on the psychological triage conducted by
the school-employed mental health professional
who looks at risk factors and warning signs to
include crisis exposure, personal vulnerabilities,
threat perceptions, and coping strategies of the
students.

Risk Factors and Warning Signs of Trauma

Crisis risk factors are variables that predict whether
a person becomes a psychological trauma victim.

Risk factors fall into three major categories: crisis exposure, vulnerabilities, and threat perceptions.

Crisis Exposure. One of the most powerful risk factors is one's physical proximity to the crisis event (e.g., where the person was physically located in relation to the incident when it occurred). Generally, the closer a student is physically to a crisis event, the greater the potential for trauma. Another strong risk factor of psychological trauma is the emotional proximity to a crisis victim. The closer the relationship and/or emotional connection to the victim(s), the more likely a child or an adolescent will experience psychological trauma.

Personal Vulnerabilities. Internal and external vulnerabilities are related to how well a child copes with the traumatic event (Brock et al., 2009). Internal vulnerabilities include factors such as avoidant coping style, poor emotional regulation, low developmental levels, poor problem-solving abilities, and significant psychological trauma history. External vulnerabilities include social connections such as family resources and extra-familial social resources. When intact, family resources serve as a protective factor; however, when parents struggle to cope or there are issues such as parental trauma, poverty, poor parenting, and the absence of physical and psychological family resources, there is a greater risk that the student's coping skills will be poor.

Threat Perceptions. The next risk factor involves the subjective experience and/or impressions of the crisis. In general, the more negative and threatening the perception of the crisis, the more likely the child may demonstrate traumatic stress reactions. In the school setting, the manner in which adults react to the trauma is of importance, as their responses have a direct influence on how students will react. If adults remain calm, students will also typically stay calm. The more negative the adult's reaction, the more likely the students will be negatively impacted, particularly among younger children.

Warning Signs. The emotional, cognitive, physical, and behavioral reactions of an individual during a crisis are warning signs that suggest that psychological trauma has occurred (Brock et al.,

2009). Initial reactions are not necessarily a reflection of psychopathology, but can be typical reactions given the crisis situations. However, when crisis reactions do not abate, but are more durable and long lasting, this may be a reflection of psychological trauma. It is important to note that, when assessing these factors and variables, it is crucial to take into account a child's/adolescent's developmental level and cultural differences. Students at varying developmental stages interpret and experience crises differently, which in turn influences their reactions and coping. As a result, reactions, coping, attitudes, and communication styles vary. Additionally, culture, ethnicity, and religious backgrounds influence crisis reactions. What may be common grief reactions in one culture may not be the same for those of different cultures and beliefs. Individuals conducting psychological triage must understand a youth's cultural differences to avoid the interpretation of these reactions as mental illness when, in fact, they may be common reactions in that particular culture or religion.

Normal Coping

It is important to understand the range of what normal coping includes. Billings and Moos (1984) identified three ways in which people may attempt to cope with crisis incidents. The first is *appraisal-focused* coping, which involves a child and/or an adolescent preparing for and logically thinking through crisis consequences. It may involve the reframing of the event and mentally holding off the trauma until they are ready to deal with it. The next domain is *problem-focused* coping. Within this domain, the individual works toward identifying crisis facts and resources in order to address problems caused by the crisis. Finally, *emotion-focused* coping involves the appropriate regulation of emotions that were generated by the crisis.

HOW TO: A GUIDE TO THE IMPLEMENTATION OF INTERVENTIONS FOR SCHOOL CRISES

Multitiered Crisis Interventions

When a crisis occurs, school crisis interventions may be categorized as falling within a multitiered model of differentiated services. A one-size-fits-all approach is not in the best interest of youth affected by trauma, as over- and/or under-responding may result in more harm (Brock, Louvar Reeves, & Nickerson, 2014). Based on the level of impact, some children may need highly directive crisis intervention supports, whereas natural support systems for other children and adolescents will be sufficient to meet their needs. The PREPaRE model is the only known comprehensive school-based crisis training model that incorporates a multitiered framework and best practices advocated for by the U.S. Departments of Education and Homeland Security (see Figure 2.2). It also aligns well with MTSS and other comprehensive school safety and educational approaches (Brock, 2011; Brock et al., 2009; Cowan et al., 2013; Reeves et al., 2011).

The PREPaRE acronym stands for the following:

P   **Prevent** and prepare for psychological trauma
R   **Reaffirm** physical health and perceptions of security and safety
E   **Evaluate** psychological trauma risk
P   **Provide** interventions
a   **a**nd
R   **Respond** to psychological needs
E   **Examine** the effectiveness of crisis prevention and intervention

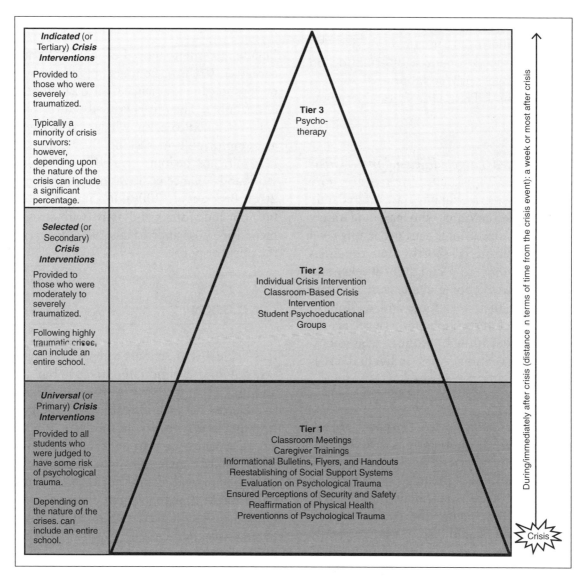

FIGURE 2.2 PREPaRE model: Multitiered crisis interventions.

Source: Brock (2011). Copyright 2011 by the National Association of School Psychologists, Bethesda, MD. Reprinted with permission of the publisher. www.nasponline.org.

Tier 1: Universal Crisis Interventions. According to the PREPaRE model, Tier 1 interventions are offered to all crisis-exposed individuals and are designed to prevent or mitigate psychological trauma and reaffirm physical health and perceptions of safety and security. Evaluating psychological trauma (psychological triage) helps to ensure that appropriate interventions are provided, such as reestablishing social support systems, providing psychoeducational information, and conducting classroom meetings. Complementary to the PREPaRE model is psychological first aid (PFA). PFA is an evidence-based approach in which school staff are trained to assist students and families in the aftermath of a crisis. It includes the core actions of: contact and engagement, safety and comfort, stabilization, information gathering, practical assistance, connection with social supports, information on coping, and linkage with collaborative services (The National Child Traumatic Stress Network, 2014).

Tier 2: Selected/Targeted/Secondary Crisis Interventions. Tier 2 crisis interventions are more prescriptive, and directive supports are offered only to children and adolescents who are moderately to severely traumatized. Interventions at this level are typically administered shortly after the crisis event (i.e., a few days to a couple of weeks) and help students address coping challenges, facilitate the processing of their reactions, and reestablish immediate coping. Interventions at this level include student psychoeducational groups, classroom-based crisis interventions, and individual crisis interventions.

Tier 3: Intensive/Indicated/Tertiary Crisis Interventions. Tier 3 interventions are offered to youth who have been severely traumatized by the crisis event and include intensive and long-term mental health treatment (i.e., PTSD). These services often require the engagement of specialized mental health supports, typically outside the school setting, and may include systems of care or wraparound services. Table 2.1 summarizes the various levels of interventions according to the PREPaRE model.

Important Considerations

It is important to examine the effectiveness of crisis preparedness through recovery efforts once a crisis has passed. This may be accomplished by interviewing crisis team members as well as faculty and staff, administering surveys to them, recording observational notes during the crisis, and having focus groups that discuss what worked and what did not. No crisis response is executed perfectly; thus, important lessons may be learned to improve future preparedness and response efforts. Brock et al. (2009), Brock (2011), and Reeves et al. (2011) have example forms to facilitate evaluation of the effectiveness of safety and crisis response efforts.

Care for the Caregiver

Finally, an often-ignored element is caring for the caregiver. Crisis responders are also exposed to the event and can experience their own emotional pain and trauma. Thus, it is critical that crisis responders are trained to acknowledge crisis reactions and are comfortable in seeking their own support to help mitigate the long-term effects of crisis response work and enhance positive coping strategies (Brock, 2011; Brock et al., 2009). It is important to identify burnout individuals and assist with stress management for those individuals directly involved with the crisis response.

CONCLUSION

It is critical that schools attend to comprehensive safe school prevention initiatives to build resilience and protective factors within youth. These protective factors help to mitigate traumatic impact and help facilitate recovery. In the event of a school crisis, crisis teams need to be trained in how to effectively execute their roles and responsibilities, and school-employed mental health professionals need to be taught how to evaluate the level of traumatic impact (psychological triage) and deliver multi-tiered crisis interventions. Ensuring that caregivers' needs are met and that comprehensive school safety and crisis initiatives and responses are evaluated for future improvement are critical to the future of ensuring the safety of students and staff.

TABLE 2.1

THE PREP<u>a</u>RE MODEL: LEVELS OF MULTITIERED CRISIS INTERVENTIONS		
Intervention	**Intervention Steps/Phases**	**Goal**
Universal/Primary		
Evaluation of psychological trauma	1. **Threat Perceptions**—determined or influenced by: • Crisis event (predictability, consequences, duration, intensity) • Physical and emotional proximity • Vulnerabilities (avoidance coping, mental illness, poor emotional control, low developmental level, trauma history, "aloneness") • Adult reactions 2. **Crisis Reactions** (mental health referral indicators) • Durable (last a week or more) • Interfere with daily functioning • Acute (panic, dissociation, extreme fright) • Increased arousal (startle, hypervigilance, disturbed sleep) • Maladaptive coping (suicidal or homicidal)	• A dynamic, ongoing process that identifies the level of impact and those individuals at risk for developing psychological trauma • Matches individual with appropriate level of intervention
Reestablishing social supports	1. **Reunification** with family and friends 2. **Returning** to familiar environments and routines	• Empower individuals to use their social support systems to facilitate natural recovery • If not sufficient in and of itself, pair with other multitiered interventions
Classroom meeting	3. **Introduce** the training 4. **Provide** crisis facts • Ensure caregivers can help children understand the crisis 5. **Answer** student questions • CAUTION: Do not give children unasked-for details 6. **Refer** (as indicated) to techniques for responding to children's crisis reactions	• Brief meetings (10–15 min) with classes/groups of students to disseminate the facts • Helps mitigate trauma generated by rumors • Begins to identify those who need additional help • "Buys time" to organize more directive crisis interventions
Targeted/Selected/Secondary		
Caregiver training (teachers and parents)	1. **Introduce** caregivers to the training 2. **Provide** crisis facts • Ensure caregivers can help children understand the crisis • CAUTION: Do not give children unasked-for details 3. **Prepare** for crisis reactions • Normalize most reactions • Identify pathological reactions and referral procedures 4. **Review** techniques for responding to crisis reactions • Review stress management and relaxation techniques • Provide bibliotherapy • Identify support systems • Specify adaptive coping strategies • Stress importance of adult reactions and empathetic responses	• Provides caregivers with knowledge they need to help children/adolescents • Provides information regarding effects of trauma exposure, adaptive and maladaptive coping, and resources

(continued)

TABLE 2.1

THE PREPaRE MODEL: LEVELS OF MULTITIERED CRISIS INTERVENTIONS *(continued)*		
Intervention	**Intervention Steps/Phases**	**Goal**

Student psychoeducational group	1. **Introduce** students to the lesson
	  • Introduce facilitators. Review process/rules
	2. **Answer** questions and dispel rumors
	  • Help students understand the crisis
	  • CAUTION: Do not give unasked-for frightening details
	3. **Prepare** students for crisis reactions
	  • Normalize most
	  • Identify pathological reactions and referral procedures
	4. **Teach** students how to manage reactions
	  • Teach stress management and relaxation techniques
	  • Identify support systems
	  • Specify adaptive coping strategies
	5. **Close**
	  • Ensure that students have crisis reaction management plans
		• Approximately 30–45 min
		• Similar to caregiver training, but focus is on self-care and secondarily how to help others cope
		• Helps students see they are not alone in their reactions
		• Emphasizes coping strategies
		• Secondary triage to identify those who may need more intensive supports

Classroom-based/ group crisis intervention	1. **Introduce** the group process
	  • Identify facilitators. Review process/rules
	2. **Provide** crisis facts and dispel rumors
	  • Help students understand the crisis
	  • CAUTION: Do not give unasked-for frightening details
	3. **Share** crisis stories
	  • Ask what happened and identify common experiences
	4. **Identify** crisis reactions
	  • Ask how students feel and behave, and identify common reactions
	5. **Empower** students
	  • Practice stress management and relaxation techniques
	  • Identify support systems
	  • Specify adaptive coping strategies
	6. **Close**
	  • Ensure that students have crisis reaction management plans
		• Achieves the same goals as the student psychoeducational group but also includes helping the students actively explore and process their individual crisis experiences
		• Share reactions
		• Should be delivered only by a trained mental health professional
		• Students are carefully selected for this level of intervention to avoid vicarious traumatization
		• Can be used when number of individuals exceeds ability to deliver 1:1 interventions and have similar crisis exposure
		• Secondary triage to identify those who may need more intensive supports

Individual crisis intervention	1. **Establish** psychological contact
	  • Introduce self
	  • Meet basic needs
	  • Demonstrate empathy, respect, and warmth
	2. **Verify** readiness to proceed
	  • Ensure student is emotionally stable and able to solve problems
	3. **Identify and prioritize** crisis problems
	  • Ask for crisis story (do not press for details)
	  • Assess lethality. Physical and safety needs come first
	  • Identify personal and social problem-solving resources
		• Primary purpose is to restore immediate coping
		• Provides physical and psychological safety
		• Provides emotional support to contain distress
		• Identifies problems and supports adapting coping
		• Secondary triage identifies those who may need more intensive supports
		• Links individuals to resources

(continued)

TABLE 2.1

THE PREPaRE MODEL: LEVELS OF MULTITIERED CRISIS INTERVENTIONS *(continued)*		
Intervention	**Intervention Steps/Phases**	**Goal**
	4. **Address** crisis problems • Ask, facilitate, then propose solutions (empower survivors) • Determine level of lethality • Determine how directive to be 5. **Evaluate** and conclude • Ensure movement toward crisis resolution	
Tier 3/Indicated/Tertiary		
Psychotherapeutic interventions	1. Identification of severe/long-lasting trauma reactions 2. Link to specialized mental health interventions (e.g., cognitive behavioral approaches, trauma-focused therapies, systematic desensitization, wraparound and/or systems of care)	• Immediate stabilization followed by short- and long-term supports to help address trauma reactions • May need to consult with and refer to professionals outside of the school setting

SELECT BIBLIOGRAPHY

Brock, S. E., & Jimerson, S. R. (Eds). (2012). *Best practices in school crisis prevention and intervention* (2nd Ed.). Bethesda, MD: National Association of School Psychologists.
This edited book covers various crisis-related topics: promoting resiliency; building prosocial skills; violence and bullying prevention; suicide prevention through postvention; crisis preparedness through recovery; legal and ethical issues; and responding to specific crises.

Brock, S. E., Nickerson, A. B., Reeves, M. A., Jimerson, S. R., Lieberman, R. A., & Feinberg, T. A. (2009). *School crisis prevention & intervention: The PREPaRE model.* Bethesda, MD: National Association of School Psychologists.
This book provides a comprehensive overview of the NASP PREPaRE model. Comprehensive safety planning; how to establish safety and crisis response teams and plans; how to provide multitiered crisis interventions; and special considerations such as media, technology, and students with special needs are included. Note: Second edition of the book is to be released in 2015.

Cowan, K. C., Vaillancourt, K., Rossen, E., & Pollitt, K. (2013). *A framework for safe and successful schools* [Brief]. Bethesda, MD: National Association of School Psychologists. Retrieved from http://www

.nasponline.org/resources/handouts/Framework_for_Safe_and_Successful_School_Environments.pdf
This joint statement provides a framework for improving school safety and increasing access to mental health supports. It advocates for a school-wide, integrated approach to school climate, safety, and learning that facilitates interprofessional collaboration and builds on a multitiered system of supports.

NASP PREPaRE. Retrieved from http://www.nasponline.org/prepare/index.aspx

National Association of School Psychologists (NASP). *Safety and crisis resources.* Retrieved from http://www.nasponline.org/resources/crisis_safety/index.aspx
This website has numerous resources to help schools prepare for and respond to a crisis. Many ready-made handouts are also available that can be immediately disseminated or adapted.

NCTSN—Psychological First Aid. Retrieved from http://www.nctsn.org/content/psychological-first-aid
This website provides resources to help individuals cope with a traumatic event. Resources for parents, schools, educators, professionals, military children, and parents are also available.

Reeves, M., Kanan, L., & Plog, A. (2010). *Comprehensive planning for safe learning environments: A school professional's guide to integrating physical and psychological safety—*

Prevention through recovery. New York, NY: Routledge.
This book provides guidance on how to establish safe learning environments using a multitiered framework that balances physical and psychological safety. Specific examples are integrated throughout.

The National Child Traumatic Stress Network (NCTSN) (2014). Retrieved from http://www.nctsn.org

REFERENCES

American Psychological Association (APA). (2013). *Diagnostic and statistical manual of mental disorder.* Arlington, VA: American Psychological Association.

Billings A. G., & Moos R. H., (1984). Coping, stress, and social resources among adults with unipolar depression. *Journal of Personality and Social Psychology, 46*(4), 877–891.

Brock, S. E. (2011). *Crisis intervention and recovery: The roles of school-based mental health professionals* (2nd ed.). Bethesda, MD: National Association of School Psychologists.

Brock, S. E., Reeves, M. L., & Nickerson, A. (2014). Best practice in school crisis intervention. In A. Thomas & J. Grimes (Eds.), *Best practices in school psychology* (6th ed., pp. 211–230). Bethesda, MD: National Association of School Psychologists.

Brock, S. E., Nickerson, A. B., Reeves, M. A., Jimerson, S. R., Lieberman, R. A, & Feinberg, T. A. (2009). *School crisis prevention & intervention: The PREPaRE model.* Bethesda, MD: National Association of School Psychologists.

Center for Effective Collaboration and Practice. (2014). *Providing intensive interventions to troubled students.* Retrieved from http://cecp.air.org/guide/actionguide/Chapter_4.asp

Charuvastra, A., & Cloitre, M. (2008). Social bonds and posttraumatic stress disorder. *Annual Review of Psychology, 59,* 301–328.

Cohen, R., Kincaid, D., & Childs, K. E. (2007). Measuring school-wide positive behavior support implementation: Development and validation of the benchmarks of quality. *Journal of Positive Behavior Interventions, 9*(4), 203–213. doi:10.1177/1098300 7070090040301

Collaborative for Academic, Social, and Emotional Learning (CASEL). (2008). *Social and emotional learning and student benefits: Implications for the safe schools/healthy students core elements.* Retrieved from http://www.promoteprevent.org/sites/www.promoteprevent.org/files/resources/SELbenefits.pdf

Cowan, K. C., Vaillancourt, K., Rossen, E., & Pollitt, K. (2013). *A framework for safe and successful schools* [Brief]. Bethesda, MD: National Association of School Psychologists. Retrieved from http://www.nasponline.org/resources/handouts/Framework_for_Safe_and_SuccessfulSchool_Environments.pdf

Durlak, J. A., Weissberg, R. P., Dymnicki, A. B., Taylor, R. D., & Schellinger, K. B. (2011). The impact of enhancing students' social and emotional learning: A meta-analysis of school-based universal interventions. *Child Development, 82*(1), 405–432.

Foa, E. B., Zinbarg, R., & Rothbaum, B. O. (1992). Uncontrollability and unpredictability in post-traumatic stress disorder: An animal model. *Psychological Bulletin, 112*(2), 218–238.

Kronenberg, M. E., Hansel, T. C., Brennan, A. M., Osofsky, H. J., Osofsky, J. D., & Lawrason, B. (2010). Children of Katrina: Lessons learned about postdisaster symptoms and recovery patterns. *Child Development, 81*(4), 1241–1259.

National Center on Response to Intervention. (2010). *Essential components of RTI—A closer look at response to intervention.* Washington, DC: U.S. Department of Education, Office of Special Education Programs, National Center on Response to Intervention. Retrieved from http://www.rti4success.org/sites/default/files/rtiessentialcomponents_042710.pdf

OSEP Technical Assistance Center on Positive Behavioral Interventions and Support. (2014). *School-wide PBIS.* Retrieved from http://www.pbis.org/school/default.aspx

Reeves, M. L., Conolly-Wilson, C., Pesce, R., Lazzaro, B., & Brock, S. (2012). Preparing for the comprehensive school crisis response. In S. Brock & S. Jimerson (Eds.), *Best practices in school crisis prevention & intervention* (2nd Ed.). Bethesda, MD: National Association of School Psychologists.

Reeves, M. L., Kanan, L., & Plog, A. (2010). Comprehensive planning for safe learning environments: *A school professional's guide to integrating physical and psychological safety—Prevention through recovery.* New York, NY: Routledge.

Reeves, M. L., Nickerson, Conolly-Wilson, C., Susan, M., Lazzaro, Jimerson, S., & Pesce, R. (2011). *PREPaRE: Crisis prevention and preparedness—Comprehensive school safety planning* (2nd Ed.). Bethesda, MD: National Association of School Psychologists.

Saylor, C. F., Belter, R., & Stokes, S. J. (1997). Children and families coping with disaster. In S. Wolchik & I. N. Sandler (Eds.), *Handbook of children's coping: Linking theory and intervention* (pp. 361–383). New York, NY: Plenum.

Schneider, T., Walker, H., & Sprague, J. (2000). *Safe school design: A handbook for educational leaders: Applying the principles of crime prevention through environmental design.* Eugene, OR: ERIC Clearinghouse on Educational Management.

Sorensen, S., Hayes, J., & Atlas, R. (2008). Understanding CPTED and situational crime prevention. In R. I. Atlas (Ed.), *21st century security and CPTED: Designing for critical infrastructure protection and crime prevention* (pp. 53–78). Boca Raton, FL: Auerbach Publications.

Sprague, J. R., & Horner, R. H. (2012). School-wide positive behavioral interventions and supports. In S. R. Jimerson, A. B. Nickerson, M. J. Mayer, & M. J. Furlong (Eds.), *Handbook of school violence and school safety: International research and practice* (2nd Ed., pp. 447–462). Mahwah, NJ: Lawrence Erlbaum.

Sprague, J. R., & Walker, H. M. (2005). *Safe and healthy schools: Practical prevention strategies.* New York, NY: Guilford Press.

U.S. Department of Education (DOE). (2009). *Overview of prevention-mitigation session.* Washington, DC: Author. Retrieved from http://www.rems.ed.gov/docs/repository/00000369.pdf

U.S. Department of Education (DOE). (2013). *Guide for developing high-quality school emergency operations plans.* Washington, DC: Author. Retrieved from http://www2.ed.gov/admins/lead/safety/emergencyplan/index.html

U.S. Department of Homeland Security. (2013). *K–12 school security checklist.* Washington, DC: Author. Retrieved from https://www.illinois.gov/ready/SiteCollectionDocuments/K–12SchoolSecurityPracticesChecklist.pdf

Evidence-Based Interventions to Support Youth Following Natural Disasters: Evidence-Based Principles and Practices

Shane R. Jimerson, Jacqueline A. Brown, and Tyler L. Renshaw

OVERVIEW

With an average of 390 occurrences each year during the past decade, most days a natural disaster (e.g., earthquake, hurricane, typhoon, wildfire, windstorm, drought, tsunami, tornado, flood, landslide, volcanic eruption) occurs somewhere in the world (Guha-Sapir, Hoyois, & Below, 2013). The Centre for Research on the Epidemiology of Disasters (CRED) maintains an Emergency Events Database (EM-DAT) that includes natural disaster events meeting at least one of the following criteria: 10 or more people reported killed; 100 or more people reported affected; declaration of a state of emergency; or a call for international assistance (CRED, 2014). Around the world, there were 5,128 natural disasters that affected human lives between 2000 and 2012 (Guha-Sapir et al., 2013). Furthermore, the scope and effects of natural disasters on humankind are vast, with estimates of approximately 3.5 billion people affected on all continents between 1991 and 2005 (International Strategy for Disaster Reduction [ISDR], 2006), impacting approximately 257 million people each year on average between 2000 and 2012 (Guha-Sapir et al., 2013). Flooding is the most frequent natural disaster (accounting for 31% of the events) and windstorms (e.g., hurricanes/typhoons, tornadoes) are also common (27%); whereas earthquakes, droughts, landslides, and wildfires occur relatively less frequently and represent successively fewer incidence rates (9%, 8%, 5%, and 3%, respectively). Windstorms, earthquakes, and tsunamis are the most deadly natural disasters, killing more than 625,000 persons around the world between 1991 and 2005 (ISDR, 2006).

Natural disasters often have extensive effects on the social/emotional, behavioral, and mental health of children and adults within the communities struck by natural disasters. There are also significant financial costs associated with natural disasters; for instance, in the United States, damage and related costs resulting from natural disasters in 2012 alone exceeded US$110 billion (National Climatic Data Center, 2012). Given that natural disasters have such adverse effects on survivors, preparation to support students and their families following such events is an important responsibility of schools.

Response efforts (e.g., local, national, international) to provide support for affected persons in the aftermath of natural disasters are particularly complicated given the array of ramifications for children and families in the affected communities. For instance, natural disasters often destroy community infrastructures essential to the provision of basic safety and services (e.g., water, electricity, food). Natural disasters often displace residents, with fatalities and casualties frequently in the hundreds or even thousands, further exacerbating individuals' stress and complicating the delivery of support services. Schools in the impact zone and surrounding areas are important settings for children and families affected by natural disasters, as they offer an organization within the community that can facilitate the maintenance of routines, recovery, and support delivery in the aftermath of traumatic events. During the past two decades, much has been learned about how children respond to natural disasters and what mental health professionals can do to facilitate the rebuilding and healing process to support children, adults, families, and schools (e.g., Kar, 2009). Thus, this chapter briefly outlines the effects of natural disasters on children and provides an overview of strategies for supporting children and adolescents following traumatic events.

ETIOLOGY AND FACTORS CONTRIBUTING TO NATURAL DISASTERS

Persons who experience a natural disaster are at increased risk for the likelihood of posttraumatic stress disorder (PTSD) symptoms (National Center for PTSD, 2000). PTSD is characterized as an anxiety reaction that emerges after witnessing or experiencing a traumatic event. Common symptoms include persistent frightening thoughts and memories, emotional numbness, or increased arousal, such as being easily startled or irritable (see Nickerson, Reeves, Brock, & Jimerson, 2009, for further information pertaining to the identifying, assessing, and treating PTSD at school). As natural disasters vary, so too will the adaptations of persons following such events. The individual's personal experience and the magnitude of human damage are associated with the likelihood of PTSD or related symptoms (Neria, Nandi, & Galea, 2008). The following section provides an overview of issues important in preparing for and responding to all types of natural disasters: relocation, family reactions and support, and coping styles.

Relocation. The frequent need for disaster survivors to relocate creates unique crises of their own. In addition to initial disaster effects (e.g., psychological and physical distress, disruption of health care), relocated families experience significant changes in their social environment, routines, sense of familiarity, and living conditions (Uscher-Pines, 2009). To facilitate relocation following natural disasters, it is recommended that several strategies can be helpful, including promoting safety and security (e.g., physical safety, water, food, shelter) and normalcy (e.g., reestablishing routines, facilitating family and community personal networks) among survivors, encouraging proactive measures to assist in coping with losses and change (e.g., connecting family members, facilitating access to support professionals), and assisting in promoting a sense of community among relocated survivors (e.g., highlighting relevant community events, facilitating communications and activities among those who have been relocated). To help facilitate the relocation process for adults, it has been suggested that parents enroll their children in school as soon as possible, facilitating maintenance of daily routines and providing opportunities for the formation of supportive peer and teacher relationships (Canter, Klotz, & Feinberg, 2005).

Parents' Reactions and Family Support. Parental reactions and family support following a natural disaster are important considerations in facilitating children's coping. Proctor and colleagues (2007) addressed the effects of an earthquake on 117 families with children in the 4- to 5-year age range. Results of analyses of pre- and postearthquake observations revealed that maternal stress significantly predicted persistent distress of girls, and that parental behavior before the earthquake moderated the relationship between the impact of the earthquake and child distress. Given that youth look to significant adults in their lives for guidance on how to manage their reactions after traumatic events, it is vital that parents provide support to their children and model adaptive behavior.

Emotional Reactivity. Preliminary findings suggest that youth with high levels of trait anxiety or negative affectivity are at increased risk of developing PTSD symptoms following a natural disaster (Weems et al., 2007). Furthermore, predisaster trait anxiety has been shown to predict postdisaster generalized anxiety disorder and depressive symptoms. In another study promoting similar conclusions, findings revealed that youth with a preexisting anxiety disorder before a major earthquake were at greater risk (relative to students without a preexisting anxiety disorder) of developing PTSD symptoms after the traumatic event (Asarnow et al., 1999).

Coping Styles. Short-term coping responses influence the process of long-term adaptations to traumatic events. Research by Zhang et al. (2010) indicates that children who exhibited a negative coping style (i.e., externalizing, internalizing, and avoidant coping strategies) before a disaster displayed increased symptoms of PTSD and other mental health problems following natural disasters. Findings from the Zhang et al. (2010) study also indicate that youth who were more directly exposed and affected by a natural disaster (i.e., observed significantly more deaths or incurred more loss in their families) were more likely to exhibit a negative coping style than students who were less directly affected. In related research, Cryder, Kilmer, Tedeschi, and Calhoun (2006) found that children's competency beliefs were significantly related to indicators of positive change experienced as a result of major natural disaster. This finding points to the importance of positive beliefs about one's competencies and future, which may influence how negatively affected youth are by the traumatic event and, in turn, how positively they cope with the crisis. Thus, in addition to providing positive social support for the youth in their care, teachers and parents would also do well to teach and model positive coping strategies to youth pre-, mid-, and postcrisis.

EVIDENCE-BASED INTERVENTIONS AND EMPIRICAL SUPPORT FOR NATURAL DISASTERS

La Greca (2008) highlighted three phases of recovery following natural disasters and offers evidence-based interventions associated with each phase. These include the *postimpact phase, short-term recovery and reconstruction phase*, and the *long-term*

recovery phase. The *postimpact phase* focuses on the immediate aftermath during the first few weeks following a natural disaster, during which brief psychological interventions are implemented to reduce or prevent psychological distress. The *short-term recovery and reconstruction phase* occurs after the first few weeks through several months or up to a year postdisaster and focuses on reducing or preventing the development of enduring psychological stressors and improving overall adaptive functioning. Finally, the *long-term recovery phase* lasts several months/ years and focuses on providing treatment to youth experiencing enduring chronic stress reactions.

La Greca (2008) describes evidence-based interventions that are used within each of these three phases of recovery. One evidence-based intervention used during the *postimpact phase* is psychological first aid (PFA; Ruzek et al., 2007). PFA aims to decrease initial distress following a disaster and supports both short- and long-term adaptive functioning through eight core helping actions, which are aimed at promoting a sense of safety, connectedness, hope, and self- and community efficacy. PFA is appropriate for individuals from various cultural backgrounds and developmental levels (Ruzek et al., 2007) and is a promising evidence-based approach as one component of a comprehensive intervention following a natural disaster (La Greca, 2008).

During the *short-term recovery phase*, psychoeducation, which includes educating parents about typical psychological reactions to disasters, in combination with cognitive behavioral therapy (CBT), has been shown to be an effective intervention (Wolmer, Laor, Dedeoglu, Siev, & Yazgan, 2005). For example, the school reactivation program (Wolmer, Laor, & Yazgan, 2003; Wolmer et al., 2005), which combines psychoeducation and CBT, significantly reduced rates of PTSD in a sample of 202 Israeli children in first through fifth grades (56% girls, 44% boys) from 32% pretreatment to 17% posttreatment, with posttreatment levels being similar to children in unaffected areas. Finally, during the *long-term recovery phase*, La Greca (2008) indicated that exposure-based CBT interventions were effective for treating more severe PTSD symptoms (e.g., March, Amaya-Jackson, Murray, & Schulte, 1998). For example, following the implementation of multi-modality trauma treatment (MMTT), children demonstrated a significant improvement on clinician-reported PTSD symptoms from pre- to postintervention, with these symptoms being maintained after 6 months (March et al., 1998). MMTT is a CBT group intervention based on emotional processing theory that embodies 18 weekly sessions, with each session including a statement of goals, review of the previous session, new information, therapist-assisted strategies and practice, and homework for the subsequent week. Examples of topics addressed in each session include providing information about PTSD, anxiety management, progressive muscle relaxation, anger, and exposure and response prevention. March and colleagues (1998) used this intervention within a single-case multiple baseline design with 17 youths in grades 4 through 9 who experienced PTSD after a single traumatic incident.

Another evidence-based treatment that is effective for long-term recovery is trauma-focused CBT (TF-CBT; Cohen, Mannarino, & Deblinger, 2010). TF-CBT is designed to decrease the effects of trauma symptoms, improve emotional and physical functioning, and reduce maladaptive functioning following a natural disaster. Cultural adaptations of TF-CBT materials are available for Native American and Latino children and treatment materials are printed in various languages (e.g., Spanish, German, and Dutch). TF-CBT can be adapted for the school setting (Jaycox et al., 2010). Jaycox and colleagues reported that children provided with TF-CBT following Hurricane Katrina showed modestly better improvement in PTSD symptoms (p = .05) than those provided with cognitive behavioral intervention for trauma in schools (CBITS; p = .24; Jaycox, 2003). CBITS is similar to TF-CBT in that it includes CBT through psychoeducation, relaxation skills, affective modulation skills, cognitive coping skills, and trauma narratives. Unlike TF-CBT, which provides conjoint parent and child sessions, CBITS is provided only to children using a group format. Another intervention that can be used to support bereaved youth within the school setting is the Mourning Child Grief Curriculum (MCGC) by Lehmann, Jimerson, and Gaasch (2001a), an effective group curriculum for bereaved teens (Jimerson & Kaufman, 2002). MCGC has been revised multiple times based on the experiences and feedback of group members and the results of pre–post behaviors/emotions reported by parents and youth. Specific details about this curriculum are provided

later in the "How to: A Guide to the Implementation of Interventions for Natural Disaster" section of this chapter.

An evidence-based approach commonly used in schools to both prepare for and respond to crises, such as natural disasters, is the PREPaRE model (Brock et al., 2009). This model provides a useful framework for developing and coordinating crisis prevention and response through five key stages: **P**reventing and preparing for crisis events, **R**eaffirming physical health and safety, **E**valuating psychological trauma, **P**roviding interventions and **R**esponding to the event, and **E**xamining the effectiveness of crisis prevention and response (Brock et al., 2009). Specific strategies targeted to include evaluating emotional relationships with the victims and physical proximity to the event, as well as personal vulnerability factors, providing psychoeducation to parents, and supporting students at the individual, group, and school-wide levels. Beyond PREPaRE, several other interventions have been shown to effectively decrease youths' distress and improve their well-being postcrisis. Furthermore, Mindfulness-Based Stress Reduction (MBSR; see "How to: A Guide to the Implementation of Interventions for Natural Disaster" section for a detailed description) is effective for addressing crisis-related symptoms. Biegel, Brown, Shapiro, and Schubert (2009) found that, when compared to a control group, adolescents receiving MBSR self-reported fewer symptoms of anxiety, depression, and somatic distress over a 5-month period.

HOW TO: A GUIDE TO THE IMPLEMENTATION OF INTERVENTIONS FOR NATURAL DISASTERS

The following section summarizes three evidence-based approaches to support children in the aftermath of a potentially traumatic event, such as a natural disaster: TF-CBT, MBSR, and the Mourning Child Grief Support Curriculum.

Trauma-Focused Cognitive Behavioral Therapy

The information in this section on TF-CBT is grounded in the work of Cohen, Mannarino, and Deblinger (2006) and Cohen et al. (2010).

TF-CBT is typically completed in 8 to 20 sessions, depending on the needs of each child and family, and the individual's ability to master each component of the treatment. Cohen and colleagues recommended that therapists implementing TF-CBT should undergo training in child development, experience assessing children and adolescents with a wide range of psychiatric disorders, and have prior training in other treatment approaches (e.g., family systems, CBT, play therapies). There are five primary goals of TF-CBT (Cohen et al., 2010): (a) master skills necessary to manage stress and improve affective, behavioral, and cognitive regulation; (b) include parents/caretakers in treatment; (c) increase the ability to cope with trauma reminders and decrease avoidance through gradual exposure; (d) use affective and cognitive processing to make meaning out of and contextualize traumatic experiences; and (e) enrich future development. The components of TF-CBT are summarized by the acronym PRACTICE: Psychoeducation and Parenting Skills, Relaxation Skills, Affective modulation, Cognitive Coping and Processing, Trauma Narrative, In Vivo Mastery of Trauma Reminders, Conjoint child–parent sessions, and Enhance Future Safety and Development (Cohen, 2014). Gradual exposure is defined as gradually increasing the intensity and duration of the child's exposure to reminders of the trauma in each sequential TF-CBT treatment component (Cohen et al., 2010) and is typically conducted through talking, writing, and other creative means that enable children and parents to cope with trauma reminders and decrease avoidant thoughts, feelings, and reminders of the traumatic event. Specific examples of how gradual exposure is integrated into the TF-CBT model are included in the sections that follow.

Psychoeducation. The therapist initially provides psychoeducation to families at the outset of treatment and continues to educate them throughout the process. At the beginning, it is important to inform families about the nature of traumatic experiences (e.g., cause, common reactions, number affected) and normalize symptoms that parents and children may be experiencing as a result of the trauma. For example, if a child exhibited a high level of trauma symptoms in the aftermath of an earthquake, it would be helpful to inform parents that (a) 6 months following an earthquake, 78% of children surveyed experienced mild to severe symptoms of PTSD (Kolaitis et al., 2003); (b) mental health symptoms such as depression, anxiety, and difficulty sleeping and eating are all common reactions; and (c) due to the lack of predictability of earthquakes, survivors may have difficulty coping and adjusting. One way to inform children about common reactions is through children's books. Although not specific to natural disasters, "A Terrible Thing Happened" by Margaret Holmes addresses common symptoms of children who have experienced a traumatic event. Furthermore, therapists should also provide psychoeducation about PTSD and its symptoms, TF-CBT and its strong empirical support, and strategies to manage current symptoms. Gradual exposure is implemented by referring to the traumatic experience by name and event (e.g., mother died from the earthquake) instead of using a euphemism (e.g., mother is at rest after the earthquake) to prevent avoidance.

Parenting Skills. Throughout the TF-CBT process, parents are viewed as pivotal change agents. This component of the process enables parents to address their own traumatic reactions, provides them with interventions similar to those being provided to their children, helps them reinforce and practice what their children are learning in treatment, and allows them to better understand their children's emotional response to treatment. Parents are taught how to engage in the following positive parenting practices by using various methods such as role-playing and modeling: (a) *child praise*—be specific, consistent, and provide praise immediately after the desired behavior has occurred; (b) *selective attention*—reinforce desired behaviors by praising positive behaviors and ignoring negative ones (e.g., temper tantrums); (c) *time-out*—interrupt the negative behavior by temporarily removing the child from the situation for a brief time, enabling the child to regain control and withdrawing adult attention; and (d) *contingency reinforcement programs*—identify desirable target behaviors and use behavioral charts to monitor and consistently reward the child for engaging in the desirable behavior. Parents are also reminded that maintaining normal routines and consistent expectations following the traumatic experience is essential to fostering youths' adaptive functioning posttrauma.

Relaxation Skills. It is common for children who have experienced trauma to exhibit accompanying psychophysiological symptoms (e.g., anxiety, sleep problems, appetite disturbance, headaches; Baggerly & Exum, 2008). Relaxation strategies are effective at treating physical symptoms, while simultaneously allowing the child to engage in positive activities and effective emotional self-regulation. Specific relaxation strategies taught include focused breathing, mindfulness, and meditation, as well as progressive muscle relaxation. Cohen et al. (2006) recommend that a relaxation plan be developed for both children and their parents, with each individual developing various relaxation strategies for scenarios where he or she experiences reminders of the trauma (e.g., school and morning routine). For example, if an earthquake occurred when the child was in math class, with his or her resulting symptoms being a stomachache and heightened anxiety whenever he or she walks by or enters his or her math class, his or her relaxation plan may include first engaging in belly breathing, then introducing progressive muscle relaxation, followed by desensitization techniques.

Affective Modulation. This component of TF-CBT enables children to practice identifying and expressing their feelings in a safe setting while building trust and therapeutic rapport with the therapist. Various tools can be used in affective modulation such as games, photographs of faces, and drawings to help children better express and understand their feelings. For example, Cohen and colleagues (2006) suggest that therapists create feeling wheels (e.g., piece of paper with a circle, with sections indicated like a pie, with emotions written in each section, and use either a spinning object in the center of the circle or dice to select the emotion for further discussion) or card games to enable the children to express a range of emotions. Parental sessions are provided to allow parents an opportunity to express their own feelings about what happened and learn how to support, understand, and encourage their children's expressions of feelings. Specific affective modulation skills are then introduced to help children engage in emotional self-regulation. These skills include: (a) *thought interruption and positive imagery*—redirect attention from upsetting thoughts and refocus it on a positive thought or mental image; (b) *positive self-talk*—recognize and verbalize how they are coping well; (c) *problem solving*—teach children how to describe the problem, identify solutions, consider likely outcomes, pick a solution, evaluate their choice, and reflect on the learning process; (d) *social skills*—encourage parents to enroll their children in a social skills group and reinforce skills learned; (e) *ensuring safety*—enable the children to practice personal safety skills that involve the parents and other community resources; and (f) *managing affective states*—teach them how to recognize when they are starting to feel distressed, select an affective modulation skill (i.e., skills that enable children to effectively express and manage their feelings; Cohen et al., 2006), such as self-talk, and develop plans for each distressing situation. Generalized exposure is used within this component of TF-CBT by having children identify and practice strategies that enable them to deal with the negative affect related to reminders of the traumatic event.

Cognitive Coping. Children are taught affective modulation skills during this component of the process, which focuses on helping them understand the connection among thoughts, feelings, and behaviors. More specifically, children are taught to examine their negative-thinking patterns to verify whether their thoughts are accurate, helpful, and make them feel better. For example, this stage often includes the use of a cognitive triangle, where children identify their feelings, distinguish between their feelings and thoughts, and generate additional thoughts that are more accurate and helpful. Furthermore, they are provided with support in changing their dysfunctional thoughts about everyday and traumatic events, which often includes discussing scenarios and having children change their feelings by brainstorming different ways of thinking about the situation. Children are also taught to identify specific maladaptive thinking patterns such as "Yes or No Yasmine" (the glass is either half full or half empty with nothing in between).

Trauma Narrative and Cognitive Processing. During several sessions, children are taught to describe in more detail what happened before, during, and after the traumatic event, along with their associated thoughts and feelings, to enable them to process negative emotions associated with the event. This process is referred to as "developing a trauma narrative." Before starting the trauma narrative, it is essential that the therapist provide children and their parents with information about the process and a rationale for why it is important to talk about what happened during the traumatic event. The trauma narrative typically involves writing down what happened in the form of a story, poem, or song that children can share with their parents. Within the narrative, children are asked to include their memories, thoughts, and feelings of what happened, the worst moment/memory of the traumatic event, as well as how they have grown since the event, and advice they would give another child. Once children create their narrative and have spoken to a greater extent about what they experienced, the therapist helps them to identify, explore, and correct inaccurate thoughts using cognitive processing, which typically involves addressing inaccurate cognitions and replacing them with more helpful thoughts.

In Vivo Mastery of Trauma Reminders. Along with the trauma narrative, children may require in vivo exposure and mastery to deal with reminders of the trauma. For example, if a tornado occurs during English class, a child may be unwilling to return to this particular class due to reminders of the event. Consequently, in vivo exposure enables the child to confront his or her fears gradually instead of avoiding English class. The student is first required to identify the feared situation (i.e., a tornado happened during English class), with a specific plan being made to help the student feel more comfortable in English class. If the child is unable to attend English class, the goal may be to first have the student stand outside the class door for 5 minutes, then step inside the classroom, and gradually increase the time spent in each stage. The child should also be praised, reassured, and rewarded for having achieved each goal.

Conjoint Child–Parent Sessions. This final intervention component involves having parents meet with a therapist to review educational information, review the trauma narrative, and engage in communication to increase children's comfort talking to their parents about their traumatic experience. The format for 1-hour sessions typically includes having the therapist meet with the child for the first 15 minutes, the parents for the second 15 minutes, and both the child and parents for the remaining 30 minutes. Before these sessions, the parents will have already heard the trauma narrative during an individual session with the therapist to ensure they are ready to hear it directly from their child. After the child reads the narrative to the parents, the parents are encouraged to praise him or her for his or her strength in writing and sharing the narrative. The child also has the opportunity to address issues of concern based on a previously prepared list, with his or her parents being given the opportunity to ask questions. Other activities may be included in these conjoint sessions, such as conflict avoidance, attributions regarding the traumatic experience, and safety planning, which may be particularly important for children who are currently exposed to dangerous situations (e.g., community violence; Cohen et al., 2010). The therapist facilitates conversations between the child and his or her parents to ensure effective communication and praises them for their successful work.

Mindfulness-Based Stress Reduction

According to Stahl and Goldstein (2010), mindfulness is defined as "being fully aware of whatever is happening in the present moment, without filters or the lens of judgment" (p. 15). There are various mindfulness strategies that are supported empirically, with three primary interventions being MBSR, Mindfulness-Based Cognitive Therapy, and Acceptance and Commitment Therapy (Burke, 2010). This section of the chapter will describe components of MBSR. MBSR typically includes weekly group sessions, home practice, as well as formal exercises (e.g., body scan, sitting, moving, walking meditations), and informal exercises (e.g., bringing mindful awareness to daily activities such as eating). Group sessions include psychoeducation about mindfulness, guided meditations, and discussions about these experiences (Burke, 2010). Although the majority of the research thus far has focused on MBSR with adults, more recent studies have adapted MBSR to be used with teens, and have found effective outcomes (e.g., Burke, 2010). Specific adaptations include reducing the length of home-based mindfulness practices from 45 minutes to 20 to 35 minutes and having psychoeducation focus on adolescent issues related to stress and behavior (e.g., self-image, life transitions, self-harming behaviors, communication, and interpersonal relationships; Biegel et al., 2009). Adolescent participants enrolled in Biegel and colleagues' 8-week (2 hours per week) MBSR treatment program also received a workbook in addition to the information discussed during group sessions and a CD with audio files for guided sitting and body scan meditations that can be performed at home. A helpful MBSR workbook that resulted from this study is *The Stress Reduction Workbook for Teens* (Biegel, 2009), which serves as a guide for conducting MBSR with adolescents.

Mindfulness-based interventions can be used for crisis situations, such as natural disasters, and implemented within the school setting for students with a range of needs (Renshaw, 2012). Renshaw (2012) provides a detailed description of how mindfulness strategies can be implemented at the school-wide, small-group, and individual level within the school setting following a crisis. At the school-wide level, all students can benefit from developing basic mindfulness skills following a crisis to provide PFA to the student population. These basic mindfulness skills may include training in breathing meditation, mindful check-in practices, and providing students with the opportunity to engage in these practices for as many as 10 minutes each day. For example, at the elementary school level, teachers may lead a 3-minute breathing meditation session at the beginning of the day and have students engage in mindful check-in—which provides students with a couple minutes to identify how they are feeling physically, emotionally, and mentally in the present moment—after lunch or before leaving school. At the small-group level, students experiencing distress following a crisis, such as a natural disaster, may be provided with small-group counseling from a mental health practitioner for 20 to 50 minutes, one to two times per week, with the goal of further enhancing their mindfulness skills and improving their overall well-being. Such counseling may involve a combination of mindfulness-based interventions, including breathing, body scan (i.e., directing one's awareness to each area of the body), and walking meditations, as well as mindful check-in practices. At the individual level, students experiencing significant levels of emotional, social, physical, and behavioral distress following a natural disaster and who have not responded to small-group intervention may require more intensive mindfulness-based therapies that focus on the development and generalization of mindfulness skills to address individual symptoms and problems.

Mourning Child Grief Support Group Curriculum

The following is a brief step-by-step description of the sessions of the Mourning Child Grief Support Group Curriculum (Lehmann et al., 2001a; Lehmann, Jimerson, & Gaasch, 2001b). This curriculum includes 10 sessions of 90 minutes each. For the most part, each session follows a standard format, including the following core elements: an opening, centering imagery, check-in, introduction to the emphasis of the session, main activities and supplementary activities, a break, and closing. Although a thorough presentation of the sessions and activities within the Mourning Child Grief Support Group Curriculum is beyond the scope of this brief chapter, all details are delineated in the curriculum materials (Lehmann et al., 2001a, 2001b).

Session 1: Getting to Know the Child and Gathering Information. The first meeting includes the caregiver and youth to discuss presenting concerns and general information that either individual would like to share. Gathering baseline information at this session with all participants is valuable because it affords an opportunity to later explore the changes in the students' adjustment.

Session 2: Telling My Story. This session is the first time the group meets together. The purpose of this session is to give the youth an opportunity to share their stories and begin to get to know each other. During this session, the group will create a joint "code of safety." Included in this code of safety is the development of an escape plan for each youth so that the group experience does not re-victimize them by forcing them to share things they do not want to share, or forcing them to hear graphic details of others' stories that may be disturbing.

Session 3: Exploring Death. This session has a dual purpose. First, it is intended to give youth a forum to talk about death. Death is a taboo topic in our culture (Samuel, 2013), and because it is taboo, there are many fears and myths that surround it. Youth have most likely learned that there are some topics that are not to be talked about, including death. This session gives the youth an opportunity to ask questions and talk about things related to death they do not understand. The second purpose of the session is to teach youth death concepts. There is frequent misinformation about death in our culture, and it is pervasive in the media, fairy tales, movies, cartoons, and stories (Samuel, 2013). Television news presentations of death typically feature sensational details (e.g., the number of deaths, violent nature of the death) that do not help youth understand the complexity or likelihood of such events, or what could be done to prevent such events from happening in the future (Meyer, 2005). In this session, youth are taught the language that surrounds death, such as "dead," "funeral," "grief," and "cemetery," as well as concepts such as "every living thing dies."

Session 4: Identifying Changes. This session is intended to teach the concept of change as it relates to grief. This session presents the concepts of change in three ways. First, it teaches the children/teens that change is a constant, as we are surrounded by change in our everyday lives. Second, when a special person dies, there can be many changes that take place in the home and in the family. There will be role changes as family members attempt to fill the roles played by the special person who died. Mood changes in the home as well as a lack of structure in the daily routine may be present for a long time when a special person dies. The session affords youth an opportunity to identify and talk about many of the changes in their families since the death. Third, this session gives youth the opportunity to talk about how they have changed since the death of another person. Special emphasis is placed on teaching the common grief reactions that are likely to occur after a special person has died. Presenting this information helps youth to see that their reactions are normal and that others their age have similar experiences.

Session 5: Memories and Remembering. This session is dedicated to helping youth share memories of their special person. All youth are given time to show pictures or items of special meaning to them. Additionally, the session encourages youth to talk about memories they have of their special person and share them with other group members. Finally, the session ends with a remembrance ceremony in which the group remembers the special people.

Session 6: Identifying and Expressing Feelings. This session helps youth to identify and talk about the feelings they have experienced since the special person's death, as well as how they personally express these feelings. During the preceding weeks, the youth have learned the language of feelings to expand their vocabulary. Weekly check-ins are meant to encourage them to talk about how they feel from the start. By this session, in which they learn that their feelings are a legitimate part of one's grief experience, they should have a good "feeling" vocabulary.

Session 7: Exploring Unfinished Business. This session is intended to introduce children/teens to the concept of "unfinished business." Unfinished business is defined as any obstacle in one's grief process that prevents its normal progression. Unfinished business can take many forms (e.g., youth not having the opportunity to say "good-bye," being excluded from some or all of the funeral rituals, or blaming oneself for the death). Each one of these topic areas is addressed in the session. Group members in all age groups are also given the opportunity to write a note to their loved one expressing all of the sentiments that they were unable to say directly to the special person before his or her death.

Session 8: Coping With Feelings. The intent of this session is to help youth learn coping strategies that will help them manage their feelings of grief in healthy ways. Youth are taught several practical techniques that they can easily take with them after they leave the group. Included in this session is a discussion about the negative implications of not finding healthy ways of expressing and managing grief.

Session 9: Learning Self-Care and Support. This session is intended to teach youth the concept of self-care and stress its importance as they grieve. Special emphasis is placed on the significance of having a strong support system during the grieving process, and practical self-care techniques are discussed. Activities help youth to identify those who provide various kinds of support in their lives, as well as any holes in their support system that might need to be filled.

Session 10: Learning to Say Good-Bye. This session is designed to allow group members to say good-bye to each other as the group ends, and review the things they learned from the group experience. An important feature of this session is affirming youths' self-esteem.

CONCLUSION

This chapter provided an overview and discussion of issues associated with specific natural disasters, generalized issues associated with most natural disasters, and evidence-based principles and practices for supporting youth following a natural disaster. The extant literature emphasizes teaching effective coping strategies, fostering supportive relationships, and helping children process their emotions to facilitate healthy adjustment in the aftermath of a natural disaster. Collaboration between school, community, state/provincial, and national organizations and agencies is necessary to respond to the many needs of children, families, and communities in the wake of natural disasters. Healthy coping in the aftermath of a natural disaster takes considerable time; however, advanced preparation and planning will enhance the immediate response and facilitate subsequent coping and healing.

SELECT BIBLIOGRAPHY

Brock, S. E., Nickerson, A. B., Reeves, M. A., Jimerson, S. R., Lieberman, R. A., & Feinberg, T. A. (2009). *School crisis prevention and intervention: The PREPaRE Model*. Bethesda, MD: National Association of School Psychologists.
This resource specifically addresses preparedness, prevention, and intervention strategies focused on the school context.

Centre for Research on the Epidemiology of Disasters (CRED). (2014). *The International Disaster Database*. Brussels, Belgium: CRED. Retrieved from http://www.emdat.be/
This resource provides updated information regarding disasters that occur throughout the world each week. Relevant information is available through the database, as well as numerous publications and links to additional resources.

Cohen, J. A., Mannarino, A. P., & Beblinger, E. (2012). *Trauma-focused CBT for children and adolescents: Treatment applications*. New York, NY: Guilford.
This book is helpful for professionals who are preparing to implement trauma-focused cognitive-behavioral therapy (TF-CBT) in a range of contexts.

U.S. Department of Homeland Security and Federal Emergency Management Agency. (2014). *Disaster preparation resources for kids, parents, and educators*. Retrieved from www.ready.gov/kids
The information on this website is updated to include contemporary resources pertaining to the preparation, response, and intervention materials for children, families, and educators.

REFERENCES

Asarnow, J., Glynn, S., Pynoos, R. S., Nahum, J., Guthrie, D., Cantwell, D. P., & Franklin, B. (1999). When the earth stops shaking: Earthquake sequelae among children diagnosed for pre-earthquake psychopathology. *Journal of the American Academy of Child and Adolescent Psychiatry, 38*(8), 1016–1023.

Baggerly, J., & Exum, H. A. (2008). Counseling children after natural disasters: Guidance for family therapists. *The American Journal of Family Therapy, 36*, 79–93.

Biegel, G. M. (2009). *The stress reduction workbook for teens: Mindfulness skills to help you deal with stress*. Oakland, CA: New Harbinger Publications, Inc.

Biegel, G. M., Brown, K. W., Shapiro, S. L., & Schubert, C. M. (2009). Mindfulness-based stress reduction for the treatment of adolescent psychiatric outpatients: A randomized clinical trial. *Journal of Consulting and Clinical Psychology, 77*(5), 855–866.

Brock, S. E., Nickerson, A. B., Reeves, M. A., Jimerson, S. R., Lieberman, R., & Feinberg, T. (2009). *School crisis prevention and intervention: The PREPaRE model*. Bethesda, MD: National Association of School Psychologists.

Burke, C. A. (2010). Mindfulness-based approaches with children and adolescents: A preliminary review of current research in an emergent field. *Journal of Child and Families Studies, 19*, 133–144. doi:10.1007/s10826–009–9282-x

Canter, A., Klotz, M. B., & Feinberg, T. (2005). *New schools for students with disabilities: Tips for families who have been relocated*. Bethesda, MD: National

Association of School Psychologists. Retrieved from www.nasponline.org

Centre for Research on the Epidemiology of Disasters (CRED). (2014). *Emergency Events Database (EM-DAT) criteria*. Brussels, Belgium: CRED. Retrieved from http://www.emdat.be

Cohen, J. A. (2014). *Trauma-focused CBT for children and adolescents. The National Child Traumatic Stress Network*. Retrieved from http://www .protectchildren.psu.edu/sites/network/files/Cohen .pdf

Cohen, J. A., Mannarino, A. P., & Deblinger, E. (2006). *Treating trauma and traumatic grief in children and adolescents*. New York, NY: Guilford.

Cohen, J. A., Mannarino, A. P., & Deblinger, E. (2010). Trauma-focused cognitive-behavioral therapy for traumatized children. In J. R. Weisz & A. Kazdin (Eds.), *Evidence-based psychotherapies for children and adolescents* (2nd ed., pp. 295–311). New York, NY: Guilford.

Cryder, C. H., Kilmer, R. P., Tedeschi, R. G., & Calhoun, L. G. (2006). An exploratory study of posttraumatic growth in children following a natural disaster. *The American Journal of Orthopsychiatry, 76*(1), 65–69.

Guha-Sapir, D., Hoyois, P., & Below, R. (2013). *Annual disaster statistical review 2012: The numbers and trends*. Brussels, Belgium: CRED.

International Strategy for Disaster Reduction (ISDR). (2006). *Disaster statistics 1991–2005*. Retrieved from http://www.unisdr.org/disaster-statistics/ introduction.htm

Jaycox, L. H. (2003). *Cognitive-behavioral intervention for trauma in schools*. Longmont, CO: Sopris West Educational Services.

Jaycox, L. H., Cohen, J. A., Mannarino, A. P., Walker, D. W., Langley, A. K., Gegenheimer, K. L.,...Schonlau, M. (2010). Children's mental health care following Hurricane Katrina: A field trial of trauma-focused psychotherapies. *Journal of Traumatic Stress, 23*(2), 223–231.

Jimerson, S. R., & Kaufman, A. (2002, June). *Evaluation of grief support services for bereaved youth: An overview and update on the UCSB project LOSS national collaborative*. Paper presented at the 2002 National Symposium on Children's Grief Support, St. Louis, MO.

Kar, N. (2009). Psychological impact of disasters on children: Review of assessment and interventions. *World Journal of Pediatrics, 5*(1), 5–11.

Kolaitis, G., Kotsopoulos, J., Tsiantis, J., Haritaki, S., Rigizou, F., Zacharaki, L.,...Katerelos, P. (2003). Posttraumatic stress reactions among children following the Athens earthquake of September 1999. *European Child & Adolescent Psychiatry, 12*(6), 273–280.

La Greca, A. M. (2008). Interventions for posttraumatic stress in children and adolescents following natural disasters and acts of terrorism. In M. C. Roberts, D. Elkin, & R. Steele (Eds.), *Handbook of evidence-based therapies for children and adolescents* (pp. 137–157). New York, NY: Springer.

Lehmann, L., Jimerson, S. R., & Gaasch, A. (2001a). *Mourning child grief support group curriculum: Middle childhood edition*. New York, NY: Routledge, Taylor & Francis.

Lehmann, L., Jimerson, S. R., & Gaasch, A. (2001b). *Teens together grief support group curriculum: Adolescence edition*. New York, NY: Routledge, Taylor & Francis.

March, J. S., Amaya-Jackson, L., Murray, M. C., & Schulte, A. (1998). Cognitive-behavioral psychotherapy for children and adolescents with posttraumatic stress disorder after a single-incident stressor. *Journal of the American Academy of Child and Adolescent Psychiatry, 37*, 585–593. Retrieved from http://www.jaacap.com

Meyer, T. P. (2005). Media portrayals of death and dying. *The Forum, 31*(2), 3–4.

National Center for PTSD. (2000). *The September 1999 earthquake in Taiwan and post-traumatic stress. A National Center for PTSD fact sheet*. White River Junction, VT: Author. Retrieved from http//www.ncptsd.org

National Climatic Data Center. (2012). *Billion dollar weather/climate events*. Retrieved from http//www .ncdc.noaa.gov/billions

Neria, Y., Nandi, A., & Galea, S. (2008). Post-traumatic stress disorder following disasters: A systematic review. *Psychological Medicine, 38*(4), 467–480.

Nickerson, A. B., Reeves, M. A., Brock, S. E., & Jimerson, S. R. (2009). *Identifying, assessing, and treating post traumatic stress disorder (PTSD) at school*. New York, NY: Springer Science.

Proctor, L. J., Fauchier, A., Oliver, P. H., Ramos, M. C., Rios, M. A., & Margolin, G. (2007). Family context and young children's responses to earthquake. *Journal of Child Psychology and Psychiatry, and Allied Disciplines, 48*(9), 941–949.

Renshaw, T. (2012). Mindfulness-based practices for crisis prevention and intervention. In S. E. Brock & S. R. Jimerson (Eds.), *Best practices in school crisis prevention and intervention* (2nd ed., pp. 401–422). Bethesda, MD: National Association of School Psychologists.

Ruzek, J. I., Brymer, M. J., Jacobs, A. K., Layne, C. M., Vernberg, E. M., & Watson, P. J. (2007). Psychological first aid. *Journal of Mental Health Counseling, 29*, 17–49. Retrieved from http://www.amhca.org/news/journal.aspx

Samuel, L. R. (2013). *Death, American style: A cultural history of dying in America*. New York, NY: Rowman & Littlefield Publishers.

Stahl, B., & Goldstein, E. (2010). *A mindfulness-based stress reduction workbook*. Oakland, CA: New Harbinger.

Uscher-Pines, L. (2009). Health effects of relocation following disaster: A systematic review of the literature. *Disasters, 33*(1), 1–22.

Weems, C. F., Pina, A. A., Costa, N. M., Watts, S. E., Taylor, L. K., & Cannon, M. F. (2007). Predisaster trait anxiety and negative affect predict posttraumatic stress in youths after hurricane Katrina. *Journal of Consulting and Clinical Psychology, 75*(1), 154–159.

Wolmer, L., Laor, N., Dedeoglu, C., Siev, J., & Yazgan, Y. (2005). Teacher-mediated intervention after disaster: A controlled three-year follow-up of children's functioning. *Journal of Child Psychology and Psychiatry, 46*, 1161–1168. Retrieved from http://www.blackwellpublishing.com/journal.asp?ref=0021–9630

Wolmer, L., Laor, N., & Yazgan, Y. (2003). School reactivation programs after disaster: Could teachers serve as clinical mediators? *Child and Adolescent Psychiatric Clinics of North America, 12*, 363–381. Retrieved from http://www.childpsych.theclinics.com/

Zhang, Y., Kong, F., Wang, L., Chen, H., Gao, X., Tan, X.,…Liu, Y. (2010). Mental health and coping styles of children and adolescent survivors one year after the 2008 Chinese earthquake. *Children and Youth Services Review, 32*, 1403–1409. doi:10.1016/j.childyouth.2010.06.009

Evidence-Based Interventions for School Violence

Lindsey M. O'Brennan and Michael James Furlong

OVERVIEW

School violence as an identified topic of public policy and scientific research emerged in the 1990s out of a more general concern about adolescents' involvement in violent crime and the occurrence of multiple victim homicides occurring on school campuses (Furlong & Morrison, 2000). As such, early school violence research focused on crime reduction and extreme forms of aggression. During the past 15 years, however, the definition of school violence has evolved in response to research about the etiology and consequences of school violence exposure. The topic of school violence has moved from its crime-prevention origins, to one that increasingly views violence as a set of behaviors that occur in and are deeply influenced by the social contexts of the school and a school's interface with the community. This expanded focus has included an interest in both violence prevention and strategies that foster safe, secure, and peaceful schools in support of optimal student development.

Definition of School Violence. Although there is no consensus on the definition of "school violence," most definitions incorporate elements articulated in those provided by the U.S. Centers for Disease Control and Prevention (CDC) and the United Nations. The CDC defines school violence as:

> Youth violence that occurs on school property, on the way to or from school or school-sponsored events, or during a school-sponsored event (and) includes...bullying, slapping, or hitting—it can cause more emotional harm than physical harm. (CDC, 2013, p. 1)

Similarly, the United Nations defines school violence as:

> The intentional use of physical force or power, threatened or actual, against oneself, another person, or against a group or community, that either results in or has a high likelihood of resulting in injury, death, psychological harm, mal-development, or deprivation. (Williams & Stelko-Pereira, 2013, p. 236)

ETIOLOGY AND FACTORS CONTRIBUTING TO SCHOOL VIOLENCE

Recent research has emphasized studying school violence topics from a social-ecological contextual model that includes multiple levels of individual and social context transactions (e.g., Boxer & Sloan-Power,

2013; Espelage & Swearer, 2004; Rutkowski, Rutkowski, & Engel, 2013; Skiba, 2014). This new emphasis also means early historical efforts to reduce "violent acts" have been supplemented by efforts to increase positive behaviors and improve school climate, factors that decrease violent acts. A dual-continua perspective represents contemporary definitions of school violence—one continuum encompasses individual aggressive and violent acts and/or experiences and a second continuum examines school contextual indicators that make violence more or less likely to occur.

INDIVIDUAL BEHAVIOR AND BELIEFS

The majority of research examining youth problem behavior has shown several demographic factors as being predictive of concurrent and later antisocial behavior (Thomas, Bierman, Thompson, Powers, & Conduct Problems Prevention Research Group, 2008). Research on gender, for example, has shown boys to be more likely to endorse physical violence to resolve interpersonal conflict than girls (Bradshaw, Sawyer, & O'Brennan, 2009; Craig & Pepler, 2003), yet adolescent girls are more likely to be the target of rumor spreading and cyberbullying than boys (O'Brennan, Furlong, O'Malley, & Jones, 2014). Research examining racial and/or ethnic differences has also revealed consistent findings that Black and Hispanic youth are more likely to engage in physical fighting (Thomas, Bierman, & Conduct Problems Prevention Research Group, 2006; Thomas et al., 2008), as well as attend schools affected by gang activity than are White students (O'Brennan, Furlong, et al., 2014).

Beyond basic demographics, youth's personal beliefs regarding violence and safety are salient correlates of school violence. For instance, youth who support aggressive retaliation (e.g., "hitting someone back if they hit you first"; Guerra, Huesmann, & Spindler, 2003) are at a heightened risk of reacting aggressively in social situations as opposed to confronting their peers in a prosocial manner. Perpetrators of aggressive behavior, bullies or bully/victims (both a perpetrator and victim of bullying), have been found to display higher levels of aggressive-impulsive behavior

than other youth (Olweus, 1993; Smokowski & Kopasz, 2005). Schwartz (2000) found that bully/victims were rated by their teachers as being hyperactive (using the Attention Deficit Hyperactive Disorders Rating Scale; DuPaul, Anastopoulos, Power, Murphy, & Barkley, 1990) and disruptive, and as having difficulties controlling their anger when provoked by their peers (using the Emotion Regulation Checklist; Shields & Cicchetti, 1997).

INTERPERSONAL RELATIONSHIPS

According to social learning theory (Bandura, 1977), the school and classroom social milieu can significantly influence the manifestation of different types of student behavior. Research by Dishion et al. warned against grouping highly aggressive students together in a classroom or school because of the increased likelihood of "deviancy training" occurring within peer groups (Dishion, McCord, & Poulin, 1999; Patterson, Dishion, & Yoerger, 2000). Deviancy training theory purports that aggressive students paired together tend to provoke and reinforce antisocial behavior (Dishion et al., 1999). This unintentional reinforcement of antisocial behavior is further compounded in that youth with a proclivity toward aggressive behavior (e.g., those involved in bullying) also tend to have poorer social skills (Smokowski & Kopasz, 2005). Previous studies suggest that bully/victims tend to provoke negative responses from their peers, are often perceived as social outcasts, are more socially avoidant, and have more negative peer interactions as compared with youth who are victims only or bullies only (Juvonen et al., 2003; O'Brennan, Bradshaw, & Sawyer, 2009). Thus, when youth who are prone to aggressive-impulsive behavior and showcase poor social skills are placed in chaotic classrooms where disruptive behavior is common, the interpersonal transactions that occur set the stage for the potential for school violence to occur.

SCHOOL CONTEXT AND CLIMATE

Social disorganization theory contends that an individual's risk for involvement in problem behavior and perceptions of the environment are influenced by contextual variables suggestive of disorder. Although some schools opt to counteract rising school violence concerns with increased security precautions (e.g., metal detectors, security guards, enhanced monitoring of student behavior), a counter movement focuses on enhancing the overall school climate. School climate, defined as the "norms, values, and expectations that support people feeling socially, emotionally and physically safe" (National School Climate Council, 2007, p. 4), is related to how students and school staff function in the school environment. For instance, a multilevel study by O'Brennan, Bradshaw, and Furlong (2014) found that teachers' positive perceptions of school climate (e.g., principal leadership, pride in school) were significantly related to lower levels of disruptive behavior among elementary school youth. Gregory et al. (2010) examined the relationship between authoritative school discipline practice, which provides both structure and support to students, and student and teacher reports on bullying and peer victimization. Multilevel results showed that there were significantly fewer bullying incidents in schools in which students believed that support from teachers and school rules were fair and consistently enforced. Although it remains unclear which of these experiences precedes the other (i.e., victimization leading to feeling unsafe vs. feeling unsafe leading to increased aggressive behavior), current research on school violence indicates that it is the combination of these factors—individual predisposition toward violence, lack of strong social bonds at school, and chaotic school environments—that sets the stage for potential incidents of school violence.

EVIDENCE-BASED INTERVENTIONS AND EMPIRICAL SUPPORT FOR SCHOOL VIOLENCE

Balance–Communication–Connectedness–Support Model

In response to the school shootings on December 14, 2012, at Sandy Hook Elementary, which resulted in the death of 20 children and 6 adults, the Interdisciplinary Group on Preventing School and Community Violence (2013) released a position statement in the *Journal of School Violence* as a call to action for educators and researchers alike. In this statement, the Interdisciplinary Group proposed an integrated pathway to safer schools, guided by four key elements: *Balance, Communication, Connectedness,* and *Support* (BCCS; see Figure 4.1).

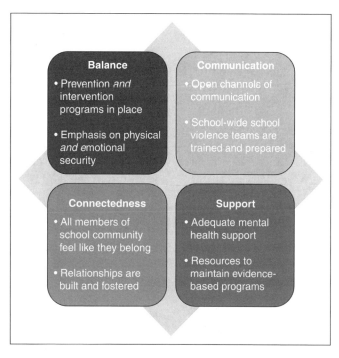

FIGURE 4.1 Balance–Communication–Connectedness–Support (BCCS) model for preventing school and community violence.

In addition, the workgroup proposed strengthened attention to school and community mental health needs, structured threat assessment approaches, revised policies on youth exposure to violent media, and increased efforts to limit inappropriate access to guns and especially, assault-type weapons. The four cornerstones of the BCCS model follow.

Balance. Often schools opt to implement intervention programs that focus on youth who have already acted on their aggressive impulses at school, whether it be a physical fight, verbal aggression toward a classmate or teacher, or defacing school property. Yet, whether it is due to limited personnel or financial resources, less attention is given to prevention programs that reduce the risk of school violence. Instead of responding to crises and solely "putting out fires," schools are encouraged to implement well-integrated prevention *and* intervention evidence-based practices that meet the needs of the entire school population, including students and staff. A balanced approach to violence prevention includes addressing physical safety, educational practices, and programs that support the social, emotional, and behavioral needs of students. Although it may be logical to control public entrances to a school by relying on metal detectors, security cameras, guards, and entry checkpoints, these strategies are unlikely to provide protection against all school-related violent attacks. Indeed, shootings have occurred in schools with strict security measures already in place; and in fact, school-associated homicides have not increased in the past 15 years (Robers, Kemp, & Truman, 2013), whereas community mass shootings have increased (from 6.4 events per year between 2000 and 2006 to 16.4 events per year between 2007 and 2013; Blair & Schweit, 2014). Efforts are needed to assemble programs that are truly *school* violence prevention programs and not general youth violence prevention programs that are conveniently administered in school settings.

Communication. The U.S. Secret Service, Federal Bureau of Investigation, and numerous researchers propose that channels of efficient, user-friendly communication, planning, and commitment throughout the school community are needed to prevent many acts of school violence (Skiba et al., n.d.). When students, staff, and parents are comfortable bringing safety concerns to the attention of school administrators, potential threats are more likely to be reported and subsequently investigated by responsible authorities. Instead of using checklists of student characteristics to detect imminent violent acts perpetrated by students, school authorities are encouraged to improve professional development activities that focus on campus safety while seeking long-term solutions that addresses the needs of at-risk students (Cornell, Allen, & Fan, 2012). Currently, the threat assessment approach with the most empirical support is the Virginia Student Threat Assessment Guidelines (VSTAG; Cornell & Sheras, 2006). Using a structured approach like the VSTAG, schools can prepare teams of staff members to use principles of threat assessment to resolve problems and conflicts identified (see Select Bibliography). Having a threat assessment team and a clear communication strategy will help schools both prevent and prepare for crises. However, schools and communities must find effective means to overcome students' reluctance to "tattle" or "snitch" by communicating to all community members that their lives or the lives of their friends might depend on seeking help for troubled individuals before problems escalate.

Connectedness. School connectedness is defined as "the belief by students that adults in the school care about their learning as well as about them as individuals" (CDC, 2009, p. 3), and has been recognized by educators and researchers as a protective and promotive factor for all school-age youth (Furlong, O'Brennan, & You, 2011; McNeely, Nonnemaker, & Blum, 2002). Schools, similar to neighborhoods, are safer places when school staff and students look out for one another, are involved in school-wide activities, and are invested in the welfare of each other. Students most at risk of delinquency and violence are often those who are most alienated from the school community. O'Brennan and colleagues (2009) found that students who were frequently involved in bullying perceived the school environment differently from those not involved in bullying, with both victims and bully/victims reporting feeling equally unsafe and disconnected from their school. Likewise, a study of middle and high school youth showed that youth reporting high levels of connectedness to their school tended to report fewer instances of peer victimization (O'Brennan & Furlong, 2010). Schools can devise opportunities for ongoing positive interactions to build positive connections with marginalized students (e.g., racial-ethnic minority, sexual minority youth), as well as foster avenues for meaningful involvement.

Support. At any given time, 5% to 7% of school-aged youth experience emotional, behavioral, and social difficulties (Pastor, Reuben, & Duran, 2012) that could benefit from support services. Roberts, Roberts, and Xing (2006) found that, among a sample of 11- to 17-year-olds, 7% reported symptoms of an anxiety disorder, 3% a mood disorder, 6% a disruptive behavior disorder, and 6% a substance-use disorder. Youths who are frequently involved in bullying (as either a victim or a bully/victim) are more likely to experience internalizing symptoms, such as depression and anxiety, than youth not frequently involved in bullying (Bond, Carlin, Thomas, Rubin, & Patton, 2001). As highlighted by these prevalence rates, many students and families experience life stresses and difficulties that must be taken seriously. A "safe" school must have the resources to maintain programs designed to address all forms of student conflict as well as the underlying mental health needs of student perpetrators and victims of violence. Safe schools implement research-based violence prevention and support programs, following a three-tier approach—universal (school-wide), targeted (at-risk students), and intensive (high-risk and high-need students).

HOW TO: A GUIDE TO THE IMPLEMENTATION OF INTERVENTIONS FOR SCHOOL VIOLENCE

The paragraphs that follow provide the key components for implementing school-based interventions guided by the BCCS integrated model.

Implementing Comprehensive School-Wide Initiatives

Regardless of how school violence is defined, an essential first step for any state or local educational agency is to delineate a comprehensive safe school plan (Furlong, Jones, Lilles, & Derzon, 2010); that is, to develop "comprehensive plans that

contribute to safe, respectful, and drug-free school environments, while promoting vital social skills and healthy childhood development" (Modzeleski et al., 2012, p. 269). A review of research suggests that successful school–community partnerships build the network and connections to positive adults that increase the time that children at risk spend in school and create more responsive and enhanced support and enrichment activities, all of which improve student academic and social-emotional outcomes (Bathgate & Silva, 2010). Working in such a collaborative fashion creates a shared family–school–community mental health agenda with greater family voice and partnership (National Association of State Mental Health Program Directors, 2002).

One example of a collaborative partnership was *Safe Schools/Healthy Students* (SS/HS), the federally funded initiative developed by the U.S. Departments of Health and Human Services, Education, and Justice. It was the largest U.S. national effort to reduce school violence and increase safety, and was grounded in the principles that school safety (a) requires a community-wide effort and (b) includes programs and services that address the developmental needs of students. The stated goals of the SS/HS projects were:

> To promote the mental health of students, to enhance academic achievement, to prevent violence and substance use, and to create safe and respectful climates through sustainable school–family–community partnerships and the use of research-based prevention and early intervention programs, policies, and procedures. (Modzeleski et al., 2012, p. 270)

The 365 school–community partnerships (see full list of SS/HS grantees via the initiative's website www.samhsa.gov/safe-schools-healthy-students) that implemented SS/HS projects between 1999 and 2013 provide examples of comprehensive, cross-agency efforts to reduce school violence and foster positive youth development.

The five core elements of these projects included:

1. *Safe school environments and violence prevention activities*—for instance, Second Step (Espelage, Low, Polanin, & Brown, 2013) is implemented to foster students' social-emotional development and reduce violence.

2. *Alcohol, tobacco, and other drug prevention activities*—many projects included prevention strategies using evidence-based programs such as Project Northland (Perry et al., 2002).
3. *Student behavioral, social, and emotional supports*—such as implementing a school-wide positive behavioral and intervention supports strategy (Pas & Bradshaw, 2012) or the check, connect, and expect intervention (Cheney et al., 2009).
4. *Mental health services*—for example, integrating efforts to foster positive behavior, school climate, and mental health services (Bradshaw, Bottiani, Osher, & Sugai, 2014) and school-wide screening for complete mental health (Furlong, Dowdy, Carnazzo, Bovery, & Kim, 2014).
5. *Early childhood social and emotional learning programs*—some schools used universal school-readiness screening as a tool for informing instruction and identifying need for additional student supports (Quirk, Furlong, Lilles, Felix, & Chin, 2011).

Each SS/HS project developed a detailed model that integrated the five core SS/HS components (for more information, see Safe School–Healthy Students Initiative, www.sshs.samhsa.gov/ given under the "Select Bibliography" section of this chapter). In addition, many states required that local educational agencies develop and annually review comprehensive safe school plans and provide resources to guide this planning process (e.g., California Department of Education, 2001; Minnesota School Safety Center Program, n.d.). For pragmatic and real-life examples of how schools designed, implemented, and evaluated balanced and/or comprehensive prevention and intervention strategies, visit the SS/HS website (www.sshs.samhsa.gov/).

Training a School Violence Team

Concerned students, parents, educators, and stakeholders in the community should attend to students' troubling behaviors that signal something is amiss. For example, if a person threatens to engage in a violent act, displays a pronounced change of mood and related social behavior, or is engaged in severe conflict with family members or coworkers, it makes sense to train teachers and school staff

who may be the first to provide assistance during a crisis. Of course, proportional and facilitative responses by school violence teams require skilled personnel operating within a planned organizational response. To ensure that school staff are well prepared, an excellent resource is the *PREPaRE: School Crisis Prevention and Intervention Training* curriculum, developed and refined by the National Association of School Psychologists (NASP; see PREPaRE: School Crisis Prevention and Intervention Training curriculum, www.nasponline.org/prepare). The PREPaRE acronym refers to the curriculum's components related to school emergencies: Prevent, Reaffirm, Evaluate, Provide and Respond, and Examine. The curriculum is aligned with the U.S. Department of Education's guidelines for emergency operations plans (U.S. Department of Education, 2013). PREPaRE was developed out of school psychologists' experiences responding to school shootings, crises, and other emergency events, and is based on the principle that a coordinated school-wide effort is needed to prevent and respond to school crises. PREPaRE helps schools establish a critical incidence command structure, plan for a school's response during a crisis, and focus resources on helping school communities manage, cope, and heal in the aftermath of traumatic events and emergencies.

Addressing Mental Health Needs

There is increasing awareness of and emphasis on the critical role of schools in addressing youth mental health as it relates to both academic success and engagement in at-risk behavior (Juszczak, Melinkovich, & Kaplan, 2003; Rones & Hoagwood, 2000). Among youth aged 8 to 15 years with a diagnosable mental disorder, only half receive treatment within the year (Greif Green et al., 2013; Merikangas et al., 2010), and as many as 70% of school-aged children with a diagnosable mental illness do not receive any treatment (Greenberg et al., 2003). However, schools are challenged by an overarching mandate to raise academic standards; school mental health programs and services are often construed as "add-ons" to the central academic mission of the educational system, which makes these programs vulnerable to being cut or given insufficient attention. In addition, educational administrators and teachers often feel inadequately resourced to provide needed mental health support for students (Weist & Paternite, 2006).

To better meet the mental health needs of school-aged youth, a growing number of collaborative partnerships between schools and community-based mental health organizations have been formed with the goal of integrating mental health services for youth and families into the school day. These collaborative efforts benefit schools and their partnering community agencies through the pooling of resources and expertise, and the implementation of integrated mental health strategies (Weist, Evans, & Lever, 2003). The Center for School-Based Mental Health (CSMH) and the National Assembly on School-Based Health Care highlight 10 key features of advancing school mental health:

1. Establish a unified, cohesive vision and a shared agenda with stakeholders;
2. Develop a centralized organizational infrastructure and accountability mechanisms to ensure implementation of the vision and action agenda;
3. Create feasible and sustainable funding models for comprehensive school mental health initiatives, including early intervention and prevention;
4. Promote an understanding among state and local educational leaders of the critical links and associations between student academic success and mental health;
5. Meaningfully engage diverse family members and youth in school mental health policy and program development;
6. Recognize the needs of culturally diverse populations and reduce disparities to access to effective school mental health services;
7. Implement preprofessional and in-service professional development for educators and school mental health personnel related to youth development, youth mental health, and best practices in school mental health;
8. Provide support for practitioners in using evidence-based school mental health strategies;
9. Coordinate equitable distribution of resources and services across schools related to ensuring student academic success, mental health, and well-being; and

10. Focus on continuous quality improvement by collecting and using outcome data to inform decision making at the local school, school district, and state levels.

Evidence of these collaborations includes the fact that, of youth who do access mental health services, 70% to 80% percent access these services in schools (Rones & Hoagwood, 2000). When students' mental health needs are effectively addressed through school-based programs, the incidence of emotional and behavioral disorders, such as attention deficit hyperactivity disorder, depression, and conduct disorder, is reduced (Hussey & Guo, 2003). Mental health programs increase student engagement in school-based preventive interventions (Greenberg, Domitrovich, Graczyk, & Zins, 2005), and less school violence is the result.

CONCLUSION

The intent of this chapter was to depict school violence intervention as a broad topic that requires comprehensive and integrated thinking about the behaviors and experiences within schools that should be considered as forms of "violence." The interventions identified provide a framework and guide to be used if and when crises occur. Within the context of this *Handbook*, the BCCS model can be paired with other interventions within schools to address crises (see Chapter 2), anger and aggression (see Chapter 12), bullying (see Chapter 13), conduct/oppositional defiant disorders (see Chapter 15), with the goal of reducing the overall occurrence and minimizing the impact of school violence.

SELECT BIBLIOGRAPHY

Handbook of school violence and school safety: International research and practice (2nd Ed.). New York, NY: Taylor & Francis.
This book includes 44 chapters that provide school safety best practice information about assessment, intervention, and policy.

PREPaRE: School crisis prevention and intervention training curriculum. Retrieved from www.nasponline.org/prepare

This is a school crises prevention and response professional development trainer-of-trainers program. It has been used extensively in schools worldwide and was developed by school psychologists who have extensive history helping schools to respond to school violence events.

Safe School–Healthy Students Initiative. Retrieved from http://www.samhsa.gov/safe-schools-healthy-students
The SS/HS initiative is the single largest effort in the United States that supports school–community collaboration to implement model strategies designed to reduce school violence. The SS/HS initiative offers a self-paced online training module as a guide to develop a detailed safe school logic model that integrates the five SS/HS core components.

U.S. Department of Education School Climate Model. Retrieved from www2.ed.gov/policy/gen/guid/school-discipline/index.html
This website includes a wide range of information and resources designed to support school's efforts to create safe and supportive school climates with current thinking of school discipline best practices.

REFERENCES

Bandura, A. (1977). *Social learning theory*. Englewood Cliffs, NJ: Prentice-Hall.

Bathgate, K., & Silva, E. (2010). Joining forces: The benefits of integrating schools and community providers. *New Directions for Youth Development, 127*, 63–73. doi:10.1002/yd.363

Blair, J. P., & Schweit, K. W. (2014). *A study of active shooter incidents, 2000–2013*. Washington, DC: Texas State University and Federal Bureau of Investigation, U.S. Department of Justice. Retrieved from http://www.fbi.gov/news/stories/2014/september/fbi-releases-study-on-active-shooter-incidents/pdfs/a-study-of-active-shooter-incidents-in-the-u.s.-between-2000-and-2013

Bond, L., Carlin, J. B., Thomas, L., Rubin, K., & Patton, G. (2001). Does bullying cause emotional problems? A prospective study of young teenagers. *British Medical Journal (Clinical research ed.), 323*(7311), 480–484.

Boxer, P., & Sloan-Power, E. (2013). Coping with violence: A comprehensive framework and implications for understanding resilience. *Trauma, Violence & Abuse, 14*(3), 209–221.

Bradshaw, C. P., Bottiani, J. H., Osher, D., & Sugai, G. (2014). The integration of positive behavioral interventions and supports and social and emotional learning. In M. D. Weist, N. A. Lever, C. P. Bradshaw, & J. Sarno Owens (Eds.), *Handbook of school mental health* (pp. 101–118). New York, NY: Springer Publishing Company.

Bradshaw, C. P., Sawyer, A. L., & O'Brennan, L. M. (2007). Bullying and peer victimization at school: Perceptual differences between students and school staff. *School Psychology Review, 36*, 361–382.

Bradshaw, C. P., Sawyer, A. L., & O'Brennan, L. M. (2009). A social disorganization perspective on bullying-related attitudes and behaviors: The influence of school context. *American Journal of Community Psychology, 43*(3–4), 204–220.

California Department of Education. (2001). *Safe schools: A planning guide for action*. Sacramento, CA: California Department of Education. Retrieved from http://colganstone.com/yahoo_site_admin/assets/docs/Safe_Schools_Pl_Guide_Wkbk_copy.61175732.pdf

Centers for Disease Control and Prevention (CDC). (2009). *School connectedness: Strategies for increasing protective factors among youth*. Atlanta, GA: U.S. Department of Health and Human Services. Retrieved from www.cdc.gov/healthyyouth/protective/pdf/connectedness.pdf

Centers for Disease Control and Prevention (CDC). (2013). *Understanding school violence*. Atlanta, GA: Author. Retrieved from www.cdc.gov/violenceprevention/pdf/school_violence_fact_sheet-a.pdf

Cheney, D., Lynass, L., Flower, A., Waugh, M., Iwaszuk, W., Mielenz, C., & Hawken, L. (2009). The Check, Connect, and Expect program: A targeted, tier 2 intervention in the schoolwide positive behavior support model. *Preventing School Failure: Alternative Education for Children and Youth, 54*, 152–158. doi:10.1080/10459880903492742

Cornell, D., & Sheras, P. (2006). *Guidelines for responding to student threats of violence book*. Longmont, CO: Sopris West.

Cornell, D. G., Allen, K., & Fan, X. (2012). A randomized controlled study of the Virginia Student Threat Assessment Guidelines in kindergarten through grade 12. *School Psychology Review, 41*, 100–115.

Craig, W. M., & Pepler, D. J. (2003). Identifying and targeting risk for involvement in bullying and victimization. *Canadian Journal of Psychiatry. Revue Canadienne de Psychiatrie, 48*(9), 577–582.

DuPaul, G. J., Anastopoulos, A. D., Power, T. J., Murphy, K., & Barkley, R. A. (1994). *AD/HD Rating Scale–IV.* Unpublished rating scale, Lehigh University.

Dishion, T. J., McCord, J., & Poulin, F. (1999). When interventions harm: Peer groups and problem behavior. *The American Psychologist, 54*(9), 755–764.

Espelage, D. L., Low, S., Polanin, J. R., & Brown, E. C. (2013). The impact of a middle school program to reduce aggression, victimization, and sexual violence. *The Journal of Adolescent Health: Official Publication of the Society for Adolescent Medicine, 53*(2), 180–186.

Espelage, D. L., & Swearer, S. M. (Eds.). (2004). *Bullying in American schools: A social-ecological perspective on prevention and intervention.* New York, NY: Routledge.

Furlong, M. J., Dowdy, E., Carnazzo, K., Bovery, B., & Kim, E. (2014). Covitality fostering the building blocks of complete mental health. *NASP Communiqué* (June issue). Retrieved from www .readperiodicals.com/201406/3346560221.html

Furlong, M. J., Jones, C., Lilles, E., & Derzon, J. (2010). Think smart, stay safe: Aligning elements within the multi-level approach to school violence prevention. In M. R. Shinn, H. M., Walker, & G. Stoner (Eds.), *Interventions for achievement and behavior problems in a three-tier model including RTI* (pp. 313–336). Bethesda, MD: National Association of School Psychologists.

Furlong, M. J., & Morrison, G. (2000). The school in school violence: Definitions and facts. *Journal of Emotional and Behavioral Disorders, 8,* 71–82. doi:10.1177/106342660000800203

Furlong, M. J., O'Brennan, L. M., & You, S. (2011). Psychometric properties of the Add Health School Connectedness Scale for 18 sociocultural groups. *Psychology in the Schools, 48,* 986–997. doi:10.1002/pits.20609.

Green, J. G., Felix, E. D., Sharkey, J. D., Furlong, M. J., & Kras, J. E. (2013). Identifying bully victims: Definitional versus behavioral approaches. *Psychological Assessment, 25*(2), 651–657.

Greenberg, M. T., Domitrovich, C. E., Graczyk, P. A., & Zins, J. E. (2005). *The study of implementation in school-based preventive interventions: Theory, research, and practice*

(Vol. 3). Rockville, MD: Center for Mental Health Services, Substance Abuse and Mental Health Services Administration.

Greenberg, M. T., Weissberg, R. P., O'Brien, M. U., Zins, J. E., Fredericks, L., Resnik, H., & Elias, M. J. (2003). Enhancing school-based prevention and youth development through coordinated social, emotional, and academic learning. *The American Psychologist, 58*(6–7), 466–474.

Gregory, A., Cornell, D., Fan, X., Sheras, P., Shih, T-H., & Huang, F. (2010). Authoritative school discipline: High school practices associated with lower bullying and victimization. *Journal of Educational Psychology, 102,* 483–496. doi:10.1037/a0018562

Guerra, N. G., Huesmann, L. R., & Spindler, A. (2003). Community violence exposure, social cognition, and aggression among urban elementary school children. *Child Development, 74*(5), 1561–1576.

Hussey, D. L., & Guo, S. (2003). Measuring behavior change in young children receiving intensive school-based mental health services. *Community Psychology, 31,* 629–639. doi:10.1002/jcop .10074

Interdisciplinary Group on Preventing School and Community Violence. (2013). December 2012 Connecticut school shooting position statement. *Journal of School Violence, 12,* 119–133. doi:10.10 80/15388220.2012.762488

Juszczak, L., Melinkovich, P., & Kaplan, D. (2003). Use of health and mental health services by adolescents across multiple delivery sites. *The Journal of Adolescent Health: Official Publication of the Society for Adolescent Medicine, 32*(6), 108–118.

Juvonen, J., Graham, S., & Schuster, M. A. (2003). Bullying among young adolescents: The strong, the weak, and the troubled. *Pediatrics, 112*(6 Pt 1), 1231–1237.

McNeely, C. A., Nonnemaker, J. M., & Blum, R. W. (2002). Promoting school connectedness: Evidence from the National Longitudinal Study of Adolescent Health. *The Journal of School Health, 72*(4), 138–146.

Merikangas, K. R., He, J. P., Burstein, M., Swanson, S. A., Avenevoli, S., Cui, L.,.... Swendsen, J. (2010). Lifetime prevalence of mental disorders in U.S. adolescents: Results from the National Comorbidity Survey Replication–Adolescent Supplement (NCS-A). *Journal of the American Academy of Child and Adolescent Psychiatry, 49*(10), 980–989.

Minnesota School Safety Center Program. (n.d.). *Comprehensive school safety guide.* Minneapolis, MN: Minnesota Department of Public Safety Division of Homeland Security and Emergency Management, Minnesota School Safety Center Program.

Modzeleski, W., Mathews-Younes, A., Arroyo, C. G., Mannix, D., Wells, M. E., Hill, G.,…Murray, S. (2012). An introduction to the Safe Schools/Healthy Students Initiative. *Evaluation and Program Planning, 35*(2), 269–272.

National Association of State Mental Health Program Directors. (2002). *Mental health, schools and families working together for all children and youth: Toward a shared agenda.* Washington, DC: U.S. Department of Education, Office of Special Education Programs.

National School Climate Council. (2007). *The school climate challenge: Narrowing the gap between school climate research and school climate policy, practice guidelines and teacher education policy.* Retrieved from www.schoolclimate.org/climate/documents/policy/school-climate-challenge-web.pdf

O'Brennan, L. M., Bradshaw, C. P., & Furlong, M. J. (2014). Influence of classroom and school climate on teacher perceptions of student problem behavior. *School Mental Health, 6*(2), 125–136.

O'Brennan, L. M., Bradshaw, C. P., & Sawyer, A. L. (2009). Examining developmental differences in the social-emotional problems among frequent bullies, victims, and bully/victims. *Psychology in the Schools, 46,* 100–115. doi:10.1002/pits.20357

O'Brennan, L. M., & Furlong, M. J. (2010). Relations between students' perceptions of school connectedness and peer victimization. *Journal of School Violence, 9,* 375–391. doi:10.1080/15388220.2010.509009

O'Brennan, L. M., Furlong, M. J., O'Malley, M. D., & Jones, C. N. (2014). The influence of school contexts and processes on violence and disruption. In P. Garner, K. James, & E. Julian (Eds.), *The Sage handbook of emotional and behavioral difficulties* (2nd Ed., pp. 165–177). London, UK: Sage. doi:10.4135/9781446247525.n12

Olweus, D. (1993). *Bullying at school.* Oxford, England: Blackwell.

Pas, E. T., & Bradshaw, C. P. (2012). Examining the association between implementation and outcomes: State-wide scale-up of school-wide positive behavior intervention and supports. *The Journal of Behavioral Health Services & Research, 39*(4), 417–433.

Pastor, P. N., Reuben, C. A., & Duran, C. R. (2012). Identifying emotional and behavioral problems in children aged 4–17 years: United States, 2001–2007. *National Health Statistics Reports,* No. 48 (February 24). Hyattsville, MD: National Center for Health Statistics.

Patterson, G. R., Dishion, T. J., & Yoerger, K. (2000). Adolescent growth in new forms of problem behavior: Macro- and micro-peer dynamics. *Prevention Science: The Official Journal of the Society for Prevention Research, 1*(1), 3–13.

Perry, C. L., Williams, C. L., Komro, K. A., Veblen-Mortenson, S., Stigler, M. H., Munson, K. A.,…Forster, J. L. (2002). Project Northland: Long-term outcomes of community action to reduce adolescent alcohol use. *Health Education Research, 17*(1), 117–132.

Quirk, M., Furlong, M. J., Lilles, E., Felix, E., & Chin, J. (2011). Preliminary development of a kindergarten school readiness assessment for Latino students. *Journal of Applied School Psychology, 27,* 77–102. doi:10.1080/15377903.2010.540518

Roberts, R. E., Roberts, C. R., & Xing, Y. (2006). Prevalence of youth-reported DSM-IV psychiatric disorders among African, European, and Mexican American adolescents. *Journal of the American Academy of Child and Adolescent Psychiatry, 45*(11), 1329–1337.

Robers, S., Kemp, J., & Truman, J. (2013). *Indicators of school crime and safety: 2012* (NCES 2013–036/NCJ 241446). Washington, DC: National Center for Education Statistics, U.S. Department of Education, and Bureau of Justice Statistics, Office of Justice Programs, U.S. Department of Justice. Retrieved from http://nces.ed.gov/pubs2013/2013036.pdf

Rones, M., & Hoagwood, K. (2000). School-based mental health services: A research review. *Clinical Child and Family Psychology Review, 3*(4), 223–241.

Rutkowski, L., Rutkowski, D., & Engel, L. (2013). Sharp contrasts at the boundaries: School violence and educational outcomes internationally. *Comparative Education Review, 57,* 232–259. doi:10.1086/669121

Schwartz, D. (2000). Subtypes of victims and aggressors in children's peer groups. *Journal of Abnormal Child Psychology, 28*(2), 181–192.

Shields, A., & Cicchetti, D. (1997). Emotion regulation among school-age children: The development and validation of a new criterion Q-sort scale. *Developmental Psychology, 33*(6), 906–916.

Skiba, R. J. (2014). The failure of zero tolerance. *Reclaiming Children and Youth, 22*(4), 27–33. Retrieved from http://search.proquest.com/docview/1658765668?accountid=14745

Skiba, R. J., Boone, K., Fontanini, A., Wu, T., Strussell, A., & Peterson, R. (2000). *Preventing school violence: A practical guide to comprehensive planning.* Bloomington, IN: Indiana Education Policy Center.

Smokowski, P. R., & Kopasz, K. H. (2005). Bullying in school: An overview of types, effects, family characteristics, and intervention strategies. *Children & Schools, 27*(2), 101–110. doi:10.1093/cs/27.2.101

Thomas, D. E., Bierman, K. L., & the Conduct Problems Prevention Research Group. (2006). The impact of classroom aggression on the development of aggressive behavior problems in children. *Development and Psychopathology, 18,* 471–487. doi:10.1017/S0954579406060251

Thomas, D. E., Bierman, K. L., Thompson, C., Powers, C. J., & the Conduct Problems Prevention Research Group. (2008). Double jeopardy: Child and school characteristics that predict aggressive-disruptive behavior in first grade. *School Psychology Review, 37,* 516–532.

U.S. Department of Education. (2013). *Guide for developing high-quality school emergency operations plans,* Washington, DC: Office of Elementary and Secondary Education, Office of Safe and Healthy Students. Retrieved from www2.ed.gov/about/offices/list/oese/oshs/rems-k-12-guide.pdf

Weist, M. D., Evans, S. W., & Lever, N. A. (Eds.). (2003). *Handbook of school mental health: Advancing practice and research.* New York, NY: Springer Publishing Company.

Weist, M. D., & Paternite, C. E. (2006). Building an interconnected policy-training practice-research agenda to advance school mental health. *Education and Treatment of Children, 29,* 173–196.

Williams, L. C., & Stelko-Pereira, A. C. (2013). Let's prevent school violence, not just bullying and peer victimization: A commentary on Finkelhor, Turner, and Hamby (2012). *Child Abuse & Neglect, 37*(4), 235–236.

Evidence-Based Interventions for Suicidal Behavior in Children and Adolescents

David N. Miller and James J. Mazza

OVERVIEW

Youth suicide is a significant public health problem both in the United States and in other countries (Centers for Disease Control and Prevention [CDC], 2012). Worldwide, an estimated 800,000 people die by suicide every year (World Health Organization, 2014), and many of these individuals are children and adolescents. Suicide is the second leading cause of death among youth between the ages of 10 and 24 years in the United States, and its rate has increased significantly during the last several decades (CDC, 2012). Although historically suicide rates have been highest among the elderly, suicide rates among children and adolescents have recently been increasing to such a marked degree that youth are now the group at highest risk for suicide in one-third of all countries in the world (CDC, 2012).

As disturbing as these statistics are, they do not adequately convey the scope of the problem of suicidal behavior among children and adolescents. Suicidal behavior—which includes suicidal ideation (i.e., thoughts about suicide), suicide-related communication (i.e., suicide threats or plans), suicide attempts, and suicide—represents a continuum of behaviors (Silverman, 2013) that affects hundreds of thousands of adolescents, young adults,

and their friends and families each year (Miller, Eckert, & Mazza, 2009). For example, for every youth who dies by suicide it is estimated that as many as 100 to 200 more make a suicide attempt and thousands more seriously contemplate taking their own lives (Miller & Eckert, 2009a). In a recent national sample involving more than 6,000 adolescents (aged 13–18 years) and their parents, the estimated lifetime prevalence rates of suicidal ideation, suicide plans, and suicide attempts were 12.1%, 4.0%, and 4.1%, respectively (Nock et al., 2013). Clearly, youth suicidal behavior is a crisis in need of urgent attention.

ETIOLOGY AND FACTORS CONTRIBUTING TO SUICIDAL BEHAVIOR IN CHILDREN AND ADOLESCENTS

Suicidal behavior is highly complex, and no single factor provides a complete explanation of why suicide, including youth suicide, occurs (U.S. Department of Health and Human Services [HHS], Office of the Surgeon General and National Action Alliance for Suicide Prevention, 2012). A comprehensive understanding of the causes of suicidal behavior among children and adolescents requires sensitivity to a broad constellation of interconnected variables, including genetic, neurobiological, social, cultural, ecological, and psychological influences (Berman, Jobes, & Silverman, 2006; Goldston et al., 2008; Wagner, 2009).

EVIDENCE-BASED INTERVENTIONS AND EMPIRICAL SUPPORT FOR YOUTH SUICIDAL BEHAVIOR

Evidence-based interventions for youth suicidal behavior include both community- and school-based approaches. Several of these interventions are described in the following sections, including means restriction, crisis hotlines and social media, psychopharmacological interventions, hospitalization, dialectical behavior therapy (DBT), and school-based suicide prevention programs.

Means Restriction

Means restriction refers to limiting the availability of or access to potentially life-threatening objects, such as firearms, bridges, tall buildings, and any medications or toxic substances that could result in a lethal overdose (Miller, 2013b). Although it is commonly believed that restricting access to lethal means in one area (e.g., restricting access to guns) will result in an increase in another nonrestricted suicide method (e.g., hanging), this typically does not occur (Lester, 2013; Miller, 2011). In fact, restricting access to lethal means has been associated with reductions in suicide and has been recommended as an important and underutilized suicide prevention strategy (Lester, 2013).

Given that most children and adolescents who die by suicide in the United States use guns as their lethal method, the issue of means restriction has particular importance when considering firearms (Miller, 2011). The evidence is clear and compelling that the presence of guns in a youth's home, especially unlocked loaded handguns, are associated with a significantly increased risk for suicide (Leenaars, 2009). Moreover, the risk resulting from guns is increased by their accessibility and number available. When guns are used in a suicide attempt, death results between 78% and 90% of the time (Berman et al., 2006). Public policy initiatives that have restricted the access to guns (especially handguns) are associated with a reduction of suicide by firearms and suicide overall, especially among youth (Leenaars, 2009). Consequently, one of the most powerful youth suicide prevention strategies is removing guns from a young person's home environment (American Psychological Association, 2013).

Because restricting access to guns is an emotionally charged issue in the United States, however, the passage of more restrictive gun laws is not likely given the current political climate (Miller, 2011). Moreover, despite the significant human and economic costs of gun violence in the United States (American Psychological Association, 2013), scientifically rigorous evaluations are not currently available for many policies that affect the access to and use of firearms. The dearth of research on gun policies is due in part to the lack of government funding on this topic, largely because of the political influence of the gun lobby (American Psychological Association, 2013). Consequently, viable and recommended strategies for preventing youth suicide, such as requiring mandatory background checks and waiting periods before making gun purchases, have been actively opposed by organizations such as the National Rifle Organization (NRA).

Crisis Hotlines and Social Media

Telephone crisis hotlines offer immediate help by providing a 24 hours, 7 days per week availability to suicidal or potentially suicidal individuals (Berman et al., 2006). Research suggests that hotlines can be beneficial to individuals who are suicidal and nonsuicidal and that youth who use them are frequently helped by them (Gould & Kalafat, 2009). Unfortunately, despite a high level of awareness regarding hotlines as a means of support, as well as reported high levels of satisfaction among those who use them, only a small number of youth access them. Moreover, males are less likely to use hotlines than females. This is problematic because, although young females attempt suicide more often than young males, the suicide rate among males is much higher than females. Additionally, many youth appear to have negative attitudes toward hotlines, especially adolescents who may be the most vulnerable to suicidal behavior (Gould & Kalafat, 2009).

In light of the accelerated rate of technology, employing greater use of the Internet and social media may be more congruent with the preferences and lifestyles of children and adolescents (Gould & Kalafat, 2009). Teenagers have been found to be as likely to access the Internet for help as they are to see a school counselor or other mental health professional, which suggests that social media can potentially play a powerful role in youth suicide prevention efforts (Gould & Kalafat, 2009). Recent advances in technology have led some hotline centers to develop crisis interventions via Facebook, Twitter, texting, and other online and social media services (Kerr, 2013). Although studies examining the effectiveness of social media for increasing help seeking among suicidal youth are not yet available, researchers are beginning to examine this technology and its possible utility in suicide prevention. Social media interventions clearly have the potential to reach and impact an unprecedented number of young people and its role in suicide prevention is therefore likely to increase.

Psychopharmacological Interventions

Although there is no medical treatment for suicide per se, psychopharmacological interventions often focus on the emotional and behavioral issues likely to be *associated* with suicidal behavior, such as bipolar disorder, posttraumatic stress disorder, conduct disorder, substance abuse, anxiety disorders, and (especially) depression. These and other mental health disorders are found typically among children and adolescents who die by suicide (Fleischmann, Bertolote, Belfer, & Beautrais, 2005), suggesting that mental health disorders increase the risk for suicide rather than directly cause it (Kaut, 2013).

Research examining the efficacy of psychopharmacological interventions indicates that the neurotransmitter serotonin is highly associated with depression and suicide attempts, and psychopharmacological interventions in the form of antidepressant medications have been effective in elevating mood and reducing rates of suicide among those highest at risk (Kaut, 2013). Norepinephrine and dopamine are also associated with depression and are affected by antidepressant medication, suggesting that receptors for these neurotransmitters might be associated with suicidal behavior as well (Kaut, 2013). Consequently,

serotonin norepinephrine reuptake inhibitors (SNRIs) are receiving increasing attention as a potentially effective antidepressant medication for youth. Research examining the effectiveness of these medications in reducing suicidal behavior among children and adolescents, however, is still needed.

Unfortunately, there is evidence that a very small percentage of children and adolescents may have an increased risk of suicidal ideation when taking selective serotonin reuptake inhibitors (SSRIs), although there is less risk with increasing age. Why this occurs is not entirely clear, but it may be that in a small subset of individuals antidepressant medication may potentially result in increased agitation, restlessness, anxiety, and possibly suicidal behavior (Joiner, 2010). Furthermore, when youth are severely depressed they may develop suicidal plans but may not have the energy to carry them out. Once they begin taking antidepressant medications and begin to feel better, they may then have the energy to follow through with their suicide plan. It is again worth noting, however, that this occurs among a very small number of children and adolescents.

Although some clinical trials have found a (slight) increase in suicidal ideation among youth taking antidepressants, an increased number of deaths by suicide have *not* been found. For example, the results of a meta-analysis of 24 controlled clinical trials involving nine antidepressant medications across approximately 4,400 pediatric patients found that there were no suicides within any of the trials, with the cumulative risk of spontaneously reported suicidal ideation being 4% for active medication and 2% for individuals taking a placebo (Hammad, Laughren, & Racoosin, 2006). Furthermore, a comprehensive literature review of this topic found evidence for a link between antidepressants and youth suicide to be "underwhelming" (Bostwick, 2006, p. 235). In fact, among individuals who are at risk for suicide, it has been suggested that *not* taking antidepressant medication will likely lead to a greater risk for suicide than using it (Joiner, 2010).

Hospitalization

Inpatient psychiatric hospitalization is currently considered the standard of care for acutely suicidal individuals, including children and adolescents (American Psychiatric Association, 2003).

The goal of inpatient psychiatric hospitalization is to effectively treat suicidal individuals so they can safely return to their communities (Galardy & Lineberry, 2013). Typically, the treatment for individuals hospitalized for suicidal behavior focuses first and foremost on risk assessment, followed by promoting optimal safety of the suicidal individual through the creation of a secure, supportive environment. Inpatient hospitalization also involves targeting and treating those modifiable risk factors believed to be contributing to the individual's suicidal ideation (Galardy & Lineberry, 2013), which may include short-term psychotherapy, medication management, or both.

Most children and adolescents who are hospitalized in the United States for suicidal behavior are not hospitalized for long—often only a day or two. This occurs for a variety of reasons, including a dramatic decline in the availability of state-funded psychiatric beds, decreased insurance reimbursement for inpatient hospitalization, the need for psychiatric beds if the patient is no longer acutely suicidal, the desire of parents to bring their child home as quickly as possible, the cost of psychiatric inpatient services, and the fact that most psychiatric involuntary holds are only for 48 to 72 hours. Given the numerous constraints and lack of consistency in follow-up care, hospitalizing suicidal youth should generally be viewed as providing containment and stabilization rather than intensive and extensive treatment (Miller, 2011). Although hospitalization may be necessary in some cases to protect an individual from self-harm, there is currently no evidence that inpatient psychiatric hospitalization reduces the frequency or the risk for suicide (Galardy & Lineberry, 2013), regardless of length of stay or whether an individual's hospitalization is voluntary or involuntary (Joiner, 2010).

Dialectical Behavior Therapy

DBT is a psychotherapeutic intervention that combines cognitive-behavior therapy with eastern mindfulness practices in conjunction with an overarching dialectical framework emphasizing the synthesis of opposites (Linehan, 1993). The fundamental dialectic in DBT is between validation and acceptance of the client as he or she is while simultaneously helping the client to change his or her thoughts and behaviors (Dimeff & Linehan, 2001).

In particular, DBT emphasizes two fundamental and related concepts: *acceptance* and *mindfulness.* In regards to acceptance, one of the goals of DBT is not to change problematic thoughts and emotions (as in traditional cognitive-behavior therapy), but rather to accept them for what they are—private experiences and not literal truth (O'Brien, Larson, & Murrell, 2008). From this perspective, acceptance is accompanied by change, but the change is of a different type than is seen in other, more traditional cognitive behavioral approaches (Linehan, 1993). Rather than encouraging clients to simply change the *content* of their thoughts, DBT therapists focus on changing the *relationship* of their clients' thoughts to their behaviors, emphasizing that thoughts are simply thoughts and not all thoughts are facts (Linehan, 2014).

In addition to embracing acceptance, the second fundamental concept in DBT is mindfulness. The practice of mindfulness involves "paying attention in a particular way; on purpose, in the present moment, and nonjudgmentally" (Kabat-Zinn, 1994, p. 4). This includes being present and nonjudgmental even in those moments and situations that are most painful and unpleasant (O'Brien et al., 2008). Engaging in mindfulness requires seven different but interrelated skills (Linehan, 2014). The first skill is being in "wise mind," which is the intersection of "reasonable" and "emotional" mind. The second set of skills is called the "what" skills: observing, describing, and participating. More specifically, "observing entails watching one's own thoughts, feelings, and behaviors without trying to change them; describing refers to the labeling of thoughts, feelings, and behaviors without judgment; and participating requires complete involvement in the present moment, without self-consciousness" (O'Brien et al., 2008, p. 21). The last three mindfulness skills are the "how" skills: being nonjudgmental, focusing on only one thing at a time ("one-mindfully"), and effectively completing the task at hand (i.e., doing what works; Linehan, 2014). For more detailed information about these processes, the reader is referred to works by Linehan (1993, 2014) and Miller, Rathus, and Linehan (2007).

The standard treatment for DBT is multifaceted and comprehensive, typically requiring weekly individual therapy, telephone consultations, group skills training, and therapist-consultation team meetings (Rojas & Rogers, 2013). DBT targets suicidal and nonsuicidal self-injurious behaviors directly as well as emotional dysregulation and other destabilizing and interfering behaviors. Like other cognitive behavioral therapies (CBTs), DBT involves the ongoing assessment of current behaviors, the clear definition of treatment goals, and the development of a collaborative working relationship between the therapist and the client (Rojas & Rogers, 2013).

There have been several published randomized control trials (RCTs) demonstrating the efficacy of DBT (e.g., Linehan et al., 2006), with many of these studies specifically addressing suicidal behavior and self-harm (Chang, Stanley, Brown, & Cunningham, 2011). DBT has demonstrated superior treatment effects in reducing suicidal crises over treatment as usual (Chang et al., 2011), and there is recent evidence that this approach can be used successfully with suicidal adolescents (Mehlum et al., 2014; Miller et al., 2007). Given the efficacy of DBT with suicidal adults and adolescents, Mazza, Dexter-Mazza, Murphy, Miller, and Rathus (2016) recently developed a universal social-emotional learning curriculum for middle and high school students based on the adaptation of many DBT skills. The close alignment of the curriculum with DBT skills and strategies holds significant promise for reaching a larger adolescent population and is currently being pilot tested.

School-Based Suicide Prevention Programs

Because children and adolescents spend much of their time in schools, educational facilities have often been viewed as ideal venues for youth suicide prevention programs (Miller, 2011). Although there is some controversy about the roles schools should play in youth suicide prevention, schools are de facto mental health facilities for the majority of school-aged youth, given the many financial, cultural, and geographical barriers that youth may experience in their attempts to access mental health services (Mazza, 2006). Initially developed in the United States in the 1970s, school-based suicide prevention programs grew rapidly during the 1980s and have continued to proliferate since that time, although their precise number is uncertain (Miller, 2011; Miller & Mazza, 2013).

Despite their clear utility, the evidence for the effectiveness of school-based suicide prevention programs is limited (Miller et al., 2009; Robinson et al., 2013) and has been hampered by a variety of methodological concerns, including a lack of RCTs (Robinson et al., 2013). To date, very few studies examining the effectiveness of school-based suicide prevention programs have demonstrated promising evidence of educational or clinical significance, identifiable components linked to statistically significant primary outcomes, and program implementation integrity (Miller et al., 2009). There is, however, emerging evidence that schools can play an important role in reducing youth suicidal behavior, and that schools with comprehensive suicide prevention programs can result in reductions in youth suicide over sustained periods of time (Zenere & Lazarus, 2009).

For example, schools can effectively promote and/or provide (a) early detection and referral-making practices; (b) help-seeking behavior; (c) education about risk factors and warning signs to students, professionals, and parents; and (d) universal, selected, and indicated interventions (Berman et al., 2006; Miller, 2011). A particularly important aspect of school-based approaches to youth suicide prevention is to teach students how and where to get help (Miller, 2011). Unfortunately, there is evidence to indicate that school-based suicide prevention programs have had a limited impact on help-seeking behavior in youth (Klimas-Dougan, Klingbeil, & Meller, 2013). A major barrier to this process is the consistent finding that youth with the highest risk for suicidal behaviors are frequently the least likely to seek help from others (Berman et al., 2006). The need for school personnel to extend themselves to students and to show their support for them is particularly important for males, given their much higher risk for dying by suicide in comparison to females.

In recent years, a public health approach to school-based suicide prevention has been increasingly viewed as a "best practice" (e.g., Mazza & Reynolds, 2008; Miller, 2011, 2012; Miller et al., 2009; Miller & Mazza, 2013). A key characteristic of a public health approach is its emphasis on prevention and the treatment of entire populations rather than individuals. Most public health models in schools make use of a three-tier model (Shinn & Walker, 2010) that collectively represents a continuum of intervention services that increase in intensity based on the corresponding responsiveness and needs of individual students. A brief guide to the implementation of a school-based, three-tier model of youth suicide prevention is provided in the following section. Readers interested in a more detailed discussion of these issues are referred to Mazza and Reynolds (2008), Miller (2011, 2012), Miller and Eckert (2009b), and Miller and Mazza (2013).

HOW TO: A GUIDE TO THE IMPLEMENTATION OF A SCHOOL-BASED SUICIDE PREVENTION PROGRAM FOR CHILDREN AND ADOLESCENTS

Universal Level (Tier 1)

The first tier is often referred to as the "universal" level because all students in a given population (e.g., all students in a classroom, school, or school district) receive a general set of interventions designed to prevent particular emotional, behavioral, social, and/or academic problems. Universal approaches attempt to reach the greatest number of students and school staff possible, with the hope of "casting a wide net" to identify the much smaller number of students who might be at risk for suicide (Berman, 2009). The primary purpose of universal suicide prevention programs is to provide practical, useful, and relevant information to students and school personnel about suicide, its prevention, and the role of the schools in those efforts.

Universal suicide prevention programs in schools generally fit into the category of curriculum-based educational programs, which aim to deliver interventions to a particular population via the school curriculum. Research has demonstrated that curriculum-based programs can lead to positive effects, including an increased knowledge among students and school staff about the risk factors and warning signs of suicide, improved attitudes toward suicidal peers, and the self-reported likelihood of help seeking (Cusimano & Sameem, 2011; Robinson et al., 2013). Curriculum-based programs also appear to be reasonably acceptable to many groups in the school community, including school superintendents (Scherff, Eckert, & Miller, 2005), high school principals (Miller, Eckert, DuPaul, & White, 1999), school psychologists (Eckert, Miller, DuPaul, &

Riley-Tillman, 2003), and students (Eckert, Miller, Riley-Tillman, & DuPaul, 2006).

School-based mental health professionals (i.e., school psychologists, school counselors, school social workers) are typically the most appropriate persons to lead universal information sessions. Topics that can and should be presented to students, faculty, and staff include dispelling common myths and misinformation about suicide. For example, some of the prominent myths about suicide that can impede suicide prevention efforts include the following: (a) asking questions or talking about suicide with children or adolescents will have a deleterious effect by actually increasing suicidal behavior; (b) suicide is caused primarily by stress and with enough of it anyone can be suicidal; (c) people who are suicidal are "crazy," "insane," or "out of their minds"; (d) if someone wants to die by suicide, there is little or nothing anyone can do to stop it; (e) people who talk about killing themselves are not "serious" about it; they are just looking for attention; (f) suicide is an impulsive act; (g) listening to certain music, watching certain movies or television shows, or playing certain video games can induce suicidal behavior; (h) suicide frequently occurs without warning; and (i) antidepressant medication can cause suicide (Joiner, 2010; Miller, 2011; Miller & Mazza, 2013).

Another topic that should be discussed within a universal framework is the various risk factors and potential warning signs of suicide. Risk factors refer to those variables that may predispose an individual to suicidal behavior (Van Orden, Witte, Selby, Bender, & Joiner, 2008). The two most prominent risk factors for suicide are (a) the presence of at least one mental health disorder, and (b) a history of previous suicidal behavior, particularly suicide attempts. Other possible risk factors for suicide include: (a) biological deficits in serotonin functioning; (b) social isolation; (c) limited access to mental health facilities; (d) poor problem solving and coping skills; (e) dysfunctional parenting or family environments; (f) parental psychopathology; (g) cultural or religious beliefs; (h) access to lethal weapons; and (i) repeated engagement in or exposure to violence (Mazza, 2006; Miller, 2011; Van Orden et al., 2008).

As opposed to risk factors, warning signs for suicide are more fluid and proximal factors that indicate a more immediate possibility of a suicidal crisis

(Van Orden et al., 2008). The American Association of Suicidology (AAS) developed a useful mnemonic for warning signs of suicide using the acronym IS PATH WARM, in which *I* is for suicidal ideation, *S* is for substance abuse, *P* is for purposelessness, *A* is for anxiety and agitation (including being unable to sleep), *T* is for trapped (as in feeling trapped), *H* is for hopeless, *W* is for withdrawal, *A* is for anger, *R* is for recklessness, and *M* is for mood fluctuations.

In addition to addressing risk factors and warning signs, universal prevention programs may also target protective factors. For example, a suicide prevention program known as Sources of Strength makes use of school leaders trained to conduct school-wide messaging among high school students. A recent outcome evaluation of Sources of Strength found that it increased perceptions of adult support for suicidal youth as well as the acceptability of seeking help for suicidal behavior among adolescents (Wyman et al., 2010).

Selected Level (Tier 2)

The second tier, often referred to as the "selected" level, comprises more intensive interventions and services for students who are identified as being at risk for suicide. One of the challenges at this level is to identify which students may be at risk. One of the most effective methods of identifying risk factors among adolescents is to use broadband self-report measures (e.g., Behavioral Assessment System for Children) at the universal level (Tier 1) that contain student IDs or names so that follow-up with identified at-risk students (Tier 2) can take place. Although many broadband measures do not directly assess suicidal behavior, the related mental health difficulties and symptoms (e.g., depression; anxiety) are often assessed. Students who are identified using these broadband measures should be followed up with more comprehensive narrow-band measures that include suicidal behavior.

In the context of self-report measures for the identification of at-risk youth, it is important to discuss proactive screening as a method for identifying those students at risk for suicidal behavior. Proactive screening via student self-report, in either Tier 1 or Tier 2, has been found to be an effective method for identifying at-risk students who are thinking about or have engaged in suicidal behavior (Mazza, 2006; Mazza & Reynolds, 2008).

Screening for suicidal behavior has its advantages and challenges, and it is important for school personnel to be aware of these issues when contemplating the use of screening procedures (for more information on this topic, see Jacob, 2009 and Miller, 2011). Perhaps the single greatest advantage of screening programs is that they are the only school-based suicide prevention programs that directly assess students. Consequently, their use can lead to the identification of youth who would likely not come to the attention of school personnel via alternative means (Miller, 2011).

For example, a recent review found that screening programs successfully identified students as being at risk for suicide who otherwise would not have come forward for help, with studies indicating that between 4% and 45% of students screened were identified as needing further supports, many of whom were subsequently linked with school- or community-based services (Robinson et al., 2013). Furthermore, screening programs do not appear to cause undue stress on those students taking part in them (Gould et al., 2005; Robinson et al., 2011), and reliable and valid screening tools are available, such as the Signs of Suicide (SOS) Suicide Prevention Program (Aseltine & DeMartino, 2004) and the Suicidal Ideation Questionnaire (SIQ; Gutierrez & Osman, 2009; Reynolds, 1987). For example, the SIQ can be used in a two-step screening process. In step 1, students can complete the SIQ, either in small or large group settings. In step 2, all students who scored above clinically significant levels on the SIQ are then individually interviewed by a school-based mental health professional (e.g., school psychologist) for a more precise assessment of suicide risk (Reynolds, 1991).

All students who are considered potentially at risk of suicidal behavior should be individually interviewed by a school-based mental health professional (e.g., school psychologist) who is adequately trained in suicide risk assessment. Examples of areas that should be explored with at-risk students include: (a) how the student currently feels; (b) past and current levels of depression, hopelessness, and suicidal ideation; (c) perceptions of possible burdensomeness and disconnection to others; (d) a history of any previous suicidal behavior, particularly suicide attempts; (e) the presence or absence of a suicide plan; (f) the degree of specificity and lethality of method in the suicide plan; (g) availability of lethal methods; (h) possibility of rescue; (i) level of support systems; and (j) reasons to live (Miller, 2011, 2013a)

Although a detailed discussion of this issue is beyond the scope of this chapter, school personnel should also be cognizant of the relationship between suicidal behavior and school shootings (Miller, 2011, 2012). Specifically, the U.S. Secret Service and the U.S. Department of Education found that 78% of school shooters exhibited a significant degree of suicidal ideation, and nearly 75% had previously threatened or attempted suicide (Vossekuil, Fein, Reddy, Borum, & Modezelski, 2002). Furthermore, four of the five most deadly school shootings in American history ended with the suicide of the perpetrator(s), and there are indications that these were planned cases of murder–suicide, in which the perpetrators fully intended to kill themselves and others (Miller & Sawka-Miller, 2015). In fact, there is increasing evidence to suggest that suicide, rather than murder, typically is the primary motivation in cases of murder–suicide (Joiner, 2014; Lankford, 2013). Consequently, when youth are suspected of being at risk for either suicidal behavior or violent behavior toward others, it would be prudent to conduct both a suicide risk assessment and a student threat assessment (Miller & Sawka-Miller, 2015).

Students who are identified as being at risk of suicidal behavior typically have significant mental health problems, particularly mood disorders (e.g., depressive disorders), substance-related disorders (e.g., alcohol and/or drug abuse), and disruptive behavioral problems, respectively (Fleischmann et al., 2005). Consequently, students receiving effective interventions for these problems may potentially result in collateral reductions to suicidal behavior as well. For example, DBT has been found to be effective for the treatment of nonsuicidal self-injury (Miller & Brock, 2010) and CBT has been demonstrated to be an effective treatment for a variety of mental health problems related to suicide, such as depression (Mazza & Reynolds, 2008) and anxiety (Huberty, 2012).

Indicated Level (Tier 3)

The third tier, referred to as the "indicated" level, is for students who are identified as having already engaged in suicidal behavior and therefore need individualized interventions. Some of these students will require immediate intervention if the risk of future suicidal behavior is imminent. In such crisis situations, the major goal is to keep the student safe and mobilize needed supports as quickly as possible. Some common steps that are involved in crisis intervention with suicidal youth include: (a) removing/restricting access to lethal means; (b) breaking confidentiality with the student and notifying parents/caregivers as well as notifying the police or other community supports as needed; (c) keeping the student supervised by an adult at all times; (d) transporting the student to a hospital or mental health facility if necessary; and (e) documenting all actions (Miller, 2011).

Tier 3 interventions for youth who are not experiencing a suicidal crisis but are still exhibiting suicidal behavior should be treated with evidence-based interventions, such as DBT and/or CBT. It is important that all students in Tier 3 have (a) a safety/crisis plan, including contact numbers of local hospitals and crisis interventions providers; (b) the number of the National Suicide Prevention Lifeline (1–800-273-TALK); (c) the numbers of their therapists outside the school; and (d) access to mental health professionals in the school who can provide appropriate therapeutic support, coping strategies, and/or crisis interventions services.

CONCLUSION

School personnel should understand that intervention programs need to account for the overall mental health and well-being of students and not simply focus on their suicidal behavior. Youth suicidal behavior does not occur in a vacuum and is likely to be an outcome of other related mental health problems and stressful life events. As such, helping children and adolescents develop effective coping strategies and skills to address their current mental health challenges and stressful life events is necessary to reduce the risk of future suicidal behavior.

SELECT BIBLIOGRAPHY

Berman, A. L., Jobes, D. A., & Silverman, M. M. (2006). *Adolescent suicide: Assessment and*

intervention, second edition. Washington, DC: American Psychological Association.
This text, which covers a variety of diagnostic, assessment, prevention, and treatment issues, provides the most comprehensive overview of adolescent suicide currently available.

Mazza, J. J., Dexter-Mazza, E. T., Murphy, H. E., Miller, A. L., & Rathus, J. L. (2016). *DBT in schools: Skills training for emotional problem solving for adolescents (DBT STEPS-A).* New York, NY: Guilford.
This book provides a curriculum for teaching problem-solving skills to middle school and high school students to help them to overcome emotional dysregulation, a common problem for adolescents exhibiting suicidal behavior.

Miller, A. L., Rathus, J. H., & Linehan, M. M. (2007). *Dialectical behavior therapy with suicidal adolescents.* New York, NY: Guilford.
This book provides the most comprehensive overview currently available for conducting dialectical behavior therapy with suicidal adolescents.

Miller, D. N. (2011). *Child and adolescent suicidal behavior: School-based prevention, assessment, and intervention.* New York, NY: Guilford.
Taking a public health approach to youth suicide prevention in the schools, this book addresses issues related to school-based suicide risk assessment, prevention, intervention, and postvention.

REFERENCES

American Psychiatric Association. (2003). Practice guidelines for the assessment and treatment of patients with suicidal behaviors. *American Journal of Psychiatry, 160*(Suppl. 11), 1–60.

American Psychological Association. (2013). *Gun violence: Prediction, prevention, and policy.* Retrieved from http://www.apa.org/pubs/info/reports/gun-violence-prevention.aspx

Aseltine, R. H., & DeMartino, R. (2004). An outcome evaluation of the SOS Suicide Prevention Program. *American Journal of Public Health, 94*(3), 446–451.

Berman, A. L. (2009). School-based suicide prevention: Research advances and practice implications. *School Psychology Review, 38,* 233–238.

Berman, A. L., Jobes, D. A., & Silverman, M. M. (2006). *Adolescent suicide: Assessment and intervention, second edition.* Washington, DC: American Psychological Association.

Bostwick, J. M. (2006). Do SSRIs cause suicide in children? The evidence is underwhelming. *Journal of Clinical Psychology, 62*(2), 235–241.

Centers for Disease Control and Prevention (CDC). (2012). *National Center for Injury Prevention and Control. WISQUARS search.* Retrieved from http://www.cdc.gov/violenceprevention/pdf/suicide-datasheet-a.PDF

Chang, N. A., Stanley, B., Brown, G. K., & Cunningham, A. (2011). Treating the suicidal patient: Cognitive therapy and dialectical behaviour therapy. In R. C. O'Connor, S. Platt, & J. Gordon (Eds.), *International handbook of suicide prevention: Research, policy, and practice* (pp. 369–382). New York, NY: John Wiley & Sons. doi:10.1002/9781119998556.ch21

Cusimano, M. D., & Sameem, M. (2011). The effectiveness of middle and high school-based suicide prevention programmes for adolescents: A systematic review. *Injury Prevention: Journal of the International Society for Child and Adolescent Injury Prevention, 17*(1), 43–49.

Dimeff, L., & Linehan, M. M. (2001). Dialectical behavior therapy in a nutshell. *The California Psychologist, 34,* 10–13.

Eckert, T. L., Miller, D. N., DuPaul, G. J., & Riley-Tillman, T. C. (2003). Adolescent suicide prevention: School psychologists' acceptability of school-based programs. *School Psychology Review, 32,* 57–76.

Eckert, T. L., Miller, D. N., Riley-Tillman, T. C., & DuPaul, G. J. (2006). Adolescent suicide prevention: Gender differences in students' perceptions of the acceptability and intrusiveness of school-based screening programs. *Journal of School Psychology, 44,* 271–285. doi:10.1016/j.jsp.2006.05.001

Fleischmann, A., Bertolote, J. M., Belfer, M., & Beautrais, A. (2005). Completed suicide and psychiatric diagnoses in young people: A critical examination of the evidence. *The American Journal of Orthopsychiatry, 75*(4), 676–683.

Galardy, C. A., & Lineberry, T. W. (2013). Hospitalization as suicide prevention. In D. Lester & J. R. Rogers (Eds.), *Suicide: A global issue, volume 2: Prevention* (pp. 91–108). Santa Barbara, CA: Praeger.

Goldston, D. B., Molock, S. D., Whitbeck, L. B., Murakami, J. L., Zayas, L. H., & Hall, G. C. (2008). Cultural considerations in adolescent suicide prevention and psychosocial treatment. *The American Psychologist, 63*(1), 14–31.

Gould, M. S., & Kalafat, J. (2009). Crisis hotlines. In D. Wasserman & C. Wasserman (Eds.), *Oxford textbook of suicidology and suicide prevention: A global perspective* (pp. 459–462). New York, NY: Oxford University Press. doi:10.1093/med/9780198570059.003.0061

Gould, M. S., Marrocco, F. A., Kleinman, M., Thomas, J. G., Mostkoff, K., Cote, J., & Davies, M. (2005). Evaluating iatrogenic risk of youth suicide screening programs: A randomized controlled trial. *Journal of American Medical Association, 293*(13), 1635–1643.

Gutierrez, P. M., & Osman, A. (2009). Getting the best return on your screening investment: Maximizing sensitivity and specificity of the Suicidal Ideation Questionnaire and Reynolds Adolescent Depression Scale. *School Psychology Review, 38,* 200–217.

Hammad, T. A., Laughren, T., & Racoosin, J. (2006). Suicidality in pediatric patients treated with antidepressant drugs. *Archives of General Psychiatry, 63*(3), 332–339.

Huberty, T. J. (2012). *Anxiety and depression in children and adolescents: Assessment, intervention, and prevention.* New York, NY: Springer. doi:10.1007/978-1-4614-3110-7

Jacob, S. (2009). Putting it all together: Implications for school psychology. *School Psychology Review, 38,* 239–243.

Joiner, T. (2010). *Myths about suicide.* Cambridge, MA: Harvard University Press.

Joiner, T. (2014). *The perversion of virtue: Understanding murder-suicide.* New York, NY: Oxford University Press.

Kabat-Zinn, J. (1994). *Wherever you go, there you are: Mindfulness meditation in everyday life.* New York, NY: Hyperion.

Kaut, K. P. (2013). Neurobiology, psychopharmacology, and the prevention of suicide. In D. Lester & J. R. Rogers (Eds.), *Suicide: A global issue, volume 2: Prevention* (pp. 27–50). Santa Barbara, CA: Praeger.

Kerr, N. A. (2013). Suicide prevention centers. In D. Lester & J. R. Rogers (Eds.), *Suicide: A global issue, volume 2: Prevention* (pp. 71–89). Santa Barbara, CA: Praeger.

Klimas-Dougan, B., Klingbeil, D. A., & Meller, S. J. (2013). The impact of universal suicide-prevention programs on the help-seeking attitudes and behaviors of youths. *Crisis: The Journal of Crisis Intervention and Suicide Prevention, 34,* 82–97.

Lankford, A. (2013). *The myth of martyrdom: What really drives suicide bombers, rampage shooters, and other self-destructive killers.* New York, NY: Palgrave Macmillan.

Leenaars, A. (2009). Gun availability and control in suicide prevention. In D. Wasserman & C. Wasserman (Eds.), *Oxford textbook of suicidology and suicide prevention* (pp. 577–581). New York, NY: Oxford University Press.

Lester, D. (2013). Preventing suicide by restricting access to methods for suicide. In D. Lester & J. R. Rogers (Eds.), *Suicide: A global issue, volume 2: Prevention* (pp. 149–168). Santa Barbara, CA: Praeger.

Linehan, M. M. (1993). *Cognitive-behavioral treatment of borderline personality disorder.* New York, NY: Guilford.

Linehan, M. M. (2014). *DBT skills training manual.* New York, NY: Guilford.

Linehan, M. M., Comtois, K. A., Murray, A. M., Brown, M. Z., Gallop, R. J., Heard, H. L., ... Lindenboim, N. (2006). Two-year randomized controlled trial and follow-up of dialectical behavior therapy vs therapy by experts for suicidal behaviors and borderline personality disorder. *Archives of General Psychiatry, 63*(7), 757–766.

Mazza, J. J. (2006). Youth suicidal behavior: A crisis in need of attention. In F. A. Villarruel & T. Luster (Eds.), *Adolescent mental health* (pp. 156–177). Westport, CT: Greenwood Publishing Group.

Mazza, J. J., Dexter-Mazza, E. T., Murphy, H. E., Miller, A. L., & Rathus, J. L. (in press). *Skills training for emotional problem solving for adolescents (STEPS-A).* New York, NY: Guilford.

Mazza, J. J., & Reynolds, W. M. (2008). School-wide approaches to prevention of and treatment for depression and suicidal behaviors. In B. Doll & J. A. Cummings (Eds.), *Transforming school mental health services* (pp. 213–241). Thousand Oaks, CA: Corwin.

Mehlum, L., Tørmoen, A. J., Ramberg, M., Haga, E., Diep, L. M., Laberg, S., ... Grøholt, B. (2014). Dialectical behavior therapy for adolescents with repeated suicidal and self-harming behavior: A randomized trial. *Journal of the American Academy of Child and Adolescent Psychiatry, 53*(10), 1082–1091.

Miller, A. L., Rathus, J. H., & Linehan, M. M. (2007). *Dialectical behavior therapy with suicidal adolescents.* New York, NY: Guilford.

Miller, D. N. (2011). *Child and adolescent suicidal behavior: School-based prevention, assessment, and intervention.* New York, NY: Guilford.

Miller, D. N. (2012). Preventing student suicide. In S. E. Brock & S. R. Jimerson (Eds.), *Best practices in school crisis prevention and intervention, second edition* (pp. 203–222). Bethesda, MD: National Association of School Psychologists.

Miller, D. N. (2013a). Assessing risk for suicide. In S. H. McConaughy (Ed.), *Clinical interviews for children and adolescents: Assessment to intervention, second edition* (pp. 208–227). New York, NY: Guilford.

Miller, D. N. (2013b). Lessons in suicide prevention from the Golden Gate Bridge: Means restriction, public health, and the school psychologist. *Contemporary School Psychology, 17,* 71–79.

Miller, D. N., & Brock, S. E. (2010). *Identifying, assessing, and treating self-injury at school.* New York, NY: Springer.

Miller, D. N., & Eckert, T. L. (2009a). Youth suicidal behavior: An introduction and overview. *School Psychology Review, 38,* 153–167.

Miller, D. N., & Eckert, T. L. (Eds.). (2009b). School-based suicide prevention: Research advances and practice implications [Special issue]. *School Psychology Review, 38*(2).

Miller, D. N., Eckert, T. L., DuPaul, G. J., & White, G. P. (1999). Adolescent suicide prevention: Acceptability of school-based programs among secondary school principals. *Suicide & Life-Threatening Behavior, 29*(1), 72–85.

Miller, D. N., Eckert, T. L., & Mazza, J. J. (2009). Suicide prevention programs in the schools· A ieview and public health perspective. *School Psychology Review, 38,* 168–188.

Miller, D. N., & Mazza, J. J. (2013). Suicide prevention programs in schools. In D. Lester & J. R. Rogers (Eds.), *Suicide: A global issue, volume 2: Prevention* (pp. 109–134). Santa Barbara, CA: Praeger.

Miller, D. N., & Sawka-Miller, K. D. (2015). Preventing school shootings: A public health approach to gun-related homicide and murder-suicide in schools. In M. B. Morris (Ed.), *Public health and harm reduction: Principles, perceptions and programs* (pp. 1–34). Hauppauge, NY: Nova Science.

Nock, M. K., Green, J. G., Hwang, I., McLaughlin, K. A., Sampson, N. A., Zaslavsky, A. M., & Kessler, R. C. (2013). Prevalence, correlates, and treatment of lifetime suicidal behavior among adolescents: Results from the National Comorbidity Survey Replication Adolescent Supplement. *JAMA Psychiatry, 70*(3), 300–310.

O'Brien, K. M., Larson, C. M., & Murrell, A. R. (2008). Third-wave behavior therapies for children and adolescents: Progress, challenges, and future directions. In L. A. Greco & S. C Hayes (Eds.), *Acceptance and mindfulness treatments for children and adolescents: A practitioner's guide* (pp. 15–35). Oakland, CA: New Harbinger.

Reynolds, W. M. (1987). *Suicidal ideation questionnaire.* Odessa, FL: Psychological Assessment Resources.

Reynolds, W. M. (1991). A school-based procedure for the identification of students at-risk for suicidal behavior. *Family and Community Health, 14,* 64–75.

Robinson, J., Cox, G., Malone, A., Williamson, M., Baldwin, G., Fletcher, K., & O'Brien, M. (2013). A systematic review of school-based interventions aimed at preventing, treating, and responding to suicide- related behavior in young people. *Crisis, 34*(3), 164–182.

Robinson, J., Pan Yuen, H., Martin, C., Hughes, A., Baksheev, G. N., Dodd, S.,... Yung, A. R. (2011). Does screening high school students for psychological distress, deliberate self-harm, or suicidal ideation cause distress—And is it acceptable? An Australian-based study. *Crisis, 32*(5), 254–263.

Rojas, E., & Rogers, J. R. (2013). Psychotherapy for suicidal clients. In D. Lester & J. R. Rogers (Eds.), *Suicide: A global issue, volume 2: Prevention* (pp. 51–69). Santa Barbara, CA: Praeger.

Scherff, A. R., Eckert, T. L., & Miller, D. N. (2005). Youth suicide prevention: A survey of public school superintendents' acceptability of school-based programs. *Suicide & Life-Threatening Behavior, 35*(2), 154–169.

Shinn, M. R., & Walker, H. M. (2010). (Eds.). *Interventions for achievement and behavior problems in a three-tier model including RTI.* Bethesda, MD: National Association of School Psychologists.

Silverman, M. M. (2013). Defining suicide and suicidal behavior. In D. Lester & J. R. Rogers (Eds.), *Suicide: A global issue, volume 1: Understanding* (pp. 1–30). Santa Barbara, CA: Praeger.

U.S. Department of Health and Human Services (HHS), Office of the Surgeon General and National

Action Alliance for Suicide Prevention (2012). *2012 National strategy for suicide prevention: Goals and objectives for action.* Washington, DC: HHS.

Van Orden, K. A., Witte, T. K., Selby, E. A., Bender, T. W., & Joiner, T. E. (2008). Suicidal behavior in youth. In J. R. Z. Abela & B. L. Hankin (Eds.), *Handbook of depression in children and adolescents* (pp. 441–465). New York, NY: Guilford Press.

Vossekuil, B., Fein, R.A., Reddy, M., Borum, R., & Modzeleski, W. (2002). *The final report and findings of the Safe School Initiative: Implications for the prevention of school attacks in the United States.* Washington, DC: Secret Service and U.S. Department of Education.

Wagner, B. M. (2009). *Suicidal behavior in children and adolescents.* New Haven, CT: Yale University Press.

World Health Organization. (2014). *Preventing suicide: A global imperative.* Geneva, Switzerland: Author.

Wyman, P. A., Brown, C. H., LoMurray, M., Schmeelk-Cone, K., Petrova, M., Yu, Q.,...Wang, W. (2010). An outcome evaluation of the Sources of Strength suicide prevention program delivered by adolescent peer leaders in high schools. *American Journal of Public Health, 100*(9), 1653–1661.

Zenere, F. J., & Lazarus, P. J. (2009). The sustained reduction of youth suicidal behavior in an urban multicultural school district. *School Psychology Review, 38*, 360–378.

Evidence-Based Interventions for Childhood Grief in Children and Adolescents

Melissa J. Hagan, Alexandra M. Ingram, and Sharlene A. Wolchik

OVERVIEW

Many children experience the death of someone close to them before the age of 18 years. Approximately 4% of youth lose a parent, 5% experience the loss of a sibling, 11% experience the death of a close friend, and 25% grieve the death of a second-degree relative, such as a grandparent (Harrison & Harrington, 2001). Although the majority of these children do not experience serious adjustment problems, some, particularly those who have experienced the death of a parent or loved one under sudden circumstances, experience problems, such as depression and post-traumatic stress reactions (Cerel, Fristad, Verducci, Weller, & Weller, 2006). For a minority of children, these mental health problems persist into adulthood (Luecken, 2008), highlighting the importance of using evidence-based interventions to help children adjust to the death of someone close to them. In this chapter, the effects of bereavement on children's functioning and the risk and protective factors that exacerbate or mitigate grief-related problems are reviewed. In addition, step-by-step instructions for two evidence-based interventions are provided for school-aged children and adolescents.

Normative Child Grief. Although it was once believed that children lack the capacity to grieve (Furman, 1973), several longitudinal studies have shown that this is not the case. Worden (2008) described four tasks of grieving in childhood that facilitate adaptive adjustment following the death of a loved one: (a) accepting the reality of the loss (i.e., *not* searching for or misidentifying the deceased person in others, minimizing their relationship with the deceased, or denying that the death occurred); (b) processing the emotional aspects of the loss by directly addressing loss-related negative emotions; (c) adjusting to an environment without the deceased, and (d) establishing a meaningful connection with the deceased in a way that allows the child to establish a new life. Importantly, no two children grieve in the same way, and stage-based grieving models, such as Worden's, do not capture every child's experience. Manifestation of grief-related behaviors and emotions depend on a multitude of factors, including the child's age, nature of the child's relationship to the deceased, circumstances surrounding the death, child's mental health history, occurrence of previous losses or traumas, child's support system and cultural and religious background, how the child was told about the death, and the extent to which the death impacts the child's routines or daily life.

Despite the number of factors that can affect how a child reacts to a death, some common patterns have been observed. For example, it is common for children's grief to come in waves, which may reflect their attempt to manage difficult and sometimes overwhelming emotions (Sood, Razdan, Weller, & Weller, 2006). Furthermore, it is common for children of all ages to show general depressive and anxiety symptoms following a loss, as well as academic problems due to difficulties with attention, concentration, and feeling different from their non-bereaved peers. For a list of grief-related symptoms observed in children and adolescents, please see Table 6.1. Notably, the manifestation of certain symptoms depends on which developmental stage the child is in. For example, bed-wetting and developmental regression (e.g., thumb sucking) are more common in early or middle childhood, and feelings of guilt and isolation are frequently experienced in adolescence.

Problematic Child Grief and Psychosocial Maladjustment. A child's grief becomes abnormal when it interferes with daily life activities or mastery of developmental competencies. Childhood *traumatic* grief refers to a condition in which children develop trauma-related symptoms that interfere with their ability to appropriately mourn a death (Cohen, Mannarino, Greenberg, Padlo, & Shipley, 2002). This is most commonly observed when children are exposed to deaths that are sudden, unexpected, or disturbing. Having a close friend or family member commit suicide is particularly traumatic. Higher rates of psychopathology have been observed in children who have lost a parent to suicide as compared with

those whose parent died of other causes (Pfeffer, Karus, Siegel, & Jiang, 2000). Traumatic grief is also more common when the death occurs in the context of a natural disaster or crisis, such as Hurricane Katrina or the September 11 World Trade Center attacks. Furthermore, when children experience the loss of someone close to them, it may result in mental health problems in adulthood. For example, Kendler, Sheth, Gardner, and Prescott (2002) found that parental bereavement in childhood was linked to low educational attainment, which in turn predicted major depression in adulthood.

ETIOLOGY AND FACTORS CONTRIBUTING TO CHILDHOOD GRIEF IN CHILDREN AND ADOLESCENTS

The likelihood that grief-related symptoms will become problematic depends on interpersonal, intrapersonal, and environmental risk and protective factors that occur before and after the death. The study of factors that influence how children adjust after the death of someone close to them has largely been focused on parental death. For example, in addition to losing a primary attachment figure, these youth face other stressors, such as family relocation, changes in household finances, depression and grief of the surviving caregiver, and increased family responsibilities (Lin, Sandler, Ayers, Wolchik, & Luecken, 2004). Perhaps most importantly, the quality of the child's relationship

TABLE 6.1

GRIEF-RELATED SYMPTOMS IN BEREAVED CHILDREN AND ADOLESCENTS		
Somatic	**Behavioral**	**Psychological**
Difficulty falling asleep	Developmental regression	Sadness
Early-morning waking	Irritability	Regret
Changes in eating	Crying	Confusion
Bed-wetting	Temper tantrums	Separation anxiety
Headaches	Withdrawal	Fear of losing others
Stomachaches	Loss of interest in play	Fear of abandonment
	Overdependence	Loss of concentration
	Increased demand for attention	Feeling guilt or blame
	Aggressive behavior	Feelings of isolation or alienation
	Obsessive caretaking of others	Developing new fears or anxieties

with the surviving caregiver has been shown to be a critical influence on child adaptation following parental death (Wolchik, Tein, Sandler, & Ayers, 2006). Parentally bereaved children with surviving caregivers who provide little warmth and acceptance, engage in ineffective discipline practices, and display high levels of grief-related distress, have an increased risk of mental health problems (e.g., Lin et al., 2004). Significantly, these children gain considerable protection from maladjustment if their caregivers model adaptive grief responses, provide both acceptance and structure, and maintain stability in the children's environment. Intrapersonal factors, such as higher levels of coping efficacy (Lin et al., 2004), adaptive control beliefs (Worden, 1996), self-esteem (e.g., Haine, Ayers, Sandler, Wolchik, & Weyer, 2003), feelings of mastery, and adaptive voluntary emotional expression (Pennebaker, Zech, & Rimé, 2001), are also protective for bereaved children.

EVIDENCE-BASED INTERVENTIONS AND EMPIRICAL SUPPORT FOR GRIEF IN CHILDREN AND ADOLESCENTS

Researchers and clinicians have recommended several strategies for working with children who have experienced the death of a loved one. For example, given that children engage in the coping and communicative behaviors modeled by caregivers and other close adults, clinicians are advised to help caregivers see that "protecting" children from all death-related information can lead them to feel isolated, confused, and mistrustful, or lead to misconceptions about the death and its circumstances (Oltjenbruns, 2001). Research suggests that caregivers can help children by talking about the deceased, providing opportunities to memorialize the deceased, remaining alert to children's grief-related feelings, and helping children find language to express these feelings (Nickman, Silverman, & Normand, 1998). Others have suggested that for school-aged children, it is important to ask what children understand, answer their questions honestly and with age-appropriate language, and let them know that they did not cause the death (Johnson, 1999).

In the following sections, two interventions are succinctly described. The Family Bereavement Program (FBP) is one of the few interventions that have been shown to improve children's adjustment in a randomized controlled trial and the only one to have examined long-term program effects. The FBP is a theory-based intervention for parentally bereaved children (ages 8–16 years) and their surviving caregivers. The FBP was designed to target modifiable risk and protective factors associated with more positive mental health outcomes in parentally bereaved youths (Ayers et al., 2014). The program is grounded in cognitive behavioral therapy and uses behavioral change methods, such as modeling and role-playing to teach skills, as well as weekly assignments and reviews of skill-related home practices (Ayers et al., 1996; Sandler et al., 1996).

A randomized controlled trial in which families were assigned to either the FBP or a self-study condition found that, compared with families in the self-study condition, those in the FBP experienced improved caregiver–child relationships, increased adaptive coping, and decreased caregiver mental health problems immediately after program completion. In addition, the FBP led to short- and long-term reductions in problematic grief (Sandler, Ma, et al., 2010) and lower internalizing and externalizing problems and higher self-esteem (Sandler, Ayers, et al., 2010). Moreover, the improvements in caregiver–child relationship quality observed immediately after the intervention were maintained 6 years later (Hagan et al., 2012).

The Grief and Trauma Intervention (GTI) has been identified by the National Registry of Evidence-Based Programs and Practices as an evidence-based intervention ready for dissemination. The program was designed for children between the ages of 7 and 12 years who experienced posttraumatic stress reactions due to death, disaster, or violence (Salloum & Overstreet, 2008). Multiple pre- and posttest studies reported that the GTI significantly decreased posttraumatic stress symptoms among children who had lost a loved one due to homicide (Salloum, 2008) and traumatic grief symptoms among children who experienced the death of someone during Hurricane Katrina (Salloum & Overstreet, 2008). A more recent study also found significant pre- to postintervention improvements in psychological distress and social support that were maintained 1 year after program completion (Salloum & Overstreet, 2012).

HOW TO: A GUIDE TO THE IMPLEMENTATION OF INTERVENTIONS FOR GRIEF IN CHILDREN AND ADOLESCENTS

Family Bereavement Program

Overall Structure and Resources Needed. The FBP consists of twelve 2-hour, concurrently run group sessions for caregivers and youth and two 1-hour individual sessions for caregivers. The individual sessions, which are held between sessions 3 and 4 and sessions 9 and 10, are used to tailor the program skills to the families' situations. Four of the 12 sessions include conjoint activities between caregivers and children. Groups, which range from 5 to 11 members, are led by two mental health professionals who use manuals that outline the activities in each session. Four rooms are needed (i.e., caregiver, adolescent and child groups, child care). The same skills are addressed in the child and adolescent groups using developmentally appropriate activities. In this chapter, we focus on the child program.

Content Overview and Format. The child component focuses on increasing self-esteem, reducing negative appraisals of stressful events, strengthening youths' relationship(s) with their caregiver(s), strengthening coping skills, and increasing adaptive emotional expression. The caregiver component aims to promote caregiver warmth and consistent discipline, increase caregiver modeling of adaptive coping responses, and reduce caregiver mental health problems. Except for the first and last sessions, group sessions have a similar format that includes review of home practice and family and/or personal goals (20–30 minutes), introduction of a new skill and rationale for using it (45–60 minutes), and skill practice (20–30 minutes). Times vary depending on the topic, number of participants, and whether there is a conjoint activity. Active learning strategies and assignment and/or review of home practice are used to increase engagement in the session material and promote use of skills in between sessions.

FBP Session Content

Session 1. In both caregiver and child components, the objectives are to share information about the grief process and its impact on family functioning, build cohesion and rapport, and normalize and validate feelings about grief-related issues. General information about the program is provided in a conjoint meeting. Children and caregivers then meet separately.

In the *caregiver group*, the content focuses on the grief process and its impact on the family. Members are encouraged to talk about grief-related issues and feelings in the family, and group leaders normalize and validate these feelings. Participants share information about their loved one's death and what they hope to gain from the program. Using the Bereavement Equation activity, group leaders show that the effects of bereavement on family functioning are greater than the sum of the parts. The activity starts with identifying the changes that the child and caregiver have experienced since the death, including modifications that have interfered with effective parenting. The group leaders help caregivers identify how the program can help with these changes. In addition, caregivers sign a participation contract that outlines how to get the most out of the program and ways to overcome barriers to participation (e.g., scheduling conflicts).

The home practice component of the program is one of the most important aspects in the contract. Caregivers are instructed to practice skills they learned in group, every week, at home with their children, and report on their home practice in the following session. This gives group leaders the opportunity to facilitate problem-solving difficulties with caregivers (i.e., newly learned skills), and to reinforce and encourage the acquisition of recent approaches. Practicing the skill activities at home helps demonstrate to caregivers that they are capable of bringing about positive changes in their families. For the full list of weekly home practice assignments, see Table 6.2. As shown, home practice is cumulative across sessions.

In the *child group*, each child shares the story of his or her parent's death (when and how the parent died, how the child found out). They then participate in the Fact or Fiction Exercise, in which they decide if statements are true or false. An example of a false statement is: "After a parent dies, all kids get over their painful feelings after about one to two months." This exercise helps normalize children's reactions and feelings and provides information on what they can expect after a parent dies. In all sessions, group leaders point out *Similarities, Normalize, Acknowledge,* and

TABLE 6.2

CUMULATIVE PRACTICE OF PROGRAM SKILLS ACROSS FBP CAREGIVER SESSIONS											
Home Practice Skills	Session										
	1	2	3	4	5	6	7	8	9	10	11
Personal and family goals	*	*	*	*	*	*	*	*	*	*	*
Family Fun Time		*	*	*	*	*	*	*	*	*	*
Catch 'em Being Good, Listening Skills: *Four Talk-to-Me's*		*	*	*	*	*	*	*	*	*	*
One-on-One Time, Listening Skills: Summary Responses				*	*	*	*	*	*	*	*
Listening Skills: Feeling Responses						*	*	*	*	*	*
Listening Skills, Guided Problem-Solving							*	*	*	*	*
Identify and challenge thinking traps								*	*	*	*
Discipline: Clear and realistic expectations, counting misbehaviors									*	*	*
Discipline: Communicate and implement change plan										*	*
Discipline: Continue and refine change plan, use anger management											*
Support child coping with stress											*

FBP, Family Bereavement Program.

*Indicates that skill is reviewed in that session.

Personalize (SNAP). Group leaders also discuss the program's goals: (a) deal with feelings of grief and loss, (b) build strong families, (c) cope with tough times, (d) share and learn new coping ideas, and (e) set and meet a personal goal. Youth are instructed to practice the program skills in between sessions. (See Table 6.3 for home practice assignments.)

Session 2. As noted in the "Overview," the *caregiver group* begins every week by reviewing the use of program skills at home and discussing progress toward short- and long-term goals. In session 2, leaders help caregivers identify hurdles they faced after the death and manageable steps to take in the next week to overcome one hurdle. Leaders also facilitate a discussion about family cycles and how caregiver and child distress can feed into one another to create a negative cycle. Family Fun Time (FFT) is introduced as an activity to change negative cycles into positive ones. FFT involves doing an inexpensive activity that family members choose together once each week. The leaders prepare the caregivers for meeting with their own children in the last part of the session to talk about how FFT will be done in their family.

In the *child group,* leaders begin by introducing how children can earn small rewards by completing their personal goals and helping other group members. Children then complete a team-building exercise to increase group rapport: two truths and one lie. Youths share this information "round robin" style and then review their personal goals in the same manner. The leaders then facilitate a discussion on how people try to hide their feelings after the death of a parent and some problems that result. Children write their own hidden feelings, and each child guesses a feeling people might hide and why (leaders should SNAP). Leaders then introduce the importance of "giving positives" (e.g., saying thank you, telling someone you love them, pointing out when a family member does something good, etc.) to other family members, help children brainstorm why people do not give positives, and review ways to give positives. Leaders end the session each week by instructing children to choose a personal goal related to what was discussed during the day's session and

TABLE 6.3

CUMULATIVE PRACTICE OF PROGRAM SKILLS ACROSS FBP CHILD/ADOLESCENT SESSIONS											
Home Practice Skills	**Session**										
	1	**2**	**3**	**4**	**5**	**6**	**7**	**8**	**9**	**10**	**11**
Give caregiver a positive		*	*								
Write one hopeful and one hurtful thought each day			*								
Replace hurtful thoughts with hopeful thoughts				*	*	*	*	*	*	*	*
Practice thinking hopeful and use hopeful thoughts reminders				*	*	*	*	*	*	*	*
Complete the personal goals worksheet					*	*	*	*	*	*	*
Share a feeling with caregiver using an *I-message*						*	*	*	*	*	*
Check off problems and negative feelings that are "Not a Kid's Job"								*	*	*	*	*
Brainstorm positive thoughts and actions to solve problems that are a kid's job to fix									*	*	*	*
Write down *You-message* thoughts and replace with *I-messages* for problem solving										*	*	*
Prepare a lesson to teach the group about a skill found to be particularly helpful											*	
Check off ways to continue using program skills after the group has ended												*

FBP, Family Bereavement Program.

*Indicates that skill is reviewed in that session.

tell them that they will report on their progress on the goal in the next session. For this week, leaders encourage children to choose a goal related to giving parents a positive.

Families then reunite for a conjoint activity. Leaders explain that, after a death, caregivers and children are often caught up in their own grief or are so busy that they forget to have fun together. Leaders introduce FFT as a weekly activity that helps strengthen relationships by building skills in group decision making, putting aside problems, and having fun. The leaders ask children to brainstorm problems that may happen during FFT (e.g., arguing) and ask the children to generate solutions to these problems.

Session 3. This session begins with a conjoint activity in which families discuss their experiences with FFT, and leaders help problem solve challenges that arose with FFT. Caregivers and children then separate into their respective groups.

In the *caregiver group*, leaders provide a rationale for the importance of good communication between caregivers and children and the value of positive reinforcement of children's good behaviors. Caregivers are given a *Catch 'Em Being Good* handout that lists positive behaviors that they might observe their children doing and are instructed to use the handout to record behaviors that the caregiver reinforced. Next, group leaders teach the first part of the Listening component: the *Four Talk to Me's*. These are: (a) be ready to listen or set aside time to listen if unable to listen at that time; (b) use good body language such as eye contact, nodding, and not engaging in another activity, (c) use open-ended questions (i.e., questions that cannot be answered with yes or no) rather than closed-ended ones; and (4) keep the child talking by showing that you are listening (e.g., "What happened next?"; "Mmm hmmm").

The *child group* begins with a team-building exercise, the Human Knot activity. After the activity, leaders discuss the ways grief can feel like a tangled knot and suggest ways to get untangled. Next, leaders engage the children in a discussion about grief-related anger, including facts about angry feelings, why they feel anger, how they show it, and ways to handle it. Then, leaders help children to identify and distinguish between *hopeful* and *hurtful thoughts* by reading stories about children dealing with problems and asking the children what hurtful and hopeful thoughts the characters might be thinking. Leaders encourage youths to be aware of their own hurtful and hopeful thoughts and provide them with a form for daily tracking. The leaders teach the event–thought–feeling link by explaining how situations lead to thoughts about the situation, which then lead to feelings. It is important that children identify thoughts and not things the character could do to make things better. It is also important to positively reframe thoughts that are actually wishful thinking, blaming, or giving up responsibility for problems.

Session 4. In the *caregiver group*, leaders present *One-on-One Time*, a regular time that caregivers spend with each child individually while providing the child undivided attention for 10 to 15 minutes. *One-on-One Time* is presented as a way to break negative cycles between caregivers and children and increase positive interactions. Caregivers are taught specific strategies for increasing their connection with the child including providing warmth, unconditional acceptance, and positive attention and avoiding advice-giving, teaching, disciplining, criticizing, and asking too many questions. Next, the leaders review the *Four Talk to Me's* and teach Listening Part 2 ("Think") and the first half of Part 3 ("Respond"). The group discusses the importance of thinking before responding to what their child has said. The leaders teach the *Summary Responses* skill, which shows whether one heard what the child had to say. To do this, caregivers summarize what they heard and check in with the child on whether they got it right.

The *child group* begins with a team-building activity, in which children have to help others in order to win, which demonstrates that families must work as a team to help each other to become stronger. Leaders then address the main focus of the session, feelings. The group discusses feelings of sadness, and leaders encourage children to share feelings by having them complete this sentence: "The times when I feel most sad about my parent's death are...." Leaders provide ideas about how to feel better and encourage children to share their coping strategies. Leaders should remember to SNAP and to not provide "quick fixes" to children's responses. Next, leaders review the event–thought–feeling connection and the previous week's thought-monitoring worksheet that children completed. "Self put downs" and "self boosters" are introduced as additional forms of hurtful and hopeful thinking, respectively, and children are shown how these strategies can affect their moods. Children complete an activity, in which they come up with self put-downs and self-boosters in response to different scenarios, and identify three self-boosters they believe about themselves. In a similar fashion, "doom and gloom thinking" and "positive thinking" are discussed and children brainstorm different examples. Leaders reinforce positive thinking by having children identify three positive thoughts that would work for them. Leaders engage children in an activity designed to show how different thoughts lead to different feelings in which children: (a) recall scenarios where they have had a problem, (b) think about using self put-downs and doom and gloom thinking, and (c) rate how they would feel on the "Feelings Scale." Children are then instructed to throw away their self put-downs and doom and gloom thinking and to repeat the exercise using positive thoughts and self-boosters.

Session 5. In the *caregiver group*, leaders teach the final section of Listening, Part 3 ("Respond"), which includes the *Feeling Responses* skill that is used to identify the feeling the child is having and to check out that understanding with the child. To increase caregivers' awareness of children's feelings and their "feelings vocabulary," they are given a list of different feelings and asked to check off the feelings that were part of recent interactions with their children. Caregivers then practice using all the listening skills. Leaders validate that good listening skills can do only so much when a caregiver has to say no to a child's request and encourage caregivers to provide the child with a reason for why they said no, avoid being critical of the child, and tell the child they appreciate that the child asked them.

In the *child group*, leaders introduce feelings of grief-related guilt and engage children in a discussion by having them complete this statement: "One thing I feel sorry or guilty about since my parent died is...." If children report no feelings of guilt or being sorry, leaders ask them to discuss *any time* they felt guilty. Leaders encourage all children to respond before asking, "What do you do to help yourself feel less guilty when you have these feelings?" Next, leaders probe for hopeful thoughts ask children how they use hopeful thoughts and assess how well they work. Leaders reinforce identifying a believable hopeful thought in almost every situation. Children work in teams to generate hopeful thoughts for four examples of hurtful thoughts and share why each hopeful thought makes sense to them. If a child seems to really believe in a hurtful thought, the leader asks, "How does it feel to believe that?" and gently challenges the child to come up with a hopeful thought that makes sense and helps the child to feel better. Leaders ask children to share other hopeful thoughts that they like and why, when they could use them, and what hurtful thoughts they might replace. Two tools are introduced to help children remember to use hopeful thoughts: (a) hopeful thoughts reminder cards (large personalized reminder cards), and (b) the rubber band technique (wearing colorful rubber bands as a reminder). Children then learn the four-step method of changing hurtful thoughts: (a) STOP and identify the feeling; (2) THINK What's the problem?; (3) BRAINSTORM hopeful thoughts and (4) CHOOSE hopeful thoughts.

Session 6. In the *caregiver group*, participants learn to use "guided problem solving" when good listening is not enough. This involves using good listening skills, brainstorming potential solutions with their child, and helping the child choose the solution that is most likely to solve the problem. Leaders also engage caregivers in a discussion about what it has been like for them to listen to their children talk about grief. In so doing, leaders continue to model listening skills and to shape caregivers' use of them.

In the *child group*, children are asked to describe two times that they shared what they were feeling with their caregiver: once when it went well and once when it went poorly. Leaders ask what made it

difficult and identify issues that can be helped by the program skills. Importantly, leaders teach the following ways to help communication with caregivers go well: (a) find the right time; (b) know what you want; (c) give an I-Message; and (d) thank your caregiver for listening. Leaders describe I-messages for sharing as including three things: (a) how you feel, (b) what happened/what you were thinking, and (c) what you want from your caregiver. Leaders model the following sentence: "I felt (what you feel) when (what happened). I just want you to listen. I don't want you to help me fix it right now, I just want to share it." Children practice using I-messages. The session ends with a conjoint activity in which caregivers use their listening skills as children share a personal memento, a meaningful object that is related to the parent who died.

Session 7. In the *caregiver group*, caregivers discuss life changes after the death of a loved one that contribute to being "blindsided by grief" and strategies for dealing with these experiences. During this session, leaders focus on developing a sense of hopefulness and competence in the group members. Leaders teach caregivers to recognize and reframe negative thoughts into helpful and hopeful ones. This process involves recognizing "thinking traps," negative thoughts that contribute to people feeling worse than is necessary and are held onto too long. Leaders teach how to change negative thoughts into thoughts that feel true and are less exaggerated. Caregivers practice this skill by considering common thinking traps related to grief and asking, "What are the facts? What do they show?" to decrease negative thinking and encourage positive thinking.

The *child group* begins with a discussion of fears and insecurities that occur after a parent dies. Children complete the sentence, "One bad thing that I worry might happen is..." and answer the question, "What ways do you find work for you to deal with feelings of fear or insecurity?" Leaders present the importance of coping with fears actively, and children are encouraged to use the stop–think–brainstorm–choose method to combat common hurtful thoughts. The leaders also discuss the importance of figuring out what problems are a child's job to fix and the tendency to feel responsible for fixing problems that are not a child's responsibility. The Backpack Activity is used to help children see the cost of assuming responsibility for problems they cannot solve. The leaders put a backpack on a group member and then fill the backpack with objects, some heavier and some lighter, that are labeled with a specific problem; some problems are not a child's job to fix, such as a caregiver being sad a lot, whereas other problems are a child's job to fix, such as getting a bad grade. After it is filled, the backpack is really heavy and leaders talk about how difficult it is to do other activities while carrying such a heavy backpack. Leaders then unload all the problems that are not a child's job to fix, showing that the weight is now much more manageable. Leaders then play a video clip taken from "Party of Five" (a TV show about five children whose parents died) to show a similar situation to what children in the group may be experiencing (e.g., a child who sees a sad caregiver feels responsible for cheering the caregiver up and neglects school work). Children process hurtful and hopeful processes they observe. Leaders teach children how to decide whether something is their responsibility or not. Children practice making these decisions using several problem scenarios.

Session 8. In the *caregiver group*, leaders set the stage for the next three sessions that focus on how to discipline children during tough times. These three sessions include information about discipline, including why it is important and difficult for bereaved caregivers to discipline effectively, and how to set clear expectations and select appropriate consequences. Throughout these sessions, it is important for leaders to help caregivers develop or increase a sense of self-efficacy and competence in regard to discipline. Leaders discuss common challenges for bereaved caregivers, roadblocks to effective discipline, and how to use discipline to teach rather than punish. Caregivers take a self-assessment in which they are given 5 to 10 discipline scenarios and choose which of four answers most closely reflects how they would react. After caregivers score their self-assessments, the leaders describe four styles of discipline (i.e., authoritarian, permissive, neglecting, and authoritative) and explain how these discipline styles affect caregiver–child relationships. The group watches videotaped scenarios depicting each style and discusses caregiver–child dynamics related to each example. Leaders teach the three Cs of discipline: Be *c*onsistent, *c*lear, and *c*alm, and discuss how realistic expectations differ for

younger and older children. Then, leaders teach the four steps of effective discipline: (a) adopt clear and realistic expectations; (b) size up the problem; (c) develop a change plan; and (d) use the plan (evaluate and reevaluate). The session ends with caregivers practicing these skills.

In the *child group*, leaders share experiences children might face after a loved one's death (e.g., dreaming about or talking to the deceased parent) and invite children to share any similar experiences they have had. This discussion is facilitated by having children complete the following questions/statements: "One thing that happens to me that I wonder about is…"; "How do you feel when this happens?" and "How do you deal with these experiences?" Leaders emphasize that this exercise is an opportunity to share with others who are especially likely to understand. If negative thoughts arise during this exercise, leaders encourage children to replace them with positive ones. This session also builds on the previous week's discussion by teaching children how to deal with problems that are in their control with the stop–think–brainstorm–choose method. This method is demonstrated using a puppet show that depicts a situation in which "Theo" acts without stopping to think first. Children practice problem solving using the stop–think–brainstorm–choose with a new step, asking, "What do I want to happen?" Leaders help children pick positive goals. Children then receive another problem scenario and come up with as many solutions as possible before choosing the option that will help them reach their goal.

Session 9. In the *caregiver group*, leaders continue teaching the three Cs of discipline and how to discipline more effectively by showing a video of two ways a mother handles the same discipline situation. Leaders explain how to be clear, consistent, and calm in discipline situations. Caregivers are taught to use positive attention when children meet expectations and reminded to use *Catch 'Em Being Good*. Guidelines for giving praise can be remembered by the acronym PRAISE. Positive attention should be *P*lentiful, *R*egular, *A*ttentive, *I*mmediate, *S*pecific, and *E*nthusiastic. Caregivers learn that when expectations are not met, different levels of consequences are appropriate for different behaviors, including ignoring minor misbehaviors, increasing supervision, allowing natural consequences to occur that allow children to learn firsthand about the effects of their own behavior, taking away meaningful privileges, and giving something unpleasant. Caregivers are taught to follow consequences with recognition of positive behaviors soon after giving the consequence to show the child they are not angry or holding a grudge. Caregivers are taught to ask themselves the following questions:

> Is it a fair consequence? Does the consequence match the broken rule? Can I consistently follow through with it? Is this a consequence that will help my child learn about the effects of his/her behavior? Is this the least harsh consequence that will control his/her behavior?

In the *child group*, leaders begin a discussion with the children about how things have changed since their parent died, things that are different that they like, and things that are difficult. Leaders then teach children how to ask for instrumental support (problem-solving help) from their caregivers. Leaders begin by modeling bad communication using You-messages such as "You are being so unfair," and explaining why statements like these can be hurtful. When discussing communication, the benefits of feeling understood are emphasized. I-messages, which have already been taught, are reviewed in the context of problem solving. Leaders model I-messages using scripted role-play scenarios. Leaders first act out a situation in which a mother and son are in a conflict because the son wants to play basketball but his mother wants him to clean his room first. The situation escalates when the mother and son continue to use You-messages. Next, children are directed to act out the same scenario, but to change the ending. The scenario shows children how I-messages can help everyone achieve their goals, and leaders coach children on how to use I-messages for problem solving using the following format: "I felt (what you feel) when (what happened). Can you help me figure out how to deal with (what happened)?" After the role-play, children discuss the differences between using You-messages and I-messages for problem solving and process concerns about using I-messages.

Session 10. In the *caregiver group*, leaders revisit the first three steps in the change plan and help caregivers troubleshoot problems with their change plans. Furthermore, the fourth step of effective discipline is taught, using the change plan, evaluating it, and reevaluating it if needed. Leaders then review the differences between effective (positive and proactive) and ineffective (negative and reactive) discipline strategies and discuss reasons to give children positive consequences for positive behaviors. A discussion then follows regarding how giving negative consequences can lead to "withdrawals," which are behaviors that keep the negative cycle going, such as commanding, crying, aggression, and whining. To prevent negative exchanges from escalating, caregivers learn to avoid responding to withdrawals with coercive behaviors and use anger management techniques. Caregivers then develop new change plans to use in the future.

The *child group* begins with a discussion about grief and how children remember the parents they lost. Leaders assure children that feeling better does not mean that they are forgetting their deceased parents and suggest ways to create memories that help them feel better. Children are taught that they will know when they are doing better when there are more positive than painful memories. Children discuss positive ways of remembering their parents by finishing the following sentences: "One thing I do to remember my parent is…" and "One thing I do to remember that helps me to feel better is…." Next, leaders review all the program skills. Children then participate in a group activity in which they pretend they are hosting a TV show, Kid Cope TV, which involves children giving advice to other children who have lost a parent. Half the group plays the role of expert and answers questions about tough situations after a parent has died. The other half plays the role of the audience and asks questions.

Session 11. In the *caregiver group*, leaders encourage caregivers to share any difficulties they are having with their change plan. The leaders also review coping strategies that have been taught in the child/adolescent component. The majority of the session is focused on how to reduce the impact of negative life events on children's outcomes. Discussion regarding situations that may be particularly upsetting for bereaved children, such as holidays and anniversaries, financial struggles, caregiver distress, and increased hours at work, are addressed. Caregivers break into small groups and talk about specific issues or situations that are difficult for their families, with leaders providing guidelines for helping children with them. For example, to help children deal with caregiver distress, leaders suggest that caregivers find a caring adult to talk to when they are distressed, tell children the basics and avoid providing unnecessary details about the situation, and remind children that the caregiver will not always be distressed. Leaders emphasize that the most important things caregivers can do to help their children with these difficult situations are to listen, model coping skills, and offer genuine reassurance.

The *child group* starts with a discussion about the changes that each child has made during the program. Children may be prompted: "What were you like then? What has changed about you?" Children demonstrate the skills they have learned by breaking into small groups and teaching a skill to each other. After group members rejoin, leaders discuss how there may be times after the program when children feel they are not handling things well. Children are encouraged to discuss what they imagine might happen in situations like holidays, their caregiver starting to date, or moving to a new school. Leaders then help children develop regular reminders to use their skills to maintain the positive changes they made during the program.

Session 12. The *caregiver group* begins with a review of the program skills and caregivers are given the opportunity to discuss concerns about them. Leaders discuss ways for caregivers to maintain the progress they have made and help caregivers take credit for the changes they have made during the program by emphasizing each family's improvements. Finally, caregivers reflect on what they have gotten out of the group.

In the *child group*, leaders give children the opportunity to talk about things they wish they could have shared with their deceased parents. Leaders encourage children to answer the question, "What's something that you wish you could have told your loved one who died, but did not get a chance to say?" Each child is encouraged to write a personal message to his or her parent, which is then attached to a balloon that will later be released. Children then answer three questions: (a) "What changes have I made and how have they helped to make my family stronger?"; (b) "How do I hope things will be in the future for my family?"; and (c) "The thing that I will miss the most about coming to this group is…?" Leaders help children process their experiences in the group while remembering to SNAP. Finally, a group picture is taken and children are given the opportunity to write each other messages in their workbooks. The children

join the caregivers for a graduation ceremony, in which children and caregivers receive diplomas and one of the leaders makes a positive statement about each person's contribution to the group. Everyone joins in a celebration party with refreshments before saying goodbye.

Grief and Trauma Intervention

The GTI is commonly implemented in schools and community-based settings after children's exposure to a traumatic, violent, or disastrous event. Here the focus is on the components most relevant to children who experienced the sudden and/or traumatic death of a loved one.

Overall Structure and Resources Needed. This group-based intervention is designed for children aged 7 to 12 years who experience moderate levels of traumatic stress after a natural disaster or traumatic event, like death of a loved one. It is recommended that groups be composed of children who experienced the loss of a loved one in the same way (i.e., homicide or natural disaster), so that common experiences can be drawn upon and subtle nuances of each child's situation may be explored. Two mental health practitioners (preferably with a master's degree) colead the 10-session group (five to six children) and meet with each child for an individual session. A 2-day training is available from the intervention developer for first-time implementers. Sessions typically last 1 hour. In addition, there is a 1-hour individual meeting between clinicians and caregivers and an individual session for teachers and school staff members.

Child group sessions begin with the clinicians reviewing the format for the day's session and offering children a light snack. Children report on the skills they practiced since the last session and are rewarded accordingly. The children also complete worksheet activities, which include drawing, writing a story, and/or a discussion, with the goal of completing a book that tells their trauma narrative by the end of the final session. Each session ends with a deep-breathing exercise and the group's ending ritual if the group has developed one.

GTI Session Content

Caregiver Session. Clinicians meet with caregivers before the group begins, or before session 4 at the latest. The primary goals are to explain the purpose of the program and gain caregivers' consent for children's participation. This is also an opportunity for clinicians to learn about the children's and caregivers' experiences and needs, provide referrals if needed, and provide education about common grief and trauma reactions in school-aged children. Caregivers also learn deep-breathing and cooldown exercises so that they may help their children use these skills.

Teacher/Staff Check-Ins. Clinicians meet individually with each teacher and school staff member who may be in a supportive or caretaking role for the children. The goals of the "check-ins" include: (a) provide psychoeducation on common reactions to death, disaster, and violence; (b) teach or review helpful coping strategies; (c) determine whether teachers and/or staff need additional support to help the children deal with the traumatic event; and (d) provide teachers and/or staff with a list of community resources (e.g., mental health and substance abuse treatment, legal services).

Child Sessions.

Session 1. During the first session, the clinicians talk about the purpose of the program, set rules for the group, and facilitate group rapport and cohesion. This session focuses on teaching children about a common reaction to death or trauma: anger, and helping children deal with anger. Children talk about recognizing signs of anger, show their own anger signs, and complete the *Anger Signs Worksheet*. Deep-breathing techniques are then taught and practiced as a way to help the body calm down. Children identify supportive adults in their lives and write these names on the *My Support People* worksheet. Finally, children identify activities they enjoy and how doing these activities has changed since the death/trauma. The clinicians encourage children to do more fun activities and talk about how these activities are related to mental and physical health. Optionally, clinicians read a short story about anger management during one of the first three sessions.

Session 2. Clinicians discuss four types of normal responses to grief and trauma: (a) thoughts, (b) feelings, (c) body reactions, and (d) behaviors, and talk about how these reactions are related to one another. Suggested teaching methods include (a) writing the categories on the board and having children provide common reactions, (b) using puppets or having children act out specific reactions, (c) telling a story about a child who experiences these reactions, or (d) using cards with feeling expressions. Next, the clinicians introduce the "My Story" book children will be creating over the course of the group through completing worksheets. Children complete the title page and choose a storytelling worksheet from the following: (a) *A Scary Thing Happened*, (b) *I Really Miss*, and (c) *When I Think About _____ I Think*....Children share only what they want to after completing their worksheets. Next, children talk about any signs of anger they noticed over the past week and about what they were angry. The clinicians then teach ways to calm down when one is angry and how to relax. Children explore different options for cooling down and complete the *Things I Can Do to Cool Myself When I Am Angry* worksheet.

Session 3. Clinicians teach anger management techniques by asking children to recall a time recently when they felt angry; children then brainstorm other ways they could have reacted and the consequences of different reactions. Clinicians acknowledge that, although children's anger after the loss of a loved one cannot be "fixed," children can learn to recognize when they feel angry, label the cause of their anger, and manage their anger in ways that won't get them into trouble. Children complete the *My Family* worksheet and/or the *Changes I Have Noticed* worksheet. They draw pictures of their families and/or of any changes that have occurred in their families since the death or traumatic event. During this activity, clinicians ask each child questions about the people in the picture to find out what the child's relationship is to each person and who provides them with emotional support.

Next, the group discusses how to deal with anniversaries or holidays by having children identify a date or holiday that may be particularly difficult for them and ways the child may be able to cope. Children learn that "old feelings" and reminders of the loss are likely to return on such occasions and that healing rituals and relaxation techniques can help during these difficult times. Finally, the idea of spirituality as a way of coping is discussed. Because spirituality may play a large or, conversely, nonexistent role in different families' lives, clinicians are respectful of the spectrum of beliefs that may exist within the group. The clinicians' main goals are to praise children for asking difficult questions related to spirituality and help them identify people in their lives with whom they could talk about spirituality. Children have the option of completing the *My Prayer, My Poem,* or *My Song* worksheet to help express themselves.

Session 4. In this session, the clinicians provide information about the specific traumatic loss around which the group was formed such as medical information for a child whose parent died of cancer. The clinicians then continue the conversation about feelings that was started in session 2, pointing out the commonality of the children's feelings. The children write down their feelings on the *My Feelings* worksheet and the clinicians encourage the children to act out different emotions for the other children to guess. Clinicians should pay special attention to addressing feelings of worry and guilt, as these are likely to be the most harmful emotions. Avoidance and reexperiencing of emotions are also addressed. After identifying the most common reactions of each child, the children draw a picture of themselves experiencing their most common emotion and write a story about the drawing. It is common for children to have feelings of wishing things were different. Because these feelings can be confusing, the clinicians encourage the children to write down questions on the *My Questions* worksheet and share them with the group if they desire. The clinicians answer the children's questions as appropriately and honestly as possible and admit if they do not know an answer. If time allows, children complete the *I Wish* worksheet with a drawing, story, and discussion.

Session 5. It is common for children to have dreams following the death of a loved one or a traumatic event. Clinicians encourage children to share whether they have been experiencing dreams, whether they were good or bad, and if these dreams were different than what they experienced before the traumatic event. Clinicians look for specific instances of *hope* and/or *bravery* in the dreams, and children complete the *I Dream* worksheet. Children who are having good dreams draw a picture and write a story depicting that dream. If children are experiencing bad dreams, they also draw a picture and write a story about their dreams. Next, they think about ways to make their dreams less scary or think of different ways the dreams could have ended. This is

done to help minimize the scariness of the dreams. Children then incorporate this piece into their stories about the dreams. The clinicians then read *Go Away Big Green Monster.* For a child having difficulty differentiating between reality and fantasy or who is experiencing frequent, intense nightmares, the clinicians meet with the child's caregiver(s) to identify ways to help the child.

Next, the clinicians discuss what it means to feel safe, help children come up with an appropriate definition of safety, and talk about what safety looks like in different contexts (e.g., home, school). Each child completes one of the following worksheets: *My Safe Place, My Safe Person,* or *My Protective Shield.* Children are encouraged to identify safe people and places in different contexts. Children who feel that they have no safe place draw and write about an imaginary safe place or complete a different worksheet. Finally, the clinicians facilitate a deep-breathing exercise and a guided-imagery exercise about feeling safe.

Session 6. This is the first of the two group sessions focused on creating a trauma narrative. As a first step, the children draw and discuss what happened during and around the death. Children choose to complete either three worksheets (*Before It Happened, When It Happened, and After It Happened*) or a single worksheet (*My Story About What Happened*). Children are encouraged to identify fun times that occurred in the *Before* portion of the narrative.

Session 6a: Individual Session. This session provides an opportunity for children to meet individually with clinicians to discuss feelings or issues that they don't feel comfortable sharing with the group. It is also an opportunity for those who missed sessions to catch up on the missed material. It is designed to be specifically tailored to the needs of each individual child; however, suggested topics include: (a) review the story of what happened from session 6; (b) complete the *My Worst Moment* worksheet and help children process difficult experiences; (c) address the child's feelings of guilt; (d) discuss possible trauma reminders and coping strategies; and (e) reinforce using relaxation techniques and practice these with the child.

Session 7. The primary goal is for children to complete the activities started in session 6 to develop a full narrative for their drawings. If a common theme emerged in the individual sessions, clinicians take time to address these topics. To facilitate children having many different ways to cope with what has happened to them, each child creates a list of at least five positive things he or she can do to feel better when experiencing grief-related negative emotions. The clinicians prepare children to anticipate the reexperiencing of these feelings, and children are encouraged to turn to their list of coping strategies when this happens. Each child's list is reviewed by the clinicians to ensure that the list includes talking to a caring and supportive person; they also help children identify additional caring and supportive individuals in their lives. Before the program ends, clinicians prepare a personalized list of coping strategies for every child.

Session 8. Children complete one of three activities in which they make a drawing about a memory of the person who died. Worksheet options include *The Thing I Miss the Most, My Favorite Memory,* or *A Happy Time Together.* After completing the drawing, children discuss the losses they have experienced and the clinicians help them better understand their losses and explore the meaning of them. To do this, the clinicians ask questions such as, "What was so special to you about _____?" Then, children are supported in writing stories about their drawings. The clinicians praise children for talking about their experiences and feelings.

Session 9. During this session, children talk about the losses they have experienced as well as positive, comforting memories. The clinicians draw from this discussion to help children complete one of two worksheets: *My Hope for the Future* or *Things About My Life That I Like.* The goal is for children to focus on the positives in their lives to build optimism and a sense of hope. The clinicians prepare children for the final meeting by explaining that the last session will include a celebration for completing the group. Some children may experience negative emotions about the group ending. To address this proactively, the clinicians initiate a discussion that encourages children to talk about difficult emotions that may come up and remind children of the coping skills they can use. Clinicians also probe for how the children have benefited from the group by reviewing the goals

of the group and having the children complete the *Grief and Trauma Intervention Review of Goals* rating sheet. Prior to the next session, clinicians organize and bind each child's "My Story" book (and if possible, type up the narratives that go with each story).

Session 10. The main goal of the final session is to help children focus on a positive vision for the present and future. Clinicians remind the children about the importance of identifying supportive and caring adults. Children are encouraged to share their "My Story" book with the identified adults. Clinicians also revisit the conversation from the first session about fun activities. Those who are not doing fun activities are reminded to develop a plan with their caregivers to do fun activities. Finally, children participate in a ceremony to celebrate completing the program. Clinicians praise children's accomplishments and give them the opportunity to talk about their experiences in the group. Children are presented with a participation certificate and their own "My Story" book. Clinicians follow up with caregivers after the session to provide any recommendations, referrals, or support that the families may need.

CONCLUSION

The majority of youth who experience the death of someone close to them will exhibit remarkable resilience; however, grief-related mental health problems may arise in a substantial minority of children. The risk of problematic functioning in children following bereavement depends upon the interpersonal, intrapersonal, and environmental risk and protective factors that occur before and after the death. By reducing risk factors and promoting individual- and family-level resources, evidence-based practices, such as those involved in the two programs described in this chapter, can help prevent the development of psychosocial problems among grieving youth.

SELECT BIBLIOGRAPHY

CTG Web. Retrieved from ctg.musc.edu
This website offers free training and resources on how to adapt trauma-focused cognitive behavior

therapy, a well-validated treatment for youth who have experienced interpersonal trauma, for treating childhood traumatic grief.

Lieberman, A. F., Compton, N., Van Horn, P., & Ghosh Ippen, C. (2003). *Losing a parent to death in the early years: Guidelines for the treatment of traumatic bereavement in infancy and early childhood.* Washington, DC: Zero to Three. *This manual provides guidelines and case examples on the application of child–parent psychotherapy to treating infants and preschool-aged children who have experienced the death of a parent.*

Webb, N. B. (2011). *Helping bereaved children: A handbook for practitioners* (3rd ed.). New York, NY: Guilford. *This Handbook offers detailed information on helping children who experience the death of family members, friends, pets, and other important figures in the child's life. In addition to providing guidance on assessing bereaved children, this handbook includes detailed clinical case examples.*

REFERENCES

Ayers, T. S., Wolchik, S. A., Sandler, I. N., Twohey, J. L., Weyer, J. L., Padget-Jones, S., ... Kriege, G. (2014). The Family Bereavement Program: Description of a theory-based prevention program for parentally-bereaved children and adolescents. *Omega: Journal of Death and Dying, 68*(4), 289–310.

Ayers, T. S., Wolchik, S. A., Weiss, L., Sandler, I. N., Jones S., Cole, E., & Barrow, S. (1996). *Family Bereavement Program: Group leader intervention manual for parent program.* Tempe, AZ: REACH Institute.

Cerel, J., Fristad, M. A., Verducci, J., Weller, R. A., & Weller, E. B. (2006). Childhood bereavement: Psychopathology in the 2 years postparental death. *Journal of the American Academy of Child and Adolescent Psychiatry, 45*(6), 681–690.

Cohen, J. A., Mannarino, A. P., Greenberg, T., Padlo, S., & Shipley, C. (2002). Childhood traumatic grief: Concepts and controversies. *Trauma, Violence, & Abuse: A Review Journal, 3*(4), 307–327.

Furman, R. A. (1973). The child's capacity for mourning. In E. J. Anthony & C. Koupernick (Eds.), *The child in his family: The impact of disease and death* (pp. 225–231). New York, NY: Wiley.

Hagan, M. J., Tein, J. Y., Sandler, I. N., Wolchik, S. A., Ayers, T. S., & Luecken, L. J. (2012). Strengthening effective parenting practices over the long term: Effects of a preventive intervention for parentally bereaved families. *Journal of Clinical Child and Adolescent Psychology: The Official Journal for the Society of Clinical Child and Adolescent Psychology, American Psychological Association, Division 53, 41*(2), 177–188.

Haine, R. A., Ayers, T. S., Sandler, I. N., Wolchik, S. A., & Weyer, J. L. (2003). Locus of control and self-esteem as stress-moderators or stress-mediators in parentally bereaved children. *Death Studies, 27*(7), 619–640.

Harrison, L., & Harrington, R. (2001). Adolescents' bereavement experiences. Prevalence, association with depressive symptoms, and use of services. *Journal of Adolescence, 24*(2), 159–169.

Johnson, J. (1999). *Keys to helping children deal with death and grief.* New York, NY: Barron's Educational Series.

Kendler, K. S., Sheth, K., Gardner, C. O., & Prescott, C. A. (2002). Childhood parental loss and risk for first-onset of major depression and alcohol dependence: The time-decay of risk and sex differences. *Psychological Medicine, 32*(7), 1187–1194.

Lin, K. K., Sandler, I. N., Ayers, T. S., Wolchik, S. A., & Luecken, L. J. (2004). Resilience in parentally bereaved children and adolescents seeking preventive services. *Journal of Clinical Child and Adolescent Psychology: The Official Journal for the Society of Clinical Child and Adolescent Psychology, American Psychological Association, Division 53, 33*(4), 673–683.

Luecken, L. J. (2008). Long-term consequences of parental death in childhood: Psychological and physiological manifestations. In M. Stroebe, R. Hansson, H. Schut, & W. Stroebe (Eds.), *Handbook of bereavement research and practice: Advances in theory and intervention* (pp. 397–416). Washington, DC: American Psychological Association.

Nickman, S. L., Silverman, P. R., & Normand, C. (1998). Children's construction of a deceased parent: The surviving parent's contribution. *The American Journal of Orthopsychiatry, 68*(1), 126–134.

Oltjenbruns, K. A. (2001). Developmental context of childhood: Grief and regrief phenomena. In M. S. Stroebe, R. O. Hansson, W. Stroebe, & H. Schut (Eds.), *Handbook of bereavement research: Consequences, coping, and care* (pp. 169–197). Washington, DC: American Psychological Association.

Pennebaker, J. W., Zech, F., & Rimé, B. (2001). Disclosing and sharing emotion: Psychological, social, and health consequences. In M. S. Stroebe, R. O. Hansson, W. Stroebe, & H. Schut (Eds.), *Handbook of bereavement research: Consequences, coping, and care* (pp. 517–543). Washington, DC: American Psychological Association.

Pfeffer, C. R., Karus, D., Siegel, K., & Jiang, H. (2000). Child survivors of parental death from cancer or suicide: Depressive and behavioral outcomes. *Psycho-Oncology, 9*(1), 1–10.

Salloum, A. (2008). Group therapy for children after homicide and violence: A pilot study. *Research on Social Work Practice, 18*(3), 198–211.

Salloum, A., & Overstreet, S. (2008). Evaluation of individual and group grief and trauma interventions for children post disaster. *Journal of Clinical Child and Adolescent Psychology: The Official Journal for the Society of Clinical Child and Adolescent Psychology, American Psychological Association, Division 53, 37*(3), 495–507.

Salloum, A., & Overstreet, S. (2012). Grief and trauma intervention for children after disaster: Exploring coping skills versus trauma narration. *Behaviour Research and Therapy, 50*(3), 169–179.

Sandler, I., Ayers, T. S., Tein, J. Y., Wolchik, S., Millsap, R., Khoo, S. T.,…Coxe, S. (2010). Six-year follow-up of a preventive intervention for parentally bereaved youths: A randomized controlled trial. *Archives of Pediatrics & Adolescent Medicine, 164*(10), 907–914.

Sandler, I. N., Ayers, T. S., Twohey, J. L., Lutzke, J. R., Li, S., & Kriege, G. (1996). *Family Bereavement Program: Group leader intervention manual for child program.* Tempe, AZ: REACH Institute.

Sandler, I. N., Ma, Y., Tein, J. Y., Ayers, T. S., Wolchik, S., Kennedy, C., & Millsap, R. (2010). Long-term effects of the family bereavement program on multiple indicators of grief in parentally bereaved children and adolescents. *Journal of Consulting and Clinical Psychology, 78*(2), 131–143.

Sood, A. B., Razdan, A., Weller, E. B., & Weller, R. A. (2006). Children's reactions to parental and sibling death. *Current Psychiatry Reports, 8*(2), 115–120.

Wolchik, S. A., Tein, J. Y., Sandler, I. N., & Ayers, T. S. (2006). Stressors, quality of the child-caregiver relationship, and children's mental health problems after parental death: The mediating role of self-system beliefs. *Journal of Abnormal Child Psychology, 34*(2), 221–238.

Worden, J. W. (1996). *Children and grief: When a parent dies.* New York, NY: Guilford.

Worden, J. W. (2008). *Grief counseling and grief therapy: A handbook for the mental health practitioner* (4th ed.). New York, NY: Springer Publishing Company.

Students With Educational Issues and Learning Disorders

Evidence-Based Interventions for Reading Disabilities in Children and Adolescents

Douglas Fuchs, Kristen L. McMaster, and Devin M. Kearns

OVERVIEW

Current Response to Intervention (RTI) models identify multitiered approaches to prevention and intervention that begin with high-quality core instruction in the general education classroom. Children generally thrive academically with such universal instruction and relatively few students require more intensive intervention (McMaster, Fuchs, Fuchs, & Compton, 2005). In the absence of high-quality core instruction, larger proportions of children requiring additional support are likely, which further strains school resources at best and, at worst, renders RTI unfeasible and incapable of meeting the students' academic needs (Noell & Gansle, 2006). Districts must consider this dilemma and make high-quality core instruction a priority.

The imperative for high-quality core instruction is emphasized both in general and in special education laws that require teachers to implement *scientific, research-based instruction* to ensure students' progress toward mastering academic standards (No Child Left Behind Act of 2001, 20 U.S.C. 6301 et seq.). Such legislation was intended to exclude poor instruction as a cause of students' serious learning problems (Individuals with Disabilities Education Act of 2004, 20 U.S.C. 140 et seq.). Despite federal mandates, few comprehensive core instructional

programs have been validated through rigorous research (Gersten et al., 2009). Thus, educators are advised to employ essential curricula that align with scientifically based principles of teaching and learning (Al Otaiba, Kosanovich-Grek, Torgesen, Hassler, & Wahl, 2005) and supplement those curricula with research-based class-wide interventions, particularly in classrooms with high proportions of students at risk of academic failure.

This chapter provides a description of peer-assisted learning strategies (PALS), a research-based classwide intervention that can be used as part of core instruction linked to multitiered models of prevention and intervention. Specifically, a description of the extent to which Reading PALS: addresses critical academic skills that align with core academic standards, provides opportunities to differentiate instruction, and has been validated as an efficacious instructional approach for diverse learners is provided.

EVIDENCE-BASED INTERVENTIONS AND EMPIRICAL SUPPORT FOR READING DISABILITIES IN CHILDREN AND ADOLESCENTS

Research-based classwide interventions ensure that students have sufficient opportunities to practice academic skills addressed in the core curriculum through differentiated instruction (Gersten et al., 2009). When selecting classwide interventions, educators should ask the following questions: (a) Does the intervention *address critical academic skills* that align with important academic standards? (b) Does the intervention *provide opportunities to differentiate instruction* for low-, average-, and high-performing learners? (c) Is the intervention efficacious for students like those in the classroom for which it is to be used, including students from diverse cultural and linguistic backgrounds, or students with disabilities?

PALS, a research-based approach, was developed by researchers at Vanderbilt University, in collaboration with teachers in Metro-Nashville (Tennessee) schools (see D. Fuchs & L. S. Fuchs, 1998 for a description of this collaboration) and is based on the Classwide Peer Tutoring (CWPT) model developed by Delquadri, Greenwood, Whorton, Carta, and Hall (1986). During the past two decades, PALS has been developed and evaluated for children in prekindergarten to high school, and separate programs for reading and mathematics.

PALS Programs Address Critical Academic Skills That Align With Core Standards

During PALS instruction, students practice critical reading skills that align with core curricula and standards at each grade level (i.e., phonological awareness [PA], letter-sound recognition, word reading, and fluency in kindergarten and first grade; reading fluency and reading comprehension in Grades 2–6). Table 7.1 provides a list of the Common Core State Standards (CCSS; National Governors Association Center for Best Practices & Council of Chief State School Officers, 2010) with corresponding PALS activities at each grade level.

Reading PALS provides students frequent opportunities to respond, engage in extended practice, and experience success in reading. PALS is implemented three times per week, for 30 to 45 minutes, depending on the grade level. Teachers typically implement PALS during reading and language arts or during independent reading time. PALS activities at each grade level are described in the following sections; additional information may be found in other publications (e.g., Fuchs & Fuchs, 2005; McMaster, Fuchs, & Fuchs, 2006).

Kindergarten Peer-Assisted Learning Strategies (K-PALS). PALS researchers worked for several consecutive years during the late 1990s with kindergarten teachers in Nashville to develop K-PALS. This researcher–teacher collaboration (described by D. Fuchs & L. S. Fuchs, 1998) included a series of evaluations of whether, and to what extent, K-PALS accelerated the progress of young children with weak-to-strong beginning reading skills. In a culminating randomized field trial (Fuchs, Fuchs, Thompson, et al., 2001), students of different skill levels who received PA + Decoding PALS outperformed those who received PA only and controls on letter–sound identification, word attack, word identification, and spelling measures. Fuchs and colleagues (2002) disaggregated the data for kindergartners with disabilities; K-PALS students with disabilities outperformed comparison students with disabilities on letter–sound recognition and word attack. Rafdal, McMaster, McConnell, Fuchs, and Fuchs (2011) replicated these findings by disaggregating data for kindergartners with disabilities from a multisite K-PALS study (Fuchs et al., 2010).

Researchers have also disaggregated the K-PALS data for English learners (ELs). McMaster, Kung, Han, and Cao (2008) examined effects of K-PALS for ELs from a variety of cultural and linguistic backgrounds in urban Midwestern classrooms. They found that ELs who received K-PALS outperformed ELs in control classrooms. Collectively, these results support the use of K-PALS as a supplement to core instruction in diverse general education classrooms.

First-Grade PALS. First-Grade PALS efficacy research has proceeded in a similar fashion to K-PALS research, but with a somewhat different focus. Researchers contrasted a decoding-only version of First-Grade PALS with a fluency-building version (PALS + Fluency; Fuchs, Fuchs, Yen, et al., 2001). Low-, average-, and high-performing students in both PALS groups outperformed their counterparts in control classrooms on measures of PA, word attack, word identification, and spelling. Furthermore, students in the PALS + Fluency group outperformed controls on measures of fluency and comprehension, supporting the added value of a fluency-building component (Fuchs, Fuchs, Yen, et al., 2001).

TABLE 7.1

READING PALS ACTIVITIES ALIGNED WITH COMMON CORE STATE STANDARDS AT EACH GRADE LEVEL		
Grade Level and Strand	**Common Core State Standards (Retrieved from http://www.corestandards.org/ELA-Literacy)**	**PALS Activity**
Kindergarten: Phonological awareness	*CCSS.ELA-Literacy.RF.K.2* Demonstrate understanding of spoken words, syllables, and sounds (phonemes). • *K.2a* Recognize and produce rhyming words. • *K.2b* Count, pronounce, blend, and segment syllables in spoken words. • *K.2c* Blend and segment onsets and rimes of single-syllable spoken words. • *K.2d* Isolate and pronounce the initial, medial vowel, and final sounds in three-phoneme (consonant–vowel–consonant) words.	Sound Play • Syllables • First sound identification • Rhyming • Guess my word (blending and segmenting) • Last sound identification
Kindergarten: Phonics and word recognition	*CCSS.ELA-Literacy.RF.K.3* Know and apply grade-level phonics and word analysis skills in decoding words. • *K.3a* Demonstrate basic knowledge of letter–sound correspondences by producing the primary or most frequent sound for each consonant. • *K.3b* Associate the short sounds with the common spellings (graphemes) for the five major vowels. • *K.3c* Read common high-frequency words by sight (e.g., *the, of, to, you, she, my, is, are, do, does*). • *K.3d* Distinguish between similarly spelled words by identifying the sounds of the letters that differ.	Decoding PALS • What sound? • What word? • Sound boxes • Reading sentences
Kindergarten: Fluency	*CCSS.ELA-Literacy.RF.K.4* Read emergent-reader texts with purpose and understanding.	Reading Decodable Books
First grade: Phonics and word recognition	*CCSS.ELA-Literacy.RF.1.3* Know and apply grade-level phonics and word analysis skills in decoding words. • *1.3a* Know the spelling-sound correspondences for common consonant digraphs (two letters that represent one sound). • *1.3b* Decode regularly spelled one-syllable words. • *1.3c* Know common vowel team conventions for representing long vowel sounds. • *1.3e* Decode two-syllable words following basic patterns by breaking the words into syllables. • *1.3f* Read words with inflectional endings. • *1.3g* Recognize and read grade-appropriate irregularly spelled words.	Sounds and Words • Saying Sounds • Sight Words • Hearing Sounds and Sounding Out • Stories • Speed Game
First Grade: Fluency	*CCSS.ELA-Literacy.RF.1.4* Read with sufficient accuracy and fluency to support comprehension. • 1.4b Read grade-level text orally with accuracy, appropriate rate, and expression.	Sounds and Words • Stories • Speed Game • Partner Reading
Grades 2–6: Fluency	*CCSS.ELA-Literacy.RF.2.4, 3.4, 4.4, 5.4* Read with sufficient accuracy and fluency to support comprehension. • 2.4a, 3.4a, 4.4a, 5.4a Read grade-level text with purpose and understanding. • 2.4a, 3.4a, 4.4a, 5.4a Read grade-level text orally with accuracy, appropriate rate, and expression. • 2.4a, 3.4a, 4.4a, 5.4a Use context to confirm or self-correct word recognition and understanding, rereading as necessary.	Partner Reading

(continued)

TABLE 7.1

READING PALS ACTIVITIES ALIGNED WITH COMMON CORE STATE STANDARDS AT EACH GRADE LEVEL *(continued)*		
Grade Level and Strand	**Common Core State Standards (Retrieved from http://www.corestandards.org/ELA-Literacy)**	**PALS Activity**
Grades 2–6: Key ideas and details	*CCSS.ELA-Literacy.RL.2.1* Ask and answer such questions as *who*, *what*, *where*, *when*, *why*, and *how* to demonstrate understanding of key details in a text.	Retell and Paragraph Shrinking
	CCSS.ELA-Literacy.RI.2.2 Identify the main topic of a multiparagraph text as well as the focus of specific paragraphs within the text.	
	CCSS.ELA-Literacy.RL.3.1 Ask and answer questions to demonstrate understanding of a text, referring explicitly to the text as the basis for the answers.	
	CCSS.ELA-Literacy.RI.3.2 Determine the main idea of a text; recount the key details and explain how they support the main idea.	
	CCSS.ELA-Literacy.RL.4.1 Refer to details and examples in a text when explaining what the text says explicitly and when drawing inferences from the text.	
	CCSS.ELA-Literacy.RI.4.2 Determine the main idea of a text and explain how it is supported by key details; summarize the text.	
	CCSS.ELA-Literacy.RI.5.2 Determine two or more main ideas of a text and explain how they are supported by key details; summarize the text.	
	CCSS.ELA-Literacy.RL.6.1 Cite textual evidence to support analysis of what the text says explicitly as well as inferences drawn from the text.	

Researchers have also demonstrated a benefit of First-Grade PALS for ELs. Calhoon, Al Otaiba, Cihak, King, and Avalos (2007) examined the effects of First-Grade PALS on the reading achievement of students in two-way bilingual immersion classrooms in the Southwest, on the border of Mexico. Findings indicated statistically significant and large effects of PALS on phonological awareness, decoding, and oral reading skills for both English-proficient students and ELs, again supporting its use in diverse classrooms.

PALS for Grades 2 to 6. Reading PALS for Grades 2 to 6 was also developed in the mid-1990s. In a randomized control trial (Fuchs et al., 1997), students from PALS classrooms on average outperformed those in control classrooms on number of words read correctly in 3 minutes, number of comprehension questions answered correctly, and number of correct maze choices on the Comprehensive Reading Assessment Battery (CRAB; Fuchs, Fuchs, & Hamlett, 1989). PALS effects were not moderated by learner type, suggesting that PALS can be used successfully in classrooms in which students with learning disabilities (LD) are included. An important caveat, however, was that 20% of PALS students with LD did *not* make marked improvement in reading, indicating that some students with LD may be in need of more intensive intervention (Fuchs et al., 1997).

PALS has also been effective for native Spanish-speaking students with and without LD in grades 3 through 6. In a randomized control trial conducted in South Texas, Saenz, Fuchs, and Fuchs (2005) assigned teachers randomly to PALS or control groups. Student participants included 132 ELs with LD and their low-, average-, and high-achieving classmates. PALS students on average outperformed control students in reading comprehension regardless of learner type.

HOW TO: A GUIDE TO THE IMPLEMENTATION OF READING INTERVENTIONS FOR CHILDREN AND ADOLESCENTS

Kindergarten PALS

K-PALS Activities. Each of the K-PALS lessons comprises three parts: (a) a teacher-directed *Sound Play* activity that provides PA practice; (b) a *Decoding Lesson* that addresses grapheme–phoneme correspondence (GPC) (*What Sound?*), sight word recognition (*Sight Words*), decoding (*Sound Boxes*), and sentence fluency (*Reading Sentences*); and (c) *Partner Reading*. In *Partner Reading*, students read in pairs using teacher-selected texts. This activity is introduced about halfway through the program.

During the Decoding Lesson, students are paired by their skill level. The first *Reader* has weaker reading skills than the student who reads second. The student who is not reading assumes the role of *Coach*. During the Decoding Lesson and Partner Reading both students assume the roles of Coach and Reader. After the Reader completes one section of the Decoding Lesson, the partners switch roles; the former Reader coaches and the former Coach reads.

Sound Play. Sound Play comprises teacher-led, 3- to 5-minute activities. Sound Play is designed to improve beginning readers' awareness of the spoken syllables, rhyming parts (vowels and trailing consonants—the sound of -*at* in *cat*; i.e., rimes), and phonemes (individual sounds—the sounds of *c, a,* and *t* in *cat*) within words. Activities change every three to six lessons and address different PA skills, as described in Table 7.2.

Teachers begin Sound Play during the introduction week, in which students learn the purpose of K-PALS, are informed that they will work in pairs to complete some K-PALS activities, and begin practicing the first Sound Play exercises. During introduction Lessons 1 and 2, Sound Play activities involve syllable clapping, a simple activity with

which most students are successful. Introduction Lessons 3 and 4 expose students to the First Sound A activity, described in Figure 7.1. The teacher repeats each Sound Play activity two or more times to ensure students master the targeted skills.

Decoding Lesson. After Sound Play, the students complete four activities using a Decoding Lesson sheet (see Figure 7.2). The teacher initiates the activities with the whole class before the students perform the activities in pairs. The teacher presents Decoding Lesson sheets using an overhead projector, a document camera, or a Smart Board. Otherwise, the Decoding Lesson can be presented on chart paper. The teacher, acting as the Coach, shows the students how to prompt Readers and how to provide corrective feedback when Readers makes mistakes. During the first few lessons, the teacher selects Coaches who are best able to model correct prompts and corrections.

What Sound? is the first activity in the Decoding Lesson. It is designed to improve recall of GPCs. In K-PALS, GPCs are taught for the 26 alphabet letters (*q* is taught as *qu* = /kw/) and the consonant digraphs *sh, ch, th,* and *ck*. During the activity, the Coach points at each grapheme (letter pattern) and the Reader identifies the associated phoneme.

The students are taught to pronounce the sounds without a trailing "uh" (IPA [International Phonetic Alphabet]: /ə/), or schwa, sound. For example, if asked to blend "kuh" (IPA: /kə/), "ah" (IPA: /æ/), and "tuh" (IPA: /tə/), a student is likely to think "cuh-att-tuh" (IPA: /kə 'æ tə/) is correct rather than *cat* (de Jong, Houter, & Nielsen, 2012). Thus, teachers must be careful with their own pronunciations.

When a Reader makes mistakes, the Coach immediately emphasizes the correct response, asks the Reader to repeat the correct response, and repeats the entire line for further clarification.

Stars, placed at intervals in the What Sound? lesson sheets (see Figure 7.2), prompt the Coach to reinforce the Reader by saying "Good work," or providing similar praise. When the Reader completes the activity, the Coach uses a pencil to mark a happy face. Afterwards, the students switch roles and the Coach becomes the Reader. When both students finish What Sound?, they proceed to the Sight Words activities without prompting from the teacher.

TABLE 7.2

K-PALS SOUND PLAY ACTIVITIES				
Activity	**Sample**	**Purpose and Procedure**	**First Lesson**	**Total Lessons**
First Sound A	Intro Lesson 3	Purpose: To identify words' initial phonemes. Procedure: Teacher says two words with target phoneme, and students choose between two pictures.	Intro 3	10
First Sound B	Lesson 5	Purpose: To identify words' initial phonemes. Procedure: Teacher says one word with target phoneme, and students choose between three pictures.	5	12
Rhyming	Lesson 9	Purpose: To identify words that rhyme. Procedure: Teacher says two words that rhyme and students choose between two pictures.	9	8
Guess My Word A	Lesson 13	Purpose: To blend phonemes to form spoken words. Procedure: Teacher says the four words that rhyme. Then, the teacher says the word's phonemes while pointing at large top boxes. Students repeat the sounds and say the word they make.	13	16
Guess My Word B	Lesson 17	Purpose: To blend phonemes to form spoken words. Procedure: Same as Guess My Word A, except words all begin with the same phoneme.	17	8

(continued)

TABLE 7.2

K-PALS SOUND PLAY ACTIVITIES *(continued)*				
Activity	**Sample**	**Purpose and Procedure**	**First Lesson**	**Total Lessons**
Guess My Word Mix	Same as earlier, with pictures that contain a variety of phonemes	Purpose: To blend phonemes to form spoken words. Procedure: Same as Guess My Word A, except words contain a variety of phonemes.	48	8
Last Sound	**Lesson 37** 	Purpose: To identify words' final phonemes. Procedure: Teacher says two words with target phoneme, and students choose between two pictures.	37	12

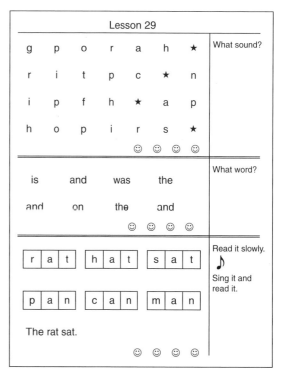

FIGURE 7.2 The Decoding Lesson sheet for K-PALS Lesson 29, the first lesson in which the students complete all four activities (What Sound?, Sight Words, Sound Boxes, and Sentences). The teacher practices the entire sheet with the whole class before they do it in pairs. For each of the three sections, both students must complete the activities before they move on to the next section. When the Reader finishes reading a section, the Coach places a slash through the happy face, and the students switch jobs.

FIGURE 7.1 First Sound A Sound Play activity. For the first item on the page, the teacher says, "*Apple, /a/*" (IPA: /æ/). *Alligator, /a/*. What starts with /a/, *hat* or *axe*? The students respond, "*Axe, /a/.*" If the students make an error, the teacher corrects the class by saying the correct answer and repeating the item.

The Sight Words activity improves students' automatic recognition of 21 high-frequency sight words taken from the Dolch list (Dolch, 1936). The procedure requires the Coach to point at a word and the Reader speaks the printed word. Each student performs Sight Words once before the pair moves on to Sound Boxes.

The Sound Boxes activity improves students' decoding—or phonics—skills using a synthetic phonics procedure; that is, matching graphemes to phonemes and blending those sounds to pronounce a word. For Sound Boxes, the letters represent individual sounds and appear in boxes (sometimes called "Elkonin boxes" after the Russian psychologist who recommended their use; Clay, 1985) to draw students' attention to the connection between letters and sounds. Both letters in a digraph occupy one box to show they create one sound. For example, the word "chop" is presented as [ch][o][p] to emphasize that the letters ch represent /ch/ (IPA: /tʃ/). The procedure requires the Coach to ask the Reader to read what is presented in the box; the Reader responds.

In Lesson 29, the Sentences activity is added. The Coach says, "Read the sentence." After students finish the Decoding Lesson, they count their marked happy faces. One point is awarded for each marked happy face. When the pair completes a point sheet, the teacher recognizes the students by asking the class to applaud the pair, and posts their completed point sheets on a K-PALS bulletin board, or displays the students' work by another method that provides appropriate recognition of their efforts.

Partner Reading. Approximately the 10th week of K-PALS, pairs begin Partner Reading with Lesson 39. The Coach reads a sentence and the Reader repeats it, which is the opposite of the Decoding Lesson order, where the Reader reads first. The Coach—who is a better reader—can provide a fluent model for the Reader, allowing the reader to benefit more from the repeated reading. Repeated reading is thought to improve reading fluency—and potentially reading comprehension—in elementary school students (e.g., O'Connor, White, & Swanson, 2007; Sindelar, Monda, & O'Shea, 1990). The teacher selects books at the "instructional level" (Burns, 2007) of the lower-performing reader, meaning the student can read the book with 93% to 97% accuracy (i.e., about 1 mistake every 20 or 25 words).

The higher-performing reader should be able to read the book at the independent level, between 98% and 100% accuracy (i.e., 1 mistake per 100 words).

During Partner Reading, if neither student knows how to say a word, the Coach raises his or her hand to gain the teacher's attention. The teacher tells the pair the word they missed. The pair repeats the word and resumes reading. When the pair finishes reading a book, they add a point to the point sheet. Pairs read a book at least six times before asking for a new book.

First-Grade Reading PALS

Overview. First-grade Reading PALS, like K-PALS, emphasizes basic skills in reading. Students focus on learning GPCs, practicing sight words, decoding, and reading fluency; however, unlike K-PALS, virtually all First-Grade PALS activities are conducted in pairs. The teacher begins each lesson by conducting a whole-class activity called *Hearing Sounds and Sounding Out.* Then, the student pairs complete the *Student Lesson*—similar to K-PALS' Decoding Lesson. After 10 weeks of First-Grade PALS implementation, teachers introduce *Partner Reading,* just as in K-PALS. The times for each activity are prescribed, and the teacher directs students when to move to the next activity.

First-Grade PALS Activities. The teacher first introduces new sounds and conducts the Hearing Sounds and Sounding Out activity with the whole class. The students complete most of the remaining activities using the Decoding Lesson sheets.

In *Teacher-Directed Hearing Sounds and Sounding Out,* the teacher leads the class in an activity that combines PA and decoding. During the Sounding Out part of the Hearing Sounds and Sounding Out activity, the teacher then points to the word and prompts the students to "sound it out" and "read it fast," pointing to each letter as the students blend the sounds in the word.

If the students make mistakes, the teacher says, for example, "Stop, that word is /kaaat/ (IPA: /kæææt/), cat. Sound it out." Students then sound the word out. Once the teacher has completed Hearing Sounds and Sounding Out, the teacher introduces new sight words the students will encounter during the Decoding Lesson. A box around the sight word signifies that it is a new sight word, as illustrated in Figure 7.2 (for "what"). Then, the students complete the Saying

Sounds, Sounding Out, and Sight Words activities for 3 minutes, 4 minutes, and 3 minutes, respectively.

The following activities are conducted with the Decoding Lesson Sheet. The Saying Sounds activity is identical to the What Sound? activity in K-PALS. The Sounding Out activity is identical to the Sounding Out part of the Teacher-Directed Hearing Sounds and Sounding Out activity. For the Sight Words activity, the Coach simply says, "Read the words," and the Reader reads them without stopping for further prompts from the Coach. Many of the First-Grade PALS sight words are grouped in phrases, and teachers often encourage their students to say the phrases together.

When a Reader completes an activity once, the Coach marks a happy face and adds five points to the point sheet. The First-Grade point sheet contains 400 points rather than 100 as in K-PALS, with points contributing to a team total. If time for the activity has not elapsed and both readers have completed the activity once, the Reader and Coach reverse roles and begin the activity again. Pairs can continue earning points and work on the same activity until the teacher's timer goes off.

After Sight Words, the teacher begins the Stories activity by presenting new *Rocket Words* necessary to read the story. Rocket Words are words the students could not decode using only the GPCs learned in First-Grade PALS that have not been taught as sight words. The teacher teaches these words as he or she would teach sight words. Then, the teacher reads the story aloud to the class as they follow along. Finally, the students return to their pairs and read the story in pairs for 5 minutes.

During the *Speed Game*, the Reader returns to the Sight Words section of the Student Lesson, and the teacher allows the Reader 30 seconds to read as much of the section as possible. As the Reader reads, the Coach corrects mistakes by saying the correct word. The Reader repeats the word and continues reading.

When the teacher's timer goes off, the Reader circles the last word read and puts his or her initials on the page. Then, the Reader reads again for 30 seconds, circles the last word, and initials. This is done a third time. If the Reader progresses further the second or third time, he or she marks an X through one of the rockets on her Speed Game chart. When the Reader completes a chart, a bookmark and a new chart are given to the Reader. A bookmark template is provided in the First-Grade PALS manual.

When the Reader finishes, the second Reader tries to beat his or her own time on the second or third reading as well. The students do not compete directly against each other, so each student has an individualized Speed Game chart. When students reach Lesson 29, the Speed Game switches from reading sight words to reading a story to emphasize passage fluency.

In week 10 of First-Grade PALS, about Lesson 30, the teacher introduces the pairs to *Partner Reading*. As in K-PALS, the text should be at the instructional level of the lower reader and the independent level of the higher reader. The students receive a happy face and five points each time they finish reading the book. They read for a total of 10 minutes during each PALS session.

Points and Teams. In First-Grade PALS, pairs are assigned to one of two teams. The teacher is careful to balance teams so that each has an equal number of stronger and weaker pairs. At the end of each week, the teacher tallies the points for each team and declares the winning team and the second-place team.

Reading PALS for Grades 2 to 6

Reading PALS for Grades 2 to 6 changes the emphasis from word recognition skills to reading fluency and reading comprehension, in line with the emphasis on these skills in the CCSS. Grade 2 to 6 PALS comprises four activities: *Partner Reading*, *Retell*, *Paragraph Shrinking*, and *Prediction Relay*. The length of each activity is prescribed, and the teacher tells the students when to move to the next activity. Pairs record points on a point sheet for completing tasks during each activity.

Students are either First Reader or Second Reader in Grade 2 to 6 PALS. The First Reader in Grade 2 to 6 PALS is the stronger reader because the texts are not controlled in terms of the words used, and it is important that the stronger reader model accurate, fluent reading for the lower-performing reader. Nonetheless, both students act as Coach and Reader, the higher-performing reader reading first and the lower-performing reader coaching first. Each pair reads a text at the instructional level of the lower-performing reader, following the same guidelines described earlier (i.e., 93%–97% accuracy for the lower-performing reader; 98%–100% accuracy for the higher-performing reader).

Grade 2 to 6 PALS has 12 training lessons, completed in the first 3 or 4 weeks of PALS implementation. After training is completed, the four activities are completely peer-directed and take a minimum of 35 minutes to complete.

Grade 2 to 6 PALS Activities. Teachers introduce students to the four activities through the 12 training lessons. These lessons are scripted, and the Grade 2 to 6 PALS manual also includes "Guiding Points" for teachers to use in lieu of scripts. We have found that students understand the lessons better and the teachers finish the lessons faster when they use the scripts.

Partner Reading. The First Reader reads for 5 minutes. The Second Reader coaches. When the teacher's timer goes off after 5 minutes, the students switch roles, starting at the same spot the First Reader began.

In Partner Reading, the Coach has two responsibilities. The Coach's primary responsibility is to follow along as the Reader reads and checks the Reader's mistakes. The Coach corrects four types of errors: adding a word or word ending; waiting longer than 4 seconds; saying a wrong word or word ending; and leaving out a word or word ending. In all cases, the Reader rereads the sentence that contained an error. The Coach's second job is to mark a point on the point sheet for each sentence the Reader reads accurately.

Retell. After Partner Reading, each pair retells what they just read for 2 minutes. The First Reader coaches and asks the Second Reader, "What happened first," and the Second Reader describes the first event in the section read. The First Reader continues asking what happened, and the Second Reader continues to retell in alignment with the text evidence emphasis in the CCSS. The students are permitted to look at the text as they retell. If the Second Reader skips an event, retells incorrectly, or gets stuck, the First Reader tells the Second Reader the answer. When Retell ends, each pair can award itself up to 10 points, depending on whether they retold all of the events in the text. Teachers provide guidance to help pairs make good decisions about the number of points they deserve.

Paragraph Shrinking. After Retell, the First Reader reads new text for 5 minutes, and the pair "shrinks" as many paragraphs as they can. To do Paragraph Shrinking, the Coach stops the pair after they read a paragraph (or several short paragraphs, when there is dialogue), and prompts the Reader to perform the three Paragraph Shrinking steps: (a) name the most important who or what; (b) tell the most important thing about the who or what; and (c) say the main idea in 10 words or less.

Prediction Relay. The final Grade 2 to 6 PALS activity requires the Reader to make a prediction, read half a page, and check the prediction by telling whether the prediction was accurate. The Coach prompts the Reader to make a prediction by asking, "What do you predict will happen next?" for fiction and "What do you predict you will learn next?" for nonfiction. After reading half a page, the Coach asks the Reader, "Did your prediction come true?" and the Reader responds simply "Yes," "No," or "I don't know yet," and continues reading. The First Reader reads new text for 5 minutes followed by the Second Reader, who also reads the new text for 5 minutes.

Mini-Lessons. After students complete training, they will need additional support to become excellent at retelling, making main-idea statements, and predicting. As a result, the Grade 2 to 6 PALS manual includes a set of short mini-lessons to improve students' skills in completing the PALS activities.

Opportunities for Differentiated Instruction

PALS was designed to accommodate academic diversity in general education classrooms (Fuchs, Fuchs, Mathes, & Simmons, 1997). Because students work in pairs, the teacher can differentiate instructional materials, pacing, and feedback to target students' individual learning needs.

As indicated, higher-performing readers are paired with lower-performing readers to practice the reading skills described earlier. Typically, the teacher rank orders all of the students in the classroom based on reading skill level, using recent progress-monitoring data. Then, the teacher divides the rank-ordered list in half, and pairs the top student from the top half with the top student from the bottom half, and so on, until all students are paired. Thus, each pair includes a stronger and a weaker reader, but the discrepancy is not so large as to introduce frustration between partners or difficulty in selecting appropriate reading materials. The teacher also takes social and behavioral skills into account, and adjusts pairs accordingly. Pairs work together for about a month, and then the teacher re-ranks the class (again using recent data) and creates new pairs so students can work with a variety of peers.

Because students work in pairs during PALS, the teacher can adjust the difficulty of each lesson according to each pair's needs. Given the relatively small discrepancy among partners, the material should be appropriate for both the stronger and weaker readers. In kindergarten and in first grade, the teacher can place pairs on earlier (or later) lessons, according to individual needs. In Grades 2 to 6, PALS is conducted with classroom reading materials (e.g., trade books, leveled readers, basal readers, or content-area texts). The teacher selects texts at the instructional level of the weaker reader. Often, teachers provide an array of texts of different genres at a given level for pairs. Students read multiple texts across the school year during PALS.

As students work with their partners, the teacher should walk around the classroom to ensure that students are following PALS procedures and reading appropriately leveled materials, and also provide individualized feedback as needed. Teachers can award additional points to pairs for engaging in specific reading behaviors (e.g., reading with expression) and social behaviors (e.g., providing help to the Reader). PALS pairs also award themselves points for completing each activity.

CONCLUSION

In this chapter, the important role of scientific, research-based, classwide intervention as part of core instruction was provided in multitiered models of prevention and intervention. PALS was highlighted as one such approach that may be used in general education elementary classrooms, each PALS component for each grade level was described, and the requisite research supporting the efficacy of PALS to improve reading outcomes for diverse learners was addressed. As with any research-based classwide intervention, PALS has the promise to benefit many, but not all children. Thus, emphasis was placed on the importance of implementing core components with fidelity to ensure that students have the opportunity to respond to high-quality PALS implementation. At the same time, it is critical to monitor the progress of students at risk of reading failure, and to make timely instructional adaptations when data indicate this need.

SELECT BIBLIOGRAPHY

Kearns, D. M., Fuchs, D., McMaster, K. L., Saenz, L., Fuchs, L. S., Yen, L., ...Smith, T. M. (2010). Factors contributing to teachers' sustained use of kindergarten peer-assisted learning strategies. *Journal of Research on Educational Effectiveness, 3*, 315–342. *This article presents factors that predict teachers' use of the K-PALS. It was found that the strongest predictors were teacher perceptions of the efficacy of K-PALS and the extent of support provided to them.*

Rafdal, B. H., McMaster, K. L., McConnell, S. R., Fuchs, D., & Fuchs, L. S. (2011). The effectiveness of kindergarten peer-assisted learning strategies for students with disabilities. *Exceptional Children, 77*, 299–316. *This study determined the effectiveness of K-PALS for students with disabilities. The researchers randomly assigned 89 kindergartners with individualized education programs (IEPs) from 47 classrooms to control (n = 9); K-PALS Level 1 (teachers received 1-day workshop; n = 19); or K-PALS Level 2 (teachers received workshop plus booster sessions; n = 19). Multivariate analysis of covariance on posttest measures of beginning reading skills indicated that K-PALS students outperformed controls on alphabetical and oral reading measures, but that no reliable between-group differences were attributable to level of support. The researchers also discuss directions for further research and implications for implementing classroom-based reading interventions for students with disabilities.*

REFERENCES

Al Otaiba, S., Kosanovich-Grek, M. L., Torgesen, J. K., Hassler, L., & Wahl, M. (2005). Reviewing core kindergarten and first-grade reading programs in light of No Child Left Behind: An exploratory study. *Reading & Writing Quarterly, 21*, 377–400.

Burns, M. K. (2007). Reading at the instructional level with children identified as learning disabled: Potential implications for response-to-intervention. *School Psychology Quarterly, 22*, 297–313.

Calhoon, M. B., Al Otaiba, S., Cihak, D., King, A., & Avalos, A. (2007). Effects of a peer-mediated program on reading skill acquisition for two-way bilingual first-grade classrooms. *Learning Disability Quarterly, 30*, 169–184.

Clay, M. (1985). *Early detection of reading difficulties.* Portsmouth, NH: Heinemann.

Delquadri, J., Greenwood, C. R., Whorton, D., Carta, J. J., & Hall, R. V. (1986). Classwide peer tutoring. *Exceptional Children, 52*(6), 535–542.

Dolch, E. W. (1936). A basic sight vocabulary. *The Elementary School Journal, 36*, 456–460.

Elbro, C., de Jong, P. F., Houter, D., & Nielsen, A.-M. (2012). From spelling pronunciation to lexical access: A second step in word decoding? *Scientific Studies of Reading, 16*, 341–359.

Fuchs, D., & Fuchs, L. S. (1998). Researchers and teachers working together to adapt instruction for diverse learners. *Learning Disabilities Research and Practice, 13*, 126–137.

Fuchs, D., & Fuchs, L. S. (2005). Peer-assisted learning strategies: Promoting word recognition, fluency, and reading comprehension in young children. *Journal of Special Education, 39*, 34–44.

Fuchs, D., Fuchs, L. S., Al Otaiba, S., Thompson, A., Yen, L., McMaster, K. N.,…Yang, N. J. (2001). K-PALS: Helping kindergartners with reading readiness: Teachers and researchers in partnerships. *TEACHING Exceptional Children, 33*, 76–80.

Fuchs, D., Fuchs, L. S., Mathes, P. H., & Simmons, D. C. (1997). Peer-assisted learning strategies: Making classrooms more responsive to diversity. *American Educational Research Journal, 34*, 174–206.

Fuchs, D., Fuchs, L. S., Thompson, A., Al Otaiba, S., Yen, L., Yang, N. J.,…O'Connor, R. E. (2001). Is reading important in reading-readiness programs? A randomized field trial with teachers as program implementers. *Journal of Educational Psychology, 93*, 251–267.

Fuchs, D., Fuchs, L. S., Thompson, A., Al Otaiba, S., Yen, L., Yang, N. J.,…O'Connor, R. E. (2002). Exploring the importance of reading programs for kindergartners with disabilities in mainstream classrooms. *Exceptional Children, 68*, 295–311.

Fuchs, D., Fuchs, L. S., Yen, L., McMaster, K., Svenson, E., Yang, N.,…King, S. (2001). Developing first-grade reading fluency through peer mediation. *TEACHING Exceptional Children, 34*, 90–93.

Fuchs, D., McMaster, K., Saenz, L., Kearns, D., Fuchs, L., Yen, L.,…Schatschneider, C. (2010). *Bringing educational innovation to scale: Top-down,* bottom-up, or a third way? Presented at the IES Conference, Washington, DC.

Fuchs, L. S., & Fuchs, D. (1998). Building a bridge across the canyon. *Learning Disability Quarterly, 21*, 99–101.

Fuchs, L. S., Fuchs, D., & Hamlett, C. L. (1989). Monitoring reading growth using student recalls: Effects of two teacher feedback systems. *Journal of Educational Research, 83*, 103–111.

Gersten, R., Compton, D., Connor, C. M., Dimino, J., Santoro, L., Linan-Thompson, S., & Tilly, W. D. (2009). *Assisting students struggling with reading: Response to intervention (RTI) and multi-tier intervention in the primary grades.* (IES Practice Guide). Washington, DC: U.S. Department of Education.

Kearns, D. M., Fuchs, D., McMaster, K. L., Saenz, L., Fuchs, L. S., Yen, L.,…Smith, T. M. (2010). Factors contributing to teachers' sustained use of kindergarten peer-assisted learning strategies. *Journal of Research on Educational Effectiveness, 3*, 315–342.

McMaster, K. L., Fuchs, D., & Fuchs, L. S. (2006). Research on peer-assisted learning strategies: The promise and limitations of peer-mediated instruction. *Reading & Writing Quarterly, 22*, 5–25.

McMaster, K. L., Fuchs, D., Fuchs, L. S., & Compton, D. L. (2005). Responding to nonresponders: An experimental field trial of identification and intervention methods. *Exceptional Children, 71*, 445.

McMaster, K. L., Kung, S., Han, I., & Cao, M. (2008). Peer-assisted learning strategies: A "tier 1" approach to promoting English learners' response to intervention. *Exceptional Children, 74*, 194–214.

National Governors Association Center for Best Practices & Council of Chief State School Officers. (2010). *Common Core State Standards for English language arts and literacy in history/social studies, science, and technical subjects.* Washington, DC: Authors.

Noell, G. H., & Gansle, K. A. (2006). Assuring the form has substance: Treatment plan implementation as the foundation of assessing response to intervention. *Assessment for Effective Intervention, 32*, 32–39.

O'Connor, R. E., White, A., & Swanson, H. L. (2007). Repeated reading versus continuous reading:

Influences on reading fluency and comprehension. *Exceptional Children, 74,* 31–46.

Rafdal, B. H., McMaster, K. L., McConnell, S. R., Fuchs, D., & Fuchs, L. S. (2011). The effectiveness of kindergarten peer-assisted learning strategies for students with disabilities. *Exceptional Children, 77,* 299–316.

Saenz, L. M., Fuchs, L. S., & Fuchs, D. (2005). Peer-assisted learning strategies for English language learners with learning disabilities. *Exceptional Children, 71,* 231–247.

Sindelar, P. T., Monda, L. E., & O'Shea, L. J. (1990). Effects of repeated readings on instructional-and mastery-level readers. *The Journal of Educational Research, 83,* 220–226.

Evidence-Based Interventions for Math Disabilities in Children and Adolescents

Kathryn E. Jaspers, Daniel F. McCleary, Lisa N. McCleary, and Christopher H. Skinner

OVERVIEW

In 2013, 42% of fourth-grade students and 36% of eighth-grade students in the United States performed at the proficient or advanced level on the mathematics National Assessment Educational Progress (NAEP) assessments, indicating that more than half of students at these grades are performing below proficient levels in math. Of most concern are the 17% of fourth-grade students and 26% of eighth-grade students who failed to meet even basic performance standards (U.S. Department of Education, National Center for Educational Statistics, 2013a). Although the percentages have shown considerable improvement since 1990, these most recent data indicate a significant need for improvement.

Prevalence rates of math disabilities (MD) are difficult to estimate. More than 2 million school-aged children in the United States are identified as having specific learning disability (SLD), which includes more than one third of students receiving special education services in the United States (U.S. Department of Education, National Center for Educational Statistics, 2013b). Exact rates of MD are not known, though earlier studies estimate that 4% to 7% of school-aged children have MD (Fuchs et al., 2005). In part, prevalence rates for MD are difficult to estimate due to

differences in the methods for determining MD. There are three primary models for determination of an SLD in the United States: IQ-achievement discrepancy, patterns of strengths and weaknesses (PSW), and Responsiveness-to-Intervention (RtI). Using an RtI model, Fuchs, Fuchs, and Compton (2012) examined data from four studies and found that approximately 4% of students could be labeled as nonresponders after receiving a mathematics intervention, which may indicate the prevalence of a math disability. Because each model involves different criteria for identification, researchers in the area of MD often use low math achievement, such as math achievement below the 10th, 16th, or 25th percentile on individually administered, standardized tests of achievement, with the absence of low IQ (i.e., not intellectually disabled) as a method for identifying students with MD for research purposes (Fuchs, Fuchs, & Compton, 2013). With such models, prevalence rates will be strongly influenced by achievement scores cutoffs.

ETIOLOGY AND FACTORS CONTRIBUTING TO MD IN CHILDREN AND ADOLESCENTS

There has been an increase in research examining the genetic and environmental influences on math ability through studies of twins. The Twin Early Development Study (TEDS) involves more than 5,000 sets of twins in the United Kingdom born between 1994 and 1996, and the Western Reserve Reading Project (WRRP) is a study of more than 300 sets of twins in the Ohio area (Hart, Petrill, Thompson, & Plomin, 2009). Although the TEDS study is larger in number, it involved only web-based measures and teacher ratings, whereas the WRRP study included individually administered, standardized measures of achievement and cognition more commonly used for the assessment of learning disabilities in the United States.

Early results from the TEDS study indicate moderate to high and significant heritability of math ability at ages 7, 9, and 10 years, with nonsignificant shared environmental influences (Hart et al., 2009; Kovas, Haworth, Petrill, & Plomin, 2007; Oliver et al., 2004). The WRRP study, in which the children were an average of 8.5 years old at the time of the first math-specific assessments and 10 years of age at the time of the second math-specific assessments, also found moderate and significant heritability of math ability. Differences from the TEDS studies emerged, however, when examining the influence of shared environment on math performance; in the WRRP study, researchers found significant influences of shared environment, though they found a "trend toward genetic influences" (Hart et al., 2009, p. 396) and a decreased environmental influence with age, which the authors noted is consistent with previous research on the increased influence of genetic factors as children age (Hart et al., 2009).

In addition to the work on the heritability of math ability, the transition from the traditional IQ-achievement discrepancy model of SLD identification toward an approach that emphasizes a PSW has supported an increased emphasis on identifying cognitive correlates of math difficulties. Researchers have found a number of cognitive processes that are often impaired in children with MD, including long-term storage and retrieval, short-term memory (including both working memory and memory span), attention and inhibitory control, set shifting, oral language skills, verbal comprehension, nonverbal problem solving, processing speed, and phonological processing (Fuchs et al., 2005; Fuchs et al., 2008; Geary, 2007; Wendling & Mather, 2009; Willcutt et al., 2013). This list of cognitive correlates is quite lengthy, which may be in part due to the large number of skills involved in mathematics (ranging from basic fact retrieval to understanding and answering word problems to geometry and measurement). Each skill may be related to different cognitive processes, and the exact nature of these relationships is not fully understood at this time. For example, one theory related to working memory deficits is that difficulty retaining information in short-term or working memory causes errors in problem solving. As evidence of this, Geary, Hoard, Byrd-Craven, Nugent, and Numtee found that children with MD are more likely to detect counting errors at the end of a counting sequence than at the beginning of a sequence, suggesting that difficulties holding information in short-term memory may be the cause of errors in calculation when problem solving (Geary et al., 2007).

The cognitive abilities found to be related to math skills may have differential impacts depending on a child's age. For example, although Fuchs and colleagues (2005) found that phonological processing was related to math performance, this was in a sample of first-grade students; in a different sample of children aged 8 to 15 years, phonemic awareness was associated only with reading disabilities and not MD (Willcutt et al., 2013). Thus, part of the difficulty in defining a math learning disability is that there are so many skills involved in mathematics (Mazzocco, 2007) that may be related to many different cognitive processes, and these cognitive processes may have different levels of importance at different ages. Though there are cognitive processes related to math skills, aptitude-by-treatment interaction researchers have found little evidence to suggest that altering cognitive processes can enhance math achievement; instead, the most effective method for improving math skills in children with disabilities is to directly target the math skills themselves (Reschly & Ysseldyke, 2002; Shapiro, 2011).

Given the cognitive correlates of math difficulties, it is not surprising that common comorbid diagnoses include reading disabilities and attention deficit hyperactivity disorder (ADHD). In a review of the literature on the comorbidity of ADHD and SLD, DuPaul, Gormley, and Laracy (2013) found a mean comorbidity of 45.1% across 17 studies. When considering just children with MD, comorbidity ranged from 5% to 30%. Comorbidity of reading and MD are significantly higher, ranging from 30% to 70% (Willcutt et al., 2013). Children with a math disability or comorbid math/reading disability are also more likely to meet criteria for a variety of internalizing and externalizing disorders such as oppositional defiant disorder (ODD), conduct disorder (CD), generalized anxiety disorder, and depression, though the increased levels of ODD and CD may be related to a subgroup of children who also meet criteria for ADHD (Willcutt et al., 2013).

EVIDENCE-BASED INTERVENTIONS AND EMPIRICAL SUPPORT FOR MD IN CHILDREN AND ADOLESCENTS

General Strategies

Although the purpose of this chapter is to highlight evidence-based mathematical interventions, instructional methods themselves cannot be overlooked. This is especially true as the application of RtI has increased focus on teachers' instructional methods and their fidelity of implementation. In addition, an exclusionary factor that Individualized Education Program (IEP) teams must consider before determining if a student qualifies for special education services is whether or not a student has received adequate instruction in reading and math. Therefore, it is important that evidence-based instructional methods are also addressed as these methods become even more vital as the academic tasks transition from concrete to abstract, requiring a great deal of mental processing and self-talk.

The National Dissemination Center for Children with Disabilities (NICHCY; Steedly, Dragoo, Arefeh, & Luke, 2008) and the National Council of Teachers of Mathematics (NCTM, 2007) identified four common instructional methods most supported by meta-analytic research on teaching mathematics: (a) systematic instruction, (b) self-instruction, (c) visual representation, and (d) peer-assisted learning. Common to each of these strategies is the need for practice and rehearsal, opportunities to respond, corrective feedback, and student engagement.

Systematic Instruction. Systematic instruction (i.e., explicit instruction and direct instruction) has been shown to have a large effect size (1.19) for students with identified disabilities and a moderate effect size (0.58) for struggling students (NCTM, 2007). Before instruction begins, the teacher assesses each student's skill level on the task and creates custom instruction to meet the individual student's needs. The teacher then overtly states the learning objective, outlines the plan to complete the objective, and follows clearly defined predetermined steps needed to complete the task. After systematic instruction, students work individually and in groups, repeating the sequence of steps taught. Other important factors to systematic instruction include the pace of the lesson, time delays for the students to process the information and provide a response, and immediate corrective feedback (Skinner, Pappas, & Davis, 2005). According to the NCTM (2007), the majority of math textbooks do not include the degree, structure, or specificity needed to meet the requirements of systematic instruction.

Self-Instruction. Self-instruction (i.e., think-alouds and self-talk) has a large effect size (0.98) for students receiving special education services (NCTM, 2007). This method is especially important with higher order math skills when problems must be solved in a sequential manner and may also help students regulate their behavior (Steedly et al., 2008). During self-instruction, students think or talk aloud (i.e., self-talk) the strategies that could be used to complete the math task (e.g., computation problem, proof, interpretation). After selecting a strategy, the student continues to verbally or metacognitively mediate each step of the process on how he or she will complete each step. A student may even write or draw the steps in place in addition to talking oneself through the process. Other important factors to effective self-instruction involve the teacher and student rehearsing how to correctly solve problems and using appropriate self-statements to identify and correct errors when such an error occurs. Again, the more opportunities the student has to engage in the activity with corrective feedback, the more likely the student is to experience success (Skinner et al., 2005; Steedly et al., 2008).

Visual Representation. Visual representation (i.e., graphic depiction and visual organizers) when used with students with disabilities has a moderate effect size (0.50). Manipulatives, pictures, number lines, and graphs can all be considered a form of visual representation (Steedly et al., 2008). The goal of visual representation is to bring abstract concepts into a more concrete form to aid students' comprehension of the problem. The effectiveness of visual representations depends largely on how specific the visual representation is to the problem, with more specific representations being more impactful (NCTM, 2007). Once more, teachers must practice using visual representations with students in order to maximize impact on learning. One of the most common visual representation methods is concrete–representational–abstract (discussed later in this chapter).

Peer-Assisted Learning. Peer-assisted learning (i.e., peer tutoring) has a moderate effect size (0.42) for students with disabilities and a large effect size (0.62) for students experiencing math difficulties (NCTM, 2007). An important aspect of peer-assisted learning is that students are placed in pairs or in groups with individuals of differing ability levels (NCTM, 2007; Steedly et al., 2008). Teachers create the materials (i.e., worksheets, flashcards, answer sheets, script, etc.) for students to use and train the students in the role of both the tutor and the tutee. This is a very structured activity in which students change roles, from tutor to tutee and vice versa, halfway through the activity. The tutor's role is to provide scaffolding as to how to complete the next step in the problem or to provide immediate corrective feedback. Some of the most common peer-assisted learning methods include classwide peer tutoring (CWPT), peer-assisted learning strategies (PALS), and reciprocal peer tutoring.

An additional model that is helpful in characterizing students' skill development is a four-stage hierarchy of skill acquisition developed by Haring and Eaton (1978). The first stage focuses on the individual attaining skill accuracy. Drilling, modeling, and cuing are the most effective interventions at this stage. The second stage is fluency (i.e., fast, accurate responding) and begins once the individual is able to accurately respond, but cannot do so quickly. Repeated practice and reinforcement are the most effective stage two interventions. Generalization (i.e., exhibiting the skill in response to a novel stimuli) of the skill occurs during the third stage of development. Effective stage three interventions include

practice responding to novel stimuli. Stage four is application (i.e., adapt the skill to meet new task demands). Application is most effectively enhanced through creative problem solving and simulation of novel situations. Using this skill acquisition hierarchy to guide intervention decisions encourages educators to consider not just what skill is deficient, but also at what level within the hierarchy a skill has been developed; this is particularly important as many of our interventions focus on skill acquisition without considering fluency, application, generalization, and maintenance of skills over time.

Early Numeracy

As our measurement tools and understanding of MD improve, educators are able to identify at-risk students at a younger age, which should allow us to prevent math skill deficits, provided we also develop interventions that target key skills in younger grades (e.g., before students are expected to fluently calculate and solve word problems). Particularly in kindergarten and early first grade, instruction often focuses on basic conceptual knowledge that will assist in students' later computation skills and application of computational skills to solve problems. Some "big topical ideas" (Clements, 2004, p. 17) in early numeracy include counting, comparing and ordering, adding to and/or taking away, composing and decomposing, grouping and place value, and equal partitioning, which are discussed in the following sections. These big ideas build upon each other, and their development serves as the base of knowledge needed for later work with numbers and operations. For example, being able to state that 4 + 2 = 6 is of little utility if students cannot understand that problem is represented by a set of four objects, a set of two objects, and when joined there are a total of six objects.

Within the area of counting, some key skills include one-to-one correspondence, knowing the names and order of the number words, cardinality (knowing that the final number counted is equal to the total number of items counted), and subitizing (knowing how many items are in a small group without having to count). Students must be able to demonstrate not only procedural understanding (being able to count) but conceptual understanding or knowing *why* the procedure works (Baroody, 2004; LeFevre et al., 2006). Counting is required for students to be able to understand comparing and ordering. The ability to compare and order (i.e., decide which of two groups is *more*) is a less demanding version of determining *how many more* are in one group than another (Clements, 2004), which is the beginning of understanding adding to and/or taking away. Focusing on these counting and quantifying skills is vital, as children with MD are more likely to use inefficient and immature strategies when solving basic math problems such as *counting all* (counting both addends beginning at 1) instead of *counting on* (starting from the larger addend and counting on) when adding (Geary, 2004).

Composing and decomposing represent the idea that a larger cardinal number can be decomposed into smaller groups in various combinations (i.e., $5 = 1 + 4$ or $2 + 3$), and smaller groups can be composed into larger numbers. A true understanding of composing and decomposing numbers is required to understand the complementary nature of addition and subtraction (i.e., $5 + 3 = 8$, so $3 + 5 = 8$ and $8 - 5 = 3$), and research has shown that this relationship between number combinations is not obvious to all children (Baroody, 1999). Young children must also learn to group items by common numbers. For example, the number 12 can be represented by 3 groups of 4. This serves as a first step to understanding place value because items are commonly grouped around sets of 10, and children must understand, for example, that the "2" in 24 represents two groups of 10 (Clements, 2004). Equal partitioning refers to decomposing a larger number into groups of equal sizes (e.g., 36 can be broken down into 12 groups of 3), a prerequisite for the development of multiplication and division (Clements, 2004).

Although the specific interventions for each requisite early numeracy/number sense skill is beyond the scope of this chapter, it is important to know that there are a plethora of early numeracy skills that may be targeted prior to and concurrently with enhancing fluency with basic facts or solving math reasoning word problems. Educators and parents must not wait until students demonstrate severe deficiencies at the math operations or problem-solving stage to begin intervening. Of great need is a research-based model of instruction for mathematics, parallel to the extensive research on early literacy skills prior to focusing on reading

of connected text (Methe & Riley-Tillman, 2008). Daly, Witt, Martens, and Dool (1997) propose the use of curriculum-based measures, work samples, and other data within a function-based model for remediating academic skills deficits.

Math Operations

Individuals with math operations deficits have difficulty with basic facts (i.e., addition, subtraction, multiplication, and division), typically due to slow and inaccurate responding. These students often engage in time-consuming strategies such as finger counting and counting hash marks. Although these strategies may result in correct responses, they tax the individual's cognitive resources and may impede the student's ability to develop automaticity (Bull & Johnston, 1997). A student's lack of fluency becomes more pronounced when math problem solving and math reasoning problems are introduced (Bryant, Bryant, & Hammill, 2000). Based on the model developed by Haring and Eaton (1978), the ideal intervention for math operations elicits review, repetition, and immediate corrective feedback. Similarly, academic researchers have demonstrated the need and superiority of interventions that encourage high rates of active, accurate, academic responding (Skinner et al., 2005). Four research-based math operations interventions that meet the aforementioned criteria are cover, copy, and compare; taped problems; interspersal; and explicit timing.

Cover, Copy, and Compare. Cover, copy, and compare (CCC) is effective at increasing the rate of correct math problems completed (Poff, McLaughlin, Derby, & King, 2012). For students who are struggling with math facts (e.g., poor accuracy and/or fluency), CCC has been found to be more effective than explicit timing (Codding et al., 2007). Research participants have primarily been composed of general education students; however, CCC has also been used with students with SLD, emotional disturbance, intellectual disabilities, and ADHD (see Joseph et al., 2012).

The CCC intervention involves creating a worksheet with math problems with answers in the left column, and one to four blank columns for the student to engage in practice. The student studies the item, covers the item with an index card or sheet of paper, and writes the problem and answer previously studied in the next column to the right. Next, the student uncovers the original stimulus and compares the individual's response to the stimulus. If the student's item matches the stimulus, then the student moves down to the next problem item. However, if the student's response is incorrect, the student engages in an overcorrection technique such as writing the problem and answer three more times in the next columns. The CCC intervention may be summarized and implemented in the following manner:

- Select a set of target math problems.
- Construct CCC worksheets.
  - Each page includes five columns.
  - The first column contains the target problems with answers, and the next four columns are blank.
  - The second column is to be used for the student to write his or her response, and the last three columns are for the student to engage in self-correction if his or her initial response was incorrect.
- Provide student with packet of CCC worksheets, pencil, and index card.
- Direct student to complete CCC problems as quickly as he or she can by studying the first problem and answer, covering it with the index card, copy the problem and answer into the second column, and compare his or her response to the original stimulus.
  - If the problem and answer are correct, the student is to continue to the next item.
  - If the problem and/or answer are incorrect, the student is to copy the problem and answer correctly three times in the next columns as a self-correct technique.
- Students can be instructed to work for a certain amount of time (e.g., 10 minutes) or complete a predetermined number of problems (e.g., complete 15 problems four times each, for a total of 60 items).
- Consider using an assessment sheet of the target problems to gauge student growth.
  - Create a math worksheet with all target problems on the page.
  - Instruct the student to complete as many problems as he or she can in 60 seconds. Calculate digits correct per minute (DCM), and graph results over time.

Taped Problems. The research on taped problems has demonstrated distinct increases in math fact fluency and sustained improvements following termination of the intervention (McCallum, Schmitt, Schneider, Rezzetano, & Skinner, 2010). Comparison studies between taped problems and CCC show taped problems to produce greater math fact fluency gains and take less time than CCC (Poncy, Skinner, & Jaspers, 2007; Poncy, Skinner, & McCallum, 2012). Taped problems is also effective with individuals with intellectual disabilities (Carroll, Skinner, Turner, McCallum, & Woodland, 2006; Poncy et al., 2007).

Taped problems worksheet packets are constructed with assessment worksheets at the front of the packet followed by the intervention "Beat the Tape" worksheets, and finally a sprint page. Each worksheet contains math problems in columns, and students are instructed to work the problems in order. Students are given explicit directions on when to start and stop work on each worksheet. Time allowed per assessment and sprint worksheets may be 30 seconds or 1 minute. On the intervention worksheets, a recording reads the math problems to the students and then provides the correct answer to each problem after a 0-, 1-, or 2-second delay after reading the problem. The students attempt to "Beat the Tape" by writing the correct answer to each problem before the correct answer is given by the recording. If the student writes an incorrect response, the student crosses out the incorrect answer and writes the correct response next to the problem item. A timed sprint page contains the same problem items as the taped problem page, but in a randomized order, and it provides the students with an opportunity to develop fluency after completing the intervention worksheets. Although researchers calculate digits correct per minute to score the assessment worksheets, students will likely find graphing their number of problems correct more meaningful. Enumerated in the following sections are the step-by-step instructions for implementing taped problems:

- Construct mutually exclusive basic math fact assessment, "Beat the Tape," and sprint pages.
  - Each page includes five columns containing the same number (e.g., 15) of math problems within each column.
  - Randomly assign target problem items to the different pages or systematically group items

(e.g., first page includes the number 2 times table and second page includes the number 3 times table).

- ○ Each "Beat the Tape" page should correspond to an assessment and a sprint page, but items should appear in a different (random) order on each page.
- Construct audio recordings for each assessment, "Beat the Tape," and sprint page.
  - ○ Assessment, "Beat the Tape," and sprint page recordings include directions to start and stop working after either 30 or 60 seconds. Directions also inform students to work down each column before moving to the next column and not to skip any problems. Students are told to work as quickly as possible without working ahead during "Beat the Tape." If a student writes an incorrect answer during "Beat the Tape," the student should cross out the incorrect answer and write the correct answer after it is delivered by the recording.
  - ○ "Beat the Tape" recordings also include the reading of each item problem followed by the reading of each correct item problem answer. The answer should be stated after a 0-second delay for the first column, 2-second delay for columns two and three, and 1-second delay for columns four and five. A 1-second delay should be given between the reading of each item answer and the following item problem.

Interspersal. Research demonstrates that students are more likely to persist on math assignments, complete a greater number of math problems, choose longer assignments for homework, and perceive less time and effort is required to complete interspersal assignments than assignments composed solely of math target items (Wildmon, Skinner, Watson, & Garrett, 2004). Interspersal is a process in which briefer and often easier items are interspersed with target items (e.g., computation facts). Typically, briefer items are interspersed with the target problems on a 1:3 ratio. For example, a student learning double-digit multiplication is given a worksheet containing a single-digit multiplication problem every fourth item. It is important to note that the interspersal intervention is additive in nature. For example, interspersal adds easier problems to a problem set without reducing the number of target items. It does not replace target items with easier items. A final note on interspersal is that the additional interspersed items should require very little time and effort to complete, and there should not be so many items that students are required to spend too much instructional time working on mastered items, otherwise the procedure could reduce learning rates (Forbes et al., 2013; Wildmon, Skinner, & McDade, 1998).

A comparison study between explicit timing and interspersal demonstrated that students completing interspersal assignments completed more problems, finished the math items within a shorter period of time, and rated the assignment as being less effortful and time consuming than explicit timing (Rhymer & Morgan, 2005). Interspersal is also useful at increasing on-task behaviors for students identified with an emotional disturbance within a self-contained classroom (Skinner, Hurst, Teeple, & Meadows, 2002). Finally, for students with SLD and low average intelligence, interspersal is particularly efficacious in enhancing the probability that students choose to engage in assigned tasks (Calderhead, Filter, & Albin, 2006; Wildmon et al., 2004).

Explicit Timing. The use of explicit timing has been shown to increase the number of problems completed per minute (Rhymer et al., 2002). Codding and colleagues (2007) compared explicit timing to CCC and found that explicit timing is the superior intervention for students whose initial fluency rate is within the instructional range. Although all the research studies exploring the effects of explicit timing included individuals with basic math fact deficits, Woodward (2006) is the only researcher who specifically included participants receiving special education services.

Explicit timing entails the instructor informing students of the total duration of the activity (e.g., 3–30 minutes) and stressing the importance of working as many problems within each 1-minute time period as possible. After providing students with math worksheets, the instructor tells the students "Pencils up, ready, begin." After 1 minute, the instructor says, "Stop." At that time, the students draw a line after the completed last item. The instructor continues giving these directions for the duration of the allotted time. Students are evaluated based on the number of correct problems or correct digits completed within each 1-minute interval. Results can be graphed to demonstrate progress and facilitate motivation.

Summary. Math operations interventions focus on automatic recall (accuracy and fluency) of basic facts, rather than conceptual understanding or application. Common aspects among the interventions reviewed include high rates of active responding. As CCC and taped problems incorporate immediate feedback, they can be used when developing both rapid and accurate responding.

Math Problem Solving

In order to solve math problems successfully, students must have knowledge of basic math skills, determine which and in what order to use an operation, and apply their knowledge in new situations. Literature reviews have identified several instructional variables that are considered effective in remediating math problem-solving skills for students with math difficulties (Gersten et al., 2009; Kroesbergen & Van Luit, 2003; Xin & Jitendra, 1999). The following are among the most consistently effective math problem-solving interventions: cognitive strategy based, schema based, and concrete–representational–abstract instruction.

Cognitive Strategy–Based Instruction. Researchers have identified cognitive strategy–based instruction as a method to improve the math problem-solving skills of students with math difficulties (Gersten et al., 2009; Kroesbergen & Van Luit, 2003; Montague, Krawec, Enders, & Dietz, 2013; Swanson, 1999). Interventions using cognitive strategy–based instruction explicitly teach students a sequence of general steps to solve a math problem. The sequence of steps helps the students identify imperative and superfluous information in a math problem. Additionally, the instruction encourages the student to self-reflect and self-evaluate as he or she follows the steps needed to solve the problem (Montague, 2008; Naglieri & Johnson, 2000). Polya's (1986) four-step math problem-solving method (i.e., understand the problem, devise a plan, carry out the plan, look back, and reflect) is an example of an intervention using cognitive strategy–based instruction.

Schema-Based Strategy Instruction. Schema-based strategy instruction is another evidence-based procedure to improve achievement in math (Fuchs & Fuchs, 2007). With some approaches, students are taught to identify important schemas found in math problems, such as identifying whether the problem requires addition or subtraction in order to find a solution. Schema-based strategy instruction includes mapping the math problem visually or graphically, providing direct instruction, and teaching students to apply self-regulation and/ or self-evaluation procedures (Jitendra et al., 2013). An example of schema-based strategy instruction is a four-step process to solve math problems investigated by Xin and Jitendra (2006). First, students are instructed to identify the math structure of the problem, including which operation needs to be used to solve the problem. Then, students map the information necessary to solve the problem on a visual representation of the word problem. Next, the students are explicitly taught a heuristic to solve the problem. Finally, the students learn to monitor their knowledge and problem-solving approach using metacognition (ability to analyze one's own higher order cognitive processes).

Concrete–Representational–Abstract Instruction. An effective method for teaching students with math difficulties, higher order math calculation skills (i.e., subtraction with regrouping, calculation with fractions, etc.), and math problem-solving skills is concrete–representational–abstract instruction (Butler, Miller, Crehan, Babbitt, & Pierce, 2003; Miller & Kaffar, 2011). Concrete–representational– abstract instruction proceeds through three phases of instruction. In the first phase of instruction, the student uses concrete manipulatives, such as base 10 blocks, to represent the problem. In the next phase, the student uses representations of the problem, such as drawings. In the final stage, the student solves the problem using the steps taught in the previous two phases, but without the concrete or visual representation of the problem. For example, the student would use only numerical symbols in the abstract level, such as 85+12, rather than manipulatives or drawings to represent the problem. In the abstract instruction phase, a mnemonic device or strategy-based instruction may be taught to help the student remember the procedure used to solve the problem (Mancl, Miller, & Kennedy,

2012). Mancl et al. used a mnemonic device in their abstract instruction phase, RENAME, designed to help students remember steps in subtraction problems when regrouping was required. The steps included: (a) read the problem; (b) examine the ones column: use the BBB sentence (i.e., bigger number on bottom means break down and trade) for ones; (c) note ones in the ones column; (d) address the tens column: use the BBB sentence for tens; (e) mark tens in the tens column; and (f) examine and note hundreds; exit with a quick check.

Summary. Explicit or direct instruction should be used to teach students a strategy or set of steps that can be used to solve most word problems (Kroesbergen & Van Luit, 2003). In addition, students are directly taught to self-monitor their problem solving as they work through the problem via metacognition. Furthermore, scaffolded prompts such as manipulatives, written steps, and visuals are also useful in helping students solve math problems efficiently and successfully.

CONCLUSION

Efforts to prevent MD may be enhanced by identifying appropriate skill development targets and validating interventions designed to enhance those skills. General models of skill development provide us with a general understanding of how different procedures should be applied across different levels of skill development. As more research in this area is conducted, educators may find that they have a pool of empirically validated interventions designed to enhance different skills (e.g., math fact fluency). Although meta-analytic studies provide guidance on which interventions educators should choose, given the individual differences of each child and adolescent, practitioners should regularly evaluate the effectiveness of their remedial procedures.

MD are not failure-to-learn problems, but learning-rate problems; students are not learning as quickly as expected. Consequently, rather than conducting comparative effectiveness studies (e.g., meta-analytic studies) that focus on amount of learning occasioned by different interventions, researchers should conduct studies that indicate which procedures cause the most rapid learning (Poncy et al., 2015). Identifying and applying procedures

that cause the most rapid learning or skill development should allow educators to prevent some MD from developing. When math deficits or disabilities do develop, knowing which interventions result in the most rapid learning will allow educators to remedy deficits more rapidly. Thus, researchers should be encouraged to develop interventions that not only work (they enhance learning) but also work better because they enhance learning rates relative to alternative interventions (Skinner, McCleary, Poncy, Cates, & Skolits, 2013).

SELECT BIBLIOGRAPHY

Lembke, E., Powell, S., Seethaler, P., & Hughes, E. (2011). *Math interventions.* Retrieved from http://ebi.missouri.edu/?page_id=983.
Lembke and colleagues provide information on an array of math interventions. The website provides intervention briefs (how to implement), evidence briefs (theoretical and empirical support documentation), and in some cases video demonstrations of the intervention being used.

Shapiro, E. S. (2011). *Academic skills problems* (4th ed.). New York, NY: Guilford.
Shapiro's seminal text provides a comprehensive description of basic skill development and procedures for assessing skill development. Also, he provides an overview of both general strategies and specific procedures for promoting mathematics skill development in students. His companion workbook provides additional materials and information designed to be used by practitioners.

Wendling, B. J., & Mather, N. (2009). *Essentials of evidence-based academic interventions.* Hoboken, NJ: John Wiley.
This book provides an overview of the most prevalent evidence-based interventions in the areas of reading, writing, and math. In addition, the authors explain the development of each academic skill.

REFERENCES

Baroody, A. J. (1999). Children's relational knowledge of addition and subtraction. *Cognition and Instruction, 17,* 137–175. doi:10.1207/S1532690XCI170201

Baroody, A. J. (2004). The developmental bases for early childhood number and operations standards.

In D. H. Clements & J. Sarama (Eds.), *Engaging young children in mathematics: Standards for early childhood mathematics education* (pp. 173–219). Mahwah, NJ: Lawrence Erlbaum.

Bryant, D. P., Bryant, B. R., & Hammill, D. D. (2000). Characteristic behaviors of students with LD who have teacher-identified math weaknesses. *Journal of Learning Disabilities, 33*(2), 168–77, 199.

Bull, R., & Johnston, R. S. (1997). Children's arithmetical difficulties: Contributions from processing speed, item identification, and short-term memory. *Journal of Experimental Child Psychology, 65*(1), 1–24.

Butler, F. M., Miller, S. P., Crehan, K., Babbitt, B., & Pierce, T. (2003). Fraction instruction for students with mathematics disabilities: Comparing two teaching sequences. *Learning Disabilities Research & Practice, 18*(2), 99–111. doi:10.1111/1540–5826.00066

Calderhead, W. J., Filter, K. J., & Albin, R. W. (2006). An investigation of incremental effects of interspersing math items on task-related behavior. *Journal of Behavioral Education, 15,* 53–67. doi:10.1007/s10864–005-9000–8

Carroll, E., Skinner, C. H., Turner, H., McCallum, E., & Woodland, S. (2006). Evaluating and comparing responsiveness to two interventions designed to enhance math-fact fluency. *School Psychology Forum: Research in Practice, 1,* 28–45.

Clements, D. H. (2004). Major themes and recommendations. In D. H. Clements & J. Sarama (Eds.), *Engaging young children in mathematics: Standards for early childhood mathematics education* (pp. 7–72). Mahwah, NJ: Lawrence Erlbaum Associates.

Codding, R. S., Shiyko, M., Russo, M., Birch, S., Fanning, E., & Jaspen, D. (2007). Comparing mathematics interventions: Does initial level of fluency predict intervention effectiveness? *Journal of School Psychology, 45,* 603–617. doi:10.1016/j.jsp.2007.06.005

Daly, E. J. III, Witt, J. C., Martens, B. K., & Dool, E. J (1997). A model for conducting a functional analysis of academic performance problems. *School Psychology Review, 26,* 554–574.

DuPaul, G. J., Gormley, M. J., & Laracy, S. D. (2013). Comorbidity of LD and ADHD: Implications of *DSM-5* for assessment and treatment. *Journal of Learning Disabilities, 46*(1), 43–51.

Forbes, B. E., Skinner, C. H., Black, M. P., Yaw, J., Booher, J., & Delisle, J. (2013). Learning rates and known-to-unknown flash-card ratios: Comparing effectiveness while holding instructional time constant. *Journal of Applied Behavior Analysis, 46*(4), 832–837.

Fuchs, L. S., Compton, D. L., Fuchs, D., Paulsen, K., Bryant, J. D., & Hamlett, C. L. (2005). The prevention, identification, and cognitive determinants of math difficulty. *Journal of Educational Psychology, 97,* 493–513. doi:10.1037/0022–0663.97.3.493

Fuchs, L. S., & Fuchs, D. (2007). Mathematical problem solving: Instructional intervention. In D. B. Berch & M. M. M. Mazzocco (Eds.), *Why is math so hard for some children? The nature and origins of mathematical learning difficulties and disabilities* (pp. 397–414). Baltimore, MD: Paul H. Brookes.

Fuchs, L. S., Fuchs, D., & Compton, D. L. (2012). The early prevention of mathematics difficulty: Its power and limitations. *Journal of Learning Disabilities, 45,* 257–269. doi:10.1177/0022219412442167

Fuchs, L. S., Fuchs, D., & Compton, D. L. (2013). Intervention effects for students with comorbid forms of learning disability: Understanding the needs of nonresponders. *Journal of Learning Disabilities, 46*(6), 534–548.

Fuchs, L. S., Fuchs, D., Stuebing, K., Fletcher, J. M., Hamlett, C. L., & Lambert, W. (2008). Problem solving and computational skill: Are they shared or distinct aspects of mathematical cognition? *Journal of Educational Psychology, 100,* 30–47. doi:10.1037/0022–0663.100.1.30

Geary, D. C. (2004). Mathematics and learning disabilities. *Journal of Learning Disabilities, 37*(1), 4–15.

Geary, D. C. (2007). An evolutionary perspective on learning disability in mathematics. *Developmental Neuropsychology, 32*(1), 471–519.

Geary, D. C., Hoard, M. K., Byrd-Craven, J., Nugent, L., & Numtee, C. (2007). Cognitive mechanisms underlying achievement deficits in children with mathematical learning disability. *Child Development, 78*(4), 1343–1359.

Gersten, R., Chard, D. J., Jayanthi, M., Baker, S. K., Morphy, P., & Flojo, J. (2009). Mathematics instruction for students with learning disabilities: A meta-analysis of instructional components. *Review of Educational Research, 79,* 1202–1242. doi:10.3102/0034654309334431

Haring, N. G., & Eaton, M. D. (1978). Systematic instructional procedures: An instructional hierarchy.

In N. G. Haring, T. C. Lovitt, M. D. Eaton, & C. L. Hansen (Eds.), *The fourth R: Research in the classroom* (pp. 23–40). Columbus, OH: Merrill.

Hart, S. A., Petrill, S. A., Thompson, L. A., & Plomin, R. (2009). The ABCs of math: A genetic analysis of mathematics and its links with reading ability and general cognitive ability. *Journal of Educational Psychology*, 101(2), 388.

Jitendra, A. K., Dupuis, D. N., Rodriguez, M. C., Zaslofsky, A. F., Slater, S., Cozine-Corroy, & Church, C. (2013). A randomized controlled trial of the impact of schema-based instruction on mathematical outcomes for third-grade students with mathematics difficulties. *The Elementary School Journal, 114*, 252–276. doi:10.1086/673199

Joseph, L. M., Konrad, M., Cates, G. Vajcner, T., Eveleigh, E., & Fishley, K. M. (2012). A meta-analytic review of the cover-copy-compare and variations of this self-management procedure. *Psychology in the Schools, 49*, 122–136. doi:10.1002/pits.20622

Kovas, Y., Haworth, C. M., Petrill, S. A., & Plomin, R. (2007). Mathematical ability of 10-year-old boys and girls: Genetic and environmental etiology of typical and low performance. *Journal of Learning Disabilities, 40*(6), 554–567.

Kroesbergen, E. H., & Van Luit, J. E. H. (2003). Mathematics interventions for children with special education needs: A meta-analysis. *Remedial and Special Education, 24*(2), 97–114. doi:10.1177/0741 9325030240020501

LeFevre, J. A., Smith-Chant, B. L., Fast, L., Skwarchuk, S. L., Sargla, E., Arnup, J. S.,…Kamawar, D. (2006). What counts as knowing? The development of conceptual and procedural knowledge of counting from kindergarten through grade 2. *Journal of Experimental Child Psychology, 93*(4), 285–303.

Mancl, D. B., Miller, S. P., & Kennedy, M. (2012). Using the concrete-representational-abstract sequence with integrated strategy instruction to teach subtraction with regrouping to students with learning disabilities. *Learning Disabilities Research & Practice, 27*, 152–166. doi:10.1111/j.1540–5826 .2012.00363.x

Mazzocco, M. M. M. (2007). Defining and differentiating mathematical learning disabilities and difficulties. In D. B. Berch & M. M. M. Mazzocco (Eds.), *Why is math so hard for some children? The nature and origins of mathematical learning difficulties and disabilities*, (pp. 7–28). Baltimore, MD: Paul H. Brookes.

McCallum, E., Schmitt, A. J., Schneider, D. L., Rezzetano, K., & Skinner, C. H. (2010). Extending research on the taped-problems intervention: Do group rewards enhance math fact fluency development? *School Psychology Forum: Research in Practice, 4*, 44–61.

Methe, S. A. & Riley-Tillman, T. C. (2008). An informed approach to selecting and designing early mathematics interventions. *School Psychology Forum: Research in Practice, 2*(3), 29–41.

Miller, S. P., & Kaffar, B. J. (2011). Developing addition with regrouping competence among second grade students with mathematics difficulties. *Investigations in Mathematics Learning, 4*(1), 25–50.

Montague, M. (2008). Self-regulation strategies to improve mathematical problem solving for students with learning disabilities. *Learning Disability Quarterly, 31*(1), 37–44. doi:10.2307/30035524

Montague, M., Krawec, J., Enders, C., & Dietz, S. (2013). The effects of cognitive strategy instruction on math problem solving of middle-school students of varying ability. *Journal of Educational Psychology.* Advance online publication. doi:10.1037/a0035176

Naglieri, J. A., & Johnson, D. (2000). Effectiveness of a cognitive strategy intervention in improving arithmetic computation based on the PASS theory. *Journal of Learning Disabilities, 33*(6), 591–597.

National Council of Teachers of Mathematics (NCTM). (2007). *Effective strategies for teaching students with difficulties in mathematics.* Retrieved from http://www.nctm.org/news/content. aspx?id=8452

Oliver, B., Harlaar, N., Hayiou Thomas, M. E., Kovas, Y., Walker, S. O., Petrill, S. A., & Plomin, R. (2004). A twin study of teacher-reported mathematics performance and low performance in 7-year-olds. *Journal of Educational Psychology, 96*, 504–517. doi:10.1037/0022–0663.96.3.504

Poff, B., McLaughlin, T. F., Derby, K. M., & King, K. (2012). Effects of cover, copy, and compare with free time in math for elementary students with severe behavior disorders. *Academic Research International, 2*, 217–228.

Polya, G. (1986). *How to solve it: A new aspect of mathematical method.* Princeton, NJ: Princeton University Press (Original work published 1945).

Poncy, B. C., Skinner, C. H., & Jaspers, K. E. (2007). Evaluating and comparing interventions designed to enhance math fact accuracy and fluency: Cover, copy, and compare versus taped problems. *Journal of Behavioral Education, 16,* 27–37. doi:10.1007/s10864–006-9025–7

Poncy, B. C., Skinner, C. H., & McCallum, E. (2012). A comparison of class-wide taped problems and cover, copy, and compare for enhancing mathematics fluency. *Psychology in the Schools, 49,* 744–755. doi:10.1002/pits.21631

Poncy, B. C., Solomon, B., Duhon, G., Skinner, C., Moore, K., & Simmons, S. (2015). An analysis of learning rate and curricular scope: Caution when choosing academic interventions based on aggregated outcomes. *School Psychology Review, 44,* 289–305.

Reschly, D. J., & Ysseldyke, J. E. (2002). Paradigm shift: The past is not the future. In A. Thomas & J. Grimes (Eds.), *Best practices in school psychology, IV* (pp. 3–20). Bethesda, MD: National Association of School Psychologists.

Rhymer, K. N., & Morgan, S. K. (2005). Comparison of the explicit timing and interspersal interventions: Analysis of problem completion rates, student preference, and teacher acceptability. *Journal of Behavioral Education, 14,* 283–303. doi:10.1007/s10864–005-8651–9

Rhymer, K. N., Skinner, C. H., Jackson, S., McNeill, S., Smith, T., & Jackson, B. (2002). The 1-minute explicit timing intervention: The influence of mathematics problem difficulty. *Journal of Instructional Psychology, 29*(4), 305–311.

Shapiro, E. S. (2011). *Academic skills problems.* New York, NY: Guilford Press.

Skinner, C. H., Hurst, K. L., Teeple, D. F., & Meadows, S. O. (2002). Increasing on-task behavior during mathematics independent seat-work in students with emotional disturbance by interspersing additional brief problems. *Psychology in the Schools, 39,* 647–659. doi:10.1002/pits.10058

Skinner, C. H., McCleary, D. F., Poncy, B. C., Cates, G. L., & Skolits, G. J., (2013). Emerging opportunities for school psychologists to enhance our remediation procedure evidence base as we apply response to intervention. *Psychology in the Schools, 50,* 272–289. doi:10.1002/pits.21676

Skinner, C. H., Pappas, D. N., & Davis, K. A. (2005). Enhancing academic engagement: Providing opportunities for responding and influencing students to choose to respond. *Psychology in the Schools, 42,* 389–403. doi:10.1002/pits.20065.

Steedly, K., Dragoo, K., Arefeh, S., & Luke, S. D. (2008). Effective mathematics instruction. *Evidence for Education, 3*(1), 1–12. Retrieved from http://www.parentcenterhub.org/wp-content/uploads/repo_items/eemath.pdf

Swanson, H. L. (1999). Reading research for students with LD: A meta-analysis of intervention outcomes. *Journal of Learning Disabilities, 32*(6), 504–532.

U.S. Department of Education, National Center for Education Statistics (2013a). *A first look: 2013 mathematics and reading* (NCES 2014-451). Retrieved from http://nces.ed.gov/nationsreportcard/subject/publications/main2013/pdf/2014451.pdf

U.S. Department of Education, National Center for Education Statistics (2013b). *Digest of education statistics, 2012* (NCES 2014-015). Retrieved from http://nces.ed.gov/fastfacts/display.asp?id=64

Wendling, B. J., & Mather, N. (2009). *Essentials of evidence-based academic interventions.* Hoboken, NJ: John Wiley.

Wildmon, M. E., Skinner, C. H., & McDade, A. (1998). Interspersing additional brief easy problems to increase assignment preference on mathematics reading problems. *Journal of Behavioral Education, 8,* 337–346. doi:10.1023/A:1022823314635

Wildmon, M. E., Skinner, C. H., Watson, T. S., & Garrett, L. S. (2004). Enhancing assignment perceptions in students with mathematics learning disabilities by including more work: An extension of interspersal research. *School Psychology Quarterly, 19,* 106–120. doi:10.1521/scpg.19.2.106.33310

Willcutt, E. G., Petrill, S. A., Wu, S., Boada, R., Defries, J. C., Olson, R. K., & Pennington, B. F. (2013). Comorbidity between reading disability and math disability: Concurrent psychopathology, functional impairment, and neuropsychological functioning. *Journal of Learning Disabilities, 46*(6), 500–516.

Woodward, J. (2006). Developing automaticity in multiplication facts: Integrating strategy instruction with timed practice drills. *Learning Disability Quarterly, 29,* 269–289. doi:10.2307/30035554

Xin, Y. P., & Jitendra, A. K. (1999). The effects of mathematical word problems for students with learning problems: A meta-analysis. *The Journal of Special Education, 32*(4), 40–78.

Xin, Y. P., & Jitendra, A. (2006). Teaching problem solving skills to middle school students with learning difficulties: Schema-based strategy instruction. In M. Montague & A. Jitendra (Eds.), *Middle school students with mathematics difficulties* (pp. 51–71). New York, NY: Guilford.

Evidence-Based Interventions for Written-Language Disorders in Children and Adolescents

Merilee McCurdy, Jill Holtz, and Julia V. Roehling

OVERVIEW

Writing is a fundamental communication skill that is important for everyday success. Children and adolescents use written language to communicate their thoughts, ideas, and knowledge to teachers in school; send messages to friends; write papers and reports; and engage in expository writing activities. Unfortunately, because of the lack of high-quality instruction, student effort and motivation, and other complex factors, many students do not acquire adequate written-language skills to ensure future success. According to the Nation's Report Card, only 33% of eighth graders and 24% of 12th graders possess "proficient" (i.e., solid academic performance) writing skills, and only 2% of eighth graders and 1% of 12th graders were considered "advanced" (i.e., superior performance; Salahu-Din, Persky, & Miller, 2008). The corpus of students included in this Report Card assessment were writing at the basic level, indicating only a partial mastery of written-language skills. Although fourth graders were not included in this evaluation, data collected for the Nation's Report Card in 2002, which did include all grade levels, yielded a similar lack of proficiency. Alarmingly, only 28% of fourth graders were writing at or above proficiency and 14% of fourth graders did not meet criteria for

basic writing skills (Persky, Daane, & Jin, 2003). Perhaps most concerning was that 94% of students with a diagnosed disability were found to be writing at a basic or below-basic level.

When considering that many students do not possess adequate writing skills, it is not surprising that there are numerous implications for individuals as they progress through school. Written-language deficits inhibit students' ability to effectively communicate their knowledge on tests, often resulting in lower grades (Graham & Perin, 2007). Additionally, students with below-average writing skills are less likely to use writing as a means to extend their learning in other classes via book reports, papers, and essays. Unfortunately, these initial deficits can go on to impact those entering college and the workforce. University faculty and future employers report concerns similar to those expressed by public school teachers. Undergraduate instructors reported that 42% of high school graduates are unprepared for the writing demands of college (Achieve, Inc., 2005). In addition, a poorly written job application can strongly impact hiring success. For example, 80% of individuals responsible for hiring reported that poorly written job application materials typically results in individuals not being offered an interview or considered for a position (National Commission on Writing, 2004). Given the difficulties associated with school progress, college preparation, and career success, it is necessary for educators and researchers to give increased attention to the development of written-language skills.

ETIOLOGY AND FACTORS CONTRIBUTING TO WRITTEN-LANGUAGE DISORDERS IN CHILDREN AND ADOLESCENTS

Writing is an exceptionally complex task composed of multiple processes. Although varied terminology is often used, theories of writing development recognize three stages of writing, including planning or prewriting, drafting or composing, and revising or editing phases (Berninger & Swanson, 1994; Flower & Hayes, 1980). These three phases are not required to occur in a predetermined order but are interconnected and ongoing throughout the writing process. For example, when required to write a story, a child/adolescent may plan a story, begin writing, and then return to revise the original plan. Editing can occur at any point during the writing process and is often repeated numerous times before producing a final draft. Given that writing is challenging for many students, there are a variety of reasons why students develop writing difficulties, including related reading concerns (Berninger, Abbott, Abbott, & Graham, 2002), poor prior instruction, lack of remedial instruction, and biological causes related to genetics and memory development (Berninger & Wolf, 2009). If children or adolescents experience any or all of these deficits, the act of writing becomes an aversive task leading to avoidant behaviors in students.

Behavioral theory states that many individuals find aversive activities punishing and may, therefore, avoid these activities. By avoiding or escaping the punishing task, the individual obtains negative reinforcement as a consequence of these behaviors (Miltenberger, 2015) and is more likely to repeat these behaviors in the future. Students with writing skill deficits may engage in these behaviors when avoiding writing tasks. For children and adolescents who do not possess proficient writing skills, writing tasks are often not enjoyable and may even be punishing. Therefore, students may choose not to complete writing assignments or activities, or they may not put forth the effort required to produce a high-quality written product (Bruning & Horn, 2000). In the classroom, these students may refuse to complete written assignments or if they do complete them, it is done with minimal effort (e.g., writes one page instead of the required five). There are several negative implications stemming from the avoidance of writing tasks, such as the reduced practice of writing skills and diminished constructive feedback from the teacher, resulting in students not associating positive reinforcement with writing, as poor effort does not result in teacher praise, passing grades, or the feelings of success for completing a difficult task (Miltenberger, 2015). Ultimately, this behavior will result in a further impairment in the student's writing deficits escalating the difficulties.

The development of strong writing skills requires many important components, such as adequate reading skills, high-quality teacher instruction, and student motivation. This chapter focuses on writing instruction/intervention and student motivation. Effective writing instruction relies on evidence-based instructional approaches for developing and increasing writing skills related to planning, drafting, and revising tasks. In addition, it is important to consider student motivation as a primary reason for students not demonstrating success with written-language tasks (Hidi & Boscolo, 2006).

EVIDENCE-BASED INTERVENTIONS AND EMPIRICAL SUPPORT FOR WRITTEN-LANGUAGE DISORDERS IN CHILDREN AND ADOLESCENTS

Two meta-analyses have informed the field of evidence-based writing instruction (Graham & Perin, 2007; Rogers & Graham, 2008). The first meta-analysis of experimental and quasi-experimental research methods (i.e., group design research; Graham & Perin, 2007) yielded effect size data indicating that strategy instruction (e.g., self-regulated strategy development [SRSD]; see the following text), summarization (e.g., Chang et al., 2002), peer assistance (e.g., MacArthur, Schwartz, & Graham, 1991), and goal setting (e.g., Page-Voth & Graham, 1999) were the most effective instructional techniques for improving writing skills for students in grades 4 to 12. The second meta-analysis included single subject designs (Rogers &

Graham, 2008), and found that percentage of non-overlapping data (PND) resulted in large to moderate effects for strategy instruction with planning, editing, and paragraph construction; teaching grammar; goal setting for productivity; and reinforcement. In both meta-analyses, strategy instruction was found to be the most effective and have the highest quality research.

Skills Development. Strategy instruction teaches a student to organize and use specific skills to master academic tasks in the classroom (Santangelo, Harris, & Graham, 2008). In its most simplified form, strategy instruction is a type of self-regulation that involves the use of mnemonics to teach students to recall and to apply important academic information. Strategy instruction has been shown to be an effective instructional technique in a variety of academic areas, particularly for students with learning disabilities (Graham & Perin, 2007). In the area of writing, the most researched intervention is SRSD (Graham & Harris, 2005; Harris & Graham, 1996). SRSD is an instructional strategy approach to writing, designed to improve a writer's knowledge, self-regulatory behaviors, and motivation.

Using a scaffolded instructional approach, SRSD teaches planning and writing skills while also targeting student motivation by addressing self-efficacy and student effort. SRSD includes six lessons, which can be individualized for each student. The lessons begin with conversations about the writing process and the student's likes and dislikes about writing. Initially, the student and adult engage in co-writing activities with the student taking more responsibility for the story as the lessons progress. By the final lesson, the student is an independent and improved writer (Danoff, Harris, & Graham, 1993; De La Paz, 1999; Graham and Harris, 1989; Tracy, Reid, & Graham, 2009), producing lengthier text with multiple story parts. For those interested in using SRSD with an individual student or groups of students, the creators of SRSD have provided detailed lesson plans (http://kc.vanderbilt.edu/projectwrite/lessonplans.html) and additional information on the Project Write website.

Motivation. As mentioned previously, many students view writing as an aversive event and therefore, have a propensity to avoid writing activities. To assist students in developing writing skills, it is necessary to address a student's motivation to engage in writing activities. Two valuable resources in this area are from Bruning and Horn (2000) and Hidi and Boscolo (2006). Each group of authors conceptualize motivation and writing in similar but slightly different ways. With an applied classroom focus, Bruning and Horn identify four factors that are critical to the development of a student's motivation to write. These factors include (a) nurturing functional beliefs about writing, (b) fostering student engagement through authentic writing goals and contexts, (c) providing a supportive context for writing, and (d) creating a positive emotional environment. In addition, Bruning and Horn identified classroom strategies related to each factor that teachers can use, such as finding writing tasks that assure student success, having students write for a variety of audiences, encouraging goal setting and monitoring of progress, and modeling positive attitudes toward writing.

Hidi and Boscolo produced a theoretical chapter that combined two bodies of research; research about writing and student motivation to identify commonalities and directions for future research. Specifically, themes were developed related to student interest of a writing topic, individual writing self-efficacy, self-regulation in writing, and the conceptualization of writing as a meaningful and social activity. Typically, writers who are interested in the topic also have high levels of self-efficacy and self-regulation. Writing instruction and interventions could be strengthened by including these components to enhance the development or remediation of writing skills.

High-quality instruction focused on skill development and student motivation to write should produce high-quality writers. This level of instruction may be enough to prevent the development of learning disabilities in many students. However, some students will not develop adequate writing skills and will require intensive intervention services to enhance writing skill development. Without early intervention services, extensive remediation may be necessary at a later point (Denton & Vaughn, 2010; Torgeson, 2000). Providing early intervention, using class-wide strategies such as the ones delineated in the following discussion, should decrease the number of students needing future assistance and remediation of written-language skills.

Summary. Writing is an important skill for success in multiple life contexts—school, work, and community—and writing instruction focused on skill development and students' motivation to write is essential for improving students' writing. Writing is a complex skill. Effective writing intervention relies on evidence-based instructional approaches for managing planning, drafting, and revising tasks. Writing interventions that allow students a choice of topics, incorporate feedback from peers, and teach self-regulation strategies are likely to enhance the development or remediation of writing skills.

HOW TO: A GUIDE TO THE IMPLEMENTATION OF INTERVENTIONS FOR WRITTEN LANGUAGE

Comprehensive Writing Program

McCurdy, Skinner, Watson, and Shriver (2008) describe a Comprehensive Writing Program (CWP) for improving the acquisition of targeted writing skills. This multicomponent CWP can be used to teach a variety of writing skills. The intervention consists of direct instruction in a targeted writing skill (i.e., complete sentences, adjectives, and compound sentences), assignment choice, daily writing practice, interdependent group contingencies with public postings of class-wide performance, and individual private feedback. The goal of this initial investigation was to apply multiple, high-quality teaching strategies to the targeted area of written language.

First, students are taught the writing skill. Instruction in the targeted skill involves (a) describing the appropriate use of the writing skill, (b) demonstrating examples of the writing skill used properly and improperly, and (c) prompting class-wide participation (i.e., choral responding) in determining the correct use of the skill. On completion of instruction, students practice using the targeted skill. As mentioned previously, students are more motivated to write about topics that are of interest to them, and thus, this intervention allows students to select their writing assignment (e.g., a choice of story starters). A class-wide goal is identified for the targeted writing skill. The class's progress is charted and posted in the classroom. Once the class meets the goal for 3 consecutive days, the class earns a group reward. In addition, students receive individual

feedback on their use of the targeted skill in their daily writing (e.g., an individual score for the target skill). Although daily individual feedback and graphing each student's progress is optional, it is recommended, as it provides the student a clear visual of the performance over time, thus incentivizing him or her to continue writing.

Materials

1. Story starters
2. Notebooks or loose-leaf paper
3. Pencils
4. Printed copies of examples and nonexamples of writing skill applications
5. Chart paper or graph paper
6. Teacher approved rewards

Intervention Steps

1. Introduce and describe the target writing skill to be learned. Example: "We are going to learn how to combine simple sentences to create compound sentences. A compound sentence consists of two independent clauses joined by a coordinating conjunction (i.e., and, but, or, yet, for, nor, so) and a comma."
2. Review how and when to use the skill. Example: "We use compound sentences when we want to connect two simple sentences that are logically related."
3. Model appropriate skill use, providing examples and nonexamples to illustrate the use of the skill.
   Examples:
   Last month was hot. August was even hotter.
   Last month was hot, **but** *August was even hotter.*
   She stayed inside. Her brother walked the dog.
   She stayed inside, **and** *her brother walked the dog.*
4. Present additional examples illustrating both correct and incorrect use of the target skill. Ask students to distinguish between examples and nonexamples of the target skill. This can be done through class-wide choral responding. Students may also be encouraged to generate their own examples.
5. Allow students an opportunity to ask questions related to the targeted writing skill. Respond to any questions.

6. On the first day the skill is taught, describe the group contingency (i.e., identified target behavior, group criterion, and group reward). Write the goal on the board, or display it using an overhead projector. In subsequent sessions, remind the class of its daily goal. Refer to the posted graph showing the class's progress with the targeted skill.

7. Provide students with at least two different story starters. Allow students to choose one of the story starters for their stories.

8. Instruct the class to plan their stories for 3 minutes. Graphic organizers (e.g., story webs) can be used to assist students as they plan. Circulate to provide assistance as students plan.

9. After students have finished planning, tell them that they will have 10 minutes to write their stories. Tell them to practice using the targeted skill in their stories.

10. After 10 minutes, tell the class to stop writing. Collect their stories.

11. Before the next session, review the students' stories and assess their progress. Calculate the class's overall score for the targeted writing skill. Provide specific, individual feedback on each student's writing performance, and calculate each student's individual score for the writing skill. Optional: Graph each student's individual progress.

12. At the next session, discuss the class's progress toward meeting the target goal. Post the class-wide progress. Return stories to students with their individual feedback and scores.

13. Once the class meets the class-wide goal for 3 consecutive days, the students earn a group reward, such as popcorn, music, or free time.

14. Move to the next goal (McCurdy et al., 2008).

Reciprocal Peer-Revision Strategy

Teaching students to revise their essays involves teaching students to manage multiple cognitive processes associated with the writing processes (e.g., reading critically, evaluating, and generating new text). Cognitive strategy instruction can be used to teach the cognitive processes involved in revising one's writing, and providing opportunities for students to provide peer feedback on essays may facilitate students' abilities to detect errors in their own writing (MacArthur, 2012). A reciprocal peer revision strategy that combines strategy instruction, peer interaction, instruction in specific evaluation criteria, and word processing has been shown to improve the students' revisions (MacArthur et al., 1991; Stoddard & MacArthur, 1993).

This intervention has teachers teach students a strategy for making revisions to a text. Teachers model the process of revision using think-aloud modeling and providing explicit instruction in revision skills. Then, teachers provide students with guided practice. Students practice evaluating sample papers and making changes to improve them. Students compose essays on the computer. Taking turns as author and editor, students work in pairs to provide each other with feedback on areas for revision (e.g., organization) as well as areas for editing (e.g., correcting punctuation). Students use the feedback they receive from their peers to make changes to the final drafts of their papers.

Materials

1. Computers with Word-processing programs
2. Prompt sheets, consisting of print copies of the nine steps in the peer-editing strategy
3. Pencils or pens
4. Computer paper
5. Writing prompts
6. Printed copies of sample essays

Intervention Steps

1. Explain to students that they will be working in pairs to learn a strategy for revising their compositions.
2. Discuss with students the characteristics of the genre in which they are writing. Example: "A descriptive essay is…"
3. Give each student a sample essay and the peer-editing procedures. Lead a discussion of the importance of revision in the overall writing process. Stress the importance of feedback and positive peer support.
4. Explain each step of the peer-editing strategy as described in what follows. Provide students with a prompt sheet that lists each of the following steps. Tell the students that they will complete

the first two steps in turn. Then each will work independently as their partner's peer editor, after which they will discuss the paper in turn.

Step 1: Listen and follow along as the author reads the first draft of his or her composition aloud.

Step 2: Tell the author what you liked best.

Step 3: Reread the paper to yourself.

Step 4: Ask yourself the following four key revision questions about the composition:

   a. *Parts?* Does it have a good beginning, middle, and ending?

   b. *Order?* Does it have a logical sequence?

   c. *Details?* Where could the writer add more details?

   d. *Clarity?* Is there any part that is hard to understand?

Step 5: Make notes on the draft based on the revision questions.

Step 6: Discuss your suggestions with the author. Begin with a positive comment.

Step 7: Work independently at the computer to revise your own paper.

Step 8: Meet again with your partner to discuss the revisions you each have made and to check each other's papers for mechanical errors.

Step 9: Work independently at the computer to make final revisions.

5. Model the strategy. Guide pairs of students through a demonstration using the sample composition. Be sure to stress the importance of positive peer support using the demonstration.

6. Assign partners. Then distribute copies of a second sample composition. Have the students practice the strategy in pairs. Circulate to provide assistance.

7. Provide students with a writing prompt. Have students compose an essay (e.g., a descriptive essay).

8. Have students work in pairs to apply the peer-editing strategy to their partner's essay. Refer students to the prompt sheets with the revision steps. Encourage students to memorize the four key words in the revision questions. Prompt positive peer-editing behaviors as needed.

9. Have students make the final revisions to their drafts.

10. Every few weeks, change student parings to allow students an opportunity to work with peer editors with a range of writing abilities (Stoddard & MacArthur, 1993).

Self-Monitoring

Self-monitoring has been shown to increase students' academic engagement during writing as well as improve the writing performance of students with learning disabilities (Harris, Graham, Reid, McElroy, & Hamby, 1994). Teaching students to self-monitor involves teaching students to self-assess the quality and/or quantity of their writing and to record their writing progress. This process involves teaching students to record their number of words written, the number of story parts included in a story, the number of story parts included in an essay, or any other indicator of writing quality (e.g., number of different sentence types, number of active verbs used, and number of ideas).

Harris and colleagues (1994) described a strategy for teaching students to write longer stories. In addition to self-monitoring, the intervention includes goal setting, graphing of student performance, and performance feedback making it particularly powerful. The intervention involves teaching students to count their total words written. Then, students are taught to record their total writing output on a chart or graph. Although Harris and colleagues describe the intervention with respect to story writing, this intervention could be used with any genre.

Materials

1. Notebooks or loose-leaf paper
2. Pencils
3. Sample student essays
4. Chart or graph paper
5. Paper with self-monitoring steps

Intervention Steps

1. First, discuss the importance of writing longer stories. Example: "Stories with more words usually tell a more complete and better story."

2. Tell the students that they will learn a strategy that will help them to write longer stories. Describe the self-monitoring strategy. Tell the students that after they finish a story, they will count the number of words they have written. Then they will record this number on a graph (e.g., bar graph). Finally, they will compare this number with the total number of words written for their last story. They will ask themselves whether they wrote more this time.

3. Model how to use strategy. Using a sample essay, demonstrate how to count the total words written (including misspelled words) and record the number on a sample graph. An overhead projector may be useful to project the story.

4. Have students practice counting the total words in one of their stories and then recording the number on a graph. (Younger children may need assistance graphing the total word count.)

5. Have students continue to record and graph their total words written for each subsequent story they write. Conference with each student to assess the student's writing progress. Monitor the student's use of the strategy with subsequent stories. Optional: Teachers may increase the effectiveness of the intervention by having students set goals for total number of words written. Students can record the goal on their charts. After writing, students can check to see if they met their goal.

SELECT BIBLIOGRAPHY

Graham, S., McKeown, D., Kiuhara, S., & Harris, K. R. (2012). A meta-analysis of writing instruction for students in elementary grades. *Journal of Educational Psychology, 104,* 879–896.
This meta-analysis examines effectiveness of elementary writing interventions tested through experimental or quasi-experimental designs. Thirteen types of interventions were included in the analysis and grouped into four overarching categories: (a) explicit teaching, (b) scaffolding students' writing, (c) alternative modes of composing, and (d) other writing activities. Recommendations for use are provided.

Harris, K. R., Graham, S., Mason, L. H., & Friedlander, B. (2008). *Powerful writing strategies for all students.* Baltimore, MD: Paul H. Brookes Publishing Co.
This book is a resource for teaching students SRSD in writing. It includes strategies for enhancing word choice; story writing; narrative, expository, and persuasive writing; revising; writing competency tests; and reading and writing informational texts. Lesson plans that educators can use to supplement their writing curriculum are provided.

Project WRITE (2009). Retrieved from http://kc.vanderbilt.edu/projectwrite
Created by researchers at Vanderbilt University, Project WRITE is an online resource for teachers of grades 1 to 3 who are interested in implementing a SRSD approach to writing instruction. The website provides a detailed overview of SRSD, as well as lesson plans and support materials for working with either individual students or classrooms.

Reid, Robert (n.d.). Retrieved from http://cehs.unl.edu/csi/
This website provides valuable teaching tools using strategy instruction. Materials are presented in seven areas: teaching strategies, lesson plans, reading, writing, mathematics, study skills, and self-regulation. Each summary paper provides step-by-step details for the use of the strategy instruction technique and an empirical citation for further research exploration.

REFERENCES

Achieve, Inc. (2005). *An action agenda for improving America's high schools.* Retrieved from http://www.achieve.org/files/actionagenda2005.pdf

Berninger, V. W., Abbott, R. D., Abbott, S. P., & Graham, S. (2002). Writing and reading: Connections between language by hand and language by eye. *Journal of Learning Disabilities, 35,* 39–56.

Berninger, V. W., & Swanson, H. L. (1994). Modifying Hayes and Flower's model of skilled writing to explain beginning and developing writing. In E. C. Butterfield (Ed.), *Children's writing: Toward a process theory of the development of writing skill* (pp. 57–83). Greenwich, CT: JAI Press.

Berninger, V. W., & Wolf, B. J. (2009). *Teaching students with dyslexia and dysgraphia: Lessons from teaching and science* (pp. 1–240). Baltimore, MD: Paul H. Brooks Publishing Co.

Bruning, R., & Horn, C. (2000). Developing motivation to write. *Educational Psychologist, 35,* 25–37.

Chang, K. E., Sung, Y. T., & Chen, I. D. (2002). The effect of concept mapping to enhance text comprehension and summarization. *Journal of Experimental Education, 71,* 5–23.

Danoff, B., Harris, K. R., & Graham, S. (1993). Incorporating strategy instruction within the writing process in the regular classroom: Effects in the writing of students with and without learning disabilities. *Journal of Reading Behavior, 25,* 295–322.

De La Paz, S. (1999). Self-regulated strategy instruction in regular education settings: Improving outcomes for students with and without learning disabilities. *Learning Disabilities Research & Practice, 14,* 92–106. doi:10.1207/sldrp1402_3

Denton, C. A., & Vaughn, S. (2010). Preventing and remediating reading difficulties: Perspectives from research. In M. R. Shinn & H. M. Walker (Eds.), *Interventions for achievement and behavior problems in a three-tier model including RTI* (pp. 469–500). Bethesda, MD: National Association of School Psychologists.

Flower, L. S., & Hayes, J. R. (1980). The dynamics of composing: Making plans and juggling constraints. In L.W. Gregg & E. R. Steinberg (Eds.), *Cognitive processes in writing* (pp. 31–50). Hillsdale, NJ: Erlbaum.

Graham, S., & Harris, K. R. (1989). Improving learning disabled students' skills at composing essays: Self-instructional strategy training. *Exceptional Children, 56,* 201–214.

Graham, S., & Harris, K. R. (2005). *Writing better: Effective strategies for teaching students with learning difficulties.* Baltimore, MD: Brookes Publishing Company.

Graham, S., & Perin, D. (2007). A meta-analysis of writing instruction for adolescent students. *Journal of Educational Psychology, 99,* 445–476. doi:10.1037/0022–0663.99.3.445

Harris, H. R., Graham, S., Reid, R., McElroy, K., & Hamby, R. S. (1994). Self-monitoring of attention versus self-monitoring of performance: Replication and cross-task comparison studies. *Learning Disability Quarterly, 17,* 121–139. doi:10.2307/1511182

Harris, K., & Graham, S. (1996). *Making the writing process work: Strategies for composition and self-regulation* (2nd ed.). Cambridge, MA: Brookline Books.

Hidi, S., & Boscolo, P. (2006). Motivation and writing. In C. A. MacArthur, S. Graham, & J. Fitzgerald (Eds.), *Handbook of writing research* (pp. 144–157). New York, NY: Guilford Press.

MacArthur, C. A. (2012). Evaluation and revision. In. V. W. Berninger (Ed.), *Past, present, and future contributions of cognitive writing research to cognitive psychology* (pp. 461–483). London: Process Press.

MacArthur, C. A., Schwartz, S. S., & Graham, S. (1991). Effects of a reciprocal peer revision strategy in special education classrooms. *Learning Disabilities Research & Practice, 6,* 201–210.

McCurdy, M., Skinner, C., Watson, S., & Shriver, M. (2008). Examining the effects of a comprehensive writing program on the writing performance of middle school students with learning disabilities in written expression. *School Psychology Quarterly, 23*(4), 571–586. doi:10.1037/1045–3830.23.4.571

Miltenberger, R. G. (2015). *Behavior modification: Principles and procedure* (5th ed.). Belmont, CA: Thomson Wadsworth.

National Commission on Writing. (2004). Writing: A ticket to work…or a ticket out. Retrieved from http://www.collegeboard.com/prod_downloads/writingcom/writing-ticket-to-work.pdf

Page-Voth, V., & Graham, S. (1999). Effects of goal setting and strategy use on the writing performance and self-efficacy of students with writing and learning problems. *Journal of Educational Psychology, 91*(2), 230–240.

Persky, H. R., Daane, M. C., & Jin, Y. (2003). *The nation's report card: Writing 2002* (NCES 2003–529). Washington, DC: U.S. Department of Education, Institute of Education Sciences, National Center for Education Statistics, Washington, DC.

Rogers, L., & Graham, S. (2008). A meta-analysis of single subject design writing intervention research. *Journal of Educational Psychology, 100,* 879–906.

Salahu-Din, D., Persky, H., & Miller, J. (2008). *The nation's report card: Writing 2007* (NCES 2008–468). Washington, DC: National Center for Education Statistics, Institute of Education Sciences, U.S. Department of Education.

Santangelo, T., Harris, K. R., & Graham, H. (2008). Using self-regulated strategy development to support students who have "trubol giting thangs into werds." *Remedial and Special Education, 29,* 78–89.

Stoddard, B., & MacArthur, C. A. (1993). A peer editor strategy: Guiding learning-disabled students in response and revision. *Research in the Teaching of English, 27,* 76–103.

Torgeson, J. K. (2000). Individual differences in response to early interventions in reading: The lingering problem of treatment resisters. *Learning Disabilities Research and Practice, 15,* 55–64.

Tracy, B., Reid, R., & Graham, S. (2009). Teaching young students strategies for planning and drafting stories: The impact of self-regulated strategy development. *The Journal of Educational Research, 102,* 323–331. doi:10.3200/JOER.102.5.323–332

Evidence-Based Interventions for Homework Compliance in Children and Adolescents

Lea A. Theodore, Bruce A. Bracken, Melissa M. Root, Melissa A. Bray, and Thomas J. Kehle

OVERVIEW

Academic work completed by students during non-school hours, most frequently at home as "homework," has long been accepted as a worthwhile endeavor and a useful teaching supplement (Bang, 2011; Cancio, West, & Young, 2004; Reinhardt, Theodore, Bray, & Kehle, 2009). Homework completion is viewed as a beneficial contributor to student learning and to the fundamental personal characteristics that underpin student academic behavior (Cooper, Robinson, & Patall, 2006). As such, homework compliance is promoted by those who believe it produces both general and specific academic and nonacademic benefits across the full-grade and student ability spectrum (Reinhardt et al., 2009).

The noted benefits of homework completion include improved retention and understanding of course content and the opportunity for students to apply newly acquired skills outside the classroom (Epstein & Van Voorhis, 2001; Rowell & Hong, 2002). Perceived nonacademic benefits include students' improved study habits, time management, self-discipline (Cooper & Valentine, 2001), self-regulation (Bembenutty, 2011), and self-efficacy (Zimmerman & Kitsantas, 2005). It is important to note that the combination of academic and nonacademic benefits

encourages learning, developing personal skills, and attaining self-attributes that promote long-term academic achievement (Epstein & Van Voorhis, 2001; Rowell & Hong, 2002; Theodore, DioGuardi, Hughes, Carlo, & Eccles, 2009). Also important is the fact that homework leads to increased parental involvement in students' education and enhances home–school collaboration among parents, teachers, and school personnel (Epstein & Van Voorhis, 2001; Patall, Cooper, & Robinson, 2008).

In contrast to the many perceived benefits mentioned, students' homework noncompliance is associated with an increased incidence of student referrals for special education, as well as diminished academic gains among students with learning disabilities (Lynch, Theodore, Bray, & Kehle, 2009). Because of the perceived detriments of failing to complete homework and the benefits of completing homework, academic interventionists would best serve the educational system by employing evidence-based interventions to enhance student homework compliance (Theodore, Bray, & Kehle, 2014).

Federal initiatives advanced over the past decade (e.g., Individuals with Disabilities Education Act, No Child Left Behind) have increasingly emphasized accountability in public education. More often than ever before, schools are being held responsible for maximizing and sustaining academic gains for all students, even those diagnosed with educational disabilities. In this climate of accountability and evidence-based practice, where student growth is paramount, homework has become an essential tool for enhancing academic achievement by expanding educational experiences beyond the classroom (Theodore et al., 2014).

This chapter promotes a greater understanding of the benefits of homework compliance while providing evidence-based expectations for appropriate homework loads, special education use of homework, and best practices in homework compliance management. The intent of this chapter is to provide readers with empirically supported strategies for helping parents and teachers maximize the benefits of student homework completion, while reducing parental and student angst associated with compliance enforcement. As such, this chapter recommends an approach to promoting collaboration between school personnel and parents to enhance students' academic competence using a multifaceted, school-based problem-solving model.

ETIOLOGY AND FACTORS CONTRIBUTING TO HOMEWORK COMPLIANCE IN CHILDREN AND ADOLESCENTS

History of Homework

Students have learned to expect that homework would be part of their academic experience for the past 200 years (Maltese, Tai, & Fan, 2012); however, the benefits of homework have been debated since the middle of the 19th century. Throughout the 1800s and early 1900s, there was little to no extant empirical support for the belief that homework enhanced student learning. Given the largely agricultural commitments of many families and communities during the late-19th and early-20th centuries, and the dependence of children as workers on family farms, homework was viewed as especially intrusive and unnecessary.

Anti-homework sentiment changed dramatically in 1957 when the Soviet Union launched the world's first earth-orbiting satellite, Sputnik, which left Americans fearing they would be left behind in the space and intercontinental missile race. With this fearsome launch of the United States' Cold War nemesis came increased public and governmental concern about whether American students were adequately prepared to compete with their international contemporaries and whether the American educational system was up to the challenge of preparing students for a technology-driven 20th century (Eren & Henderson, 2011). As a result of these concerns, the U.S. federal and state governments increased funding for education and set higher educational expectations and standards; homework was viewed as instrumental for improving student achievement and accelerating academic mastery. Not surprising to many, evaluation-oriented educational researchers began to report that increase in student homework resulted in higher student achievement (Maltese et al., 2012).

The social upheaval of the 1960s and 1970s, including populous reactions against the Vietnam War, shifted public attention away from education and homework and toward an emphasis on personal and social freedoms (Keith, Diamond-Hallam, & Fine, 2004), as well as students' school deportment and truancy (Maltese et al., 2012). *A Nation at Risk: The Imperative for Educational Reform* (National Commission on Excellence in Education, 1983) and *What Works* (DoE, 1986) raised concerns once more about perceived waning excellence of America's students during the 1980s. As with the Sputnik era, homework was viewed as a means to enhance educational achievement, ensure global competition, and improve the economic competitiveness of the United States.

As the 21st century ushered in the new millennium, yet another anti-homework movement was initiated by parents who feared that long school days and excessive homework were causing their children undue stress (Cooper et al., 2006; Keith et al., 2004). The cyclical nature of the merit of homework continues, and it appears that when the United States faces difficult economic times or an uncertain political future, public interest in more rigorous academic standards prevails, which corresponds with public acceptance of and educators' increase in homework (Theodore et al., 2014).

Purposes of Homework

Homework serves four primary instructional purposes: practice, preparation, extension, and integration (Power, Karutsis, & Habboushe, 2001). Accepting the inherent usefulness of these homework purposes increases the likelihood that parents and students will follow through on homework compliance. A brief definition of each homework purpose follows:

Practice homework reinforces instructional practices and methods taught to students in school through rote practice at home.

Preparation homework prepares students for content that teachers will present in upcoming lessons and serves as an advanced organizer for future lessons.

Extension homework helps students generalize newly acquired information and skills for application in different situations and contexts.

Integration homework facilitates students' combination of disparate skills and concepts to create a more comprehensive final outcome (Cooper et al., 2006).

Appropriate Amounts of Homework

There is an optimal amount of homework for maximal effective learning. The key factors in determining the most beneficial amount of homework is to match the amount of assigned work with the subject matter and students' grade levels. The National Education Association and the National Parent Teacher Association (National Education Association, 2013) recommended a heuristic for determining homework allocations for elementary grade students: 10-minute increase in homework per grade level, beginning with 10 minutes of homework for first-grade students; second, third, and fourth graders, then, would be expected to complete 20, 30, and 40 minutes of homework per night, respectively. Because assignments vary in complexity and duration (e.g., semester-long projects), homework times for high school students would be expected to differ day to day (Brock, Lapp, Flood, Fisher, & Tao, 2007). High school seniors, because of multiple subjects and college-bound expectations, might expect 2 or more hours of homework each night (Cooper & Valentine, 2001).

Special Education and Homework

Students with attention and learning problems experience significant difficulty completing homework, which further exacerbates their academic difficulties. Moreover, homework noncompliance for these populations increases conflicts between parents and children, increases students' risk for anxiety and depressive disorders, and often results in less effective relationships between students and their peers and between parents and teachers (Lynch et al., 2009; Power, Werba, Watkins, Angelucci, & Eiraldi, 2006; Sheridan, 2009). Special education students struggle with homework in part because of less cognitive ability and greater inattention and impaired concentration, which lead to incorrect recording of assignments, difficulty completing assignments, and making frequent careless errors (Bryan, Burstein, & Bryan, 2001). Furthermore, students with attention and learning difficulties often experience inordinate frustration and a sense of failure that negatively influences their productivity, motivation to initiate homework, and likelihood of completing assignments (Lynch et al., 2009). These interpersonal issues further contribute to declines in academic achievement, lowered grades, increased risk for dropping out of school, and lower levels of employment (Sheridan, 2009).

Given the negative implications stemming from homework noncompliance, students with attention and learning problems need additional opportunities for practice to promote learning within the classroom, with less schoolwork sent home. In this manner, briefer homework assignments serve to reinforce prior learning and strengthen the nonacademic benefits that homework provides, coupled with less frustration and angst (Theodore et al., 2014).

EVIDENCE-BASED INTERVENTIONS AND EMPIRICAL SUPPORT FOR HOMEWORK COMPLIANCE IN CHILDREN AND ADOLESCENTS

Research has shown the positive influential effects of homework on the learning process and overall academic achievement. The relationship between homework and scholastic performance is moderated by grade level, with students in high school evidencing the greatest effects on achievement (Cooper & Valentine, 2001), as demonstrated by test scores and grades, particularly for the subject area of mathematics (Eren & Henderson, 2011). Although the academic benefits of homework are most apparent during the high school years, due to the increased curricular demands and greater reliance on work to be completed after school hours for mastery, the positive effects of homework are manifest in younger students as well (Cooper et al., 2006; Power et al., 2006; Zimmerman & Kitsantas, 2005). For young children, homework provides myriad opportunities for the development of proper study habits and self-discipline, the promotion of independent problem-solving and positive academic attitudes, and the involvement of families in their children's schooling and educational progress (Cooper et al., 2006; Power et al., 2006). These nonacademic benefits contribute to long-term academic achievement.

To augment the retention and learning of classroom material, numerous research-based interventions and strategies have been designed to enhance homework performance in children and adolescents. These approaches have focused on how schools, teachers, and parents may become active participants in assisting students' long-term understanding of academic material and educational success. Although the literature base is still evolving, school-based strategies, effective parent–teacher communication, the provision of clear expectations, and accommodations, incentives, and remedial policies, have all been shown to improve homework performance and compliance.

HOW TO: A GUIDE TO THE IMPLEMENTATION OF INTERVENTIONS FOR HOMEWORK COMPLIANCE IN CHILDREN AND ADOLESCENTS

A primary goal of all educators is to facilitate the acquisition of student knowledge and enhance the overall academic functioning of students. When students fail to complete homework assignments, their academic performance and attitudes toward learning may be negatively affected (Theodore et al., 2014). Because homework is primarily within the purview of classroom teachers, school psychologists, counselors, and administrators typically support teachers and parents in homework compliance as consultants.

This chapter proposes universal, targeted, and intensive evidence-based strategies to enhance homework compliance. To this end, a three-level approach to homework management follows (Table 10.1):

Preparative Homework: Setting Expectations

In collaboration with administrators, teachers, and parents, interventionists should promote the following preparative approaches to enhance students' homework compliance:

- Provide policies to students and their parents that make clear expectations for homework completion, as well as consequences for late and missed assignments.
- Institute a homework hotline that students can call to ask questions about assignments (Dawson, 2008).
- Develop a homework management system within the school such as Edline or Moodle.
- Establish a classroom posting at the beginning of the academic year to inform students and parents of the manner in which homework will be assigned and how it will be collected (Cooper & Valentine, 2001).
- Ensure that homework assignments are unambiguous so that students know what is expected of them when completing assignments at home. Classroom teachers should regularly: (a) describe the purpose of each assignment, (b) post the assignment on the board or send an assignment sheet home, (c) provide instructions for completing the assignment and provide examples, (d) remind students before the assignment due date when it is due, and (e) communicate how assignments will be graded (Dawson, 2008).
- Assign homework that extends lessons taught in class to the home context (Bembenutty, 2011).
- Consider the developmental rule of thumb to determine appropriate amounts of homework for each grade level, following the Cooper and Valentine (2001) guidelines.
- Provide students with tips for organizing and completing homework independently.
- Correct homework in a timely manner to enhance student learning and comprehension of course content.

Parental Roles. Parents have an important role in the homework-monitoring process. They have the opportunity to establish homework routines and

TABLE 10.1

A MODEL FOR HOMEWORK COMPLIANCE

Preparative Homework: Setting Expectations

Schools:

- Provide clear homework policies to parents and students
- Implement a homework hotline
- Develop a website devoted to addressing questions, posting resources, displaying class assignments

Teachers:

- Establish a routine of when homework will be a assigned and when it will be collected
- Clearly state the homework assignment
  - ○ Announce the purpose of the assignment
  - ○ Write the assignment on the board
  - ○ Provide explicit instructions regarding how to complete the assignment
  - ○ Provide examples
  - ○ Remind students of assignment due dates
  - ○ Inform students how the work will be graded
- Make homework meaningful to students by tying assignment to class instruction
- Be mindful of developmentally appropriate amounts of homework (the 10-minute rule)
- Provide feedback in a timely manner
- Implement the flipped classroom

Parents:

- Establish homework routines at home
  - ○ Identify a quiet area away from distractions where homework may be completed
  - ○ Designate a specific time that homework is to be completed
  - ○ Ensure that there are materials needed to complete the homework
- Communicate with your child's teacher
- Talk to your child about the assignments
- Monitor your child while he or she completes the work

Homework Compliance: Maximizing Student, Parent, and Teacher Involvement

Schools:

- Organize an after-school homework club

Teachers:

- In collaboration with interventionists:
  - ○ Teach students organizational strategies
  - ○ Help students develop good study habits
  - ○ Teach students appropriate study skills
  - ○ Tailor assignment to the skill level of the student
  - ○ Identify whether academic tutoring is warranted
- Provide homework accommodations
- Use incentive systems
- Implement a class-wide contingency for homework management

Parents:

- Continue communication with teachers
  - ○ School–home logs
  - ○ Daily report cards

Remedial Homework: Enforcing Homework Compliance

Interventionists in collaboration with teachers may:

- Conduct a functional behavioral assessment to determine why a student is not completing homework
- Develop individually tailored behavioral management plans

expectations at home during the early grades to communicate to their children a strong message that academic success is important. These early-established homework routines inculcate in students a reassuring sense of stability that becomes part of the children's behavioral repertoire (Dawson, 2010). Parents can facilitate the homework compliance process by implementing the following recommendations:

- Identify a quiet place in the home where students can effectively complete homework.
- Ensure necessary educational materials are available for students to complete homework assignments (e.g., paper, pencils, crayons, scissors).
- Specify a time when homework is to be completed each day (e.g., immediately after school, after dinner). Parents or teachers should provide children with a homework planner where assignments can be recorded; a homework planner also facilitates and encourages communication with teachers (Dawson, 2008). Moreover, both teachers and parents should "sign off" on homework to ensure supervision at school and home.
- Parents should monitor homework completion, be available to answer their children's questions, evaluate completed work, and help their children prepare for exams (Keith & Keith, 2006).
- Parental involvement in homework completion should be as indirect and minimally involved as possible. To encourage students to become independent learners, parents should "provide the minimum help necessary for the child to be successful" (Dawson, 2008, p. 1079).

Homework Compliance: Maximizing Student, Parent, and Teacher Involvement

Students who require parent and teacher involvement at this level are not making sufficient progress with homework compliance. Therefore, focused and intensive strategies designed to facilitate homework compliance are warranted and should be implemented.

Tutoring. Parents and teachers should consider whether additional academic support personnel are needed to assist with homework compliance, such as home-based or school-based tutors. Classroom teachers can develop assignments tailored to the skill level of their students that can be implemented with the assistance of tutors. Specific tutorial assignments can be created to address academic areas in need of remediation, and students' academic progress may be further facilitated at home with parental (or professional) tutoring. Tutors can also provide requisite structure and encouragement to ensure homework completion (Keith & Keith, 2006).

After-School Interventions. Counselors and teachers often coordinate after-hours homework opportunities for students who require additional assistance. Organizing an after-school homework club wherein multiple students complete assigned work together with a trained peer tutor or under the supervision of supporting teachers and/or administrators is one approach that has been shown to work well (Keith & Keith, 2006).

Effective Parent–Teacher Communication. Students' homework should be monitored carefully by parents and teachers to ensure compliance. Such collaboration between parents and teachers is necessary to ensure that at-risk students comply with homework completion expectations. Providing consistency across children's primary contexts, parents and teachers can better coordinate efforts and collaborate meaningfully to promote student success (Sheridan, 2009). As such, home–school logs or daily report cards may facilitate communication about the student's progress between settings. In addition to written communications, weekly or monthly phone calls and parent conferences to discuss students' homework progress enhance the home–school partnership, and ultimately, homework performance.

Accommodations. Classroom teachers can provide meaningful accommodations to facilitate homework compliance. Following is a list of suggestions teachers can employ to help students grapple with homework assignments:

- Divide assignments into small and more easily managed tasks.
- Modify the number and kinds of assignments.
- Provide students with a peer tutor to help with homework.
- Provide students with work samples to which they can refer.
- Help students complete some homework before they leave school.
- Provide time during the school day to work on homework assignments.

- Grade homework without penalizing students for handwriting or spelling errors.
- Allow students to complete some homework for extra credit.
- Assign less homework initially and gradually increase the amount as the student becomes more proficient.

Incentives. Students may also benefit from incentive systems that use positive reinforcement to encourage homework compliance, such as allowing computer time or other activities students find reinforcing (Dawson, 2010).

Group Contingencies. Group-oriented contingencies, which may be categorized as "independent," "interdependent," or "dependent," can be used to target the same behaviors, criteria, and reinforcements for all students in the class (Theodore et al., 2009). Several common group contingency approaches follow:

- *Independent group contingencies* are established when the standards for reinforcement are the same for the entire class, but rewards are based on an individual student's performance.
- *Interdependent group contingencies* employ the same reward for an entire class based on the class meeting an identified criterion. Teachers may use class averages, high and low student performances, the performance of the entire class, and division of the class into teams to determine which contingency will be reinforced (Theodore, Bray, Kehle, & DioGuardi, 2003).
- *Dependent group contingencies* reinforce the entire class based on the performance of a single student or a couple of targeted students.

Group contingencies are particularly attractive because they make efficient use of teacher time and resources. Group contingencies are easy to employ because the teacher must manage only one contingency program at a time (Lynch et al., 2009; Theodore et al., 2014). Research has shown that all three group contingency types are effective in improving homework compliance (Lynch et al., 2009; Reinhardt et al., 2009; Theodore et al., 2009; Theodore et al., 2014). Therefore, the choice of which contingency approach to employ depends largely on teacher preferences and characteristics of the class.

Remedial Homework: Enforcing Homework Compliance

Services provided at this level typically consist of interventions for students for whom earlier strategies were unsuccessful. At this juncture, the student's academic functioning has been negatively affected and homework compliance is minimal. Students who do not complete their homework or do not turn in assignments may require more intensive support from classroom teachers and parents. Although there are many reasons why homework noncompliance exists, teachers and parents must work collaboratively to identify and overcome those reasons (Theodore et al., 2014).

Individually tailored interventions should be designed to meet the unique needs of each student by addressing the reasons for homework noncompliance. Prior to developing an effective behavioral management plan, it is important to understand the function of the student's behavior. Functional behavioral assessments can be used to identify the reason(s) for student homework noncompliance or failing to turn in assignments. In this endeavor it is beneficial to review the student's academic records (i.e., grades, attendance, and medical and social history); interview parents, teachers, and the student; as well as observe the student in multiple contexts (Steege & Watson, 2009). It is essential to determine the function of the homework noncompliance so effective interventions can be employed to help the student be successful.

Once the functional rationale for homework noncompliance has been determined, behavioral management strategies (e.g., behavioral plans, homework charts, and token economy systems) may be employed to improve the homework compliance. It is important to involve students in the planning of their own interventions and the selection of possible reinforcers (Theodore et al., 2014). When developing interventions, students should understand how the intervention will work, when it will be employed, what the cost will be, the reinforcers that are available, the points/tokens needed to earn rewards, and when points/tokens may be redeemed for rewards. Particularly noteworthy is that rewards may need to be changed from time to time to maintain reinforcing potency (Pfiffner, Barkley, & DuPaul, 2006). Effective rewards vary student to student, so different rewards will be reinforcing for different students.

CONCLUSION

Homework has been a long continued practice in schools because researchers and teachers alike have attested to its benefits. In an era of increased accountability, homework is influential in the learning process because in part it allows for a daily evaluation of student gains. It is commonly accepted that students who engage in homework have higher grades on average than students who do not complete homework (Cooper et al., 2006). Further, a well-established positive relationship exists between homework completion and academic achievement, with homework providing greater academic benefits to children in middle and high schools as compared to elementary-aged students (Zimmerman & Kitsantas, 2005).

Although homework at the lower grade levels appears to minimally influence academic achievement, it has been shown to be helpful for shaping students' educational values and beliefs, as well as promoting personal responsibility and independence (e.g., the development of good study habits, self-discipline, and time-management skills). Homework also serves to encourage curiosity outside of the classroom, and educational curiosity leads to improved attitudes toward school (Epstein & Van Voorhis, 2001).

Given the significant implications of homework completion, it is incumbent upon educators to work collaboratively with parents to support children with homework compliance. This valuable endeavor may be best accomplished by providing teachers, parents, and students with effective, evidence-based homework-related strategies, interventions, and accommodations to enhance their overall academic functioning.

SELECT BIBLIOGRAPHY

Bryan, T., Burstein, K., & Bryan, J. (2001). Students with learning disabilities: Homework problems and promising practices. *Educational Psychologist, 36,* 167–180.
The authors discuss how students diagnosed with a learning disability struggle with homework. The article provides useful strategies and suggestions for how to improve overall homework performance for students with disabilities.

Dawson, P. (2010). Homework: A guide for parents. In A. Canter, S. Carroll, L. Paige, & I. Romero (Eds.), *Helping children at home and school III: Handouts from your school psychologist* (pp. S2H11–1–S2H11–4). Bethesda, MD: National Association of School Psychologists.
This chapter provides an overview of homework benefits including a comprehensive discussion of practical strategies designed to improve homework completion and accuracy.

Theodore, L. A., Bray, M. A., & Kehle, T. J. (2014). Best practices in facilitating homework management in schools. In P. L. Harrison & A. Thomas (Eds.), *Best practices in school psychology VI (student-level services)* (pp. 83–96). *Best Practices VI.* Silver Springs, MD: National Association of School Psychologists.
This is an excellent resource for practitioners and parents. Research-based interventions and guidelines for implementing these homework strategies are discussed. A comprehensive chapter that addresses all aspects of homework management, including the history and best practices of homework, for mental health practitioners, parents, and teachers.

REFERENCES

Bang, H. J. (2011). Promising homework practices: Teachers' perspectives on making homework work for newcomer immigrant students. *The High School Journal, 95*(2), 3–31. doi:10.1353/hsj.2012.0001

Bembenutty, H. (2011). Meaningful and maladaptive homework practices: The role of self-efficacy and self-regulation. *Journal of Advanced Academics, 22,* 448–473. doi:10.1177/1932202X1102200304

Brock, C. H., Lapp, D., Flood, J., Fisher, D., & Tao, K. (2007). Does homework matter? An investigation of teacher perceptions about homework practices for children from nondominant backgrounds. *Urban Education, 42,* 349–372.

Bryan, T., Burstein, K., & Bryan, J. (2001). Students with learning disabilities: Homework problems and promising practices. *Educational Psychologist, 36,* 167–180. doi:10.1207/S15326985EP3603_3

Cancio, E. J., West, R. P., & Young, R. K. (2004). Improving mathematics homework completion and accuracy of students with EBD through self-management and parent participation. *Journal of Emotional and Behavioral Disorders, 12,* 9–22. doi:10.1177/10634266040120010201

Cooper, H., Robinson, J., & Patall, E. (2006). Does homework improve academic achievement? A synthesis of research, 1987–2003. *Review of Educational Research, 76,* 1–62. doi:10.3102/00346543076001001

Cooper, H., & Valentine, J. C., (2001). Using research to answer practical questions about homework. *Educational Psychologist, 36,* 143–153. doi:10.1207/S15326985EP3603_1

Dawson, P. (2008). Best practices in managing homework. In A. Thomas & J. Grimes (Eds.), *Best practices in school psychology V* (pp. 1073–1084). Bethesda, MD: National Association of School Psychologists.

Dawson, P. (2010). Homework: A guide for parents. In A. Canter, S. Carroll, L. Paige, & I. Romero (Eds.), *Helping children at home and school III: Handouts from your school psychologist* (pp. S2H11–1– S2H11–4). Bethesda, MD: National Association of School Psychologists.

Epstein, J. L., & Van Voorhis, F. L. (2001). More than minutes: Teachers' roles in designing homework. *Educational Psychologist, 36,* 181–194. doi:10.1207/S15326985EP3603_4

Eren, O., & Henderson, D. J. (2011). Are we wasting our children's time by giving them more homework? *Economics of Education Review, 30,* 950–961.

Keith, T. Z., Diamond-Hallam, C., & Fine, J. G. (2004). Longitudinal effects of in-school and out-of-school homework on high school grades. *School Psychology Quarterly, 19,* 187–211. doi:10.1521/scpq.19.3.187.40278

Keith, T. Z., & Keith, P. B. (2006). Homework. In G. G. Bear & K. M. Minke (Eds.), *Children's needs III: Development, prevention, and intervention* (pp. 615–629). Bethesda, MD: National Association of School Psychologists.

Lynch, A., Theodore, L. A., Bray, M. A., & Kehle, T. J. (2009). A comparison of group-oriented contingencies and randomized reinforcers to improve homework completion and accuracy for students with disabilities. *School Psychology Review, 38,* 307–324.

Maltese, A. V., Tai, R. H., & Fan, X. (2012). When is homework worth the time? Evaluating the association between homework and achievement in high school science and math. *The High School Journal, 96*(1), 52–71. doi:10.1353/hsj.2012.0015

National Commission on Excellence in Education. (1983). *A nation at risk: The imperative for educational reform.* Washington, DC: U.S. Government Printing Office.

National Education Association. (2013). *Research spotlight on homework.* Retrieved from http://www.nea.org/tools/16938.htm

Patall, E. A., Cooper, H., & Robinson, J. C. (2008). Parent involvement in homework: A research synthesis. *Review of Educational Research, 78,* 1039–1101. doi:10.3102/0034654308325185

Pfiffner, L. J., Barkley, R. A., & DuPaul, G. J. (2006). Treatment of ADHD in school settings. In R. A. Barkley (Ed.), *Attention deficit hyperactivity disorder: A handbook for diagnosis and treatment* (3rd ed., pp. 547–589). New York, NY: Guilford.

Power, T. J., Karutsis, J. L., & Habboushe, D. F. (2001). *Homework success for children with ADHD: A family-school intervention program.* New York, NY: Guilford.

Power, T. J., Werba, B. E., Watkins, M. W., Angelucci, J. G., & Eiraldi, R. B. (2006). Patterns of parent-reported homework problems among ADHD-referred and non-referred children. *School Psychology Quarterly, 21,* 13–33. doi:10.1521/scpq.2006.21.1.13

Reinhardt, D., Theodore, L. A., Bray, M. A., & Kehle, T. J. (2009). Improving homework accuracy: Interdependent group contingencies and randomized components. *Psychology in the Schools, 46,* 471–488. doi:10.1002/pits.20391

Rowell, L., & Hong, E. (2002). The role of school counselors in homework intervention. *Professional School Counseling, 5,* 285–291.

Sheridan, S. M. (2009). Homework interventions for children with attention and learning problems: Where is the "home" in "homework?" *School Psychology Review, 38,* 334–337.

Steege, M. W., & Watson, T. S. (2009). *Conducting school-based functional behavioral assessments: A practitioner's guide* (2nd ed.). New York, NY: Guilford.

Theodore, L. A., Bray, M. A., & Kehle, T. J. (2014). Best practices in facilitating homework management in schools. In P. L. Harrison & A. Thomas (Eds.), *Best practices in school psychology VI* (student-level services), (pp. 83–96). *Best practices* VI. Silver Springs, MD: National Association of School Psychologists.

Theodore, L. A., Bray, M. A., Kehle, T. J., & DioGuardi, R. J. (2003). Contemporary review of group-oriented contingencies for disruptive behavior. *Journal of Applied School Psychology, 20,* 79–101. doi:10.1300/J370v20n01_06

Theodore, L. A., DioGuardi, R. J., Hughes, T. L., Carlo, M., & Eccles, D. (2009). A class-wide intervention for improving homework performance. *Journal of Educational and*

Psychological Consultation, 19, 275–299. doi:10.1080/10474410902888657

U.S. Department of Education (DoE). (1986). *What works.* Washington, DC: Author.

Zimmerman, B. J., & Kitsantas, A. (2005). Homework practices and academic achievement: The mediating role of self-efficacy and perceived responsibility beliefs. *Contemporary Educational Psychology, 30,* 397–417. doi:10.1016/j.cedpsych.2005.05.003

Evidence-Based Interventions for Working With Culturally Diverse Children and Families

Margaret R. Rogers and Elisabeth C. O'Bryon

OVERVIEW

As the nation's latest educational reform and legislative initiatives are heard in nightly news stories, other changes—just as significant and transformative—are underway, but seem less likely to capture headlines. One such change concerns shifts occurring in the racial, ethnic, and linguistic makeup of the United States. An examination of past census reports and projections highlights the increasing diversity within the United States. In 1991, racial and ethnic minority group members made up about 20% of the U.S. population (U.S. Census Bureau, 1991); by 2000, the percentage of individuals of color grew to about 31%. As reported in the 2010 census, 36% of the U.S. population was identified as people of color (Humes, Jones, & Ramirez, 2011). Moreover, the most recent U.S. Census shows that Latinos surpassed African Americans as the largest minority group, representing about 17% of the population (U.S. Census Bureau, 2014). A finer grain analysis of the census data revealed that minorities comprise the majority of the population in four states (i.e., California, Hawaii, New Mexico, and Texas) and the District of Columbia and seven states are approaching a minority majority (i.e., Arizona, Florida, Georgia, Maryland, Nevada, New Jersey, and New York; Humes et al., 2011). The latest projections suggest that the U.S. population will become minority majority by 2043 (U.S. Census Bureau, 2012).

The demographic changes happening nationwide are also transforming the student body of our public schools. In 2001, 60% of students in prekindergarten to 12th grade self-identified as non-Hispanic White; 17% identified as African American; 17% identified as Latino; 4% as Asian American; 1% as American Indian; and less than 1% of the students were identified as multiracial (Kena et al., 2014). As of 2014, Whites no longer represent the majority of students within public schools (Hussar & Bailey, 2013). By 2023, student enrollments are projected to decrease for Whites to 45%, African Americans to 15%, and American Indians to less than 1%, whereas Latino students will increase to 30%, Asian Americans to 5%, and multiracial students to 4% (Kena et al., 2014). These demographic changes are widespread and observed across every major region of the country and the majority of U.S. states. Regionally, a closer look at the data shows varying concentrations of students by race and ethnicity, with the greatest shifts occurring among non-Hispanic Whites, whose enrollment declines are largest in the West, and Latinos, whose enrollments have grown most noticeably in the South (Kena et al., 2014).

The most recent demographic changes seem largely propelled by a growing immigrant population. The region or country of origin for recent immigrants varies, but four dominate, including Latin America (especially Mexico), Asia, Europe, and Africa. Immigrants constitute approximately 13% of the U.S. population, and while a modest segment of society, the numbers have special significance for the school-aged population (American Psychological Association, Presidential Task Force on Immigration, 2013). At present, about 25% of school-aged youth have at least one parent who is a recent immigrant (Nwosu, Batalova, & Auclair, 2014). Historically, immigrants have immigrated to a handful of states (e.g., California, Florida, Illinois), but recent waves of immigrants have settled across the United States (APA, Presidential Task Force on Immigration, 2013). This pattern of expanded migration brings children of immigrants into schools that have limited histories with culturally and linguistically diverse (CLD) families, and likely lack familiarity with the specific needs, issues, and adaptations necessary to create successful transitions and educational experiences for immigrant students. One of the primary challenges facing schools is addressing the needs of children who speak English as a second language. Among those students who are 5 years of age and older, approximately 21% are "English language learners" (ELLs), and their most common first languages are Spanish, Chinese, Tagalog, and Vietnamese (Ryan, 2013).

Given the increasing cultural and linguistic diversity of the school-aged population, mental health professionals across the country must develop unique knowledge and skills to meet these students' social, educational, and emotional needs, and help educators make necessary system-wide adjustments. Recent reports show that 97% of school psychologists deliver services to a racially and ethnically diverse clientele (Curtis, Castillo, & Gelley, 2012). Concurrent with their educational needs, evidence suggests that diverse youth face disparities in health care and mental health care. A recent meta-analysis found disparities in health and health care for diverse children that were "extensive, pervasive, and persistent" in access, use, and quality of care, among other indicators (Flores

and The Committee on Pediatric Research, 2010, p. 979). In terms of mental health care, Cook, Barry, and Busch's (2013) longitudinal analysis of records for more than 30,000 African American, Latino, and White children found a marked disparity in care between the ethnic groups, with African Americans and Latinos seeking care half as often as Whites. With respect to educational outcomes, the findings are mixed, with Asian Americans outpacing all other racial and ethnic groups in 4-year high school graduation rates at 93%, followed by non-Hispanic Whites at 85%, Latinos at 76%, and African Americans and American Indians at 68% (Kena et al., 2014).

Other education-related statistics are as noteworthy for select student groups. For example, African American students are disproportionately identified as in need of special education services for intellectual deficiencies and emotional disturbance in comparison with students of other racial and ethnic groups (National Association of School Psychologists, 2013). In addition, one in every six African American children is suspended from school, a rate more than three times their White counterparts (Losen & Gillespie, 2012), reflecting a long-standing history of disparate disciplinary treatment of children of color in U.S. schools (Skiba et al., 2011). The noted disparities are just a sampling of those data available and represent a small portion of information practitioners need to understand the context of service provision for diverse youth. In light of these data, mental health professionals will need a specialized skill set to work with culturally diverse children and families. This skill set includes considering the entire ecosystem, understanding the public and social policies that impact families' circumstances, the nature of disparities families face, the systemic changes needed to create equitable systems of care and education, and the processes required to ensure equity. In the following sections, information on the best ways of providing optimal services for CLD children and their families is laid out. In addition, the chapter addresses the status of empirically supported methods for providing care, what is presently known about best practices in care, and then the chapter closes with a bibliography of readings and resources to assist mental health professionals in delivering high-quality services.

ETIOLOGY AND FACTORS CONTRIBUTING TO WORKING WITH CULTURALLY DIVERSE CHILDREN AND FAMILIES

When working with CLD children and families, mental health professionals must consider several factors that affect how care is provided, the families' engagement in care, the need for intervention, and overall service delivery (i.e., type and scope of services). Despite the challenges and complexities involved in service provision, professionals have an ethical and professional responsibility to appropriately assess and intervene when diverse students struggle.

Socioeconomic Status

One factor that significantly influences child well-being is whether the child is raised in a low-socioeconomic-status household. Poverty has consistently been identified as a social and cognitive risk factor among culturally diverse families (Sirin, 2005). A recent meta-analysis revealed a significant relationship between socioeconomic status and literacy and language, aggression, and internalizing behaviors (Letourneau, Duffet-Leger, Levac, Watson, & Young-Morris, 2011). Practitioners must identify whether and how factors associated with low socioeconomic status are implicated in the display of academic, social, and emotional problems. Moreover, mental health professionals must determine whether an identified problem is caused by a disability or sociocultural issues. A disproportionate number of students from poor backgrounds receive special education services (Shifrer, Muller, & Callahan 2011), which highlights the challenge of distinguishing between the influences of economic factors from those of a true disability.

English Learner Status

Recent census data show that more than 300 languages are spoken in the public schools nationwide. Understanding how to effectively support ELLs is critical given that many struggle academically (Aud et al., 2011) and socially (Edl, Jones, & Estell, 2008). Mental health professionals (as well as teachers) are tasked with the challenge of parsing out whether difficulties experienced by ELLs merit language-related intervention (e.g., scaffolded language support and cooperative learning opportunities) or more intensive intervention (e.g., special education services). Assessing language proficiency (Rhodes, Ochoa, & Ortiz, 2005); acquiring relevant background information (e.g., prior schooling, experience with native and second language; O'Bryon, 2014); and selecting and using appropriate assessment tools (Fernandez, Boccaccini, & Noland, 2007) are considered best practices when working with ELLs. Importantly, identifying and using interventions shown to be effective with children from diverse linguistic backgrounds are imperative.

Immigration and Acculturative Stress

Immigrants who are adjusting to a new culture may experience acculturative stress when exposed to changes in language, values, and customs (Romero & Branscome, 2014). Family members are likely to acculturate at different rates and in different ways, which can pose unique challenges for them (Suárez-Orozco et al., 2012). The stress associated with the process of acculturation can lead to internalizing problems, as well as learning difficulties and adjustment problems (Scribner, 2002). Appropriately identifying the level of acculturation and related stresses enables practitioners to identify appropriate supports to implement. Interventions shown to promote positive outcomes include those that target social and emotional skill development (Bal & Perzigian, 2013), engage families in school–home partnerships (Crosnoe, 2013), and share targeted information about college pathways (Suárez-Orozco, Suárez-Orozco, & Todorova, 2008).

Trust Issues and Use of Advocacy

An important, albeit typically unspoken, issue concerns CLD clients' perceptions and beliefs about mental health practitioners and treatment. Practitioners are advised to consider not only clients' perceptions about mental health, illness, and well-being, but also how institutional responses influence clients' responsiveness to mental health care. For well informed clients, this history may form a backdrop of ill will, apprehension, and deep-seated mistrust of Western mainstream mental health providers, their research, and their services. From the Tuskegee syphilis experiment

(Mays, 2012), to the repeated mistreatment of Native Americans (Hodge, 2012), and the exploitation of Sri Lankan children by researchers following the tsunami of 2004 (Watters, 2012), our history includes research and treatment abuses of vulnerable people at the hands of the medical and psychological establishment, often in the name of science. As such, clients may not trust researchers and service providers whom they see as representing the establishment, including helping professionals. Consequently, practitioners need to be deliberate in establishing trust and a positive working alliance with diverse clients and their families. Special attention needs to be paid to the basic steps of building trust including being dependable, following through with promised communications and resources, listening intently, being empathetic, and being informed about and taking steps to address the broader sociopolitical context of clients' life circumstances and presenting problems.

With respect to this latter point, professionals must develop a sense of how social inequalities are embedded in the broader institutional (e.g., unjust treatment by organizations such as the government and corporations) and structural (e.g., when one particular group is given unequal status as compared with others) systems in the United States, both past and present, to fully understand the factors that differentially affect diverse families. Social inequalities or the uneven distribution of resources are often difficult to identify (Fisher, 2014), yet are a powerful force in people's lives. Understanding these inequities can help practitioners see points of vulnerability, obstacles, stressors, and pressures that affect CLD families day to day and over time. In the schools, knowing how to assess school climate is critical, especially as it relates to discipline (U.S. Department of Justice and U.S. Department of Education, 2014), zero tolerance policies (Nelson, 2008), dropout prevention programs, safe schools programs, grade retention policies, and so on.

Helping professionals should know how structural inequalities affect CLD children and their families and the kinds of prejudice and discrimination families face. Individuals working in school settings who wish to right an injustice involving a CLD youngster may do so by advocating in the face of entrenched, inequitable educational policies and practices. Although advocating as school employees, professionals must also attend to the terms of their employment contract, which may place limitations on public statements. In such cases, court cases involving free speech are relevant. As described in Jacob, Decker, and Hartshorne (2011), two relevant U.S. Supreme Court cases are *Pickering v. Board of Education of Township High School District 205, Will County* (1968), and *Garcetti v. Ceballos* (2006). The *Pickering* ruling allows school employees to make public remarks critical of school policy, whereas the *Garcetti* ruling restricts those rights when the employee does so in a professional capacity as part of his or her position. Thus, in cases involving advocating for righting inequities, practitioners working in schools are advised to (a) state the child's needs; (b) clarify the changes needed to address the needs; (c) emphasize the advantages to the child, family, and system for making the changes; (d) link the changes required to the educational values espoused within the system; and (e) engage professional (e.g., colleagues and professional organizations) resources to support the changes. Practitioners will need to maintain a positive approach, be doggedly persistent, and make the case for change first by privately approaching school administrators (Jacob et al., 2011).

EVIDENCE-BASED INTERVENTIONS AND EMPIRICAL SUPPORT FOR WORKING WITH CULTURALLY DIVERSE CHILDREN AND FAMILIES

The evidence-based practice movement has become a professional priority given the importance of identifying effective interventions that can enhance service delivery to children, adolescents, and adults (Kratochwill & Shernoff, 2004). Although standards for evidence-based interventions (EBI) exist, such as multiple randomized control trials and evidence of large effect sizes (Kumpfer, Magalhaes, & Xie, 2012), all interventions are not "created equal" and a deliberate and intentional decision-making process is needed when determining whether and how to use an EBI with the population of interest. Appropriately considering *why* an intervention worked (i.e., under what conditions? with what sample?) is critical (Ingraham & Oka, 2006), especially when determining how to apply the EBI research to diverse clients.

Given concern over how cultural diversity may influence the effectiveness of an EBI, a debate exists regarding the extent to which an intervention must consider culture in order to be appropriate and effective for diverse clients. That is, whether the sole inclusion of individuals from minority backgrounds in efficacy and effectiveness trials is adequate (Hohmann & Parron, 1996), or more extensive modifications in the treatment and delivery processes that increase the cultural relevance are needed (Smith, Domenech Rodriguez, & Bernal, 2011). Researchers in the latter camp warn of the risks associated with disseminating treatments that do not systematically consider cultural values of specific groups (Calzada, 2010). Specifically, they assert that failing to fully engage the individual targeted for intervention will likely compromise positive outcomes (Calzada, 2010).

Cultural adaptation procedures are a potential solution to the challenge of identifying and appropriately using interventions that are both evidence based and culturally responsive (Bernal, Jimenez-Chafey, & Domenech Rodriguez, 2009). Cultural adaptation has been defined as "the systematic modification of an evidence-based treatment or intervention protocol to consider language, culture, and context in such a way that is compatible with the client's cultural patterns, meanings, and values" (Bernal et al., 2009, p. 362). Castro-Olivo and Merrell (2012) summarize general guidelines for culturally adapting evidence-based practices into two key recommendations: first, to familiarize yourself with your target population; and second, to adapt delivery methods to best reach the target populations.

Meta-analytic research on the effects of culturally adapted interventions has revealed that interventions intended for a specific cultural group were more effective than those provided to client groups from a number of different cultural backgrounds (Griner & Smith, 2006; Smith et al., 2011) and that more cultural adaptations result in better treatment outcomes (Smith et al., 2011). In addition, interventions conducted in clients' native languages were twice as effective as those conducted in English (Griner & Smith, 2006). These findings have important implications for determining which intervention to use with diverse clients. However, although positive outcomes have been associated with adapted interventions, additional research directly comparing adapted versus standard interventions is still needed (Miranda et al., 2005).

HOW TO: A GUIDE TO THE IMPLEMENTATION OF INTERVENTIONS FOR CULTURALLY DIVERSE CHILDREN AND FAMILIES

Training in Cultural Competence

A first step in providing high-quality, culturally tailored services is effective training. Acquiring cultural competencies requires exposure to a curriculum that fully embeds theory and research about diverse clients into all courses and training experiences. Proctor and Meyers (2014) stress the importance of building such competencies in trainee attitudes, knowledge, and skills. Such an approach allows for students and/or practitioners to benefit from iterations of critical self-reflection, direct instruction of relevant skills, exposure to relevant illustrations and dilemmas, applied practice, and corrective feedback. Several resources are available to help faculty embed cultural competencies into their training program's curricula and an especially useful recent illustrative publication is listed in this chapter's bibliography.

Assessment

Appropriately assessing children from diverse cultural and linguistic backgrounds and the contexts within which they reside and are educated involves careful attention to several factors throughout the assessment process. The considerations begin early in the process and include thoughtful collection of information about resources and stressors in the broad environment (locale, neighborhood, school district policies, school building policies, classroom policies, social, educational, language and culture related, etc.), components of the mental health environment (school climate, teacher–student relationships, parent–child relationships, peer relationships, status in relationships; Cohen & Lotan, 2004; Ysseldyke, Lekwa, Kingbeil, & Cormier, 2012), and features of the instructional environment (curriculum, instruction and pedagogy, etc.; Sleeter & Delgado Bernal, 2004; Ysseldyke et al., 2012). Assessment also includes intentional decision making about instrument selection, including the following: (a) Has the measure been normed with a representative sample of children? and (b) Are there cultural and/or linguistic demands that would disadvantage the child being evaluated (Rhodes et al., 2005)? These questions have important implications as research has shown a linear, inverse relationship between English-language proficiency and performance on assessments requiring higher levels of English-language development and knowledge of mainstream culture (Sotelo-Dynega, Ortiz, Flanagan, & Chaplin, 2013). The validity of an assessment is compromised when the results are influenced more by the cultural and/or linguistic demands of the task than the construct of interest.

Assessments with children from diverse backgrounds may also require the use of interpreters, which can introduce bias and error to the testing process if not used appropriately. A study of bilingual school psychologists revealed that only 5% of participants had preservice training in working with interpreters, and many used them inappropriately by working with untrained interpreters and using interpreters to translate standardized instruments (O'Bryon & Rogers, 2010). Knowledge and use of best practices include briefing the interpreter before the assessment, discussing any technical terms that are part of the assessment, discussing confidentiality, and practicing with the interpreter (Lopez, 2002; Scribner, 2002). Results obtained with interpreters should be highlighted in psychological reports, and used cautiously (Rogers et al., 1999). Psychologists must ensure that the decisions informed by their results (e.g., special education eligibility, intervention programs) are appropriate and fair.

Intervening With Diverse Families

Although limited in scope, existing intervention and prevention research with diverse families have identified key considerations that can inform service delivery. First, it is critical to consider the wants and needs of the community of interest. For example, do families want a traditional parenting class, a traditional class in Spanish, or a culturally targeted class (Domenech Rodriguez, Baumann, & Schwartz, 2011)? The answer to this question will inform whether families are delivered an intervention "as is," a cultural adaptation, or a newly developed intervention. A second consideration is whether the intervention aligns with the cultural values of the families who are the target of the intervention. Calzada, Basil, and Fernandez (2012) found that Latina mothers considered some evidence-based parenting strategies acceptable (praise and social rewards), whereas others were objectionable and not aligned with cultural norms and beliefs (selective ignoring in public and the elimination of spanking). Knowledge and understanding of families' cultural values are essential.

A third consideration involves an examination of whether and how researchers have involved the community of interest in the process of culturally adapting an intervention. The value of working closely with the community in the cultural adaptation process has been consistently underscored, given the unique insights and contributions possible from families who are the target of the intervention. In one study, researchers partnered with community organizations (a mental health agency, a behavioral health clinic, and a faith-based community organization) to increase families' access and comfort with the intervention (Valdez, Padilla, Moore, & Magana, 2013), and in another, researchers formed a participatory research partnership with an American Indian community to effectively develop and evaluate their intervention (Goodkind, LaNoue, Lee, Freeland, & Freund, 2012). Available research identifies positive outcomes associated with the cultural adaptation of family-focused intervention and prevention efforts. These include increases in cultural identity, self-esteem, positive coping strategies, quality of life, and social adjustment in a community-based health intervention for American Indian families (Goodkind et al., 2012). They also include improved psychological functioning, increased family and marital support, and enhanced family functioning in an intervention for Latina immigrant mothers with depression and their families (Valdez et al., 2013); and meaningful improvements in recruitment and retention efforts in a family-skills intervention adapted for African American, Hispanic, Asian/Pacific Islander, and American Indian families (Kumpfer, Alvarado, Smith, & Bellamy, 2002).

Intervening in the Schools

It is also critical that practitioners have a deep knowledge and understanding of school-based interventions with demonstrated positive effects for diverse student populations. An important first step is to examine the student populations represented in the available intervention research. For example, the Good Behavior Game, a classroom behavioral intervention, has undergone extensive efficacy testing and positive student outcomes have been shown with urban, low-income, English learner, and international populations (Nolan, Houlihan, Wanzek, & Jenson, 2014). Research on school-based interventions designed for specific student groups can also inform high-quality service delivery (e.g., see Wood, Chiu, Hwang, Jacobs, and Ifekwunigwe [2008] for a discussion of culturally adapting cognitive behavioral therapy for use with Mexican American youth). Meta-analyses also provide valuable insight and guidance for those working in diverse schools. For example, a comparison of six core reading curricula on oral reading fluency growth found that growth trajectories for curricula varied based on the students' socioeconomic background (Crowe, Connor, & Petscher, 2009). Finally, it is important to underscore that using EBI is critical when working within a response to intervention (RTI, a tiered process that allows for the early identification of struggling students as well as the provision of supports and interventions) framework in schools. For psychologists, there is an ethical responsibility to consider students' diverse characteristics when identifying appropriate interventions (Burns, Jacob, & Wagner, 2008).

CONCLUSION

Understanding and effectively applying best practices for working with diverse children and families are imperative for psychologists delivering services in today's diverse schools and communities. Unfortunately, much of the extant research on children from minority backgrounds has taken a deficit perspective, shedding more light on the challenges and struggles of CLD youth than on strengths, adaptations, and positive accomplishments (Cabrera, Beeghly, & Eisenberg, 2012). This chapter has highlighted what we presently know are the key elements to consider in providing effective services to CLD clients, spanning both client-centered issues (i.e., language status, acculturation status, etc.) and

context issues (i.e., status of empirically based services, etc.) based on the best available evidence.

In order to provide high-quality services, we *implore* practitioners to conduct and seek out the most up-to-date, rigorous research to inform their practice, especially as our understanding of between- and within-group differences grows and as research uncovers needed insight into the factors associated with the positive development of diverse students within intersecting contexts. We use the term "implore" here with intention for those readers who are school psychologists, given the results of a recent survey of 54 members of the Society for the Study of School Psychology (i.e., McIntosh, Martinez, Ty, & McClain, 2013) who were asked to identify topics in school psychology they considered to be most significant, most exciting, and those they thought would guide the future of the field. Notably, among the six major categories and 17 minor categories of their responses, delivering services to CLD clients did not make either list of major or minor categories. We hope the present chapter redresses this oversight and helps us to provide guidance in what is most surely the real future of the field.

SELECT BIBLIOGRAPHY

Castro-Olivo, S. M., & Merrell, K. W. (2012). Validating cultural adaptations of a school-based social-emotional learning programme for use with Latino immigrant adolescents. *Advances in School Mental Health Promotion, 5*, 78–92.
This article elucidates the cultural adaptation process of how an existing SEL program was adapted for use with a Spanish-speaking recent-immigrant high school population.

Lopez, E. C., & Bursztyn, A. M. (2013). Future challenges and opportunities: Toward culturally responsive training in school psychology. *Psychology in the Schools, 50*, 212–228.
This is an excellent resource that integrates a multicultural framework with the latest ethical standards published by the National Association of School Psychologists. The article provides explicit examples of how culturally relevant knowledge and skills relate to the 10 NASP domains and gives multiculturally keyed resources (research articles, names of well-respected scholars, excellent examples of issues and practical applications) that faculty can use to guide curricular changes.

The Education Alliance at Brown University (information available at www.brown.edu/academics/education-alliance/teaching-diverse-learners)
This contains several useful resources for helping educators and mental health professionals transform their services to serve ELL students effectively. Helpful information is provided about assessing ELLs' elementary literacy, teaching and learning strategies, policy, and ELLs' families and communities—all resources designed to improve instruction and enhance the equity of the school environment for ELL students.

REFERENCES

American Psychological Association, Presidential Task Force on Immigration. (2013). *Working with immigrant-origin clients: An update for mental health professionals.* Washington, DC: American Psychological Association. Retrieved from http://www.apa.org/topics/immigration/immigration-report-professionals.pdf

Aud, S., Hussar, W., Kena, G., Bianco, K., Frohlich, L., Kemp, J., & Tahan, K. (2011). *The condition of education 2011* (NCES 2011–033). U.S. Department of Education, National Center for Education Statistics. Washington DC: U.S. Government Printing Office.

Bal, A., & Perzigian, A. (2013). Evidence-based interventions for immigrant students experiencing behavioral and academic problems: A systemic review of the literature. *Education and Treatment of Children, 36,* 5–28.

Bernal, G., Jimenez-Chafey, M. I., & Domenech Rodriguez, M. M. (2009). Cultural adaptation of treatments: A resource for considering culture in evidence-based practice. *Professional Psychology: Research and Practice, 40,* 361–368. doi:10.1037/a0016401

Burns, M. K., Jacob, S., & Wagner, A. R. (2008). Ethical and legal issues associated with using response-to-intervention to assess learning disabilities. *Journal of School Psychology, 43,* 263–279. doi:10.1016/j.jsp.2007.06.001

Cabrera, N. J., Beeghly, M., & Eisenberg, N. (2012). Positive development of minority children: Introduction to the special issue. *Child Development Perspectives, 6,* 207–209.

Calzada, E. J. (2010). Bringing culture into parent training with Latinos. *Cognitive and Behavioral Practice, 17,* 167–175. doi:10.1016/j.cpbra.2010.01.003

Calzada, E. J., Basil, S., & Fernandez, Y. (2012). What Latina mothers think of evidence-based parenting practices: A qualitative study of treatment acceptability. *Cognitive and Behavioral Practice, 20,* 362–374.

Castro-Olivo, S. M., & Merrell, K. W. (2012). Validating cultural adaptations of a school-based social-emotional learning programme for use with Latino immigrant adolescents. *Advances in School Mental Health Promotion, 5,* 78–92.

Cohen, E. G., & Lotan, R. A. (2004). Equity in heterogeneous classrooms. In J. A. Banks, & C. A. McGee Banks (Eds.), *Handbook of research on multicultural education* (2nd ed., pp. 736–750). San Francisco, CA: Jossey-Bass.

Cook, B., Barry, C. L., & Busch, S. H. (2013). Racial/ethnic disparity trends in children's mental health care access and expenditures from 2002 to 2007. *Health and Educational Trust, 48,* 129–149. doi:10.1111/j.1475–6773.2012.01439.x

Crosnoe, R. (2013). *Preparing the children of immigrants for early academic success.* Washington, DC: Migration Policy Institute.

Crowe, E. C., Connor, C. M., & Petscher, Y. (2009). Examining the core: Relations among reading curricula, poverty, and first through third grade reading achievement. *Journal of School Psychology, 47,* 187–214. doi:10.1016/j.jsp.2009.02.002

Curtis, M. J., Castillo, J. M., & Gelley, C. (2012). School psychology 2010: Demographics, employment, and the context for professional practices: Part 1. *Communique, 40,* 28–29.

Domenech Rodriguez, M. M., Baumann, A. A., & Schwartz, A. L. (2011). Cultural adaptation of an evidence-based intervention: From theory to practice in a Latino/a community context. *American Journal of Community Psychology, 47,* 170–186. doi:10.1007/s10464–010-9371-4

Edl, H. M., Jones, M. H., & Estell, D. B. (2008). Ethnicity and English proficiency: Teacher perceptions of academic and interpersonal competence in European American and Latino students. *School Psychology Review, 37,* 38–45.

Fernandez, K., Boccaccini, M. T., & Noland, R. M. (2007). Professionally responsible test selection for Spanish-speaking clients: A four-step approach for identifying and selecting translated tests. *Professional Psychology: Research and Practice, 38,* 363–374.

Fisher, C. B. (2014). Multicultural ethics in professional psychology practice, consulting, and training. In F. T. L. Leong (Ed.), *APA handbook of multicultural psychology* (pp. 35–57). Washington, DC: American Psychological Association.

Flores, G., & The Committee on Pediatric Research. (2010). Racial and ethnic disparities in the health and health care of children. *Pediatrics, 125,* 979–1020. doi:10.1542/peds.2010–0188

Goodkind, J., LaNoue, M., Lee, C., Freeland, L., & Freund, R. (2012). Feasibility, acceptability, and initial findings from a community-based cultural mental health intervention for American Indian youth and their families. *Journal of Community Psychology, 40,* 381–405. doi:10.1002/jcop.20517

Griner, D., & Smith, T. B. (2006). Culturally adapted mental health interventions: A meta-analytic review. *Psychotherapy: Theory, Research, Practice, Training, 43,* 531–548.

Hodge, F. S. (2012). No meaningful apology for American Indian unethical research abuses. *Ethics and Behavior, 22,* 431–444.

Hohmann, A. A., & Parron, D. L. (1996). How the new NIH guidelines on inclusion of woman and minorities apply: Efficacy trials, effectiveness trials, and validity. *Journal of Consulting and Clinical Psychology, 64,* 851–855.

Humes, K. R., Jones, N. A., & Ramirez, R. R. (2011). *Overview of race and Hispanic origin: 2010.* Washington, DC: U.S. Department of Commerce, Economics and Statistics Administration, U.S. Census Bureau.

Hussar, W. J., & Bailey, T. M. (2013). *Projections of education statistics to 2022* (NCES 2014–051). U.S. Department of Education, National Center for Education Statistics. Washington, DC: U.S. Government Printing Office.

Ingraham, C. L., & Oka, E. R. (2006). Multicultural issues in evidence-based interventions. *Journal of Applied School Psychology, 22,* 127–149. doi:10.1300/J370v22n02_07

Jacob, S., Decker, D. M., & Hartshorne, T. S. (2011). *Ethics and law for school psychologists* (6th ed.). Hoboken, NJ: Wiley.

Kena, G., Aud, S., Johnson, F., Wang, X., Zhang, J., Rathbun, A.,…Kristapovich, P. (2014). *The condition of education 2014* (NCES 2014–083). Washington, DC: U.S. Department of Education, National Center for Education Statistics.

Kratochwill, T. R., & Shernoff, E. S. (2004). Evidence-based practice: Promoting evidence-based interventions in school psychology. *School Psychology Review, 31,* 34–48. doi:10.1016/j.jsp.2004.08.001

Kumpfer, K. L., Alvarado, R., Smith, P., & Bellamy, N. (2002). Cultural sensitivity and adaptation in family-based prevention interventions. *Prevention Science, 3,* 241–246.

Kumpfer, K. L., Magalhaes, C., & Xie, J. (2012). Cultural adaptations of evidence-based family interventions to strengthen families and improve children's developmental outcomes. *European Journal of Developmental Psychology, 9,* 104–116.

Letourneau, N., Duffet-Leger, L., Levac, L., Watson, B., & Young-Morris, C. (2011). Socioeconomic status and child development: A meta-analysis. *Journal of Emotional and Behavioral Disorders, 20,* 1–14.

Lopez, E. C. (2002). Best practices in working with school interpreters to deliver psychological services to children and families. In A. Thomas & J. Grimes (Eds.), *Best practices in school psychology IV* (pp. 1419–1432). Washington, DC: National Association of School Psychologists.

Losen, D. J., & Gillespie, J. (2012). *Opportunities suspended: The disparate impact of disciplinary exclusion from school.* Retrieved from The Civil Rights Project at UCLA website http//www.civilrightsproject.ucla.edu

Mays, V. M. (2012). The legacy of the U.S. public health service study of untreated syphilis in African American men at Tuskegee on the Affordable Care Act and health care reform fifteen years after President Clinton's apology. *Ethics and Behavior, 22,* 411–418.

McIntosh, K., Martinez, R. S., Ty, S. V., & McClain, M. B. (2013). Scientific research in school psychology: Leading researchers weigh in on its past, present, and future. *Journal of School Psychology, 51,* 267–318. doi:10.1016/j.jsp2013.04.003

Miranda, J., Bernal, G., Lau, A., Kohn, L., Hwang, W., & LaFromboise, T. (2005). State of the science on psychosocial interventions for ethnic minorities. *American Review of Clinical Psychology, 1,* 113–142.

National Association of School Psychologists. (2013). *Racial and ethnic disproportionality in education* [Position statement]. Bethesda, MD: National Association of School Psychologists, Author.

Nelson, A. C. (2008). The impact of zero tolerance school discipline policies: Issues of exclusionary discipline. *Communique, 37*, 33.

Nolan, J. D., Houlihan, D., Wanzek, M., & Jenson, W. R. (2014). The Good Behavior Game: A classroom behavior intervention effective across cultures. *School Psychology International, 35*, 191–205. doi:10.1177/0143034312471473

Nwosu, C., Batalova, J., & Auclair, G. (2014). *Frequently requested statistics on immigrants and immigration in the United States*. Migration Policy Institute. Retrieved from http://www.migrationpolicy.org/article/frequently-requested-statistics-immigrants-and-immigration-united-states#7

O'Bryon, E. C. (2014). Challenges and complexities in the assessment of the bilingual student. In A. B. Clinton (Ed.), *Assessing bilingual children in context: An integrated approach* (pp. 7–24). Washington, DC: American Psychological Association.

O'Bryon, E. C., & Rogers, M. R. (2010). Bilingual school psychologists' assessment practices with English language learners. *Psychology in the Schools, 47*, 1018–1034. doi:10.1002/pits.20521

Proctor, S. L., & Meyers, J. (2014). Best practices in primary prevention in diverse schools and communities. In P. L. Harrison, & A. Thomas (Eds.), *Best practices in school psychology: Foundations* (pp. 1–15). Bethesda, MD: National Association of School Psychologists.

Rhodes, R. L., Ochoa, S. H., & Ortiz, S. O. (2005). *Assessing culturally and linguistically diverse students: A practical guide*. New York: Guilford Press.

Rogers, M. R., Ingraham, C., Bursztyn, A., Cajigas-Segredo, N., Esquivel, G., Hess, R.,…Lopez, E. C. (1999). Providing psychological services to racially, ethnically, culturally, and linguistically diverse individuals in the schools: Recommendations for practice. *School Psychology International, 20*, 243–264.

Romero, P. A., & Branscome, J. (2014). Acculturation and sociocognitive factors. In A. B. Clinton (Ed.), *Assessing bilingual children in context: An integrated approach* (pp. 191–214). Washington, DC: American Psychological Association.

Ryan, C. (2013). *Language use in the United States: 2011*. Washington, DC: U.S. Department of Commerce, Economics and Statistics Administration, U.S. Census Bureau.

Scribner, A. P. (2002). Best assessment and intervention practices with second language learners. In A. Thomas & J. Grimes (Eds.), *Best practices in school psychology IV* (pp. 1485–1499). Washington, DC: National Association of School Psychologists.

Shifrer, D., Muller, C., & Callahan, R. (2011). Disproportionality and learning disabilities: Parsing apart race, socioeconomic status, and language. *Journal of Learning Disabilities, 44*, 246–257.

Sirin, S. R. (2005). Socioeconomic status and academic achievement: A meta-analytic review of research. *Review of Educational Research, 75*, 417–453. doi:10.3102/00346543075003417

Skiba, R. J., Horner, R. H., Chung, C.-G., Rausch, M. K., May, S. L., & Tobin, T. (2011). Race is not neutral: A national investigation of African American and Latino disproportionality in school discipline. *School Psychology Review, 40*, 85–107. doi:2011–07091-006

Sleeter, C. E., & Delgado Bernal, D. (2004). Critical pedagogy, critical race theory, and antiracist education. In J. A. Banks (Ed.), *Handbook of research on multicultural education* (2nd ed., pp. 240–258). San Francisco, CA: Jossey-Bass.

Smith, T. B., Domenech Rodriguez, M., & Bernal, G. (2011). Culture. *Journal of Clinical Psychology, 67*, 166–175.

Sotelo-Dynega, M., Ortiz, S. O., Flanagan, D. P., & Chaplin, W. F. (2013). English language proficiency and test performance: An evaluation of bilingual students with the Woodcock Johnson III Tests of Cognitive Abilities. *Psychology in the Schools, 50*, 781–797. doi:10.1002/pits.21706

Suárez-Orozco, C., Birman, D., Casas, J. M., Nakamura, N., Tummala-Narra, P., Zarate, M., & Vasquez, M. (2012). *Crossroads: The psychology of immigration in the new century. Report of the APA Presidential Task Force on Immigration*. Washington, DC: APA Public Interest Directorate.

Suárez-Orozco, C., Suárez-Orozco, M. M., & Todorova, I. (2008). *Learning a new land: Immigrant students in American society*. Cambridge, MA: Harvard University Press.

U.S. Census Bureau. (1991). *1990 Census of population, general populations characteristics*. Washington, DC: U.S. Department of Commerce, Economics and Statistics Administration, U.S. Census Bureau.

U.S. Census Bureau. (2012). *U.S. Census bureau projections show a slower growing, older, more diverse nation a half century from now.* United States Census Bureau Newsroom released December 12, 2012.

U.S. Census Bureau. (2014). *U.S. Census Bureau: State and county quick facts.* Data derived from population estimate, American community survey, census of population and housing, state and county housing unit estimates, county business patterns, nonemployer statistics, economic census, survey of business owners, building permits. Released May 16, 2014.

U.S. Department of Justice and U.S. Department of Education. (2014). *Dear colleague letter: Nondiscriminatory administration of school discipline.* Washington, DC: Office of Civil Rights, U.S. Department of Education.

Valdez, C. R., Padilla, B., Moore, S. M., & Magana, S. (2013). Feasibility, acceptability, and preliminary outcomes of the Fortaleza Familiares intervention for Latino families facing maternal depression. *Family Process, 52,* 394–410. doi:10.1111/famp.12033

Watters, E. (2012). The wave that brought PTSD to Sri Lanka. In *Crazy like us: The globalization of the American psyche* (pp. 65–125). New York, NY: Simon & Schuster, Inc.

Wood, J. J., Chiu, A. W., Hwang, W., Jacobs, J., & Ifekwunigwe, M. (2008). Adapting cognitive-behavioral therapy for Mexican American students with anxiety disorders: Recommendations for school psychologists. *School Psychology Quarterly, 23,* 515–532. doi:10.1037/1045–3830.23.4.515

Ysseldyke, J., Lekwa, A. J., Kingbeil, D. A., & Cormier, D. C. (2012). Assessment of ecological factors as an integral part of academic and mental health consultation. *Journal of Educational and Psychological Consultation, 22,* 21–43. doi:10.1080 /10474412.2011.649641

PART

IV

Children and Adolescents With Childhood Psychopathologies

12

Evidence-Based Interventions for Anger and Aggression in Children and Adolescents

Tracy Evian Waasdorp, W. John Monopoli, Danielle Centeno, and Stephen S. Leff

OVERVIEW

Peer aggression is a pervasive and costly problem in schools. Although prevalence rates vary across studies, research indicates that many youth are either involved with or witness peer aggression (Wang, Iannotti, & Nansel, 2009; Welsh et al., 2008), with at least 30% of youth experiencing ongoing bullying at school (Robers, Kemp, Truman, & Snyder, 2013). Schools are in a particularly important position to prevent and intervene with aggressive behaviors given that youth spend so much time each school day within this context. In fact, most states have passed laws related to the prevention of aggressive and bullying behaviors (Limber & Small, 2003), sparking an increased focus on school-based intervention programming (Ttofi & Farrington, 2011). Despite laws and policies aimed at preventing aggression and bullying within schools, states often do not have specific and systematic recommendations for ensuring that effective programs chosen match the specific needs of a school, are implemented as intended, and are evaluated on aggression reduction outcomes.

Peer aggression includes behaviors that are negative and intend to cause harm to another peer. For instance, there are several different types of aggression. Physical aggression, which consists of hitting or pushing others, and verbal aggression, which includes threatening, name-calling, and teasing, have long been recognized as the most common forms of aggression, especially among boys (Card, Stucky, Sawalani, & Little, 2008). These forms are often referred to as "overt aggression" in the literature. However, when girls aggress against their peers, they are more likely to use relational forms of aggression (Crick, Ostrov, & Kawabata, 2007). "Relational aggression" is the manipulation of peer relationships and reputations as the means to harm other youth (Crick & Grotpeter, 1995). Given the steady increase in the use of electronic and social media by youth, it is not surprising that peers are increasingly using electronics and social media to aggress (Waasdorp, Horowitz-Johnson, & Leff, in press), which is often called "cyber aggression/bullying" (Kiriakidis & Kavoura, 2010). Although aggression exists on a continuum, meaning that all children exhibit some aggression under certain circumstances, when the aggressive behavior is repeated over time and perpetrated by someone with higher social status than the victim of lower social status, this by definition is "bullying" (Ttofi & Farrington, 2011).

All forms of aggressive behavior have been associated with various maladaptive outcomes throughout childhood and adolescence such as increased substance use, (Becker, Luebbe, Stoppelbein, Greening, & Fite, 2012) academic underachievement, (Fite, Hendrickson, Rubens, Gabrielli, & Evans, 2013), and negative peer relationships (Crick, Murray-Close, & Woods, 2005; Lansford, Malone, Dodge, Pettit, & Bates, 2010). For instance, a number of research studies have found that physical aggressors have higher rates of certain psychiatric disorders such as attention deficit hyperactivity disorder (ADHD), oppositional defiant disorder (ODD), and conduct disorder (Becker, et al., 2012; Zalecki & Hinshaw, 2004); relational aggression also appears to be related to ADHD symptoms (Zalecki & Hinshaw, 2004), and possibly features of borderline personality disorder (Crick et al., 2005) and/or mood disorders (Card et al., 2008; Spieker et al., 2012). Victims of aggressive behavior are at an increased risk for experiencing internalizing symptoms, such as anxiety, depression, and feelings of loneliness, as well as academic difficulties (Polanin, Espelage, & Pigott, 2012; Waasdorp, Pas, O'Brennan, & Bradshaw, 2011; Williams, Fredland, Han, Campbell, & Kub, 2009).

However, it is important to note that aggression can also be adaptive in some circumstances. For instance, many proactive youth find aggressive behavior to be reinforcing such as using relational aggression to achieve social goals (Waasdorp, Baker, Paskewich, & Leff, 2013). Moreover, research shows that there is some evidence that boys' use of physical aggression is associated with increased social status (Waasdorp, et al., 2013; Xie, Li, Boucher, Hutchins, & Cairns, 2006), yet for girls, the use of relational aggression may be associated with increased social status, especially within urban, high-risk environments. Furthermore, youth who specifically use relational aggression are often seen as leaders among peers (Waasdorp et al., 2013). This presents an additional challenge for intervention programs, as programs need to consider ways in which to make alternative behavioral choices more attractive to these youth.

ETIOLOGY AND FACTORS CONTRIBUTING TO ANGER AND AGGRESSION IN CHILDREN AND ADOLESCENTS

To determine best-practice strategies to prevent and intervene with aggressive behavior, it is crucial to understand the etiology of anger and aggression. Recent research suggests that genetics plays a significant role in the development of aggression, as twin studies and meta-analytic reviews estimate heritability as being between 40% and 60% (Burt, 2009; Wang, Niv, Tuvblad, Raine, & Baker, 2013). For instance, although the environment can exacerbate a genetic predisposition for aggression, it can also mitigate its effects, such as research findings indicating that strict parental monitoring in adolescence may diminish the effects of a gene associated with externalizing problems (e.g., aggression, disruptive behavior; Dick et al., 2009). This suggests that, although children may be predisposed to exhibiting behavioral problems, interactions with the environment can determine the extent to which they do.

Environmental influences in the development of aggression have primarily been discussed within the context of Bronfenbrenner's social ecological theory, which views behavior as the result of interactions with several systems influencing the child's development (Bronfenbrenner, 1992). For instance, a lack of emotional support from parents, or witnessing parents using verbal aggression during arguments has been associated with increased aggression (Barboza et al., 2009; Ferguson, San Miguel, & Hartley, 2009). Even more distal contexts, such as the school and neighborhood, can influence whether a child is aggressive. Research shows that children who perceive the school climate as unsafe are more likely to aggress or bully their peers (Goldweber, Waasdorp, & Bradshaw, 2013; Lindstrom Johnson, Waasdorp, Debnam, & Bradshaw, 2013) and children who witness violence in their neighborhoods are also more likely to use aggression to resolve conflicts (Farrell, Mehari, Kramer-Kuhn, & Goncy, 2014).

Research also suggests a link between physiological reactivity to provocations and aggression. Higher reactivity (e.g., higher blood pressure and heart rate) to relational (threats related to social status or relationships) as well as instrumental provocations (e.g., threats related to dominance or physical safety) have been associated with relational aggression (e.g., Murray-Close & Crick, 2007). This suggests the importance of emotion regulation for coping with stress and anger in prevention and intervention programs. These skills are often coupled with social-cognitive retraining strategies based upon Crick and Dodge (1994) social information processing model of aggressive behaviors. For instance, Crick and Dodge identified five steps of social information processing: (a) identification of cues regarding social context and emotion; (b) interpretation of others' intentions; (c) goal adoption; (d) consideration of possible behavioral responses; and (e) actual behavioral response. Children who demonstrate high levels of physical aggression have deficits at each step of this model. Children who demonstrate high levels of relational aggression show deficits mainly in the interpretation phase, as they may mistake a neutral overture for a negative one (Godleski & Ostrov, 2010). As such, similar social-cognitive retraining and emotion regulation are thought to be an appropriate approach to help decrease relational as well as physical aggression (Leff & Waasdorp, 2013).

EVIDENCE-BASED INTERVENTIONS AND EMPIRICAL SUPPORT FOR ANGER AND AGGRESSION IN CHILDREN AND ADOLESCENTS

Many aggression prevention programs are rooted in the ecological framework of development (Bronfenbrenner, 1979), with programming occurring across many settings in the school, and include both school staff and parents. In fact, studies show that intervention programs most effectively reduce aggression when they are multicomponent, have school-wide policies, include the entire school body and parents in trainings and/or meetings, and increase playground supervision (Polanin, et al., 2012; Ttofi & Farrington, 2011). Further, aggression and bullying prevention programs often focus on changing malleable individual factors, such as social-cognitive processing, within the context of broader support across a range of different settings including the peer group, diverse school personnel, and home setting. Taking a multifaceted approach focusing on the individual child in the context of his

or her peer group, school, and community appears to have the best chance for changing aggressive behaviors and the overall school climate. Given these considerations, our reviews of programs focus primarily upon malleable individual, school, and community factors within three well-respected programs.

Coping Power; Walk Away, Ignore, Talk, Seek Help (WITS); and Preventing Relational Aggression in Schools Everyday (PRAISE) are three evidence-based interventions that focus on aggression and victimization prevention. These programs were chosen because they are based on strong psychological theory, use empirically supported techniques, and have demonstrated promising effects across a range of outcome variables. These programs have been evaluated in a randomized trial or well-designed quasi-experimental study (with a control group); address aggression in a multifaceted manner; and utilize novel approaches to engage youth and those supporting youth (e.g., teachers, parents, community leaders) in aggression prevention programming.

The Coping Power program, developed from the previously evaluated Anger Coping Program (Lochman, 1992), was one of the first small-group interventions that was effective in changing youth's physically aggressive behavior. Coping Power is one of the oldest and most well-respected evidence-based programs for physical aggression, and it has been conducted for more than 20 years and across many different parts of the country. Recently, Coping Power was updated to include additional youth sessions and a parent-training component that continue to show success. Studies show that Coping Power produces lower rates of delinquent behaviors and substance use postintervention and at a 1-year follow-up (Lochman & Wells, 2003, 2004), along with lower self-reported substance use, improved social competence, and behavioral improvement (i.e., self-regulation, self-control, and impulse control), as rated by the teacher (Lochman & Wells, 2002). All manuals and materials, which include training guides for both the child and the parent components for Coping Power, are available on the Internet (www.copingpower.com) for review and require a fee.

The WITS program was developed through a collaboration of elementary school educators, community-based nonprofit organizations, and university-based developmental psychologists (Leadbeater & Hoglund, 2006). WITS was included because of its unique emphasis on victimization and community engagement. WITS takes an inclusive, multisetting approach to reducing peer victimization and enhancing children's social skills at the school and classroom level (Leadbeater & Hoglund, 2006) by incorporating many important adults from the community (police) into the intervention. WITS, unlike most aggression interventions, is one of a few that focuses primarily on victimization (of relational and physical aggression) as opposed to perpetration. Furthermore, WITS addresses sibling and parental relationships, which is an important, yet often overlooked, component in aggressive interventions. Program materials are also available on the Internet, where some materials will require a fee (www.witsprogram.ca).

The PRAISE program was developed from the Friend to Friend program (F2F; Leff et al., 2007; Leff et al., 2009), an evidence-based, small-group intervention that reduced urban African American girls' relationally aggressive behaviors. PRAISE was developed through a partnership-based approach, known as participatory action research (PAR), for blending empirically based strategies from F2F with feedback from urban students, teachers, parents, and administrators (Leff et al., 2010). Through this process, PRAISE was adapted into a classroom-based prevention program designed to reduce overt and relational aggression for urban youth. PRAISE was selected due to its use of a partnership-based approach to contextualize a program to specifically meet the needs of urban African American youth as well as its strong focus on relational aggression. Given that PRAISE was developed by using PAR to meet the needs of under-resourced urban schools, it is not surprising that the intervention was found to be very applicable and relatable for those living within the urban school settings. This is a strength of PRAISE as few aggression prevention programs were designed to specifically and effectively meet the needs of minority youth, with a strong focus on all forms of aggression, especially relational forms. Research on PRAISE shows increase in knowledge of social information processing, better anger-management techniques and lower levels of relational and overt aggression, especially among girls (Leff et al., 2010).

In summary, although common themes are addressed throughout the programs, the implementation styles and modes of operation vary by intervention. Information regarding implementation of all three programs can be found in Table 12.1. A step-by-step guideline for implementation of each evidence-based intervention is given in the subsequent sections.

HOW TO: A GUIDE TO THE IMPLEMENTATION OF INTERVENTIONS FOR ANGER AND AGGRESSION IN CHILDREN AND ADOLESCENTS

Coping Power[1]

- Small-group format of four to six physically aggressive third to seventh graders
  o 34 sessions over 15 to 18 months with individual sessions approximately every 2 months
- School counselors can facilitate the sessions
  o Facilitators receive 10 hours of training and have weekly supervision

Session Design: Year 1—Implementation of Child Program of Coping Power

- Session 1: Introductions and developing group structure
  o Introduce the program and discuss the expectations of the youth while developing group rules and a point system.
- Sessions 2 to 3: Goal setting
  o Explain barriers to goal setting and develop a "buddy system" where students are paired together to help maintain and achieve goals.
- Session 4: Study skills
  o Discuss how to improve academic skills and develop new educational skills to use at home.
- Sessions 5 and 6: Feelings identification
  o Acknowledge different components of emotional states, identifying situational triggers, discussing difficulty with expressing feelings, and recognizing cues or levels of anger.
- Session 7: Coping with anger
  o Review methods of dealing with anger and begin the use of anger coping or self-control strategies.

TABLE 12.1

DETAILS OF SELECTED PROGRAMS

Title of Program	Mode of Operation	Theorized Population for Program	Implementation	Materials/Instructional Strategies	Targeted Behaviors/Skills	Assessment
Coping Power (Lochman, et al., 2013)	• School & community-wide	• 3rd–7th grade	• 34-session therapy group	• Videotaping; including problem-solving video and role-plays	• Reduction of aggressive behavior	• Coder rating of engagement for therapist
	• Closed, small group	• 4–6 children per group with two group leaders	• 50–60 min., weekly for 16–18 months	• Workbook; activity sheets and homework assignments	• Coping with peer pressure	• Teacher and parent ratings of behavioral problems
	• Dual-component (child/parent)		• A graduate-level research staff member and a school counselor conduct the child component • Two graduate-level research staff members conduct the parent component	• Point system with incentives for following rules and positive participation	• Improve social competence	• Self-report of substance use and delinquent behavior
	• Inclusion is assessment based		• Children are expected to have brief individual session every 4–6 weeks • Booster sessions; six follow-up sessions	• Manual available online; fee required	• Prevent substance abuse	• Self and parent reports of mediating processes
Walk away, Ignore, Talk, Seek help (WITS, Leadbeater et al., 2003)	• School & community-wide	• K–3rd grade	• Read three or more WITS books, implement three or more WITS classroom activities	• Literature & activities to reinforce your WITS, police liaison visit class	• Reduction/prevention of victimization	• Parent and teacher reports of child social competence
	• Universal prevention	• U.S. & Canadian	• Teachers, principals, playground assistants, librarians	• Activity books, siblings pamphlets to take home	• Promote positive conflict resolution strategies	• Self-report of peer victimization

(continued)

147

TABLE 12.1

DETAILS OF SELECTED PROGRAMS (continued)

Title of Program	Mode of Operation	Theorized Population for Program	Implementation	Materials/Instructional Strategies	Targeted Behaviors/Skills	Assessment
		• SES & ethnically diverse • Boys & girls	• Adults receive 2-hour in-service training	• WITS posters • Manual available online	• Increase social responsibility school- & community-wide	• Parent and teacher reports of aggression and emotional problems
PReventing Aggression In Schools Everyday (PRAISE; Leff et al., 2010)	• School based • Universal prevention (though has been examined for at-risk youth)	• 3rd–5th grade • Urban elementary schools • Boys and girls	• 20 classroom sessions • 40 min., two times per week • Bachelors- and masters-level facilitators partner with teachers to implement intervention • Facilitators trained by a licensed psychologist (4 hours per week for 2 months) • Booster sessions; session follow-up	• Culturally relevant cartoons & videos to depict SIP skills, perspective-taking, bystander of aggression • Role-play • Discussions • Manual & integrity monitoring sheets available	• Identifying physiological signs of arousal, & applying SIP skills to a range of social situations • Promoting empathy and positive bystander behavior • Decrease relational & physical aggression • Improve problem solving • Increase prosocial behaviors • Gain leadership skills	• Integrity monitoring sheets • Knowledge of social problem solving; Attributional processing • Teacher report of aggression • Self-report of peer sympathy

- Sessions 8 to 10: Using self-statements for anger coping
  - Reinforce self-talk, distraction training, and how to use these skills in classroom.
- Session 11: Relaxation and barriers to self-control
  - Teach self-control through deep breathing and identify barriers to the use of self-control.
- Sessions 12 to 14: Perspective taking
  - Identify different perspectives in social situations, applying problem-solving skills to these situations, and discussing the idea of accidental issues.
- Session 15: Problem solving
  - Introduce problem solving and describe how to "pick apart" problems in order to resolve them.
- Sessions 16 to 19: Social problem solving
  - Identify and evaluate choices when dealing with a problem and reinforce persistence when problem solving can be effective.
- Sessions 20 to 22: Group project
  - Create, film, and view the videotape, done by group members, which is used to demonstrate the use of strategies.

Session Design: Year 2—Child Program
- Sessions 23 and 24: Review
  - Discuss and review group structure and purpose along with strategies learned over the course of the previous year.
- Session 25: Applying social problem solving to teacher conflict
  - Discuss teacher perspective and practice the use of problem-solving skills when dealing with teacher conflict.
- Session 26: Applying social problem solving to friendship development
  - Practice the skill to help youth in joining a group activity or making friends.
- Session 27: Applying social problem solving to group entry
  - Demonstrate skills associated with group entry and peer negotiation.
- Session 28: Applying problem-solving strategies to sibling conflict
  - Identify issues related to sibling conflict and role-play alternative solutions.

- Session 29: Applying social problem solving to peer pressure
  - Discuss what peer pressure is, why it works, and how to resist it.
- Session 30: Developing skills to refuse peer pressure
  - Use role-play to develop refusal skills. These skills include, but are not limited to, leaving the situation, saying "no thanks," or suggesting a better idea.
- Session 31: Problem solving related to neighborhood and/or community problems
  - Practice the use of problem-solving skills with neighborhood problems and define group status.
- Session 32: Peer pressure poster created
  - Create a poster to reinforce public commitment to use of refusal skills.
- Session 33: Developing positive relationships
  - Identify strengths and discuss good leadership qualities.
- Session 34: Termination
  - Review skills learned; hand out certificates of completion; and plan an end-of-the-year party.

Walk Away, Ignore, Talk, Seek Help

- Determine if WITS is the best fit for your school (please see the description given earlier in the chapter).
  - Review the WITS program for a good fit between schools goals and objectives.
- Learn how to use the WITS program.
  - Visit the website where staff can complete an accreditation program.
  - School staff who are interested in being WITS leaders can earn accreditation through a 90-minute program, which is accessible on the Internet (www.witsprogram.ca).
- Obtain WITS resources and share them.
  - Order WITS guides, lesson plans, videos, or posters that are reflective of the needs of the staff using the program and ensure that the resources are easily accessible.
- Identify a community leader for your school.
  - Partner with community member(s), such as a police officer, firefighter, paramedic, athlete, or elder and invite them to participate in the training program.

- Conduct the swearing-in ceremony and tug-of-help at your school.
  - Organize a special assembly, to be at the beginning of the school year, and led by the community leader(s).
- Integrate WITS strategies into daily classroom.
  - Begin the use of WITS resources and materials during classroom activities.
  - WITS strategies are integrated into literacy lessons with teachers or other school staff implementing at least three WITS lesson plans throughout a school year (e.g. reading a story book that focuses on a specific form of bullying; Hoglund, Hosan, & Leadbeater, 2012).
- Arrange follow-up visits.
  - Invite community leader(s) to make regular visits to the classroom(s) throughout the year. This time can be used to discuss WITS strategies and distribute WITS reminder gifts to students.
- Invite parents to participate.
  - Send home a WITS pamphlet to parents to introduce the program and hold a WITS information night.
- Sustain the momentum.
  - Continue the use of WITS by having staff members discuss these skills with other members of the school and organize school-wide activities related to WITS.

Preventing Relational Aggression in Schools Everyday

- Classroom-based intervention led by a master's-level clinician combined with the classroom teacher
- Sessions 1 and 2: Introduction to program and friendship problems
  - Introduce the program's premise of students being "friendship detectives" who learn to identify and handle different types of friendship problems.
- Sessions 3 and 4: Feelings identification—using "Face, Body and other Information" (FBI-Self)
  - Discuss where friendship problems happen (at school), describing feelings and learning how to deal with friendship problems by identifying feelings with the use of FBI-Self.
- Sessions 5 and 6: Strategies for coping with anger—"Cool it before action" (CIA)

- Explain and practice the use of CIA strategies to stay calm when getting angry. These strategies include: self-talk, counting to 10, deep breaths, and imagery.
- Sessions 7: Interpreting intent of aggression—FBI-Other
  - Teach the use of FBI-Other to help understand how another child is feeling by looking at the child's face, body, and other information.
- Session 8: Interpreting intent of aggression—FBI-Other to assume an accident (AAA)
  - Review all previously discussed strategies along with introducing AAA, which asks participating students, unless 100% sure that a child did something on purpose, should assume an accident.
- Session 9: Choosing a response to aggressive behaviors
  - Review choices, or options, that group members can choose when responding to a friendship problem.
- Session 10: Introducing rumors as a friendship problem
  - Discuss the types of rumors, why children may start them, and the consequences of rumors.
- Sessions 11 and 12: Cyberbullying
  - Review cyberbullying, how it is different from other forms of bullying, and how to use PRAISE strategies to handle cyberbullying situations.
- Sessions 13 and 14: Understanding empathy
  - Introduce the concept of empathy and why it is important to identify feelings of others.
- Sessions 15 and 16: Perspective taking
  - Discuss the difficulties and benefits of perspective taking and conduct a two-sided vase exercise that demonstrates taking someone else's perspective into consideration when problem solving.
- Sessions 17 and 18: Being a positive bystander
  - Review the role of a positive bystander and what barriers to being a positive bystander may be.
- Session 19: Developing a class plan to prevent friendship problems
  - Review strategies through the use of a jeopardy game and develop class rules and strategies to help when dealing with friendship problems after PRAISE.

- Session 20: Termination and wrap up
  - Fine-tune the class plan, review all materials, and hand out certificates of achievement.

Challenges to Program Success

There are several important things to consider when deciding on an evidence-based program for implementation within your school or community-based setting. A best-practice program is effective within a particular setting only when: (a) it is based on solid psychological theory and empirically based strategies (such as the three programs highlighted within this chapter); (b) the program is considered a good match by key stakeholders within the particular school or community setting in which it is intended to be implemented; and (c) the program can be implemented with strong fidelity, that is, in a systematic manner following structured manuals and guidelines (Durlak & DuPre, 2008; Weare & Nind, 2011). The second and third points are related to one another because a best-practice program that is "dropped" into a setting that is not a particularly good match for implementation and/or without having appropriate school and community buy-in is not likely to be successful. Coping Power is a targeted intervention for physically and overtly aggressive youth that has shown strong success in reducing self-reported substance use and physically aggressive and impulsive behaviors. Thus, it would be highly recommended for use with schools having these types of problems. In contrast, it does not focus on relational or cyber forms and it is a relatively time-intensive program, which may make this less feasible to implement for some schools. WITS has a strong focus on relational victimization (as opposed to perpetration) and is intended for younger children (e.g., elementary aged, K-4) and for schools where there is active community engagement and involvement in the program. It includes lessons related to all forms of aggression and/or victimization, with rigorous research studies underway to examine the effectiveness of the program.

CONCLUSION

A best-practice program that never makes it out of the box it is packaged in, or a program that is implemented in a nontraditional manner is unlikely to have success. Instead, we recommend careful consideration of the needs of a particular school or community and how that best matches to a program designed to meet those needs. Having local champions endorse the program is also an important aspect of program buy-in and sustainability.

NOTE

1. Details are provided for the primary (youth group) component; however, details of the parent component of the programs can be found in Lochman and Wells (2003); Lochman, Wells, Qu, and Chen (2013); Wells, Lenhardt, and Lochman (1996), and http://www.copingpower.com

SELECT BIBLIOGRAPHY

Leff, S. S., & Waasdorp, T. E. (2013). Effect of aggression and bullying on children and adolescents: Implications for prevention and intervention. *Current Psychiatry Reports, 15*(3), 343–343. doi:http://dx.doi .org/10.1007/s11920–012–0343–2
This article reviews the literature on aggression and bullying among school-age youth. It highlights considerations for intervening and preventing these behaviors with implications for psychiatrists and other mental health professionals.

http://www.stopbullying.gov/
This website is managed by the U.S. Department of Health and Human Services. It provides evidence-based information regarding definitions of bullying and cyber bullying, who is at risk, prevention, and intervention.

Hymel, S., McClure, R., Miller, M., Shumka, E., & Trach, J. (2015). Addressing school bullying: Insights from theories of group processes. *Journal of Applied Developmental Psychology, 37,* 16–24. doi:http://dx.doi .org/10.1016/j.appdev. 2014.11.008
Although not cited in this chapter, this article discusses the importance of viewing school bullying as a group and systemic problem and not a dyadic (bully and victim) problem, which is proving to be the most effective way to decrease bullying and victimization.

REFERENCES

Barboza, G. E., Schiamberg, L. B., Oehmke, J., Korzeniewski, S. J., Post, L. A., & Heraux, C. G. (2009). Individual characteristics and the multiple contexts of adolescent bullying: An ecological perspective. *Journal of Youth and Adolescence*, *38*(1), 101–121.

Becker, S. P., Luebbe, A. M., Stoppelbein, L., Greening, L., & Fite, P. J. (2012). Aggression among children with ADHD, anxiety, or co-occurring symptoms: Competing exacerbation and attenuation hypotheses. *Journal of Abnormal Child Psychology*, *40*(4), 527–542.

Bronfenbrenner, U. (1979). *The ecology of human development: Experiments by nature and design.* Cambridge, MA: Harvard University Press.

Bronfenbrenner, U. (1992). Ecological systems theory. In R. Vasta (Ed.), *Six theories of child development: Revised formulations and current issues* (pp. 187–249). London, England: Jessica Kingsley.

Burt, S. A. (2009). Rethinking environmental contributions to child and adolescent psychopathology: A meta-analysis of shared environmental influences. *Psychological Bulletin*, *135*(4), 608–637.

Card, N. A., Stucky, B. D., Sawalani, G. M., & Little, T. D. (2008). Direct and indirect aggression during childhood and adolescence: A meta-analytic review of gender differences, intercorrelations, and relations to maladjustment. *Child Development*, *79*(5), 1185–1229.

Crick, N. R., & Dodge, K. A. (1994). A review and reformulation of social information processing mechanisms in children's social adjustment. *Psychological Bulletin, 115*, 74–101.

Crick, N. R., & Grotpeter, J. K. (1995). Relational aggression, gender, and social-psychological adjustment. *Child Development*, *66*(3), 710–722.

Crick, N. R., Murray-Close, D., & Woods, K. (2005). Borderline personality features in childhood: A short-term longitudinal study. *Development and Psychopathology*, *17*(4), 1051–1070.

Crick, N. R., Ostrov, J. M., & Kawabata, Y. (2007). Relational aggression and gender: An overview. In D. J. Flannery, A. T. Vazsonyi, & I. D. Waldman (Eds.), *The Cambridge handbook of violent behavior and aggression* (pp. 245–259). New York, NY: Cambridge.

Dick, D. M., Latendresse, S. J., Lansford, J. E., Budde, J. P., Goate, A., Dodge, K. A., Pettit, G. S., & Bates, J. E. (2009). Role of GABRA2 in trajectories of externalizing behavior across development and evidence of moderation by parental monitoring. *Archives of General Psychiatry*, *66*(6), 649–657.

Durlak, J. A., & DuPre, E. P. (2008). Implementation matters: A review of research on the influence of implementation on program outcomes and the factors affecting implementation. *American Journal of Community Psychology*, *41*(3–4), 327–350.

Farrell, A. D., Mehari, K. R., Kramer-Kuhn, A., & Goncy, E. A. (2014). The impact of victimization and witnessing violence on physical aggression among high-risk adolescents. *Child Development*, *85*(4), 1694–1710.

Ferguson, C. J., San Miguel, C., & Hartley, R. D. (2009). A multivariate analysis of youth violence and aggression: The influence of family, peers, depression, and media violence. *The Journal of Pediatrics*, *155*(6), 904–908.e3.

Fite, P. J., Hendrickson, M., Rubens, S. L., Gabrielli, J., & Evans, S. (2013). The role of peer rejection in the link between reactive aggression and academic performance. *Child & Youth Care Forum*, *42*(3), 193–205.

Godleski, S. A., & Ostrov, J. M. (2010). Relational aggression and hostile attribution biases: Testing multiple statistical methods and models. *Journal of Abnormal Child Psychology*, *38*(4), 447–458.

Goldweber, A., Waasdorp, T. E., & Bradshaw, C. P. (2013). Examining the link between forms of bullying behaviors and perceptions of safety and belonging among secondary school students. *Journal of School Psychology*, *51*(4), 469–485.

Hoglund, W. L., Hosan, N. E., & Leadbeater, B. J. (2012). Using your wits: A 6-year follow-up of a peer victimization prevention program. *School Psychology Review*, *41*(2), 193–214.

Johnson, L. S., Waasdorp, T. E., Debnam, K., & Bradshaw, C. P. (2013). The role of bystander perceptions and school climate in influencing victims' responses to bullying: To retaliate or seek support? *Journal of Criminology, 2013*, 10. doi:10.1155/2013/780460.

Kiriakidis, S. P., & Kavoura, A. (2010). Cyberbullying: A review of the literature on harassment through the Internet and other electronic means. *Family & Community Health*, *33*(2), 82–93.

Lansford, J. E., Malone, P. S., Dodge, K. A., Pettit, G. S., & Bates, J. E. (2010). Developmental cascades of peer rejection, social information processing biases, and aggression during middle childhood. *Development and Psychopathology, 22*(3), 593–602.

Leadbeater, B., & Hoglund, W. (2006). Changing the social contexts of peer victimization. *Journal of the Canadian Academy of Child and Adolescent Psychiatry, 15*(1), 21–26.

Leff, S. S., Angelucci, J., Goldstein, A. B., Cardaciotto, L., Paskewich, B., & Grossman, M. B. (2007). Using a participatory action research model to create a school-based intervention program for relationally aggressive girls—the friend to friend program. In J. E. Zins, M. J. Elias & C. A. Maher (Eds.), *Bullying, victimization, and peer harassment: A handbook of prevention and intervention.* (pp. 199–218). New York, NY: Haworth Press.

Leff, S. S., Gullan, R. L., Paskewich, B. S., Abdul-Kabir, S., Jawad, A. F., Grossman, M.,…Power, T. J. (2009). An initial evaluation of a culturally adapted social problem-solving and relational aggression prevention program for urban African American relationally aggressive girls. *Journal of Prevention & Intervention in the Community, 37*(4), 260–274.

Leff, S. S., & Waasdorp, T. E. (2013). Effect of aggression and bullying on children and adolescents: Implications for prevention and intervention. *Current Psychiatry Reports, 15*(3), 343–343. doi:http://dx.doi .org/10.1007/s11920–012-0343–2

Leff, S. S., Waasdorp, T. E., Paskewich, B., Gullan, R. L., Jawad, A. F., Macevoy, J. P.,…Power, T. J. (2010). The preventing relational aggression in schools everyday program: A preliminary evaluation of acceptability and impact. *School Psychology Review, 39*(4), 569–587.

Limber, S. P., & Small, M. A. (2003). State laws and policies to address bullying in schools. *School Psychology Review, 32*(3), 445–455.

Lochman, J. E. (1992). Cognitive-behavioral intervention with aggressive boys: Three-year follow-up and preventive effects. *Journal of Consulting and Clinical Psychology, 60*(3), 426–432.

Lochman, J. E., & Wells, K. C. (2002). The Coping Power program at the middle-school transition: Universal and indicated prevention effects. *Psychology of Addictive Behaviors: Journal of the Society of Psychologists in Addictive Behaviors, 16*(4 Suppl), S40–S54.

Lochman, J. E., & Wells, K. C. (2003). Effectiveness of the coping power program and of classroom intervention with aggressive children: Outcomes at a 1-year follow-up. *Behavior Therapy, 34*(4), 493–515.

Lochman, J. E., & Wells, K. C. (2004). The coping power program for preadolescent aggressive boys and their parents: Outcome effects at the 1-year follow-up. *Journal of Consulting and Clinical Psychology, 72*(4), 571–578.

Lochman, J. E., Wells, K. C., Qu, L., & Chen, L. (2013). Three-year follow-up of coping power intervention effects: Evidence of neighborhood moderation? *Prevention Science: The Official Journal of the Society for Prevention Research, 14*(4), 364–376.

Murray-Close, D., & Crick, N. R. (2007). Gender differences in the association between cardiovascular reactivity and aggressive conduct. *International Journal of Psychophysiology: Official Journal of the International Organization of Psychophysiology, 65*(2), 103–113.

Polanin, J. R., Espelage, D. L., & Pigott, T. D. (2012). A meta-analysis of school-based bullying prevention programs' effects on bystander intervention behavior. *School Psychology Review, 41*(1), 47–65.

Robers, S., Kemp, J., Truman, J., & Snyder, T. D. (2013). *Indicators of school crime and safety: 2012* (nces 2013–036/ncj 241446). Retrieved from http://nces .ed.gov/programs/crimeindicators/ crimeindicators2012/index.asp

Spieker, S. J., Campbell, S. B., Vandergrift, N., Pierce, K. M., Cauffman, E., Susman, E. J., & Roisman, G. I.; the NICHD Early Child Care Research Network. (2012). Relational aggression in middle childhood: Predictors and adolescent outcomes. *Social Development (Oxford, England), 21*(2), 354–375.

Ttofi, M. M., & Farrington, D. P. (2011). Effectiveness of school-based programs to reduce bullying: A systematic and meta-analytic review. *Journal of Experimental Criminology, 7*(1), 27–56. doi:10.1007/s11292–010-9109–1

Waasdorp, T. E., Baker, C. N., Paskewich, B. S., & Leff, S. S. (2013). The association between forms of aggression, leadership, and social status among urban youth. *Journal of Youth and Adolescence, 42*(2), 263–274.

Waasdorp, T. E., Horowitz-Johnson, Z., & Leff, S. S. (in press). Cyberbullying across the lifespan: Risk factors and consequences. In C. P. Bradshaw (Ed.), *Handbook of bullying prevention: A lifecourse perspective*. National Association of Social Workers (NASW) Press.

Waasdorp, T. E., Pas, E. T., O'Brennan, L. M., & Bradshaw, C. P. (2011). A multilevel perspective on the climate of bullying: Discrepancies among students, school staff, and parents. *Journal of School Violence*, 10(2), 115–132.

Wang, J., Iannotti, R. J., & Nansel, T. R. (2009). School bullying among adolescents in the United States: Physical, verbal, relational, and cyber. *The Journal of Adolescent Health: Official Publication of the Society for Adolescent Medicine*, 45(4), 368–375.

Wang, P., Niv, S., Tuvblad, C., Raine, A., & Baker, L. A. (2013). The genetic and environmental overlap between aggressive and non-aggressive antisocial behavior in children and adolescents using the self-report delinquency interview (SR-DI). *Journal of Criminal Justice*, 41(5), 277–284.

Weare, K., & Nind, M. (2011). Mental health promotion and problem prevention in schools: What does the evidence say? *Health Promotion International*, 26(Suppl. 1), i29–i69. doi:10.1093/heapro/dar075

Welsh, B. C., Loeber, R., Stevens, B. R., Stouthamer-Loeber, M., Cohen, M. A., & Farrington, D. P. (2008). Costs of juvenile crime in urban areas: A longitudinal perspective. *Youth Violence and Juvenile Justice*, 6(1), 3–27.

Williams, J. R., Fredland, N., Han, H. R., Campbell, J. C., & Kub, J. E. (2009). Relational aggression and adverse psychosocial and physical health symptoms among urban adolescents. *Public Health Nursing*, 26(6), 489–499.

Xie, H., Li, Y., Boucher, S. M., Hutchins, B. C., & Cairns, B. D. (2006). What makes a girl (or a boy) popular (or unpopular)? African American children's perceptions and developmental differences. *Developmental Psychology*, 42(4), 599–612.

Zalecki, C. A., & Hinshaw, S. P. (2004). Overt and relational aggression in girls with attention deficit hyperactivity disorder. *Journal of Clinical Child and Adolescent Psychology: The Official Journal for the Society of Clinical Child and Adolescent Psychology, American Psychological Association, Division 53*, 33(1), 125–137.

Evidence-Based Interventions for Bullying Among Children and Adolescents

Susan M. Swearer, Scott M. Fluke, Sara E. Gonzalez, and Zachary R. Myers

OVERVIEW

School bullying and peer victimization are pervasive phenomena that affect many youth. Although bullying is viewed as an important public health problem and the most frequent form of school violence, many inconsistencies in defining and assessing bullying still exist (Swearer, Siebecker, Johnsen-Frerichs, & Wang, 2010), hindering the comparability of research in assessment, prevention, and intervention strategies (Gladden, Vivolo-Kantor, Hamburger, & Lumpkin, 2014). As an effort to increase consistency of measurement and distinguish bullying from other forms of misbehavior or types of aggression, the Centers for Disease Control and Prevention (CDC) along with the U.S. Department of Education have provided a uniform definition and description of the types of bullying. According to the CDC report, bullying is:

> Any unwanted aggressive behavior(s) by another youth or group of youths who are not siblings or current dating partners that involves an observed or perceived power imbalance and is repeated multiple times or is highly likely to be repeated. Bullying may inflict harm or distress on the targeted youth including physical, psychological, social, or educational harm. (p. 7)

Thus, students are victimized when they are highly likely to be a repeated target of intentional negative actions by one or more students who are perceived by the victim to be more verbally, physically, socially, or psychologically powerful.

As described by Gladden et al. (2014), bullying can include both direct and indirect forms. Direct bullying is a relatively open aggressive act on the targeted youth, whereas indirect bullying is not directly communicated to the student being targeted (i.e., spreading rumors). Moreover, physical (e.g., hitting, kicking, punching, and pushing), verbal (e.g., taunting, name calling, threats, and offensive written notes or hand gestures), relational (e.g., spreading rumors and posting embarrassing images/comments in a physical or electronic space without the target's permission), and damage to property (e.g., destroying target's property in his or her presence and deleting personal electronic information) have been identified as specific forms or dimensions of bullying (Gladden et al., 2014). To add yet another layer to this complex social dynamic, bullying involvement cannot be parsed into neat categorical labels. Bullying happens across a continuum where students involved do not necessarily have fixed roles, but rather fluctuate between being a perpetrator of bullying behaviors, being a target, being both a perpetrator and a target, being a bystander, or having no involvement at all (Ryoo, Wang, & Swearer, 2014; Swearer, Collins, Radliff, & Wang, 2011).

Bullying is increasingly recognized as a prevalent phenomenon with recent research finding approximately 30% of youth reporting being victims of bullying (DeVoe & Murphy, 2011). However, until data from national and longitudinal studies have been systematically gathered and a uniform definition is used, prevalence rates will not be definitive; instead, the use of local and state data, in order to inform bullying intervention efforts, is recommended (Evans, Fraser, & Cotter, 2014). Thus, bullying represents a significant problem for youth involved, in any role along the continuum, and is associated with a plethora of negative outcomes (i.e., depression, anxiety, and isolation; O'Brennan, Bradshaw, & Sawyer, 2009). Additionally, there are numerous individual, peer, school, familial, and community factors that influence bullying, all of which have an impact on youth perceptions of school climate and overall social–emotional functioning (Swearer, Espelage, Vaillancourt, & Hymel, 2010).

ETIOLOGY AND FACTORS CONTRIBUTING TO BULLYING AMONG CHILDREN AND ADOLESCENTS

Bullying is a complex social relationship problem. Practitioners must think of bullying beyond just an issue between an individual bully and his or her victim. Instead, bullying must be conceptualized as being "multiply-determined and multiply-influenced" (Swearer & Espelage, 2011, p. 4). That is, bullying follows the principle of equifinality (Cicchetti & Rogosch, 1996), meaning that a variety of factors can ultimately lead to involvement in the bullying dynamic. Thus, there is no single cause of bullying behaviors.

The social–ecological model of bullying (Swearer & Doll, 2001) has been proposed as an ecological theory examining the multitude of factors that contribute to involvement in bullying. Expanding from Bronfenbrenner's seminal work on social–ecological theory (Bronfenbrenner, 1979), the social–ecological model of bullying describes a series of interrelated systems in which

youths interact with their environment. Variables at the individual, family, peer group, school, community, and culture levels have been shown to predict involvement in the bullying continuum, whether as a bully, bully-victim, victim, bystander, or a combination of roles.

Some individual factors are not subject to change, but are still important to understand in predicting bullying. Males are more likely to engage in physical bullying than females, and males engage in similar levels of social bullying as females (Card, Stucky, Sawalani, & Little, 2008; Underwood & Rosen, 2011). Bullying is most prevalent among middle school youth, particularly after students' transition into a new building or social group (Pellegrini & Long, 2002). Some individual causes are amenable to change. Preexisting high levels of anxiety and/ or depression, impulsivity, lack of empathy, and pro-bullying attitudes predicted involvement in bullying (Lee, 2011). At the family level, youth from homes where there are high levels of aggression and violence are more likely to engage in bullying (Bowes, Arseneault, Maughan, Taylor, & Moffitt, 2009). Additionally, authoritarian parenting styles increase the risk of involvement in bullying, as children are often not taught effective problem-solving strategies (Rodriguez, 2010).

Peer and school factors play a critical role in bullying. At the peer level, youth often engage in bullying as a means to gain popularity or social attention (Pellegrini & Long, 2002; Ross & Horner, 2009). Aggressive youth are also prone to spending time with aggressive peers who may model and reinforce bullying (i.e., homophily; Espelage, Holt, & Henkel, 2003). Bystanders can also play a causal role in bullying. When bystanders passively observe bullying or actively reinforce the perpetrator (e.g., laughing and joining in), bullying is seen as more acceptable and thus more likely to recur (Gini, Pozzoli, Borghi, & Franzoni, 2008; Ross & Horner, 2009). At the school level, effective behavior management systems can reduce bullying behavior (Lee, 2011), while lack of supervision can increase the likelihood of bullying (Vaillancourt et al., 2010).

The community and cultural levels of the social–ecological model include broader factors that lead to involvement in bullying. Research on these broad factors is difficult, and thus limited data are available. However, cultural factors, such as involvement in gangs (Espelage & Swearer, 2010) and religious ideology (Khoury-Kassabri, Benbenishty, Astor, & Zeria, 2004), were found to predict school aggression. Lack of access to mental health resources and lack of community resources, such as youth camps or parks, may play a role as well (Lee, 2011).

The social–ecological model underscores the assertion that bullying is a complex phenomenon that cannot be explained by a simple cause and effect relationship. Instead, practitioners must consider the entire ecology of youth in order to understand why bullying is happening. Factors at each level make up the etiology of bullying, and successful interventions are likely to be those that address multiple levels in a comprehensive fashion.

EVIDENCE-BASED INTERVENTIONS AND EMPIRICAL SUPPORT FOR BULLYING AMONG CHILDREN AND ADOLESCENTS

Consistent with an increase in research on bullying over the past two decades, bullying prevention and intervention programming has also dramatically increased. Although there exists a plethora of antibullying curricula, books, workshops, plays, movies, and assemblies that are marketed to school personnel, few of these programs include any formal research evaluation. This is troubling, as schools are buying and implementing anti-bullying programming that does not have scientific data that support their effectiveness. Fortunately, bullying prevention and intervention researchers are turning their attention to program evaluation in addition to conducting basic research. A recent meta-analysis suggested that several programs have had a positive impact (Ttofi & Farrington, 2011) and a body of research is building for the support of Positive Behavioral Interventions and Supports (PBIS; www.pbis.org) and for the Collaborative for Academic, Social, and Emotional Learning (CASEL; www.casel.org). In the next section of this chapter, we review the research on *Expect Respect*, *Second Step*, and the *RULER* program, curricula with outcome data from U.S. schools.

HOW TO: A GUIDE TO THE IMPLEMENTATION OF INTERVENTIONS FOR BULLYING AMONG CHILDREN AND ADOLESCENTS

Expect Respect: Bullying Prevention in PBIS

PBIS is an evidence-based framework for reducing a wide variety of problem behavior in school settings (Bradshaw, Mitchell, & Leaf, 2010; Flannery, Fenning, Kato, & McIntosh, 2014). Bullying prevention within the PBIS framework typically follows the Expect Respect curriculum (Nese, Horner, Dickey, Stiller, & Tomlanovich, 2014). The Expect Respect curriculum is available to download for no charge from the PBIS website (www.pbis.org), is designed for use with middle or high school students, and is implemented school-wide (Stiller, Nese, Tomlanovich, Horner, & Ross, 2013). A curriculum built on the same behavioral principles as Expect Respect is also available for elementary schools (Ross, Horner, & Stiller, 2014).

Expect Respect is based on research demonstrating that bullying is frequently reinforced by social attention (Ross & Horner, 2009). Therefore, if social attention can be decreased or removed when bullying occurs, bullying should stop and it is less likely to reoccur in the future. To accomplish this goal, Expect Respect seeks to teach five core skills to students (Stiller et al., 2013). These skills are taught through direct instruction, guided feedback, and role-plays, and include:

1. The ability to discriminate between respectful and disrespectful behavior
2. The ability to use a predetermined "stop phrase" if someone is being disrespectful to the student
3. The ability to use a stop phrase if someone is being disrespectful to another student
4. The ability to respond with an appropriate "stop strategy" if asked to stop by another student
5. The ability to seek help appropriately from adults when needed

The following steps can be employed to implement the Expect Respect curriculum:

1. *Implement school-wide PBIS procedures.* Implementing PBIS school-wide is a large undertaking. However, effective use of PBIS procedures

can lead to significant academic and behavioral gains for the student body (Bradshaw et al., 2010). Expect Respect is built on the same principles as PBIS, and is most likely to be effective at reducing bullying in a school that is already using a PBIS framework (Stiller et al., 2013).

2. *Develop a school-wide stop signal.* The school-wide stop signal serves as a visual and auditory cue for bullying perpetrators and bystanders that a behavior is disrespectful. The signal must be used school-wide to ensure that all students understand what the signal means. Furthermore, the signal should be short, developmentally appropriate, and easy to remember in order to maximize the likelihood that it will be used by students (Ross et al., 2014). The signal should include both a physical gesture (e.g., a raised hand or the "time-out" signal) and a verbal response (e.g., "stop," "that's enough," "quit it").

3. *Teach all faculty and staff the* Expect Respect *procedures.* In order for faculty and staff to teach students the Expect Respect curriculum, they must first understand it themselves as well as gain confidence that the program will work (i.e., staff "buy-in" must be obtained). All school personnel are expected to participate in the program, including teachers, administrators, office staff, and support staff (Stiller et al., 2013). This allows students to report bullying situations to any adult and to be confident that every staff member will respond in a consistent fashion. To accomplish this, two all-staff training sessions should be conducted. During the first training session, faculty and staff engage in discussions about modeling respect, the etiology and consequences of bullying behaviors, and discriminating between respectful and disrespectful behaviors, including which behaviors warrant specific adult intervention (e.g., ignoring, intervening, or making an office referral). During the second staff-training session, staff are taught how to respond to reports of bullying and other disrespectful behavior. Staff receive direct instruction on using reflective listening, supportive statements, and working with students to develop the next steps toward a solution (Stiller et al., 2013). Importantly, staff are taught to follow up with the student after a report is made to ensure that the selected strategy was effective.

4. *Create a student advisory team.* Student buy-in is a critical component of school-wide behavioral interventions, particularly when students are encouraged to intervene in the bullying behaviors of other students. Accordingly, a student advisory team should be created to assist staff in developing program materials and procedures, including the stop signal. The student advisory team should consist of approximately 8 to 15 students with strong leadership skills, strong social skills, and who are well liked and popular among their peers. The student advisory team can serve as models for prosocial and assertive behaviors for the rest of the student body.

5. *Teach all students the* Expect Respect *curriculum.* Students are taught about bullying and how to respond to bullying using three 45-minute sessions, taught to classroom-sized groups. Each lesson consists of group discussion, practice, role plays, and guided feedback. The first lesson serves as an introduction to the program and addresses why bullying behavior happens, strategies to respond to bullying behavior, when and how to use the stop signal, and how to respond when others use the stop signal on them. The second lesson uses a short, scripted play to teach students how to respond when others are being bullied (i.e., how to be an effective bystander). Students are taught why bystander behavior is important, how to use the stop signal as a bystander, how to help the person being bullied to leave the situation, and how to provide social support (Stiller et al., 2013). In the third lesson, students view YouTube videos that demonstrate prosocial and bullying behaviors. Using these videos, students discuss how they would respond as each person involved. Students are also taught how to seek help appropriately from adults. Finally, students are encouraged to create their own Expect Respect materials, including artwork, videos, or other media to help spread awareness of the program among the student body.

6. *Conduct booster sessions at regular intervals.* Successful school-wide interventions are more likely to be effective when students are frequently reminded of expectations (Stiller et al., 2013). Lesson plans for booster sessions for the Expect Respect curriculum are provided to remind students of the strategies taught during

the initial lessons, as well as to provide instruction for new students. Booster sessions should be conducted at least annually. Booster sessions consist of three 45-minute lessons taught at the classroom-level, and each closely mirrors the initial teaching lessons.

***Strengths and Weaknesses of* Expect Respect.** The primary strength of the Expect Respect program is its integration with PBIS. Many schools across the country have already implemented PBIS and may find it relatively simple to implement Expect Respect alongside other PBIS initiatives. Another strength of the program is its cost, as it is currently free. Importantly, Expect Respect is built to address what research has shown to be one of the root causes of bullying behaviors—peer attention. However, it is likely that not all students who are engaging in bullying do so for peer attention. Expect Respect may not be as effective in reducing bullying behaviors among students for whom peer attention is not the motivating factor. Finally, Expect Respect requires significant time investment and teacher and student buy-in to implement with fidelity.

The *Second Step* Bullying Prevention Unit

The *Second Step* Bullying Prevention Unit is a research-based program that seeks to inform and provide strategies to youth, school staff, and families to reduce bullying behaviors. Based on the social–ecological model of bullying (Swearer & Espelage, 2011), the bullying prevention unit is designed to address beliefs incorporated in multiple levels and individuals, including the students, their parents, and the school staff. The program uses both student- and adult-focused components to address several short- and long-term goals related to bullying, including improved class and school climate, increased student reporting and responding to bullying behaviors, and increased staff knowledge and responses to bullying situations. Its predecessor, the *Steps to Respect* program, was deemed one of the few evidence-based bullying prevention programs because of several well-designed studies surrounding its effectiveness (Brown, Low, Smith, & Haggerty, 2011). Therefore, it is important to note that the *Second Step* Bullying Prevention Unit includes all *Steps*

to Respect components (Committee for Children, 2013).

Although it is a separate program, the *Second Step* Bully Prevention Unit is designed to be implemented in tandem with the *Second Step: Skills for Social and Academic Success* social and emotional curriculum. This social emotional learning (SEL) curriculum includes numerous topics that are related to bullying prevention, including problem solving, friendship skills, and building empathy. Combined, these two programs can effectively address bullying-specific concerns, as well as build overall social and emotional skills for all students. It is recommended that the Bullying Prevention Unit be implemented after first addressing the "Skills for Learning" section in the general *Second Step* program.

The *Second Step* Bullying Prevention Unit incorporates four core components to effectively address bullying behaviors:

1. Training all school staff members
2. Teaching all bullying prevention unit lessons to classrooms of students
3. Following through by completing provided activities on positive classroom climate
4. Engaging families with provided "Home Link" activities

These components have all been found to impact bullying behaviors. For example, positive school climate and teacher perceptions of administrative support for bullying intervention have been associated with lower levels of reported bullying (Espelage, Polanin, & Low, 2014; Gage, Prykanowski, & Larson, 2014). Therefore, it is important not only to address the student components that contribute to a positive school climate, but the staff components as well.

Implementation of the following steps may be employed in a school for the *Second Step* Bullying Prevention Unit.

School Staff Training. In order to effectively address bullying, all school staff must be trained on how to recognize, report, and respond to bullying behaviors. This allows students to feel confident in reporting bullying to any adult in the school, no matter their position. The bullying prevention unit includes three separate trainings for school staff members to address these issues. All trainings are provided online and can be accessed through the Committee for Children's website (http://secondstep.org).

- *Principals and program coordinators*: This training provides information on bullying policies and procedures, as well as how to effectively communicate this information to school staff and families.
- *All school staff training*: This training provides all school staff and personnel with information on how to recognize, respond to, and report bullying. School staff are also provided with strategies for developing plans to address both perpetrators and victims of bullying.
- *Teachers and counselors*: This training provides teachers and counselors with information on the curriculum notebook, teaching each classroom lesson, following through with classroom climate activities, and strategies and activities to involve families.

Student Lessons. The bullying prevention unit provides school staff with separate lessons plans for younger (kindergarten through grade 3) and older (grades 4 and 5) students. The K–third-grade program seeks to prevent bullying through education surrounding what bullying is, how to recognize and report it, and what to do when one sees bullying happen. The fourth- and fifth-grade program also incorporates these topics, but focuses primarily on teaching and empowering bystanders on how to intervene in both traditional and cyberbullying. Each curriculum includes five weekly classroom lessons that last 30 minutes each. Lessons are scripted and incorporate engaging materials, such as videos and activities on the provided DVD, as well as teacher-led classroom activities.

Kindergarten Through Grade Three. Following is a description of lessons for young children:

- *Introductory lesson (develop classroom rules)*: In this introductory lesson, students discuss how their words and actions can be safe and respectful.
- *Lesson 1 (recognizing bullying)*: During this lesson, students learn what bullying is and how to identify bullying behaviors through examples.

- *Lesson 2 (reporting bullying)*: Students learn how to report bullying, the difference between tattling on peers and reporting, and how to identify adults to whom they can report bullying.
- *Lesson 3 (refusing bullying)*: Students learn how to refuse to join in or be the targets of bullying by using assertive skills in bullying scenarios.
- *Lesson 4 (bystander power)*: Finally, students learn the definition of a bystander and skills bystanders can use to stop bullying when it occurs.

Grades 4 and 5. Following are lessons appropriate for use with older children:

- *Introductory lesson (class rules)*: Similar to the K–3 curriculum, students learn how to identify and demonstrate how their actions and words can be respectful and responsible.
- *Lesson 1 (recognizing, reporting, and refusing bullying)*: Students learn the definition and types of bullying, discuss the need to report bullying to adults, and learn ways to refuse bullying when it occurs.
- *Lesson 2 (bystander power)*: Students learn what a bystander to bullying is and how bystanders can act to both stop bullying when it occurs and help the person who is being victimized.
- *Lesson 3 (bystander's responsibility)*: Students learn how bystanders can also make bullying worse by joining in or ignoring the behavior. Students then discuss how bystanders can positively respond when faced with bullying.
- *Lesson 4 (bystanders to cyber bullying)*: Students learn to recognize cyberbullying and the various forms it can take (e.g., social media and texting). Students then learn how to support others who are being victimized through cyberbullying.

Engaging Families. The last component of the *Second Step* Bullying Prevention Unit involves incorporating the students' families in activities and discussions of bullying. Each classroom lesson also includes a related Home Link activity to be done by the parents and their child. By sharing the same message and information on bullying both at home and at school, the child learns that bullying is an unacceptable behavior, no matter the environment.

- *Family letter*: A provided family letter is sent home before implementing the bullying prevention unit. This letter explains to the students' families what the program consists of and that behavioral change requires work at home as well. Parents are also provided with an activation key to access information on the Committee for Children website.

- *Home Link activities*: Each classroom lesson also includes a Home Link activity on the same topic taught at school. These activities encourage discussion between the child and his or her family on the various topics surrounding bullying.

In assessing the *Second Step* Bullying Prevention Unit, it is clear that the authors have combined key features from their previous evidence-based program and the literature into an effective bullying prevention program. The involvement and training of the whole school staff helps ensure that every adult in the building knows how to recognize and respond to bullying. In addition, the incorporation of the program into comprehensive social and emotional learning not only teaches more effective skills for reducing bullying, but also promotes healthy social development and a better school climate. Finally, involving parents through structured activities helps promote antibullying attitudes and policies across environments. However, the incorporation of the bullying prevention unit within the general *Second Step* curriculum requires the ability to commit time and resources to both programs. School staff and administration should assess their availability of resources to implement the program with fidelity. Overall, the *Second Step* Bullying Prevention Unit provides research-based strategies and activities for both children and the adults involved in their lives.

RULER Program

Intervention programs that focus on SEL aim to increase awareness of self and others by integrating thoughts, emotions, and behaviors; effective decision making; and behavioral management that, when implemented in the schools, cultivate social competence, school safety, and conflict resolution skills (Brackett & Rivers, 2014b). *RULER* is a SEL program endorsed by the CASEL that aligns with common core standards (CASEL, 2014). Additionally, as it targets the underlying causes of bullying and victimization, lack of emotional understanding and self-regulation, *RULER* also fosters a bullying-free school environment (Brackett & Rivers, 2014a). *RULER*, with the goal of promoting emotional literacy, integrates emotional intelligence into the daily classroom routines from preschool to high school by teaching those involved how to *Recognize, Understand, Label, Express,* and *Regulate* emotions (i.e., five key skills of the program; Brackett & Rivers, 2014b).

Although *RULER* stems from the ability model of emotional intelligence proposed by Salovey and Mayer (1990), it adds a unique component by focusing on the development of emotional intelligence as a product of formal instruction (Brackett & Rivers, 2014b), integrated into the academic curriculum (e.g., analyzing emotional aspects of academic tasks and current events; evaluating how characters and historical figures managed their feelings) via a literacy-based, skill-building approach (Rivers, Brackett, Reyes, Elbertson, & Salovey, 2013).

Implementing the *RULER* program within a school or school district will increase students' emotional literacy as they master the *RULER* skills by acquiring knowledge and skills on emotions, being in a safe environment with potential to experience a myriad of emotions, having the opportunity to practice and receive feedback on their skills, and having repeated contact with adults who have undergone the *RULER* training and will serve as examples in applying the *RULER* skills (Rivers et al., 2013). Information about ways to prepare a school or school district to adopt the *RULER* program can be found at their website: www.theRULERapproach.org.

In order for the *RULER* program to be successfully implemented, school personnel or a school district must undergo three separate phases. Once the interactive training phases are completed, teachers and students will be able to put into practice the 16 lessons and daily implementation sessions within the Anchor Tools along with the 75 lessons of the Feeling Words Curriculum (Yale Center for Emotional Intelligence, 2013).

Phase 1. As described by the Yale Center for Emotional Intelligence (2013), Phase 1 requires stakeholders (i.e., superintendents, school leaders, teachers, and staff) from a school to receive 4 days of explicit instruction to become *RULER* trainers, facilitating the development of the requisite knowledge and skills needed to train others at their schools. Through hands-on sessions, skill-building exercises, and resources (i.e., presentation slides, training books, and lesson plans), this initial group will be trained in the Anchors of Emotional Intelligence. In order for this first step to be successful and to ensure long-term sustainability, trainers are paired with a certified *RULER* coach with whom they meet several times a year. Coaching sessions include sharing of successes and challenges and training via didactic instruction, role-playing exercises, lesson design, observation of instruction, and feedback (Hagelskamp, Brackett, Rivers, & Salovey, 2013). In order to ensure there is a base understanding of emotion-related concepts and healthy relationships within the classroom, the four Anchor tools need to be used to assess feelings and moods of both teachers and students in order to determine activities and strategies for a successful day at school.

The Anchors of Intelligence, as described by Brackett and Rivers (2014b), are:

1. *Charter*: A mission statement is written by all members of the learning community in order to document shared goals and values that define appropriate behaviors that foster feelings of empowerment and respect and how to man-age emotions when these behaviors are not displayed. A faculty charter and individual class-room charters need to be created.
2. *Mood Meter*: The Mood Meter is designed as a self-awareness tool to assess the learning com-munity's feelings. This tool is depicted as a graph representing levels of feelings ranging from unpleasant to pleasant on the *x*-axis and levels of energy from low to high on the *y*-axis and is a downloadable app (Brackett & Kremenitzer, 2011).
3. *Meta-Moment*: By being preventative rather than reactive with emotions, taking a meta-moment helps students and stakeholders improve self-reflection and regulation. The meta-moment encourages individuals to imagine their best self in the situation and then to use strategies to respond appropriately.

Phase 2. Once a school has completed Phase 1 and the foundation of the Anchor Tools has been set, the *RULER* trainers go to a 3-day training to learn and practice the skills they will need to integrate the Feeling Words Curriculum into the academic curricula (Yale Center for Emotional Intelligence, 2013) and to provide learners with a rich "feelings" vocabulary they can use in academic learning, peer relationships, and personal growth (Rivers & Brackett, 2011). The developers of the program note that teaching language tools leads to more effective communication (Yale Center for Emotional Intelligence, 2013); hence, this curriculum aims to encourage the learning community to express the full range of human emotions. Feeling words are nested within larger word families and arranged by grade levels ranging from basic emotions to more complex self-evaluative emotions (Brackett & Rivers, 2014b). For example, the "angry" family for third, fourth, and fifth graders includes the words "enraged," "annoyed," and "aggressively." Teachers follow five steps for each feeling word unit every 2 to 3 weeks throughout the school year. According to Brackett and Kremenitzer (2011), the steps for every lesson entail describing the feeling word and the associated five steps:

1. *Personal association*: link new and prior knowledge
2. *Academic and real world*: use the feeling word to understand course material and current events
3. *School–home partnership*: introduce the feeling word to family members
4. *Creative connection*: evoke the feeling word through art and/or drama
5. *Strategy building*: discuss how to express and regulate the feeling word

Phase 3. *RULER* is a self-perpetuating program guaranteeing direct knowledge about the Anchors and the Feelings Word Curriculum by having selected staff trained as *RULER* trainers (Yale Center for Emotional Intelligence, 2013). This, along with ongoing support from a dynamic online platform, permits that, by the end of Phase 2, schools are ready to thrive as a *RULER* school.

When considering pros and cons of the use of the *RULER* approach in a school, the main issue that may arise is that it is not a bullying-specific intervention program. Hence, it does not teach students explicitly what bullying is, how to recog-nize when it is happening, and ways the student could intervene for themselves or someone else. However, as explained previously, the program focuses on teaching how to recognize, understand, label, express, and regulate emotions; therefore, it provides a broader set of skills that can assist students in more facets than solely bullying situations. Additionally, in support of the program, it is a whole-school, structured curriculum approach that can be readily embedded into the academic curriculum. Finally, a drawback in trying to successfully put into effect the program within a school is the high cost of trainings during each phase of implementation.

Although it can be overwhelming for educators and practitioners to wade through the vast array of anti-bullying curricula, books, workshops, plays, movies, and assemblies, the good news is that research is increasingly seen as a critical part of program development and evaluation—closing the research-to-practice gap in bullying prevention and intervention.

CONCLUSION

School bullying and peer victimization are pervasive phenomena that affect many youth. Although bullying is viewed as an important public health problem and the most frequent form of school violence, many inconsistencies in defining and assessing bullying still exist. Bullying can include both direct (e.g., openly aggressive acts on targeted youth) and indirect (e.g., spreading rumors) forms. Moreover, physical (e.g., hitting, kicking, punching, and pushing), verbal (e.g., taunting, name calling, threats, and offensive written notes or hand gestures), relational (e.g., posting embarrassing images/comments in a physical or electronic space without the target's permission), and damage to property (e.g., destroying target's property in his or her presence and deleting personal electronic information) have been identified as specific forms or dimensions of bullying. To add yet another layer to this complex social dynamic, bullying happens across a continuum where students involved do not necessarily have fixed roles, but rather fluctuate between being a perpetrator of bullying behaviors, being a target, being both a perpetrator and a target, being a bystander, or having no involvement at all. Thus, bullying represents a significant problem for youth involved, in any role along the

continuum, and is associated with a plethora of negative outcomes.

There is no single cause for bullying behaviors. Consistent with an increase in research on bullying over the past two decades, bullying prevention and intervention programming has also dramatically increased. Research within this bailiwick has evolved to program evaluation in addition to conducting basic research. Specific interventions, including *Expect Respect*, *Second Step*, and the *RULER* program, are provided for step-by-step implementation by mental health professionals in the hopes of ameliorating this serious epidemic and enhancing the academic, behavioral, social, and emotional functioning of children and adolescents.

SELECT BIBLIOGRAPHY

Brackett, M. A., & Rivers, S. E. (2014). Transforming students' lives with social and emotional learning. In R. Pekrun, & L. Linnenbring-Garcia (Eds.), *International handbook of emotions in education* (pp. 368–388). New York, NY: Routledge.
This chapter examines the features and examples of social and emotional learning programs. Additionally, the chapter describes the RULER approach to social and emotional learning including its components and implementation of the program.

Jimerson, S. R., Swearer, S. M., & Espelage, D. L. (2010). *Handbook of bullying in schools: An international perspective.* New York, NY: Routledge.
This book takes an in-depth look at bullying research from around the globe. Chapters focus on bullying and related constructs (e.g., school climate), assessment of bullying, and investigations of prevention and intervention programs to reduce bullying behaviors.

Rigby, K. (2012). *Bullying interventions in schools: Six basic approaches.* Chichester, UK: Wiley-Blackwell.
This book addresses six intervention methods for addressing bullying, including traditional discipline, interventions that strengthen the victim, mediation, restorative justice, support groups, and the method of shared concern.

Swearer, S. M., Espelage, D. L., & Napolitano, S. A. (2009). *Bullying prevention & intervention: Realistic strategies for schools.* New York, NY: Guilford Press.
This book provides school staff with practical strategies that can be used in their classrooms to

reduce bullying. The authors provide information and examples of bullying at different grade levels, as well as steps for schools to develop an antibullying policy.

REFERENCES

Bowes, L., Arseneault, L., Maughan, B., Taylor, A., & Moffitt, T. E. (2009). School, neighborhood, and family factors are associated with children's bullying involvement: A nationally representative longitudinal study. *Journal of American Academy of Child and Adolescent Psychiatry, 48*, 45–553. doi:10.1097/CHI.0b013e31819cb017

Brackett, M., & Kremenitzer, J. (Eds.). (2011). *Creating emotionally literate classrooms*. Port Chester, NY: Dude Publishing.

Brackett, M., & Rivers, S. (2014a). Preventing bullying with emotional intelligence. *Education Week, 33*. Retrieved from http://www.edweek.org/ew/articles/2014/02/19/21brackett_ep.h33.html

Brackett, M., & Rivers, S. (2014b). Transforming students' lives with social and emotional learning. In R. Pekrun & L. Linnenbrink-Garcia (Eds.), *International handbook of emotions in education* (pp. 368–389). New York, NY: Routledge.

Bradshaw, C. P., Mitchell, M. M., & Leaf, P. J. (2010). Examining the effects of schoolwide positive behavioral interventions and supports on student outcomes: Results from a randomized controlled effectiveness trial in elementary schools. *Journal of Positive Behavior Interventions, 12*, 133–148. doi:10.1177/1098300709334798

Bronfenbrenner, U. (1979). *The ecology of human development: Experiments by nature and design*. Cambridge, MA: Harvard University Press.

Brown, E. C., Low, S., Smith, B. H., & Haggerty, K. P. (2011). Outcomes from a school-randomized controlled trial of steps to respect: A bullying prevention program. *School Psychology Review, 40*, 423–443. Retrieved from http://www.nasponline.org/publications/spr/index-list.aspx

Card, N. A., Stucky, B. D., Sawalani, G. M., & Little, T. D. (2008). Direct and indirect aggression during childhood and adolescence: A meta-analytic review of gender differences, intercorrelations, and relationships to maladjustment. *Child Development, 79*, 1185–1229. doi:10.1111/j.1467–8624.2008.01184.x

Cicchetti, D., & Rogosch, F. A. (1996). Equifinality and multifinality in developmental psychopathology.

Development and Psychopathology, 8, 597–600. doi:10.1017/S0954579400007318

Collaborative for Academic, Social, and Emotional Learning (CASEL). (2014). *RULER*: Program design and implementation support. Retrieved from http://www.casel.org/guide/programs/ruler

Committee for Children. (2013). *Bullying prevention unit: Review of research*. Retrieved from http://www.cfchildren.org/Portals/0/SS_BPU/BPU_DOC/Review_of_Research_BPU.pdf

DeVoe, J., & Murphy, C. (2011). *Student reports of bullying and cyber-bullying: Results from the 2009 School Crime Supplement to the National Crime Victimization Survey (NCES 2011–336)*. U.S. Department of Education, National Center for Education Statistics. Washington, DC: U.S. Government Printing Office.

Espelage, D. L., Holt, M. K., & Henkel, R. R. (2003). Examination of peer group contextual effects on aggression during early adolescence. *Child Development, 74*, 205–220. doi:10.1111/1467–8624.00531

Espelage, D. L., Polanin, J. R., & Low, S. K. (2014). Teacher and staff perceptions of school environment as predictors of student aggression, victimization, and willingness to intervene in bullying situations. *School Psychology Quarterly, 29*, 287–305. doi:10.1037/spq0000072

Espelage, D. L., & Swearer, S. M. (2010). A social-ecological model for bullying prevention and intervention: Understanding the impact of adults in the social ecology of youngsters. In S. R. Jimerson, S. M. Swearer, & D. L. Espelage (Eds.), *Handbook of bullying in schools: An international perspective* (pp. 61–72). New York, NY: Routledge.

Evans, C., Fraser, M., & Cotter, K. (2014). The effectiveness of school-based bullying prevention programs: A systematic review. *Aggression and Violent Behavior, 19*, 532–544. doi:10.1016/j.avb.2014.07.004

Flannery, K. B., Fenning, P., Kato, M. M., & McIntosh, K. (2014). Effects of school-wide positive behavioral interventions and supports and fidelity of implementation on problem behavior in high schools. *School Psychology Quarterly, 29*, 111–124. doi:10.1037/spq0000039

Gage, N. A., Prykanowski, D. A., & Larson, A. (2014). School climate and bullying victimization: A latent class growth model analysis. *School Psychology Quarterly, 29*, 256–271. doi:10.1037/spq0000064

Gini, G., Pozzoli, T., Borghi, F., & Franzoni, L. (2008). The role of bystanders in students' perception of bullying and sense of safety. *Journal of School Psychology, 46,* 617–638. doi:10.1016/j.jsp.2008.02.001

Gladden, R. M., Vivolo-Kantor, A. M., Hamburger, M. E., & Lumpkin, C. D. (2014). *Bullying surveillance among youths: Uniform definitions for public health and recommended data elements, Version 1.0.* Atlanta, GA: National Center for Injury Prevention and Control, Centers for Disease Control and Prevention and U.S. Department of Education.

Hagelskamp, C., Brackett, M., Rivers, S., & Salovey, P. (2013). Improving classroom quality with the *RULER* approach to social and emotional learning: Proximal and distal outcomes. *American Journal of Community Psychology, 51,* 530–543. doi:10.1007/s10464–013-9570-x

Khoury-Kassabri, M., Benbenishty, R., Astor, R., & Zeria, A. (2004). The contributions of community, family, and school variables to student victimization. *American Journal of Community Psychology, 34,* 187–204. doi:10.1007/s10464–004-7414–4

Lee, C. (2011). An ecological systems approach to bullying behaviors among middle school students in the United States. *Journal of Interpersonal Violence, 26,* 1664–1693. doi:10.1177/0886260510370591

Nese, R. N. T., Horner, R. H., Dickey, C. R., Stiller, B., & Tomlanovich, A. (2014). Decreasing bullying behaviors in middle school: *Expect Respect. School Psychology Quarterly, 29,* 272–286. doi:10.1037/spq0000070

O'Brennan, L. M., Bradshaw, C. P., & Sawyer, A. L. (2009). Examining developmental differences in the social–emotional problems among frequent bullies, victims, and bully/victims. *Psychology in the Schools, 46,* 100–115. doi:10.1002/pits.20357

Pellegrini, A. D., & Long, J. D. (2002). A longitudinal study of bullying, dominance, and victimization during the transition from primary to secondary school. *British Journal of Developmental Psychology, 20,* 259–280. doi:10.1348/026151002166442

Rivers, S., & Brackett, M. (2011). Achieving standards in the English language arts (and more): Using the *RULER* approach to social and emotional learning. *Reading & Writing Quarterly, 27,* 75–100. doi:10.1080/10573569.2011.532715

Rivers, S. E., Brackett, M. A., Reyes, M. R., Elbertson, N. A., & Salovey, P. (2013). Improving the social and emotional climate of classrooms: A clustered randomized controlled trial testing the *RULER* approach. *Prevention Science, 14,* 77–87. doi:10.1007/s11121–012-0305–2

Rodriguez, C. M. (2010). Parent–child aggression: Association with child abuse potential and parenting styles. *Violence and Victims, 25,* 728–741. doi:10.1891/0886–6708.25.6.728

Ross, S. W., & Horner, R. H. (2009). Bully prevention in positive behavior support. *Journal of Applied Behavior Analysis, 42,* 747–759. doi:10.1901/jaba.2009.42–747

Ross, S., Horner, R., & Stiller, B. (2014). Bully prevention in positive behavior support. Retrieved from http://www.pbis.org/common/cms/files/pbisresources/pbsbullyprevention.pdf

Ryoo, J. H., Wang, C., & Swearer, S. M. (2014). Examination of the change in latent statuses in bullying behaviors across time. *School Psychology Quarterly, 30*(1), 105–122. doi:10.1037/spq0000082

Salovey, P., & Mayer, J. D. (1990). Emotional intelligence. *Imagination, Cognition, and Personality, 9,* 185–211. doi:10.2190/DUGG-P24E-52WK-6CDG

Stiller, B. C., Nese, R. N. T., Tomlanovich, A. K., Horner, R. H., & Ross, S. W. (2013). Bullying and harassment prevention in positive behavior support: *Expect Respect.* Retrieved from http://www.pbis.org/common/cms/files/pbisresources/2013_02_18_final_covr_manual_123x.pdf

Swearer, S. M., Collins, A., Radliff, K. H., & Wang, C. (2011). Internalizing problems in students involved in bullying and victimization. In D. Espelage, & S. Swearer (Eds.), *Bullying in North American schools* (2nd ed., pp. 45–61). New York, NY: Routledge.

Swearer, S. M., Espelage, D., Vaillancourt, T., & Hymel, S. (2010). What can be done about school bullying? Linking research to educational practice. *Educational Researcher, 39,* 38–47. doi:10.3102/0013189X09357622

Swearer, S. M., Siebecker, A., Johnsen-Frerichs, L., & Wang, C. (2010). Assessment of bullying/victimization: The problem of comparability across studies and across methods. In S. Jimerson, S. Swearer, & D. Espelage (Eds.), *Handbook of bullying in schools: An international perspective* (pp. 305–327). New York, NY: Routledge.

Swearer, S. M., & Doll, B. (2001). Bullying in schools: An ecological framework. *Journal of Emotional Abuse, 2,* 7–23. doi:10.1300/J135v02n02_02

Swearer, S. M., & Espelage, D. L. (2011). Expanding the social–ecological framework of bullying among youth: Lessons learned from the past and directions for the future. In D. L. Espelage & S. M. Swearer (Eds.), *Bullying in North American schools* (2nd ed., pp. 3–10). New York, NY: Routledge.

Ttofi, M. M., & Farrington, D. P. (2011). Effectiveness of school-based programs to reduce bullying: A systematic and meta-analytic review. *Journal of Experimental Criminology, 7*(1), 27–56. doi: 10.1007/s11292-010-9109-1

Underwood, M. K., & Rosen, L. H. (2011). Gender and bullying: Moving beyond mean differences to consider conceptions of bullying, processes by which bullying unfolds, and cyberbullying. In D. Espelage & S. M. Swearer (Eds.), *Bullying in North American schools* (2nd ed., pp. 13–22). New York, NY: Routledge.

Vaillancourt, T., Brittain, H., Bennett, L., Arnocky, S., McDougall, P., Hymel, S.,…Cunningham, L. (2010). Places to avoid: Population-based study of student reports of unsafe and high bullying areas at school. *Canadian Journal of School Psychology, 25*, 40–54. doi:10.1177/0829573509358686

Yale Center for Emotional Intelligence. (2013). *RULER* overview: How *RULER* becomes an integral and enduring part of your school or district. Retrieved from http://ei.yale.edu/RULER/RULER-overview

Evidence-Based Interventions for Attention Deficit Hyperactivity Disorder in Children and Adolescents

George J. DuPaul, Georgia D. Belk, and Kristina Puzino

OVERVIEW

Attention deficit hyperactivity disorder (ADHD) is one of the most commonly diagnosed behavior disorders in childhood and continues to be evident in 2.5% of adults (American Psychiatric Association [APA], 2013), making it a lifetime disorder. According to estimates reported by the Centers for Disease Control and Prevention (CDC, 2013), ADHD affects approximately 3% to 10% of the population, and males are nearly three times more likely to be affected by the disorder than females (CDC, 2013; Barkley, 2015; Visser et al., 2014).

According to the *Diagnostic and Statistical Manual of Mental Disorders* (5th ed.; *DSM-5*; APA, 2013), symptoms of ADHD include inattention and hyperactivity-impulsivity. These core symptoms put individuals at risk for the development of additional functional problems, including academic underachievement, poor peer relationships, aggression, and noncompliance (Barkley, 2015). Aggressive behaviors are often linked to extraneous functional difficulties that are experienced by individuals diagnosed with ADHD, such as difficulty with peer relationships and cross-context stressors such as parent and teacher stress, drug use, and antisocial behaviors (e.g., stealing, vandalism; Barkley, 2015). Furthermore, ADHD symptoms can cause stress for both parents and teachers, particularly for families and teachers interacting with young boys with ADHD, and even more so when ADHD symptoms are coupled with opposition/defiance and/or aggressive behaviors (Theule, Wiener, Tannock, & Jenkins, 2013).

By definition, the symptomatic behaviors comprising ADHD must be associated with some impairment in academic or social functioning in order for diagnostic criteria to be met (APA, 2013). Thus, students with ADHD typically underachieve academically with a deficit of approximately 0.60 to 0.75 standard deviation units on achievement tests relative to non-ADHD classmates (Frazier, Youngstrom, Glutting, & Watkins, 2007). In addition, children and adolescents with ADHD are more likely to repeat a grade, to be referred and identified for special education services, suspended, and drop out of school relative to students without disabilities (Barkley, Fischer, Smallish, & Fletcher, 2006; Frazier et al., 2007; Kent et al., 2011). ADHD symptoms also are frequently associated with impairments in social relationships. Specifically, students with ADHD typically have difficulties interacting with peers and adult authority figures as well as struggle to make and keep same-age friends (Stormont, 2001). Not surprisingly, youth with this disorder are more likely to be rejected by peers than are their non-ADHD classmates (Hoza, 2007).

There is no single cause of ADHD as a myriad of factors may result in ADHD symptomology (Nigg, 2006). As such, it is important to understand what treatments are available for practitioners and how to implement these treatments appropriately and effectively. Further, ADHD may present itself differently across individuals, so there is not necessarily a "one-fits-all" treatment.

ETIOLOGY AND FACTORS CONTRIBUTING TO ADHD IN CHILDREN AND ADOLESCENTS

There is no single risk factor that fully accounts for the development of ADHD. Rather, a variety of different risks and risk pathways, both genetic and environmental, may all lead to similar clinical presentations. The following section elucidates the potential causal variables that have been identified, including neurobiological factors, hereditary influences, and environmental toxins.

Neurobiological Variables

Researchers have considered neurobiological factors to have a strong etiological influence (Thapar, Cooper, Eyre, & Langley, 2013). Previous research has demonstrated structural differences in the brains of individuals with ADHD compared with those without the disorder. For example, abnormalities may be present in the fronto-striatal neural circuit of the brain (Nigg, 2006) as well as cerebellar regions, splenium of the corpus callosum, and right caudate (Valera, Faraone, Murray, & Seidman, 2007). Additionally, studies have found an overall reduction in the size of the prefrontal cortex among children with ADHD (Wolosin, Richardson, Hennessey, Denckla, & Mostofsky, 2009). The prefrontal cortex is largely responsible for executive functioning, which involves inhibition of behavior and impulse control. The neurotransmitters, dopamine and norepinephrine, which are especially prevalent in the prefrontal cortex, seem to play a pivotal role in the development of ADHD. Such neurotransmitters are responsible for reward-motivated behavior as well as stimulatory processes in the body. Providing supports for this claim, studies demonstrate that medication used to treat ADHD temporarily increases the availability of dopamine in the synaptic cleft (Stein et al., 2005).

Hereditary Influences

Empirical evidence indicates that ADHD has a strong genetic component. For example, twin studies suggest that the concordance rate between monozygotic twins is 50% to 80%, whereas concordance rates between dizygotic twins is only 33% (Bradley & Golden, 2001; Larsson, Larsson, & Lichtenstein, 2004). Family studies demonstrate that children of parents with ADHD are more likely to develop this disorder than children of parents without ADHD (Nigg, 2006).When compared with healthy controls, siblings of children with ADHD are three to five times more likely to have the diagnosis (Faraone et al., 1995). Although genetic factors explain approximately 80% of the variance in the symptomatology of ADHD, environmental factors also play a significant role (Larsson et al., 2004). Nonshared environmental factors, experiences unique to each child, may be important in predicting ADHD symptomology. Specifically, nonshared environmental factors refer to the environmental influences that produce behavioral differences among siblings living in the same household (e.g., sibling differences in accidents, illnesses, peer-group affiliations, hobbies and other extracurricular activities, and differential parental treatment). The significance of nonshared environments increases as children enter adolescence and gain autonomy regarding their friendships, classes, hobbies, and daily schedules. Alternatively, shared environmental experiences explain little to no variance in children's ADHD symptoms (Larsson et al., 2004).

Even though twin studies demonstrate that ADHD is a highly heritable condition, molecular genetics studies suggest that the genetic makeup of ADHD is complex. Evidence indicates four genes in particular in the etiology of the disorder: dopamine receptor, D1, D4, and D5 genes, and the dopamine transporter gene, when compared with non-ADHD samples (Waldman & Gizer, 2006). Nevertheless, no single gene has been found to account for more than a very small amount of variance in ADHD symptoms. Thus, it is best to view this disorder as being influenced to a small degree by many genes (Hinshaw & Scheffler, 2014).

Environmental Toxins

Certain environmental toxins, prenatal, and perinatal factors have been related to the development of ADHD symptoms. Specifically, lead poisoning and exposure to pesticides during infancy and early childhood may damage the neural systems presumed to underlie ADHD (Nigg, 2006). In addition, researchers have found a significant relationship between maternal smoking (Milberger, Biederman, Faraone, Chen, & Jones, 1996) or prenatal exposure to nicotine and smoke products (Mick, Biederman, Faraone, Sayer, & Kleinman, 2002) during pregnancy and low birth weight as well as the development of ADHD (Mick, Biederman, Prince, Fischer, & Faraone, 2002). It appears that environmental toxins may deprive the fetus of adequate oxygen, which may compromise brain development, resulting in an increased risk for ADHD.

Taken together, research demonstrates that ADHD is not caused by any single factor. Consistent with a diathesis-stress model, ADHD may be best conceptualized as a disorder that results from the interaction of biological vulnerability and exposure to stressful and/or challenging environments (e.g., classrooms, other settings that require sustained attention and impulse control in order to perform). As such, interventions to ameliorate putative neurobiological deficits and modify environmental stimuli may be necessary to improve student functioning.

EVIDENCE-BASED INTERVENTIONS AND EMPIRICAL SUPPORT FOR ADHD IN CHILDREN AND ADOLESCENTS

The most effective treatments for ADHD include psychotropic medications (chiefly central nervous system [CNS] stimulants), behavioral interventions implemented at home and/or school, academic support strategies, and self-regulation interventions (DuPaul & Stoner, 2014). CNS stimulants used to treat ADHD include methylphenidate (e.g., Ritalin), dextroamphetamine (e.g., Dexedrine), lisdexamfetamine (e.g., Vyvanse), and mixed amphetamine compounds (e.g., Adderall). Hundreds of studies over the past several decades have documented that CNS stimulants lead to improvements in attention, hyperactivity-impulsivity, compliance with rules, aggression, and classroom productivity for the majority of children with ADHD receiving pharmacotherapy (for review, see Barkley, 2015). Numerous double-blind empirical investigations and meta-analyses indicate that stimulants are associated with large effects on ADHD symptoms and associated disruptive behavior with much smaller effects on academic performance and achievement (e.g., Faraone & Buitelaar, 2010; MTA Cooperative Group, 1999). In fact, the most prudent conclusion is that, although stimulants are the single-best treatment to reduce ADHD symptoms, these compounds do not necessarily lead to notable improvement in academic or social functioning. Thus, stimulants and other psychotropic medications may be necessary for treating many students with ADHD; however, pharmacotherapy is never sufficient and must be paired with other interventions to optimize outcomes (American Academy of Pediatrics, 2011).

Behavioral interventions implemented in home and school settings are also effective in addressing ADHD symptoms and associated behavior control difficulties. As described later in the chapter, behavioral interventions involve manipulation of environmental events (i.e., antecedents and consequences) to alter the probability of a specific behavior occurring. Specific behavioral interventions that have been studied for the treatment of ADHD include token reinforcement (e.g., point systems or token economies), response cost, and time-out from positive reinforcement (DuPaul & Stoner, 2014). Typically, parents and teachers receive training and support in implementation of behavioral strategies from a psychologist or other mental health professional. Parents and teachers may also collaborate on daily report card or home–school communication programs wherein behaviors at school are reinforced by parents later in the day (Owens et al., 2012). Several systematic reviews and meta-analyses have shown behavioral interventions to have moderate to large effects on inattentive, hyperactive-impulsive, disruptive, and aggressive behaviors as well as moderate to large effects on associated academic and social difficulties (Evans, Owens, & Bunford, 2014; Fabiano et al., 2009).

Several programs for providing parental education in behavioral modification strategies have been developed (e.g., Eyberg et al., 2001; Sonuga-Barke, Daley, Thompson, Laver-Bradbury, & Weeks, 2001) for specific use with children diagnosed with ADHD and related behavioral disorders. Although various parental education programs differ slightly in content and approach, they share common elements including: (a) helping parents to understand challenging behaviors (e.g., noncompliance) as a function of environmental antecedent and consequent events, (b) assisting parents in structuring home expectations and routines to be clear and consistent, (c) supporting parents in the use of contingent positive reinforcement strategies such as token reinforcement (e.g., point systems), (d) advising parents to use punishment strategies (e.g., time-out from positive reinforcement) in a limited fashion with a strong emphasis on positive reinforcement, and (e) helping parents to extend behavioral strategies to community and school settings. Controlled empirical studies have demonstrated the positive effects of behavioral parental education on child compliance, aggression, and oppositional behavior, and, as such, this is considered a well-established treatment for ADHD (Evans et al., 2014).

In similar fashion, the application of behavioral principles in classroom settings has been associated with significant improvements in the on-task behavior, social interactions, and academic productivity of students with ADHD (Barkley, 2015; DuPaul & Stoner, 2014; Evans et al., 2014). A recent meta-analysis of 60 outcome studies published between 1996 and 2010 showed classroom-based contingency management to be associated with moderate to large effects in behavior along with small to moderate effects on academic performance for children with ADHD (DuPaul, Eckert, & Vilardo, 2012). In fact, effect sizes for attention and behavioral control were nearly as large as those for stimulant medication and larger for academic outcomes than pharmacotherapy.

Although studied far less extensively than stimulant medication and behavioral intervention, two other approaches have been found effective for treating the symptoms and impairment associated with ADHD. Academic interventions such as explicit instruction, computer-assisted instruction, and peer tutoring have shown positive effects for both behavioral and academic functioning (DuPaul et al., 2012). It seems that directly targeting areas of impairment (e.g., academic productivity and accuracy) may indirectly improve classroom behavior. Similarly, several single-subject design studies have shown that self-regulation strategies (e.g., self-monitoring, self-evaluation) improve classroom behavior and work completion for students with ADHD (DuPaul et al., 2012; Reid, Trout, & Schartz, 2005). More extensive randomized clinical trials of academic and self-regulation interventions are necessary to more firmly establish the efficacy of these strategies for treating ADHD. Nevertheless, extant findings are promising and practitioners should certainly consider including these treatments as part of a multimodal intervention protocol.

HOW TO: A GUIDE TO THE IMPLEMENTATION OF INTERVENTIONS FOR ADHD IN CHILDREN AND ADOLESCENTS

Behavioral Interventions

Behavioral treatments have been successfully applied to children with ADHD to facilitate the management of disruptive behavior, inattention, social skill building, and academic performance (Fabiano et al., 2009). Classroom behavioral modification methods have demonstrated promise in reducing symptom levels and/or related behavioral and emotional difficulties. Classroom contingency management is grounded in learning theory and incorporates classical conditioning, operant conditioning, cognitive behavioral theory, and social learning principles (O'Leary, Becker, Evans, & Saudargas, 1969). Many of these techniques emphasize operant procedures in which the antecedents and consequences of the child's behavior are manipulated to increase the desired behavior and decrease undesired behavior. Assessment of antecedent and consequent events is used to analyze behavior and design interventions. Behavioral modification strategies can be used in the child's home, school, and other relevant environments (e.g., playground). One example of classroom contingency management is a token economy system in which tokens are administered to immediately reinforce target behavior and exchanged later for backup reinforcers.

Step-by-Step Implementation of Token Economy System in Classroom

Step 1. Select behavior to target for change by operationally defining the problem using a functional behavioral assessment (FBA). The following methods constitute an FBA. Initial assessment is required to determine the behavior to be changed and to ensure that the function of the target behavior is being directly addressed in intervention. The teacher should engage in the process of gathering and interpreting assessment information to develop a hypothesis about why the behavior is occurring. Doing this will provide a clear link between assessment and intervention techniques. The functions of behavior are determined by understanding the events that occur before and after the behavior. Specifically, the teacher should identify relevant antecedents (i.e., variables that set the stage for the target behavior) and relevant consequences (i.e., variables that strengthen and maintain the target behavior). Next, the target behavior should be defined in specific, observable, and measurable terms. (Non-example: "Tim is a hyperactive student; Example: "Tim frequently gets out of his seat. When in his seat, he frequently taps his pencil and looks at other students rather than doing his work.") Each individual who is part of the students' everyday life (i.e., school staff and parents) need to be involved in planning and implementation of the intervention.

Step 2. Select tokens and develop a method for management. A record-keeping system is needed to keep track of tokens earned and spent. An individual laminated "bank" can display the student's name in which the teacher can easily write and erase as token totals change throughout the day. The location of the bank and the actual tokens are important to consider. Posting the bank in the classroom enables the student to receive important feedback in a timely manner. Tokens can include objects such as play money, marbles, pennies, plastic chips, or stickers. Alternatively, depending on the developmental status of the student, concrete reinforcers may not be beneficial. For instance, concrete reinforcers are necessary for young children and elementary students, but not appropriate for middle and high school students. For older children, a point system, or behavioral contract method should be used. Ultimately, tokens should be easily dispensed, difficult for the student to forge or reproduce, and safe to use.

Step 3. Identify powerful backup reinforcers (rewards). Once the token economy system is in place, the students will periodically exchange their tokens for backup reinforcers (i.e., rewards). Depending on the frequency of the target behavior and the student's age, the student can exchange his or her tokens at the end of each school day or the end of the school week. In order for the reinforcer to be motivating, the student should perceive the reinforcer as desirable and worth working for. To determine what reinforcer will be most motivating, the student should complete a reinforcement survey. This can be done by simply asking the student what he or she would like to earn in the areas of activities, privileges, objects, and edibles. In addition, teachers can observe students in their free time to see what activities or objects they enjoy.

Step 4. Establish goals. Determine the number of tokens that can be earned for displaying appropriate behavior and deemed necessary to obtain a reinforcer. The reinforcer should be selected by reviewing the reinforcement survey, and determining what is most rewarding and motivating to the student. In addition, decide on the cost of each reinforcer. It is important to initially set the goal at a level that is easily achieved and then gradually increase the goal as performance improves. For instance, if costs are too low, the student can attain reinforcers too quickly, and potentially lose motivation to perform the appropriate behavior. In contrast, if the cost is too high, the student may be incapable of attaining the reinforcers and, as a result, choose to give up.

Step 5. Explain the intervention to the child. At a neutral time and place (e.g., homeroom at beginning of school day), discuss how the token economy system works. Specifically, identify where and when it will be in effect, how to be successful, and the goals for earning the reinforcers. Careful discussion and role-playing to demonstrate the details of how to implement the intervention are recommended. Furthermore, communicating the details of the intervention with parents is important. Decide when tokens will be exchanged for reinforcers (i.e., daily or weekly; at the end of the day or before lunch). Given that students with ADHD frequently are impulsive, the shorter the delay between token receipt and exchange for backup reinforcement, the better. Students will likely anticipate the opportunity to exchange their token for reinforcers; therefore, consistency with the exchange plan is critical.

Step 6. Teacher provides reinforcers, when necessary. The delivery of tokens should be accompanied by praise that specifically describes the behavior that resulted in the earning of a token. The token and praise should not cause interruption and should be delivered quickly. The teacher should systematically review the child's progress toward the goal with the student. Consequences for both achieving and not achieving the goal are discussed.

Step 7. Progress monitoring and altering the program. If and when the child's behavior improves to a desired level for a certain period of time, the program should be altered. To maintain the student's interest and motivation, increases to the number of tokens required for a reinforcer can be made. Additionally, new target behaviors can be substituted once the previous one has been consistently achieved. In addition, teachers can lengthen time covered by the system (i.e., incorporating morning and afternoon activities instead of just morning activities) or implement the system in a new setting or a new time of the day. If alterations are made, the teacher must explain the changes and new expectations to the student.

Prior to implementing a token economy system with a child with ADHD, several considerations should be noted. Initially, improvements made in the location in which the token economy system was implemented are situational and may not generalize to other settings. If contingency management techniques are consistently executed in other settings through effective communication, generalization can be achieved. In addition, maintenance of treatment gains heavily depends on consistent implementation over long periods of time. Furthermore, the success or failure of a classroom contingency management system relies on the teacher's personality (attitudes), compatibility and/or relationship between the student and teacher, and the teacher's philosophy of child behavioral management. The time available for the teacher to devote to the implementation is important to consider. If teachers have limited time, it is suggested to keep the token economy system as simple as possible, or request an aid to assist in the classroom.

Academic Interventions

As students with ADHD frequently experience academic impairment, they may require interventions that directly address skill and/or performance deficits. Among the support strategies available, the most prominent academic interventions for students with this disorder include explicit instruction, computer-assisted instruction, and peer tutoring (DuPaul & Stoner, 2014).

Explicit Instruction. Explicit instruction involves the systematic presentation of academic skills with ample opportunities for students to respond and receive feedback and reinforcement. Teaching using explicit instruction principles involves (a) providing clear information regarding what is to be learned; (b) instructing skills in small increments using multiple, concrete examples; (c) assessing student skill attainment on a continuous basis; and (d) providing opportunities for active student participation (Nelson, Benner, & Mooney, 2008). There are five key elements of explicit instruction including (a) daily review and prerequisite skill check, (b) teaching of new content, (c) guided practice, (d) independent practice, and (e) weekly/monthly review of skill attainment (Nelson, Benner, & Bohaty, 2014). Although the impact of explicit instruction on the academic achievement of students with ADHD has not been directly evaluated, there are a plethora of studies supporting this teaching approach for children and adolescents with emotional and behavioral disorders (for review and extended discussion see Nelson et al., 2014).

Computer Technology. Computer technology can be used to support the acquisition, practice, and retention of academic skills. Computer-assisted instruction has most frequently been used as a supplement to or in lieu of independent seatwork wherein students practice math and reading skills using computer software rather than paper and pencil. Several single-subject design studies have shown computer-assisted instruction (e.g., Math Blaster) to be associated with gains in attention and skill acquisition for students with ADHD relative to typical seatwork conditions (Mautone, DuPaul, & Jitendra, 2005; Ota & DuPaul, 2002).

Peer-Tutoring Strategies. A variety of peer-tutoring strategies have been developed; however, all involve having students working on academic material in pairs, practicing academic skills in a structured format, and delivering frequent, immediate feedback to each other under teacher supervision. The most widely studied form of peer tutoring is classwide peer tutoring (CWPT; Greenwood, Delquadri, & Carta, 1988), which has been found to improve the on-task behavior and academic performance of students with ADHD (DuPaul, Ervin, Hook, & McGoey, 1998). As an example of the implementation of an academic intervention, the steps for CWPT are presented for use in an elementary school classroom that includes one or more students with ADHD.

Step-by-Step Implementation of CWPT

Step 1. Choose subject matter for CWPT. Peer tutoring can be used to promote skill acquisition and retention in math, reading, and/or spelling. A typical CWPT session lasts 15 to 20 minutes and teachers must decide whether to use this strategy in one, two, or three subject areas. One option is to use CWPT for alternate subject areas across days (e.g., math on Monday, reading on Tuesday).

Step 2. Divide classroom into two "teams" and within teams divide students into pair groups. CWPT involves the participation of every student in the classroom. This is a significant advantage for its use in supporting students with ADHD as it does not isolate or stigmatize any single student and it is a strategy that may improve academic performance for all students. Teachers should strive to form teams that are relatively equal in academic achievement and to assign students who follow classroom rules and are at least average academic performers as tutoring partners for students with ADHD.

Step 3. Train class in CWPT procedures. One or two practice sessions are needed for teachers to guide students through the steps of CWPT, including (a) tutor presenting academic items (e.g., math problems, reading passage) to tutee, (b) tutor reinforcing correct answers with praise and points (e.g., two points for each correct answer), (c) tutor immediately correcting error and offering tutee chance to practice correct

answer three times, (d) tutor reinforcing corrected response with praise and one point, (e) tutor presenting items until signaled by teacher to stop, and (f) students change roles (i.e., tutor becomes tutee and vice versa) and repeat CWPT procedures until signaled by teacher to stop.

Step 4. Implement CWPT for one or more subjects on a regular basis. CWPT should be implemented on a daily basis for 15 to 20 minutes. During the tutoring sessions, teachers should visit tutoring pairs and praise those who are following CWPT procedures. Teachers award bonus points to pairs who are working effectively together. A timer is used to signal when tutoring roles are reversed (e.g., after 10 minutes) and when the tutoring session is complete (e.g., after 20 minutes).

Step 5. Chart progress and provide feedback/reinforcement to students. At the conclusion of each CWPT session, teachers record the number of points earned by each tutoring pair and enter these values on a chart that is visible to the classroom. Points are tallied for each team and student efforts and/or improvements are praised. At the end of the week, the team with the most points is applauded by the other team. Typically, no other rewards beyond praise and recognition are necessary.

Step 6. Modify teams and student pairings, as necessary. Team composition and student pairs may be changed on a weekly basis to ensure that performance is relatively equal across teams and to build positive relationships across students. It is particularly important to rotate pairings for students with ADHD to avoid interpersonal conflicts and/or frustrations that may arise given the social challenges that many students with this disorder face.

Self-Monitoring

Self-monitoring is a commonly used intervention strategy for students with ADHD that is couched within self-regulation interventions. These types of interventions involve high levels of input from the individual and vary in how they are used, including evaluating behavior to predetermined criteria, reinforcing the action of meeting self-regulation goals, and self-monitoring of behavior (Reid, Trout, & Schartz, 2005). The process of self-monitoring involves observing and recording one's behaviors and successful self-monitoring includes two basic steps. First, the student must determine if the target behavior has occurred and following that determination he or she must record that occurrence or nonoccurrence (Mace, Belfiore, & Hutchinson, 2001). The act of self-monitoring can be accomplished through the use of many techniques and can be structured to fit within the individual's setting. Furthermore, this strategy has been shown to be effective with a wide range of ages and in multiple settings such as school and work (Gulchak, 2008). Typically, individuals using a self-monitoring method are trained to evaluate their own behaviors and record these behaviors, using data sheets and/ or some other type of recording device, such as a counter. As described in the following sections, the methods used to self-monitor are determined by the targeted behavior as well as the developmental level of the individual, with practical considerations also taken into account. For example, attention or on-task behavior may be targeted for students who are frequently distracted and have trouble sustaining attention to class activities. Alternatively, task performance (i.e., accuracy of completed worksheet items) may be targeted for students whose primary difficulty is completion of assignments or who tend to rush through assignments.

Training an individual to self-monitor their behavior can focus on either the self-monitoring of attention (SMA) or the self-monitoring of performance (SMP; Reid, Trout, & Schartz, 2005). SMA involves individuals assessing the degree to which they are paying attention to a particular task. Alternatively, SMP is concerned with assessing the quality and/or quantity of performance on a task (e.g., academic assignment).

SMA is often used to increase an individual's on-task performance by prompting him or her to attend to the task at hand. In general, this style of self-monitoring involves using a specified prompt that the individual recognizes as a cue, at which point he or she evaluates whether or not the appropriate level of attention is being paid to the task. The steps included in successfully implementing a SMA intervention are as follows:

Step 1. Identify the target task. Determine the target task that the student should be attending to. This may be an assignment, class, period in the day, or other targeted task. All parties involved (e.g., student, teacher, aide, or other provider) should be informed as to when this task or period starts and when it ends so that there is no confusion about when the student should be self-monitoring attention.

Step 2. Decide on an effective prompt and prompt schedule. Student should receive prompts at regular intervals to self-monitor task-related attention. The prompt should be determined by the student and whomever he or she is working with and may include a sound prompt, a determined passage of time, or another applicable and appropriate prompt (e.g., visual cue from teacher).

Step 3. Teach self-monitoring and expectations. After deciding on a prompt, the student should be explicitly taught how to self-monitor his or her on-task behavior when the prompt occurs. If, for example, the goal is to increase the student's on-task behavior in a specific classroom when an auditory cue occurs, he or she should be taught what is expected of him or her during the class period (e.g., working on assigned material) so that he or she can meet the criteria and successfully self-monitor his or her on-task behavior.

Step 4. Record behavior. The student records whether or not the on-task or attending behavior is occurring. The essence of self-monitoring teaches the student to evaluate whether or not he or she is engaging in the targeted behavior or not and recording it. Documentation can be done in multiple ways; either with pencil and paper, electronic devices, or another method that fits the need of the setting (see Figure 14.1 for an example). Initially, an observer should also record if the student is engaging in the targeted behavior. This should be done to establish (a) whether the procedure should be altered to better suit the situation or needs of the student, (b) whether additional training is required, and (c) the accuracy of the student's self-monitoring.

Step 5. Implement the self-monitoring intervention. Once this skill has been thoroughly taught and the student understands how to self-monitor his or her on-task behavior and attention, the intervention can be implemented. When the cue occurs, the student should evaluate if he or she is appropriately

Self-Monitoring Form for: _____			
Date: _____			
Did I meet my goal for … ?			
Math	Paying **attention** to assigned work	Yes	No
	Following the classroom **rules**	Yes	No
Reading	Paying **attention** to assigned work	Yes	No
	Following the classroom **rules**	Yes	No
Science	Paying **attention** to assigned work	Yes	No
	Following the classroom **rules**	Yes	No
History	Paying **attention** to assigned work	Yes	No
	Following the classroom **rules**	Yes	No
_____	Paying **attention** to assigned work	Yes	No
	Following the classroom **rules**	Yes	No
Goal (number of "Yes"):		**Total "Yes":** *Goal met?*	
		Yes	No
Signed: _____ _____ _____			
Student *Teacher* *Parent*			
Date: _____			

FIGURE 14.1 The self-monitoring form illustrates one way for students to independently record if they are meeting predetermined goals, in this case, goals related to attention (or on-task behavior) as well as general classroom behavior.

exhibiting the on-task/attending behavior that was taught and record the occurrence or nonoccurrence of that behavior in a predetermined manner.

Step 6. Graph recorded behavior. Behavior should be graphed on an ongoing basis. This allows the teacher, parent, student, and/or other interested parties to better understand how the targeted behavior is changing over time as a function of the self-monitoring intervention and if the latter is having the desired effect.

SMP can also increase the occurrence of positive behaviors in students with ADHD. These interventions focus on completion of tasks and/or the accuracy of task performance and can address multiple behaviors and academic or work skills. The steps included in successfully implementing a SMP intervention are similar to those of a SMA intervention but differ in some ways. The steps are as follows:

Step 1. Identify the target behavior. Determine the target behavior that the student should be focusing on. Performance in this case may include domains such as number of problems completed, accuracy of work, or skills (e.g., organization or materials

management). Similar to SMA, SMP may occur in a specific time period or class and this should be established with all parties involved.

Step 2. Decide on an effective prompt and prompt schedule. In the same way that SMA uses prompts, SMP also uses prompts to cue self-monitoring. As described previously, the prompt should be determined in conjunction with the student and whomever he or she is working with. These prompts may include verbal or auditory prompts, the passage of time, visual prompts, or other applicable and appropriate prompts.

Step 3. Teach self-monitoring and expectations. After deciding on a prompt, the student should be explicitly taught how to self-monitor his or her targeted performance when the prompt occurs. If, for example, the goal is to increase the student's planning skills at the end of the school day during a specified time, he or she should be taught what is expected of him or her (e.g., to write down homework assignments and upcoming tests/quizzes) so that all criteria can be met and he or she can monitor his or her planning.

Step 4. Record behavior. The next step is to record the performance of the targeted behavior. Students must be taught to evaluate whether or not they are performing the targeted behavior and record this via pencil and paper, an electronic device, or with another method that is appropriate (see Figure 14.2 for an example). An observer should also record if the student is performing the behavior to establish whether or not the procedure should be altered or trained again to better suit the situation or needs of the student and to establish the accuracy of the student's self-monitoring.

Step 5. Implement the self-monitoring intervention. Once the performance of this skill has been taught and the student understands how to self-monitor his or her performance, the intervention can be implemented. At the onset of the cue, the student should evaluate if he or she is performing the behavior that was taught and record the occurrence or nonoccurrence of that behavior in a predetermined manner.

Step 6. Graph recorded behavior. The student or teacher should graph the performance on an

Completed?	Science (*or:* Monday)	Math (Tuesday)	English (Wednesday)	History (Thursday)	Special (Friday)
Homework/tests/events written in planner					
Binder is free of loose papers					
Materials for class/home work in book bag					
Papers in the appropriate section of binder/folder					

FIGURE 14.2 The self-monitoring form illustrates one way for students to independently record if they are meeting predetermined goals, in this case, goals related to organization and planning.

ongoing basis. This provides better understanding of how the targeted behavior is changing over time as a function of the self-monitoring intervention and if it is having the desired effect.

school personnel to consistently implement behavioral, academic, and self-regulation interventions across settings to optimize children's educational and psychological functioning.

CONCLUSION

ADHD is a chronic neurodevelopmental disorder that is associated with significant academic and/or social impairment over time and across settings. Thus, a long-term, multifaceted approach is needed to successfully treat symptoms and impairment at home, school, and community environments. The most effective treatments are CNS-stimulant medications, behavior modification, academic interventions, and self-regulation strategies. In particular, stimulants and behavioral interventions are considered well-established treatments for ADHD. Although stimulant medication is the single-best treatment for reducing ADHD symptoms, it is rarely, if ever, sufficient especially in addressing the multiple academic and/or social impairments experienced by individuals with this disorder. Thus, the combination of stimulant medication, behavioral interventions at home and school, as well as academic support and/or self-regulation strategies represent the optimal treatment approach for most children and adolescents with ADHD. Mental health professionals should assist families and

SELECT BIBLIOGRAPHY

Barkley, R. A. (Ed.). (2015). *Attention-deficit/ hyperactivity disorder: A handbook for diagnosis and treatment* (4th ed.). New York, NY: Guilford. *This is the most comprehensive compendium of research-based information on all aspects of ADHD, including etiology, diagnosis, and treatment. Authors provide clinically relevant information from medical, psychological, and educational perspectives.*

Children and Adults with ADHD (CHADD). Retrieved from www.chadd.org
CHADD is a national advocacy group for individuals with ADHD. The site includes many helpful fact sheets and other informative resources for parents, teachers, and mental health professionals working with children and adolescents with ADHD.

Evans, S. W., Owens, J. S., & Bunford, N. (2014). Evidence-based psychosocial treatments for children and adolescents with attention-deficit/hyperactivity disorder. *Journal of Clinical Child and Adolescent Psychology: The Official Journal for the Society of Clinical Child and Adolescent Psychology, American Psychological Association, Division 53, 43*(4), 527–551.

This article provides a comprehensive literature review regarding effective psychosocial treatment strategies for children and adolescents with ADHD.

National Resource Center for ADHD. Retrieved from www.help4ADHD.org
Funded by the CDC, this website includes helpful information and resources for parents and teachers working with students with ADHD as well as information for individuals with ADHD.

Reid, R., & Johnson, J. (2012). *Teacher's guide to ADHD.* New York, NY: Guilford.
This is another outstanding resource for general and special education teachers who work with students with ADHD. The emphasis in this book is on educational strategies that will improve academic functioning of children and adolescents with ADHD.

REFERENCES

American Academy of Pediatrics. (2011). ADHD: Clinical practice guideline for the diagnosis, evaluation, and treatment of attention-deficit/hyperactivity disorder in children and adolescents. *Pediatrics, 128,* 1007–1022. doi:10.1542/peds.2011-2654

American Psychiatric Association (APA). (2013). *Diagnostic and statistical manual of mental disorders* (5th ed.). Washington, DC: Author.

Barkley, R. A. (Ed.) (2015). *Attention-deficit/hyperactivity disorder: A handbook for diagnosis and treatment* (3rd ed.). New York, NY: Guilford.

Barkley, R. A., Fischer, M., Smallish, L., & Fletcher, K. (2006). Young adult outcome of hyperactive children: Adaptive functioning in major life activities. *Journal of the American Academy of Child and Adolescent Psychiatry, 45*(2), 192–202.

Bradley, J. D., & Golden, C. J. (2001). Biological contributions to the presentation and understanding of attention-deficit/hyperactivity disorder: A review. *Clinical Psychology Review, 21*(6), 907–929.

Centers for Disease Control and Prevention (CDC). (2013, May 17). Mental health surveillance among children-United States, 2005–2011. *Morbidity and Mortality Weekly Report, 62*(Suppl. 2), 1–35.

DuPaul, G. J., Eckert, T. L., & Vilardo, B. (2012). The effects of school-based interventions for attention deficit hyperactivity disorder: A meta-analysis 1996–2010. *School Psychology Review, 41,* 387–412.

DuPaul, G. J., Ervin, R. A., Hook, C. L., & McGoey, K. E. (1998). Peer tutoring for children with attention deficit hyperactivity disorder: Effects on classroom behavior and academic performance. *Journal of Applied Behavior Analysis, 31*(4), 579–592.

DuPaul, G. J., & Stoner, G. (2014). *ADHD in the schools: Assessment and intervention strategies* (3rd ed.). New York, NY: Guilford.

Evans, S. W., Owens, J. S., & Bunford, N. (2014). Evidence-based psychosocial treatments for children and adolescents with attention-deficit/hyperactivity disorder. *Journal of Clinical Child and Adolescent Psychology: The Official Journal for the Society of Clinical Child and Adolescent Psychology, American Psychological Association, Division 53, 43*(4), 527–551.

Eyberg, S. M., Funderburk, B. W., Hembree-Kigin, T. L., McNeil, C. B., Querido, J. G., & Hood, K. K. (2001). Parent-child interaction therapy with behavior problem children: One and two year maintenance of treatment effects in the family. *Child and Family Behavior Therapy, 23,* 1–20. doi:10.1300/J019v23n04_01

Fabiano, G. A., Pelham, W. E., Coles, E. K., Gnagy, E. M., Chronis-Tuscano, A., & O'Connor, B. C. (2009). A meta-analysis of behavioral treatments for attention-deficit/hyperactivity disorder. *Clinical Psychology Review, 29*(2), 129–140.

Faraone, S. V., & Buitelaar, J. (2010). Comparing the efficacy of stimulants for ADHD in children and adolescents using meta-analysis. *European Child & Adolescent Psychiatry, 19*(4), 353–364.

Faraone, S. V., Biederman, J., Chen, W. J., Milberger, S., Warburton, R., & Tsuang, M. T. (1995). Genetic heterogeneity in attention-deficit hyperactivity disorder (ADHD): Gender, psychiatric comorbidity, and maternal ADHD. *Journal of Abnormal Psychology, 104*(2), 334–345.

Frazier, T. W., Youngstrom, E. A., Glutting, J. J., & Watkins, M. W. (2007). ADHD and achievement: Meta-analysis of the child, adolescent, and adult literatures and a concomitant study with college students. *Journal of Learning Disabilities, 40*(1), 49–65.

Greenwood, C. R., Delquadri, J., & Carta, J. J. (1988). *Classwide peer tutoring.* Seattle, WA: Educational Achievement Systems.

Gulchak, D. J. (2008). Using a mobile handheld computer to teach a student with an emotional and behavioral disorder to self-monitor attention. *Education and Treatment of Children, 31*(4), 567–581. doi:10.1353/etc.0.0028

Hinshaw, S. P., & Scheffler, R. M. (2014). *The ADHD explosion: Myths, medication, money, and today's push for performance.* New York, NY: Oxford University Press.

Hoza, B. (2007). Peer functioning in children with ADHD. *Journal of Pediatric Psychology, 32*(6), 655–663.

Kent, K. M., Pelham, W. E., Molina, B. S., Sibley, M. H., Waschbusch, D. A., Yu, J., … Karch, K. M. (2011). The academic experience of male high school students with ADHD. *Journal of Abnormal Child Psychology, 39*(3), 451–462.

Larsson, J. O., Larsson, H., & Lichtenstein, P. (2004). Genetic and environmental contributions to stability and change of ADHD symptoms between 8 and 13 years of age: A longitudinal twin study. *Journal of the American Academy of Child and Adolescent Psychiatry, 43*(10), 1267–1275.

Mace, F. C, Belfiore, P. J., & Hutchinson, J. M. (2001). Operant theory and research on self-regulation. In B. J. Zimmerman & D. H. Schunk (Eds.), *Self-regulated learning and academic achievement: Theoretical perspectives* (2nd ed., pp. 39–65). Mahwah, NJ: Lawrence Erlbaum.

Mautone, J. A., DuPaul, G. J., & Jitendra, A. K. (2005). The effects of computer-assisted instruction on the mathematics performance and classroom behavior of children with ADHD. *Journal of Attention Disorders, 9*(1), 301–312.

Mick, E., Biederman, J., Faraone, S. V., Sayer, J., & Kleinman, S. (2002). Case-control study of attention-deficit hyperactivity disorder and maternal smoking, alcohol use, and drug use during pregnancy. *Journal of the American Academy of Child and Adolescent Psychiatry, 41*(4), 378–385.

Mick, E., Biederman, J., Prince, J., Fischer, M. J., & Faraone, S. V. (2002). Impact of low birth weight on attention-deficit hyperactivity disorder. *Journal of Developmental and Behavioral Pediatrics, 23*(1), 16–22.

Milberger, S., Biederman, J., Faraone, S. V., Chen, L., & Jones, J. (1996). Is maternal smoking during pregnancy a risk factor for attention deficit hyperactivity disorder in children? *The American Journal of Psychiatry, 153*(9), 1138–1142.

MTA Cooperative Group. (1999). A 14–month randomized clinical trial of treatment strategies for attention-deficit/hyperactivity disorder. *Archives of General Psychiatry, 56*, 1073–1086. doi:10.1001/archpsyc.56.12.1073

Nelson, J. R., Benner, G. J., & Bohaty, J. (2014). Addressing the academic problems and challenges of students with emotional and behavioral disorders. In H. M. Walker & F. M. Gresham (Eds.), *Handbook of evidence-based practices for emotional and behavioral disorders: Applications in schools* (pp. 363–377). New York, NY: Guilford.

Nelson, J. R., Benner, G. J., & Mooney, P. (2008). *Instructional practices for students with behavioral disorders: Strategies for reading, writing, and math.* New York, NY: Guilford.

Nigg, J. T. (2006). *What causes ADHD? Understanding what goes wrong and why.* New York, NY: Guilford.

O'Leary, K. D., Becker, W. C., Evans, M. B., & Saudargas, R. A. (1969). A token reinforcement program in a public school: A replication and systematic analysis. *Journal of Applied Behavior Analysis, 2*(1), 3–13.

Ota, K. R., & DuPaul, G. J. (2002). Task engagement and mathematics performance in children with attention deficit hyperactivity disorder: Effects of supplemental computer instruction. *School Psychology Quarterly, 17*, 242–257. doi:10.1521/scpq.17.3.242.20881

Owens, J. S., Holdaway, A. S., Zoromski, A. K., Evans, S. W., Himawan, L. K., Girio-Herrera, E., & Murphy, C. E. (2012). Incremental benefits of a daily report card intervention over time for youth with disruptive behavior. *Behavior Therapy, 43*(4), 848–861.

Reid. R., Trout, A. L., & Schartz, M. (2005). Self-regulation interventions for children with attention deficit/hyperactivity disorder. *Exceptional Children, 71*(4), 361–377.

Sonuga-Barke, E. J., Daley, D., Thompson, M., Laver-Bradbury, C., & Weeks, A. (2001). Parent-based therapies for preschool attention-deficit/hyperactivity disorder: A randomized, controlled trial with a community sample. *Journal of the American Academy of Child and Adolescent Psychiatry, 40*(4), 402–408.

Stein, M. A., Waldman, I. D., Sarampote, C. S., Seymour, K. E., Robb, A. S., Conlon, C., … Cook,

E. H. (2005). Dopamine transporter genotype and methylphenidate dose response in children with ADHD. *Neuropsychopharmacology: Official Publication of the American College of Neuropsychopharmacology, 30*(7), 1374–1382.

Stormont, M. (2001). Social outcomes of children with ADHD: Contributing factors and implications for practice. *Psychology in the Schools, 38,* 521–531. doi:10.1002/pits.1040

Thapar, A., Cooper, M., Eyre, O., & Langley, K. (2013). What have we learnt about the causes of ADHD? *Journal of Child Psychology and Psychiatry, and Allied Disciplines, 54*(1), 3–16.

Theule, J., Wiener, J., Tannock, R., & Jenkins, J. M. (2013). Parenting stress in families of children with ADHD: A meta-analysis. *Journal of Emotional and Behavioral Disorders, 21,* 3–17. doi:10.1177/1063426610387433

Valera, E. M., Faraone, S. V., Murray, K. E., & Seidman, L. J. (2007). Meta-analysis of structural imaging findings in attention-deficit/hyperactivity disorder. *Biological Psychiatry, 61*(12), 1361–1369.

Visser, S. N., Danielson, M. L., Bitsko, R. H., Holbrook, J. R., Kogan, M. D., Ghandour, R. M.,...Blumberg, S. J. (2014). Trends in the parent-report of health care provider-diagnosed and medicated attention-deficit/hyperactivity disorder: United States, 2003–2011. *Journal of the American Academy of Child and Adolescent Psychiatry, 53*(1), 34–46.e2.

Waldman, I. D., & Gizer, I. R. (2006). The genetics of attention deficit hyperactivity disorder. *Clinical Psychology Review, 26*(4), 396–432.

Wolosin, S. M., Richardson, M. E., Hennessey, J. G., Denckla, M. B., & Mostofsky, S. H. (2009). Abnormal cerebral cortex structure in children with ADHD. *Human Brain Mapping, 30*(1), 175–184.

Evidence-Based Interventions for Oppositional Defiant Disorder in Children and Adolescents

Jeffrey D. Burke and Rolf Loeber

OVERVIEW

Oppositional defiant disorder (ODD) is characterized by chronic problems with noncompliance and defiance, antagonism, and irritability, typically having an onset in early childhood. Children with ODD struggle in family and peer interactions (Burke, Pardini, & Loeber, 2008; Tseng, Kawabata, & Gau, 2011), in social settings (Burke, Rowe, & Boylan, 2014; Burke, Waldman, & Lahey, 2010; Munkvold, Lundervold, & Manger, 2011; van Lier & Koot, 2010), and academically (Harpold et al., 2007). Significantly, they are at increased risk of comorbid depression, anxiety, attention deficit hyperactivity disorder (ADHD), and conduct disorder (CD). Research indicates that the negative outcomes stemming from ODD (i.e., familial and social impairment; risk for other psychopathology) persist into adulthood (Burke, Rowe, & Boylan, 2014; Burke & Stepp, 2012; Leadbeater et al., 2012). Despite these broad and enduring deleterious consequences, several factors have limited the recognition of the significance of the disorder. In particular, the perception that ODD is exclusively a behavioral disorder of childhood, primarily associated with problematic parent–child interactions, has shaped the development and focus of commonly available interventions. Furthermore, parents may be more reluctant to seek appropriate services for children with ODD if they perceive that their child's behavior serves as an indicator of poor parenting.

ODD was first formalized as a diagnostic category in the *Diagnostic and Statistical Manual of Mental Disorders* (3rd ed.; *DSM-III*; American Psychiatric Association [APA], 1980) and has historically been characterized as a behavioral disorder. A prohibition against assigning a diagnosis of CD was implemented because of a belief that, if the criteria for CD were met, the criteria for ODD would also likely be met. The perceived association between ODD and CD on the part of researchers and practitioners has been so great that relatively little information exists about the course of ODD independent of CD (Burke, Waldman, & Lahey, 2010). Some scholars have questioned whether ODD should even be maintained as a distinct disorder (Moffitt et al., 2008).

ODD Symptoms. A fundamental understanding of ODD requires awareness of the symptoms of the disorder, which include often losing temper, being touchy or easily annoyed, being angry and resentful, defiant or noncompliant, arguing with those in authority, annoying others, blaming others and not taking accountability for their actions, and being spiteful or vindictive toward others (APA,

2013). In particular, it is important to understand how these symptoms function to identify a distinct condition and a distinct population of children. A focus on oppositional and defiant aspects of the disorder, without due recognition of other features such as persisting irritability or anger may obscure key distinctions between ODD and other behavioral disorders. A restricted understanding of the breadth of the symptoms would also risk diagnosing children who are oppositional where such behavior is developmentally appropriate for their age, and otherwise do not meet criteria for the disorder.

Without a full appreciation of the symptoms, one might feel justified in conceptualizing ODD as indicative of nothing more than mild antisocial behavior. For example, the item "often actively defies [...] authority figures or [...] rules" (APA, 2013, p. 462) manifestly includes rule-breaking behavior, which could be seen as the foundation from which more discrete antisocial behaviors might arise. Indeed, rule breaking was previously a much more prominent feature of ODD; *DSM-III* (APA, 1980) included only five symptoms of ODD, the first of which was "violations of minor rules." As with any disorder, however, it is faulty to draw such conclusions from the consideration of a single symptom. ODD does mark an increased risk for the development of antisocial behavior, but a robust evidence base illustrates that ODD denotes a risk for affective psychopathology as well. In fact, ODD substantially explains the comorbidity often seen between behavioral disorders and affective disorders (Burke & Loeber, 2010; Copeland, Shanahan, Costello, & Angold, 2009).

Furthermore, there are important distinctions between ODD and other categories of behavioral psychopathology as well. In particular, ODD does not include aggressive behaviors among its symptoms, nor do those symptoms include violations of the law, whereas CD consists of a set of discrete antisocial behaviors that include status offenses (e.g., skipping school), property violations (e.g., vandalism and theft), and aggression. It is most distinctive of ODD that it also includes a dimension of affectively oriented symptoms commonly referred to as "irritability" (e.g., Burke et al., 2014; discussed more extensively in the following), which are not present in the other antisocial behavioral disorders described in the *Diagnostic and Statistical Manual of Mental Disorders* (5th ed.; *DSM-5*; APA, 2013). Although interventions for

ODD are often applied to CD or to aggressive behavior as well, such broad interventions may be inappropriate to the treatment of ODD, and may not suitably address the irritability dimension of ODD.

Beyond the differences evident in the content of the symptoms, empirical evidence further supports the distinction between ODD and other behavioral disorders. Studies consistently find that ODD symptoms reflect a separate dimension from CD, ADHD, and other forms of psychopathology (e.g., Bezdjian et al., 2011; Burns, Boe, Walsh, Sommers-Flanagan, & Teegarden, 2001; Frick et al., 1993; Hartman et al., 2001). Studies have also identified multiple dimensions within ODD—consistently one irritability dimension with either one or two behavioral dimensions (e.g., Aebi et al., 2010; Burke, 2012; Burke et al., 2010, 2014; Stringaris & Goodman, 2009a). These dimensions have significant implications for the development of comorbid conditions associated with ODD, discussed as follows.

The irritability dimension of ODD, which includes symptoms of anger, being touchy or easily annoyed, and frequently losing one's temper, likely affects interactions with others more generally, while also impacting parent–child interactions. A significant change to the *DSM-5* description of ODD was a reflection of these dimensions in the criteria for the disorder. Additional changes to the *DSM-5* also demonstrate an understanding that this is not a disorder limited to childhood or to poor parent–child interactions. For example, the symptoms now include language indicating problematic adult interactions with authority figures. The revised symptoms in the *DSM-5* include relationships beyond that of parents and children, and likely reflect the nature of interactions with others into adulthood (Burke, Rowe, & Boylan, 2014). The symptoms of the disorder have always included features pertinent to relationships other than that between parent and child. Blaming others, irritating others, and being spiteful or vindictive pertain to behaviors that impede the development of positive and prosocial peer relationships, and clearly are not limited to interactions between children.

ODD Prevalence. ODD is among the most prevalent disorders in childhood. Epidemiological studies find cross-sectional rates ranging from as low as 1% to as high as 15% (Boylan, Vaillancourt, Boyle, & Szatmari, 2007; Maughan, Rowe,

Messer, Goodman, & Meltzer, 2004), varying by gender, age, types of measures used, and differences in samples. Across studies, most estimates fall between 3% and 6% (Boylan et al., 2007). A lifetime prevalence rate of 10.2% was found using retrospective report among adults (Nock, Kazdin, Hiripi, & Kessler, 2007). The prevalence rate does not vary by cultures or geographic regions (Canino, Polanczyk, Bauermeister, Rhode, & Frick, 2010).

Prevalence Rates by Gender. In childhood, prevalence rates vary by gender, with boys being diagnosed two to three times the rate of girls. This difference narrows with development caused by the increasing rates of ODD among girls (Boylan et al., 2007). Retrospective lifetime prevalence estimates reported by Nock et al. (2007) show a modest difference between men (11.2%) and women (9.2%).

Leadbeater and colleagues (2012) examined ODD symptoms from adolescence through young adulthood and found further support for differences in developmental trajectories for men and women. Young men showed a stable trajectory through age 24 years, whereas women showed increasing symptoms through late adolescence, followed by a decline into young adulthood (Leadbeater et al., 2012). Although young men tended to show higher mean symptoms of ODD than women between the ages of 12 and 24, these differences rarely reached a significant level. Thus, differences in rates of ODD between boys and girls are most apparent in childhood, but increasing rates among girls result in largely similar rates of ODD by adolescence. No studies have examined rates of ODD symptoms, let alone gender differences, beyond young adulthood.

Prevalence in Clinic Populations. ODD is extremely common in clinic samples of children, with rates of ODD among children in clinics as high as 65% (Boylan et al., 2007). In part, high rates in clinical samples may be associated with the high salience of ODD behaviors in parents (Teagle, 2002). ODD behaviors are associated with parental burden (Bussing, Gary, et al., 2003), resulting in parents' decisions to seek treatment for their child (Bussing, Zima, et al., 2003). ODD also exerts a negative influence on parenting behaviors, leading to an increase in poor communication, coercive interactions, lower parental involvement, and reduced disciplinary efforts (Burke et al., 2008).

Comorbidity. ODD is a disorder with high rates of comorbidity with other psychopathology, including ADHD, CD, depression, and anxiety (Burke, Loeber, & Birmaher, 2002). The association between ODD and depression (Burke, Loeber, Lahey, & Rathouz, 2005; Copeland et al., 2009) is so robust that ODD may serve as a better predictor of depression than depression itself. In a community sample, after accounting for depression, anxiety, CD, and other comorbid conditions, only ODD in childhood predicted depression in adulthood. In the same sample, ODD and anxiety disorders in adolescence—but not depression—predicted adult depression (Copeland et al., 2009). Ultimately, it appears that a historical focus on a theoretical link between CD and depression (e.g., Puig-Antich, 1982) may have resulted from a failure to consider ODD. Other adult outcomes associated with ODD have included borderline personality disorder in young men (Burke & Stepp, 2012) and women (Stepp, Burke, Hipwell, & Loeber, 2012) and neuroticism (Burke, 2012).

The comorbidity of ODD with behavioral and affective disorders appears to be accounted for by the aforementioned dimensions among the symptoms of ODD (Burke, 2012; Burke et al., 2014; Burke, Hipwell, & Loeber, 2010; Burke & Loeber, 2010; Lavigne et al., 2014; Rowe, Costello, Angold, Copeland, & Maughan, 2010; Stringaris & Goodman, 2009b). Irritability serves as a risk factor for developing problems with depression and anxiety (Burke, 2012; Burke et al., 2010; Rowe et al., 2010; Stringaris & Goodman, 2009a,b). This risk is circumscribed, in that the irritability dimension of ODD has been shown not to predict subsequent problems with bipolar disorder (Stringaris, Cohen, Pine, & Leibenluft, 2009), borderline personality disorder (Burke & Stepp, 2012), ADHD (Dougherty et al., 2013; Krieger et al., 2013), and conduct problems (Whelan, Stringaris, Maughan, & Barker, 2013). Furthermore, the presence of mood and anxiety problems, but not behavioral psychopathology or substance use among parents, has been found to predict irritability in children (Dougherty et al., 2013; Krieger et al., 2013). Genetic evidence, reviewed in the following, may help to illustrate the intergenerational linkage between the irritability dimension of ODD and affective disorders.

Research has begun to identify limitations to the hierarchical developmental model in which

ODD leads to CD, and conversely in which CD arises from ODD (e.g., *Diagnostic and Statistical Manual of Mental Disorders* [4th ed.; *DSM-IV*; APA, 1994]). Only a minority of children with ODD—approximately one third at most—will go on to develop CD (Burke et al., 2010; Rowe et al., 2010). There may also be important gender differences in these developmental pathways; ODD may serve as a risk factor for CD in boys but not girls (Rowe et al., 2010). Furthermore, evidence suggests that up to half of youth who meet the criteria for CD may not have previously met the criteria for ODD, and that the ODD-to-CD pathway is less frequent as children develop into adolescence (Rowe et al., 2010). Finally, ODD differs from CD in that it does not itself predict antisocial personality disorder (APD; Burke, Lahey, & Waldman, 2010; Lahey, Loeber, Burke, & Applegate, 2005).

ETIOLOGY AND FACTORS CONTRIBUTING TO ODD IN CHILDREN AND ADOLESCENTS

Several factors have been identified as etiologically relevant to ODD. Theories of the development of ODD have focused on parenting practices and/or parent–child relationships. For example, Patterson's (1982) coercion model suggests that some behavioral problems arise when a parent issues a command, the child responds in a noncompliant manner, and the parent gives in. This reinforces the child's disobedience because the parents conceded to the child, making it more likely that such behaviors are repeated in the future. Patterson's model was not developed specifically for ODD, but theoretically explains ODD behaviors. Burke et al. (2008) found that parental reluctance to discipline the unacceptable behavior of their children led to increasing levels of ODD. That study also suggested that children with ODD had more control over parental behavior. Thus, how parents respond impacts the progression of ODD.

Genetics

Consistent with the idea that ODD is not simply a function of parent–child interactions, evidence strongly suggests biological contributions. Studies suggest that between 40% and 60% of variability in ODD may be explained by a genetic liability (Dick, Viken, Kaprio, Pulkkinen, & Rose, 2005; Rowe, Rijsdijk, Maughan, Eley, & Hosang, 2008). These studies consistently find that the remainder of the variability in ODD is explained by non-shared environmental factors (those that make twins more different from one another) and that shared environmental factors common to both twins explain essentially none of the variability in ODD. Research has identified unique genetic influences that differentiate ODD from CD and ADHD (Dick et al., 2005; Rowe et al., 2008). Where comorbidity is observed between these disorders, it appears to be due, at least in part, to common genetic influences (Dick et al., 2005).

Two studies have used behavioral genetic analyses to focus on the irritability dimension of ODD. The association observed at the phenotypic level between the irritability dimension of ODD and depression and anxiety has a genetic component (Savage et al., 2015; Stringaris, Zavos, Leibenluft, Maughan, & Eley, 2012). The links between behavioral dimensions of ODD and other behavioral disorders are influenced by separate and distinct genetic factors (Stringaris et al., 2012). These results highlight the importance of assessing for irritability in the context of ODD and provide evidence for a possible mechanism explaining developmental linkages between irritability and depression. In sum, genetics plays a role in ODD, including behavioral problems and coexisting internalizing difficulties, such as anxiety and depression.

EVIDENCE-BASED INTERVENTIONS AND EMPIRICAL SUPPORT FOR ODD IN CHILDREN AND ADOLESCENTS

There are many intervention models that address ODD-related behaviors. A comprehensive review of the literature on psychosocial evidence-based interventions (EBI) for disruptive behavioral problems (Eyberg, Nelson, & Boggs, 2008) identified 34 studies that met criteria as having been well conducted. From these studies, one treatment model was determined to be "well established," and 15 others were rated as "probably efficacious," based on criteria established by a task force on promotion and dissemination of psychological procedures (Chambless & Hollon, 1998).

Of course, the provider looking for an EBI for ODD will not find all 16 models to be appropriate treatment for a given child, as the models vary in intensity and in delivery. Thus, it is important to select an intervention that is suitable to the child, the problems, and the context. Multidimensional treatment foster care (MTFC; Chamberlain & Smith, 2003), for instance, is appropriate only for children being placed outside of the home. Multisystemic therapy (MST; Henggeler & Lee, 2003) was developed for juvenile delinquent populations (e.g., Olsson, 2010) and would not be well matched to the needs of an ODD population outside of such a facility.

The available treatment models differ more in terms of the age of the population for which they were designed than they do in terms of the features of the disorders they target. The interventions also differ in terms of intended severity of the behavioral problem, so that treatments established for younger children also target a lower severity of behavioral problems. For example, many of the models identified by Eyberg et al. (2008) have been developed for application in early childhood, including Parent–Child Interaction Therapy (PCIT, ages 2–7 years; Brinkmeyer & Eyberg, 2003); Helping the Noncompliant Child (ages 3–8 years; Forehand & McMahon, 1981); and the Incredible Years (ages 2–8 or 2–10 years for the parent component; Webster-Stratton & Reid, 2003). Because of the tendency to collapse interventions across ODD and CD and the lack of distinct ODD-specific treatment models, relatively fewer treatment options are available for treating an adolescent who struggles with ODD and does not also show more severe behavioral problems like aggression or CD.

Overall, although there are clearly a number of treatment models available for children with disruptive behavior problems, they have been developed largely to target dimensions of behaviors (e.g., noncompliance, aggression, and violence) rather than targeting disorders in particular. There are developmental periods, variations in severity of need, and varying contextual factors that are not comprehensively addressed by established treatment models. Mental health providers need to match the needs of children and families to an appropriate evidence-based intervention.

HOW TO: A GUIDE TO THE IMPLEMENTATION OF INTERVENTIONS FOR ODD IN CHILDREN AND ADOLESCENTS

To illustrate variations on types of interventions for ODD, three models reflecting somewhat different treatment modalities (dyadic observation and live instruction, group-based treatment, and individual parent-management training) are discussed. Despite differences in the format and delivery of these treatment models, commonalities across them illustrate key steps involved when treating ODD, and specifics of each model will be used to exemplify each step. The first of these models, PCIT (Brinkmeyer & Eyberg, 2003; Zisser & Eyberg, 2010), has been demonstrated as efficacious for children between the ages of 2 and 7 years. It is delivered as individual outpatient therapy, but is distinguished by having the therapist directly observing from another room while providing feedback and instruction to parents.

Second, the Incredible Years Program (Webster-Stratton & Reid, 2003) has several modules, covering a range of ages from 0 to 13 years, and is developed for parents, children, and teachers. The parenting program (Webster-Stratton, 1981) has been expanded to provide specific program curricula for infants (0–1 years), toddlers (1–3 years), preschool children (3–6 years), and school-aged (6–13 years) children. The intervention is designed to be delivered in small-group sessions, which make use of group discussion and video vignettes modeling social learning.

Finally, a third example is parent management training. Russell Barkley's parent-management training program (Defiant Children; Barkley, 2013) presents a clear and well-structured 10-step program for individual work with parents of children who show problems with oppositional and defiant behavior. The conceptual model underlying the intervention posits four contributing factors to defiant children's behavior: (a) disrupted parenting, (b) child characteristics (e.g., negative temperament), (c) parental characteristics (e.g., adult ADHD), and (d) social ecology (e.g., marital conflict or divorce). Additionally, coercion theory (Patterson, 1982) is integral to the model.

Step 1. Ensure that the initial assessment provides sufficient information regarding antecedents and consequences pertinent to ODD-related behaviors, understanding the contexts and environments in which the behaviors occur and the environmental responses following the behaviors. As noted previously, sufficient attention should be given during the assessment to irritability symptoms typical of the child. Additionally, it is important to fully understand the nature of prior disciplinary efforts taken at home, school, or in other settings. This is crucial, because often the child has shown at least partially successful response to prior strategies, which may simply have needed some fine-tuning in order to be maximally effective. Relatedly, it is important to be aware that parents may describe, in shorthand, prior disciplinary strategies that have failed (e.g., "We've tried time-out and that did not work."). Often, when these assertions are probed further, it turns out that the parent employed the strategy in a fashion that undermined the effort, such as continuing to engage with the child during time-out.

Step 2. Provide psychoeducation to orient parents regarding ODD and the work to come. This must include a discussion about basic behavioral principles, especially regarding the use of reinforcement and punishment strategies. Parents should be educated regarding how ODD behaviors originate and are maintained. Parents may express resistance to the concept of rewarding, or even bribing, children for doing something they should be doing naturally. They may also view reinforcement as involving only tangible, or even monetary, reinforcers. These views should be gently challenged during psychoeducation, and will likely need to be addressed throughout the initial intervention period. If parents report the use of physical punishment, initial psychoeducation should include a discussion of evidence of the limited effectiveness and potential harmful outcomes associated with these practices, especially in contrast to the empirically supported techniques that the therapist will train them to employ.

Step 3. Establish nurturing and positive parent–child interactions. When parents and children first engage in services, they are typically at a peak of stressful, unrewarding, and negative interactions and mutually rewarding and positive interactions are minimal. First steps in therapy involve breaking these entrenched patterns by having parents focus on providing praise (i.e., catch children being good) and engaging in nondirective activities with children. Concepts regarding punishment or response cost are not introduced early in sessions.

In PCIT, this step is reflected in the initial focus on child-directed interaction. During child-directed interaction, the therapist instructs the parent to respond to the child's behavior and to resist any efforts to direct or control the child's activities. Parents are instructed to refrain from issuing commands, asking questions, or expressing critical thoughts or comments. The therapist provides training, practice, and guidance for parents in the use of techniques such as praising of children's desirable behavior, using reflection to express the child's statements back to them, and simply providing descriptive statements of the child's behaviors. Parents are provided with instructional material and given daily practice activities. In coaching sessions, the therapist provides guidance, support, and direction for parents in using these skills. The therapist may focus particular attention on techniques that have proven to be especially difficult for the parent. As therapy progresses in this stage, parents are taught to use differential attention to desirable behaviors while ignoring negative behaviors, to help shape parental nurturance, and to provide a foundation for shaping desirable child behaviors. More problematic child behaviors (e.g., hitting others or throwing objects) are met with a suspension of the play activity until the child reestablishes appropriate behavioral control. The child-directed phase of the intervention continues until parents demonstrate mastery of the techniques.

In both the Incredible Years Program and Barkley's Defiant Children models, initial steps include working with parents to enhance their attention to positive or desirable behavior on the part of children. During periods in which a high frequency of distressing interactions occurs, parents may lose sight of the fact that children are not always engaging in undesirable behavior. Catching a child being good is a technique that helps parents to provide positive reinforcement for desirable behavior, such as playing quietly, that might otherwise go unremarked on. Parent training in the use of practices of basic contingent responding to desirable behavior with praise, ignoring nonsignificant noxious or undesirable behaviors, and selective attention to preferred behavior helps to provide a strong focus on increasing the frequency of reinforcement of desirable behavior.

Step 4. Increase authoritative parenting and child compliance. Building on the foundation established during the initial phase of treatment, parental skills are further developed in this step. In PCIT, treatment moves from child-directed to parent-directed interactions. The parent-directed interaction phase of treatment continues to include positive attention to desirable child behaviors, but introduces parental direction of activities. Parents are guided to be consistent and calm in responding to children's behaviors. They are taught to use clear and direct positive commands. The therapist provides education regarding how to use commands that are appropriate to the child's age.

In the Incredible Years Program, this step of treatment involves helping parents to establish and maintain reliable routines, develop and maintain clear and consistent household rules, give clear and effective commands, and enhance their application of appropriate reinforcement procedures. The Defiant Children Program includes modules to train parents in the use of a behavioral program, with tokens or points as reinforcers for a specific set of targeted behaviors. Subsequent to the successful introduction of the program, parents are instructed about response cost procedures for a highly circumscribed set of undesirable behaviors, and train parents how to implement response cost appropriately. Finally, once positive behaviors are mastered, parents are trained to generalize time-out to misbehavior in other settings and with other individuals.

Across models, this step includes the introduction of the use of time-out procedures. Time-out is commonly misunderstood but is exceptionally powerful, so careful consideration is given to training parents in this procedure. Time-out represents a removal from all reinforcement; parents may not initially appreciate that even unpleasant or conflict-laden interactions may serve as reinforcement and thus undermine the effectiveness of time-out. Parents are instructed to establish and employ a consistent protocol including the location for time-out. Once implemented, parents are trained to see the time-out protocol through without acquiescence.

Step 5. Improve parental use of personal anger management and problem-solving skills and reduce parental stress. Parental effectiveness is impaired when parental personal resources are taxed and stress is high. Although listed as Step 5 in this sequence, attention to parental concerns should occur from initial assessment throughout the intervention. A transition in focus may occur, however, from addressing clear impediments to success during the initial stages to a focus on encouraging parents to engage in ongoing self-care in order to maximize their effectiveness with their children. Concerns that may need to be addressed early on include marital conflict and parental psychopathology. Efforts to change children's behavior benefit greatly from having all caregivers on board and working collaboratively. Parental conflict reduces consistency in parenting behaviors, and children may take advantage of parental disagreement to the detriment of the intervention.

As noted by Barkley (2013) and in the literature reviewed earlier, behavioral problems often have a strong heritability component, suggesting that parents may be struggling with similar disruptions in functioning that their child is experiencing. Attention to parental ADHD, including pharmacotherapy, may reduce parental impulsive decision making and inattention that could undermine consistency. The Incredible Years Program includes a specific program to enhance parental personal control and reduce parental stress. This program, entitled ADVANCE, focuses on substituting positive parental self-talk for angry and self-defeating statements. The program builds effective communication skills and problem-solving skills for adults and highlights strengthening self-care behaviors including the use of social supports.

The three selected programs are not the only established treatment programs pertinent to intervention for ODD. They represent several variations in treatment modalities, such as the use of group versus individualized treatment protocols; individualized protocols for parents, children, and teachers; and the use of direct observation and real-time feedback. Common to these interventions, and to established treatments for ODD more broadly, are a reliance on behavioral principles, training parents in the use of behaviorally based techniques, efforts to improve communication and to foster supportive parent–child interactions.

Given the emerging focus on irritability as a distinguishable component of ODD (e.g., Burke et al., 2014) and the implications of this dimension for children's outcomes over the near and long term (Burke, 2012; Burke et al., 2010; Rowe et al., 2010; Stringaris & Goodman, 2009b; Whelan et al., 2013), it is clear that interventions for ODD should include an increased focus in the assessment of irritability and other behavioral problems. Treatment should incorporate specific elements that focus on the reduction of irritability where this is identified as a concern for a particular child. Further validation will be required to ensure that interventions sufficiently reduce irritability and help to prevent the development of depression and anxiety.

CONCLUSION

ODD is a distressing disorder involving elements of noncompliance, noxious or antagonizing behaviors, and irritability. The general historical perspective of ODD as essentially a milder form of CD has likely hindered the necessary research and clinical attention it deserved. Recent research has shown that ODD impacts children's functioning beyond simply conflict with parents. ODD and its outcomes persist beyond childhood, and it contributes to affective psychopathology as well. Distinguishable dimensions of ODD include an irritability component as well as one or more related behavioral components. Mental health professionals should ensure that their assessment is sufficient to identify the presence of irritability; specific treatment efforts to address irritability may help to reduce later problems with mood and anxiety disorders. There are several well-established treatment models pertinent to ODD, and these offer some variety in treatment modalities. However, existing treatments are typically generalized to disruptive behaviors rather than being specific to ODD. Existing treatments may need to be augmented, or new treatments developed, to specifically address irritability and its risk for affective psychopathology. Existing treatments focus on the childhood years; relatively less guidance exists for working with adolescents with ODD. No known treatments have been advanced yet for treating ODD behaviors in adulthood.

SELECT BIBLIOGRAPHY

Barkley, R. A. (2013). *Defiant children* (3rd ed.). New York, NY: Guilford.
Russell Barkley's Defiant Children *is a clinician's manual that describes a straightforward, empirically supported and theoretically grounded approach to working with parents and children struggling with defiant and noncompliant behavior. Also available are Barkley's books written for parents of defiant children and defiant teens.*

Lochman, J. E., Evans, S. C., Burke, J. D., Roberts, M. C., Fite, P. J., Reed, G. M., . . . Elena Garralda, M. (2015). An empirically based alternative to *DSM-5*'s disruptive mood dysregulation disorder for ICD-11. *World Psychiatry, 14,* 30–33. doi:10.1002/wps.20176
Lochman and colleagues (2015) present a comprehensive but concise review of the empirical literature regarding the irritability dimension of ODD. The review focuses on explaining the decision to include a new diagnostic specifier for ODD (with irritability) in the upcoming revision of the International Classification of Diseases (ICD) instead of the new DSM-5 category of Disruptive Mood Dysregulation Disorder.

REFERENCES

Aebi, M., Muller, U. C., Asherson, P., Banaschewski, T., Buitelaar, J., Ebstein, R., . . . Steinhausen, H. C. (2010). Predictability of oppositional defiant disorder and symptom dimensions in children and adolescents with ADHD combined type. *Psychological Medicine, 40,* 2089–2100. doi:10.1017/S0033291710000590

American Psychiatric Association. (1980). *Diagnostic and statistical manual of mental disorders* (3rd ed.). Washington, DC: American Psychiatric Association.

American Psychiatric Association (APA). (1994). *Diagnostic and statistical manual of mental disorders* (4th ed.). Washington, DC: American Psychiatric Association.

American Psychiatric Association (APA). (2013). *Diagnostic and statistical manual of mental disorders* (5th ed.). Arlington, VA: American Psychiatric Publishing.

Barkley, R. A. (2013). *Defiant children* (3rd ed.). New York, NY: Guilford.

Bezdjian, S., Krueger, R. F., Derringer, J., Malone, S., McGue, M., & Iacono, W. G. (2011). The structure of *DSM-IV* ADHD, ODD, and CD criteria in adolescent boys: A hierarchical approach. *Psychiatry Research, 188,* 411–421. doi:10.1016/j.psychres.2011.02.027

Boylan, K., Vaillancourt, T., Boyle, M., & Szatmari, P. (2007). Comorbidity of internalizing disorders in children with oppositional defiant disorder. *European Child & Adolescent Psychiatry, 16,* 484–494. doi:10.1007/s00787–007–0624–1

Brinkmeyer, M. Y., & Eyberg, S. M. (2003). Parent–child interaction therapy for oppositional children. In A. E. Kazdin & J. R. Weisz (Eds.), *Evidenced-based psychotherapies for children and adolescents* (pp. 204–223). New York, NY: Guilford.

Burke, J. D. (2012). An affective dimension within oppositional defiant disorder symptoms among boys: Personality and psychopathology outcomes into early adulthood. *Journal of Child Psychology & Psychiatry, 53,* 1176–1183. doi:10.1111/j.1469–7610.2012.02598.x

Burke, J. D., Boylan, K., Rowe, R., Duku, E., Stepp, S. D., Hipwell, A. E., & Waldman, I. D. (2014). Identifying the irritability dimension of ODD: Application of a modified bifactor model across five large community samples of children. *Journal of Abnormal Psychology, 123,* 841–851. doi:10.1037/a0037898

Burke, J. D., Hipwell, A. E., & Loeber, R. (2010). Dimensions of oppositional defiant disorder as predictors of depression and conduct disorder in preadolescent girls. *Journal of the American Academy of Child & Adolescent Psychiatry, 49,* 484–492. doi:10.1097/00004583–201005000–00009

Burke, J. D., & Loeber, R. (2010). Oppositional defiant disorder and the explanation of the comorbidity between behavioral disorders and depression. *Clinical Psychology: Science and Practice, 17,* 319–326. doi:10.1111/j.1468–2850.2010.01223.x

Burke, J. D., Loeber, R., & Birmaher, B. (2002). Oppositional defiant and conduct disorder: A review of the past 10 years, Part II. *Journal of the American Academy of Child and Adolescent Psychiatry, 41,* 1275–1293. doi:10.1097/01.Chi.0000024839.60748.E8

Burke, J. D., Loeber, R., Lahey, B. B., & Rathouz, P. J. (2005). Developmental transitions among affective and behavioral disorders in adolescent boys. *Journal of Child Psychology and Psychiatry, 46,* 1200–1210. doi:10.1111/j.1469–7610.2005.00422.x

Burke, J. D., Pardini, D. A., & Loeber, R. (2008). Reciprocal relationships between parenting behavior and disruptive psychopathology from childhood through adolescence. *Journal of Abnormal Child Psychology, 36,* 679–692. doi:10.1007/s10802–008–9219–7

Burke, J. D., Rowe, R., & Boylan, K. (2014). Functional outcomes of child and adolescent ODD in young adult men. *Journal of Child Psychiatry and Psychology, 55,* 264–272. doi:10.1111/jcpp.12150

Burke, J. D., & Stepp, S. D. (2012). Adolescent disruptive behavior and borderline personality disorder symptoms in young adult men. *Journal of Abnormal Child Psychology, 40,* 35–44. doi:10.1007/s10802–011–9558–7

Burke, J. D., Waldman, I., & Lahey, B. B. (2010). Predictive validity of childhood oppositional defiant disorder and conduct disorder: Implications for the *DSM-V. Journal of Abnormal Psychology, 119,* 739–751. doi:2010–19345–001 [pii] 10.1037/a0019708

Burns, G. L., Boe, B., Walsh, J. A., Sommers-Flanagan, R., & Teegarden, L. A. (2001). A confirmatory factor analysis on the *DSM-IV* ADHD and ODD symptoms: What is the best model for the organization of these symptoms? *Journal of Abnormal Child Psychology, 29,* 339–349.

Bussing, R., Gary, F. A., Mason, D. M., Leon, C. E., Sinha, K., & Garvan, C. W. (2003). Child temperament, ADHD, and caregiver strain: Exploring relationships in an epidemiological sample. *Journal of the American Academy of Child and Adolescent Psychiatry, 42,* 184–192. doi:10.1097/00004583–200302000–00012

Bussing, R., Zima, B. T., Gary, F. A., Mason, D. M., Leon, C. E., Sinha, K., & Garvan, C. W. (2003). Social networks, caregiver strain, and utilization of mental health services among elementary school students at high risk for ADHD. *Journal of the American Academy of Child and Adolescent Psychiatry, 42,* 842–850. doi:10.1097/01.Chi.0000046876.27264.Bf

Canino, G., Polanczyk, G., Bauermeister, J. J., Rohde, L. A., & Frick, P. J. (2010). Does the prevalence of CD and ODD vary across cultures? *Social Psychiatry and Psychiatric Epidemiology, 45,* 695–704. doi:10.1007/s00127–010-0242-y

Chambless, D. L., & Hollon, S. D. (1998). Defining empirically supported therapies. *Journal of Consulting and Clinical Psychology, 66,* 7.

Copeland, W. E., Shanahan, L., Costello, E. J., & Angold, A. (2009). Childhood and adolescent psychiatric disorders as predictors of young adult disorders. *Archives of General Psychiatry, 66,* 764–772.

Dick, D. M., Viken, R. J., Kaprio, J., Pulkkinen, L., & Rose, R. J. (2005). Understanding the covariation among childhood externalizing symptoms: Genetic and environmental influences on conduct disorder, attention deficit hyperactivity disorder, and oppositional defiant disorder symptoms. *Journal of Abnormal Child Psychology, 33,* 219–229.

Dougherty, L. R., Smith, V. C., Bufford, S. J., Stringaris, A., Leibenluft, E., Carlson, G. A., & Klein, D. N. (2013). Preschool irritability: Longitudinal associations with psychiatric disorders at age 6 and parental psychopathology. *Journal of the American Academy of Child and Adolescent Psychiatry, 52,* 1304–1313.

Eyberg, S. M., Nelson, M. M., & Boggs, S. R. (2008). Evidence-based psychosocial treatments for children and adolescents with disruptive behavior. *Journal of Clinical Child and Adolescent Psychology, 37,* 215–237. doi:792194652 [pii] 10.1080/15374410701820117

Forehand, R. L., & McMahon, R. J. (1981). *Helping the noncompliant child: A clinician's guide to parent training.* New York, NY: Guilford.

Frick, P. J., Lahey, B. B., Loeber, R., Tannenbaum, L., Vanhorn, Y., Christ, M. A. G.,…Hanson, K. (1993). Oppositional defiant disorder and conduct disorder—A meta-analytic review of factor-analyses and cross-validation in a clinic sample. *Clinical Psychology Review, 13*(4), 319–340. doi:10.1016/0272–7358(93)90016-F

Harpold, T., Biederman, J., Gignac, M., Hammerness, P., Surman, C., Potter, A., & Mick, E. (2007). Is oppositional defiant disorder a meaningful diagnosis in adults? Results from a large sample of adults with ADHD. *Journal of Nervous and Mental Disease, 195,* 601–605. doi:10.1097/NMD.0b013e318093f448 00005053-200707000-00008 [pii]

Hartman, C. A., Hox, J., Mellenbergh, G. J., Boyle, M. H., Offord, D. R., Racine, Y.,…Sergeant, J. A. (2001). *DSM-IV* internal construct validity: When a taxonomy meets data. *Journal of Child Psychology and Psychiatry and Allied Disciplines, 42*(6), 817–836. doi:10.1111/1469–7610.00778

Henggeler, S. W., & Lee, T. (2003). Multisystemic treatment of serious clinical problems. In A. E. Kazdin & J. R. Weisz (Eds.), *Evidence-based psychotherapies for children and adolescents* (pp. 301–322). New York, NY: Guilford Press, xix, 475 pp.

Krieger, F. V., Polanczyk, G. V., Goodman, R., Rohde, L. A., Graeff-Martins, A. S., Salum, G.,…Stringaris, A. (2013). Dimensions of oppositionality in a Brazilian community sample: Testing the *DSM-5* proposal and etiological links. *Journal of the American Academy of Child and Adolescent Psychiatry, 52*(4), 389–400.

Lahey, B. B., Loeber, R., Burke, J. D., & Applegate, B. (2005). Predicting future antisocial personality disorder in males from a clinical assessment in childhood. *Journal of Consulting and Clinical Psychology, 73*(3), 389–399. doi:2005–06517-002 [pii] 10.1037/0022–006X.73.3.389

Lavigne, J. V., Bryant, F. B., Hopkins, J., & Gouze, K. R. (2014). Dimensions of oppositional defiant disorder in young children: Model comparisons, gender and longitudinal invariance. *Journal of Abnormal Child Psychology, 43*(3), 1–17. doi:10.1007/s10802–014-9919–0

Leadbeater, B., Thompson, K., & Gruppuso, V. (2012). Co-occurring trajectories of symptoms of anxiety, depression, and oppositional defiance from adolescence to young adulthood. *Journal of Clinical Child and Adolescent Psychology, 41*(6), 719–730. doi:10.1080/15374416.2012.694608

Maughan, B., Rowe, R., Messer, J., Goodman, R., & Meltzer, H. (2004). Conduct disorder and oppositional defiant disorder in a national sample: Developmental epidemiology. *Journal of Child Psychology and Psychiatry, 45*(3), 609–621.

Moffitt, T. E., Arseneault, L., Jaffee, S. R., Kim-Cohen, J., Koenen, K. C., Odgers, C. L.,…Viding, E. (2008). Research review: *DSM-V* conduct disorder: Research needs for an evidence base. *Journal of Child Psychology and Psychiatry, 49*(1), 3–33. doi:10.1111/j.1469–7610.2007.01823.x

Munkvold, L. H., Lundervold, A. J., & Manger, T. (2011). Oppositional defiant disorder: Gender differences in co-occurring symptoms of mental health problems in a general population of children. *Journal of Abnormal Child Psychology, 39*(4), 577–587. doi:10.1007/s10802–011-9486–6

Nock, M. K., Kazdin, A. E., Hiripi, E., & Kessler, R. C. (2007). Lifetime prevalence, correlates, and persistence of oppositional defiant disorder: Results from the national comorbidity survey replication. *Journal of Child Psychology and Psychiatry, and Allied Disciplines, 48*(7), 703–713. doi:JCPP1733 [pii]

Olsson, T. M. (2010). Intervening in youth problem behavior in Sweden: A pragmatic cost analysis of MST from a randomized trial with conduct disordered youth. *International Journal of Social Welfare, 19*(2), 194–205.

Patterson, G. R. (1982). *A social learning approach, volume 3: Coercive family process.* Eugene, OR: Castalia Publishing Company.

Puig-Antich, J. (1982). Major depression and conduct disorder in prepuberty. *Journal of the American Academy of Child Psychiatry, 21*(2), 118–128.

Rowe, R., Costello, E. J., Angold, A., Copeland, W. E., & Maughan, B. (2010). Developmental pathways in oppositional defiant disorder and conduct disorder. *Journal of Abnormal Psychology, 119*(4), 726–738. doi:2010–23724-004 [pii] 10.1037/a0020798

Rowe, R., Rijsdijk, F. V., Maughan, B., Eley, T. C., & Hosang, G. M. (2008). Heterogeneity in antisocial behaviours and comorbidity with depressed mood: A behavioural genetic approach. *Journal of Child Psychology and Psychiatry, 49*, 526–534. doi:10.1111/j.1469–7610.2008.01834.x

Savage, J., Verhulst, B., Copeland, W., Althoff, R. R., Lichtenstein, P., & Roberson-Nay, R. (2015). A genetically informed study of the longitudinal relation between irritability and anxious/depressed symptoms. *Journal of the American Academy of Child & Adolescent Psychiatry, 54*(5), 377–384.

Stepp, S. D., Burke, J. D., Hipwell, A. E., & Loeber, R. (2012). Trajectories of attention deficit hyperactivity disorder and oppositional defiant disorder symptoms as precursors of borderline personality disorder symptoms in adolescent girls. *Journal of Abnormal Child Psychology, 40*, 7–20. doi:10.1007/s10802–011-9530–6

Stringaris, A., Cohen, P., Pine, D.S., & Leibenluft, E. (2009). Adult outcomes of youth irritability: A 20-year prospective community-based study. *American Journal of Psychiatry, 166*, 1048–1054.

Stringaris, A., & Goodman, R. (2009a). Three dimensions of oppositionality in youth. *Journal of Child Psychology and Psychiatry, 50*(3), 216–223. doi:JCPP1989 [pii] 10.1111/j.1469–7610.2008.01989.x

Stringaris, A., & Goodman, R. (2009b). Longitudinal outcome of youth oppositionality: Irritable, headstrong, and hurtful behaviors have distinctive predictions. *Journal of the American Academy of Child and Adolescent Psychiatry, 48*(4), 404–412. doi:10.1097/CHI.0b013e3181984f30 00004583–200904000-00009 [pii]

Stringaris, A., Zavos, H., Leibenluft, E., Maughan, B., & Eley, T. C. (2012). Adolescent irritability: Phenotypic associations and genetic links with depressed mood. *American Journal of Psychiatry, 169*(1), 47–54. doi:10.1176/appi.ajp.2011.10101549

Teagle, S. E. (2002). Parental problem recognition and child mental health service use. *Mental Health Services Research, 4*(4), 257–266.

Tseng, W.-L., Kawabata, Y., & Gau, S. S.-F. (2011). Social adjustment among Taiwanese children with symptoms of ADHD, ODD, and ADHD comorbid with ODD. *Child Psychiatry and Human Development, 42*(2), 134–151.

van Lier, P. A. C., & Koot, H. M. (2010). Developmental cascades of peer relations and symptoms of externalizing and internalizing problems from kindergarten to fourth-grade elementary school. *Development and Psychopathology, 22*(3), 569–582.

Webster-Stratton, C. (1981). Modification of mothers' behaviors and attitudes through videotape modeling group discussion program. *Behavior Therapy, 12*, 634–642.

Webster-Stratton, C., & Reid, M. (2003). The Incredible Years parents, teachers, and children training series: A multifaceted treatment approach for young children with conduct problems. In A. E. Kazdin & J. R. Weisz (Eds.), *Evidenced-based psychotherapies for children and adolescents* (pp. 224–240). New York, NY: Guilford.

Whelan, Y. M., Stringaris, A., Maughan, B., & Barker, E. D. (2013). Developmental continuity of oppositional defiant disorder subdimensions at ages 8, 10, and 13 years and their distinct psychiatric outcomes at age 16 years. *Journal of the American Academy of Child and Adolescent Psychiatry, 52*(9), 961–969. doi:10.1016/j.jaac.2013.06.013

Zisser, A., & Eyberg, S. M. (2010). Treating oppositional behavior in children using parent–child interaction therapy. In A. E. Kazdin & J. R. Weisz (Eds.), *Evidence-based psychotherapies for children and adolescents* (2nd ed., pp. 179–193). New York, NY: Guilford.

Evidence-Based Interventions for Conduct Disorder in Children and Adolescents

Debra Hyatt-Burkhart, Jered B. Kolbert, and Laura M. Crothers

OVERVIEW

The hallmark of conduct disorder is a "repetitive and persistent pattern of behavior in which the basic rights of others or major age-appropriate societal norms or rules are violated" (American Psychiatric Association [APA], 2013, p. 472). Conduct disorder in childhood and adolescence is considered to be a significant mental health concern because of its connection to numerous other social, emotional, and academic outcomes, both in terms of concurrent (e.g., school failure and dropout) and future functioning (e.g., unemployment, early, inadequate parenting; Farmer, Compton, Bums, & Robertson, 2002; Frick, Ray, Thornton, & Kahn, 2014; Odgers et al., 2007, 2008). Among the disorders that affect the academic, social, emotional, and behavioral functioning of youth, conduct disorder is one of the most difficult to treat. Therefore, in this chapter, although attention will be paid to the description of and risk factors for conduct disorder, the primary focus is on the examination and explanation of the treatment strategies for the disorder. Three evidence-based interventions will be more thoroughly reviewed for practitioners interested in the adoption of these treatment strategies.

Symptoms, Prevalence, and Comorbidity of Conduct Disorder

There are four main groupings of behavior for conduct disorder: (a) aggressive conduct that results in or threatens physical harm to people or animals (e.g., bullying, threatening, or intimidating others); (b) nonaggressive conduct that causes property loss or damage (e.g., fire setting to cause serious damage); (c) deceitfulness or theft (e.g., breaking into someone else's house, building, or car); and (d) serious rule violations (e.g., truancy from school, beginning before the age of 13 years; APA, 2013). For the criteria for conduct disorder to be met, three or more characteristic behaviors must have occurred within the past 12 months, with at least one behavior present in the past 6 months. The behavioral disturbance must cause clinically significant impairment in social, academic, or occupational functioning, and is usually present in several settings, including home, school, or in the community.

In the *Diagnostic and Statistical Manual of Mental Disorders* (5th ed.; *DSM-5*; APA, 2013), there are three subtypes of conduct disorder that are provided based on the age at onset, all of which can occur in a mild, moderate, or severe form

(APA, 2013). When there is insufficient information to determine age at onset, an unspecified-onset subtype is used. Individuals who meet the criteria for childhood-onset conduct disorder are typically male, demonstrate physical aggression toward others, have disturbed peer relationships, meet the criteria for oppositional defiant disorder during early childhood, meet the full criteria for conduct disorder before puberty, and are likely to have persistent conduct disorder into adulthood. Children with childhood-onset type appear to be more likely to be concurrently diagnosed with attention deficit hyperactivity disorder (ADHD) or other neurodevelopmental disorders. Other comorbid conditions to conduct disorder include substance use (Farmer et al., 2002), anxiety disorders (Connor, McLaughlin, & Jeffers-Terry, 2008), and depressive disorders (Turgay, 2005).

Individuals with adolescent-onset type are less likely than individuals with child-onset type to display aggressive behaviors, and typically have more normative peer relationships, although they tend to demonstrate conduct problems alongside of peers. They are less likely than those with the childhood-onset type to demonstrate the disorder into adulthood; the ratio of males to females with conduct disorder is also more equivalent in adolescent-onset than in childhood-onset types. Moreover, the 1-year population prevalence estimates for conduct disorder range from 2% to more than 10%, with a median of 4%. Conduct disorder seems to occur equally among cultural, racial, and ethnic groups, although it is more common among males, with estimates ranging from 2.1% to 8.8% for males and from 0% to 1.4% for females (APA, 2013; Maughan, Rowe, Messer, Goodman, & Meltzer, 2004).

A new contribution to the diagnosis of conduct disorder in the *DSM-5* is the specifier of conduct disorder with a callous-unemotional (CU) presentation. In order to meet the criteria for this specifier, a child must have demonstrated at least two of four CU symptoms (lack of remorse or guilt, callous-lack of empathy, lack of concern about performance, shallow or deficient affect) persistently over 12 months, and in multiple relationships. CU traits are positively correlated with measures of fearless or thrill-seeking behaviors and negatively related with measures of trait anxiety or neuroticism and with sensitivity to punishment (Buitelaar

et al., 2013). The subtyping of conduct disorder based on CU traits is because of their relative stability in childhood and adolescence, their association with the severity of conduct problems, delinquency or aggression, and their increased heritability in comparison to low CU antisocial behavior.

ETIOLOGY AND FACTORS CONTRIBUTING TO CONDUCT DISORDER IN CHILDREN AND ADOLESCENTS

The next section examines the role of genetic, neurological, and environmental factors implicated in the development of conduct disorder.

Underlying Neurological Causes

There appear to be several neurological features and conditions that serve as risk factors for conduct disorder symptomatology. First, left amgydala activation levels appear to be lower in conduct-disordered children and adolescents than in average youngsters in response to fear or threat (Fairchild et al., 2011). Second, researchers have found differential neural activity in the prefrontal areas of the brain in conduct-disordered adolescents in comparison with control groups, specifically in the right dorsal anterior cingulated cortex (Fairchild et al., 2011). Furthermore, evidence of frontal cortex dysfunction and executive functioning deficits have been found among adolescents with conduct disorder symptomatology (Fairchild et al., 2011). Third, slower brain waves, greater wave amplitude, shorter latency periods, temporal lobe seizures, and lower resting heart and electrodermal resting levels have been associated with conduct disorder in children and adolescents (Mpofu, 2002). Lower cortisol levels have been found in both male and female children and adolescents diagnosed with conduct disorder (Oosterlaan, Geurts, Knol, & Sergeant, 2005). Finally, there are neurochemical factors that have been associated with conduct disorder, including low or poorly modulated levels of the neurotransmitters, serotonin and norepinephrine, and the behavioral activation and inhibition functions of the hypothalamic–pituitary–adrenal (HPA) axis (Mpofu, 2002).

Underlying Genetic Causes

The research literature suggests that there are numerous genetic influences that are associated with conduct disorder. In studies of twins, genetics has been found to be a modest to substantial contributor in the manifestation of conduct disorder (Singh & Waldman, 2010). Genome linkage analysis yielded several regions on chromosomes 19 and 2 that may contain genes that present a risk for conduct disorder. Difficult temperament levels at the age of 3 years are predictive of the development of conduct disorder in adolescence, and a CU personality style (lack of empathy, remorselessness, and shallow affect) is associated with delinquency and conduct-disordered behavior in both males and females (Pardini, Obradovic, & Loeber, 2006). Finally, the propensity for risk taking, low reactions to threatening and emotional stimuli, reduced sensitivity to cues of punishment, and low levels of conscience and moral development are temperamental traits that appear to be common in adolescents diagnosed with conduct disorder (Frick, 2004; Frick et al., 2003).

Underlying Environmental Causes

There are several environmental risk factors that have been associated with the development of conduct disorder in children and adolescents. First, there are parental, familial, and social risk factors that may render children vulnerable to developing antisocial behaviors. For example, maternal antisocial behaviors, young maternal age at first birth, maternal depression, authoritarian parenting, negative parenting, maternal permissiveness, poor educational background, exposure to consistent poverty, and frequent family transitions, as well as biological risk factors such as birth complications, maternal illness during pregnancy, and parental temperament problems have been found to be related to the onset of conduct disorder (Kim-Cohen, Moffitt, Taylor, Pawlby, & Caspi, 2005). Second, poor attachment between a mother and the infant during the first 12 to 18 months of life has been found to be a predictor of aggression and antisocial behavior in children in some studies (DeVito & Hopkins, 2001), whereas other investigations have yielded no predictive relationship between attachment and the severity or diagnosis of disruptive behavior disorders (Speltz, DeKlyen, Calderon, Greenberg, & Fisher, 1999). Third, school factors, such as attending classes in which there is little focus on academic work, low teacher expectancies for students, and lack of teacher availability to address problems that students encounter, as well as peer rejection and negative peer relationships are associated with the development of conduct disorder (Barton, 2003). Fourth, community factors, such as low socioeconomic status (SES), community disorganization, high crime rates and neighborhood violence, living in (low-income) community housing, the presence of neighborhood adults involved in crime, the availability of drugs, high unemployment rates, and exposure to prejudice (Barton, 2003) may be risk factors that heighten an individual's likelihood of developing antisocial behaviors. Fifth, child physical and sexual abuse and early exposure to victimization seem to predispose children to exhibit aggressive, conduct-disordered behavior (Dodge, Pettit, Bates, & Valente, 1995; Hilarksi, 2004). Finally, environmental toxins, such as pre- and postnatal tobacco exposure and exposure to lead, have been associated with increased odds of developing conduct disorder (Braun et al., 2008).

Understanding the Confluence of Risk Factors

Three conceptual models have been presented as frameworks for understanding the confluence of the numerous risk factors for conduct disorder: additive, interactive, and transactional. The additive model suggests that multiple factors must be considered in the diagnosis and treatment of conduct disorder. Deater-Deckard, Dodge, Bates, and Petit (1996) revealed that a model comprising 20 different biological, contextual, and life-experience factors during preschool demonstrated only weak associations with conduct 5 years later, but the cumulative risk, including all factors, accounted for nearly half of the variance in conduct problems. Interactive models propose that certain risk factors operate only in the presence or absence of other risk factors. Such diathesis-stress models have been supported and further enhance the understanding of the development of conduct disorder. For instance, research reveals that the risk associated with family and neighborhood poverty may be moderated by parental supervision (Pettit,

Laird, Bates, & Dodge, 1997). Although both the additive and the interactive models have empirical support and may predict antisocial outcomes, these models offer little explanation regarding the processes or development of conduct disorder over time. The transactional-ecological developmental model offers a developmental explanation, postulating that the contact between the individual and his or her environment involves reciprocal interaction through which each influences the other (Sameroff, 1995). This model can account for the social and cognitive states of the individual while recognizing that behavior is highly contextual (Bronfenbrenner, 1979; Sameroff, 1995). Indeed, Henggeler, Schoenwald, Borduin, Rowland, and Cunningham's (1996) review of the research literature of aggression in youth revealed that "serious antisocial behavior is multidetermined by the reciprocal interplay of characteristics of the individual youth and the key social systems in which youths are embedded (i.e., family, peer, social, neighborhood, and community)" (pp. 6–7).

Conclusion Regarding Etiology of Conduct Disorder

A comprehensive review of the literature indicates that there is not one single developmental trajectory that leads to conduct disorder, but rather an evolution through periods of quiescence and more dynamic increases over time (Patterson & Yoerger, 2002). The current consensus regarding the etiology of conduct disorder is reflected in a transactional-ecological developmental model that incorporates the dynamic and reciprocal influences of biological, individual, and contextual factors over time.

EVIDENCE-BASED INTERVENTIONS AND EMPIRICAL SUPPORT FOR OPPOSITIONAL DEFIANT DISORDER IN CHILDREN AND ADOLESCENTS

Externalizing disorders in children are difficult to treat and, if not successfully ameliorated, are associated with lifelong disturbance in adulthood that may include criminal behavior, poor mental health, and low socioeconomic status (Farmer

et al., 2002). Buitelaar et al. (2013) emphasize that treatment for conduct disorder must be: (a) multimodal, (b) involve a family-based and social systems–based approach, and (c) focus on multiple foci over long periods of time. The first level of interventions that should be considered is nonmedical psychosocial interventions, such as parental management training (PMT) and individual skill-building opportunities (e.g., social skills and anger management training). Psychosocial treatment programs such as multisystemic therapy (MST), functional family therapy (FFT), and multidimensional treatment foster care that combine PMT, structural family therapies, and skill-building appear to have a moderate to large-effect size in reducing aggression and symptoms of conduct disorder. However, psychosocial treatment approaches have significant limitations, including a declining-effect size of PMT with increasing age, low generalizability of treatment benefits, and obstacles such as high-dropout rates, parental psychopathology, and poor parental motivation. Additionally, psychosocial treatments appear to be particularly beneficial with children with high levels of impulsive aggression, whereas children with high CU traits appear to be less responsive to these interventions (Buitelaar et al., 2013).

Although best practice procedures for the treatment of conduct disorder indicate that psychosocial or nonmedical interventions should be attempted first, there is support for the use of psychotropic agents to target common behaviors inherent to those diagnosed with conduct disorder (Buitelaar et al., 2013). The use of such agents remains under study, but the following medications have been shown to reduce primarily aggressive and impulsive behaviors that are common in the sequelae of conduct disorder.

Psychostimulants, generally used in the treatment of ADHD, which is a common comorbid condition of conduct disorder, have been shown to reduce aggression in a number of studies. Meta-analyses of these trials indicated that stimulants had a mean-effect size of 0.78 to 0.84 on aggressive behaviors (Buitelaar et al., 2013). Additionally, the use of paroxetine, a selective serotonin reuptake inhibitor (SSRI), has also shown promise in the reduction of aggressive and impulsive behaviors in those with conduct disorder (Cherek, Lane, Pietras, & Steinberg, 2002). Perhaps the most researched psychotropic medication that is used for the treatment of conduct disorder is risperidone. Connor and colleagues (2008) reference five methodologically controlled trials of risperidone in their study of quetiapine for the same treatment purpose. These studies, which involved 400 pediatric participants, all found some support for risperidone as compared with placebo specifically to target aggressive behaviors (Connor et al., 2008). Connor et al. (2008) also found, although in a small study, similar support for the use of quetiapine in adolescents with conduct disorder. Finally, in Buitelaar et al. (2013) review of mood stabilizers—most notably lithium—a moderate-effect size (0.4) was detected in reducing aggressive symptoms, although the potential side effects and need for careful blood level monitoring often deter prescription of such agents. In summary, the use of psychotropic medications to reduce the symptoms patterns common in youth with a diagnosis of conduct disorder remains controversial and under significant study, but their place as a potentially valuable treatment option cannot be ignored.

HOW TO: A GUIDE TO THE IMPLEMENTATION OF INTERVENTIONS FOR CONDUCT DISORDER IN CHILDREN AND ADOLESCENTS

As the evidence base regarding the treatment options has grown for conditions such as conduct disorder, those interventions that are comprehensive and multifaceted have emerged as most efficacious (Frick, 2012). Hence, what follows is a discussion of three evidence-based interventions that incorporate comprehensive and systemic interventions in the treatment of conduct disorder. The implementation for each intervention is described in detail. It is essential to note that the evidence base for the efficacy of these models exists, in part, because of the fidelity to these models in application. These "blueprint" programs manualize treatment interventions in a way that provides the ability to replicate treatment and increase provider consistency, which enhances the strength of the evidence base. As such, in order to implement the methods described in the following sections, practitioners would need to undertake the training and supervision required by each program in order to competently adopt the use of the program in their own settings.

Multisystemic Therapy

Among the most-researched interventions for conduct disorder, MST is a family-, home-, and community-based treatment intervention that uses Bronfenbrenner's (1979) social ecological model (Henggeler, Schoenwald, Borduin, Rowland, & Cunningham, 2009) as its premise. From this framework, the disturbance of emotion and conduct present in individuals with conduct disorder is conceptualized as inherently influenced by the reciprocal interchange between the individuals' spheres of interaction (e.g., school, peers, parents, larger society) and their influence on one another (Henggeler & Borduin, 1990; Henggeler & Sheidow, 2012). The implementation of MST is performed by qualified mental health professionals who are extensively trained in the model (a minimum of 5 days) and who receive weekly supervision, periodic retraining (quarterly), and regular consultation regarding the use of the model (Henggeler, Melton, Brondino, Scherer, & Hanley, 1997). Fidelity to the model is monitored through the Therapist Adherence Measure (TAM; Henggeler & Borduin, 1990) as the integrity of the model is a key component of its status as an evidence-based intervention.

In application, the interventions used in MST are drawn from several theoretical perspectives, which are incorporated with the intent to enhance and complement the components of Bronfenbrenner's (1979) theory. Specifically, the components of cognitive behavioral theory, social learning theory, Minuchin's (1974) structural family therapy, and Haley's (1987) strategic formulation are all acknowledged as integral to MST's treatment process (Henggeler & Sheidow, 2012). MST is implemented in a team format with master's level therapists and a supervisor who has had more advanced academic training (either a postmaster's certificate or PhD) and experience with using the model. Therapists generally maintain a caseload between four and six families with whom treatment lasts from 4 to 6 months. Contact is based on family need and individual assessment and usually occurs several times per week with 24 hour per day/7 day per week availability on the part of the therapists who provide services in the youth's most natural and convenient settings (e.g., home, school, and community; Henggeler & Sheidow, 2012; Henggeler et al., 1997).

Interventions with MST are family rather than treatment provider driven and families are perceived as full collaborators within the therapeutic process. According to Henggeler et al. (1997), treatment is guided by nine principles that operationalize MST:

1. The primary purpose of assessment is to understand the fit between the identified problems and their broader systemic context.
2. Therapeutic contacts should emphasize the positive and should use systemic strengths as levers for change.
3. Interventions should be designed to promote responsible behavior and decrease irresponsible behavior among family members.
4. Interventions should be present focused and action oriented, targeting specific and well-defined problems.
5. Interventions should target sequences of behavior within or between multiple systems that maintain identified problems.
6. Interventions should be developmentally appropriate and fit the developmental needs of the youth.
7. Interventions should be designed to require daily or weekly effort by family members.
8. Intervention effectiveness is evaluated continuously from multiple perspectives, with providers assuming accountability for overcoming barriers to successful outcomes.
9. Interventions should be designed to promote treatment generalization and long-term maintenance of therapeutic change by empowering caregivers to address family members' needs across multiple systemic contexts (Henggeler et al. (1997, p. 832).

These principles are not prescriptive, but instead reflect the overall approach of the interventions. In application, the interventions are varied based on the individual needs of the youth. Interventions are strength based and build on the protective factors present in the system, as well as on the skills and competencies of the individual family members (Henggeler et al., 2009). Areas for development

may include parent competencies, problem-solving skills, vocational direction, and the establishment of an appropriate social support network. The developers of MST have created comprehensive treatment manuals that delineate systemic and individual interventions that build proficiencies in both caregivers and youth so as to reduce the common disruptive behaviors of conduct disorder (Baglivio, Jackowiski, Greenwald, & Wolff, 2014). Practitioners who wish to explore the use of this model should seek out these materials, which are beyond the scope of this chapter.

Parent Management Training

Another comprehensive, multifaceted, evidence-based approach to the treatment of conduct disorder is PMT. This model originated from the Oregon Social Learning Center and is based on social interaction learning theory, which is an ecological perspective that views behavior as a function of a child's social environment, of which parenting practices are integral (Forgatch & Patterson, 2010). Contextual factors within the family (e.g., divorce, poverty, mental illness, substance abuse, scarcity of resources), community (e.g., marginalization, discrimination, trauma), and the individual (e.g., attachment, personality, temperament, comorbid conditions) are viewed as having a possibly derailing effect on healthy development (Forgatch & Patterson, 2010). Parents are perceived as being in a strong and unique position from which to intervene to interrupt unhealthy trajectories and correct these possible derailments (Forgatch & Patterson, 2010). The clinical focus of PMT is to improve parenting practices by assisting parents in replacing ineffective, coercive patterns of interaction, which often lead to misconduct and aggressive behaviors, with positive parenting methods (Baumann, Rodríguez, Amador, Forgatch, & Parra-Cardona, 2014; Forgatch & Patterson, 2010).

Within the PMT model, Forgatch and Patterson (2010) delineate five components or dimensions on which interventions or teaching are centered:

1. Skill encouragement, which incorporates the concept of scaffolding on the part of the parents in order to help children to build competencies with new, more appropriate expressions

2. Limit setting, where parents encourage prosocial behavior by employing appropriate consequences
3. Monitoring of activities, which include peer interactions, level of adult supervision, and school performance
4. Problem solving, which involves the identification of targets, developing plans for achievement, techniques for evaluation, and mechanisms to revise targets
5. Positive parental involvement, which consists of increasing and enhancing ways in which parents demonstrate warmth, affection, and love

Generally, these components are approached in a systematic fashion and are viewed as a cumulative, skill-building continuum that is designed to increase positive parent–child interactions and decrease conduct-disordered behaviors. Mental health practitioners also focus on assisting parents in giving effective directions, developing effective communication and active listening skills, and modeling these skills for their children so they may be generalized by the youth into practice outside of the family (Forgatch & Patterson, 2010).

Clinicians who wish to practice PMT–Oregon model (PMTO) must participate in extensive training, which follows a full transfer model (Baumann et al., 2014). In application, the model is highly structured and training is centered on teaching clinicians to promote unified parenting, assist in the development of effective parenting practices, work through resistance to the changes, and engage parents in active learning through role-plays and other experientially based activities (Implementation Sciences International Incorporated, PMTO, retrieved from www.isii.net/index.html). Generally, families meet with their therapists on a weekly basis in either a group or an individual format (25–30 sessions for individuals or 14 sessions for group formats; Forgatch & Patterson, 2010). Both of these platforms typically follow a similar format that proceeds as follows: initial check-in, review of the previous week's homework or application assignments, introduction of new material, practice of new material, and finally, a wrap-up and assignment of homework/application for the next week (Forgatch & Patterson, 2010). Although the program is structured and somewhat prescribed, tailoring of specific interventions and assignments is based on the individual family's needs as assessed at the beginning of treatment. As with MST, fidelity to the model is essential in maintaining its evidence base. Practitioners receive continued training, supervision, and coaching in the model as they practice and are evaluated regarding their fidelity through the Fidelity of Implementation Rating System (Knutson, Forgatch, & Rains, 2009).

Functional Family Therapy

The final set of evidence-based interventions that we address is FFT, which is a family prevention and intervention program specifically designed for work with adolescents with oppositional defiant and conduct disorder (Zazzali et al., 2008). Similar to MST, FFT is a structured community- and home-based family intervention (Baglivio et al., 2014); a systematic clinical model that has developed through a process identified as "model integration" (Alexander, Sexton, & Robbins, 2002). Although "integrated" through the incorporation of concepts from communication, behavioral, systems, cognitive, and, most recently, social constructivist theories, FFT remains primarily relationally focused (Sexton & Alexander, 2003).

An adolescent's symptomatic behavior is viewed as serving a function within the family system and therapy is primarily concerned with restructuring family relationships and dynamics so that these functions can be undertaken through more effective or constructive means (Keiley, 2002; Sexton & Alexander, 2003). Three major constructs form the core of FFT: (a) the nature of clinical problems, (b) the relational functioning of the family system, and (c) the core mechanisms of successful therapeutic change (Sexton & Alexander, 2003). Clinicians are charged with viewing problem behaviors through a lens that promotes contextual consideration of family strengths and risks, systemic conceptualization of clients, and therapy as a systematic, phase-implemented process (Sexton & Alexander, 2004).

In implementation, FFT is prescribed and systematic. Described by Sexton and Alexander (2003) as "phasic," the clinical model is divided into three distinct periods of intervention. Phase one is engagement and motivation, which involves the targeted goals of developing alliances among family members, and having the therapists "join" with each family member; decreasing conflict, negative interactions, and blame; establishing a family focus toward the presenting issues; and increasing hope for change (Sexton & Alexander, 2004). In essence, the therapist's task during this phase is to establish rapport and reduce family conflict with the belief in the possibility for positive change that can be manifested within the system. One of the primary tools employed by therapists in this phase is "reframing." Reframing involves helping family members reconceptualize negative behaviors from a standpoint of functionality, not merely "badness." An example may be helping parents to view their child's tantrum behaviors as an effective way to nonverbally communicate distress. Such reframes help to describe the function of the behavior in less negative terms, which can help to reduce negative perceptions and blame, thereby opening avenues for change. During this phase, the clinicians assess the reduction in negativity and the increase in hope for change in preparation to move on to the next phase of intervention.

Once phase one is complete, phase two, which is behavioral change, can begin. This phase has four primary goals: (a) changing individual and family risk patterns; (b) incorporating activities within and outside therapy sessions; (c) providing interventions that match the unique relational functions of the family; and (d) promoting change that is obtainable for the family within its context (Sexton & Alexander, 2004). The ultimate hope for outcomes in phase two is to decrease risks and increase competencies in communication patterns (between family members and the external system), increase effective parenting skills (appropriate rewards and consequences, limit setting), and to increase conflict management (Sexton & Alexander, 2004).

Clinicians in this phase are actively engaged in establishing clear behavioral goals and implementing interventions designed to help the family achieve these goals. For example, a family may have a goal to decrease conflicts stemming from miscommunication. As such, the clinician may establish objectives regarding the development of clear, noncoercive instructions. In the sessions, work toward developing an understanding of how that behavior looks in practice would be coupled with out-of-session homework to reinforce the gains made in the session (Sexton & Alexander,

2004). Not unlike many other family therapy approaches, skill deficits are identified, reframed, redirected, practiced, and evaluated during this phase. In addition to the development of effective communication skills, some of the common foci of the behavioral change phase of FFT are assisting parents in employing positive parenting skills, increasing problem-solving skills, and increasing the ability to engage in appropriate conflict resolution (Sexton & Alexander, 2004). As in phase one, the clinician is required to engage in assessment to measure progress in attaining these goals. Assessment is completed through clinician observation, gathering of family feedback, and through the use of standardized assessment tools provided through the model.

The final phase of the model is the generalization phase, in which the clinicians assist the family in applying the skills and behaviors that have been learned to other systems (Sexton & Alexander, 2004). Special attention is paid in helping the family maintain the gains that have been made in treatment and assisting the family to establish a network of support from within the natural community resources (Sexton & Alexander, 2003, 2004). Here, the clinician is assisting the family to be self-sufficient in the implementation of the skills that have been previously learned and is connecting the family to resources that will help the family sustain the gains made post discharge from services. High-quality aftercare planning is essential, especially for youth involved in the juvenile justice system in which recidivism rates for those diagnosed with conduct problems are quite high (Baglivio et al., 2014).

In implementation, FFT is generally a short-term, time-limited intervention that involves 12 to 14 structured sessions that occur over a 3- to 5-month time frame (Sexton & Alexander, 2004). It also involves an intensive 1 year to 18 months of training period for both clinicians and supervisors with substantial commitments to future training and assessment of adherence to the model. Again, this expected fidelity and rigorous training are essential to the evidence base of this "blueprint" model program. Of note is the availability of the FFT clinician's training manual in the public domain. Those who are interested in this model are able to access detailed descriptions and the manual quite easily through a simple Internet search. A link to the manual is provided at the end of this chapter.

CONCLUSION

In this chapter, the symptoms, prevalence, and comorbid conditions of conduct disorder were presented, followed by the etiology of this externalizing behavioral problem of childhood and adolescence. In the discussion of the etiology of conduct disorder, neurological, genetic, and environmental contributions to the disorder were reviewed, and the confluence for these risk factors was also presented, followed by a brief summary of the interventions that have been used to treat conduct disorder. Finally, an in-depth review of three evidence-based treatment strategies for conduct disorder was presented. Although there is some cause for optimism in the burgeoning empirically supported literature base to treat conduct disorder, it remains among the most intractable behavioral problems in childhood and adolescence, and future study is clearly needed to support children and their families struggling with this significant externalizing behavioral problem.

SELECT BIBLIOGRAPHY

Buitelaar, J. K., Smeets, K. C., Herpers, P., Scheepers, F., Glennon, J., & Rommelse, N. N. (2013). Conduct disorders. *European Child & Adolescent Psychiatry, 22* (Suppl. 1), S49–S54.
In this article, the authors provide a concise but thorough overview of conduct disorder as described in the DSM-5, including a discussion of general treatment approaches, psychological interventions, and medical interventions.

Eyberg, S. M., Nelson, M. M., & Boggs, S. R. (2008). Evidence-based psychosocial treatments for children and adolescents with disruptive behavior. *Journal of Clinical Child and Adolescent Psychology, 37*(1), 215–237.
Eyeberg and colleagues provide a literature review from 1996 to 2007 regarding 16 evidence-based (and nine possibly efficacious) psychosocial treatments for child and adolescent disruptive behavior, including oppositional defiant disorder and conduct disorder.

Henggeler, S. W., & Sheidow, A. J. (2012). Empirically supported family-based treatments for conduct disorder and delinquency in adolescents. *Journal of Marital and Family Therapy, 38*(1), 30–58.
This article provides a summary and evaluation of the models of multisystemic therapy, functional family therapy, multidimensional treatment foster care, and brief strategic family therapy in family-based treatments for conduct disorder and delinquency in adolescents.

REFERENCES

Alexander, J., Sexton, T., & Robbins, M. (2002). The developmental status of family therapy in family psychology intervention science. In H. S. Liddle, D. Santsiteban, R. Levant, & J. Bray (Eds.), *Family psychology intervention science* (pp. 17–40). Washington, DC: American Psychological Association.

American Psychiatric Association (APA). (2013). *Diagnostic and statistical manual of mental disorders* (5th ed.). Arlington, VA: American Psychiatric Publishing.

Baglivio, M., Jackowiski, K., Greenwald, M., & Wolff, K. (2014). Comparison of multisystemic therapy and functional family therapy effectiveness: A multiyear statewide propensity score matching analysis of juvenile offenders. *Criminal Justice and Behavior, 41*, 1033–1056.

Barton, J. (2003). Conduct disorder: Intervention and prevention. *International Journal of Mental Health Promotion, 5*, 32–41.

Baumann, A. A., Domenech Rodríguez, M. M., Amador, N. G., Forgatch, M. S., & Parra-Cardona, J. R. (2014). Parent Management Training-Oregon model (PMTO™) in Mexico City: Integrating cultural adaptation activities in an implementation model. *Clinical Psychology: A Publication of the Division of Clinical Psychology of the American Psychological Association, 21*(1), 32–47.

Braun, J. M., Froehlich, T. E., Daniels, J. L., Dietrich, K. N., Hornung, R., Auinger, P., & Lanphear, B. P. (2008). Association of environmental toxicants and conduct disorder in U.S. children: NHANES 2001–2004. *Environmental Health Perspectives, 116*(7), 956–962.

Bronfenbrenner, U. (1979). *The ecology of human development: Experiments by nature and design.* Cambridge, MA: Harvard University Press.

Buitelaar, J. K., Smeets, K. C., Herpers, P., Scheepers, F., Glennon, J., & Rommelse, N. N. (2013). Conduct disorders. *European Child & Adolescent Psychiatry, 22* (Suppl 1), S49–S54.

Cherek, D. R., Lane, S. D., Pietras, C. J., & Steinberg, J. L. (2002). Effects of chronic paroxetine administration on measures of aggressive and impulsive responses of adult males with a history of conduct disorder. *Psychopharmacology, 159*(3), 266–274.

Connor, D. F., McLaughlin, T. J., & Jeffers-Terry, M. (2008). Randomized controlled pilot study of quetiapine in the treatment of adolescent conduct disorder. *Journal of Child and Adolescent Psychopharmacology, 18*(2), 140–156.

Deater-Deckard, K., Dodge, K., Bates, J. E., & Petit, G. S. (1996). Physical discipline among African American and European American mothers: Links to children's externalizing behaviors. *Developmental Psychology, 32*, 1065–1072.

DeVito, C., & Hopkins, J. (2001). Attachment, parenting, and marital dissatisfaction as predictors of disruptive behavior in preschoolers. *Development and Psychopathology, 13*(2), 215–231.

Dodge, K. A., Pettit, G. S., Bates, J. E., & Valente, E. (1995). Social information-processing patterns partially mediate the effect of early physical abuse on later conduct problems. *Journal of Abnormal Psychology, 104*(4), 632–643.

Fairchild, G., Passamonti, L., Hurford, G., Hagan, C. C., von dem Hagen, E. A., van Goozen, S. H.,…Calder, A. J. (2011). Brain structure abnormalities in early-onset and adolescent-onset conduct disorder. *The American Journal of Psychiatry, 168*(6), 624–633.

Farmer, E. M., Compton, S. N., Bums, B. J., & Robertson, E. (2002). Review of the evidence base for treatment of childhood psychopathology: Externalizing disorders. *Journal of Consulting and Clinical Psychology, 70*(6), 1267–1302.

Forgatch, M., & Patterson, G. (2010). Parent management training-Oregon model: An intervention for antisocial behavior in children and adolescents. In J. R. Weisz & A. E. Kazdin (Eds.), *Evidence-based psychotherapies for children and adolescents* (2nd ed., pp. 159–178). New York, NY: Guilford.

Frick, P. J. (2004). Developmental pathways to conduct disorder: Implications for serving youth who show severe aggressive and antisocial behavior. *Psychology in the Schools, 41*, 823–834.

Frick, P. J. (2012). Developmental pathways to conduct disorder: Implications for future directions in research, assessment, and treatment. *Journal of Clinical Child and Adolescent Psychology, 41*, 378–389.

Frick, P. J., Cornell, A. H., Bodin, S. D., Dane, H. E., Barry, C. T., & Loney, B. R. (2003). Callous-

unemotional traits and developmental pathways to severe conduct problems. *Developmental Psychology, 39*(2), 246–260.

Frick, P. J., Ray, J. V., Thornton, L. C., & Kahn, R. E. (2014). Annual research review: A developmental psychopathology approach to understanding callous-unemotional traits in children and adolescents with serious conduct problems. *Journal of Child Psychology and Psychiatry, and Allied Disciplines, 55*(6), 532–548.

Haley, J. (1987). *Problem-solving therapy: New strategies for effective family therapy.* San Francisco, CA: Jossey-Bass.

Henggeler, S., & Borduin, C. M. (1990). *Family therapy and beyond: A multisystemic approach to treating the behavior problems of children and adolescents.* Pacific Grove, CA: Brooks Cole.

Henggeler, S. W., Melton, G. B., Brondino, M. J., Scherer, D. G., & Hanley, J. H. (1997). Multisystemic therapy with violent and chronic juvenile offenders and their families: The role of treatment fidelity in successful dissemination. *Journal of Consulting and Clinical Psychology, 65*(5), 821–833.

Henggeler, S. W., Schoenwald, S. K., Borduin, C. M., Rowland, M. D., & Cunningham, P. B. (1996). *Multisystemic treatment of antisocial behavior in children and adolescents.* New York, NY: Guilford Press.

Henggeler, S. W., Schoenwald, S. K., Borduin, C. M., Rowland, M. D., & Cunningham, P. B. (2009). *Multisystemic therapy for antisocial behavior in children and adolescents* (2nd ed.). New York, NY: Guilford Press.

Henggeler, S. W., & Sheidow, A. J. (2012). Empirically supported family-based treatments for conduct disorder and delinquency in adolescents. *Journal of Marital and Family Therapy, 38*(1), 30–58.

Hilarski, C. (2004). Child and adolescent substance abuse: Risk factors, assessment, and treatment. *Journal of Evidence-based Social Work, 1*, 79–97.

Keiley, M. K. (2002). Attachment and affect regulation: A framework for family treatment of conduct disorder. *Family Process, 41*(3), 477–493.

Kim-Cohen, J., Moffitt, T. E., Taylor, A., Pawlby, S. J., & Caspi, A. (2005). Maternal depression and children's antisocial behavior: Nature and nurture effects. *Archives of General Psychiatry, 62*(2), 173–181.

Knutson, N., Forgatch, M., & Rains, L. (2009). *Fidelity of implementation rating system (FIMP): The training manual for PMTO.* Eugene, OR: PE Oregon Social Learning Center.

Maughan, B., Rowe, R., Messer, J., Goodman, R., & Meltzer, H. (2004). Conduct disorder and oppositional defiant disorder in a national sample: Developmental epidemiology. *Journal of Child Psychology and Psychiatry, and Allied Disciplines, 45*(3), 609–621.

Minuchin, S. (1974). *Families and family therapy.* Cambridge, MA: Harvard University Press.

Mpofu, E. (2002). Psychopharmacology in the treatment of conduct disorder children and adolescents: Rationale, prospects, and ethics. *South African Journal of Psychology, 32,* 9–21.

Odgers, C. L., Caspi, A., Broadbent, J. M., Dickson, N., Hancox, R. J., Harrington, H.,…Moffitt, T. E. (2007). Prediction of differential adult health burden by conduct problem subtypes in males. *Archives of General Psychiatry, 64*(4), 476–484.

Odgers, C. L., Moffitt, T. E., Broadbent, J. M., Dickson, N., Hancox, R. J., Harrington, H.,…Caspi, A. (2008). Female and male antisocial trajectories: From childhood origins to adult outcomes. *Development and Psychopathology, 20*(2), 673–716.

Oosterlaan, J., Geurts, H. M., Knol, D. L., & Sergeant, J. A. (2005). Low basal salivary cortisol is associated with teacher-reported symptoms of conduct disorder. *Psychiatry Research, 134*(1), 1–10.

Pardini, D., Obradovic, J., & Loeber, R. (2006). Interpersonal callousness, hyperactivity/impulsivity, inattention, and conduct problems as precursors to delinquency persistence in boys: A comparison of three grade-based cohorts. *Journal of Clinical Child and Adolescent Psychology, 35*(1), 46–59.

Patterson, G. R., & Yoerger, K. (2002). A developmental model for early- and late-onset delinquency. In J. B. Reid, G. R. Patterson, & J. Snyder (Eds.), *Antisocial behavior in children and adolescents: A developmental analysis and model for intervention* (pp. 147–172). Washington, DC: American Psychological Association.

Pettit, G. S., Laird, R. D., Bates, J. E., & Dodge, K. A. (1997). Patterns of after-school care in middle childhood: Risk factors and developmental outcomes. *Merrill-Palmer Quarterly, 43,* 515–538.

Sameroff, A. J. (1995). General systems theories and developmental psychopathology. In D. Cicchetti & D. Cohen (Eds.), *Developmental psychopathology* (pp. 659–689). New York, NY: John Wiley.

Sexton, T. L., & Alexander, J. F. (2003). Functional family therapy: A mature clinical model for working with at risk adolescents and their families. In M. Robbins, T. Sexton, & G. Weeks (Eds.), *Handbook of family therapy: The science and practice of working with families and couples* (pp. 323–348). New York, NY: Routledge.

Sexton, T. L., & Alexander, J. F. (2004*). Functional family therapy clinical training manual.* Baltimore, MD: Annie E. Casey Foundation.

Singh, A. L., & Waldman, I. D. (2010). The etiology of associations between negative emotionality and childhood externalizing disorders. *Journal of Abnormal Psychology, 119*(2), 376–388.

Speltz, M. L., DeKlyen, M., Calderon, R., Greenberg, M. T., & Fisher, P. A. (1999). Neuropsychological characteristics and test behaviors of boys with early onset conduct problems. *Journal of Abnormal Psychology, 108*(2), 315–325.

Turgay, A. (2005). Treatment of comorbidity in conduct disorder with attention-deficit hyperactivity disorder (ADHD). *Essential Psychopharmacology, 6*(5), 277–290.

Zazzali, J. L., Sherbourne, C., Hoagwood, K. E., Greene, D., Bigley, M. F., & Sexton, T. L. (2008). The adoption and implementation of an evidence-based practice in child and family mental health services organizations: A pilot study of functional family therapy in New York State. *Administration and Policy in Mental Health, 35*(1–2), 38–49.

Evidence-Based Interventions for Children and Adolescents With Emotional and Behavioral Disorders

Tammy L. Hughes, Michael E. Tansy, and Corrine Fallon

OVERVIEW

Treating emotional and behavioral disorders in children and adolescents is a complex issue; that is, practitioners must understand children's typical patterns of social, emotional, and cognitive development and determine what is responsible for having taken the referred child off that "normal" path. The purpose of intervention is to promote developmentally appropriate growth, even if a child's development occurs slower than his or her age-mates. To foster developmentally appropriate growth, practitioners must understand what drives the child's problem behaviors, which is often difficult and requires several considerations. First, a systematic social–emotional–behavioral assessment is needed to collect relevant information, determine the nature of the problem, and inform intervention planning. For the most challenging students, the process often includes a time-consuming and labor-intensive evaluation. Second, parents and school teams tend to seek immediate, yet simple, solutions—which are ineffective and short-lived. Practitioners must be prepared to explain why more complex intervention plans are preferable, despite their more demanding requirements of everyone involved. Third, although educational and behavioral services must be individualized for students, many classrooms and individualized educational programs (IEPs) do not provide personalized

and differentiated support because the unique needs of the child are not well understood and articulated or because demands for classroom uniformity compete with and supersede specific student needs. Mental health professionals must explain why students with emotional or behavioral disorders require personalized intervention plans regardless of the preference for well-worn classroom strategies. Finally, *how*, *when*, and *what* treatment is provided is complicated by the idiosyncratic practices of the school and family contexts. That is, because service provision is guided by special education eligibility categories, and often takes precedence over the unique psychological and psychiatric needs of students, familiarity with the social and political context surrounding educating special needs children is essential.

Samuel Kirk (1962) introduced the term "social maladjustment" to education and differentiated children with an emotional disturbance (i.e., where problematic behaviors were characterized by inner tension, anxiety, neuroticism, and psychosis) from those with social maladjustment (i.e., where problematic behaviors were characterized by incorrigibility, truancy, and quarrelsomeness). Congress modified Bower's (1981) elaboration of Kirk's distinction, resulting in a definition that includes reference to social maladjustment:

A condition exhibiting one or more of the following characteristics over a long period of time and to a marked degree that adversely affects a child's educational performance: (a) An inability to learn that cannot be explained by intellectual, sensory, or health factors; (b) An inability to build or maintain satisfactory interpersonal relationships with peers and teachers; (c) Inappropriate types of behavior or feelings under normal circumstances; (d) A general pervasive mood of unhappiness or depression; and (e) A tendency to develop physical symptoms or fears associated with personal or school problems. The term includes schizophrenia. The term does not apply to children who are socially maladjusted, unless it is determined that they have an emotional disturbance. (Sec. 300.8 of the Individuals with Disabilities Education Act, 2004)

Soon after its adoption, educators began to debate the utility of a definition that does not include an additional definition of social maladjustment.

Social maladjustment has historically also been synonymous with the *Diagnostic and Statistical Manual of Mental Disorders* (DSM) diagnoses of conduct disorder, antisocial personality disorder, and oppositional-defiant disorder. Unfortunately, many emotionally and behaviorally disordered children who need, would benefit from, and are eligible for special education services are excluded from services because school teams fail to identify qualified students (Kauffman, Mock, & Simpson, 2007). This exclusionary practice results in lower emotional disturbance (ED) identification rates than originally anticipated; a disproportionality that has remained stable since 1976 when Office of Special Education Programs (OSEP) began collecting data (Oswald & Coutinho, 1995).

A more contemporary definition of emotional disability and social maladjustment asks practitioners to identify and understand the needs of three subgroups of children with social, emotional, and behavioral problems (Hughes et al., 2013). First, there are children with internalizing disorders, such as depressive, anxiety, and somatization disorders. Although these internalizers' symptoms adversely affect their academic achievement and their ability to function in school, these children often fail to be identified because they tend not to disrupt the educational setting (Tandon, Cardeli, & Luby, 2009), which results in a lag in identification and treatment (Tandon et al., 2009). Second, there are two subgroups of children

with externalizing disorders; those who engage in disruptive behavior in a reactive way (Constenbader & Buntaine, 1999) and those whose disruptive behavior is intentional, purposeful, and consciously mediated (Theodore, Akin-Little, & Little, 2004). Although these two groups of externalizing disordered children are different and their differences are measureable (Gacono & Hughes, 2004), school personnel have been very slow to appreciate the importance of distinguishing between these groups.

Externalizing children, even those who meet the criteria for a conduct disorder, should be considered emotionally disturbed if their problematic behaviors are directed by emotions that are reactive, labile, and dysregulated (Gacono & Hughes, 2004; Hughes, Tansy, & Wisniewski, 2013). Children engaging in disruptive behavior that is intentional, purposeful, consciously mediated, and characterized by callous and unemotional traits should be considered socially maladjusted. However, all children with severely disruptive social, emotional, and behavioral problems should receive treatment. Accordingly, because the function of their behavior is distinctively different, they need different treatment approaches.

The *DSM-5* (American Psychiatric Association [APA], 2013) now offers diagnostic criteria that include an observable, behavioral threshold for the diagnosis of conduct disorder and provide a specifier for conduct-disordered children with callous and unemotional traits. This distinction is important because callous and unemotional children show poorer outcomes (Barry, Frick, Golmaryami, & Rivera-Hudson, 2013) and require different treatments (Frick, Ray, Thornton, & Kahn, 2014).

Correct conceptualization of these three groups (i.e., internalizing disordered emotionally disabled children, externalizing disordered emotionally disabled children, and externalizing disordered socially maladjusted children) is critical for correctly determining special education eligibility and developing evidence-based intervention protocols to address their needs. Special education eligibility and placement is critical because it relates to the manner in which behaviors and discipline are managed. Specifically, it is inappropriate, and inconsistent with special education law, to punish a child for behaviors that are a manifestation of their disability. For internalizing disordered emotionally disabled children and externalizing disordered emotionally disabled children, managing problematic behaviors is an issue that must be addressed through the IEP process. Particularly for externalizing disordered emotionally disabled children a comprehensive (multimodal) functional behavior assessment and behavioral intervention plan should be developed to determine appropriate interventions to promote age-appropriate emotion regulation. In contrast, the externalizing disordered socially maladjusted children need treatment strategies that hold them accountable for their behaviors in addition to their treatment.

The National Association of School Psychologists recently provided a position statement (www .nasponline.org/publications/cq/42/5/callous.aspx) highlighting the importance of schools partnering with others in the comprehensive treatment of youth with callous and unemotional traits. School-based treatments can be offered through general education and alternative education initiatives in coordination with multisystemic family or coordinated community interventions. Understanding that special education eligibility is not required for providing services (Hughes & Bray, 2004), and, in the case of callous and unemotional students, is contraindicated.

ETIOLOGY AND FACTORS CONTRIBUTING TO EMOTIONAL AND BEHAVIORAL DISORDERS

The diathesis-stress model (Ingram & Luxton, 2005) explains psychopathology as a combination of a person's vulnerability (e.g., biology and genetics) and exposure to stress. Simply put, when a person's stress exceeds their capacity to cope, underlying difficulties (e.g., disease or disorder) become apparent. It is the balance between stressors and coping that accounts for the onset and continuation of mental health and other medical disorders.

For children with emotionally driven internalizing disorders, general risk factors include family history, early exposure to stress and traumatic experiences, and being female and adolescent. The risk of children developing an anxiety disorder is increased if the child experiences chronic or serious illness. Children with significant loss, attention problems, learning problems, or conduct disorders face increased risk of developing depression.

For youth with externalizing disorders, general risk factors include family history, frontal lobe dysfunction (i.e., attention deficit/hyperactivity disorder and other learning problems), child abuse, family dysfunction, parental substance abuse, and exposure to poverty. Children with emotionally driven externalizing behaviors are often at increased risk by the presence of anxiety and depressive symptoms that predate or are co-occurring with the conduct problems. Families tend to experience conflict and the children experience emotional distress (e.g., remorse, guilt, and shame) over their aggressive and destructive behaviors. In contrast, children with externalizing symptoms with callous and unemotional traits typically respond poorly to punishment and others' distress. They often display low levels of anxiety and fear, and high levels of thrill-seeking personality traits.

For youth with externalizing problems, the presence of callous and unemotional traits must be considered for treatment planning. When developing intervention plans it is important to consider what approach works best for children within a disability category. Evidence-based practice identifies interventions that have demonstrated effectiveness with groups of children sharing a diagnosis. For example, cognitive and behavioral treatments are especially effective for children with anxiety and depression. However, practitioners must adjust interventions because individuals may have very different causes for shared symptoms, and children are entitled to *individualized* educational programs.

EVIDENCE-BASED INTERVENTIONS AND EMPIRICAL SUPPORT FOR CHILDREN AND ADOLESCENTS WITH EBD

Substance Abuse and Mental Health Services Administration (SAMHSA, 2012) provides a list of promising evidence-based practices. What matters *most* for effective services is the match between the intervention and every child's specific needs. School teams must:

1. Distinguish between problem behaviors and age-appropriate behaviors

2. Determine the requisite skills needed for adequate development
3. Determine the specific strengths and deficits this child possesses

Once the child's *individual* needs are identified, interventions can be selected and implemented, the child's progress can be monitored, and adjustments to the intervention can be made as needed.

- Consider whether the planned assessment will capture the relevant information needed to develop an appropriate intervention plan. Even though antecedents and consequences of a behavior may be considered, the essential personality traits that drive behaviors must also be considered. To effectively intervene with a callous and unemotional child, one must assess and consider personality traits.
- Resist the urge to select generic interventions. School teams are at risk for selecting generic interventions with children with conduct problems without a nuanced understanding of the nature of the child's problems.
- Move beyond a categorical (e.g., emotional disturbance), diagnosis-related approach when selecting interventions. Complicated cases require school teams to select interventions based on demonstrated effectiveness for correcting the identified cause(s) of the behavior (e.g., a functional approach).

Because challenging children requires structural and functional intervention selection, a generic list of interventions is insufficient.

Age-Appropriate Child Development

Evidence-based interventions facilitate social–emotional development. From this perspective, a child's healthy development and effective learning are what determine the efficacy of an intervention.

It is useful to think of behavioral development as similar to academic development. In both skill domains, there is an ordered sequence to skill acquisition. One cannot expect a child to understand complex skills if he or she does not possess prerequisite, underpinning skills. Continuing with the academic analogy, a child may not understand addition if he or she does not understand the number line. Similarly, it is unreasonable to expect a child to learn behavioral control when the child is unable to identify, understand, and manage his or her emotions. Simply rewarding appropriate behavior without teaching foundational emotion management skills will not likely prepare the child for life as an adult where these skills are necessary, yet unlikely to be routinely and systematically coupled with reinforcement by an external agent. To further the academic example, modern curricula do not reward a child for memorizing multiplication tables. Although memorization may be useful for a test and in generating automatic responses, it is more useful to understand how multiplication is related to addition and division, and to use that information to reason about how numbers and math concepts are related. In this way, behavioral control is essential and what a child will be judged on; intervention is like the curriculum including requisite substeps, material presented in a variety of formats, and the practice and feedback needed to obtain mastery. As with children who have academic delays, children with social–emotional skill delays have development that is slow and in much need of remediation; however, the key to understanding and changing pathological behavior rests in learning theory. Whereas psychopathology labels children's skill deficits, learning theory offers a pathway to remediating emotional and behavioral skill deficits within developmental, learning theory, and psychoeducational contexts.

Emotional Development. Emotional regulation may be thought of as being distributed along a bell-curve. Although some children are very emotional and others seem to suffer from shallow affect, most children demonstrate developmentally appropriate capacity for emotional experiences, including expression and regulation. In general, emotional regulation is possible after adequate emotion identification, comprehension, and expression are accomplished. As with many skill sets, typical children show similar-to-adult skills by the age of 12 years; however, under stress, previously developed skills may fail or go unused when needed.

Some emotions are experienced from birth and include interest, distress, disgust, contentment, anger, sadness, joy, surprise, and fear. More complex emotions are grounded within the child's familial, cultural, and social experiences and result in complex self-conscious feelings such as embarrassment, envy, guilt, pride, and shame. A child's temperament and its match with his or her caregiver's personality is thought to influence the child's ease of learning, including emotional learning. A good-enough match between parent and child facilitates learning whereas a poor match can impede learning. As children mature, complementary parent and teacher matches facilitate learning. During adolescence, peers become a dominant influence on the child's emotional development. Indeed, emotional regulation is grounded in social interactions in which early attachment figures lay the groundwork for how the child comes to understand interactions with others. Social development is reviewed in a later section.

The first step in the acquisition of emotional regulation is learning to identify one's emotions, emotional identification. Emotion identification requires the child to experience the emotion, including (a) identifying, (b) verbalizing, and (c) describing its source. Often, children who experience abuse or neglect have significant impairments in identification of emotions. These children's emotions may have been ignored or punished by their parents. Trauma experiences may interfere with their memory retrieval routes. Their emotions may be undifferentiated, whereas their emotional experience is felt as generally positive or negative, yet without complexity or clear purpose. As they mature, children can associate different emotional valences (i.e., positive and negative emotions) with different targets (e.g., one, two, or three people). Until about 5 years of age most children have no awareness of experiencing two simultaneous emotions (e.g., anger and sadness). The stages of emotional development of young children include: (a) some awareness that two emotions can occur at same time; (b) the ability to identify and express the same valence (+/+) or (−/−) toward different people, simultaneously; (c) the beginning of feelings of different valence (+/−) toward different targets; and (d) feelings of different valence (+/−) simultaneously toward the same target. Treatments selected to promote emotional identification focus on helping the child experience and label emotions. For young children, identification may occur through scenarios laden with emotional contexts in which children can discuss actors' feelings and why they might feel the way they do. For older children, bibliotherapy and classroom assignments (e.g., age-appropriate current events) can provide contexts for identifying and processing emotional experiences. Children often have difficulty understanding how events are related to an emotional experience, the residual nature of emotions, and how experiences can result in lasting feelings throughout the day or when they think about others. As such, interventions need to support the development of these additional skills. As the child's skills mature, interventions should encourage children to process emotional material.

A useful way to conceptualize how an intervention plan should proceed includes: (a) ensuring a clear understanding about how emotions develop in and are experienced by all people; (b) determining various therapeutic emotional experiences (e.g., various levels of intensity and contexts) required for children to practice how they think and react to emotionally charged material; and (c) ensuring there is a meaningful emotional support so children can expand their skills and gain mastery.

Step two involves the acquisition of emotional expression; that is, the appropriate display or communication of feelings. Not only do we want children to feel, we also want them to express their feelings in a socially appropriate manner. Being angry may be understandable; however, hitting is not generally considered an accepted form of anger expression. For young children, interventions should focus on emotional intensity. Too much intensity, too impulsive responding (e.g., stop and think strategies), or too little intensity (e.g., low assertiveness) should be differentiated and addressed. Adolescents need to apply display rules, such as looking pleased and saying thank you even when they have received a disappointing gift. Interventions in this area often focus on acknowledging emotional experiences and teaching expressions appropriate to various contexts (e.g., how is anger expressed toward a peer, toward an adult, and toward a stranger). Emotional regulation is the ability to identify inner experiences and express them appropriately for the context. This skill requires coordinating temperamental style with feelings and experiences, along with evaluating internal feelings and environmental demands.

Developmentally, children progress from external regulation (e.g., parent soothing an upset child) to internal regulation (e.g., using cognitive and behavioral strategies to sooth oneself). Typically, one's internal regulation is learned via observation, modeling, imitation, practicing self-control, and ultimately self-regulation. Positive behavioral support programs promote self-regulation and are useful for most children; however, some children require the explicit interventions listed earlier. Only when these aforementioned prerequisite skills are established is emotional regulation possible.

Children with internalizing behavioral disorders often have difficulty expressing emotions (e.g., inappropriate intensity, withdrawing, or avoiding others when stressed). Children with emotionally driven externalizing behavioral disorders often have problems with excessive expression of emotional reactions (e.g., inappropriate intensity, screaming, hitting, and biting when stressed). Children with externalizing behaviors associated with callous and unemotional traits typically do not show emotional dysregulation, unless they are also emotionally disturbed.

Social Development. As noted previously, attachment and context of parenting relationships are early learning experiences that provide templates for how children learn to understand and participate in subsequent relationships. Parents who are responsive to their children help establish expectations about the responsiveness of the others when they are distressed. In contrast, problematic parenting sets a pattern of irregular, nonexistent or contingent support from others, and sometimes, even with people who are loved ones, relationships may include hostility, domination, and violence. Children are first socialized through family experiences and then, as they mature into adolescence, by their peer group.

The functional social skills required for self-regulation include cooperation, assertiveness, responsibility, empathy, and self-control (CARES; Gresham & Elliott, 1990). Because children are not born with these skills, they must acquire them. Some children have difficulty displaying more than one emotional skill at a time (e.g., assertiveness and cooperation); others require practice calibrating when one skill should be emphasized and when another should be deemphasized. Interventions designed to teach these skills are useful after early childhood relationships have been established on a solid foundational self-identity. Specifically, interventions need to focus on developing self-esteem and self-efficacy.

Children with internalizing behavioral disorders are often delayed in social relations (e.g., when there is a history of underdeveloped social support systems and they do not yet view others as a source of support, relationships may not be reciprocal). Children with emotionally driven externalizing behavioral disorders often lag behind in their self-definition (e.g., they tend to be self-focused), which may appear to be antisocial behaviors, narcissistic tendencies, obsessive compulsive symptoms, or insufficient consideration of others. Children with externalizing behaviors associated with callous and unemotional traits are delayed in their ability to integrate the expressions of others (e.g., especially feelings) and are developmentally lagging in their ability to be selfless; rather they are overly self-focused (e.g., they display a reward-dominate approach where they consider their gains above consideration of others).

Cognitive Development. Cognitive development refers to how a child perceives, thinks, and draws conclusions about his or her world. Specifically, cognitive thought includes (a) bringing information in to the mind, (b) the processing of that material, and (c) making decisions. Good cognitive development is evident when a child is able to have and use relevant information effectively at the point of performance.

The learning brain is one that gathers relevant information to increase survival. Like other areas of development, the formation of fundamental cognitive structures is begun via exchanges between the baby and the baby's parents. Social interactions, experiences, and language-based exchanges expand, articulate, and develop basic structures. For example, children exposed to language-rich environments not only know more words and their meanings but also develop more fluidity and flexibility in how words are used. Similarly, increased social exchanges broaden the child's contextual understanding of nonverbal and cultural communications. When children are socially isolated or have interpersonal deficits, cognitive development can also be stunted. Also, children with poor emotional control can find themselves with fewer social opportunities; taken together it is important to note that children who have deficits in all areas are likely to develop the greatest delays and require the most comprehensive intervention plans.

Cognitive structures include schemas and working memory. Cognitive schemas are organizational categories where relevant knowledge about a particular issue is held. Elaborated schemas connect concepts together well. For example, a child may be able to identify the differences between a student and a teacher. An elaborated schema may indicate that, although different, students and teachers are also the same as they are both people. Children with restricted experiences benefit from interventions that increase their exposure to life events as well as interpretations of these life events that aid in understanding. For children with mild delays, bibliotherapy, elaborated discussions, and ongoing feedback may satisfactorily assist age-appropriate schema development. For children with significantly delayed schemas (e.g., "I had to hit him, he made me mad") or distorted schemas (e.g., "Fat girls are worthless"), new schemas need to be developed. Cognitive behavioral therapy is a particularly effective intervention for developing, repairing, or introducing healthier rival schemas. However, interventions involving the development of new or rival schemas must consider cognitive capacity. Although memory deficits can be itself a unique problem, when short-term memory is overloaded, new learning does not occur, new schemas are not developed, and existing problem schemas are not updated. Traumatized and neglected children struggle with focusing on the relevant information or may be overly focused on irrelevant details. Abused children may need revised schemas that are contradictory to their life experiences or parental injunctions (e.g., "Don't trust anyone outside of this family" or "Never forget that"). The mental effort needed to revise these schemas can result in cognitive overload. Practitioners will note a need for slowly moving through therapeutic protocols in order to help children learn to manage the acquisition of new thought structures.

Cognitive processing involves the intersection of the information that the child is taking in from the environment and his or her personal psychology (e.g., the child's learning history). Because a child's background and experiences greatly influence the patterns he or she expects, even when good cognitive material is available, the child's learning history informs schemas with which to interpret the material, modifying how the child interprets, understands, experiences, and retains memory of an experience. For this reason, existing maladaptive schemas resist change and are maintained, often, in the face of healthier, more adaptive possibilities. These narratives can result in social problem-solving deficits. Social problem solving is defined as solving real-world social problems as they occur. They are not restricted to social interactions, but rather reference problems in the social environment. In contrast to a specific thinking error held by an individual, as discussed earlier, problematic narratives restrict the child's motivation, ability to generate potential solutions, preferred coping styles, decision making, and, ultimately, the ability to implement effective solutions.

Interventions that address social problem solving often use zone of proximal development (Vygotsky, 1934) to modify and improve narratives, leading to successful social experiences. These interventions teach the child how to evaluate social situations, and practice solution generation, decision making, and strategies for applying new skills. Some children may be good at generating solutions but be poor at implementing them, whereas others may have the opposite set of skills. Cognitive conclusions are the finalized thoughts or ideas held by the child after input and thinking have occurred. Problematic conclusions are often biased attributions or inappropriate deference. Biased attributions are the systemic error that is applied in the child's reasoning or explanation about why something has happened. Classic biased attributions include: (a) fundamental attribution bias—other peoples' bad behavior is the result of an internal characteristic (e.g., they are a jerk)—if I have bad behavior it is because of an understandable circumstance (e.g., external cause); (b) false consensus bias—other people think, feel, and behave the same way I do; (c) confirmatory bias—once the child has made a conclusion about something, he or she continues to look for more evidence to support his or her position, among other problematic attributions. Cognitive behavioral interventions that challenge the thinking errors that maintain dysfunctional cognitive conclusions and that identify unconscious erroneous leaps in logic are useful.

Children with internalizing behavioral disorders demonstrate various cognitive errors, such as selective abstraction (e.g., focusing on incomplete information), dichotomous thinking (e.g., that a person is either good or bad), and arbitrary inference (e.g., drawing erroneous conclusions without evidence). Children with emotionally driven externalizing behavior disorders also show a wide range of cognitive errors. Commonly, they maintain a hostile attribution bias where the intent of others is interpreted as purposefully aggressive even when the precipitating event is ambiguous. Children with externalizing behaviors associated with callous and unemotional traits harbor unique cognitive errors reviewed in the following discussion.

Callous and Unemotional Traits. The development of the "moral emotions" of guilt, shame, and embarrassment is central to the acquisition of empathy, morality, and moral behavior. They begin to develop at about the age of 3 years and are directly related to a sense of responsibility and recognition of violating moral standards. Moral emotions come from recognition of the effect of one's actions on another person and can be modified through intervention.

Conduct-disordered children with callous and unemotional traits have deficits in the development of their moral emotions as they possess low levels of fearfulness, low levels of anxiety, and high levels of thrill seeking. Moreover, they often fail to respond to distress in others. Therefore, their feelings are not integrated into their decision making or actions. Their ability to take others' perspectives is delayed, too, but improves with treatment. Indeed, cognitive behavioral treatments can be appropriate for this group. It is important to note that emotional empathy deficits seem to be uniquely associated with callous and unemotional traits and are distinct from deficits associated with poor cognitive perspective taking and theory of mind (e.g., what is the other person thinking or feeling) deficits that are shown by children with an autism spectrum disorder (ASD). Furthermore, children with conduct disorder but without callous and unemotional traits do not show emotional or cognitive empathy deficits (Frick et al., 2014). These children suffer other cognitive deficits, including poor responses to punishment cues, failing to predict that punishment would be a result of their behavior, positive associations with deviant values (e.g., aggression is an acceptable way to acquire needs) and moral transgressions (e.g., my priorities matter more than the damage my acts may cause others). Highly callous and unemotional children do not benefit from traditional mental health services; however, modest success has been achieved by reaching children at very early ages, aiding parents with specific parenting strategies, tailoring treatments to address empathy deficits (e.g., how to read the emotions of others, why the emotions of others matter, and how to use that information in one's own decision making) and coordinating comprehensive school, community, and parenting treatments for a very sustained period.

Developmental Maturity Considered

As skills develop and stabilize, *interpersonal intelligence* (the ability to understand other people, what motivates them, how they work, and how to work cooperatively with them) and *intrapersonal intelligence* (the capacity to form an accurate, coherent, realistic, differentiated model of oneself to be able to use that model to operate effectively in life) form *emotional intelligence*. Emotional intelligence involves the ability to monitor one's own *and* others' emotions, to discriminate among them, and to use the information to guide one's thinking and actions. Emotional intelligence involves *self-awareness* (observing oneself and recognizing feelings as they happen), *managing emotions* (handling feelings so that they are appropriately expressed including being able to realize what is behind a feeling and finding ways to handle fears, anxieties, anger, and sadness), *handling relationships* (managing emotions in others and demonstrating social competence and social skills), *motivating oneself* (channeling emotions in the service of a goal, emotional self-control, delay of gratification and managing impulses), and *empathy* (sensitivity to others' feelings and concerns and taking their perspective and appreciating the differences in how people feel about things).

Interventions that do not address these complex, dynamic, and interactive systems often fail to achieve meaningful change for children with emotional and behavioral disorders (Curtis, Ronan, & Borduin, 2004). Because many evidence-based interventions use generic terms and promise comprehensive results, many school teams, erroneously, believe that selecting an intervention involved the simple straightforward task of picking an intervention from a list. Given the aforementioned review of development, it is anticipated that school teams can better proceed in selecting interventions.

HOW TO: A GUIDE TO THE IMPLEMENTATION OF INTERVENTIONS FOR EMOTIONAL AND BEHAVIORAL DISTURBANCE IN CHILDREN AND ADOLESCENTS

Once school teams are comfortable with conceptualizing the nature of the child's difficulties and have selected interventions based on the skill deficit that they seek to develop, they may refine implementation practices using chapters throughout the *Handbook of Applied Interventions for Children and Adolescents*. Practitioners should combine the skills learned from the evidence-based interventions for each disorder, and modify them as needed to address specific individual needs related to an emotional disturbance. However, independent of any psychological or educational diagnosis, at its core psychoeducational interventions call for the development of prosocial skills in children.

An intervention that addresses a skill deficit is good; an intervention program that comprehensively addresses foundational skills, including each specific deficit as well as any additional or related issues, is better. Although academic success is central to school functioning, each child's social, emotional, and behavioral needs should be weighed carefully. Furthermore, because children with social and emotional disorders are unique, and the context of the school buildings varies, teams must supplement or adjust even the most comprehensive intervention programs.

Importantly, the team should articulate a rationale for the intervention. That is: (a) *What is the child's deficit*? (b) *How will this intervention help develop skills*? and (c) *What is the outcome that is expected*? Please see Table 17.1 for an example of an effective planning session.

Using this approach, teams will be better able to address children who progress slowly as they may know how to think and reason about interventions rather than simply apply them. Additionally, there are resources (e.g., searchable databases) that facilitate treatment options; a list of those is provided at the end of this chapter.

Most children identified as emotionally disabled benefit from schooling in general education classes for part or all of the day. However, at times, based on the student's response to intervention (RTI),

TABLE 17.1

EFFECTIVE PLANNING EXAMPLE				
Example Question: What is the problem behavior?	*Example Question:* What is driving the problem behavior?	*Example Question:* How will this intervention help develop skills?	*Example Question:* What is the outcome that is expected?	*Example Question:* Who is responsible for implementation?
Example Response: Withdraws from class participation	*Example Response:* Emotional expression difficulty	*Example Response:* Emotional expression will be taught via the Coping Cat intervention.	*Example Response:* Improved expression of feelings (communication) and assertiveness	*Example Response:* School psychologist will provide group 40 minutes twice a week for at least 16 sessions.
Example Support Data: Parents report fear of group work. Teacher indicated she understands class activities but can refuse to participate.	*Example Support Data:* This child can identify feelings and knows that she is anxious and worried. She does not yet express anxiety appropriately.	*Example Support Data:* This intervention focuses on talking about nervous thoughts and feelings; relaxation techniques are used to promote emotional expression.	*Example Support Data:* Teaching skills to manage feelings (e.g., relaxation)	*Example Support Data:* Daily report card will be provided by teacher. Weekly progress monitoring will be completed by the child and shared with parents.

self-contained settings are required. Regardless of educational setting, emotionally disabled students benefit from a program that coordinates school-wide positive behavior interventions and support (PBIS) plans with individualized educational programs. If, however, the school-wide program and IEP conflict, the child's needs should be the top priority.

As is the case with academic interventions, behavioral interventions need to match the child's developmental skill level in order to build success. The mixture of known-to-unknown material should be about 70% known to 30% unknown, otherwise the student's frustration levels will be too high. For example, if the child acknowledges feelings (e.g., arousal) but cannot name his or her emotion, you know that you are starting at the beginning of the sequence. If the child knows that he or she is angry but fails to express anger in a socially appropriate manner, teach developmentally appropriate anger expression. Teaching the child that suppressing emotions is less beneficial than processing emotional material and acting in a manner that gets his or her needs met.

CONCLUSION

Most children identified as socially maladjusted benefit from treatment and schooling provided in alternative education classes. Alternative education effectively separates children with an emotional disability from those with social maladjustment because children with social maladjustment tend to manipulate those around them to acquire gains for themselves. Placing this group in proximity to children who are emotionally or socially vulnerable is problematic. Of particular issue is the need to be able to apply discipline strategies that keep socially maladjusted students—who can control their behaviors, especially when it is to their advantage—accountable. Moreover, when schools identify children as emotionally disturbed exclusively by virtue of their socially maladjusted behavior, they provide an opportunity for these students to continue to engage in these problematic behaviors. Furthermore, by engaging in this practice, schools provide socially maladjusted students a setting where problematic behaviors are more likely to

occur as they may not be held accountable for their behavior as such behavior would be considered a manifestation of their disability.

Three psychosocial intervention approaches are effective for all youth with conduct problems: parent training, contingency management, and cognitive behavioral skill training, particularly parent training. However, parent training interventions and other forms of behavioral therapy are less effective for children with calloused and unemotional conduct problems than their peers with conduct problems without calloused and unemotional traits. Traditional behavioral approaches (e.g., teaching caregivers effective discipline strategies such as time-out) are undermined by the characteristic insensitivity to punishment among these youth. Punishment is contraindicated for children with calloused and unemotional traits because they often respond by escalating levels of anger, revenge, and reactive aggression. Although these factors can make intervening with these youth challenging, some interventions improve their behavior, including reward-based behavioral strategies (e.g., descriptive praise). This suggests that evidence-based interventions for conduct problems may be modified to better fit the reward-dominant response styles of calloused and unemotional children. To illustrate, Kimonis and Armstrong's (2012) adaptation of Parent–Child Interaction Therapy (Zisser & Eyberg, 2010) to include an adjunctive token economy successfully reduced conduct problems to below clinically significant levels in a young boy with high callous and unemotional traits.

The promise of desired student outcomes resulting from evidence-based interventions is in the hands of educators who implement and maintain the intervention effectively. Critical to this outcome is selecting teachers who are open to and invested in the intervention, as well as providing adequate training, coaching, and support for the teacher. Additionally, regular assessment about the fidelity with which the treatment is administered and using fidelity-related data to improve the implementation and maintenance efforts are important (Fixsen, Naoom, Blase, Friedman, & Wallace, 2005). Of issue is the tendency to modify evidence-based interventions to fit the realities of the practice setting. As such, many treatments are edited and thus the tie to successful student outcomes can be compromised.

In addition to knowing what to do is the issue of knowing what to stop doing. Pushing out "problem" children to alternative educational settings and failing to provide treatment is common. New educational initiatives are expanding service provision to include children who are at risk and may not be considered disabled. Furthermore, nonspecial education issues such as drug and alcohol use, teen pregnancy, and obesity are priorities, and treatment programs are delivered in school–community partnerships. Practitioners prepared to address these complexities are important leaders in the school building.

SELECT BIBLIOGRAPHY

Child Trends. Retrieved from http://www.childtrends.org
This site offers a searchable database of interventions that can be tailored (e.g., by population, demographics, health and mental health need) to match the child you are trying to help.

National Registry of Evidence-based Programs and Practices (NREPP). Retrieved from http://www.nrepp.samhsa.gov
This is a searchable database for researching alternatives in intervention planning. This database provides access to program reviews as well as a description of the program, which can help practitioners determine if the intervention would be possible given the restrictions of their setting.

Research Roundup on Conduct Disorder
This is a summary of the recent addition of a specifier to the diagnosis of conduct disorder (CD) in the DSM-5. A complete review of the extant literature can be found at http://www.apapracticecentral.org/update/2014/02-27/conduct-disorder.aspx

REFERENCES

American Psychiatric Association. (2013). *Diagnostic and statistical manual of mental disorders* (5th ed., pp. 469–472). Arlington, VA: American Psychiatric Publishing.

Barry, C. T., Frick, P. J., Golmaryami, F. N., & Rivera-Hudson, N. (2013). Evidence-based assessment of conduct disorder: Current considerations and preparation for *DSM-5*. *Professional Psychology: Research and Practice, 44*(1), 56–63. doi:10.1037/a0029202

Bower, E. M. (1981). *Early identification of emotionally handicapped children in school* (3rd ed.). Springfield, IL: Charles C. Thomas.

Curtis, N. M., Ronan, K. R., & Borduin, C. M. (2004). Multisystemic treatment: A meta-analysis of outcome studies. *Journal of Family Psychology, 18*(3), 411–419.

Costenbader, V., & Buntaine, R. (1999) Diagnostic discrimination between social maladjustment and emotional disturbance: An empirical study. *Journal of Emotional and Behavioral Disorders, 7,* 2–7.

Fixsen, D. L., Naoom, S. F., Blase, K. A., Friedman, R. M., & Wallace, F. (2005). *Implementation research: A synthesis of the literature.* Tampa, FL: University of South Florida, Louis de la Parte Florida Mental Health Institute, The National Implementation Research Network (FMHI Publication #231).

Frick, P. J., Ray, J. V., Thornton, L. C., & Kahn, R. E. (2014). Can callous–unemotional traits enhance the understanding, diagnosis, and treatment of serious conduct problems in children and adolescents? A comprehensive review. *Psychological Bulletin, 140*(1), 1–57

Gacono, C. B., & Hughes, T. L. (2004). Differentiating emotional disturbance from social maladjustment: Assessing psychopathology in aggressive youth. *Psychology in the Schools, 41*(8), 849–860.

Gresham, F. M., & Elliott, S. N. (1990). *Social skills rating system manual.* Circle Pines, MN: American Guidance Service.

Hughes, T. L., & Bray, M. A. (2004). Differentiation of emotional disturbance and social maladjustment. *Psychology in the Schools, 41,* 819–822.

Hughes, T. L., Tansy, M., & Wisniewski, K. G. (2013). Oppositional defiant disorder and conduct disorder in the classroom. In J. B. Kolbert & L. M. Crothers (Eds.), *Understanding and managing behaviors of children with psychological disorders: A reference for classroom teachers* (pp. 229–268). New York, NY: Continuum Publishers.

Individuals With Disabilities Education Act. (2004). 20 U.S.C. § 1400.

Ingram, R. E., & Luxton, D. D. (2005). Vulnerability-stress models. In B. L. Hankin & J. R. Z. Abela (Eds.), *Development of psychopathology: A vulnerability stress perspective* (pp. 32–46). Thousand Oaks, CA: Sage.

Kauffman, J. M., Mock, D. R., & Simpson, R. L. (2007). Problems related to underservice of students with emotional or behavioral disorders. *Behavioral Disorders, 33,* 43–57.

Kimonis, E. R., & Armstrong, K. (2012). Adapting parent–child interaction therapy to treat severe conduct problems with callous-unemotional traits: A case study. *Clinical Case Studies, 11*(3), 234–252.

Kirk, S. (1962). *Educating exceptional children.* Boston, MA: Houghton Mifflin.

Oswald, D. P., & Coutinho, M. J. (1995). Identification and placement of students with serious emotional disturbance. Part I: Correlates of state child-count data. *Journal of Emotional and Behavioral Disorders, 3*(4), 224–229.

U.S. Department of Health and Human Services Substance Abuse and Mental Health Services Administration Center for Behavioral Health Statistics and Quality (2012). *Results from the 2011 National Survey on Drug Use and Health: Summary of National Findings.* Rockville, MD: Author. Retrieved from http://archive.samhsa.gov/data/NSDUH/2k11results/nsduhresults2011.pdf downloaded 4.24.2016

Tandon, M., Cardeli, E., & Luby, J. (2009). Internalizing disorders in early childhood: A review of depressive and anxiety disorders. *Child Adolescent Psychiatry Clinic North America, 18,* 593–610. doi:10.1016/j.chc.2009.03.004

Theodore, L. A., Akin-Little, A., & Little, S. (2004). Evaluating the differential treatment of emotional disturbance and social maladjustment. *Psychology in the Schools, 41,* 879–886.

U.S. Department of Health and Human Services Substance Abuse and Mental Health Services Administration Center for Behavioral Health Statistics and Quality. (2012). *Results from the 2011 National Survey on Drug Use and Health: Summary of National Findings.* Rockville, MD: Author. Retrieved from http://archive.samhsa.gov/data/NSDUH/2k11results/nsduhresults2011.pdf

Vygotsky, L. (1934). *Thought and language.* Cambridge, MA: MIT Press.

Zisser, A. R., & Eyberg, S. M. (2010). Parent-child interaction therapy and the treatment of disruptive behavior disorders. In A. E. Kazdin & J. R. Weisz (Eds.), *Evidence-based psychotherapies for children and adolescents* (2nd ed., pp. 179–193). New York, NY: Guilford Press.

Evidence-Based Interventions for Obsessive-Compulsive Disorder in Children and Adolescents

Sophia Zavrou, Brittany M. Rudy, and Eric A. Storch[1]

OVERVIEW

The purpose of this chapter is to describe three evidence-based interventions for youth diagnosed with obsessive-compulsive disorder (OCD). OCD is defined as the presence of obsessions and/or compulsions that are time-consuming and/or cause clinically significant distress or impairment in functioning (American Psychiatric Association [APA], 2013). Obsessions are characterized by recurrent, unwanted, and persistent thoughts, images, and impulses whereas compulsions are repetitive, ritualistic behaviors or covert acts that are performed in response to obsessions or to alleviate distress (APA, 2013). The content of the obsessions and compulsions varies among individuals with OCD; however, there are five themes that are commonly experienced across both children and adults: contamination, symmetry/ordering, forbidden or taboo thoughts, harm, and hoarding[2] (Leckman et al., 1997). Both adults and children with OCD vary in terms of insight related to the accuracy of their dysfunctional beliefs, ranging from acknowledging the fact that the beliefs are irrational to being completely convinced the beliefs are true. In children, especially below 7 years of age, appropriate lack of metacognition oftentimes contributes to limited insight into the irrationality of their beliefs (Lewin et al., 2010; Storch, Milsom, et al., 2008).

OCD prevalence rates range from 1% to 2% of children and adolescents (Zohar et al., 1997), with males diagnosed more frequently than females in childhood. Notably, OCD becomes more gender balanced into adolescence and adulthood (Tükel et al., 2005). Approximately 80% of people with OCD report symptom onset during childhood (Pauls et al., 1995). Pediatric OCD confers significant functional impairment (Piacentini, Bergman, Keller, & McCracken, 2003) and reduced life quality (Lack et al., 2009) with sustained functional impairment for those who are inadequately treated (Rapaport, Clary, Fayyad, & Endicott, 2005).

Comorbid diagnoses are common among youth with OCD (Storch, Merlo, Larson, Geffken, et al., 2008) and serve to compound impairment (Storch, Larson et al., 2010; Storch, Larson, et al., 2008). Common comorbid disorders include anxiety disorders (Farrell, Barrett, & Piacentini, 2006), tic disorders (i.e., Tourette disorder; Storch, Stigge-Kaufman, et al., 2008), attention deficit hyperactivity disorder (ADHD; Geller, 2006), disruptive behavior disorders (Farrell et al., 2006), and major depressive disorder (Storch et al., 2012).

ETIOLOGY AND FACTORS CONTRIBUTING TO OCD IN CHILDREN AND ADOLESCENTS

The etiology of OCD is multidetermined with behavioral, cognitive, genetic, and biological factors being implicated. Each will be briefly reviewed in the following sections but see Hettema, Neale, and Kendler (2001) for a more comprehensive discussion of genetic and biological factors. Behaviorally, the symptoms of OCD appear to be a learned response to anxiety or discomfort, maintained by negative reinforcement (Lewin et al., 2014). Individuals with OCD engage in compulsions to alleviate anxiety/distress related to their obsessions. Once the compulsions are performed, the distress is diminished, thereby negatively reinforcing the individual for ritual engagement and increasing the chance of further symptom reliance. Avoidance of anxiety-provoking stimuli or situations that trigger obsessions or compulsions is similarly maintained through the mechanisms of negative reinforcement, with each successfully avoided situation strengthening the avoidance response. With repeated pairings, the connection between behavior and anxiety alleviation strengthens, making the learned response harder to eliminate.

Cognitive models of OCD purport that this disorder is associated with cognitive misappraisals and distorted patterns of thinking. Specifically, OCD is believed to be related to the following domains of cognition: inflated responsibility, overimportance of thoughts, control of thoughts, overestimation of threat, intolerance of uncertainty, and perfectionism (Obsessive-Compulsive Cognition's Working Group, 1997, 2001). Maladaptive cognitive distortions provoke distress, which motivate engagement in ritualistic behavior/avoidance.

There is evidence supporting a genetic component to OCD (Kirkby, 2003), with rates of OCD being significantly higher among relatives of participants with OCD as compared with control participants (Hettema, Neale, & Kendler, 2001). OCD has been associated with dysfunction in the orbitofrontal cortex, anterior cingulate cortex, basal ganglia, and thalamus (Neel et al., 2002). Studies have shown cortico-striato-thalamo-cortical circuitry dysfunction in the brains of people with OCD (Saxena & Rauch, 2000). Although further research is needed to clarify the role of neurotransmitter abnormalities in the pathophysiology of OCD, the effects of serotonergic drugs on obsessive-compulsive symptoms may suggest serotonin plays a role in pathogenesis and illness expression (Goddard et al., 2008). Dopamine and glutamate have also been implicated in OCD, though to a lesser extent (Wu, Hanna, Rosenberg, & Arnold, 2012). Furthermore, in recent years, abrupt-onset pediatric OCD has been associated with various infectious agents and a postinfectious autoimmune syndrome. A small subgroup of children with OCD, given the label PANDAS (pediatric autoimmune neuropsychiatric disorders associated with streptococcal infections), experience sudden onset of symptoms of an episodic nature, following infection with Group A beta-hemolytic streptococci (Murphy et al., 2012).

EVIDENCE-BASED INTERVENTIONS AND EMPIRICAL SUPPORT FOR OCD IN CHILDREN AND ADOLESCENTS

The American Academy of Child and Adolescent Psychiatry (AACAP) Practice parameters recommend cognitive behavioral therapy (CBT) with exposure and response prevention (ERP) monotherapy for the treatment of children with mild to moderate OCD and combined CBT and pharmacotherapy for severe cases of OCD (AACAP, 2012). Multiple studies have demonstrated the efficacy of CBT with ERP for the treatment of pediatric OCD, with ERP demonstrating superiority to placebo (POTS, 2004), attention-control conditions (Freeman et al., 2014; Piacentini et al., 2011), and pharmacotherapy (POTS, 2004; Storch et al., 2013). Results are similarly robust when delivered in various formats, including group (Barrett et al., 2004) and intensively (Storch et al., 2007b). In ERP, individuals are gradually and systematically exposed to anxiety-provoking situations or stimuli while refraining from engaging in any rituals or avoidance behaviors (see Bouton, 2004). Repeated exposures lead to habituation, or the experience of decreased anxiety/distress, when in the presence of the previously fearful situation. In this way, the child learns that the anxiety/distress decreases on its own without need for avoidance or compulsive behaviors.

The family should be meaningfully included in the treatment of pediatric OCD for a variety of reasons (Storch, 2014). First, family inclusion can decrease symptom accommodation, which is very common in pediatric OCD (Lebowitz et al., 2013; Storch et al., 2007a). This is very important as accommodation unfortunately often maintains anxious symptomology and, therefore, has been linked to poorer treatment outcomes (Merlo et al., 2009; Storch, Björgvinsson, et al., 2010). Second, with family involvement, parents can learn to act as "coaches" during home exposures (Merlo et al., 2009) and therefore can facilitate completion of homework assignments. In the treatment of pediatric OCD, parents can also help children generalize treatment gains to novel situations or situations that cannot be practiced in session. Finally, it is important to include parents in the treatment as child–parent reports can be discrepant in terms of reporting symptoms and their severity. Having both parent and child reports results in a more comprehensive and accurate picture of the child's symptomology, which facilitates the treatment process.

Therapists can incorporate various techniques with traditional ERP to make treatment more appropriate for the child's clinical presentation. Therapists may implement parenting strategies and behavioral modification techniques to help parents deal with temper tantrums related to anxious oppositionality. Families can facilitate the use of reinforcers for successful completion of exposure exercises to increase motivation (see Davis & Ollendick, 2005). Furthermore, incorporating parents into participant modeling can be very helpful in the treatment of young children (Bouton, 2004). Recent studies have shown efficacious results when using these components with traditional ERP, especially when treating young children, in decreasing obsessive-compulsive symptoms, as well as in reducing family accommodation and oppositional behaviors related to anxiety (Lewin et al., 2014; Merlo et al., 2009).

Psychopharmacological studies support the use of selective serotonin reuptake inhibitors (SSRIs) in the treatment of pediatric OCD. A meta-analysis has shown superiority of SSRIs to placebo for treating youth with OCD (Geller et al., 2003), although effect sizes are modest and smaller than for CBT. Studies generally show a response rate

of ~50% for youth receiving SSRI monotherapy (POTS, 2004). However, youth treated with medication only often continue to exhibit clinically significant symptoms even after an adequate medication trial (Riddle et al., 2001) and few youth achieve remission with SRI therapy alone (POTS, 2004). Although CBT should always be provided as a first-line intervention, research supports the augmentation of SRI treatment with ERP (POTS-II, 2011; Storch, Lehmkuhl, et al., 2010). Furthermore, pharmacotherapy may not be as acceptable to parents as CBT.

HOW TO: A GUIDE TO THE IMPLEMENTATION OF INTERVENTIONS FOR OCD IN CHILDREN AND ADOLESCENTS

This section provides a detailed description of three evidenced-based interventions for pediatric OCD. Treatment guidelines for pediatric OCD suggest the most efficacious treatment is CBT with ERP, either alone or in combination with pharmacotherapy for the most severe cases (AACAP, 2012). Therefore, we describe three successful CBT interventions: CBT with ERP, family-based CBT with ERP, and cognitive therapy interventions that can be used in conjunction with ERP.

CBT With ERP

The primary component of graduated ERP includes placing the child in increasingly fearful situations and having him or her resist completion of compulsive behaviors to alleviate anxiety/distress, thereby promoting habituation and extinction learning. In conducting ERP, the primary goals of session one are to provide psychoeducation and treatment rationale, and establish treatment goals. The treating clinician should provide information, including reasons surrounding the presence and purpose of OCD (e.g., biological bases, environmental factors), definitions for obsessions and compulsions, and a description of habituation and extinction learning to ensure understanding of OCD and anxiety as well as the purpose of ERP. Creative examples such as the idea of jumping into the deep end of a pool for the first time (i.e., the first time one jumps, the act of jumping may appear scary

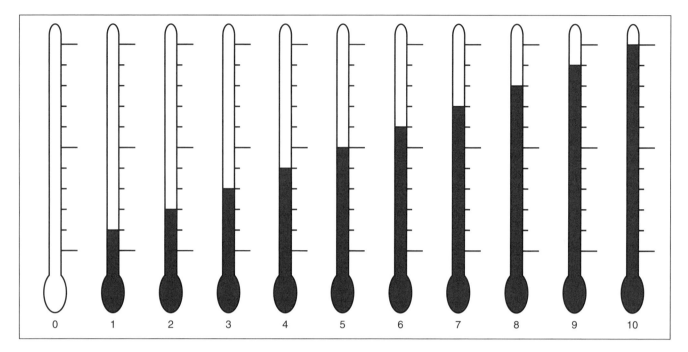

FIGURE 18.1 Fear thermometer.

and cause anxiety; however, after the person jumps a few times, the act of jumping is no longer scary and does not cause anxiety—habituation occurs—in fact, it likely becomes fun for the person) may be used to communicate rationale for extinction learning in lay terms. It may be useful to provide visual aids, drawings, and/or handouts to help the child understand the process of anxiety and the necessity of exposure to facilitate habituation and decrease compulsive behaviors.

The purpose of session two is to complete the child's fear hierarchy, and address any remaining questions regarding psychoeducation and treatment. The fear hierarchy is a graduated list of fearful situations that elicit obsessions and are usually met with avoidance and/or compulsive behaviors. Feared situations that make up fear hierarchies are usually rated from 0 to 10 (or 100) with 0 being no distress/no difficulty resisting compulsions and 10 being very severe fear and anxiety/extreme difficulty resisting compulsions. A fear thermometer is often used with children to help orient anxiety/distress ratings visually (see Figure 18.1).

The goal of the therapist during hierarchy creation should be to establish a range of low-, moderate-, and high-level situations that are relatively evenly balanced, though a greater number

of moderate to difficult situations may be listed. This list is used as the basis for future exposure sessions and should be sufficiently detailed (e.g., a minimum of 10–15 items) whereas remaining open to modification throughout the treatment process. For an example of a fear hierarchy, see Table 18.1.

During session three, the treating clinician should select a low-level exposure activity to complete with the child. Using the hierarchy in Table 18.1 as an example, the therapist would ask the child to touch the office doorknob without washing or using sanitizer. After the child touches the doorknob, the therapist should check in with the child every 1 to 2 minutes by asking the child to rate the level of distress experienced. The therapist and child should remain in the situation until the distress dissipates. The therapist and child can discuss the anxiety/distress and the obsessions that accompany the situation, but reassurance and distraction techniques, such as thinking of relaxing thoughts, switching topics, and so forth, should *not* be utilized. It is important for the child to experience and manage the anxiety/distress and notice how, over time, it dissipates, in order for habituation to occur. It is appropriate to repeat the activity just completed once the anxiety/distress decreases to an "acceptable level." An acceptable level will vary by child and is up to the therapist's judgment, but typical

TABLE 18.1

SAMPLE FEAR HIERARCHY			
Rating	Feared Situation	Obsession	Exposure Examples
10	Going to bed without taking a shower	My bed will get dirty	Take a shower once a day in the morning
10	Taking a shower less than three times per day		Take one shower per day
8	Using the same bath towel without washing	My towel gets dirty after I have used it once	Use the same bath towel without washing for 5 days
8	Using dirty hand towels	Hand towels have germs	Use same hand towel as other people without washing for 3 consecutive days
7	Touching bathroom floor	Bathroom floor is dirty	Touch bathroom floor without washing
7	Eating food items that touch the floor	The floor has germs and is dirty	Put food on floor for patient to pick up and eat
6	Eating food items that touch "unclean" surfaces	The food will get infected with germs	Put goldfish, pretzels, etc. on surfaces in office for patient to eat
6	Shaking hands with people	I will get their germs	Walk around and shake hands with others
5	Touching bathroom sinks	I will get infected by toilet germs	Touch bathroom sink without washing
5	Touching and using kitchen items for food without (re)washing first	Items may be dirty and infect the food	Touch items in kitchen. Then put food on items in kitchen without washing items (items are previously washed) and eat
5	Touching toys that other children have used	Toys will spread germs	Touch toys other children have used without washing
4	Touching the floor	The floor is dirty and has germs	Touch floor without washing
3	Touching a doorknob	Doors have germs and are dirty	Touch doorknob without washing

guidelines suggest a rating of 3 or below on a 0 to 10 scale for items rated higher than 5, and 10 for less distress-provoking stimuli. Each exposure should be repeated multiple times during a session and/or as homework to ensure habituation and successful learning that the feared outcome does not take place. During the first few sessions, when exposures consist of easy hierarchy items, the clinician may be able to address more than one hierarchy item. However, as exposure difficulty increases, each session focuses on only one hierarchy item.

Should the child refuse to participate in the activity when it is described, the therapist may negotiate a modified, slightly easier exposure activity. For instance, the therapist may touch the doorknob and then touch the child's arm, facilitating "spread of germs" but not direct contact with the germ surface. Other variations, although not ideal, that may be necessary depending on the difficulty experienced in refraining from compulsions include attempting to increase the time between the activity and the compulsion. For instance, the therapist may ask the child to touch the doorknob and wait several minutes before using hand sanitizer. Then, the therapist would repeat the activity, asking the child to wait a longer duration before sanitizing, and then again with an even longer wait. Similarly, the therapist may ask the child to hold his or her hand on the doorknob for increasing intervals. For children, framing exposures in the form of games (e.g., "Can the child beat his/her last time for going without sanitizing?"; "Who can touch the most 'dirty' objects in 1 minute, the therapist or the child?") may be helpful to engage the child in therapy and motivate him or her to complete the task.

The therapist should vary the activity in session as much as possible. For instance, the therapist should have the child touch more than one doorknob in the office. Once the child has successfully conquered a particular activity on his or her hierarchy in session, he or she should be instructed to practice the same activity at home. Varying exposure activities and practicing at home provide opportunities for generalization and maintenance. Homework should be given at the end of each session for the child to complete activities mirroring those completed in session. For instance, for session three, homework could consist of having the child touch doorknobs repeatedly each day without washing with homework assignments lasting up to 60 minutes per day.

The remainder of therapy sessions should be similar to session three. The basic format of a 50-minute session involves an interval update (5 minutes), homework review (5 minutes), exposure task (30–35 minutes), and finally, discussion of homework and goals for the between-session interval. During each session, the therapist and child should pick one or more activities (depending on difficulty, child motivation, and time) to complete in session. The child rates his or her anxiety/distress for each exposure and the activity is repeated until it can be performed with minimal distress. For instance, during session four, the therapist may ask the child to repeatedly touch toys used by other children for the first task and touch utensils in the office kitchen for the second task. It is important that the child's distress level decrease sufficiently prior to ending each activity. It may be necessary and/or beneficial to plan extra time around exposure activities, particularly those that are more difficult, to assure that sufficient distress reduction occurs.

Progress monitoring is suggested throughout the therapy process, and it may be useful to gauge progress in therapy and time to termination every four to five sessions. The Children's Yale-Brown Obsessive Compulsive Scale (Scahill et al., 1997) is one possible clinician-administered option, or alternatively, a self-reported measure of symptom severity (e.g., Children's Florida Obsessive Compulsive Inventory (C-FOCI); Storch et al., 2009) or impairment (e.g., Child Obsessive-Compulsive Impact Scale (COIS); Piacentini et al., 2003) can be used. The child's hierarchy may be altered to include newly developed feared triggers or those not previously deemed as significantly interfering. Conducting ERP requires creativity and planning in facilitating exposures that elicit anxiety/distress in controlled situations, as well as adaptability to adjust sessions and exposure activities to meet the child at his or her level of anxiety/distress and most current/interfering symptoms.

Although uncommon, some children with OCD experience intrusive thoughts or images that are not always accompanied by compulsive behaviors or triggered by certain situations. These thoughts may seem nonsensical or improbable, but are usually extremely distressing to the child. Such obsessions can be addressed through mental exposures. For instance, if a child has an intrusive thought of "I may have offended God," a possible exposure would be to have him or her repeat the thought aloud, record the thought and listen to the recording, or write the thought over and over, until anxiety/distress related to the thought itself decreases. This allows the child to experience the anxiety/distress and uncertainty that the thought elicits and then habituate to it.

Conversely, some children may experience compulsions, often accompanied by a "just not right" (JNR) feeling, that are not connected to specific obsessive thoughts. Exposure activities may include attempting to replicate the JNR feeling and refraining from the compulsion. For instance, if a child feels the need to repeat walking in and out of doorways until if feels "right," the exposure activity would be to ask the child to walk through different doors only once. Hoarding is another example of a compulsive behavior that may not always be accompanied by obsessive thoughts. Exposure activities for hoarding may include making an item hierarchy and discarding increasingly more difficult items in session and at home, and/or being exposed to the chance to acquire preferred items while refraining from doing so.

Family-Based CBT With ERP

When treating OCD in children, regardless of age but particularly with very young children, family involvement in treatment is recommended. Children are often not the initiators of the treatment process and may require external motivation for treatment participation and compliance. Furthermore, children often include their families in rituals, perpetuating the negative reinforcement cycle of symptoms and creating a family-wide need for intervention. Family accommodation occurs when family members engage in activities that interfere with their own lives to prevent the child from experiencing anxiety/distress and/or from engaging in oppositional and tantrum behaviors (e.g., providing reassurance, receiving confessions, opening doors for the child, cleaning surfaces before the child uses them).

Children who experience significant anxiety/distress and/or ritualized behaviors often demonstrate accompanying anxious oppositional behaviors, such as temper tantrums (e.g., screaming, hitting, kicking), refusal to participate in activities, or even attempts to run or flee to avoid feared situations (Storch, Merlo, Larson, Marien, et al., 2008). Session one in family-based CBT with ERP is identical to the first session of traditional ERP described above with the exception that specific time is set aside to discuss parental roles in treatment. It may also be useful to have one or more parent-only sessions following session one, particularly when treating younger children and/or those who demonstrate oppositional behaviors, to provide further education on implementation of behavioral strategies and reduction of accommodation. As part of the parent-only session(s), parents should be taught acceptable and unacceptable behavioral responses to anxiety/distress, and how to handle each set of responses with basic parenting strategies. Such strategies include praise and rewards for brave behavior, ignoring nondestructive negative behaviors (e.g., whining), and implementation of a structured time-out protocol for defiance and tantrum behaviors. See Barkley (1997) and McNeil et al. (1999) for a complete discussion of structured time-out protocols. Parents should also be educated on the role of excessive reassurance (e.g., responding repeatedly to anxious questions,

especially "what if" questions) and accommodation behaviors in maintaining distress. Parents should be encouraged to gradually remove accommodation at home. A parent-only session is also a good time to address any remaining questions about the treatment process and/or information provided before exposure sessions begin.

Remaining sessions are structured similarly to traditional ERP, with the only difference being that parents or primary caregivers have considerable involvement in the treatment and eventually transition to becoming the leaders of exposure activities (with therapist coaching). Notably, this does not differ much from more traditional ERP. Once exposure sessions begin, certain behavioral techniques such as participant modeling, reinforced practice, and contingency management or response cost techniques are generally incorporated into treatment to address complicating family factors. Participant modeling is a technique that involves a child observing another individual interacting with a feared situation or stimulus in a nonfearful way. Participant modeling may be utilized by the therapist; however, it may also be helpful for parents to engage in participant modeling in session and at home during practice activities and homework. For instance, if the exposure activity is to touch the doorknob with a bare hand and refrain from washing, the therapist may have the child's parent touch the doorknob without sanitizing to demonstrate lack of danger and acceptability of the task. The parent may then touch the child or ask the child to touch the doorknob, without sanitizing. Having the parents model the exposure activities for their child fully engages them in the therapy process, teaching them how to become their child's coach, which is particularly useful for home practice and generalization.

Provision of external motivation through reinforced practice, or the provision of reinforcement of small gains for participating in exposure activities can be especially helpful, given common lack of insight and internally motivating factors in children who experience anxiety/distress. Using another example from Table 18.1, the therapist may tell the child that, once he or she eats a cracker that has been set on the desk, he or she may earn a sticker or checkmark, with three stickers/checkmarks adding to equal a prize at the end of session. The prize may be a fun activity or game, playground time, or a small toy. Combining these techniques, each time a new activity is suggested, the parent completes the activity first, followed by the child, and once the child completes the activity, he or she earns a small reward. Although it is typically suggested that the child and his or her parents or primary caregiver attend sessions without other family members, in certain circumstances, siblings and other family members can also participate in exposure activities, using participant modeling and similar techniques. Such involvement is significant in educating other family members about OCD and ERP, teaching them the necessary skills for managing the child's symptoms and the role of family accommodation. This is particularly important for family members who are considered "contaminants" by the child with OCD. For instance, if a sibling was sick, and the child experiences obsessions related to contamination with the sibling's possessions, the therapist may have the child touch or use his or her sibling's toys. Similarly, if a child believes a family member is "dirty," then the therapist may ask this family member to touch the child's possessions or play with his or her toys. Continued family involvement in treatment and gradual transition to parent-led exposures, particularly at home, is an eventual goal of therapy. In doing so, the therapist is not only teaching the child to manage his or her anxiety/distress, but also teaching the family appropriate responses to anxiety/distress and how to reduce interference with family functioning at home.

Cognitive Interventions

Cognitive strategies may be employed in the treatment of OCD to enhance ERP and provide the child with ways to adaptively respond to obsessions and compulsions. Cognitive interventions that have been found to be effective in OCD treatment and discussed in this section include "bossing back OCD," constructive self-talk, cognitive restructuring, cultivating nonattachment, and worry time (POTS, 2004; Piacentini et al., 2011). "Bossing back OCD" is often used at the beginning of treatment to help set the goals for treatment and increase motivation for exposures. This cognitive strategy aims at externalizing the problem so that parents or the child are not blamed for the symptoms. Additionally, it helps create an alliance between the parents, child, and therapist who

will work together to minimize or eliminate OCD symptoms. The first step in "bossing back OCD" is having the child externalize OCD by acknowledging and labeling when OCD symptoms occur. In young children, it may be helpful for the child to choose a name for OCD that will be used throughout the treatment (e.g., the monster). Subsequently, the child uses this strategy during treatment to identify instances of OCD controlling his or her life. Helpful questions therapists can use throughout the treatment include, "When did OCD [or child's chosen name] boss you around this week?" "Did you talk back to OCD this week?" and "Who helped you talk back to OCD?" Children can also "talk back to OCD" during an exposure by saying, for example, "I won't listen to you OCD; I'm the boss" (March & Mulle, 1998).

Cultivating nonattachment is another helpful cognitive intervention and it includes accepting the presence of the OCD-related thought but letting it pass through one's mind without need for further exploration or action. In cultivating nonattachment, children are taught four self-statements in an attempt to externalize OCD and allow them to recognize it as the enemy (March & Mulle, 1998). First, children learn to attribute the thoughts to OCD by saying, for example, "It's just OCD talking again." The second self-statement is, "My brain is hiccupping again," used to recognize the biological underpinnings of OCD. Then, children learn to view OCD thoughts as meaningless (e.g., "These hiccups are not important."). The final self-statement emphasizes the fact that these thoughts will go away without the need for specific action (e.g., "I'll do something fun until OCD goes away."). These self-statements encourage the child to pay attention to what "OCD says" but allow the thoughts to subside on their own. This cognitive strategy should be distinguished from actively attempting to block anxiety-provoking thoughts, which may itself exacerbate OCD symptoms by virtue of trying to suppress a cognition.

Constructive self-talk is used to combat anxiety/distress related to negative self-statements, being critical toward oneself, and pessimism about being free of OCD symptoms. The main technique used is replacing such maladaptive cognitions with realistic self-talk that focuses on the child's ability to fight OCD. For example, a child who is pessimistic about his or her ability to complete an exposure can be taught to tell himself or herself, "I can do this! I can handle the anxiety/distress. I've done it before." Additionally, children may learn to remind themselves that, even though they are very anxious/distressed at the beginning of the exposure, the anxiety/distress will eventually decrease. It is interesting to note that evidence suggests that reducing the negative self-talk or negative patterns of thinking is more important than increasing positive self-talk, a phenomenon called "the power of non-negative thinking" (Kendall, 1984). Therefore, the therapist must focus on reducing and replacing negative thoughts and statements with more constructive self-talk rather than merely introducing or increasing positive statements.

Another effective strategy is cognitive restructuring. Cognitive restructuring involves teaching the child to identify the nature of his or her distress-provoking thoughts, and helping the child analyze the validity of his or her thoughts. The first step in cognitive restructuring is helping the child learn to identify thoughts and understand the relationship between thoughts and feelings. Then, the therapist helps the child evaluate the validity and/or accuracy of anxiogenic thoughts. Finally, the child learns to challenge inaccurate thoughts and replace them with more realistic and/or accurate ones.

An example of a cognitive restructuring strategy is estimating the likelihood of the occurrence of the dreaded event. Imagine that a child is afraid a meteor will hit Earth and the only way to prevent this from happening is for him to rub the back of his parents' couch every time he enters the living room. In this example, the therapist can help the patient estimate the likelihood of a meteor hitting Earth with the aim of decreasing the child's fear and therefore, need to engage in a compulsion, upon seeing that the probability of this event happening is minuscule. An alternative strategy would be to analyze the patient's personal responsibility for the dreaded event. For example, if a child is afraid of being the cause of his mother getting cancer, then the therapist can ask the child why he thinks he would be responsible for such an event. Subsequently, the therapist and child can challenge feelings of personal responsibility by discussing whether this thought is logical and/or even medically possible. In challenging personal responsibility for a dreaded event, the therapist and patient can create a list of factors that contribute to the occurrence of the event and put a numerical value

on the contribution of each factor. By the end of this exercise, the child will see that his or her contribution is significantly smaller than initially thought. Sometimes, obsessions can be challenged by exploring the link between the compulsion and the prevention of the dreaded event to reveal the lack of logical connection between the two. For example, "How would you rubbing the couch change a meteor's course?" When using cognitive restructuring, it is helpful to label the initial anxiety-provoking thought as being what "OCD thinks" so as to externalize the thought and decrease the child's resistance to challenging it.

Another cognitive restructuring technique involves asking the child to become a detective and look for clues about the credibility of anxiety-provoking thoughts. In order to use this strategy, the therapist explains that anxiety is our body's alarm system, alerting us of danger in the environment. However, the child is told that our alarm system sometimes is activated when there is no real danger (false alarm). Children are taught to act as detectives when the body alarm system is activated to ascertain whether it is a real or false alarm. In making this decision, children are to look for evidence of real danger in the environment. Helpful questions in the investigation include, "Has this ever happened before?" "What is the evidence it won't happen?" and "Are there any facts to support my thought?" This technique is especially useful during exposures as children experience anxiety/distress in these situations. A child who engages in frequent hand washing due to fears of contamination can, for example, use this strategy when his body alarm system causes him to feel anxious/distressed about contracting a disease. During the exposure, the child can "look for evidence" that either supports or refutes the anxiety-provoking thought.

The final cognitive intervention discussed herein is worry time, which can be used with children who experience great amounts of excessive worry, most often in the form of "what if" or related questions/obsessions. Because of the fact that exposures may be difficult to implement with such children given the future focus of such "what if" obsessions, worry time provides a successful way of managing anxiety levels and augmenting exposure treatment. Worry time refers to setting aside 10 to 15 minutes a day for parents and the child to discuss certain obsessional worries. During worry time, the child is encouraged to expose himself or herself to the mental obsessions (see ERP section) and if necessary, to use his or her detective skills, discussed above, to challenge worries. In addition, the child may be encouraged to problem solve worries if possible. This technique is helpful in diminishing overall anxiety associated with obsessional worries throughout the day as worries are "saved" for worry time. Parents should be instructed to engage in a fun activity with their child at the end of worry time as a reward and to help the child continue with his or her day.

CONCLUSION

The purpose of this chapter was to describe three evidence-based interventions for the treatment of OCD in children and adolescents. Current treatment guidelines for OCD suggest that the most efficacious treatment is CBT with ERP alone for mild to moderate cases, or CBT with ERP in combination with pharmacotherapy for moderate to severe cases (American Academy of Child and Adolescent Psychiatry, 2012). Therefore, this chapter described three CBT interventions that have been shown to be effective in the treatment of OCD, namely CBT with ERP, family-based CBT with ERP, and cognitive interventions. Clinicians should consider the child's age, developmental level, and family situation in deciding whether to conduct CBT in an individual or family format, and whether cognitive interventions would be helpful in enhancing ERP.

NOTES

1. This research was supported by a Fulbright Scholar award to the last author. The findings and conclusions in this report are those of the authors and do not necessarily represent the official position of the Fulbright Scholar Program, Council for International Exchange of Scholars, and Institute of International Education. Correspondence concerning this article should be addressed to Eric Storch, PhD.
2. In *Diagnostic and Statistical Manual of Mental Disorders* (5th ed.; *DSM–5*; APA, 2013), hoarding is classified as a separate disorder except in rare cases when the hoarding behaviors are a consequence of obsessions or compulsions in the context of OCD.

SELECT BIBLIOGRAPHY

Chansky, T. E. (2001). *Freeing your child from obsessive-compulsive disorder*. New York, NY: Three Rivers Press.
This is a guide for parents on understanding and overcoming OCD in their children and adolescents. It includes cognitive behavioral techniques for helping families deal with their children's symptoms and decrease family accommodation.

Piacentini, J., Langley, A., & Roblek, T. (2007). *Cognitive-behavioral treatment of childhood OCD*. New York, NY: Oxford University Press.
In this book, the authors outline a 12-session, CBT treatment for OCD in children and adolescents that combines individual and family therapy.

Storch, E. A., & McKay, D. (2014). *Obsessive-compulsive disorder and its spectrum: A lifespan approach*. Washington, DC: American Psychiatric Association.
This book reviews the existing literature on OCD and OCD-spectrum disorders (OCSDs), focusing largely on assessment and treatment. The book takes a life-span approach, meaning it looks at OCD and OCSDs across different age groups. This book is beneficial for clinicians as well as researchers.

Storch, E. A., Murphy, T. K., & Geffken, G. (2007). *Handbook of child and adolescent OCD*. Hillsdale, NJ: Lawrence Erlbaum.
This Handbook provides a comprehensive review of the literature on OCD in children and adolescents, including effective treatments, etiology, and assessment. It is very useful for mental health professionals.

REFERENCES

American Academy of Child and Adolescent Psychiatry (AACAP). (2012). Practice parameter for the assessment and treatment of children and adolescents with obsessive-compulsive disorder. *Journal of the American Academy of Child and Adolescent Psychiatry, 51*(1), 98–113. doi:http://dx.doi .org/10.1016/j.jaac.2011.09.019

American Psychiatric Association (APA). (2013). *Diagnostic and statistical manual of mental disorders* (5th ed.). Arlington, VA: American Psychiatric Publishing. Retrieved from 10.1176/appi .books.9780890425596.744053

Barkley, R. A. (1997). *Defiant children: A clinician's manual for assessment and parent training*. New York, NY: Guilford Press.

Barrett, P., Healy-Farrell, L., & March, J. S. (2004). Cognitive-behavioral family treatment of childhood obsessive-compulsive disorder: A controlled trial. *Journal of the American Academy of Child and Adolescent Psychiatry, 43*(1), 46–62.

Bouton, M. E. (2004). Context and behavioral processes in extinction. *Learning & Memory, 11*(5), 485–494.

Davis, T. E., & Ollendick, T. H. (2005). Empirically supported treatments for specific phobia in children: Do efficacious treatments address the components of a phobic response? *Clinical Psychology: Science and Practice, 12*, 144–160. doi:10.1093/clipsy.bpi018

Farrell, L., Barrett, P., & Piacentini, J. (2006). Obsessive-compulsive disorder across the developmental trajectory: Clinical correlates in children, adolescents, and adults. *Behavior Change, 23*, 103–120. doi:http://dx.doi.org/10.1375/bech.23.2.103

Freeman, J., Sapyta, J., Garcia, A., Compton, S., Khanna, M., Flessner, C., . . . Franklin, M. (2014). Family-based treatment of early childhood obsessive-compulsive disorder. The Pediatric Obsessive-Compulsive Disorder Treatment Study for Young Children (POTS Jr)—A randomized clinical trial. *JAMA Psychiatry, 71*(6), 689–698. doi: 10.1001/jamapsychiatry.2014.170

Geller, D. A. (2006). Obsessive-compulsive and spectrum disorders in children and adolescents. *Psychiatric Clinics of North America, 29*(2), 353–370. doi: http://dx.doi.org/10.1016/j.psc.2006.02.012

Geller, D. A., Biederman, J., Stewart, S. E., Mullin, B., Martin, A., Spencer, T., & Faraone, S. V. (2003). Which SSRI? A meta-analysis of pharmacotherapy trials in pediatric obsessive-compulsive disorder. *The American Journal of Psychiatry, 160*(11), 1919–1928.

Goddard, A. W., Shekhar, A., Whiteman, A. F., & McDougle, C. J. (2008). Serotoninergic mechanisms in the treatment of obsessive-compulsive disorder. *Drug Discovery Today, 13*(7–8), 325–332.

Hettema, J. M., Neale, M. C., & Kendler, K. S. (2001). A review and meta-analysis of the genetic epidemiology of anxiety disorders. *The American Journal of Psychiatry, 158*(10), 1568–1578.

Kendall, P. C. (1984). Behavioral assessment and methodology. In G. T. Wilson, C. M. Franks, K. D. Brownell, & P. C. Kendall (Eds.), *Annual review of behavior therapy: Theory and practice* (pp. 39–94). New York, NY: Guilford Press.

Kirkby, K. C. (2003). Obsessive-compulsive disorder: Towards better understanding and outcomes. *Current Opinions in Psychiatry, 16*, 49–55. doi:10.1097/00001504–200301000-00011

Lack, C. W., Storch, E. A., Keeley, M. L., Geffken, G. R., Ricketts, E. D., Murphy, T. K., & Goodman, W. K. (2009). Quality of life in children and adolescents with obsessive-compulsive disorder: Base rates, parent-child agreement, and clinical correlates. *Social Psychiatry and Psychiatric Epidemiology, 44*(11), 935–942.

Lebowitz, E. R., Woolston, J., Bar-Haim, Y., Calvocoressi, L., Dauser, C., Warnick, E.,…Leckman, J. F. (2013). Family accommodation in pediatric anxiety disorders. *Depression and Anxiety, 30*(1), 47–54.

Leckman, J. F., Grice, D. E., Boardman, J., Zhang, H., Vitale, A., Bondi, C.,…Pauls, D. L. (1997). Symptoms of obsessive-compulsive disorder. *The American Journal of Psychiatry, 154*(7), 911–917.

Lewin, A. B., Bergman, R. L., Peris, T. S., Chang, S., McCracken, J. T., & Piacentini, J. (2010). Correlates of insight among youth with obsessive-compulsive disorder. *Journal of Child Psychology and Psychiatry, and Allied Disciplines, 51*(5), 603–611.

Lewin, A. B., Park, J. M., Jones, A. M., Crawford, E. A., De Nadai, A. S., Menzel, J.,…Storch, E. A. (2014). Family-based exposure and response prevention therapy for preschool-aged children with obsessive-compulsive disorder: A pilot randomized controlled trial. *Behaviour Research and Therapy, 56*, 30–38.

March, J. S., & Mulle, K. (1998). *OCD in children and adolescents: A cognitive-behavioral treatment manual.* New York, NY: Guilford Press.

McNeil, C. B., Capage, L. C., Bahl, A., & Blanc, H. (1999). Importance of early intervention for disruptive behavior problems: Comparison of treatment and waitlist-control groups. *Early Education and Development, 10*, 445–454. doi:http://dx.doi.org/10.1207/s15566935eed1004_2

Merlo, L. J., Lehmkuhl, H. D., Geffken, G. R., & Storch, E. A. (2009). Decreased family accommodation associated with improved therapy outcome in pediatric obsessive-compulsive disorder. *Journal of Consulting and Clinical Psychology, 77*(2), 355–360.

Murphy, T. K., Storch, E. A., Lewin, A. B., Edge, P. J., & Goodman, W. K. (2012). Clinical factors associated with pediatric autoimmune neuropsychiatric disorders associated with streptococcal infections. *The Journal of Pediatrics, 160*(2), 314–319.

Neel, J. L., Stevens, V. M., & Stewart, J. E. (2002). Obsessive-compulsive disorder: Identification, neurobiology, and treatment. *The Journal of the American Osteopathic Association, 102*(2), 81–86.

Obsessive-Compulsive Cognition's Working Group. (1997). Cognitive assessment of obsessive-compulsive disorder. *Behaviour Research and Therapy, 35*, 667–681. doi:10.1016/S0005–7967(97)00017-X

Obsessive-Compulsive Cognition's Working Group. (2001). Development and initial validation of the Obsessive Beliefs Questionnaire and the Interpretation of Intrusions Inventory. *Behaviour Research and Therapy, 39*, 987–1006. doi:10.1016/S0005–7967(00)00085–1

Pauls, D. L., Alsobrook, J. P. II, Goodman, W., Rasmussen, S., & Leckman, J. F. (1995). A family study of obsessive-compulsive disorder. *American Journal of Psychiatry, 152*, 76–84. Retrieved from http://ajp.psychiatryonline.org/doi/abs/10.1176/ajp.152.1.76

Pediatric OCD Treatment Study (POTS) Team. (2004). Cognitive-behavioral therapy, sertraline, and their combination for children and adolescents with obsessive-compulsive disorder: The Pediatric OCD Treatment Study randomized controlled trial. *Journal of the American Medical Association, 292*, 1969–1976. doi:10.1001/jama.292.16.1969

Pediatric OCD Treatment Study II Team (POTS-II). (2011). Cognitive behavior therapy augmentation of pharmacotherapy in pediatric obsessive-compulsive disorder: The Pediatric OCD Treatment Study II randomized controlled trial. *Journal of the American Medical Association, 306*(11), 1224–1232. doi:10.1001/jama.2011.1344

Piacentini, J., Bergman, R. L., Chang, S., Langley, A., Peris, T., Wood, J. J., & McCracken, J. (2011). Controlled comparison of family cognitive behavioral therapy and psychoeducation/relaxation training for child obsessive-compulsive disorder. *Journal of the American Academy of Child and Adolescent Psychiatry, 50*(11), 1149–1161.

Piacentini, J., Bergman, R. L., Keller, M., & McCracken, J. (2003). Functional impairment in children and adolescents with obsessive-compulsive disorder. *Journal of Child and Adolescent Psychopharmacology, 13* (Suppl. 1), S61–S69.

Rapaport, M. H., Clary, C., Fayyad, R., & Endicott, J. (2005). Quality-of-life impairment in depressive and anxiety disorders. *American Journal of Psychiatry, 162*, 1171–1178. Retrieved from http://ajp.psychiatryonline.org/doi/abs/10.1176/appi.ajp.162.6.1171

Riddle, M. A., Reeve, E. A., Yaryura-Tobias, J. A., Yang, H. M., Claghorn, J. L., Gaffney, G.,…Walkup, J. T. (2001). Fluvoxamine for children and adolescents with obsessive-compulsive disorder: A randomized, controlled, multicenter trial. *Journal of the American Academy of Child and Adolescent Psychiatry, 40*, 222–229. doi:http://dx.doi.org/10.1097/00004583–200102000-00017

Saxena, S., & Rauch, S. L. (2000). Functional neuroimaging and the neuroanatomy of obsessive-compulsive disorder. *Psychiatric Clinics of North America, 23*, 563–586. Retrieved from http://www.psych.theclinics.com/issues?issue_key=S0193–953X(05)X7011–3

Scahill, L., Riddle, M. A., McSwiggin-Hardin, M., Ort, S. I., King, R. A., Goodman, W.….Leckman, J. F. (1997). Children's Yale-Brown Obsessive Compulsive Scale: Reliability and validity. *Journal of the American Academy of Child and Adolescent Psychiatry, 36*, 844–852. doi:http://dx.doi.org/10.1097/00004583–199706000-00023

Storch, E. A. (2014). Can we improve psychosocial treatments for child anxiety? *Depression and Anxiety, 31*(7), 539–541.

Storch, E. A., Björgvinsson, T., Riemann, B., Lewin, A. B., Morales, M. J., & Murphy, T. K. (2010). Factors associated with poor response in cognitive-behavioral therapy for pediatric obsessive-compulsive disorder. *Bulletin of the Menninger Clinic, 74*(2), 167–185.

Storch, E. A., Bussing, R., Small, B. J., Geffken, G. R., McNamara, J. P., Rahman, O.,…Murphy, T. K. (2013). Randomized, placebo-controlled trial of cognitive-behavioral therapy alone or combined with sertraline in the treatment of pediatric obsessive-compulsive disorder. *Behaviour Research and Therapy, 51*(12), 823–829.

Storch, E. A., Geffken, G. R., Merlo, L. J., Jacob, M. L., Murphy, T. K., Goodman, W. K.,…Grabill, K. (2007a). Family accommodation in pediatric obsessive-compulsive disorder. *Journal of Clinical Child and Adolescent Psychology, 36*, 207–216. doi:10.1080/15374410701277929

Storch, E. A., Geffken, G. R., Merlo, L. J., Mann, G., Duke, D., Munson, M., A...Goodman, W. K. (2007b). Family-based cognitive-behavioral therapy for pediatric obsessive-compulsive disorder: Comparison of intensive and weekly approaches. *Journal of the American Academy of Child and Adolescent Psychiatry, 46*(4), 469–478.

Storch, E. A., Khanna, M., Merlo, L. J., Loew, B. A., Franklin, M., Reid, J. M., & Murphy, T. K. (2009). Children's Florida obsessive compulsive inventory: Psychometric properties and feasibility of a self-report measure of obsessive–compulsive symptoms in youth. *Child Psychiatry and Human Development, 4*, 467–483. doi:10.1007/s10578-009-0138-9

Storch, E. A., Larson, M. J., Merlo, L. J., Keeley, M. L., Jacob, M. L., Geffken, G. R.,...Goodman, W. K. (2008). Comorbidity of pediatric obsessive–compulsive disorder and anxiety disorders: Impact on symptom severity and impairment. *Journal of Psychopathology and Behavioral Assessment, 30*(2), 111–120. doi:10.1007/s10862-007-9057-x

Storch, E. A., Larson, M. J., Muroff, J., Caporino, N., Geller, D., Reid, J. M.,...Murphy, T. K. (2010). Predictors of functional impairment in pediatric obsessive-compulsive disorder. *Journal of Anxiety Disorders, 24*(2), 275–283. doi:10.1016/j.janxdis.2009.12.004

Storch, E. A., Lehmkuhl, H. D., Ricketts, E., Geffken, G. R., Marien, W., & Murphy, T. K. (2010). An open trial of intensive family-based cognitive-behavioral therapy in youth with obsessive-compulsive disorder who are medication partial responders or nonresponders. *Journal of Clinical Child and Adolescent Psychology, 39*(2), 260–268.

Storch, E. A., Lewin, A. B., Larson, M. J., Geffken, G. R., Murphy, T. K., & Geller, D. A. (2012). Depression in youth with obsessive-compulsive disorder: Clinical phenomenology and correlates. *Psychiatry Research, 196*(1), 83–89.

Storch, E. A., Merlo, L. J., Larson, M. J., Geffken, G. R., Lehmkuhl, H. D., Jacob, M. L.,...Goodman, W. K. (2008). Impact of comorbidity on cognitive-behavioral therapy response in pediatric obsessive-compulsive disorder. *Journal of the American Academy of Child and Adolescent Psychiatry, 47*(5), 583–592.

Storch, E. A., Merlo, L. J., Larson, M. J., Marien, W. E., Geffken, G. R., Jacob, M. L.,...Murphy, T. K. (2008). Clinical features associated with treatment-resistant pediatric obsessive-compulsive disorder. *Comprehensive Psychiatry, 49*(1), 35–42.

Storch, E. A., Milsom, V. A., Merlo, L. J., Larson, M., Geffken, G. R., Jacob, M. L.,...Goodman, W. K. (2008). Insight in pediatric obsessive-compulsive disorder: Associations with clinical presentation. *Psychiatry Research, 160*(2), 212–220.

Storch, E. A., Stigge-Kaufman, D., Marien, W. E., Sajid, M., Jacob, M. L., Geffken, G. R.,...Murphy, T. K. (2008). Obsessive-compulsive disorder in youth with and without a chronic tic disorder. *Depression and Anxiety, 25*, 761–767. doi:10.1002/da.20304

Tükel, R., Ertekin, E., Batmaz, S., Alyanak, F., Sözen, A., Aslantas, B.,...Ozyildirim, I. (2005). Influence of age of onset on clinical features in obsessive-compulsive disorder. *Depression and Anxiety, 21*(3), 112–117.

Wu, K., Hanna, G. L., Rosenberg, D. R., & Arnold, P. D. (2012). The role of glutamate signaling in the pathogenesis and treatment of obsessive-compulsive disorder. *Pharmacology, Biochemistry, and Behavior, 100*(4), 726–735.

Zohar, A. H., Pauls, D. L., Ratzoni, G., Apter, A., Dycian, A., Binder, M.,...Cohen, D. J. (1997). Obsessive-compulsive disorder with and without tics in an epidemiological sample of adolescents. *American Journal of Psychiatry, 154*(2), 274–276. Retrieved from http://ajp.psychiatryonline.org/doi/abs/10.1176/ajp.154.2.274

Evidence-Based Interventions for Social Anxiety Disorder in Children and Adolescents

Jeremy S. Peterman, Nina D. Shiffrin, Erika A. Crawford, Elana R. Kagan, Kendra L. Read, and Philip C. Kendall

OVERVIEW

Social anxiety disorder (SAD), formerly known as "social phobia" in the *Diagnostic and Statistical Manual of Mental Disorders* (4th ed., text rev.; *DSM-IV-TR*; American Psychiatric Association [APA], 2000), is one of the most common psychological disorders in youth, with an estimated yearly prevalence rate between 1.6% and 2.8% (Merikangas, Nakamura, & Kessler, 2009). SAD is characterized by a marked fear or anxiety about social situations in which the child or adolescent perceives that he or she may be scrutinized by others. A diagnosis requires symptomatology lasting for at least 6 months. Youth with SAD are concerned that they will be humiliated or rejected, and thus, these youth typically avoid social situations or endure them with extreme distress. The most recent version of the *Diagnostic and Statistical Manual of Mental Disorders* (5th ed., *DSM-5*; APA, 2013) stipulates that social situations are almost always anxiety provoking, and may be accompanied by symptoms of crying, tantrums, freezing, and/or shrinking. The child or adolescent's fear must be out of proportion to the actual threat posed by the social situation and cause prolonged distress or functional impairment to meet diagnostic criteria (APA, 2013).

Such distress and impairment in youth manifest in several ways, including withdrawal from extracurricular activities and social events, reticence to join or participate in conversations with peers, reluctance to speak in class, hesitancy in conducting group work or providing oral presentations, anxiety about eating in front of others or using a public restroom, avoidance in speaking or texting on the phone, difficulty asserting oneself, or speaking to strangers and adults (APA, 2013; Beidel, Turner, & Morris, 1999). Research supports that children and adolescents with SAD have fewer friends, less intimate relationships, reduced extracurricular involvement, and lower levels of social support than their peers (LaGreca & Lopez, 1998). Their fears and avoidance result in loneliness, dysphoria, and inadequate social skills (Beidel et al., 1999). If untreated, these difficulties may persist into adulthood, with a continued negative impact on both occupational and social functioning. Social anxiety in adolescence is also predictive of later anxiety, depressive episodes, substance abuse, and educational underachievement (Woodward & Ferguson, 2001).

The onset of SAD typically occurs in adolescence, with 75% of individuals experiencing symptoms between the ages of 8 and 15 years (Kessler, Chiu, Delmer, & Walters, 2005). Additionally, early onset is associated with increased symptom severity and greater resistance to treatment. With respect to gender, rates of SAD in childhood are similar for both males and females. However, during adolescence, rates of SAD increase in females but not in males, creating a gender imbalance that continues into adulthood, perhaps because of genetic or environmental differences (APA, 2013; Kessler et al., 2005). In addition, more than 60% of youth with SAD have a comorbid disorder, most commonly another anxiety disorder (Beidel et al., 1999; Kendall et al., 2010). SAD is also associated with mood disorders, disruptive behaviors, eating disorders, and substance abuse disorders (Merikangas et al., 2009).

Given the early onset and deleterious effects of SAD, there is great value in developing effective treatments that target social anxiety in youth. This chapter reviews the current state of treatment for youth with SAD, beginning with a brief discussion of the etiology of social anxiety, followed by an overview of the empirical support for cognitive behavioral interventions. Finally, an in-depth review of three empirically supported interventions for social anxiety in youth is provided. The chapter closes with a suggested list of further readings and resources for those interested in additional information.

ETIOLOGY AND FACTORS RELATED TO SAD IN CHILDREN AND ADOLESCENTS

Many factors, including genetic, neurobiological, cognitive, and environmental, have been implicated in the development of SAD. However, no single factor perfectly predicts SAD; rather, a biopsychosocial model has been proposed to explain its etiology.

Genetics and Neurobiology

The genetic contribution to SAD is well established, with 30% to 50% of the variance being explained through heritability in twin studies (Kimbrel, 2008). Additionally, children of parents with SAD show an elevated risk of developing SAD, and conversely, children with SAD are more likely to have socially anxious parents (Rapee & Spence, 2004), likely accountable by gene–environment interactions. Additionally, it is believed that children inherit behavioral and neurobiological characteristics (i.e., temperament, shyness, activation levels of implicated brain regions) rather than a specific gene or group of "social anxiety" genes (Stein & Stein, 2008).

Low dopamine receptor binding in the striatum has been observed in adults with SAD as well as reduced dopamine transporter density (Marcin & Nemeroff, 2003). Serotonin and norepinephrine have also been connected with SAD, but findings have been mixed. Acute increases in serotonin are associated with increases in anxiety in adults, while long-term use of medication that increases the availability of serotonin (selective serotonin reuptake inhibitors [SSRIs]) is associated with reductions in anxiety (Ledley, Erwin, Morrison, & Heimberg, 2013). Some studies have found increased levels of norepinephrine in individuals with SAD, although other studies have not found this association. Nevertheless, serotonin–norepinephrine reuptake inhibitors have been found to be as efficacious in the treatment of SAD as SSRIs (Liebowitz, Gelenberg, & Munjack, 2005). Additionally, the amygdala, hippocampus, and prefrontal cortex have been implicated in the evaluation of social threat situations (Ledley et al., 2013). In adolescents, activation of the amygdala has demonstrated selective increases in activation to socially threatening information (Killgore & Yurgelun-Todd, 2005). Anxious adolescents have also demonstrated increased activation of the ventromedial prefrontal cortex (vmPFC) in response to a peer evaluation task and to fearful or angry faces, with higher anxiety associated with stronger connectivity between the vmPFC and amygdala (Blackford & Pine, 2012).

Temperament, considered an innate trait, has been linked with the development of SAD in youth. Infants and toddlers who display fear and resistance when encountering new or unfamiliar situations and/or people (e.g., appear withdrawn, show restraint and few approach behaviors) are considered to have a behaviorally inhibited temperament (Hitchcock, Chavira, & Stein, 2009). Longitudinal research has demonstrated that behavioral inhibition predicts shy behavior in preschool-aged children and SAD in later childhood and early adolescence (Kagan, 2002; Pérez-Edgar et al., 2010).

Family Environment

Young children with insecure attachment patterns are more likely to be diagnosed with SAD later in their lives (Ledley et al., 2013). Additionally, adults with SAD recall that their parents were overprotective, inconsistent in parenting (e.g., mixed in attentiveness and reinforcement), and insensitive with regard to emotional support (Neal & Edelmann, 2003). Children may learn anxious and avoidant behavior through parental modeling (Burstein & Ginsburg, 2010). Parents with an authoritarian parenting style or who model anxious behaviors may undermine the child's self-efficacy, restrict opportunities for socializing, and promote a pattern of avoidance behaviors that maintain anxiety.

Cognitive Biases

Similar to adults with SAD, children as young as 8 years demonstrate cognitive biases in social information processing and in their thoughts, attitudes, and beliefs (Rapee & Spence, 2004). For example, children with SAD anticipate fewer positive outcomes during social experiences, evaluate themselves more negatively, and endorse more negative cognitions than do their nonanxious counterparts (Alfano, Beidel, & Turner, 2006). Socially anxious children are also more likely to have negative interpretations of socially ambiguous situations and to display an attentional bias toward threatening social information (Kimbrel, 2008).

Negative Life Events

Negative life events in childhood (e.g., divorce; family conflict; parent psychopathology; and sexual, physical, and/or emotional abuse) have been found to be associated with SAD (Rapee & Spence, 2004). Some of these negative life events may be linked to peer problems (e.g., reduced quality of friendships, popularity, and withdrawal from social situations). Although research is largely correlational, children with SAD experience fewer positive outcomes in their peer interactions and report a higher frequency of aversive social experiences (i.e., rejection, exclusion, and neglect) than do nonanxious youth (Neal & Edelmann, 2003). Correspondingly, lower levels of peer acceptance are predictive of increased social anxiety in adolescents (Tillfors, Persson, Willen, &

Burk, 2012), and poorer social functioning is associated with more severe anxiety (Settipani & Kendall, 2013). Additionally, approximately half of adults with SAD report traumatic social experiences in childhood and adolescence (Kimbrel, 2008). Finally, there is also evidence that children with SAD may have deficits in social skills (e.g., nonverbal communication and perspective taking), which may contribute to their vulnerability in experiencing positive interactions with others (Tillfors et al., 2012).

EVIDENCE-BASED INTERVENTIONS AND EMPIRICAL SUPPORT FOR CHILDREN AND ADOLESCENTS WITH SAD

Fortunately, there are several treatments with strong empirical support for SAD. The most efficacious psychological treatment for SAD is cognitive behavioral therapy (CBT). The Division of Clinical Psychology of the American Psychological Association (APA) considers CBT a "well established" intervention for anxious youth (Hollon & Beck, 2013). CBT for SAD involves providing psychoeducation about social anxiety, teaching patients skills to regulate their anxious thoughts and feelings, guiding patients through behavioral exposures to previously avoided situations, and in some cases, social skills training. Of the various formats of CBT for SAD, the Coping Cat (Kendall & Hedtke, 2006) has received the most empirical support. The Coping Cat is designed to provide CBT in an individual format for children aged 7 to 13 years with a variety of anxiety disorders, including SAD. The Coping Cat has been adapted to be developmentally appropriate for adolescents aged 14 to 17 years, known as the C.A.T. Project (Kendall, Choudhury, Hudson, & Webb, 2002). Both the Coping Cat and C.A.T. Project's efficacy has been demonstrated in multiple randomized trials (Kendall, 1994; Kendall et al., 1997; Walkup et al., 2008). Compared with waitlist conditions, youth receiving Coping Cat experienced greater reductions in anxiety, fear, depression, negative thoughts, externalizing behavioral problems, improved social behaviors, and a perceived sense of coping ability with feared situations (Kendall, 1994). In the largest efficacy trial for CBT on youth anxiety to date (488 youth), researchers compared CBT (Coping Cat/C.A.T. project), sertraline, a combination of CBT and sertraline (Zoloft), and a pill placebo. The percentage of children who were rated as very much or much improved was 60% for CBT, 55% for sertraline, 81% for combination, and 24% for placebo, and most of these gains were maintained at a 36-week follow-up (Piacentini et al., 2014; Walkup et al., 2008). However, despite the demonstrated efficacy, SAD has, in some studies, been associated with poorer outcome and maintenance of gains relative to other anxiety disorders (Kerns, Read, Klugman, & Kendall, 2013).

In addition to the individual format of the *Coping Cat, C.A.T. Project,* and related programs, there are several efficacious treatments utilizing a family- or group-based intervention rather than an individual format (Ishikawa, Okawajima, Matusuoka, & Sakano, 2007). Reductions in anxiety are comparable for individual-, group-, and family-based CBT (Flannery-Schroeder & Kendall, 2000; Kendall, Hudson, Gosch, Flannery-Schroeder, & Suveg, 2008; Manassiss et al., 2002). *Coping Cat* has also been adapted into a computer-assisted program known as *Camp-Cope-A-Lot,* which has shown significant reductions in child anxiety (Khanna & Kendall, 2010).

Group treatment may be beneficial for some youth with SAD (Flannery-Schroeder & Kendall, 2000). Several group-based CBT treatments have been developed. *Cognitive Behavioral Group Therapy for Adolescents* (CBGT-A) was developed for adolescents with social anxiety and includes training in social skills and social problem solving in addition to general coping skills and exposures (Albano & Dibartolo, 2007).

Another empirically supported treatment, *Social Effectiveness Therapy for Children and Adolescents* (SET-C), combines individual exposures to the feared stimulus, group treatment, and social skills training for anxious youth and results in enhanced social skills, increased social interaction, and reduced social anxiety (Beidel, Turner, & Morris, 2003). Across patients in individual *Coping Cat* treatment, or group-based treatments including CBTG-A or SET-C, treatment gains in social anxiety were maintained at least 5 years later and were associated with decreased substance use and depression (Garcia-Lopez et al., 2006; Kendall, Safford, Flannery-Schroeder, & Webb, 2004). Although the aforementioned interventions focus on children and adolescents aged 7 to 17 years,

cognitive behavioral treatments are currently being evaluated for both very young children with social anxiety (Comer et al., 2012) and adolescents with social anxiety as they emerge into adulthood (Albano, 2014).

HOW TO: A GUIDE TO THE IMPLEMENTATION OF INTERVENTIONS FOR CHILDREN AND ADOLESCENTS WITH SAD

Three empirically supported treatments for socially anxious youth are outlined and discussed in detail in the following section: (a) The *Coping Cat,* (b) CBGT-A, and (c) SET-C. Although there is substantial overlap among these treatments, unique features of each protocol are highlighted.

The Coping Cat

The *Coping Cat* is a 16- to 20-session individual CBT with two major components: (a) psychoeducation/skill building and (b) exposures to feared stimuli/situations. In the first part of treatment, youth (a) develop an awareness of their anxious thoughts, feelings, and behaviors and (b) learn anxiety modulation techniques. The early stage of treatment is organized around the FEAR plan: a four-step process to help children and adolescents cope with anxiety. The FEAR plan consists of Feeling Frightened?, Expecting Bad Things to Happen?, Actions and Attitudes that Can Help, Results and Rewards. Each step is reviewed in detail in the following text. Once youth have learned the FEAR plan, they move to the exposure phase where children apply learned skills to anxiety-provoking situations. Common to all CBT for childhood anxiety, exposure is at the heart of treatment. It is often communicated to youth and parents that, although the first half of treatment creates a foundation of skills (e.g., relaxation, coping thoughts, and problem solving), substantial behavioral change may not occur until the exposure stage of treatment. In other words, psychoeducation and skill building are used to *prepare* youth to exposure, not serve as a substitute for it. Additionally, throughout the *Coping Cat* manual there are sections marked as "Flex." These signal opportunities to tailor the therapy to the child's individual presentation and set of interests.

Youth are given a *Coping Cat* workbook to accompany treatment. Between sessions, children and adolescents complete homework assignments known as STIC tasks (Show That I Can). Early STIC tasks focus on self-monitoring of anxiety and practicing skills, whereas later STIC tasks are at-home exposures. Youth receive points or stickers for completed STIC tasks, tracked in a section in the workbook entitled "The Bank." Points earned in the Bank are later exchanged for prizes. If a STIC task was not initiated, the youth and therapist complete it at the beginning of session.

Sessions 1 to 4: Psychoeducation. The first session of *Coping Cat* is largely devoted to introducing the treatment and building rapport with the child or adolescent. Therapists first meet with the family to discuss treatment expectations, general session structure, and other practical issues (e.g., confidentiality). Therapists provide youth and parents with a general overview of anxiety, including its evolutionary roots, its prevalence rates, and its definition by *DSM* criteria. Afterwards, the therapist meets with the child individually to play a "get to know you game." For example, in the Ungame, youth and therapists alternate drawing cards with personal questions and answering them (e.g., "What is your favorite food?" "What do you like to do for fun?"). Rapport building with older children is often less structured and more conversational. Therapists also use the initial session to define important terms for youth, such as "anxiety" and "coping," and note that therapy helps children and adolescents confront and cope with anxiety-provoking situations, rather than eliminate all anxiety. Therapists also use appropriate self-disclosure about times they have felt anxious and how they coped. In doing so, therapists normalize anxiety, introduce that anxiety exists along a continuum, and model coping behavior.

The second and third sessions focus on building an emotional awareness. In session 2, youth are asked to recall as many emotions as they can, including nonfear emotions. Children learn that similar behaviors or physiological reactions (e.g., heart palpitations) can be related to different emotions (anger or fear). Afterwards, the therapist and child or adolescent discuss how they can detect specific feelings based on others' facial and bodily cues. Thus, youth learn to differentiate between different emotions and read nonverbal body language. These lessons are strengthened through experiential activities. For example, youth can make a Feelings Dictionary in which they cut out pictures of faces from magazines, paste them to a piece of construction paper, and label emotions based on facial expressions. Session 3 emphasizes youth's own physiological reaction to anxiety. Therapists help children and adolescents identify what happens in their bodies when they become anxious (e.g., heart beats fast, sweating, and dizziness) and how it may relate to a specific stimulus or anxiety-provoking situation. Youth can also draw pictures of their bodies, coloring in the parts that feel uncomfortable when they are anxious.

Within the initial sessions, therapists introduce the subjective units of distress scale (SUDS) to youth. The scale ranges from 0 to 8 and is used to measure how anxious the child feels in a given situation. Children and adolescents are encouraged to create a personalized SUDS scale on a piece of paper (e.g., least to most favorite color). Therapists later use the SUDS scale to guide the construction of a fear hierarchy. The fear hierarchy arranges the youth's anxiety-provoking situations on a gradient, with scarier (e.g., higher SUDS) situations at the top. Therapists spend time with the youth to rate tasks and break down complex situations (e.g., attending school) into smaller ones on the hierarchy (e.g., giving a presentation or asking a question in class; see Table 19.1).

At this point youth are taught the F-step: Feeling frightened? Here, children and adolescents are asked to identify how they feel in a given situation through rating their SUDS and identifying anxious bodily cues. Session 4 marks the first of two parent-only appointments. Therapists answer parents' questions about treatment, discuss the CBT model, and amend the fear hierarchy.

Sessions 5 to 9: Skill Building. Session 5 covers the first of three anxiety regulation skills: relaxation. Therapists assist children and adolescents to distinguish differences in how their bodies feel when tense versus relaxed. For example, the

TABLE 19.1

SAMPLE FEAR AND AVOIDANCE HIERARCHY	
Situation	SUDS (Fear Rating)
Delivering an oral report in front of the class	8
Asking (in person) someone from school to hang out	8
Texting someone from school to hang out	7
Sending a male acquaintance a text to say "hi"	6
Sending a female acquaintance a text to say "hi"	5
Putting a photo of myself on Facebook	5
Getting my picture taken, putting photo on refrigerator	4
Raising my hand in class to answer a question	4
Staying after school to ask teacher for help	3
Saying "hi" to a classmate in the hallways	3
Nodding my head to a classmate in the hallways	2
Eating in front of others at school	2
Ordering for myself at a restaurant	1

SUDS, subjective units of distress scale.

therapist may use the metaphor of cooked versus uncooked spaghetti:

> When we feel anxious we can be rigid and stiff like a strand of uncooked spaghetti (therapist stands very straight, encourages child to do the same). How does that feel to you? This feeling can make us feel even more nervous. But when we are relaxed, we're more like cooked spaghetti (therapist flops down on chair in relaxed manner, encourages child to do the same). Now how does that feel?

The therapist reviews relaxation techniques, including deep breathing and progressive muscle relaxation (PMR). In the former, youth are instructed to inhale slowly through their nose, hold their breath for 3 to 5 seconds, and exhale through their mouths. PMR teaches individuals to tense isolated muscle groups for 5 seconds and then release them to relax (e.g., see Ollendick & Cerny, 1981). For instance, youth are trained to tighten their fists as if they are squeezing a lemon to make lemonade, followed by a quick release. Therapists make personalized recordings using relaxation scripts that combine deep breathing and head-to-toe PMR, to be taken home and practiced as homework. In the following session, children and adolescents shift from feelings to thoughts. First, therapists help youth recognize anxious thoughts, also known as "negative self-talk." Given the prior emphasis on teaching feelings, the therapist reminds children that thoughts are distinct but related (e.g., "Thoughts are the talk in your head/what you say to yourself; feelings happen in your body."). To accomplish this, the therapist and child scan cartoon pictures of ambiguous situations and assess what the character may be thinking in a "thought bubble." Here, youth are taught the E-step of the FEAR plan: Expecting bad things to happen? Accordingly, youth record their anxious thoughts regarding a given anxiety-provoking situation. After identification of thoughts, children are encouraged to ask (and answer) questions to challenge their anxious self-talk. Common challenging questions include: Do I know for sure this will happen? Do I have evidence it will happen? Can I cope with the worst-case situation? Coping thoughts are derived from this line of questions and answers, and used as self-statements to manage anxiety-provoking situations. Examples of coping thoughts are: "I've done it before and I can do it again" and "Everyone makes mistakes." Finally, individual coping thoughts can be recorded on index cards for the youth to take home.

Following relaxation and coping thoughts, the third skill youth learn is problem solving (session 7). Problem solving teaches youth to implement a series of steps to meet a particular goal: (a) identify the situation, (b) list all possible solutions (no matter how silly), (c) cross out the solutions that are likely not to work (examining the pros and cons and why they may be unfeasible), (d) choose one or two from the remaining solutions, and (e) carry the solution out and assess how it went. The therapist reviews these steps with a low anxiety-provoking situation (e.g., you are about to leave for school but cannot find your shoes), and later applies the steps to a situation from the youth's hierarchy of anxiety-provoking situations. Now, children and adolescents have completed the A-step: Actions and attitudes that help, which involves using the tools they learned in the skill-building phase.

Session 8 finishes the FEAR plan with the R-step: Results and Rewards. In "results," youth reflect on how they did coping in an anxiety-provoking situation. Did they practice the FEAR plan; did they cope; or did they avoid? Importantly, the therapist emphasizes coping and putting forth effort over perfect outcomes. If there was significant avoidance, the therapist should praise efforts, assess how aware the youth were of the avoidance, understand others' involvement in avoidance (i.e., parents), conduct a brief functional analysis that may have contributed to avoidance, and problem-solve ways that children can approach the situation in the future with reduced avoidance. Additionally, the therapist elicits a list of rewards that the youth will be able to earn in the next stage of treatment. In session 9, the therapist again meets with parents to explain exposure and familiarize them with the FEAR steps.

Sessions 10 and Beyond: Exposure. In the first exposure session, the therapist explains the rationale of exposure including the principle of habituation. Youth are told, in language that they can understand, that exposures will assess the validity of their catastrophic thoughts in the form of controlled experiments. The therapist may begin by giving children and adolescents the choice of two to three situations that are low on the fear hierarchy; the process of exposure is meant to be gradual. Before conducting the exposure, the youth and therapist apply the FEAR plan to the situation. An example FEAR plan for paying someone a compliment may be: F—butterflies in stomach and SUDS at a 3, E—person will think my compliment is not genuine, A—coping thought "I like when people compliment me," R—did I give the compliment? If so, tell myself "good job!"

At the beginning of the exposure:

- The therapist elicits the youth's SUDS and continues to do so for approximately 1- to 2-minute intervals.
- Exposure continues until SUDS have decreased by 50%.
- It is paramount that the therapist monitors and limits subtle avoidance behaviors during

exposure (e.g., not making eye contact, speaking only to familiar peers).
- After the exposure, the therapist provides feedback on the youth's participation.
- Likewise, the therapist can show the child or adolescent the pattern of SUDS, assess whether the feared outcome occurred (and if so, did the child cope), and praise and reward effort.

Exposures are completed both in session and at home. As successes build for the youth, so does the difficulty of exposure. Once certain therapy goals are met and the situations on the hierarchy are no longer avoided, therapy reaches closure. In the final sessions, the therapist and youth reflect on gains. The therapist can videotape children and adolescents making a commercial about the FEAR plan and ways to cope with anxiety. The therapist also meets with the families to discuss relapse prevention and to plan for ways to address challenges in the coming months. In the end, the therapist celebrates each youth's achievements with his or her family and presents the youth with a certificate of achievement.

Cognitive Behavioral Group Therapy for Adolescents

Like *Coping Cat*, CBGT-A is a 16- to 20-session protocol that is divided into skills building and exposure phases of treatment. However, CBGT-A differs in a few ways. First, CBGT-A is a group therapy for approximately five to six participants and is led by two co-therapists. Second, CBGT-A is specifically designed for socially anxious youth, whereas *Coping Cat* treats a wider variety of anxiety disorders. Third, CBGT-A contains specific modules for social skills training to address social deficits. Snack time breaks are built into sessions for youth to socialize and practice therapy skills with peers. Finally, this treatment is specifically designed for adolescents and the delivery of the content is comparable to adult interventions for social anxiety. Sessions in CBGT-A begin with youth completing relevant assessment forms (unique to the manual), including their Fear Hierarchies. Afterwards, sessions involve a review of homework (e.g., self-monitoring anxious thoughts, cognitive restructuring, and exposures) as well as a brief quiz on material from the prior week.

Session 1: Psychoeducation.

- The first session begins with introductions from therapists and group members.
- A therapist provides expectations for therapy (e.g., attendance policy, participation, and confidentiality) as well as the rationale for therapy.
- Therapists elicit anxiety-provoking social situations from youth with an emphasis on physiological symptoms and avoidance behaviors. Physiological symptoms may include heart palpitations, dizziness, sweating, or shaking among others. Avoidance behaviors can be obvious, such as leaving a party early or not attending school on picture day. They may also be more subtle, such as holding back an opinion in a conversation, eating only food that will not spill in front of others, or avoiding eye contact or speaking softly with others. Therapists may also disclose social anxiety from their own lives. This activity helps one to normalize anxiety and illustrate similarities across group members. It also leads into a conversation about the short-term benefits and long-term consequences of avoidance.
- In the first snack time practice, youth separate themselves from the group and have a more casual conversation with peers on a one-to-one basis, introducing themselves and sharing personal information with their peers.

Sessions 2 to 3: Cognitive Component.

- Session 2 provides education about the three components of anxiety (thoughts, feelings, and behaviors) and how they interact with one another.
- Therapists discuss situations from the teenagers' lives to illustrate the three-component model.
- Time is devoted to establishing concrete and feasible goals for each group member.
- For homework, youth self-monitor anxious situations by noting their accompanying thoughts, feelings, and behaviors using a worksheet.
- In the next session, youth learn to challenge anxious thoughts. Therapists present the concept of automatic thoughts (ATs) by role-playing an encounter between two teenagers who just met at school. Mental health professionals express ATs to the group between verbal exchanges.
- Youth also learn to challenge and label ATs with cognitive distortions such as all-or-nothing thinking, mind reading, fortune telling/catastrophizing, overgeneralizing, labeling, filtering, and overestimating. In doing so, youth become "detectives" and assess for evidence to confirm or deny their ATs.
- Akin to coping thoughts in the *Coping Cat*, each youth ultimately derives a rational response, a positive self-statement that helps him or her to facilitate approach behaviors.

Sessions 4 to 6: Problem Solving and Skill Training.

- Session 4 recaps the four-step model of cognitive restructuring: identifying thoughts, questioning the validity of the prediction, countering ATs with a rational response, and using self-reinforcement.
- The session also introduces problem solving, which parallels the steps taught in the *Coping Cat*.
- The subsequent session is focused on social skills training. Cotherapists role-play an interaction between a socially skilled and unskilled teen. The exercise highlights important nonverbal (e.g., eye contact, bored facial expression) and verbal skills (e.g., interrupting, not asking questions) that help promote social interactions. Consequently, youth learn the five-stage model for social skills training: (a) identifying the skill to be corrected, (b) imagining practicing the skill (may also practice alone in front of a mirror), (c) imagining difficulties that may arise when practicing and what coping strategies to use to address them, (d) practicing the skill with a partner, and (e) self-reinforcing oneself (e.g., praise) for the effort in practicing the skill with another person.
- In session 6, youth practice the five-stage model by interacting with a conversation partner in front of the group. Therapists provide feedback about specific social skills. The rest of the session is devoted to assertiveness training. Once again, co-therapists use role-play to demonstrate ATs that occur in a conversation that would require assertiveness. Youth apply the three-component model to situations they are afraid to assert themselves, challenge ATs and develop rational responses, and then use the five-stage model for social skills training to increase assertiveness.

Sessions 7 to 8: Review and Preparation for Exposure. To prepare for the second phase of treatment in session 7, participants take turns leading the group to explain a specific skill that was learned in treatment. Youth also identify sources of social support (e.g., friends, coaches, and counselors) that they can turn to when help is needed. Barriers to accessing social support are identified and problem solving is used to overcome them. Group members also reflect on the support they would like from parents and on challenges to their relationships. In session 8, attentive listening and perspective taking are highlighted. Youth role-play situations in dyads where one member plays the parent of the other (and then students switch). This exercise helps youth sympathize with their parents, understand how social anxiety may contribute to misunderstandings, and practice active listening by using reflective sentences and asking for clarification. The exercise is later replicated between the child and his or her actual parent.

Session 9 and Beyond: Exposure and Relapse Prevention. Exposures are conducted in a manner similar to those in *Coping Cat*. The first exposure involves the therapist selecting an adolescent with moderate social anxiety.[1] The situation and goals for the exposure are clearly defined. The therapist guides the youth in the four-step process of cognitive restructuring beforehand. The exposure is then done in front of the group with SUDS tracked throughout (e.g., every 1–2 minutes, although the length of time can vary depending on the therapist's preference or context of the exposure). Afterward, the youth interprets his or her SUDS curve, assesses if the feared outcome occurred, determines whether the exposure goal(s) were met, and acknowledges the link between thoughts and feelings. Additionally, group members provide constructive feedback. Children and adolescents are encouraged to practice the exposure at least three times between sessions. Over time, exposures gradually increase in difficulty and may include outside participants. Typically, two exposures are completed each session.

In the final sessions, relapse prevention is addressed. Youth are encouraged to continue practicing skills and plans are made for future situations when the youth may be vulnerable. Additionally, plans are made to keep the children or adolescents interpersonally connected through planned social activities. In the last session, the group processes any feelings of sadness associated with termination and celebrates with a pizza party.

Social Effectiveness Therapy for Children and Adolescents

A developmental extension of the initial adult SAD therapeutic manual, the SET-C is a 25-session, 12-week group therapy program designed to address social anxiety, behavioral avoidance, and social skills deficits for youth between the ages of 8 and 16 years. Similar to CBTG-A, the SET-C program includes psychoeducation about social anxiety, social skills training, and in vivo behavioral exposure with the end goals of increasing social engagement, competency, and self-efficacy while decreasing anxiety. Interestingly, this program specifically does not include a cognitive component, citing early research that youth with SAD often have difficulty identifying anxious cognitions (e.g., Spence, Donovan, Brechman-Toussaint, 2000). Although this program is designed to be a group treatment for youth of generally the same chronological or developmental level (approximately four to six youths per group), flexible implementation allows for program components to be delivered individually. In terms of setting, the nature of the treatment components allows for it to be administered within inpatient, outpatient, or school-based settings. In general, the SET-C treatment comprises three components: an Educational Session (one session), Social Skills Training with Peer Generalization, and In Vivo Exposure. Following the Educational Session, sessions occur twice per week, with 1 day devoted to social skills, and 1 day to exposure.

Session 1: Educational Session. The first session of the SET-C manualized program comprises an initial meeting for both youth and parents enrolled in the treatment group. The purpose of this initial meeting is to provide psychoeducation regarding the nature of anxiety and fear within a social context, as well as information about the structure of treatment. The roles of youth and parents within treatment are discussed, including emphasis on the need for attendance, participation in all treatment components, and involvement and consistency with reward systems. Similar to other interventions for children and adolescents with anxiety, parents are often called upon to participate in the treatment by facilitating youths' participation in social events, tolerating their children's distress, and rewarding their efforts to cope with anxiety.

Given the group nature of treatment, confidentiality is also emphasized.

Weeks 2 to 13: Social Skills Training. The second component of the SET-C program targets the improvement or refinement of social skills for socially anxious youth, delivered within a 12-week group format for approximately 90 minutes per session, followed by 90 minutes of Peer Generalization activities that occur later that same day (see the following discussion). This component comprises a series of social skills exercises divided into two facets, Social Environment Awareness and Interpersonal Skill Enhancement, social difficulties thought to be specific to anxious youth (Beidel, Turner, & Morris, 1999, 2000). Social Environment Awareness (4 weeks) includes instruction on the nuts and bolts of how, when, and why social interactions occur (e.g., recognition of social cues and how to start a conversation). The Interpersonal Skill Enhancement portion (7 weeks) includes the instruction of the mechanics of verbal and nonverbal interaction within specific scenarios (e.g., where to meet friends, giving and receiving compliments, and appropriate assertiveness). In the delivery of each skill, the clinician engages in five specific procedures, including didactic instruction of the skill, modeling of the skill by the clinician, behavioral rehearsal of all group members to a specified criterion through the use of role-play exercises, corrective feedback, and positive reinforcement. Behavioral rehearsal is identified as a crucial aspect of this aspect of training, given the ability of youth to practice particular skills within a controlled and instructive environment. Of note, despite the use of corrective feedback when necessary during behavioral rehearsal, positive reinforcement should be given for any participation in social activities, even participation during the instructional portion of the session.

Peer Generalization Events. Following each social skills session, socially anxious youth enrolled in the Peer Generalization experiences meet with same-aged, nonanxious peers in natural settings for approximately 90 minutes. Nonanxious peers, identified by adults who know them in the community, are recruited from the community to specifically assist in the engagement of socially anxious youth during this facet of the treatment program. All nonanxious peers and their parents are coached on confidentiality before engaging in Peer Generalization experiences. These experiences can be tailored to the needs and interests of the group (e.g., visiting arcades, eating a meal together, or going to the zoo). However, the Peer Generalization experiences are intended to approximate typical peer interactions for their age group. The purpose of these Peer Generalization experiences is to provide socially anxious youth with opportunities to further practice their social skills and improve the generalization of targeted lessons into the lives of children and youth. Generally, the same number of age-matched peers are recruited to facilitate typical social interactions. Furthermore, Peer Generalization sessions allow for the provision of positive reinforcement of socially anxious youth by positive peer role models. Peers are specifically tasked with engaging socially anxious youth in conversation and remaining with them for the duration of the 90-minute exercise. The primary goal of these activities is for anxious youth to practice sustained engagement with peers, including specific skills reviewed in their Social Skills session earlier that day. The use of these peer interaction activities also allows the clinician to observe each youth's interaction with peers in order to identify further areas of social difficulty. Parents are not encouraged to attend the Peer Generalization activities given their status as safety and avoidance figures for SAD youth.

Weeks 2 to 13: In Vivo Exposure. In Vivo Exposure in anxiety-provoking situations is presented concurrently with the 12-week social skills training component of the treatment. These exposures are implemented in addition to the Peer Generalization activities that inherently constitute an element of behavioral exposure. However, the specific In Vivo Exposure component of SET-C includes more formalized, clinician-assisted execution of exposure activities on an individual basis. Similar to other social anxiety interventions, these exposure tasks occur in or out of the clinic in order to best approximate each youth's specific fears or feared environments. These sessions last approximately 60 to 90 minutes, depending on the nature of the fear addressed. Before engagement in exposure, clinicians are advised to conduct behavioral analysis in order to best understand each youth's core fears and subsequent responses. A youth's behaviors and environmental responses will aid the clinician in structuring exposure sessions to best address these fears and discourage avoidance. In the first exposure session, clinicians can solicit information regarding feared situations from the youth directly to construct a fear hierarchy. Following this understanding, youth are introduced to the rationale behind exposure, homework tasks, and positive reinforcement schedules. Similar to other CBT programs, youth are encouraged to remain in feared situations during exposure until their distress level has reduced by approximately 50%. At the end of session, the youths and their parents agree on challenges to be completed over the upcoming week and sign a Weekly Reward Contract to be fulfilled on completion of at-home exposures.

Wrapping Up. The final sessions involve review of skills learned throughout the program in order to bolster learned skills and enhance the likelihood of generalization. In the final group social skills session, clinicians lead a skills practice and review session in a party scenario, which allows youth to simultaneously practice social skills (e.g., joining in conversations and giving compliments) while celebrating their accomplishments throughout the program. The clinicians are also encouraged to lead a discussion about what situations youth may practice in the future.

CONCLUSION

Despite SAD's pervasiveness and multiple causes, efficacious cognitive behavioral treatment exists and is effective. In fact, mental health professionals have a choice of three empirically supported interventions that may be tailored to the youth's clinical presentation. Despite different emphases, there are more similarities than differences across these interventions. Regardless of the specific manual used, the application of empirically supported treatments combined with a therapist's flexibility and clinical skills will provide high-level care for socially anxious youth.

NOTE

1. In later exposures, therapists rely on adolescents volunteering for exposure.

SELECT BIBLIOGRAPHY

Chansky, T. (2004). *Freeing your child from anxiety: Powerful, practical solutions to overcoming your child's fears, worries, and phobias.* New York, NY: Broadway
This is a book for parents that helps them to differentiate normative versus clinical anxiety. It explains different anxiety diagnoses and etiology, and provides parenting strategies for managing youth anxiety. The book can be used on its own or as an adjunct to CBT.

Kendall, P. C., & Hedtke, K. A. (2006) *Cognitive-behavioral therapy for anxious children: Therapist manual* (3rd ed.). Ardmore, PA: Workbook Publishing
Coping Cat is a manualized CBT program for youth with social phobia, generalized anxiety disorder, and separation anxiety disorder. It is the most empirically supported of the anxiety treatments. A version for teenagers exists as well (e.g., "the C.A.T. Project").

Kendall, P. C., & Khanna, M. S. (2008). *CBT4CBT: Computer-based training to become a cognitive-behavioral therapist [DVD].* Ardmore, PA: Workbook Publishing Inc.
CBT4CBT is a CD-based platform that trains clinicians to deliver empirically supported treatment for social phobia and related anxiety disorders. CBT4CBT includes outlines and videos to help clinicians gain proficiency in CBT for anxiety.

REFERENCES

Albano, A. M. (2014). *A developmental approach to treating anxiety and depression in the transitional years (ages 18–25).* Paper presented at Anxiety and Depression Association of America, Chicago, IL.

Albano, A. M., & DiBartolo, P. M. (2007). *Cognitive behavioral therapy for social phobia in adolescents: Stand up, speak out therapist guide.* New York, NY: Oxford University Press.

Alfano, C. A., Beidel, D. C., & Turner, S. M. (2006). Cognitive correlates of social phobia among children and adolescents. *Journal of Abnormal Child Psychology, 34,* 189–201. doi:10.1007/s10802-005-9012-9

American Psychiatric Association (APA). (2000). *Diagnostic and statistical manual of mental disorders* (4th ed., text rev.). Washington, DC: Author

American Psychiatric Association (APA). (2013). *Diagnostic and statistical manual of mental disorders* (5th ed.). Arlington, VA: American Psychiatric Publishing.

Beidel, D. C., Turner, S. M., & Morris, T. L. (1999). Psychopathology of childhood social phobia. *Journal of the American Academy of Child and Adolescent Psychiatry, 38,* 643–650. doi:10.1097.00004583–199906000-00010

Beidel, D. C., Turner, S. M., & Morris, T. L. (2000). Behavioral treatment of childhood social phobia. *Journal of Consulting and Clinical Psychology, 68,* 1072–1080. doi:10.1037/0022–006X.68.6.1072

Beidel, D. C., Turner, S. M., & Morris, T. L. (2003). *Social effectiveness therapy for children and adolescents (SET-C).* Toronto, Ontario: Multi-Health Systems.

Blackford, J. U., & Pine, D. S. (2012). Neural substrates of childhood anxiety disorders: A review of neuroimaging findings. *Child and Adolescent Psychiatric Clinics of North America, 21,* 501–525. doi:10.1016/j.chc.2012.05.002

Burstein, M., and Ginsburg, G. S. (2010). The effect of parental modeling of anxious behaviors and cognitions in school-aged children: An experimental pilot study. *Behaviour Research and Therapy, 48,* 506–515. doi:10.1016/j.brat.2010.02.006

Comer, J. S., Puliafico, A., Aschenbrand, S. G., McKnight, K., Robin, J. A., Goldfine, M. E., & Albano, A. M. (2012). A pilot feasibility evaluation of the CALM program for anxiety disorders in early childhood. *Journal of Anxiety Disorders, 26,* 40–49. doi:10.1016/j.janxdis.2011.08.011

Flannery-Schroeder, E. C., & Kendall, P. C. (2000). Group and individual cognitive-behavioral treatments for youth with anxiety disorders: A randomized clinical trial. *Cognitive Therapy and Research, 20,* 251–278. doi:10.1023/A:1005500219286

Garcia-Lopez, L. J, Oliveraes, J., Beidel, D., Albano, A. M., Turner, S., & Rosa, A. I. (2006). Efficacy of three treatment protocols for adolescents with social anxiety disorder: A 5-year follow-up assessment. *Journal of Anxiety Disorders, 20,* 175–191. doi:10.1016/j.janxdis.2005.01.003

Hitchcock, C. A., Chavira, D. A., and Stein, M. B. (2009). Recent findings in social phobia among children and adolescents. *The Israel Journal of Psychiatry and Related Sciences, 46,* 34–44.

Hollon, D. S., & Beck, A. T. (2013). Cognitive and cognitive-behavioral therapies. In M. J.

Lambert (Ed.), *Bergin and Garfield's handbook of psychotherapy and behavior change* (6th ed., pp. 393–442). New York, NY: Wiley.

Ishikawa, S., Okawajima, I., Matusuoka, H., & Sakano, Y. (2007). Cognitive behavioural therapy for anxiety disorders in children and adolescents: A meta-analysis. *Child and Adolescent Mental Health, 12,* 164–172. doi:10.1111/j.1475–3588.2006.00433.x

Kagan, J. (2002). Childhood predictors of states of anxiety. *Dialogues in Clinical Neuroscience, 4,* 287–293.

Kendall, P. C. (1994). Treating anxiety disorders in children: Results of a randomized clinical trial. *Journal of Consulting and Clinical Psychology, 62,* 100–110. doi:10.1037/0022–006X.62.1.100

Kendall, P. C., Choudhury, M., Hudson, J., & Webb, A. (2002). *The C.A.T. Project Manual: For the cognitive behavioral treatment of anxious adolescents.* Ardmore, PA: Workbook Publishing.

Kendall, P. C., Compton, S. N., Walkup, J. T., Birmaher, B., Albano, A., Sherrill, J.,…Piacentini, J. (2010). Clinical characteristics of anxiety disordered youth. *Journal of Anxiety Disorders, 24,* 360–365. doi:10.1016/j.janxdis.2010.01.009

Kendall, P. C., Flannery-Schroeder, E., Panichelli-Mendel, S. M., Southam-Gerow, M., Henin, M., & Warman, M. (1997). Therapy for youths with anxiety disorders: A second randomized clinical trial. *Journal of Consulting and Clinical Psychology, 65,* 366–380. doi:10.1037/0022–006X.65.3.366

Kendall, P. C., & Hedtke, K. A. (2006). *Cognitive-behavioral therapy for anxious children: Therapist manual* (3rd ed.). Ardmore, PA: Workbook Publishing.

Kendall, P. C., Hudson, J. L., Gosch, E., Flannery-Schroeder, E., & Suveg, C. (2008). Cogntive-behavioral therapy for anxiety disordered youth: A randomized clinical trial evaluation child and family modalities. *Journal of Consulting and Clinical Psychology, 76,* 282–297. doi:10.1037/0022–006X.76.2.282

Kendall, P. C., Safford, S., Flannery-Schroeder, E., & Webb, A. (2004). Child anxiety treatment: Outcomes in adolescence and impact on substance use and depression at 7.4-year follow up. *Journal of Consulting and Clinical Psychology, 72,* 276–287. doi:10.1037/0022–006X.72.2.276

Kerns, C. M., Read, K. L., Klugman, J., & Kendall, P. C. (2013). Cognitive behavioral therapy for youth with social anxiety: Differential short and long-term treatment outcomes. *Journal of Anxiety Disorders, 27,* 210–215. doi:10.1016/j.janxdis.2013.01.009

Kessler, R. C., Chiu, W. T., Demler, O., & Walters, E. E. (2005). Prevalence, severity, and comorbidity of twelve-month *DSM-IV* disorders in the National Comorbidity Survey Replication (NCS-R). *Archives of General Psychiatry, 62,* 617–627. doi:10.1001/archpsyc.62.6.617

Khanna, M. S., & Kendall, P. C. (2010). Computer-assisted cognitive behavioral therapy for child anxiety: Results of a randomized clinical trial. *Journal of Consulting and Clinical Psychology, 78,* 737–745. doi:10.1037/a0019739

Killgore, D. S., & Yurgelun-Todd, D. A. (2005). Social anxiety predicts amygdala activation in adolescents viewing fearful faces. *Developmental Neuroscience, 16,* 1671–1675. doi:10.1097/01.wnr.0000180143.99267.bd

Kimbrel, N. A. (2008). A model of the development and maintenance of generalized social phobia. *Clinical Psychology Review, 28,* 592–612. doi:10.1016/j.cpr.2007.08.003

LaGreca, A. M., & Lopez, N. (1998). Social anxiety among adolescents: Linkages with peer relations and friendships. *Journal of Abnormal Child Psychology, 26,* 83–94.

Ledley, D. R., Erwin, B. A., Morrison, A. S., & Heimberg, R. G. (2013). Social anxiety disorder. In W. E. Craighead, D. J. Miklowitz, & L. W. Craighead (Eds.), *Psychopathology: History, diagnosis, and empirical foundations* (2nd ed., pp. 147–192). Hoboken, NJ: Wiley.

Liebowitz, M. R., Gelenberg, A. J., & Munjack, D. (2005). Venlafaxine extended release vs. placebo and paroxetine in social anxiety disorder. *Archives of General Psychiatry, 62*(2), 190–198.

Manassiss, K. Menlowitz, S. L, Scapillato, D., Avery, D., Fiskenbaum, S., Freiire, M.,...Owens, M. (2002). Group and individual cognitive-behavioral therapy for youth anxiety disorders: A randomized trial. *Journal of the American Academy of Child and Adolescent Psychiatry, 41,* 1423–1430. doi:10.1097/00004583-200212000-00013

Marcin, M. S., and Nemeroff, C. B. (2003). The neurobiology of social anxiety disorder: The relevance of fear and anxiety. *Acta Psychiatrica Scandinavica, 108,* 51–64. doi:10.1034/j.1600–0447.108.s417.4.x

Merikangas, K. R., Nakamura, E. F., & Kessler, R. C. (2009). Epidemiology of mental disorders in children and adolescents. *Dialogues in Clinical Neuroscience, 11,* 7–20.

Neal, J. A., & Edelmann, R. J. (2003). The etiology of social phobia: Toward a developmental profile. *Clinical Psychology Review, 23,* 761–786. doi:10.1016/S0272–7358(03)00076-X

Ollendick, T. H., & Cerny, J. A. (1981). *Clinical behavior therapy with children.* New York, NY: Plenum.

Pérez-Edgar, K., McDermott, J., Korelitz, K., Degnan, K. A., Curby, T. W., Pine, D. S., & Fox, N. A. (2010). Patterns of sustained attention in infancy shape the developmental trajectory of social behavior from toddlerhood through adolescence. *Developmental Psychology, 46,* 1723–1730. doi:10.1037/a0021064

Piacentini, J., Bennett, S., Compton, S. N., Kendall, P. C., Birmaher, B., Albano, A. M.,...Walkup, J. (2014). 24- and 36-week outcomes for the child/adolescent anxiety multimodal study (CAMS). *Journal of the American Academy of Child & Adolescent Psychiatry, 53,* 297–310. doi:10.1016/j.jaac.2013.11.010

Rapee, R. M., & Spence, S. H. (2004). The etiology of social phobia: Empirical evidence and an initial model. *Clinical Psychology Review, 24,* 737–767. doi:10.1016/j.cpr.2004.06.004

Settipani, C. A., & Kendall, P. C. (2013). Social functioning in youth with anxiety disorders: Association with anxiety severity and outcomes from cognitive-behavioral therapy. *Child Psychiatry and Human Development, 44,* 1–18. doi:10.1007/s10578–012-0307–0

Spence, S. H., Donovan, C., & Brechman-Toussaint, M. (2000). The treatment of childhood social phobia: The effectiveness of a social skills training-based, cognitive-behavioural intervention, with and without parental involvement. *Journal of Child Psychology and Psychiatry, 41,* 713–726.

Stein, M. B., & Stein, D. J. (2008). Social anxiety disorder. *Lancet, 371,* 1115–1125. doi:10.1016/S0140–6736(08)60488–2

Tillfors, M., Persson, S., Willén, M., & Burk, W. J. (2012). Prospective links between social anxiety and adolescent peer relations. *Journal of Adolescence, 35,* 1255–1263. doi:10.1016/j.adolescence.2012.04.008

Walkup, J. T., Albano, A. M., Piacentini, J., Bimaher, B., Compton, S. N., Sherrill, J. T.,…Kendall, P. C. (2008). Cognitive behavioral therapy, sertraline, or a combination in childhood anxiety. *New England Journal of Medicine, 359,* 2753–2766. doi:10.1056/NEJMx110064

Woodward, L. J., & Ferguson, D. M. (2001). Life course outcomes of young people with anxiety disorders in adolescence. *Journal of American Academy of Child and Adolescent Psychiatry, 40,* 1086–1093. doi:10.1097/0000 4583-200109000-00018

Evidence-Based Interventions for Selective Mutism for Children and Adolescents

Thomas J. Kehle, Marisa A. del Campo, Melissa M. Root, Melissa A. Bray, Lea A. Theodore, and Bruce A. Bracken

OVERVIEW

As indicated in the American Psychiatric Association's *Diagnostic and Statistical Manual of Mental Disorders* (5th ed.; *DSM-5*; APA, 2013), selective mutism (SM) is considered an anxiety disorder characterized by "consistent failure to speak in specific social situations in which there is an expectation for speaking (e.g., at school) despite speaking in other situations" (APA, 2013, p. 195). This speech disturbance impedes major life functions, such as learning, working, or communicating socially, for a minimum of 1 month. This disorder is caused neither by an unfamiliarity with the language used in a specific social situation nor by a communication disorder (APA, 2013). SM may co-occur with a variety of emotional responses, including "excessive shyness, fear of social embarrassment, social isolation and withdrawal, clinging, compulsive traits, negativism, temper tantrums, or mild oppositional behavior" (APA, 2013, p. 195). Intentional vomiting and enuresis also co-occur with SM (Kehle, Bray, Root, & Theodore, 2016). SM occurs in approximately 0.03% to 1% of the population, with similar prevalence rates across ethnicities and gender (APA, 2013).

Because of a substantial overlap between SM and social anxiety disorder (SAD), it is widely believed that the disorders may have similar genetic etiologies; however, Stein et al. (2011), on the basis of one study, questioned the merits of the *DSM-5* (APA, 2013) reclassification of SM under SAD. Stein et al. (2011) suggested that there may be "considerable heterogeneity in the SM syndrome such that some forms are more closely allied with the autism spectrum disorder" (ASD) (p. 830) and consequently proposed an umbrella term "social inhibition disorders" that more aptly addresses the complexity of the relationship between SM, SAD, and ASD.

Children with SM do not speak in certain settings, most often in school or school-related situations. Consequently, their academic and social competencies are often compromised. Although these children typically speak in their homes with parents and siblings, they may refuse to speak when others are present. In some cases, they will make very unusual discriminations for speaking even in the home setting. For instance, there have been cases in which children with SM refuse to speak with male relatives in any setting (Kehle, Bray, Root, & Theodore, in press).

SM typically has an onset before the child is 5 years of age; however, the condition may not be noticed until the child enters school where expectations for peer and teacher interactions are fundamental (APA, 2013). Also, as suggested in the *DSM-5* (APA, 2013), some individuals who have SM may idiosyncratically "outgrow" the disorder, thus leaving the long-term prognosis unknown.

ETIOLOGY AND FACTORS CONTRIBUTING TO SM IN CHILDREN AND ADOLESCENTS

The etiology of SM is varied and probably multifaceted and likely a heterogeneous condition (Oerbeck, Johansen, Lundahl, & Kristensen, 2012). As previously mentioned, most often these children, in addition to being selectively mute, will be diagnosed with SAD. Stein et al. (2011) noted that, given the extensive familial overlap between SM and SAD, SM should be categorized as a form of SAD with roots developed during the childhood years. Additionally, a genetic component to the etiology of the disorder has been postulated by Black and Uhde (1995), with a relationship that appears among not only SM and SAD, but social communication, language disorders, and ASD as well (Stein et al., 2011). Thus, it appears that there exists a partially shared pathophysiology and genetic basis between SM, SAD, and ASD.

Beyond the association between SAD and ASD, several additional comorbidities have been noted. For example, Freeman et al. (2004) noted that as many as 18% of those with SM exhibit obsessive-compulsive behaviors. Expressive language and motor delays are also frequently reported among children who suppress their speech in particular settings (Steinhausen & Juzi, 1996). However, according to the *DSM-5* (APA, 2013) classification, children who meet the criteria for other communication disorders are currently excluded from the diagnosis of SM.

The extent to which environmental factors play a role in the development of SM is not entirely clear. In some cases, parents of children with SM, because of their often-present social inhibition (e.g., Black & Uhde, 1995), may inadvertently model reticence. Furthermore, parents of children with SM are frequently characterized as overprotective or as more controlling than parents whose children have been diagnosed with other anxiety disorders (APA, 2013). Higher rates of marital discord (Elizur & Perednik, 2003; Remschmidt et al., 2001) and lower levels of social interaction have also been noted among the families of children with SM (Vecchio & Kearney, 2005). Sometimes the onset of SM can be linked to a precipitating stressful event, but this appears to be true for only a minority of cases (Black & Uhde, 1995; Steinhausen & Juzi, 1996). SM can be conceived as a learned behavior that is maintained through practice and reinforcement (Kehle, Madaus, Baratta, & Bray, 1998; Schill, Kratochwill, & Gardner, 1996), which results in SM becoming more resistant to remediation over time (Kehle et al., 1998). Thus, early identification and intervention are recommended to mitigate potential effects on children's social development and educational progress (Schwartz, Freedy, & Sheridan, 2006).

Cross-culturally, there appears to be a higher rate of SM among bilingual and immigrant children (Bergman, Piacentini, & McCracken, 2002; Elizur & Perednik, 2003), resulting in bilingual children being diagnosed with SM, on the whole, representing an etiologically distinct subgroup. In particular, Elizur and Perednik (2003) found that social anxiety was more common in children with SM of immigrant backgrounds as compared to other children with SM. Although social anxiety was more prevalent among these children, they were less likely to have comorbid neurodevelopmental disorders or delays (Elizur & Perednik, 2003). It is probable that the process of second-language acquisition influences the development of SM for some children. In particular, it has been proposed that hearing different languages in private and public settings may confuse the child and cause communication hesitance (Elizur & Perednik, 2003). Clearly, a label of SM is not applicable if a child's lack of speech is the result of an inability to speak the language. It should also be noted that it is normal for individuals acquiring a new language to pass through a nonverbal period in the second language; for children aged 3 to 8 years, this phase is typically not longer than 6 months (Toppelberg, Tabors, Coggins, Lum, & Burger, 2005). Additional factors, such as acculturation processes, minority status, and lack of confidence with the acquired language, may further elevate fear of speaking in social situations in children who have the propensity for social anxiety (Viana, Beidel, & Rabian, 2009).

EVIDENCE-BASED INTERVENTIONS AND EMPIRICAL SUPPORT FOR SM IN CHILDREN AND ADOLESCENTS

Hultquist's (1995) early review on the treatments for SM ranged from psychotherapy to self-modeling; however, Hultquist noted that, "Wergeland believes psychoanalytical therapy with mute children can be demanding and lengthy, as well as exasperating and intolerable for some therapists" (1995, p. 102) in that "talking," the basic component of psychodynamic approaches, is not present in the child who has SM. Hultquist (1995) also cited play therapy as a possibly effective approach, noting studies by Weininger (1987) and Barlow, Strother, and Landreth (1986). The theory behind play therapy is that it occurs in a stress-free environment that presents little pressure for speech production (Hultquist, 1995). Drug therapies involving the antidepressants of sertraline and fluoxetine (Black & Uhde, 1995; Carlson, Kratochwill, & Johnston, 1999; Kehle et al., 1998) also have been shown to be effective. However, the most common treatment for SM is a behavioral management strategy that incorporates stimulus fading, generalization, desensitization, and extinction (Hultquist, 1995). This intervention approach for SM has been corroborated by Watson and Kramer (1992), noting that behavioral interventions conducted simultaneously were the most effective, efficient, and generalizable. Additionally, they suggested that strength of reinforcement schedule (e.g., variable ratio) would better maintain fluent speech over time.

Viana, Beidel, and Rabian (2009) conducted a 15-year review covering literature published between 1992 and 2007. They noted that existing studies had not employed randomized controlled trials because of the rarity of the disorder; rather, single-case experimental designs were more prominent in the literature. Results indicated a clear advantage of behavioral interventions that included contingency management, in which reinforcement is contingent on verbal responding; shaping, in which successive approximations toward the desired verbal behavior are reinforced;

stimulus fading and systematic desensitization, which involve the gradual inclusion of other individuals, usually classmates, on the condition the child with SM continues appropriate speech; and self-modeling, in which a child with SM is shown an edited video that appears to depict him or her speaking in the target setting. Such behaviorally based techniques appear to be the most effective interventions currently being used. As mentioned previously, using several of these strategies in combination tends to result in more immediate and seemingly permanent remission of SM.

A systematic analysis of treatment models conducted by Pionek-Stone, Kratochwill, Sladeczek, and Serlin (2002) supported the efficacy of combining multiple behavioral treatments. The study investigated the following predictions: (a) some form of treatment for SM would be more effective than baseline; (b) behavioral approaches would be more effective than other psychological treatments; and (c) different forms of behavioral treatments (e.g., modeling, cognitive behavioral therapy) would differ in effectiveness. The authors reported that "due to the lack of quantifiable data for the other treatment models" they could conclude only that behavior therapy is more effective than no treatment (p. 184). They also found that "treatment programs that draw upon techniques from applied behavior analysis [such as positive reinforcement, contingency management, shaping, and stimulus fading] or a combined behavioral approach [such as modeling with positive reinforcement]" (p. 187) yielded equally effective results.

Kehle, Madaus, Baratta, and Bray (1998) have experienced success in remediating SM using their augmented self-modeling technique that packages many of the aforementioned applied behavioral strategies with cognitive behavioral strategies, such as self-modeling. These techniques are also combined with the use of pharmacological agents, if the behavioral strategies do not result in adequate remission.

HOW TO: A GUIDE TO THE IMPLEMENTATION OF INTERVENTIONS FOR SM IN CHILDREN AND ADOLESCENTS

Kehle and his colleagues have successfully employed *Augmented Video Self-Modeling* with dozens of children with SM. The following section outlines the typical treatment plan that they most often used to promote normal and expected speech across varied settings.

Video Self-Modeling

Video self-modeling (VSM) is the use of video to depict the child as a model engaged in appropriate and exemplary behavior as a treatment to improve target behaviors. VSM is derived from social learning theory and relies on modeling and observational learning. The more similar the model is to the observer, the more effective the intervention. VSM has been implicated in altering memories and cognitions related to the target behavior (Margiano, Kehle, Bray, Nastasi, & DeWees, 2009). For example, as Kehle, Hintze, and DuPaul (1997) postulated, self-efficacy appears to improve as modeling the behavior occurs.

The rationale for combining self-modeling with other techniques is that SM is remediated most efficiently when multiple behavioral techniques are employed simultaneously (Watson & Kramer, 1992). According to Watson and Kramer (1992), using solely one technique will not adequately address the antecedents and consequences that maintain the nonverbal behavior. Pionek-Stone, Kratochwill, Sladeczek, and Serlin (2002) concurred with Watson and Kramer (1992), noting that using multiple behavioral techniques in combination appears to be the most efficacious in treating SM.

Augmented VSM typically involves rehearsal, successive approximations, self-reinforcement, mystery motivators, the spacing effect, stimulus fading, peer expectations, shaping, and contingency management. For illustrative purposes, the steps presented in this section have been applied in many cases in which the children speak fluently in the home, but exhibit SM in school. Typically, construction of the self-modeling video includes the following steps (taken from Kehle, Bray, Byer-Alcorace, Theodore, & Kovac, 2012):

1. Consultation with the parent to develop approximately 10 to 12 questions to be used to create the VSM videos. These questions should be appropriate for use in the classroom setting.
2. Consultation with the parent on practicing the questions at home to increase the child with SM's fluency in responding to the questions.
3. Instruction to the parent on the use of *successive approximations*. This technique involves asking the same 10 to 12 questions to the child at increasing closeness to the school.
4. Video recording of the classroom teacher, during a regular class session, asking these questions to the child and several classmates.
5. Video recording of the parent asking the same questions to the child after school on the same day and in the same classroom. Only the person recording the session, ideally the parent, along with the child should be present in the classroom. The video should focus only on the child.
6. Construction of one 12- to 15-minute edited intervention video depicting the child appearing to respond to the teacher's questions during the regular classroom setting. This depiction is accomplished by splicing the two videos together to show the teacher asking the questions and the child answering. Combining the two videos can be done easily with simple online editing software. Be certain to show only exemplary behavior of the child on the final film.
7. Consultation with the parent regarding small rewards that are appealing to the child, which will be used during intervention. These rewards should be wrapped in gender-neutral wrapping paper and placed in a basket.
8. Consultation with the parent and teacher regarding the use of a "mystery motivator" in the classroom. A mystery motivator is a desired but unknown object being used as a reinforcer for appropriate behavior. Place the mystery motivator, or a picture of it, in an envelope labeled with a large question mark and the child's name printed on the front. The mystery motivator reinforcer is typically larger in value to the child than the rewards identified in step 7. Tape the labeled envelope to the wall at the front of the classroom. Inform the child that the mystery motivator envelope contains something highly desirable and that the contents of the envelope can be obtained as soon as the desired behavior is present, as shown on the VSM video (i.e., asking the teacher, in normal conversational tone, to be allowed to have the contents of the mystery motivator envelope). The mystery motivator is designed to increase the value of the reinforcement by increasing the child's anticipation, similar to the enticing effects of a wrapped present.

9. On the first day of the intervention in a room that is preferably away from the classroom, show the first 2- to 3-minute segment of the edited VSM video to the child. Place the basket of wrapped reinforcers within sight of the child and the video. Use "self-controlled reinforcement," which involves allowing the child to view a 2- to 3-minute segment of the edited VSM video and pause the video when the child views himself or herself verbally responding to the teacher's questions. Allow the child to then select one of the wrapped presents. The pause and self-controlled reinforcement should occur only when the VSM video shows evidence of the child responding to the teacher. If the video player is not manageable by the child, an adult should pause the video after the child says "Stop" when seeing himself or herself on the video responding to the teacher. It may be beneficial to instruct the child to then say, "Please stop," "Please stop the video," and so on to increase verbal behaviors. Another adult member of the school community should be present when the child views the VSM video to facilitate *generalization*.

10. Subsequent intervention sessions should be spaced approximately 4 to 6 days apart. "The *spacing effect*—which refers to the finding that for a given amount of study time, spaced presentations yield substantially better learning than do massed presentations—is one of the most remarkable phenomena to emerge from laboratory research on learning" (Dempster, 1988, p. 627). "In many cases, two spaced presentations are about twice as effective as two massed presentations" (Dempster, 1988, p. 627). In self-modeling research, the VSM videos are typically presented on several occasions that are spaced several days apart. To date, the effect of the 4- to 6-day spacing of the viewing of the VSM videos has not been investigated. There likely exists an optimal number of viewings with a preferred delay time between viewings, but none have been identified at this time. It is additionally assumed that, by showing different segments of the VSM video to the child, each viewing will increase the child's attention to and interest in the VSM video, which would theoretically yield a greater effect.

11. On the second VSM video viewing day, show the child with SM a different 2- to 3-minute segment of the VSM video. Continue use of the self-controlled reinforcement. In place of the adult school community member, have another student present in the room during the viewing. This student, preferably a classmate and friend of the child with SM, should be allowed to choose a wrapped gift at the end of the session. After unwrapping the gift, have the student describe what he or she received to the child with SM. Instruct the children to put the presents in their backpacks upon reentrance to the classroom. The other classmates will almost immediately become aware that the friend received a gift for helping you and the child with SM, which will increase their interest in assisting also. Be certain that you have parental permission to involve the child with SM's classmates as observers and permission to give them the presents.

12. During the third through sixth VSM video viewing days, increase the number of classmate observers to two and then three. If possible, use different students during each session to facilitate *generalization*. All of the classmate observers should be allowed to select a wrapped present at the end of the session. If the child with SM is talking during the viewing sessions, ask the child to describe to the other students the present that was unwrapped. At some point during the intervention, given the child with SM's permission, show the entire 12- to 15-minute VSM video to the class in order to establish *positive peer expectations*.

13. Whenever the child with SM asks for the "mystery motivator," give it and allow it to be opened immediately. At the time the child opens the envelope, ask the child to please describe the present to his or her classmates.

CONCLUSION

SM is a relatively rare disorder characterized by failure to speak in a particular social setting whereas fluent speech occurs in a different setting. According to *DSM-5* (APA, 2013), it is considered to be an anxiety disorder and may coexist with SAD and ASD. Longevity of the disorder is not definitively known, but some children may cease showing symptomology as they age. Although a variety of interventions have been used with SM, behaviorally based techniques are the most successful. Combining these techniques has been shown to be the most effective treatment for SM. Augmented VSM, which combines multiple treatments including modeling, the spacing effect, self-reinforcement, generalization, mystery motivator, and positive peer expectations, is a highly effective package for the remediation of SM in children.

SELECT BIBLIOGRAPHY

Kehle, T. J., Bray, M. A., Byer-Alcorace, G. F., Theodore, L. A., & Kovac, L. (2012). Augmented self-modeling as an intervention for selective mutism. *Psychology in the Schools, 49,* 93–103. doi:10.1002/pits.21589
This article offers a parental perspective on SM as well as an outline of the predominant treatments in the field. These include behavior modification, cognitive behavioral therapy, psychopharmacological interventions, psychodynamic and family therapies, and augmented self-modeling.

Kehle, T. J., Madaus, M. M. R., Baratta, V. S., & Bray, M. A. (1998). Augmented self-modeling as a treatment for children with selective mutism. *Journal of School Psychology, 36,* 247–260. doi:10.1016/S0022–4405(98)00013–2
This research article describes the use of augmented self-modeling to remediate SM in three children. All three cases were studied using single-case AB design.

Pionek-Stone, B., Kratochwill, T. R., Sladeczek, I., & Serlin, R. C. (2002) Treatment of selective mutism: A best-evidence synthesis. *School Psychology Quarterly, 17,* 168–190. doi:10.1521/scpq.17.2.168.20857
This research article includes an exhaustive review of all SM studies in the literature. It contains a description of common therapies. Effect sizes are calculated for all studies that meet the search and inclusion criteria. Treatments that use applied behavioral analysis or a combination of behavioral treatments like self-modeling with positive reinforcement are recommended.

REFERENCES

American Psychiatric Association (APA). (2013). *Diagnostic and statistical manual of mental disorders* (5th ed.). Arlington, VA: American Psychiatric Publishing.

Barlow, K. Strother, J., & Landreth, G. (1986). Sibling group play therapy: An effective alternative with an electively mute child. *The School Counselor, 1,* 44–60.

Bergman, R. L., Piacentini, J., & McCracken, J. T. (2002). Prevalence and description of selective mutism in a school-based sample. *Journal of the American Academy of Child and Adolescent Psychiatry, 41*(8), 938–946.

Black, B., & Uhde, T. W. (1995). Psychiatric characteristics of children with selective mutism: A pilot study. *Journal of the American Academy of Child and Adolescent Psychiatry, 34*(7), 847–856.

Carlson, J. S., Kratochwill, T. R., & Johnston, H. F. (1999). Sertraline treatment of 5 children diagnosed with selective mutism: A single-case research trial. *Journal of Child and Adolescent Psychopharmacology, 9*(4), 293–306.

Dempster, F. N. (1988). The spacing effect: A case study in the failure to apply the results of psychological research. *American Psychologist, 43,* 627. doi:10.1037/0003–066X.43.8.627

Elizur, Y., & Perednik, R. (2003). Prevalence and description of selective mutism in immigrant and native families: A controlled study. *Journal of the American Academy of Child and Adolescent Psychiatry, 42*(12), 1451–1459.

Freeman, J. B., Garcia, A. M., Miller, L. M., Dow, S. P., & Leonard, H. L. (2004). Selective mutism. In T. L. Morris & J. S. March (Eds.), *Anxiety disorders in children and adolescents* (pp. 280–301). New York, NY: Guilford Press.

Hultquist, A. M. (1995) Selective mutism: Causes and interventions. *Journal of Emotional and Behavioral Disorders, 3,* 100–107. doi:10.1177/106342669500300205

Kehle, T. J., Bray, M. A., Byer-Alcorace, G. F., Theodore, L. A., & Kovac, L. (2012). Augmented self-modeling as an intervention for selective mutism. *Psychology in the Schools, 49,* 93–103. doi:10.1002/pits.21589

Kehle, T. J., Bray, M. A., Root, M. M., & Theodore, L. A. (2016). Single case methodology: Patients with selective mutism. *Research Methods Cases*. CA: Sage.

Kehle, T. J., Hintze, J. M., & DuPaul, G. J. (1997). *Selective mutism*. In T. Alex, G. Bear, & K. Minke (Eds.), *Children's needs II: Development, problems and alternatives* (pp. 329–337). Bethesda, MD: National Association of School Psychologists.

Kehle, T. J., Madaus, M. M. R., Baratta, V. S., & Bray, M. A. (1998). Augmented self-modeling as a treatment for children with selective mutism. *Journal of School Psychology, 36*, 247–260. doi:10.1016/S0022–4405(98)00013–2

Margiano, S. G., Kehle, T. J., Bray, M. A., Nastasi, B. K., & DeWees, K. (2009). Examination of the effects of self-modeling on autobiographical memory. *Canadian Journal of School Psychology, 24*, 203–221. doi:10.1177/0829573509343096

Oerbeck, B., Johansen, J., Lundahl, K., & Kristensen, H. (2012). Selective mutism: A home- and kindergarten-based intervention for children 3–5 years: A pilot study. *Clinical Child Psychology and Psychiatry, 17*(3), 370–383.

Pionek-Stone, B., Kratochwill, T. R., Sladeczek, I., & Serlin, R. C. (2002) Treatment of selective mutism: A best-evidence synthesis. *School Psychology Quarterly, 17*, 168–190. doi:10.1521/scpq.17.2.168.20857

Remschmidt, H., Poller, M., Herpertz-Dahlmann, B., Hennighausen, K., & Gutenbrunner, C. (2001). A follow-up study of 45 patients with elective mutism. *European Archives of Psychiatry and Clinical Neuroscience, 251*(6), 284–296.

Schill, M. T., Kratochwill, T. R., & Gardner, W. I. (1996). An assessment protocol for selective mutism: Analogue assessment using parents as facilitators. *Journal of School Psychologists, 34*, 1–21. doi:10.1016/0022–4405(95)00023–2

Schwartz, R. H., Freedy, A. S., & Sheridan, M. J. (2006). Selective mutism: Are primary care physicians missing the silence? *Clinical Pediatrics, 45*, 43–48. doi:10.1177/000992280604500107

Stein, M. B., Yang, B. Z., Chavira, D. A., Hitchcock, C. A., Sung, S. C., Shipon-Blum, E., & Gelernter, J. (2011). A common genetic variant in the neurexin superfamily member CNTNAP2 is associated with increased risk for selective mutism and social anxiety-related traits. *Biological Psychiatry, 69*(9), 825–831.

Steinhausen, H. C., & Juzi, C. (1996). Elective mutism: An analysis of 100 cases. *Journal of the American Academy of Child and Adolescent Psychiatry, 35*(5), 606–614.

Toppelberg, C. O., Tabors, P., Coggins, A., Lum, K., & Burger, C. (2005). Differential diagnosis of selective mutism in bilingual children. *Journal of the American Academy of Child and Adolescent Psychiatry, 44*(6), 592–595.

Vecchio, J. L., & Kearney, C. A. (2005). Selective mutism in children: Comparison to youths with and without anxiety disorders. *Journal of Psychopathology and Behavioral Assessment, 27*, 31–37. doi:10.1007/s10862–005-3263–1

Viana, A. G., Beidel, D. C., & Rabian, B. (2009). Selective mutism: a review and integration of the last 15 years. *Clinical Psychology Review, 29*(1), 57–67.

Watson, T. S., & Kramer, J. J. (1992). Multimethod behavioral treatment of long-term selective mutism. *Psychology in the Schools, 29*, 359–366. doi:0.1002/1520–6807(199210)29:4<359::AID-PITS2310290409>3.0.CO;2–6

Weininger, O. (1987). Electively mute children: A therapeutic approach. *Journal of the Melanie Klein Society, 5*, 25–42.

Evidence-Based Interventions for Separation Anxiety Disorder in Children and Adolescents

John S. Carlson and Allison Siroky

OVERVIEW

Anxiety disorders are the most common mental health conditions to impact school-aged children (United States Department of Health and Human Services, 1999). A particular diagnostic subtype termed "separation anxiety disorder" accounts for the majority of referrals seen within child and adolescent psychological service delivery systems including schools. As indicated by the subtype name, children diagnosed with this type of anxiety condition present with irrational fears when separating or anticipating separation from attachment figures (i.e., parents and caregivers) or the home setting. Excessive fear/worry, avoidance/escape, and emergence of somatic symptoms (e.g., vomiting and headaches) before, during, or after separation characterize separation anxiety disorder.

According to the *Diagnostic and Statistical Manual of Mental Disorders* (5th ed.; *DSM-5*; American Psychiatric Association [APA], 2013), evidence of *at least three* out of eight separation-related criteria must be met from the following: (a) distress when separating or anticipating separation from the attachment figure, (b) fear of harm to or loss of the attachment figure, (c) worry about a potentially dangerous event that may result in separation, (d) refusal to be

away from home caused by fear of separation, (e) reluctance to be left alone without the presence of the attachment figure, (f) refusal to sleep away from home or without the attachment figure, (g) repeated nightmares about separation, and (h) complaints about physical ailments in anticipation of or in response to actual separation from attachment figures. Indicators of *impairment in social or academic functioning* resulting from these symptoms must be evident given that separation anxiety symptoms are normal and are present in about half the childhood population (Figueroa, Soutullo, Ono, & Saito, 2012). In addition, *persistent symptoms over at least a 1-month* period must be observed before meeting diagnostic criteria, as transitions and life events (e.g., moving, new school, new friends, and medical illness) can be associated with acute symptoms of separation anxiety. Cultural considerations (e.g., school entry practices, sleeping arrangements, level of parent supervision, and family system beliefs pertaining to children's independence) are also important when making a diagnosis of separation anxiety disorder.

It is important to recognize that anxiety related to separation from an attachment figure is developmentally appropriate when children are infants and as they develop through the preschool years (ages 0–5 years). The ability to appropriately regulate one's emotions and fears about separating on a consistent basis is generally not expected before 3 to 4 years of age (Angelosante, Ostrowski, & Chizkov, 2013). In addition, overgeneralization of harmless events such as a headache or nightmare can appear similar to or promote separation anxiety symptoms (Eisen et al., 2011). Assessing developmentally inappropriate responses (i.e., both quality and quantity of the symptoms) to separating from an attachment figure through a functional behavior assessment is a key component of the diagnostic process.

Childhood-onset separation anxiety disorder usually begins before 13 years of age and peaks between the ages of 7 and 9 years. Rarely is the condition diagnosed before age 5 years given the normality of anxiety associated with separation before formal school entry (Figueroa et al., 2012). Lifetime prevalence of childhood separation anxiety disorder is estimated between 3% and 5% and varies by gender (girl–boy ratio of 2:1) and age, with a mean average age of onset at 9 years (Angelosante et al., 2013; Eisen et al., 2011). Prevalence rates typically decline as children get older with onset in adolescence atypical, yet lifetime prevalence estimates for adult separation anxiety disorder are surprisingly high at 6.6% (Shear, Jin, Ruscio, Walters, & Kessler, 2006). This highlights the importance and rationale for its recent inclusion in *DSM-5*.

Part of the unique challenge associated with assessment and intervention of separation anxiety disorder is the commonalities and overlapping symptoms with a number of other childhood anxiety disorders. Specifically, avoidance behavior, problems sleeping, and somatic symptoms associated with separation anxiety are also commonly seen in generalized anxiety disorder and social anxiety disorder (Mohatt, Bennett, & Walkup, 2014). Characteristics of oppositional defiant disorder and school refusal behavior are common secondary symptoms given the intensity of avoidance that a child might undertake to prevent him or her from feeling anxious. Severe forms of school refusal behavior often have nothing to do with an attachment figure and instead may be linked to symptoms of depression or agoraphobia (i.e., fear of being in dangerous places or in a setting where it may be difficult to escape a situational threat).

The developmental connection between childhood separation anxiety disorder and adolescent/

adult panic disorder has also been well documented in the literature. Close attention to potential commonalities in symptom presentation and emergence of additional symptoms of anxiety, depression, oppositionality, and even disruptive behavior disorders is necessary. Isolating the specific setting, behavior, and/or cognitive antecedents associated with children's fears of anticipated or real separation is essential to differential diagnosis and treatment planning.

Associated features of separation anxiety include parent–child dysfunction, school attendance difficulties, and challenges to social functioning (APA, 2013). Early intervention is an important step in preventing later developmental challenges from impacting the functioning of a child presenting with subclinical symptoms of separation anxiety. Recognition of the etiological characteristics can help one to identify those at risk. Specifically, a number of biopsychosocial factors are believed to play a role in the development and maintenance of separation anxiety disorder.

ETIOLOGY AND FACTORS CONTRIBUTING TO SEPARATION ANXIETY DISORDER IN CHILDREN AND ADOLESCENTS

Biological (e.g., genetic vulnerability for anxiety and temperamental characteristics associated with behavior inhibition) and environmental factors (e.g., family/attachment figure characteristics, early experiences, and family stressors) play a role in the development of separation anxiety disorder. For example, a parent who presents to his or her behaviorly inhibited child (e.g., socially avoidant, slow-to-warm to new situations or people) as overprotective or overattentive, or has a low anxiety tolerance, may unknowingly promote a child's anxiousness around times of separation.

Anxiety-provoking interactions within new or perceived fearful situations can be reciprocally reinforcing to both the parent and the child. Such patterns of interaction make treatment of separation challenges difficult. The persistent and chronic nature of dysfunctional parent–child interactions that have developed across years of a child's life may not be problematic until expectations for separation (e.g., formal schooling, parents' need to be away) increase (Drake & Ginsburg, 2012). The complex etiology and interaction of biology, psychology, and the social environment associated with children who present with a severe expression of separation anxiety result in an internalizing disorder that is reinforced by a child's environment (e.g., attachment figure). These challenges may be unremitting without a multimodal approach (i.e., biological, psychological, and ecological), especially in those cases where psychosocial treatments used in isolation (i.e., cognitive behavioral therapy [CBT], parent training) fail to reduce symptoms or improve functioning (Eisen et al., 2011).

A number of considerations are essential when assessing children's separation anxiety symptoms for the purpose of developing an appropriate treatment strategy that meets the unique needs of the child and his or her family. These include biological factors, such as a child's temperament. Additional considerations include processes associated with children's cognitions as well as family system variables. In addition, assessing parental mental health, including anxiety and depressive symptoms, is important. A familial system of social support and available resources to promote positive parenting practices should be an important target of treatment planning. Finally, acute and chronic life events impacting the child or family should be examined.

EVIDENCE-BASED INTERVENTIONS AND EMPIRICAL SUPPORT FOR SEPARATION ANXIETY DISORDER IN CHILDREN AND ADOLESCENTS

Evidence-based interventions for children and adolescents with separation anxiety disorder closely align to the risk factors and etiologies presented previously. These interventions include CBT, family therapy, pharmacological treatments, or a combination of these biopsychosocial therapies. Given the important role that attachment figures (e.g., parents and caregivers) play with separation anxiety disorder, it is essential that these individuals are integrally involved in both treatment planning and implementation. Numerous programs and treatments have been developed and empirically tested to determine their clinical efficacy for children

identified as having anxiety disorders (e.g., generalized, social, separation, and specific phobias), yet a paucity of investigations specific to youth with separation anxiety disorder exists.

Cognitive Behavioral Therapy

Research points to CBT as the most favorable method for effective and appropriate treatment for childhood anxiety (Nauta & Emmelkamp, 2012). Through this psychological treatment approach, youth learn to identify anxious thoughts/*cognitions* and practice replacing previous maladaptive patterns of *behavior* with more adaptive ones. Specific attention is given to reduction of both (a) irrational fears associated with separation and (b) avoidant behaviors associated with separation. Fundamental components of CBT include psychoeducation, cognitive restructuring, exposure therapy, relaxation strategies, reduction of avoidance, behavior modeling, social skills training, and homework assignments. CBT can be done individually or within a small group format.

Individual CBT. Individual CBT focuses primarily on treating the child who experiences symptoms of anxiety. Active parental involvement helps one to carry out the treatment program within the home setting. Kendall (1990) was one of the first to develop a manualized CBT program called "Coping Cat" for childhood anxiety disorders. Coping Cat teaches children how to (a) restructure negative or anxious thoughts about separating from an attachment figure and (b) how to use adaptive coping strategies through graded exposure to anticipated or actual situations (e.g., going to school, going to sleep, and being away from parents). Efficacy studies highlight significant gains for participants with separation anxiety disorder, as well as generalized anxiety and social anxiety. For example, remission rates for Coping Cat range from 64% to 77% (Kendall, 1994), with even higher rates reported in long-term follow-up investigations (Kendall, Safford, Flannery-Schroeder, & Webb, 2004).

Walkup and colleagues (2008) demonstrated that the majority of children (60%) benefit from CBT when compared with children randomly assigned to a wait-list control group (23%). Maintenance of treatment gains and further improvements in functioning after only 12 to 16 weeks of CBT have been reported in studies that have followed youth for up to 9 years after treatment (Seligman & Ollendick, 2011). These improvements have been reported for youth presenting with varied comorbid conditions and across different ethnic and cultural groups.

Group CBT. Although potentially less efficacious in clinical settings (Bodden et al., 2008), group CBT may be implemented more frequently in practical settings (e.g., schools and day camps) and is another promising option for the treatment of separation anxiety disorder. Group-based treatment is both time- and cost-effective (Eisen et al., 2011). Considering the prevalence of separation anxiety disorders among school-aged children, this approach may be ideal within a tiered model of service delivery. For example, the FRIENDS (*F*eelings, *R*elax, *I*nner Helpful Thoughts, *E*xplore Solutions, *N*ow Reward Self, *D*on't Forget to Practice, *S*tay Cool!) program (Barrett, Lowry-Webster, & Turner, 2000) not only provides targeted support for groups of children with anxiety, but also incorporates elements of interpersonal therapy, universal preventive care, and parental education. Children and families in the FRIENDS program learn to identify feelings first and to employ relaxation techniques before, during, or after anxiety-provoking situations. Over the course of 10 weekly sessions, they also practice managing their thoughts, problem solving with one another, and giving or receiving rewards for appropriate behaviors. In a randomized controlled trial, a majority of participants receiving the FRIENDS program no longer met diagnostic criteria (69%) compared with 6% of their peers not treated (Shortt, Barrett, & Fox, 2001).

Intensive group-based treatments in the form of weeklong camps have also been developed to treat anxiety. One example, the Child Anxiety Multi-day Program (CAMP; Santucci, Ehrenreich, Trosper, Bennett, & Pincus, 2009) was created specifically for school-aged girls diagnosed with separation anxiety disorder. CAMP involves the use of peer support within a socially active setting. Results from a recent randomized controlled trial of CAMP showed significant improvements in clinical severity and parent-reported symptoms of children's separation anxiety (Santucci & Ehrenreich-May, 2013).

Commonalities across the various individual and group CBT approaches include specific instruction, development of a hierarchy of feared situations, exposure to the fear hierarchy, and the use of homework exercises (Seligman & Ollendick, 2011). Generalization and maintenance of treatment gains ultimately occur through guided practice, as therapists show parents or children how to carry out exposure activities in new contexts outside of the clinic, and continual progress monitoring. Skill development is reinforced through behavior rehearsal involving modeling and role playing. Group approaches, in theory, may be more advantageous than individual approaches given the potential benefits associated with peer reinforcement and practice. Yet, fear of social scrutiny within a peer group may be contraindicated for a subset of those who present with both social and separation anxiety disorders.

Family-Based Treatment

Parental behaviors (e.g., unintended reinforcement of child's anxiety) and parenting style (e.g., overprotective) are associated with increased risk for childhood anxiety, including separation anxiety disorder (Drake & Ginsburg, 2012). Treatment methods that emphasize parent–child relationships or strengthen the family system may be especially beneficial to children experiencing separation anxiety (Eisen et al., 2011). Family-based treatment programs typically work with the family as a whole. Yet, sometimes these are modified to include only anxious children and their parents/caregivers or may focus only on caregivers. Parent-training programs, for example, do not involve direct intervention with the child but instead work with parents to develop positive and appropriate parenting techniques (Eisen, Raleigh, & Neuhoff, 2008). One of the more popular and effective family-based treatments for separation anxiety disorder is Parent–Child Interaction Therapy (PCIT; Eyberg, 1988).

Parent–Child Interaction Therapy. Although originally intended for children with oppositional defiant or conduct disorders, PCIT has been adapted to address the needs of children with separation anxiety disorder (Choate, Pincus, Eyberg, & Barlow, 2006; Pincus, Eyberg, & Choate, 2005). Two phases are involved: Child-Directed Interaction (CDI) and Parent-Directed Interaction (PDI). During CDI, children initiate play and discussion. Parents are trained to participate in these interactions and given continuous feedback by therapists through "bug in the ear" devices. In the PDI phase, parents lead discussion and play while remaining attentive to their child's needs. When implementing PCIT with children with separation anxiety disorder, a third Bravery-Directed Interaction (BDI) phase is often supplemented after the first CDI phase. BDI emphasizes cognitive behavior strategies such as psychoeducation, development of a fear hierarchy, and a reward system to be used with exposure activities. Investigations of PCIT for separation anxiety disorder show promising results across multiple trials (Choate et al., 2006; Pincus, Santucci, Ehrenreich, & Eyberg, 2008).

Adaptations to PCIT. To address concerns that traditional PCIT may be beyond the developmental level of young children (i.e., age 7 years or younger), Puliafico, Comer, and Albano (2008) adapted PCIT to treat anxiety in children between the ages of 3 and 8 years using the CALM (Coaching Approach behavior and Leading by Modeling) program. Much like PCIT adaptation for separation anxiety disorder, the second phase of the CALM program includes exposure activities to help parents promote "brave behaviors" as they receive therapist feedback during sessions (Comer et al., 2012). However, the CALM program does not include the third PDI phase.

Alternative Family-Based Treatments. A recent study compared a family-based treatment program called Separation Anxiety Family Therapy (SAFT; German: *TrennungsAngstprogramm Für Familien* [TAFF]; Schneider et al., 2011) with the Coping Cat program in a randomized controlled trial with 64 children between the ages of 8 and 13 years with separation anxiety disorder. SAFT (German: TAFF) differs from Coping Cat in that it includes disorder-specific materials for participating youth and a CBT-based parent-training component. Although a slightly greater percentage of the SAFT (German: TAFF) group compared with the Coping Cat group no longer met criteria for separation anxiety disorder, these differences were not statistically significant (Schneider et al., 2013). Benefits of additional parent training such as SAFT may best be determined by the context and characteristics of the family (Bodden et al., 2008).

Pharmacological Treatment

The use of pharmacological treatments for childhood anxiety disorders may be considered for children who fail to respond to evidence-based psychosocial treatments. The cost-effectiveness, ease of access, and overall success in alleviating anxious symptoms contribute to the popularity of anxiety medications (Reinblatt & Riddle, 2007). Yet, no medication holds the Food and Drug Administration (FDA) approval for treatment of separation anxiety disorder. Despite this indication, selective serotonin reuptake inhibitors (SSRIs) such as fluoxetine and sertraline are often used "off-label." SSRIs are currently the most favorable pharmacological treatments for anxiety disorders, including separation anxiety disorder (Eisen et al., 2011). The side effects associated with SSRIs (e.g., headaches and stomachaches) typically are mild and short-lived (Figueroa et al., 2012). Numerous studies (e.g., Segool & Carlson, 2008; Walkup et al., 2008) suggest that SSRIs in combination with CBT can be very effective in treating obsessive fears and worries, so reductions can be made in avoidant behavior. Individual child or family circumstances must be taken into consideration when deciding if a pharmacological approach to treating separation anxiety symptoms is an appropriate and necessary adjunct to psychosocial treatments (e.g., parental training and CBT).

HOW TO: A GUIDE TO THE IMPLEMENTATION OF INTERVENTIONS FOR SEPARATION ANXIETY DISORDERS IN CHILDREN AND ADOLESCENTS

Step-by-step instructions for how to carry out the three primary evidence-based treatments for separation anxiety disorder are presented. First, individual and group approaches to implementing a six-step CBT intervention are addressed. Next, a five-step approach to carrying out a parent-training program is reviewed. Finally, a five-step approach to evaluating the costs and benefits of using a psychopharmacological treatment (i.e., SSRIs) for children and adolescents with separation anxiety disorder is provided.

Intervention 1: CBT

Developmental considerations are important to assess when making decisions about how best to intervene with children experiencing significant dysfunction as a result of separation anxiety symptoms. CBT requires a child to work closely with an adult therapist to question and alter his or her thoughts, feelings, and actions. Children as young as 8 years have been shown to benefit significantly from this psychosocial treatment approach. Younger children may also benefit, but often need their parents to support and remind them as they work through treatment beyond the therapy session. A six-step approach to CBT is provided and can be carried out in either group or individual format.

Step 1: Psychoeducation. Children and parents must initially learn that thoughts, feelings, and behaviors have profound influences on one another. During this phase, specific information about the disorder should be discussed. Although CBT focuses primarily on the individual child or groups of children who demonstrate separation anxiety symptoms, it is essential to weave parent-training procedures into each of these steps. For example, in this first step, children are taught how to monitor and track their thoughts, feelings, and behaviors so that they can see problematic patterns of behavior and situations that induce their symptoms. Parents too learn to examine their responses before and following conditions that lead to children's separation anxiety symptoms. Based on the information provided through these activities, an individualized treatment plan is developed.

Step 2: Relaxation. To learn about the process of how anxiety emerges, children are first taught about the physiological symptoms of anxiousness (e.g., rapid or shallow breathing, shakiness, tense muscles, increased heart rate, sweaty palms, stomach sensations sometimes referred to as "butterflies," needing to use the bathroom, dizziness, and crying). Many times these bodily reactions to anxiety lead to entrenched somatic symptoms (e.g., nausea and vomiting) and complaints (e.g., headaches). The physiological symptoms associated with anxiety need to be initially addressed and targeted before tackling additional changes in cognitions and behaviors.

When children begin to feel anxious or worried, they are taught to apply specific relaxation techniques to calm themselves. These techniques are introduced in therapy and sessions should allow time to practice these techniques so that they can be readily employed in real-life avoidance situations. Relaxation techniques include tensing and releasing muscle groups throughout the body (progressive muscle relaxation), thinking about doing things successfully (positive imagery), engaging in deep/abdominal breathing techniques (diaphragmatic breathing), and teaching the body to respond to thoughts/words (autogenic training).

Step 3: Exposure/Avoidance Prevention. After children can effectively practice relaxation, they need to begin pairing these techniques with their anxious thoughts and feelings. Early on in treatment, children and the therapist should work together to develop a plan for exposure activities and avoidance prevention. Through exposure, children encounter anxiety-provoking situations and practices reframing their negative cognitions. This approach teaches them to replace their previous response to fearful situations (avoidance) with more adaptive cognitions and behaviors. Asking children to think logically about their anxious thoughts or beliefs (e.g., What do I believe will happen? How likely is it this outcome will occur?) may serve as an additional step to break their habit of avoiding separation.

Step 4: Systematic Desensitization. Children receiving CBT for anxiety are typically introduced to anxiety-provoking situations slowly, rather than all at once. Systematic desensitization is a technique that involves the development of a fear hierarchy to guide exposure activities over the course of treatment. The fear hierarchy is a list of situations or events that trigger the child's anxiety, ranked from least to most fearful. For example, a child with separation anxiety might list "parents leaving the room for 10 minutes" at the bottom of his or her fear hierarchy and "parents going on vacation for 10 days" near the top. The therapist and child will attempt to work through each situation on the hierarchy via exposure activities as treatment progresses. Each successive step is reinforced.

Step 5: Role-Playing/Practice. Initial sessions will likely require additional time for introducing and explaining the aforementioned techniques. After the child is comfortable with these, the remainder of treatment will focus on in-session practice. The therapist may use various behavior strategies including modeling, in vivo exposure, role playing, relaxation training, and reinforced practice (i.e., rewards for positive responses to situations) to encourage children to move forward on their fear hierarchy. In some cases, children will respond well to modeling as they see others separate from their parents successfully. Films or live models can be used, but the child will need to attempt the exposure activity soon after watching the model.

Rating scales may also help the child and therapist to evaluate the success of the coping strategies/plan. Before an exposure activity, ask the child to rate his or her feelings of fear/anxiety on a predetermined scale. Then, ask the child to use this scale immediately after he or she successfully completes the activity and compare results. Ideally, the child will see that his or her anxiety decreased even after facing the fearful situation. In addition, a system of reinforcement is generally effective in promoting continued success. A child creates a list of rewards for his or her behavior after meeting a specified goal or step on his or her fear hierarchy ladder.

Step 6: Maintenance/Generalization. In the final stage of treatment, children can begin practice coping with anxiety beyond the clinic. Children, often with the help of their parents, receive assignments to conduct exposure exercises across various settings (e.g., home, school, and in the community). Assignments require children to enter previously avoided situations and typically are a part of their fear hierarchy. Parents can adapt a previous reward system to focus on the successful completion of these activities. It will be important to provide consistent praise and feedback to children throughout treatment. During the last session, review any and all improvements since treatment onset to reinforce their efforts. Discuss with parents strategies for encouraging continued progress and preventing relapse through booster sessions.

Intervention 2: Parent Training

Parental behaviors and practices may have a significant impact on a child's emotional and psychological well-being. As the parent–child dynamic is reciprocal in nature, children who show distress in certain situations can actually shape parental behaviors. In turn, parents may feel the need to protect their child from experiencing anxiety, and children learn that the only way to reduce their worry is by avoiding fearful situations. In some cases, parents may even feel anxious themselves and make little effort to hide this in front of their children. For these families, a parent-directed training program may be a favorable treatment option. This guide presents the basic structure of a parent-training program for families affected by separation anxiety.

Step 1: Assessment. In the first session, parents will report the severity of their child's separation anxiety through questions such as: In which situations does my child appear most anxious? What does my child say or ask? What is my child trying to avoid? What does my child think is going to happen? This initial evaluation targets the frequency, excessiveness, and antecedents of the separation anxiety to help identify triggers or environmental stressors that contribute to the child's fear of separation. The extent to which the anxiety impairs the child's functioning across settings (e.g., school, social, and familial) should also be noted. Rating scales such as the Multidimensional Anxiety Scale for Children-Second Edition (MASC-2; March, 2013) comprehensively assess for anxiety disorder symptoms in children 8 years and older (e.g., separation anxiety/phobia, social anxiety, and generalized anxiety) and provide a report that links symptoms to potential interventions. As anxiety treatment does not follow a "one size fits all" rule, the general focus and pace of interventions must be then individualized to meet the needs of each family. Finally, it helps to have parents think critically about the goals of the intervention (e.g., expected changes in parenting practices or child behaviors) and use them as a reference for post-treatment review.

Step 2: Identifying Systems of Reinforcement for Parental and Child Behavior. Within the first two sessions, parents need to identify existing parenting practices and systems of reinforcement. Some parents may not understand that their behaviors can actually encourage or exacerbate their child's anxiety. For example, a child who is markedly distressed when his or her parent is running a few minutes late may feel relief when the parent greets him or her with more affection than usual. Although warm parenting is recommended no matter the context, children who receive excessive attention after expressing anxiety may come to associate anxious behaviors with increased parental attention.

Other parental accommodations, like allowing the child to stay home or sleep in the parents' bed each night, can also encourage anxious behaviors. This is often referred to as the "cycle of avoidance" and should be explained to parents early on. Parents have a natural desire to step in for their child to relieve his or her worries or fears. However, doing so might actually increase a child's dependence on the parent and it inadvertently suggests to the child that distress is an appropriate response to such events. When parents remove the fearful stimulus (separation), this negatively reinforces the child to avoid the same stimulus next time. Once parents learn about behaviors that might exacerbate their child's anxiety, they should reflect on their own parenting practices. Parents might benefit from an activity that asks them to write down common reactions to their child's anxiety, followed by careful consideration of the intent and outcome of each behavior. Problematic behaviors can turn into points of intervention during later sessions in which parents focus on interrupting this cycle of avoidance.

Step 3: Reducing Parental Fears and Worries. In addition to identifying specific parental behaviors, parents should recognize how their personal fears and worries influence their child's anxiety. Educate parents on the general nature of anxiety (i.e., potential causes, course, prevalence, and comorbidity) and how it is typically treated. As anxiety does have a major genetic component, parents of anxious children will often be anxious themselves. Work with parents to foster *realistic thinking* and reduce worrisome thoughts. Realistic thinkers recognize that situations do not directly influence their emotions; their beliefs about a situation do. Anxiety is typically a result of overestimating the likelihood of a negative event occurring or assuming the worst possible outcome.

Instruct parents to list their own fears, especially those related to separating with their child, and their initial thoughts about fearful events.

Have them think realistically about these events by responding to questions like: How likely is it that this event will happen? What is the worst that could happen? Could I cope with this if it were to happen? The goal is not to remove the fear entirely, but to reduce the associated negative beliefs. Once parents effectively employ realistic thinking during treatment, they can teach their child how to think realistically as well. Children can also list fearful situations, identify initial beliefs, consider the "evidence" by reflecting on past experience, and reevaluate their worries after thinking critically.

Step 4: Altering Entrenched and Pervasive Patterns of Parental Behavior. After parents have clearly identified maladaptive thoughts or actions, they are ready to actively attempt to shape their patterns of behavior. Changing less-helpful parenting responses must be targeted. These may include excessive reassurance, overly intrusive parenting, failing to provide the child with appropriate choices, allowing avoidance, or general impatience. Again, parents need to reflect on antecedents that prompt the use of these strategies and recall common outcomes. For example, consider what a child might learn if parents direct them to behave in a certain way in the face of anxiety (e.g., "don't cry", "calm down"). Replace specific behaviors with more positive approaches to coping with their child's anxiety such as rewarding brave (i.e., nonanxious) behaviors, ignoring maladaptive behaviors (e.g., throwing tantrums and asking too many questions), prompting their child to cope constructively, and modeling appropriate behaviors. These positive parenting strategies are to be practiced consistently.

A majority of parent-training sessions will involve role-play activities to allow parents to work on their reactions before and after separating with their child. Therapists will provide extensive guidance at the beginning of treatment, but will eventually help parents learn to initiate these exercises on their own and complete out-of-session assignments. Through training, parents learn to model appropriate responses to separation, and children may start to recognize that separation is less fearful than anticipated. Teaching parents how to properly regulate emotions and use a problem-solving approach will also prepare them for dealing with their child's separation anxiety at any given moment.

Step 5: Practicing and Processing Changes in Parent–Child Interaction. Improving parent–child interactions must be emphasized. For example, in PCIT parents first learn how to engage in child-directed play where the main focus is on the child's behaviors. Parents learn to use "PRIDE" skills: Praise, Reflection, Imitation, Description of behavior, and Enthusiasm. These skills direct parents to engage in activities of their child's interest. During this activity, parents are asked to avoid questions or directives. Instead, they are encouraged to describe or reflect on their child's behavior, following by an appropriate statement of praise. For example, while a child and parent draw pictures together, the parent might state, "I see you are drawing a big, yellow sun. Great work!" Therapists may observe interactions and provide feedback on parental behaviors.

Parents may also be trained on how to practice exposure activities at home. They can work with their child to develop a fear hierarchy by listing anxiety-provoking events in order from least to most fearful. Together, the family will encounter each event and apply relaxation or coping strategies to reduce feelings of anxiety, progressing gradually up the hierarchy. During each exercise, parents should prompt children to think realistically. They should also respond appropriately to their child's anxiety, repeat exercises if needed, and consistently reward positive gains. Scheduled exposures with therapist guidance are suggested, though spontaneous practice will help the family generalize strategies to new contexts.

Intervention 3: Adjunctive Psychopharmacological Treatment

The third intervention targets the small number of cases that fail to respond to CBT and/or parent-training techniques. Psychopharmacological treatment is believed to be an important adjunct for those cases of separation anxiety disorder cases that are resistant to psychosocial interventions. Children who are good candidates for this intervention have a family history of what can be considered a genetic/biological component to their anxiety disorder. A step-by-step approach follows for mental health practitioners and parents to use when physicians are considering, selecting, monitoring, and discontinuing an adjunctive pharmacological treatment to psychosocial treatments. Specifically, a six-session intervention around medication evaluation issues (Carlson & Shahidullah, 2014) is warranted for cases where it is necessary to turn to an intensive biopsychosocial approach to treating separation anxiety disorder.

Step 1 (Week 1—Treatment Planning/ Implementation). It is essential to identify the stakeholders impacted by a decision to treat symptoms with an SSRI (e.g., child, parents, school staff, and treating practitioner). Important questions need to be answered, such as: Who needs to know what, when, and how? How can these important stakeholders help to observe for emergent target or side effects? How do stakeholders communicate and how often? Next, the therapist will need to conduct a diagnostic interview and identify specific areas of dysfunction (e.g., obsessive thoughts/rumination, severe avoidant behavior, major emotional or behavior distress at the perceived or real point of separation) through screening and assessment. Additional information should be assessed including family history of anxiety issues and specifically hypothesized genetic and/or environmental transmission. Each of these factors may contribute to a general inference for why psychosocial treatment alone was ineffective and whether pharmacological treatment will be sufficient for treating severe symptoms. In developing the treatment plan, the therapist will select target behaviors for treatment and operationalize them for parents and children to understand. These behaviors guide the treatment plan and will be used within a progress-monitoring plan. Both baseline data and targeted goals or expectations for these behaviors need to be defined as well. Parents, teachers, and the treating physician should all be involved in the creation and continued monitoring of the treatment plan. Brief rating scales or daily report cards can be particularly effective and efficient for use in monitoring the child's response to treatment.

The treating physician will make an initial dosage determination and should review possible side effects with the child/family. During this first meeting, the physician provides general guidelines for when a treatment response is typically seen (i.e., 4–8 weeks for SSRI treatment). A plan to provide, continue, or reinstate a parallel set of psychosocial interventions (e.g., CBT and parental training) will then be developed and implemented over the next 8 to 12 weeks with a follow-up visit scheduled after about 4 weeks from treatment onset.

Step 2 (Week 5—Progress Monitoring: Initial Adjustments). Before this follow-up visit, the treating practitioner should gather data of the child's progress collected by parents and teachers. A brief summary and graphical representation of target behavior data will be helpful when explaining the child's progress to the treating physician.

If necessary, dosage changes may be considered during this clinic visit but should be supported by parental and child interviews. Typically, side effects which may have emerged during the initial week of medication treatment will have shown signs of diminishing before this 1-month follow-up visit. On reviewing the child's growth over the past 4 weeks, targeted treatment response is observed/reported by parents, teachers, or other stakeholders. Depending on these reports, treatment modifications to adapt to the individual child's needs can be considered and implemented. Once all stakeholders are aware of the plan for the remainder of treatment, a follow-up visit about 8 weeks following treatment onset will be scheduled.

Step 3 (Week 9—Progress Monitoring: Additional Adjustments). Similar to the previous meeting, the treating mental health professional will once again present data collected by parents and teachers to the treating physician. In this session, there should be substantial evidence of how the child has been responding to treatment. Treatment modifications (e.g., dosage increase) will be necessary if the child's functioning remains at baseline levels. If symptoms of separation anxiety are starting to decline, the remaining course of treatment is determined and initial thoughts on treatment termination may be discussed. While considering treatment termination, it is important to keep in mind the initial goals for medication treatment (frequency, duration, intensity of targeted behaviors and symptoms) that were developed during the baseline visit at week 1.

Step 4 (Week 13—Progress Monitoring: Maintenance). At this point in treatment, the child should be responding successfully to the current plan. The focus shifts now from determining an appropriate plan to maintaining any positive gains and encouraging further progress. Data provided by parents and teachers will be gathered once again by the treating helping professional and summarized for presentation to the child's physician. In the event that the child remains at baseline levels of functioning, other treatment modifications (e.g., switch to alternate medication in SSRI category or a non-SSRI) need to be considered. For children who do show positive responses to the current treatment plan, previous data collection procedures are reduced and global assessment of functioning through interviewing is typically used within subsequent physician visits. Using a variety of data sources, final decisions should be made pertaining to treatment modifications or discontinuation of adjunctive psychosocial treatments. The treating physician will work with the family to establish the frequency of additional clinic visits.

Step 5 (Week 36—Treatment Discontinuation). A clear plan for discontinuing medication treatment should now be in place by the treating physician and communicated to all stakeholders involved in the child's treatment plan. CBT/parent-training booster sessions should be scheduled with the helping professional to reinforce continuation of adaptive responses to previously feared separations. As with pharmacological treatment, psychosocial booster sessions may be scheduled more frequently at first (i.e., weekly or every other week), but should slowly taper off as the child continues to respond or progress positively. This decision will also require critical consideration of the child's age, previous level of impairment, and response to past psychosocial treatments (Perwien & Bernstein, 2004).

CONCLUSION

Temporary discomfort when separating from a parent is developmentally appropriate for most children. With time and warm parenting, this fear will eventually subside. However, when a child becomes persistently distressed about having to separate from his or her caregiver, this may be cause for concern. Although no singular cause of separation anxiety has been identified, researchers suggest that this disorder may result from an interaction among individual biological, psychological, and social factors. In turn, a multi-faceted etiological perspective on separation anxiety disorder leads to various evidence-based approaches to intervention. In this review, CBT, parent training, and adjunctive psychopharmaoclogical treatment were reviewed and outlined in detail. Across all three of these treatments, it is essential to work collaboratively and communicate effectively with all stakeholders involved. Clear articulation of current and expected levels of target behaviors is crucial. Progress monitoring for treatment modification, continuation, and termination are necessary requirements of each of these step-by-step approaches.

SELECT BIBLIOGRAPHY

Boston Children's Hospital. (2016). *Separation anxiety disorder in children*. Retrieved from http://www.childrenshospital.org/health-topics/conditions/separation-anxiety-disorder
This is an informative website tailored for parents with children with separation anxiety disorder. Parents will find in-depth descriptions about anxiety in general, as well as sample questions to discuss with the child's primary doctor, treatment options, and links to resources for more information.

Grills-Taquechel, A. E., & Ollendick, T. H. (2013). *Phobic and anxiety disorders in children and adolescents*. Cambridge, MA: Hogrefe.
This brief guide to childhood and adolescent anxiety disorders may be helpful for therapists, parents, or other interested readers. The book provides parent-friendly descriptions of each disorder, along with considerations regarding etiology, diagnosis, and treatment.

Massachusetts General Hospital, School Psychiatry Program and MADI Resource Center. (2010). *Separation anxiety disorder*. Retrieved from www2.massgeneral.org/schoolpsychiatry/info_separationanxiety.asp
This is a website for parents, professionals, and teachers devoted to providing resources and support to parents of children diagnosed with separation anxiety disorder. It includes assessment and treatment resources for use by professionals and teachers.

Rapee, R., Wignall, A., Spence, S., Cobham, V., & Lyneham, H. (2008). *Helping your anxious child: A step-by-step guide for parents*. Oakland, CA: New Harbinger.
Intended for parents and written by experts in childhood anxiety, this book is an excellent resource for parents who wish to understand typical thoughts processes for children with anxiety. The authors provide parents with a systematic process for reducing their child's anxious thoughts or behaviors.

REFERENCES

American Psychiatric Association (APA). (2013). *Diagnostic and statistical manual of mental disorders* (5th ed.) Arlington, VA: American Psychiatric Publishing.

Angelosante, A. G., Ostrowski, M. A., & Chizkov, R. R. (2013). Separation anxiety disorder. In R. A. Vasa & A. K. Roy (Eds.), *Pediatric anxiety disorders: A clinical guide* (pp. 119–142). New York, NY: Springer Publishing Company.

Appelboom-Geerts, K. C. (2008). Child versus family cognitive-behavior therapy in clinically anxious youth: An efficacy and partial effectiveness study. *Journal of the American Academy of Child & Adolescent Psychiatry, 47*, 1384–1394.

Barrett, P. M., Lowry-Webster, H., & Turner, C. (2000). *FRIENDS program for children: Group leaders manual*. Brisbane, QLD: Australian Academic Press.

Bodden, D. H., Bögels, S. M., Nauta, M. H., De Haan, E., Ringrose, J., Appelboom, C.,...Shahidullah, J. D. (2014). Best practices in assessing the effects of psychotropic medications on student performance. In P. L. Harrison & A. Thomas (Eds.), *Best practices in school psychology: Systems-level services* (pp. 361–374). Bethesda, MD: National Association of School Psychologists.

Choate, M. L., Pincus, D. B., Eyberg, S. M., & Barlow, D. H. (2006). Parent–child interaction therapy for treatment of separation anxiety disorder in young children: A pilot study. *Cognitive and Behavioral Practice, 12*, 126–135. doi:10.1016/S1077-7229(05)80047-1

Comer, J. S., Puliafico, A. C., Aschenbrand, S. G., McKnight, K., Robin, J. A., Goldfine, M. E., & Albano, A. M. (2012). A pilot feasibility evaluation of the CALM Program for anxiety disorders in early childhood. *Journal of Anxiety Disorders, 26*, 40–49. doi:10.1016/j.janxdis.2011.08.011

Drake, K. L., & Ginsburg, G. S. (2012). Family factors in the development, treatment, and prevention of childhood anxiety disorders. *Clinical Child and Family Psychology Review, 15,* 144–162. doi:10.1007/s10567–011-0109–0

Eisen, A. R., Raleigh, H., & Neuhoff, C. C. (2008). The unique impact of parent training for separation anxiety disorder in children. *Behavior Therapy, 39,* 195–206. doi:10.1016/j.beth.2007.07.004

Eisen, A. R., Sussman, J. M., Schmidt, T., Mason, L., Hausler, L. A., & Hashim, R. (2011). Separation anxiety disorder. In D. McKay & E. A. Storch (Eds.), *Handbook of child and adolescent anxiety disorders* (pp. 245–259). New York, NY: Springer Publishing Company.

Eyberg, S. M. (1988). Parent–child interaction therapy: Integration of traditional and behavior concerns. *Child and Family Behavior Therapy, 10,* 33–46.

Figueroa, A., Soutullo, C., Ono, Y., & Saito, K. (2012). Separation anxiety. In J. M. Rey (Ed.), *IACAPAP e-textbook of child and adolescent mental health* (F.2). Geneva, Switzerland: International Association for Child and Adolescent Psychiatry and Allied Professions.

Kendall, P. C. (1990). *Coping cat workbook.* Ardmore, PA: Workbook Publishing.

Kendall, P. C. (1994). Treating anxiety disorders in children: Results of a randomized clinical trial. *Journal of Consulting and Clinical Psychology, 62,* 100–110. doi:10.1037/0022–006X.62.1.100

Kendall, P. C., Safford, S., Flannery-Schroeder, E., & Webb, A. (2004). Child anxiety treatment: Outcomes in adolescence and impact on substance use and depression at 7.4-year follow-up. *Journal of Consulting and Clinical Psychology, 72,* 276. doi:10.1037/0022–006X.72.2.276

March, J. S. (2013). *Multidimensional anxiety scale for children* (2nd ed.). North Tonawanda, NY: Multi-Health Systems Inc.

Mohatt, J., Bennett, S. M., & Walkup, J. T. (2014). Treatment of separation, generalized, and social anxiety disorders in youth. *American Journal of Psychiatry, 171,* 741–748. doi:10.1176/appi.ajp.2014.13101337

Nauta, M. H., & Emmelkamp, P. M. G. (2012). *Separation anxiety disorder. Handbook of evidence-based practice in clinical psychology.* New York, NY: Wiley.

Perwien, A. R., & Bernstein, G. A. (2004). *Separation anxiety disorder.* New York, NY: Oxford University Press.

Pincus, D. B., Eyberg, S. M., & Choate, M. L. (2005). Adapting parent–child interaction therapy for young children with separation anxiety disorder. *Education and Treatment of Children, 28,* 163–181. doi:10.1016/j.chc.2012.05.005

Pincus, D. B., Santucci, L. C., Ehrenreich, J. T., & Eyberg, S. M. (2008). The implementation of modified parent–child interaction therapy for youth with separation anxiety disorder. *Cognitive and Behavioral Practice, 15,* 118–125. doi:10.1016/j.cbpra.2007.08.002

Puliafico, A. C., Comer, J. S., & Albano, A. M. (2008). *Coaching approach behavior and leading by modeling: The CALM Program for anxious preschoolers.* New York, NY: Columbia University.

Reinblatt, S. P., & Riddle, M. A. (2007). The pharmacological management of childhood anxiety disorders: A review. *Psychopharmacology, 191,* 67–86. doi:10.1007/s00213–006-0644–4

Santucci, L. C., Ehrenreich, J. T., Trosper, S. E., Bennett, S. M., & Pincus, D. B. (2009). Development and preliminary evaluation of a one-week summer treatment program for separation anxiety disorder. *Cognitive and Behavioral Practice, 16,* 317–331. doi:10.1016/j.cbpra.2008.12.005

Santucci, L. C., & Ehrenreich-May, J. (2013). A randomized controlled trial of the child anxiety multi-day program (CAMP) for separation anxiety disorder. *Child Psychiatry and Human Development, 44,* 439–451. doi:10.1007/s10578–012-0338–6

Schneider, S., Blatter-Meunier, J., Herren, C., Adornetto, C., In Albon, T., & Lavallee, K. (2011). Disorder-specific cognitive-behavior therapy for separation anxiety disorder in young children: A randomized waiting-list-controlled trial. *Psychotherapy and Psychosomatics, 80,* 206–215. doi:10.1159/000323444

Schneider, S., Blatter-Meunier, J., Herren, C., In Albon, T., Adornetto, C., Meyer, A., & Lavallee, K. L. (2013). The efficacy of a family-based cognitive-behavior treatment for separation anxiety disorder in children aged 8–13: A randomized comparison with a general anxiety program. *Journal of Consulting and Clinical Psychology, 81,* 932–940. doi:10.1037/a0032678

Segool, N. K., & Carlson, J. S. (2008). Efficacy of cognitive-behavior and pharmacological treatments for children with social anxiety. *Depression and Anxiety, 25,* 620–631. doi:10.1002/da.20410

Seligman, L. D., & Ollendick, T. H. (2011). Cognitive behavior therapy for anxiety disorders in youth. *Child and Adolescent Psychiatric Clinics of North America, 20*, 217–238. doi:10.1016/j.chc.2011.01.003

Shear, K., Jin, R., Ruscio, A., Walters, E., & Kessler, R. (2006). Prevalence and correlates of estimated DSM-IV child and adult separation anxiety disorder in the National Comorbidity Survey Replication. *American Journal of Psychiatry, 163*, 1074–1083.

Shortt, A. L., Barrett, P. M., & Fox, T. L. (2001). Evaluating the FRIENDS program: A cognitive-behavior group treatment for anxious children and their parents. *Journal of Clinical Child Psychology, 30*, 525–535. doi:10.1207/S15374424JCCP3004_09

U.S. Department of Health and Human Services. (1999). *Mental health: A report of the surgeon general.* Washington, DC: National Institute of Mental Health. Retrieved from http://profiles.nlm.nih.gov/ps/access/NNBBHS.pdf

Walkup, J. T., Albano, A. M., Piacentini, J., Birmaher, B., Compton, S. N., Sherrill, J. T.,...Kendall, P. C. (2008). Cognitive behavior therapy, sertraline, or a combination in childhood anxiety. *New England Journal of Medicine, 359*, 2753–2766. doi:10.1056/NEJMoa0804633

Evidence-Based Interventions for Specific Phobias in Children and Adolescents

Maria G. Fraire, Thorhildur Halldorsdottir, and Thomas H. Ollendick

OVERVIEW

A specific phobia is characterized by an excessive and persistent fear of a specific object (e.g., dogs, spiders, costume characters) or situation (e.g., being alone in the dark, heights, thunderstorms) that almost always provokes a negative avoidant response. According to the fifth edition of the *Diagnostic and Statistical Manual of Mental Disorders* (American Psychiatric Association [APA], 2013), specific phobias are categorized into five subtypes: animal, natural environment, situational, blood–injection–injury, and other type. The phobic object or situation is actively avoided and/or elicits intense distress for the child or adolescent. Although some fear may be developmentally (e.g., fear of strangers as an infant) or situationally appropriate (e.g., fear of petting a strange animal without knowing it is safe), a specific phobia elicits a response that is out of proportion to the actual danger posed by the phobic object or situation. Fear may be manifested in children by yelling, crying, tantrums, freezing, or clinging to caretakers (APA, 2013); in adolescents, it may present in the form of a panic attack (e.g., rapid breathing, sweating, heightened heart rate, shaking, and fear of losing control; Essau, Conradt, & Petermann, 2000).

A diagnosis of specific phobia requires significant interference in the child's daily functioning while simultaneously negatively affecting the family. A child with a specific phobia may miss out on sleepovers, play-dates, sports, and school functions, whereas families of children with specific phobias may find themselves avoiding vacations, parks, carnivals, parades, and parties. For example, a child with a fear of dogs may avoid parks and other outdoor areas, avoid spending time with friends who have dogs, and parents of the child may have to call ahead if they are visiting to either ensure there are no dogs or request the dogs be kept away from the child during the visit. A child with a specific phobia of thunderstorms may frequently check the weather, become agitated and distracted at school if a storm commences, and may refuse to leave the house during a storm. These behaviors may result in a ripple effect and adversely affect the child's familial and social relationships. For example, a child may begin turning down birthday invitations if he or she has a specific phobia of dogs and knows there will be a dog at the party. Similarly, an adolescent may become distracted while taking a test, because he or she sees clouds outside the window and worry a storm is coming. Finally, a family may not be able to take a trip to an amusement park because their child is afraid of costume characters. Notably, this disorder significantly impacts a child's academic, behavioral, and social and emotional functioning, results in extreme fear and anxiety and avoidance of the phobic stimulus, and an overall lower quality of life.

Approximately 5% of children and 16% of adolescents are diagnosed as having a specific phobia, with females having a greater likelihood of being affected (APA, 2013). Treatment of specific phobias in children is particularly important because phobias may persist over the course of a lifetime (Öst, 1997), and may result in other disorders such as anxiety, mood, and substance-use problems (Kendall, Safford, Flannery-Schroeder, & Webb, 2004). It is clear that specific phobias have the potential to affect individuals throughout their entire lives.

Comorbidity rates between specific phobias and other disorders are lower in community samples than in clinical samples (Ollendick, King, & Muris, 2002). Research has shown that school-aged children and adolescents in community samples with specific phobias are more likely to have a sole diagnosis of specific phobia (i.e., not comorbid with other anxiety or mood disorders). However, youth referred to clinics for treatment are more likely to have other coexisting disorders (e.g., anxiety disorders, depressive disorders, substance abuse). These data indicate the level of severity and impairment children and adolescents experience prior to seeking treatment (Essau et al., 2000; Ollendick et al., 2002).

ETIOLOGY AND FACTORS CONTRIBUTING TO SPECIFIC PHOBIAS IN CHILDREN AND ADOLESCENTS

As with most other forms of child and adolescent psychopathology, multiple pathways can lead to the development of a specific phobia; thus, most researchers support the notion of multiple pathogenic factors contributing to the disorder. Specifically, the acquisition of a specific phobia tends to be the result of the complex interplay between genetic and environmental influences. As such, Ollendick (1979) suggests that phobias are overdetermined.

Heritability is thought to play a modest but significant role in the development of specific phobias, with up to one third of the variance of specific phobias explained by genetic factors (Distel et al., 2008; Hettema et al., 2005). It has been well documented that anxiety disorders, including specific phobias, run in families. For instance, studies have found that first-degree relatives of individuals with a specific

phobia are more likely to also suffer from a specific phobia themselves than relatives of individuals without a specific phobia (Van Houtem et al., 2013). Similarly, children of parents with a specific phobia are also more likely to have the disorder compared to the children of parents without the disorder (Hughes et al., 2009).

Although it is evident that genetic vulnerability plays a role in the etiology of specific phobias, heritability alone does not fully explain the acquisition of specific phobias as many individuals with a family history of anxiety do not go on to develop this disorder. Environmental factors also contribute greatly to the etiology of specific phobias. That is, learning experiences, typically aversive or traumatic experiences, surrounding phobic stimuli can contribute to the acquisition of fear. Studies have found that environmental influences may explain up to 70% of the variance associated with a specific phobia (Hettema et al., 2005). Through classical conditioning, fear of a harmless situation can be acquired if the situation is repeatedly linked with a frightening stimulus (e.g., Eelen & Vervliet, 2006). One of the earliest and most cited illustrations of this was conducted by Watson and Rayner (1920; see Ollendick, Sherman, Muris, & King, 2012, for a current analysis of this seminal case) on a 9-month-old toddler referred to as Little Albert. In brief, Little Albert was initially a curious young boy who did not display any overt signs of fear in the presence of a white rat (neutral stimulus). However, the researchers repeatedly paired the presence of the rat with a loud noise (unconditional stimulus), which subsequently elicited fear (unconditional response) in Little Albert. After several pairings of the stimuli, Little Albert learned to fear (conditional response) the sight of the rat. The fear elicited by the loud noise had become associated with the rat. The study also demonstrated that learned fear can generalize to stimuli that have similar physical qualities. For instance, Little Albert also displayed signs of fear in the presence of a white rabbit and a white mask after the conditioning trials. Generalization of fear is commonly seen in clinical settings. As an example, an individual with a specific phobia of dogs may also develop a fear of cats or other small animals through generalization.

Watson and Rayner's (1920) early findings with this case study have been replicated with different neutral and unconditional stimuli. However, there are some stipulations to classical conditioning in the development of fear. First, avoidance of the phobic stimulus is crucial to prevent the extinction of the fear response (Mowrer, 1960). That is, if a child or an adolescent does not avoid the conditioned stimulus, the association will be weakened. Second, individuals are evolutionarily predisposed to develop a fear of certain type of stimuli more readily than other stimuli (for review, see Coelho & Purkis, 2009). For instance, it is more likely that an individual will acquire a fear of spiders than mushrooms, although some mushrooms are poisonous. Still, the principles of classical conditioning are the foundation for the most effective psychotherapies for treating specific phobias (see later in the chapter for evidence-based interventions).

Although classical conditioning may help explain the development of many specific phobias, not all phobias have a distinct conditioning event associated with their onset (Davey, 1992). There are many cases in which children and adolescents with a diagnosis of a specific phobia have not had any direct contact with the phobic stimulus. In these cases, indirect pathways, such as observational learning and information learning (or threat information transmission), play a significant role in the acquisition of fear. Observational learning refers to learning that occurs vicariously through observing other people's actions toward a stimulus (Rachman, 1978). In addition to the many psychological studies supporting the role of observational learning in the development of specific phobias (e.g., Coelho & Purkis, 2009), functional magnetic resonance imaging (fMRI) studies have found activation in the bilateral amygdala (a neural substrate associated with emotional processing and motivation) during a vicarious experience of social observation (Olsson & Phelps, 2004).

Information learning is another indirect pathway to developing a phobia (Rachman, 1978). This pathway includes hearing that a stimulus or situation may be dangerous or be accompanied by a negative consequence. In one of the many interesting studies on the effect of negative information, children acquired a fear of novel Australian animals after hearing negative information about the species, whereas a decline in fear was observed in youth who received positive information about the animals (Muris & Field, 2010).

Again, it is important to recognize that the acquisition of a specific phobia is a complex process with multiple pathways. Most fears are attributed to more than one cause and oftentimes involve a combination of conditioning, modeling, and information processing (for review, see Coelho & Purkis, 2009; Ollendick, 1979).

EVIDENCE-BASED INTERVENTIONS AND EMPIRICAL SUPPORT FOR SPECIFIC PHOBIAS IN CHILDREN AND ADOLESCENTS

A critical component to effective treatment includes a thorough, evidence-based assessment (Davis & Ollendick, 2005), including the evaluation of subjective fear ratings (e.g., "How afraid of dogs are you?"), cognitions ("What do you think will happen to you?"), behavioral responses ("What do you do?"), and physiological responses ("What happens inside your body when you see or are around the dog?"). Typically, at least one caregiver and the child/adolescent are both involved in the assessment process, with the assessment tailored in a developmentally appropriate way. Ideally, assessment of a specific phobia would include a semi-structured clinical interview (e.g., Anxiety Disorders Interview Schedule; Silverman & Albano, 1996), a functional behavioral analysis (FBA), and a behavioral approach task (Silverman & Ollendick, 2005).

With respect to the assessment process, the clinical interview provides in-depth information regarding the specific phobia and on other internalizing and externalizing disorders that may have implications for the case conceptualization and successful implementation of the treatment (see Fraire & Ollendick, 2013; Halldorsdottir & Ollendick, 2014). FBA is tailored to the child's specific phobia and is composed of questions focused on the specifics of the feared phobic object and/or situation, how the child responds in the presence of the object and/or situation, what the child avoids due to his or her fear, and how parents respond (see Table 22.1 for an example).

A behavioral approach task (Ost, Svensson, Hellström, & Lindwall, 2001) involves exposure to the feared object and/or situation in a controlled environment. The child or the adolescent is given the option to participate (e.g., "Behind this closed door there is a dog on a leash.") and the clinician observes how the child/adolescent is able to handle initial exposure to the phobic stimulus. This information is important because it informs case conceptualization

TABLE 22.1

EXPOSURE IDEAS	
Feared Object/Situation	**Exposure Ideas**
Dogs	• Different breeds, colors, and sizes • Engage in fun activities (e.g., play fetch, do tricks, feed treats) • Walk the dog on a leash • Practice with dog walking toward child
Dark and/or dark/alone	• Hide and seek • Hide glow sticks • Shadow puppets • Child guesses noises and investigates
Costume characters	• Child wears costume • See person put on costume • Have a familiar person put on a costume • Play games with a costumed character (e.g., toss a ball, play with balloons, play hide and seek, go on parade)
Weather	• Watch videos of varying intensity • Use strobe light and wind machine to simulate storms • Science experiments that mimic tornados/water spouts • Study clouds • Find fun games to play in the rain/mud
Heights	• Climbing a ladder • Looking out high windows • Traveling up/down elevators • Carnival rides

and treatment planning (see Ollendick et al., 2009; Ost et al., 2001).

In this chapter, cognitive behavioral therapy (CBT) and one-session treatment (OST), a specific variant of CBT, is discussed in detail, as well as the role parents may play in the treatment process (Ollendick et al., in press). In addition, systematic desensitization, which has historically been used to treat specific phobias in children and adolescents, is commented on briefly.

HOW TO: A GUIDE TO THE IMPLEMENTATION OF INTERVENTIONS IN SPECIFIC PHOBIAS IN CHILDREN AND ADOLESCENTS

CBT: Multiple Sessions (8–12 Hourly Sessions)

CBT focuses on how thoughts, behaviors, and emotions are interrelated and how they are associated with the phobic object or situation. Cognitively,

automatic negative thoughts are identified and modified (e.g., recognizing maladaptive thoughts, challenging and/or replacing negative thoughts). Behaviorally, avoidance and safety behaviors are identified and an exposure hierarchy is developed to gradually expose the child or the adolescent to the feared object and/or situation. An exposure hierarchy is a list of situations ranked from easiest to hardest for the child or the adolescent to engage in, due to their specific phobia. The exposure hierarchy aids the case conceptualization and provides the foundation for the exposure exercises. The combination of cognitive and behavioral components, along with regular homework assignments, results in a reduction in anxiety. For example, a child with a specific phobia of costume characters learns to identify negative automatic thoughts (e.g., "The character will hurt me.") and challenge these thoughts, (e.g., "It's never happened before." and "I have been safe.") and an exposure hierarchy is developed ranging from the child dressing up in his or her own costume to going on parade with a group of costume characters. See Table 22.1 for potential exposure ideas.

Session 1: Assessment and Hierarchy Building.

- Understanding the fear from the child's point of view is critical to developing a treatment plan that includes cognitive coping and the design of a hierarchy for exposures. See Table 22.2 for a list of potential questions.
- The child is integral to building the hierarchy in order to have the child's input and ensure situations on the hierarchy are relevant to the fear. Constructing a hierarchy involves beginning with the easiest situation (including things the child may have been able to do with variable success before) and building toward the most difficult situation the child can imagine. Using a visual thermometer (e.g., the 0–8 scale from the Anxiety Disorders Interview Schedule or a 0–10 scale) will help the child put the feared situations

in an ascending order. See Table 22.3 for a sample hierarchy.

Between-sessions assignment (i.e., homework): Act like a detective and gather more information about aspects of the fear that are not yet a part of the hierarchy or recognized safety behaviors (e.g., track if the child is asking his mom to call a friend to make sure a dog is kept away from the child during a visit), so the safety behavior can be addressed in session.

Session 2: Psychoeducation and Coping Skills.

- Provide education regarding phobias generally and with respect to the feared object or situation specifically (e.g., different facts about dogs, where thunder comes from, why the dark is good), and the treatment approach. In particular, it is important to highlight the relationship between thoughts, feelings, and behaviors. For children and adolescents, it is helpful to explain

TABLE 22.2

FUNCTIONAL BEHAVIORAL ANALYSIS FOR SPECIFIC PHOBIA OF DOGS	
Content Area	**Sample Questions**
Specifics about the feared object	• Does the size/breed/color of the dog matter? • Are there certain features that are especially scary (e.g., teeth, paws, eyes, ears, color)? • Does the energy level of the dog matter? • Does it matter if the dog is on or off a leash? • Does it matter if the child has met the dog before?
Associated thoughts	• What does the child think the dog will do (e.g., bark, bite, chase, attack)? • How often does the child have these thoughts?
Associated child behaviors	• What will the child do if he or she sees a dog (e.g., run away, scream, cry, freeze)? • Are there places the child does not go, because of his or her fear of dogs (e.g., parks, friends' houses)?
Child's physiological response	• How does the child's body feel when he or she sees a dog (e.g., heart race, feel shaky, trouble breathing, muscles tenses)?
Caregiver responses	• How does the caregiver respond when the child is distressed? • Provide reassurance? • Facilitate avoidance? • Encourage bravery?
Child safety behaviors	• Hiding behind parents • Carrying safety objects (e.g., carrying blanket or favorite stuffed toy) • Asking a sibling to go with him everywhere

TABLE 22.3

SAMPLE HIERARCHY FOR BEES	
Easy	1 Looking at a still picture of a bee 2 Listening to audio of bees buzzing 3 Watching short video clips of bees
Moderate	4 Sitting in a room 1 foot from a jar with a bee 5 Placing hand on the jar with a bee 6 Sitting 1 ft away when the lid is taken off the jar 7 Being next to the jar with the lid off
Hard	8 Being in the room with a bee in the corner 9 Being outside in a park near a bush with a bee 10 Being outside in a park near a bush with multiple bees

how often being told, "don't be afraid" has not worked, but we have evidence to support that changing how we *think* (cognitions) and the things we *do* (behaviors) alter the way we *feel* (the cognitive triangle).

- Explain to the child/adolescent that they have control in the exposures. Control is given to the child/adolescent by having them dictate the pace of the exposures and they are involved in coming up with the exposure exercises. It is explained there will not be any surprises and steps of the hierarchy will be moved through gradually.
- Coping skills (i.e., relaxation skills) empower the child if he or she is unexpectedly confronted with the feared situation. It is important to convey to the child or the adolescent (and parents) that coping skills should *not* be used during planned exposures. In order for exposures to be effective, anxiety must be experienced, so the child or the adolescent learns what they fear does not actually happen. This allows for new learning about the feared object and/or situation to occur. However, having a coping skill that the child or the adolescent may use to calm down or regulate themselves emotionally if they are in their feared situation (e.g., a dog suddenly runs up to them in a park) are helpful in treatment and provide a tool which children and adolescents may rely on in the present and future to deal with the phobia.
- *Deep breathing:*
  - Teach the child to take in a deep breath for 5 seconds, in through his or her nose and then blow all the air out through his or her mouth

for 10 seconds. As a general rule of thumb, the child or the adolescent should spend twice as much time expelling air as breathing in. For younger children, telling them to envision blowing up a large balloon can be useful.
- *Lemon squeezes:*
  - Teach the child to squeeze his or her fists tight, holding them for 10 seconds, then releasing. This should be repeated at least three times, or until the child feels he or she has regained some control.
- *Positive thoughts:*
  - Help the child find a phrase he or she likes and feels comfortable with. It is important the child comes up with the phrase without coaching, to increase the likelihood he or she will use it.
    - Examples include:
      - "I can do this."
      - "I am strong."
      - "I got this."
      - "I can handle this."
- *Thought challenging:*
  - Has the event that is the basis of the phobic belief happened before?
  - What are the chances the phobic belief will occur?
  - Thought challenging will be most effective during exposures, but can be practiced when not exposed to the phobic object as well.

Between-sessions assignment (i.e., homework): Coping skills should be practiced each day; it helps the child to have a set time to practice so that coping skills can be incorporated into their regular routine.

Session 3 and Beyond: Begin Gradual Exposures and Continue for the Number of Sessions Required for Any One Child—Usually 8 to 12 Sessions.

- Number of exposure sessions required will vary from child to child. Some children will master their fears more quickly than others and require fewer sessions (e.g., two to four), whereas other children require more sessions (e.g., five to ten).
- Exposures will be most effective if they can be practiced in session (described later in the chapter). This will involve creative thinking and planning to be able to have the objects on hand (e.g., animals, bugs, spiders, costumes) or elicit the situations (e.g., dark rooms, video or sound clips of storms, heights).
- Exposures begin in a slow and gradual way, beginning with the least-feared item on the hierarchy. How quickly a child moves through the hierarchy varies by the child and the situation. Therefore, each hierarchy is tailored to the individual needs of the child or the adolescent. Usually, only one exposure step is repeated throughout the session until the child has a sense of mastery and control over that step. Alternatively, in some instances, multiple steps in the hierarchy may be achieved in one session, depending on how quickly the child begins to master the steps.
- Exposures can occur in multiple ways:
  o Distance: Gradually approaching the feared object
  o Time: Gradually increasing the amount of time in a feared situation
  o Modeling: Observing someone else interact with the feared object
    ■ Participant modeling (hand-over-hand): The therapist physically guiding the child specifically on how to approach an object (e.g., the therapist petting the dog while the child's hand is on the therapist's shoulder and then elbow and then hand)
- Thought challenging occurs throughout the exposure session:
  o Is the event anticipated in the phobic belief actually occurring?
  o What is actually happening in the situation?
  o Is it as bad as the child anticipated?

Between-sessions assignment (i.e., homework): Help the child and parents plan for exposures to be practiced between sessions. It is best to begin practicing at home with a step the child/adolescent has already mastered before moving to a more difficult step.

Final Session: Review Skills, Review Learning That Occurred Over the Course of Treatment, Relapse Prevention.

- The last session should be a review session. This includes reviewing coping skills, the cognitive triangle, and ensuring that the child has an idea of what to do if a new feared situation occurs (relapse prevention). One way to do this is to ask the child how he or she would help a friend through a fear and look for him or her to provide answers about gradual exposure and thought challenging.

One-Session Treatment

Given that the OST (Ollendick et al., 2009; Öst & Ollendick, 2001; Öst et al., 2001) is an intensive CBT intervention, there are many similarities between OST and traditional CBT described earlier. For instance, both include gradual exposures, participant modeling, and eliciting and/or challenging negative cognitions. However, as the name implies, OST occurs in one single session that is designed to be 3 hours in duration and that includes a greater emphasis placed on exposures than in the traditional CBT approach. The length of the session allows exposures to be done in an intensive yet graduated way, while being able to move through multiple phases of a hierarchy in that single session.

- *Functional analysis (45 minutes)*
  o Similar to traditional CBT, the first session focuses on rapport building and conducting a functional analysis. In the functional analysis, information about the child's avoidance and maladaptive cognitions is gathered to devise gradual exposures tailored to the child's fear (see Table 22.1 for helpful questions for the functional analysis).
  o Following the functional analysis, the rationale and structure of treatment are explained to the child or the adolescent and questions regarding the treatment are answered. During

this time, given the child's severe fear and avoidance of the phobic object or situation, it is important that the clinician highlight the gradual nature of the exposures to ensure that the child will remain motivated for treatment and return to the clinic for the 3-hour treatment session. An emphasis should be placed on how the clinician and child will work together during the exposures and the child will never experience more fear than he or she can handle (e.g., "We will work together as a team on overcoming your fear when you come back to the clinic. Although you may experience fear during treatment, we will never break your personal record of being fearful around the phobic object or situation and you will never experience more fear than you can handle.").

o If the caregiver(s) is an active participant throughout the OST, two clinicians are preferable: one child clinician and one parent clinician. In the parent-augmented protocol, the parent clinician also provides the caregiver with psychoeducation on anxiety in addition to gathering information surrounding the child's fear and avoidance of the phobic stimuli. More specifically, the parent learns about the etiology of specific phobias and the *Three Component Model of Specific Phobias* is introduced. That is, anxiety and fear are explained through the interaction of thoughts, physical feelings, and behaviors and parents are taught to break down their child's phobia into these three parts. During the treatment, the model is revisited and parents observe the child clinician target each component. After observing, parents practice themselves targeting each component to help decrease the child's fear of the phobic stimuli.

- *One-session treatment (3 hours)*
  o Approximately 1 week after the functional analysis is conducted, the family returns for the treatment session.
  o Exposures begin in a gradual way. The gradual nature of the treatment is essential and the initial exposure should be carefully devised based on the functional assessment and the child's fear level. As an example, an initial exposure for one child with a fear of dogs may be observing a small dog on a leash from across the room, whereas another child with a more severe phobia may need to begin by looking at photos and videos of dogs (see Table 22.3 for ideas for gradual exposures).

o Psychoeducation and cognitive challenging should occur concurrently with the exposures. Specifically, the child is provided with factual information on the phobic stimuli and assisted in the cognitive challenge of thoughts and beliefs associated with the feared stimulus while gradually being exposed to the phobic stimuli. As an example for a child fearful of the dark, while playing with glow sticks in a dimly lit room, the clinician can educate the child on why it is dark at night and inform him that most burglaries occur during the day when no one is home.

o Participant modeling is a key component in developing graduated exposures. As noted earlier, this involves the child or the adolescent learning a new response to the phobic object or situation through observing a model (typically the clinician) interact with the object or situation and that the feared consequence does not occur. Importantly, participant modeling also involves having the child "participate" in the exposure with the model (i.e., therapist) in some way. For example, a child with a specific phobia of dogs, who believes a dog will bite, not only observes a model interacting with a dog and does not get bitten but the child also places his or her hand on the clinician's shoulder while the clinician pets the dog. When the child's fear level decreases somewhat, he or she is encouraged to gradually come closer to the dog through participant modeling. The next step, for instance, would be the child placing his or her hand on top of the clinician's hand while the clinician pets the dog. Finally, the child is encouraged to pet the dog independently alongside the therapist.

o Clinicians should be creative in the development of exposures and create a game or fun activity out of the exposure whenever possible. As an example, a game for a child who is fearful of costume characters could be playing a board game, "monkey in the middle" or take turns blowing and catching bubbles with a costume character.

○ In the parent-augmented condition (Ollendick et al., in press), as in the standard OST, the child works with a mental health professional in gradual exposures to the phobic stimuli. Meanwhile, the caregiver and parent clinician observe the treatment behind a one-way mirror. As noted earlier, in addition to observing exposures, the caregiver receives coaching in strategies to reinforce appropriate approach behavior and decrease avoidance and distress associated with the phobic object. The caregiver is also assisted in designing exposures for the child after treatment and utilizing a reward system to motivate exposures. In the last hour of the session, the parent joins the child clinician and the child to transfer control of the exposures to the parent by practicing the skills they have observed.

○ Before ending the session, it is important to advise the caregiver that some regression is expected when beginning exposures at home after treatment. Therefore, the caregiver should be encouraged to take "a few steps back" in the exposure hierarchy from where treatment left off to increase the chance of successful exposures. For instance, if the child's final in-session exposure of being fearful of the dark involves mimicking going to sleep in a dark room by himself or herself the initial exposure at home may involve hiding glow sticks in the dark at home or staying in a dark room for a limited amount of time based on the child's fear level prior to expecting the child to successfully go to bed in a dark room at home. This will increase the child's likelihood of succeeding and also minimize the caregiver interpreting the child's fear as oppositionality (Ollendick et al., in press).

• *Follow-up*
○ Following treatment, it may be beneficial for the clinician to contact the caregiver for brief phone consultations once a week for 4 consecutive weeks to determine how the child is doing and advise the family on continued exposures.

Systematic Desensitization (8–12 Sessions)

Systematic desensitization is based on classical conditioning theory. Specifically, a phobic response is thought to be "weakened" through the introduction of an antianxiety response (i.e., relaxation) in the presence of the feared stimulus (Wolpe, 1958). Exposure to the feared object or situation is gradual, so relaxation becomes the new learned response instead of anxiety, and is either imaginal or in vivo, although research suggests that in vivo exposure may be superior to imaginal exposure (Ollendick & King, 1998). For example, a child with a specific phobia of being in the dark alone learns relaxation skills such as diaphragmatic breathing or progressive muscle relaxation (PMR). Once he or she masters the relaxation skills, he or she is gradually exposed to being in the dark alone for increasing intervals of time, while using the relaxation skills to replace the anxiety response. Systematic desensitization occurs over several sessions beginning with the development of a fear hierarchy and relaxation training before moving on to the exposures (e.g., Davison, 1968).

Session 1: Development of a Fear Hierarchy.

• Similar to the CBT and OST, the initial session is focused on developing a fear hierarchy.

Session 2: Relaxation Training.

• The child receives training in deep breathing (see earlier) or PMR. (Ollendick & Cerny, 1981). PMR is typically a clinician-guided relaxation in which the clinician provides instructions to alternate the tensing and relaxing of targeting specific muscle groups of the body one at a time. Systematically all major muscle groups are targeted in the tensing and then relaxing with a duration of about 30 minutes. During PMR, the clinician provides a brief introduction of the task. (E.g., "Close your eyes while we do some relaxation exercises together. We are going to take turns tensing and relaxing different parts of our bodies. While we do this, keep breathing in through your nose slowly and out through your mouth.") Subsequently, the clinician gives detailed instructions on tensing and relaxing different muscle groups. (E.g., "Let's start with our toes and work our way up the body. Think about your toes and your feet. Now squeeze your feet and toes tight while we count to 5. 1, 2, 3, 4, 5 and relax your feet and your toes. Feel your feet relaxing. Now think about your legs. Straighten them and squeeze all the muscles in your legs while we count to 5.") This continues until each large muscle group in the body has been targeted.

Session 3 and Beyond: Counterconditioning, Which May Take 8 to 12 Sessions.

- The child is engaged in the relaxation technique, either deep breathing or PMR.
- When the child is deeply relaxed, gradual exposures (imaginal or in vivo) begin starting with the least feared item on the fear hierarchy. Desensitization is thought to have occurred after meeting the criterion of 15 seconds without any signs of anxiety. Once relaxed and desensitized to the phobic stimuli, the child moves on to the second least feared item on the fear hierarchy. This continues until the child has become desensitized to the most anxiety-provoking item on the fear hierarchy.
- Number of sessions will depend on the child's fear level and how quickly desensitization occurs (e.g., typically 8–12 sessions).

CONCLUSION

This chapter provides an introduction to specific phobias, their etiology, and a brief overview of three evidence-based treatment approaches: CBT, OST as a variant of CBT, and systematic desensitization. Overlapping themes in these treatment approaches include thorough evidence-based assessment, building a fear hierarchy, gradual exposure, cognitive challenges, and homework. Clinical judgment should inform which treatment approach will be the most effective for the child or the adolescent. Factors to consider should include cognitive developmental level (i.e., younger children may benefit from a more behavioral emphasis than cognitive) and family schedule (i.e., whether weekly sessions or a 3-hour intensive is more feasible). Working to overcome fears may enhance the overall quality of life for the child, adolescent, and their families.

SELECT BIBLIOGRAPHY

Ollendick, T. H., King, N. J., & Muris, P. (2002). Fears and phobias in children: Phenomenology, epidemisology, and aetiology. *Child and Adolescent Mental Health*, 7(3), 98–106.
This discusses how genetic influences, temperamental predispositions, parental psychopathology, parenting practices, and individual conditioning histories contribute to the development and maintenance of childhood phobias. It provides an in-depth overview and understanding of phobias, which is important information for a clinician to have when developing case conceptualizations.

Ollendick, T. H., Ost, L. G., Reuterskiöld, L., Costa, N., Cederlund, R., Sirbu, C.,…Jarrett, M. A. (2009). One-session treatment of specific phobias in youth: A randomized clinical trial in the United States and Sweden. *Journal of Consulting and Clinical Psychology*, 77(3), 504–516.
This article explains the development of OST for children/ adolescents and provides empirical support for the treatment via a randomized control trial study. The article provides the reader with additional information regarding OST sessions.

Silverman, W. K., Pina, A. A., & Viswesvaran, C. (2008). Evidence-based psychosocial treatments for phobic and anxiety disorders in children and adolescents. *Journal of Clinical Child and Adolescent Psychology: The Official Journal for the Society of Clinical Child and Adolescent Psychology, American Psychological Association, Division 53*, 37(1), 105–130.
This article provides an overview of empirically supported treatments for youth with anxiety disorders. The article discusses individual and group treatments, as well as the role parents may or may not play in the treatment process.

REFERENCES

American Psychiatric Association (APA). (2013). *Diagnostic and statistical manual of mental disorders* (5th ed.). Washington, DC: American Pyschiatric Association.

Coelho, C. M., & Purkis, H. (2009). The origins of specific phobias: Influential theories and current perspectives. *Review of General Psychology, 13*, 335–348. doi:10.1037/a0017759

Davey, G. C. L. (1992). Classical conditioning and the acquisition of human fears and phobias: A review and synthesis of the literature. *Advances in Behavior Research and Therapy, 14*, 29–66. doi:10.1016/0146–6402(92)90010-L

Davis, T. E., & Ollendick, T. H. (2005). Empirically supported treatments for specific phobia in children: Do efficacious treatments address components of a phobic response? *Clinical Psychology: Science and Practice, 12*, 144–160. doi:10.1093/clipsy.bpi018

Davison, G. C. (1968). Systematic desensitization as a counter-conditioning process. *Journal of Abnormal Psychology, 73*(2), 91–99.

Distel, M. A., Vink, J. M., Willemsen, G., Middeldorp, C. M., Merckelbach, H. L., & Boomsma, D. I. (2008). Heritability of self-reported phobic fear. *Behavior Genetics, 38*(1), 24–33.

Eelen, P., & Vervliet, B. (2006). Fear conditioning and clinical implications: What can we learn from the past? In M. Craske, D. Hermans, & D. Vansteenwegen (Eds.), *Fear and learning: From basic processes to clinical implications* (pp. 17–35). Washington, DC: American Psychological Association.

Essau, C. A., Conradt, J., & Petermann, F. (2000). Frequency, comorbidity, and psychosocial impairment of specific phobia in adolescents. *Journal of Clinical Child Psychology, 29*(2), 221–231.

Fraire, M. G., & Ollendick, T. H. (2013). Anxiety and oppositional defiant disorder: A transdiagnostic conceptualization. *Clinical Psychology Review, 33*(2), 229–240.

Halldorsdottir, T., & Ollendick, T. H. (2014). Comorbid ADHD: Implications for the treatment of anxiety disorders in children and adolescents. *Cognitive and Behavioral Practice, 21*, 310–322. doi:10.1016/j.cbpra.2013.08.003

Hettema, J. M., Prescott, C. A., Myers, J. M., Neale, M. C., & Kendler, K. S. (2005). The structure of genetic and environmental risk factors for anxiety disorders in men and women. *Archives of General Psychiatry, 62*(2), 182–189.

Hughes, A. A., Furr, J. M., Sood, E. D., Barmish, A. J., & Kendall, P. C. (2009). Anxiety, mood, and substance use disorders in parents of children with anxiety disorders. *Child Psychiatry and Human Development, 40*(3), 405–419.

Kendall, P. C., Safford, S., Flannery-Schroeder, E., & Webb, A. (2004). Child anxiety treatment: Outcomes in adolescence and impact on substance use and depression at 7.4-year follow-up. *Journal of Consulting and Clinical Psychology, 72*(2), 276–287.

Mowrer, O. H. (1960). *Learning theory and the symbolic processes*. London: Wiley.

Muris, P., & Field, A. P. (2010). The role of verbal threat information in the development of childhood fear. "Beware the Jabberwock!" *Clinical Child and Family Psychology Review, 13*(2), 129–150.

Ollendick, T. H. (1979). Fear reduction techniques with children. In M. Hersen, R. M. Eisler, & P. M. Miller (Eds.), *Progress in behavior modification* (Vol. 8, pp. 127–168). New York, NY: Academic Press.

Ollendick, T. H., & King, N. J. (1998). Empirically supported treatments for children with phobic and anxiety disorders: Current status. *Journal of Clinical Child Psychology, 27*(2), 157–167.

Ollendick, T. H., King, N. J., & Muris, P. (2002). Fears and phobias in children: Phenomenology, epidemiology, and aetiology. *Child and Adolescent Mental Health, 7*(3), 98–106. doi:10.1111/1475–3588.00019

Ollendick, T. H., Ost, L. G., Reuterskiöld, L., Costa, N., Cederlund, R., Sirbu, C.,... Jarrett, M. A. (2009). One-session treatment of specific phobias in youth: A randomized clinical trial in the United States and Sweden. *Journal of Consulting and Clinical Psychology, 77*(3), 504–516.

Ollendick, T. H., Sherman, T. M., Muris, P., & King, N. J. (2012). Conditioned emotional reactions: Beyond Watson and Rayner's Little Albert. In A. Slater and P. Quinn (Eds.), *Developmental psychology: Revisiting the classic studies* (pp. 24–35). London: Sage.

Olsson, A., & Phelps, E. A. (2004). Learned fear of "unseen" faces after Pavlovian, observational, and instructed fear. *Psychological Science, 15*(12), 822–828.

Öst, L. G. (1997). Rapid treatment of specific phobias. In G. C. L. Davey (Ed.), *Phobias: A handbook of theory, research and treatment* (pp. 227–247). Oxford, England: Wiley.

Öst, L. G., & Ollendick, T. H. (2001). *Manual for the one-session treatment of specific phobias in children and adolescents*. Unpublished manual.

Öst, L. G., Svensson, L., Hellström, K., & Lindwall, R. (2001). One-session treatment of specific phobias in youths: A randomized clinical trial. *Journal of Consulting and Clinical Psychology, 69*(5), 814.

Rachman, S. J. (1978). An anatomy of obsessions. *Behaviour Analysis and Modification, 2*(4), 253–278.

Silverman, W. K., & Albano, A. M. (1996). *Manual for the ADIS-IV-C/P*. New York, NY: Psychological Corporation.

Silverman, W. K., & Ollendick, T. H. (2005). Evidence-based assessment of anxiety and its disorders in children and adolescents. *Journal of Clinical Child and Adolescent Psychology: The Official Journal for the Society of Clinical Child and Adolescent Psychology, American Psychological Association, Division 53, 34*(3), 380–411.

Van Houtem, C. M., Laine, M. L., Boomsma, D. I., Ligthart, L., van Wijk, A. J., & De Jongh, A. (2013). A review and meta-analysis of the heritability of specific phobia subtypes and corresponding fears. *Journal of Anxiety Disorders, 27*(4), 379–388.

Watson, J. B., & Rayner, R. (1920). Conditioned emotional reactions. *Journal of Experimental Psychology, 3*(1), 1–14.

Wolpe, J. (1958). *Psychotherapy by reciprocal inhibition*. Stanford, CA: Stanford University Press.

Evidence-Based Interventions for School Refusal Behavior in Children and Adolescents

Christopher A. Kearney and Kyleigh K. Sheldon

OVERVIEW

School attendance is an important foundational competency of children and adolescents because it is essential for academic achievement, social connectedness, civic learning, work, and work-related skills. Unfortunately, school absenteeism and eventual school dropout are rampant in American schools. The rate of chronic school absenteeism, missing more than 10% of school days in an academic year, is approximately 15% (Balfanz & Byrnes, 2012). Moreover, absenteeism data from the National Center for Education Statistics (2006) reveal that 19% of fourth graders and 20% of eighth graders missed at least 3 days of school in the month that was considered.

School absenteeism refers to physical absence from school, but school refusal behavior refers more broadly to child-motivated refusal to attend school. School refusal behavior includes complete absence from school, chronic tardiness or skipped classes, morning home misbehaviors in an attempt to miss school, and school-based distress that precipitates a child's pleas for release from school or future nonattendance (Kearney & Silverman, 1996). School refusal behavior represents a continuum of school attendance problems that can vary by severity, frequency, intensity, and chronicity.

The prevalence rates of school refusal behavior range from 28% to 34% (Pina, Zerr, Gonzales, & Ortiz, 2009). In addition to school refusal behavior, school withdrawal is a result of parent-motivated school absenteeism, where parents deliberately keep a child home from school. School withdrawal is often evident in cases involving parent psychopathology (e.g., anxiety, depression, and substance use disorder), maltreatment, custody disputes, or dependence on the child for economic, child-care, or other family support (Kearney, 2008a). In contrast to school withdrawal, this chapter focuses on child-motivated school refusal behavior.

School refusal behavior can affect any school-aged child (i.e., 5–17 years), but the highest average rates of absenteeism occur among 10- to 13-year olds, when youth enter middle school and face an overall increase in demands, especially with academic and social challenges (Neild, Balfanz, & Herzog, 2007). School refusal behavior differs little by ethnicity, but school dropout rates tend to be highest for Hispanics (Kaufman, Alt, & Chapman, 2004). Rates of school absenteeism are elevated for students who have disabilities, are English language learners (ELL), and are from lower socioeconomic homes (e.g., those eligible for free/reduced lunch). Males, students in low-income families, children and adolescents who are employed, and youth with 11 to 12 years of education are at greater risk of dropping out of school than other subgroups (National Center for Education Statistics, 2006).

Youth with school refusal behavior evince substantial heterogeneity in behavioral characteristics or symptoms. This population is notably high in internalizing behavioral problems, such as general and social anxiety, fear, worry, depression, self-consciousness, fatigue, and somatic complaints (Suveg, Aschenbrand, & Kendall, 2005). In addition to internalizing issues, common externalizing behavioral problems among this group include noncompliance, defiance, running away from school or home, tantrums, and aggression (Dube & Orpinas, 2009). Common comorbid disorders for youth with school refusal behavior include anxiety disorders (especially separation anxiety disorder), depression, and oppositional defiant and conduct disorders (Kearney & Albano, 2004). Furthermore, medical conditions may be associated with school refusal behavior, particularly conditions related to pain (e.g., migraine headaches) or respiratory distress such as asthma (Kearney & Bensaheb, 2006).

ETIOLOGY AND FACTORS CONTRIBUTING TO SCHOOL REFUSAL BEHAVIOR IN CHILDREN AND ADOLESCENTS

Risk factors for school refusal behavior are varied and include a host of child-, parent-, family-, peer-, school-, and community-based factors (see Kearney [2008b] for a full review and citations). Primary child-based risk factors for school refusal behavior include a youth's extensive employment outside of school, previous grade retention, poor health, limited academic proficiency, pregnancy, trauma, and underdeveloped social and academic skills; these factors are in addition to the psychopathology and medical problems discussed previously. Key parent-based risk factors for child school refusal behavior include low expectations of school performance or attendance, overly permissive or authoritarian parenting styles, poor communication with school officials, lack of involvement and supervision, and psychopathology such as substance use disorder.

Family-based risk factors for child school refusal behavior include interpersonal dynamics such as enmeshment, isolation, and conflict; homelessness and poverty; ethnic differences from school personnel; and stressful family situations or transitions, such as divorce, illness, or unemployment. With respect to peers, risk factors for child school refusal include proximity to deviant peers, limited participation in extracurricular activities, bullying or other forms of victimization, and support for alluring activities outside of school, such as substance use.

School-based risk factors for school refusal behavior include poor school climate (including poor student–teacher relationships); violence; teacher absences; poor monitoring of attendance; inflexible curricula not tailored to student academic needs; inadequate responsiveness to diversity issues; and inconsistent, minimal, or highly punitive methods to address absenteeism (e.g., immediate referral to the juvenile justice system). Many school districts employ suspension or expulsion to address school attendance problems, but these methods paradoxically lead to greater absenteeism and delinquent behavior (Monahan, VanDerhei, Bechtold, & Cauffman, 2014). These "heavy handed" methods tend to disengage a child from school, including its beneficial services. Community-based risk factors for school refusal behavior include economic factors (e.g., plentiful jobs not needing a high school diploma), lack of transportation and social and educational support services, and disorganized or unsafe neighborhoods.

The etiology of school refusal behavior also includes variables that maintain the behavior over time. Kearney and Silverman (1996) described various functions of school refusal behavior based on negative and/or positive reinforcement of proximal behaviors. In this model, many youth continue to refuse attending school to (a) avoid school-based stimuli that provoke a general sense of negative affectivity (anxiety and depression), (b) escape aversive social and/or evaluative situations at school (e.g., physical education class), (c) seek attention from significant others, such as parents, and/or (d) pursue tangible reinforcers outside of school, such as time with friends. The initial two functions refer to school refusal behavior maintained by negative reinforcement, or a desire to reduce distress associated with school by not attending (i.e., bullying). The latter two functions refer to school refusal behavior maintained by positive reinforcement, or a desire to pursue more alluring activities outside of school. Assessment and treatment of school refusal behavior often include a consideration of the forms and functions of the behavior as well as the contextual risk factors discussed earlier (Kearney & Albano, 2007).

EVIDENCE-BASED INTERVENTIONS AND EMPIRICAL SUPPORT FOR SCHOOL REFUSAL BEHAVIOR IN CHILDREN AND ADOLESCENTS

Interventions for school refusal behavior can be arranged along a multitiered system similar to a Response to Intervention (RtI) model (Clark & Alvarez, 2010). RtI involves problem-solving-based interventions that focus on prevention (Tier 1), early intervention for emerging cases (Tier 2), and intense intervention for severe cases (Tier 3). In addition, given the severity of the psychopathological, familial, legal, academic, and other problems associated with the school refusal population, interventions are designed for very severe and chronic cases of school absenteeism, which may represent a de facto Tier 4 strategy. Evidence-based interventions for each of the RtI tiers are discussed as follows.

Tier 1

Tier 1 strategies have been designed specifically for school absenteeism and related causal issues (e.g., bullying and school safety) that boost school attendance. The universal strategies that Tier 1 provides are school-wide or district-wide and are directed toward all students with continuous progress monitoring. One Tier 1 strategy that is relevant to school absenteeism includes programs to enhance school climate, such as Positive Behavioral Interventions and Support (PBIS). PBIS promotes clear behavioral expectations for all students, rewards and skill development for prosocial behaviors that are monitored and reinforced on consistent basis, consistent progress monitoring of disciplinary data, and evidence-based academic and behavioral interventions (Bradshaw, Koth, Thornton, & Leaf, 2009). Such a program could be extended to school attendance by increasing parental and student awareness of absenteeism policies (e.g., via newsletters and e-mail), monitoring patterns in attendance data, rewarding attendance school-wide, and providing nuanced responses to different forms of absenteeism (Kearney & Graczyk, 2014).

A second Tier 1 strategy designed to reduce absenteeism rates includes safety-oriented approaches to reduce violence and bullying, health-based approaches to minimize illness and boost medical care and specialized educational services, school-based mental health services, and social and emotional learning programs. Programs that include parental involvement, an essential factor in school attendance, can include bridging language and cultural differences between parents and school personnel by using interpreters or introducing cultural diversity curricula into the school (Garcia-Gracia, 2008). School readiness and orientation programs and educating school faculty and staff about early warning signs of school refusal behavior are helpful as well. Finally, task forces may be developed to review attendance and suspension policies, develop more flexible responses to different forms of absenteeism, and coordinate with community agencies to streamline educational and social services (Bye, Alvarez, Haynes, & Sweigart, 2010).

Tier 2

Tier 2 strategies are intended to address emerging cases of school refusal behavior (e.g., initial absences, skipped classes, tardiness, morning misbehaviors to avoid school, and substantial distress about school). Cognitive behavioral interventions designed for Tier 2 cases are generally effective (Pina et al., 2009). Treatment components include gradual reintroduction to school, cognitive restructuring, anxiety management techniques to reduce physical symptoms, parent-based contingency management, and consultation with school personnel. Online interventions to help students manage anxiety symptoms have been designed and show promising outcomes (Heyne, Sauter, Ollendick, Van Widenfelt, & Westenberg, 2014).

Kearney and Albano (2007) outlined a prescriptive treatment model for school refusal behavior based on the primary function or reason that a particular child refuses school. For youth refusing school to avoid school-based stimuli that trigger negative affectivity (i.e., symptoms of anxiety and depression), treatment primarily includes somatic management exercises (e.g., relaxation training and breathing exercises) and exposure-based practices that gradually reintroduce a child to school for 1 hour or class at a time. For youth refusing school to escape aversive social and/or evaluative situations, treatment is similar to the first function but also includes cognitive restructuring to modify unrealistic thoughts in these situations.

For youth who refuse school for attention, parent-based treatment includes modifying parental commands toward greater clarity and brevity. A command such as "Get ready for school," for example, could be modified to "Pick up your backpack." Other tactics include developing regular but flexible morning routines (and daytime and evening routines as necessary), ignoring minor inappropriate behaviors, assigning incentives and disincentives for attendance and absenteeism, and reducing excessive reassurance-seeking behavior. For youth who refuse school for tangible rewards outside of school (e.g., time with friends), family-based treatment includes contingency contracting to establish incentives for attendance, family communication and problem-solving training, peer refusal skills training to decline offers to miss school, and escorts to school and class as necessary (Kearney, 2008c). In addition, pairing a student with a positive student role model and providing the child with a teacher mentor can be beneficial in increasing the student's school attendance (Dubois, Portillo, Rhodes, Silverthorn, & Valentine, 2011; White & Kelly, 2010).

Tier 3

Tier 3 strategies are designed to address severe and chronic cases of school refusal behavior that have extended beyond a legal limit for truancy (e.g., 10 absences in a 15-week period). Tier 3 strategies include an expansion of Tier 2 strategies such as extended family or marital therapy, psychoeducational assessment with individualized educational plans, and modified academic schedules. Parent or youth psychopathology (e.g., substance use and depression) is often more serious at this level as well and must be addressed. Tier 3 cases also contain legal and financial ramifications for parents, such as having to go to court.

Tier 3 strategies often include alternative educational programs to allow students to accrue academic credit at a modified pace or in a setting tailored to their academic and behavioral needs. Alternative educational programs include segregated learning facilities with close supervision, apprenticeships in vocational or technical trades,

or career academies that teach skills relevant to a local community, such as tourism (Detgen & Alfeld, 2011). Alternative schooling methods can apply and include hybrid home-based instruction with in-school work, extended class time, evening or part-time classes, summer coursework, and other nontraditional options (Dupper, 2008).

Beyond Tier 3

Many school-based and mental health professionals are faced with cases of absenteeism that have lasted for many years and that involve severe levels of anxiety, depression, externalizing behavioral problems, and/or substance use, among other issues. These cases usually involve substantial family conflict and little contact with school officials. Intervention at this level involves several months of sustained coordination across educational and social service agencies and may include in-home visits, inpatient or other hospital settings with academic tutoring, intense family therapy, and medication as necessary (see, e.g., the Adolescent Treatment and Learning Alternative Services [ATLAS] program in Markham, Ontario, Canada: www.msh.on.ca/node/1166). Finally, treatment must include realistic end-state goals, such as partial attendance that may not necessarily include full reintegration into a regular classroom setting or on-time graduation.

HOW TO: A GUIDE TO THE IMPLEMENTATION OF INTERVENTIONS FOR SCHOOL REFUSAL BEHAVIOR IN CHILDREN AND ADOLESCENTS

This section of the chapter contains a step-by-step process for several evidence-based interventions that address school refusal behavior in youth, including (a) child-based therapy that focuses on anxiety management, (b) parent- and family-based therapy that focuses on contingency management, and (c) a broader approach that incorporates school personnel and other professionals.

Anxiety Management

Anxiety management protocols for school refusal behavior have been designed and tested for youth of various ages. Integral components were described previously and are presented here in an annotated format. The goal of this approach is to alleviate anxiety-based somatic symptoms, modify troublesome cognitions related to school attendance (especially social and/or evaluative situations), and help children reintegrate gradually into their schools.

Initial Stages

- Psychoeducation is the first part of treatment, explaining to both the child and parents about school refusal behavior, the related aspects of anxiety, particularly anxiety related to overall school absenteeism and anxiety related to the child's specific issues. A discussion should also include a conversation regarding the physical, cognitive, and behavioral components of anxiety. A common trajectory in children with school refusal behavior begins with somatic symptoms early in the morning (e.g., upset stomach, jitteriness, and increased heart rate), followed by invasive thoughts about not wanting to attend school, fears of aversive situations at school (e.g., social embarrassment), and avoidance wishes to stay home. These negative thoughts lead to avoidant behaviors, such as asking parents to be allowed to stay home.
- Outline the rationale to parents and children for the therapy process following psychoeducation. Examples of related topics include somatic management techniques for physical anxiety symptoms, cognitive restructuring for anxiety-based thoughts, and exposure-based practices for school avoidance. In addition, therapists must decide on the pace of the therapeutic process and how slowly or quickly the child can be reintegrated into his or her school (in collaboration with school officials).
- Consult with school personnel about procedures that can be put in place to facilitate the child's reintegration into the school. Such procedures may include increased supervision by school officials, initial part-time schedule, academic work sent home for the child to complete, regular parent–school official communication, tutoring or other assistance for make-up work, and peer and nursing support.

Initial Intervention

- Begin the formal therapy process by instructing the child in relaxation and breathing exercises.

Relaxation training can come in many forms but often includes tension-release muscle exercises that focus on a progressive relaxation of various body parts (e.g., stomach, face, jaw, shoulders, hands, arms, and legs). Breathing retraining can focus on deep diaphragmatic breathing that emphasizes inhaling slowly and fully through the nose and exhaling slowly through the mouth. Mental imagery, such as picturing a tire or a balloon inflating and deflating may be useful for younger children. The child should be encouraged to practice these exercises daily and especially during times of increased anxiety.

- If the child is older or has well-developed intellectual and verbal development, cognitive restructuring may be used in conjunction with somatic control exercises to help modify unrealistic thoughts that interfere with school attendance. Cognitive restructuring focuses on altering common distortions, such as personalization, mindreading, and catastrophization. Cognitive restructuring can include dispute handles (e.g., "Am I 100% sure this will happen?") to help youth challenge unrealistic and anxiety-provoking thoughts and substitute them with more realistic thoughts. A child who enters a classroom assuming that others are snickering at him or her may challenge this thought to include alternative explanations for the perception.

Later Intervention

- Exposure-based practice can follow to help children gradually reintegrate into school. A rule of thumb is to increase attendance 1 hour or one class period per week at a minimum, though a more accelerated pace can be attempted in more urgent cases involving immediate risk of academic failure or court referral. A common schedule is to have the child attend school for 1 hour or one class in the morning as school starts and then leave for home to complete academic work during the remaining school hours. Exposure-based practice occurs in conjunction with the somatic control exercises and cognitive restructuring processes so that youth can manage symptoms and lessen fear of negative consequences for attendance. Exposure-based practice can begin as well in the afternoon, at lunchtime, for a favorite class, or in a school area such as the library that does not yet involve classroom attendance.

- Several weeks may be needed to reintegrate the child into school, with attempts made to ensure that academic progress is maintained and that the child is fully integrated with peers. Follow-up contact by a clinician should be conducted regularly for 4 weeks on full reintegration to school to assess for anxiety and somatic symptoms, continuation of effective therapy techniques, and attendance.

Contingency Management

Therapy for school refusal behavior can also involve contingency management procedures. Many youth refuse school for attention from significant others or to pursue tangible rewards outside of school. Treatment in these cases focuses primarily on the parents or the family in general (defined by the parents and the child refusing school). Effective therapy differs depending on the age of the child. Elementary school-aged children benefit from therapy that focuses predominantly on the parents, but middle and high school students benefit more than younger students from inclusion in the therapeutic process. The goal of this approach is to enhance parental oversight and control, increase student incentives for school attendance, and minimize incentives for absences.

First Stages

- Therapists must outline the treatment components for the parents and/or family members and decide on the pace of the child's reintegration to school. Intervention must be tailored to the needs of the child and his or her family. Therapists must also provide a rationale for the therapeutic process to the parents and youth, and the attention-based or tangible incentives designed by the parents. Therapists must consult with school personnel as necessary to coordinate timelines, schedules, academic work, and credit accumulation.
- Therapists should help parents establish a morning routine for the child that includes a regularly scheduled time to rise, eat breakfast, dress, wash, and finish other school preparation behaviors. Defining timelines needed for each task should

include some flexibility (e.g., if a task typically takes 10 minutes, assign 15–20 minutes to the activity). Arrange the morning routine so that, as the child completes required tasks, time is available before departure for a rewarding event (e.g., watching television and reading).

Beginning Intervention

- Work with parents to modify instructions given to their child (especially during the morning routine), focusing on brevity and clarity and minimizing lecturing, criticizing, negotiating, and bribing. A command such as "Get ready for school," for example, could be reformulated into smaller and more frequent commands such as "Put your materials in your backpack" or "Finish brushing your teeth in 5 minutes."
- Parents need to ignore (i.e., extinguish) or downplay minor child complaints or noncompliant behavior; in particular, requests to avoid school, minor somatic complaints, excessive reassurance-seeking behavior, and dawdling. Finally, parents should conduct all farewell affection at home and not at the point of separation at school. Specifically, parents should say "goodbye" at the bus stop, and if parents drive their children to school, they should separate from them at the entryway of the school building; that is, parents should not be allowed to enter the school building. School personnel may call the parents in an hour or so to let them know how their child is doing.
- For younger children whose refusal to attend school may be attention based, it is important to develop rewards for school attendance that include social reinforcers (e.g., special time with parents or other family members). Conversely, school absenteeism or intense morning misbehaviors must have consequences associated with them, such as requiring an early bedtime or completion of solitary chores. It is important to recognize that rewards and consequences must be delivered consistently for interventions to work.

Later Intervention

- Pursue a gradual school reintegration schedule for younger children that may introduce one additional hour or class per week. Consult with school officials to develop a plan so that the child does not leave the school campus prematurely to go home (e.g., extra supervision by school officials).

- For adolescents, a contingency contracting approach can enhance family problem-solving and communication skills and increase tangible but appropriate incentives for school attendance and disincentives for school absenteeism. Initial contracts may involve school preparation behaviors or academic work at home but can later include attendance as the target behavior.

- Work with adolescents and parents to design attendance contracts that are at least 1 week in length and specify incentives and disincentives. Emphasize contracts to which all parties will agree and be willing to implement. An example might include a contract that requires full-time school attendance for the week in exchange for time with friends on the weekend (and, conversely, loss of social time if there are any absences or tardiness). Adolescents may also earn the opportunity to conduct paid chores based on school attendance.

- Contracts are useful but can deteriorate if a youth does not fulfill attendance obligations because peers are encouraging the student to miss school. Peer refusal skills training are useful in helping youth decline offers to miss school in socially acceptable ways. A student may decline an offer to miss school so that extended time with friends is allowed on the weekend. Consult with school personnel about changes in class schedules to minimize risk for early departure from campus. Escorting youth to school as well as from each class may enhance the likelihood of attendance and, thus, contract rewards.

- Special arrangements may be necessary in chronic cases of school refusal behavior, such as part-time credit accrual, adjunct additional psychopathology, family transitions such as divorce, and assessment and intervention for learning-based problems.

Tier 3

Many cases of school absenteeism are severe and chronic, perhaps lasting several years, placing the child and/or adolescent at especially high risk for school dropout. These cases may involve lack of parental involvement, associated psychopathology (e.g., substance use), contextual factors (see the previous discussion), extended absenteeism, and extensive family conflict. Intervention for these cases is typically multifaceted and innovative, with an eye toward realistic goals that may not include full reintegration into a regular classroom setting. The general goal of this approach is to enhance the student's functioning to the point that some attendance and course credit accrual is possible, thereby increasing the probability the student will graduate from school.

- Explore alternative academic settings that focus on part-time and/or supervised attendance as well as academic work. Consult with school personnel about options for vocational or technical skills training, part-time instruction combined with home-based study, or career academies. Explore options that are suitable for school officials, parents, and the child or adolescent, and establish a timeline for school attendance and course credit accrual.

- Assess and address obstacles to regular school attendance that include transportation difficulties, mistrust of school officials, ethnic and language differences, deviant peer involvement, school-based threats, and medical problems.

- Explore an expansion of Tier 2 strategies, particularly mental health strategies designed to address severe child or parental psychopathology, substance use, disruptive behavioral disorders, undiagnosed learning disorders, trauma-based events, suicidality, family dynamics and parenting skills and other issues that often must be addressed before school attendance is considered.

- Pursue inpatient and related facilities designed to specifically address severe psychopathology and attendance issues. Such facilities generally emphasize home visits, independent but supervised coursework, after-school activities with peers, cognitive behavioral and family therapy, community activities, and individualized instruction.

- Use social media and online resources (e.g., Skype) to help connect families, school officials, therapists, and other important figures. Relatedly, employ strategies to increase parental involvement in their child's education, including school-based events that encourage parental participation and attendance (Hornby, 2011).

- Discover ways to integrate family needs so meetings with multiple professionals occur in one setting to reduce parental concerns of stigma, transportation, and so on. Integrating such professionals as probation officers, therapists, social workers, housing and unemployment officials, and guidance counselors and school psychologists, among others, will help parents greatly.

- Employ legal strategies such as referral to a truancy court or juvenile detention agency when appropriate and when such a referral is likely to result in a greater probability of success. Pursue implementing a truancy court and academic remediation plan in conjunction with school personnel to engage school personnel and increase parental involvement, with an eye toward school-based sanctions that include reintegration.

- Pursue multisystemic therapy that involves home-based strategies to enhance family support and functioning, reduce association with deviant peers, boost social and academic skills, and address mental disorders (Henggeler, Schoenwald, Borduin, Rowland, & Cunningham, 2009).

- Become involved in broader interventions as needed, such as treatment services at a truancy court, multidisciplinary teams to address severe cases of school refusal behavior, and consultation with community agencies to coordinate social services.

- Explore whether district-wide changes in school attendance policies should be revisited to reflect a more nuanced approach to responding to absenteeism as well as establishing multidisciplinary strategies to address extreme cases of school refusal behavior.

CONCLUSION

School refusal behavior is a complex but common problem that requires a combination of interventions at a multitiered level. Mental health and other professionals who work with children and adolescents who exhibit school refusal behaviors must be prepared to address various behavioral symptoms, problematic family dynamics, and other contextual variables to develop innovative and individualized treatment strategies. In addition, school refusal behavior is a problem that demands a multidisciplinary approach among clinicians and school personnel. At a minimum, therapists must work closely in concert with schools to develop a treatment plan that will likely include at least initial part-time attendance, cooperation and assistance from teachers and others, academic remediation, and increased parental involvement. An expansion of Tier 1 strategies must be adopted as well to help prevent so many youth from entering Tier 2 and higher levels of school refusal behavior.

SELECT BIBLIOGRAPHY

Balfanz, R., & Byrnes, V. (2012). *Chronic absenteeism: Summarizing what we know from nationally available data.* Baltimore, MD: Johns Hopkins University.
This reference provides a broad overview of truancy and factors that lead to extensive school absenteeism and dropout.

Bye, L., Alvarez, M. E., Haynes, J., & Sweigart, C. E. (2010). *Truancy prevention and intervention: A practical guide.* New York, NY: Oxford University Press.
This reference provides an overview of Tier 1 strategies to help prevent school absenteeism before it worsens.

Kearney, C. A., & Graczyk, P. A. (2014). A response to intervention model to promote school attendance and decrease school absenteeism. *Child and Youth Care Forum, 43,* 1–25. doi:10.1007/s10566–013–9222–1
This reference provides an overview of an RtI model of school absenteeism with suggestions for interventions at various tiers.

REFERENCES

Balfanz, R., & Byrnes, V. (2012). *Chronic absenteeism: Summarizing what we know from nationally available data.* Baltimore, MD: Johns Hopkins University.

Bradshaw, C. P., Koth, C. W., Thornton, L. A., & Leaf, P. J. (2009). Altering school climate through school-wide Positive Behavioral Interventions and Supports: Findings from a group-randomized effectiveness trial. *Prevention Science, 10*, 100–115. doi:10.1007/s11121–008-0114–9

Bridgeland, J. M., Dilulio, J. J., & Morison, K. B. (2006). *The silent epidemic: Perspectives of high school dropouts.* Seattle, WA: Bill and Melinda Gates Foundation.

Bye, L., Alvarez, M. E., Haynes, J., & Sweigart, C. E. (2010). *Truancy prevention and intervention: A practical guide.* New York, NY: Oxford University Press.

Clark, J. P., & Alvarez, M. E. (Eds.). (2010). *Response to intervention: A guide for school social workers.* New York, NY: Oxford University Press.

Detgen, A., & Alfeld, C. (2011). *Replication of a career academy model: The Georgia Central Educational Center and four replication sites.* Washington, DC: U.S. Department of Education, Institute of Education Sciences, National Center for Education Evaluation and Regional Assistance, Regional Educational Laboratory Southeast.

Dube, S. R., & Orpinas, P. (2009). Understanding excessive school absenteeism as school refusal behavior. *Children and Schools, 31*, 87–95. doi:10.1093/cs/31.2.87

DuBois, D. L., Portillo, N., Rhodes, J. E., Silverthorn, N., & Valentine, J. C. (2011). How effective are mentoring programs for youth? A systematic assessment of the evidence. *Psychological Science in the Public Interest, 12*, 57–91. doi:10.1177/1529100611414806

Dupper, D. R. (2008). Guides for designing and establishing alternative school programs for dropout prevention. In C. Franklin, M. B. Harris, & P. Allen-Meares (Eds.), *The school practitioner's concise companion to preventing dropout and attendance problems* (pp. 23–34). New York, NY: Oxford University Press.

Garcia-Gracia, M. (2008). Role of secondary schools in the face of student absenteeism: A study of schools in socially underprivileged areas. *International Journal of Inclusive Education, 12*, 263–280. doi:10.1080/13603110601103204

Henggeler, S. W., Schoenwald, S. K., Borduin, C. M., Rowland, M. D., & Cunningham, P. B. (2009). *Multisystemic therapy for antisocial behavior in children and adolescents* (2nd ed.). New York, NY: Guilford.

Heyne, D., Sauter, F. M., Ollendick, T. H., Van Widenfelt, B. M., & Westenberg, P. M. (2014). Developmentally sensitive cognitive behavioral therapy for adolescent school refusal: Rationale and case illustration. *Clinical Child and Family Psychology Review, 17*, 191–215. doi:10.1007/s10567–013-0160–0

Hornby, G. (2011). *Parental involvement in childhood education: Building effective school–family partnerships.* New York, NY: Springer.

Kaufman, P., Alt, M. N., & Chapman, C. (2004). *Dropout rates in the United States: 2001 (NCES 2005–046).* Washington, DC: U.S. Government Printing Office.

Kearney, C. A. (2008a). School absenteeism and school refusal behavior in youth: A contemporary review. *Clinical Psychology Review, 28*, 451–471. doi:10.1016/j.cpr.2007.07.012

Kearney, C. A. (2008b). An interdisciplinary model of school absenteeism in youth to inform professional practice and public policy. *Educational Psychology Review, 20*, 257–282. doi:10.1007/s10648–008-9078–3

Kearney, C. A. (2008c). *Helping school refusing children and their parents: A guide for school-based professionals.* New York, NY: Oxford University Press.

Kearney, C. A., & Albano, A. M. (2004). The functional profiles of school refusal behavior: Diagnostic aspects. *Behavior Modification, 28*, 147–161. doi:10.1177/0145445503259263

Kearney, C. A., & Albano, A. M. (2007). *When children refuse school: A cognitive-behavioral therapy approach/therapist guide* (2nd ed.). New York, NY: Oxford University Press.

Kearney, C. A., & Bensaheb, A. (2006). School absenteeism and school refusal behavior: A review and suggestions for school-based health professionals. *Journal of School Health, 76*, 3–7. doi:10.1111/j.1746–1561.2006.00060.x

Kearney, C. A., & Graczyk, P. A. (2014). A response to intervention model to promote school attendance and decrease school absenteeism. *Child and Youth Care Forum, 43*, 1–25. doi:10.1007/s10566–013-9222–1

Kearney, C. A., & Silverman, W. K. (1996). The evolution and reconciliation of taxonomic strategies for school refusal behavior. *Clinical Psychology: Science and Practice, 3*, 339–354. doi:10.1111/j.1468–2850.1996.tb00087.x

Monahan, K. C., VanDerhei, S., Bechtold, J., & Cauffman, E. (2014). From the school yard to the squad car: School discipline, truancy, and arrest. *Journal of Youth and Adolescence, 43*, 1110–1122. doi:10.1007/s10964–014-0103–1

National Center for Education Statistics. (2006). *The condition of education 2006*. Washington, DC: U.S. Department of Education.

Neild, R. C., Balfanz, R., & Herzog, L. (2007). An early warning system. *Educational Leadership, 65*, 28–33.

Pina, A. A., Zerr, A. A., Gonzales, N. A., & Ortiz, C. D. (2009). Psychosocial interventions for school refusal behavior in children and adolescents. *Child Development Perspectives, 3*, 11–20. doi:10.1111/j.1750–8606.2008.00070.x

Suveg, C., Aschenbrand, S. G., & Kendall, P. C. (2005). Separation anxiety disorder, panic disorder, and school refusal. *Child and Adolescent Psychiatric Clinics of North America, 14*, 773–795. doi:10.1016/j.chc.2005.05.005

White, S. W., & Kelly, F. D. (2010). The school counselor's role in school dropout prevention. *Journal of Counseling and Development, 88*, 227–235. doi:10.1002/j.1556–6678.2010.tb00014.x

Evidence-Based Interventions for Major Depressive Disorder in Children and Adolescents

Kevin D. Stark, Leah A. Wang, and Kelly N. Banneyer

OVERVIEW

Depression is a chronic, recurring disorder that impacts children's academic, interpersonal, and family functioning (Garber & Horowitz, 2002; Keller, 2003). According to the *Diagnostic and statistical manual of mental disorders* (5th ed.; *DSM-5*; American Psychiatric Association [APA], 2013), a child diagnosed with major depressive disorder (MDD) must experience a depressed or irritable mood and/or a loss of interest or pleasure along with three or more of the following symptoms: significant weight loss or decrease in appetite, insomnia, or hypersomnia, psychomotor agitation or retardation, fatigue or lack of energy, feelings of worthlessness or guilt, decreased concentration or indecisiveness, or recurrent thoughts of death or suicide. These symptoms must be present for at least a period of 2 weeks. In addition, children may experience some of the following symptoms: persistent sad or irritable mood, frequent vague and nonspecific physical complaints, frequent absences from school or poor performance in school, being bored, alcohol or substance abuse, increased irritability, anger or hostility, or reckless behavior (APA, 2013). Overall prevalence rates for depression in childhood range from about 1% to 3% (Costello, Erklani, & Angold, 2006) and increase to approximately 8.3% during adolescence (SAMHSA, 2009). Increases in depression during adolescence are likely because of developmental factors including hormonal and neurobiological changes (Andersen & Teicher, 2008), sexual maturation, and an increase in emotional intensity. For example, the prefrontal cortex and dopaminergic reward systems, which are necessary to regulate these more complex emotions, continue to develop until late adolescence or early adulthood. For this reason, many adolescents lack sufficient coping resources and are vulnerable to developing depression (Davey, Yücel, & Allen, 2008).

The goal of this chapter is to present an overview of three evidence-based programs designed to decrease depressive symptoms in children and/or adolescents. The chapter begins with a brief overview of the etiology of depression. Next, it presents a description of a cognitive behavioral therapy (CBT) intervention designed to be delivered in a group format, an individual interpersonal intervention, and an individual behavioral activation (BA) intervention that includes a great deal of parental involvement. Finally, the chapter concludes with a brief discussion of universal therapeutic techniques to be incorporated into work with depressed youth regardless of the therapeutic orientation or treatment strategy.

ETIOLOGY AND FACTORS CONTRIBUTING TO MDD IN CHILDREN AND ADOLESCENTS

There is no single gene or specific environmental event that is known to cause depression. The general consensus in the field is that the etiology of depression is based on a combination of biological, cognitive, and environmental factors. Several conceptual models have emerged and have been investigated. For a more thorough description of these models, see Kazdin and Marciano (1998). Proponents of biological models have used twin studies to examine the influence of heredity and genes in the development of depression. The heritability of MDD is likely to be in the range of 31% to 42% (Sullivan, Neale, & Kendler, 2000). Research has demonstrated that depression runs in families, but a bidirectional influence between depressed parents and children suggests that genes are not solely responsible for the onset and presence of depression. Researchers of neurobiological models have investigated the role of different neurotransmitters and brain regions associated with depression. Most research has emphasized the role of serotonin, acetylcholine, and dopamine. Investigators have also found changes in frontal lobe activity in depressed patients (Stuss, Gow, & Hetherington, 1992).

The cognitive model posits that depression develops owing to distorted belief systems and perceptual and attributional styles. Specifically, depressed patients demonstrate negative beliefs about the self, world, and future (Beck, 1967). Behavioral models focus on learned responses to environmental stimuli and concomitant behavioral deficits. The interpersonal models, although sometimes encompassed by behavioral models, are unique in that they examine early parent–child relationships and how family messages and interactional styles may contribute to later depression. Finally, socioenvironmental models propose that stressful environmental events, such as the death of a loved one, may trigger depressive symptomatology.

HOW TO: A GUIDE TO THE IMPLEMENTATION OF INTERVENTIONS FOR MDD IN CHILDREN AND ADOLESCENTS

The following sections outline three depression treatments for youth. In addition to having an evidence base, the three were chosen based on their varied theoretical orientations, populations served, and suggested settings and formats for implementation.

ACTION: A Cognitive Behavioral Treatment for Depressed Youth

The ACTION program is a manualized program that is based on a cognitive behavioral model of depression. The name ACTION reminds participants to: Always find something to do to feel better, Catch the positive, Think of it as a problem to be solved, Inspect the situation, Open themselves to the positive, and Never get stuck in the negative muck. It is appropriate for males and females and for children and adolescents. However, the activities, coping skills, and illustrations in the treatment materials were designed for children between 9 and 13 years old. The program was originally implemented with same-gender groups in elementary and middle school settings. ACTION is a group treatment that uses a structured therapist manual (Stark, Schnoebelen, Simpson, et al., 2007) and workbook (Stark, Simpson, Schnoebelen, et al., 2007). The treatment is designed to be a fun and engaging approach to teaching skills to manage depressive symptoms, interpersonal difficulties, and personal stressors. Skills are taught through didactic presentations and activities, are rehearsed during in-session activities, and are applied through therapeutic homework. Each of the 20 group and two individual meetings last approximately 60 minutes and should occur twice per week for 11 weeks. Refer to Table 24.1 for a summary of the objectives for each group meeting. This program's intense schedule was a developmental consideration and likely contributes to its efficacy. The schedule should be adhered to whenever possible as children tend to remember more of the material and complete more therapeutic homework when meetings are conducted twice per week. Although designed as a group treatment, the program could be easily adapted for individual clients. However, interviews with participants suggest that children feel part of the program's effectiveness is attributable to the group implementation format.

There are four primary treatment components to ACTION: (a) affective education, (b) coping skills training (BA), (c) problem-solving training, and (d) cognitive restructuring. The first component, affective education, teaches children to use the "3Bs" (Brain, Body, and Behavior) to identify

TABLE 24.1

Meeting #	Objectives
OBJECTIVES FOR EACH MEETING OF THE ACTION TREATMENT PROGRAM FOR YOUTH DEPRESSION	
1	Discuss parameters of meetings, introduce counselors and children, establish rationale for treatment, discuss confidentiality, establish group rules, build group cohesion, establish within group incentive system
2	Introduce chat time and agenda setting, establish pragmatics of completing homework, introduce mood meter and take ACTION list, complete coping activity
3	Discuss importance of thinking about meetings and doing practice, introduce various therapeutic components including: catch the positive diaries, affective education, and coping strategies
Individual meeting 1	*Review therapeutic concepts, develop individual treatment goals*
4	Extend group cohesion, review participant goals discuss application of coping strategies, complete coping skills activity together
5	Experience impact of coping skills activity; introduce, extend, and apply problem solving; emphasize brainstorming step of problem solving
6	Demonstrate the role of cognition in emotion and behavior, introduce connection of thoughts to feelings, complete coping skills activity
7	Apply problem solving to real-life situations, practice brainstorming activity, experience coping skills activity
8	Apply problem solving to teasing, experience coping skills activity
9	Apply problem solving to interpersonal problems, experience coping skills activity
Individual meeting 2	*Review therapeutic concepts, identify common negative thoughts, individualize catch the positive diaries, introduce cognitive restructuring*
10	Prepare for and practice cognitive restructuring, experience coping skills activity
11	Introduce how perceptions are constructed, illustrate how depression distorts thinking, provide rationale for changing negative thoughts
12	Practice identifying negative thoughts of group members, explore participant strengths through self-map activity, practice cognitive restructuring
13	Practice identifying negative thoughts, continue identifying strengths for self-maps, practice cognitive restructuring with questions using alternative interpretations
14	Continue with negative thoughts, adding strengths to self-maps, and cognitive restructuring
15	Continue with negative thoughts and adding strengths to self-maps, introduce examining evidence as a tool for cognitive restructuring
16	Continue activities from sessions 12–15 begin to prepare for termination
17	Review and add to self-maps, integrate and apply cognitive restructuring, continue preparing for termination
18	Review and add to self-maps, integrate and apply learned skills, continue preparing for termination
19	Complete empowerment activity using completed self-maps, prepare for group termination
20	Say goodbye to the group, say goodbye to negative thoughts and feelings, terminate

their emotional experiences. By attending to their thoughts (Brain), the sensations in their bodies (Body), and their own actions (Behavior), children become acutely more aware of their emotions. Over the course of therapy, they also become more aware of *changes* in their emotions and more skilled at using the identified changes as cues to engage in coping, problem solving, or cognitive restructuring. Activities completed within meetings and as homework help children become more aware of their personal experiences and the links between their thoughts, behaviors, and emotions.

The second treatment component is coping skills training. As depressed youth often experience undesirable situations that are not within their control (and thus cannot be changed by them), they are taught to take action. Participants learn to recognize when something bad is happening that they cannot change, and to do something to help improve their mood and other depressive symptoms. Children experience the benefits of coping skills as they complete coping activities during at least seven of the first nine meetings. Children are taught to use five broad categories of coping strategies, including: (a) do something fun and distracting, (b) do something soothing and relaxing, (c) do something that expends a lot of energy, (d) spend time with friends, and (e) change the way you are thinking. These strategies came from focus groups composed of especially resilient children. Therapists should introduce a variety of activities from each of the coping categories over the course of these meetings and encourage the children to experiment with different ones to find what works best for them. A crucial component of the ACTION program is this coping practice. In each session, therapists evaluate the mood within the group at the start of the meeting and then choose a coping skill that leads to an improvement. Children rate their moods, complete the activity, and then re-rate their moods. The changes and experiences are processed to address why the activity produced an improvement in mood and what the children can do to replicate the outcome outside of the group meetings. The therapist encourages use of coping skills outside of meetings through the children's workbooks that provide a guide for self-monitoring and activity scheduling. Thus, this strategy is also a form of BA.

The third treatment component is problem-solving training. Problem solving is an overarching philosophy of the treatment program; participants learn to view depressive symptoms as representing problems to be solved. They also learn to recognize when undesirable situations that occur within their lives can be changed or managed, and are within their control. If change is deemed to be within their control, then they are instructed to use problem solving. The therapist teaches children a five-step problem-solving procedure to change undesirable situations and thus reduce distress and accompanying emotional upset. Becoming proficient at problem solving also promotes self-efficacy. It is important to note that children are reminded that, if change is not within their control, they should use coping skills to manage their emotional reactions. Therapists should not hesitate to encourage children to use coping skills along with problem solving. For example, a child may use coping skills to elevate his or her mood to feel well enough to use problem solving. By the middle of treatment, children typically are proficient at using coping and problem-solving skills, which enables them to focus on identifying and changing negative thoughts.

The fourth treatment component is cognitive restructuring. In this part of the ACTION program, children learn that depression comes partly from having negative thoughts that are not based in reality. Depressed youth are taught to recognize and then evaluate negative thoughts using a number of cognitive restructuring strategies. The therapist uses both within session activities and therapeutic homework exercises to teach children to be "Thought Judges" who evaluate the validity of their negative thoughts. In ACTION, Thought Judges use the following two questions: (a) What is another way of looking at it? and (b) What is the evidence? Children are taught that some thoughts are not only false, but also constructed and can be changed. Once they can recognize negative thoughts as likely false, the therapist should help them learn to "talk back" to these thoughts by arguing against them. For example, for a child who has the negative thought "I'm helpless," the therapist could point to evidence supporting a belief in personal efficacy. If a depressed child's negative thought is realistic and reflects a situation that can be changed, then the child is encouraged to use problem solving to develop and follow a plan that produces improvement. If the situation is real but cannot be changed, then a coping strategy is used to manage feelings about the situation.

The ACTION program also includes a parent-training component. This component is a hybrid of parent training and family therapy (eight group meetings with children attending four sessions). In addition, there are two individual family meetings. The objective of the parental intervention is to teach parents the same skills their children are learning so they can apply the skills to their own lives, be better models, and help their children apply new skills. The parental intervention is designed to change the family environment so it is more positive and also to modify parent–child interactions that develop and maintain a depressive style of thinking. Parent training is effective only to the extent that parents attend meetings. The more personal contact the therapist has with the caregiver, the more likely the caregiver will participate in the sessions. Failure of even one parent to attend the group parent-training meetings has adverse effects on the child, contributing to the depressed child's perception he or she is unlovable, worthless, and that nothing is going to change the current situation.

Summary. ACTION is a developmentally appropriate and engaging CBT treatment that is experiential in nature. It engages depressed youth in activities that are designed to teach them coping, problem solving, and cognitive restructuring skills. Practicing skills in the group and experiencing the benefits of treatment in session combats children's pessimism, increases treatment credibility, and builds self-efficacy. With these new skills, children can both change the stressors in their lives (through problem solving) and moderate the impact of the stressors they cannot change (through coping and cognitive restructuring). As children get more proficient at using the skills, they see changes in their lives. As their experience of the world changes, so do their cognitions. New beliefs that they are lovable, worthy, and efficacious lead to long-term improvements. Parent training augments treatment to help produce a positive, healthy environment that encourages skill usage and the development of positive core beliefs.

Interpersonal Therapy for Adolescents

Interpersonal Psychotherapy for Depressed Adolescents (IPT-A; see Mufson, Dorta, Moreau, & Weissman, 2004) is derived from interpersonal theory and is a downward extension of interpersonal therapy approaches developed for adults. Research examining outcomes of IPT-A for adolescents with depressive symptoms suggests that it is an efficacious treatment modality (Mufson, Dorta, Wickramaratne, et al., 2004; Mufson, Weissman, Moreau, & Garfinkel, 1999; Rosselló & Bernal, 1999). Mufson and colleagues (1999) found that, in comparison to clinical monitoring, IPT-A was superior at reducing depressive symptoms, increasing depression recovery rates, and increasing treatment retention. Moreover, adolescents who received IPT-A showed improved social functioning and interpersonal problem solving. Mufson, Dorta, Olfson, Weissman, and Hoagwood (2004) also examined the efficacy of IPT-A in school-based mental health clinics to determine whether IPT-A could be successfully implemented in community settings and delivered by community-based clinicians. Results demonstrated that adolescents treated with IPT-A in the school-based mental health clinics showed greater symptom reduction and improvement than adolescents in the treatment-as-usual condition (Mufson, Dorta, Olfson, et al., 2004).

There are two primary goals of IPT-A. One is to reduce depressive symptoms; the other is to improve aspects of interpersonal functioning that may cause or maintain the depressive symptoms. For example, adolescents may have relationship difficulties such as confiding in people with whom they are close. To accomplish these two primary goals, the adolescent and therapist identify one or two problem areas that may contribute to or exacerbate depression and work toward improving interpersonal functioning within that context. Problem areas may involve grief, interpersonal disputes, adolescent role transitions, or interpersonal deficits.

IPT-A is a 12-week individual treatment plan, with the therapist and adolescent meeting once per week. Parental involvement is encouraged in IPT-A; parents are considered collaborative therapists. Each session begins with a "check-in" to assess the adolescent's depressive symptoms, assessment of suicidal risk, and mood rating. Treatment is divided into an initial phase, middle phase, and termination phase of about four sessions each. The following sections identify goals and session content for each of the phases.

Initial Phase. During the initial phase, the therapist aids the adolescent in identifying problem areas, providing a rationale for treatment, negotiating and signing a formal therapeutic contract, and defining the adolescent's role in therapy. The therapist educates the adolescent and the adolescent's parents about depression to facilitate an understanding of the disorder and its implications. Additionally, the therapist works with the adolescent to ensure that he or she is socially engaged with family, in school, and with friends. The therapist should ask parents to encourage their child's participation in as many regular activities as possible. Thus, psychoeducation and BA are used as primary treatment strategies during the first phase of treatment.

Objectives. There are seven objectives for the initial phase of treatment (see Table 24.2). These objectives should all be achieved during the first four sessions. The first two objectives should be achieved in the first session (see identified tasks in the following section).

Tasks. To complete the first two objectives in the initial stage, the following six tasks should be completed during the first session: confirm patient suitability for IPT-A, psychoeducation about depression, explain treatment options, explain limited "sick role," introduce principles of IPT-A, and obtain commitment to treatment. To assess whether the patient is a good fit for this therapeutic approach, the therapist should review the patient's depressive symptoms. Reviewing the adolescent's symptoms helps confirm the diagnosis, normalize symptoms of depression for the patient, put the symptoms in an interpersonal context, and demonstrate the active role that both the patient and therapist will have in treatment. The therapist should provide a thorough assessment evaluating symptoms in multiple domains of functioning. Furthermore, giving the adolescent a "limited sick role" helps to conceptualize depression as an illness, which allows the adolescent to feel less pressure to perform daily activities at the same level as someone not suffering from depression.

Middle Phase. The middle phase of treatment usually consists of sessions five through eight. The focus of this phase is achieving the primary goals of treatment. At this point in treatment, the adolescent actively provides information and experiences within each problem area. The therapist also allows the adolescent to choose topics of discussion related to the problem areas.

During the middle phase of treatment, the nature of each previously identified problem is clarified, effective strategies for attacking the problems are determined, and relevant intervention plans are developed and implemented. When developing plans, an overarching goal is to improve interpersonal functioning. Adolescents are also taught to monitor the experience of depressive symptoms and their emotional experiences. Thus, self-monitoring and problem solving about interpersonal difficulties are the primary treatment strategies used during the middle phase of treatment.

Objectives. The middle phase of treatment has three objectives: (a) further clarify the problem area(s), (b) identify strategies to improve the problem area(s), and (c) implement interventions to resolve the problem area(s). To achieve these therapeutic

TABLE 24.2

OBJECTIVES FOR THE INITIAL PHASE OF IPT-A	
Objective #	Objectives
1	Confirm diagnosis
2	Psychoeducation
3	Interpersonal inventory. For this step, the therapist first creates a list of the current and past significant relationships in the patient's life. Next, the two discuss the most significant relationships in some depth.
4	Identify interpersonal difficulties
5	Explain theory and goals
6	Explain expected roles of patient and therapist in treatment
7	Prepare for middle phase

objectives, the therapist employs the following techniques: exploratory questioning, encouragement of affect, linking affect with events, clarification of conflicts, communication analysis, and behavioral change techniques, such as role playing.

Tasks. The therapist should accomplish the following tasks in order to achieve the goals for the middle phase of treatment: monitor depressive symptoms, allow patient to discuss topics related to problem area(s), monitor feelings and encourage self-disclosure of affective state, schedule regular meetings with the youth's parents, and maintain alliance with parents. If there is no symptom reduction as a result of the intervention, the therapist should consider suggesting adjunctive treatment, such as pharmacotherapy.

Termination Phase. Sessions 9 to 12 comprise the termination phase, or the final phase of treatment. The therapist should remind the adolescent of the termination date at least 2 to 4 weeks before the cessation of treatment.

Objectives. The foremost objectives of this phase are to prepare the adolescent for termination and to establish a sense of personal competence for managing future problems. During this phase, the therapist should review the course of treatment, work with the adolescent to prepare for interpersonal stress after treatment, and assess the need for continued treatment. The two should discuss the adolescent's reaction to the prospect of ending therapy and emphasize progress the adolescent has made toward developing feelings of competence.

Tasks. The therapist should complete the following tasks during the termination phase of treatment: assess feelings about treatment termination, review signs of reemerging depression, distinguish interpersonal strengths, review stressful interpersonal situations, review helpful strategies, discuss applying strategies to future situations, and determine need for continued treatment.

Summary. The overarching objectives of IPT-A are to reduce depressive symptoms and improve interpersonal functioning. This occurs through interpersonal skills training, BA, and using problem solving in an interpersonal context. The intervention

is divided into three phases that can be conceptualized as psychoeducation and interpersonal problem identification, interpersonal skill building and application, and mastery of interpersonal skills and building a sense of interpersonal efficacy. Parents are engaged in the treatment as collaborative therapists.

BA for Depression

Behavioral activation (BA) has its roots in CBT; it stemmed from a desire to examine whether BA alone could be an efficacious alternative to traditional CBT involving both cognitive and behavioral interventions (Jacobson et al., 1996). Dimidjian and colleagues (2006) reported that for more severely depressed adults, BA worked just as well as antidepressant medication and had some advantages over cognitive therapy. BA is an idiographic treatment based on the premise that specific avoidant behaviors maintain depression for each individual by inhibiting opportunities for positive reinforcement. BA designed specifically for adolescents is quite new. McCauley and colleagues (2006) published the first results examining the efficacy of the Adolescent Behavioral Activation Program (A-BAP) as compared with evidence-based practice for depression (CBT or IPT-A). Researchers showed that there were no significant differences across treatment conditions over a 12-week period, and that both groups showed significant improvement over time (McCauley et al., 2006). Within the A-BAP group, of the 27 children who completed a posttreatment diagnostic interview (Kiddie-SADS [K-SADS]; Kaufman et al., 1997), 21 were rated as no longer meeting criteria for a depressive disorder.

The goal of BA therapy for adolescents is to collaboratively identify the internal and external barriers to experiencing rewards and achieving goals, and work to systematically overcome these barriers by increasingly practicing approach behavior rather than avoidance (McCauley, Schloredt, Gudmundsen, Martell, & Dimidjian, 2011). In order to increase positive behaviors, the therapist serves the role of coach for the adolescent and his or her parents, and, in addition to providing didactic information each session, helps plan specific BA "Try it out" practice to be completed between meetings.

BA treatment for adolescents is designed to take place in 12 sessions, over about 16 weeks, with the therapist meeting with the adolescent and parents during each session. Parental involvement in BA treatment for adolescents is deemed absolutely essential. Some sessions include time for the therapist to meet with the adolescent and parents together, but most meetings require separate time with each, with the majority of the time allotted for the adolescent and therapist alone. The treatment is divided into five phases of two to four sessions each (Getting Started, Getting Active, Core Skills, Practice & Application, and Relapse Prevention & Termination). The following sections outline goals and session content summarizing each of the phases outlined in the McCauley et al. (2011) treatment manual.

Getting Started (Two Sessions). During this initial phase of treatment, the therapist begins to create a functional case conceptualization of the adolescent's depression, provides the rationale for BA treatment to both the adolescent and his or her parents, and discusses the outline of treatment, structure of sessions, and roles of each participant in treatment (i.e., therapist as coach, adolescent as his or her partner, and parent as support person). The therapist also asks the adolescent to complete a weekly assessment monitoring his or her mood. As in all sessions, the therapist uses specific worksheets to assist teaching and application during the initial phase.

Getting Active (Two Sessions). Sessions begin with collaborative agenda setting. In the didactic portion of session 3, the idea of using activity to improve mood is introduced. In session 4, the didactic content explores functional assessment, positive and negative reinforcement, and helping adolescents understand their behavior. In-session BA activities are used along with mood ratings so that adolescents have the opportunity to experience how activities can influence mood positively. The therapist also asks adolescents to track their activities. Parent meetings center on how to support a depressed teen by managing one's own stress, having realistic expectations, and validating the child's experience.

Core Skills (Four Sessions). During this phase of treatment, the therapist teaches the core skills of BA. The authors outline specific strategies used with the parents and adolescents in this phase of treatment (see Table 24.3). As before, handouts related to each topic are available from the authors to supplement each meeting.

Individualized Application/Practice (Three–Seven Sessions). The focus of the next treatment phase is to help the adolescents generalize and practice the skills they have learned and support them in setting and working toward goals that lead to improved mood. In the first of these sessions, the therapist reviews mood data from the past weeks in treatment and works collaboratively to outline a detailed plan of the treatment goals, including an estimate of how many more sessions will be needed. The next sessions focus on carrying out this collaboratively developed plan, and the therapist encourages the adolescent to use rewards for engaging in activating behaviors between meetings. As before, the teen is assigned a "Try it out" homework practice at each meeting.

Moving Forward: Relapse Prevention and Termination (One Session). The final BA session centers on creating an individualized Plan for Moving Forward to help the adolescent manage triggers, recognize the onset of depressive symptoms in the future, and manage any setbacks. In this final session, the adolescent completes the Doing What Works worksheet, which includes identifying personal triggers, signs of regression (both physical and behavioral), plans for what to do if regression occurs, and a list of support people who can help.

Summary. The goal of BA therapy for adolescents is to collaboratively identify the internal and external barriers to experiencing rewards and achieving goals, and work to systematically overcome those barriers by increasingly practicing approach behavior rather than avoidance. The primary treatment strategy used to help participants achieve their goals of improved mood is activity scheduling. Through self-monitoring of mood and engagement in pleasant activities, adolescents are taught that there is a connection between how they feel and what they do. The more they are actively engaged in pleasurable activities, the better they feel. In addition, a variety of behavioral strategies are employed to help the children achieve their goals and eliminate stress in their lives. Parental involvement and therapeutic homework are critical components of this treatment.

TABLE 24.3

CORE SKILLS OF BEHAVIORAL ACTIVATION		
Core Skill	**Adolescent Goals**	**Parent Goals**
Session 5: Problem Solving	Use COPE to handle challenging situations and manage stress: CALM down and CLARIFY the problem and emotional triggers, generate OPTIONS, pick one and try it (PERFORM), and EVALUATE how it went.	Learn and practice active listening strategies: Demonstrate interest, ask clarifying questions, reflect feelings, and paraphrase.
Session 6: Goal Setting	Learn to set SMART goals: Specifically stated, Measurable, Appealing, Realistic, and Timed. Begin to identify graded mini-steps on the way to achieving a goal.	Learn additional methods for being supportive; Set specific goals, begin to monitor and rate performance on implementing supportive behaviors.
Session 7: Identifying Barriers	Learn to recognize and differentiate between internal and external barriers to achieving goals, and begin to plan how to get around these barriers; Attempt to shift behavior to be more goal-directed and less mood-directed.	Adolescents and parents together: Adolescent shares goals with parents and group works to identify specific measurable ways parents can support adolescent's goals.
Session 8: Overcoming Avoidance	Introduce TRAP (Trigger Response Avoidance-Pattern) and TRAC (Trigger Response Alternative-Coping) to encourage teens to get out of the TRAP of depression being maintained by avoidance and back on a goal-directed TRAC.	Review all session content and skills presented to date, ask how providing support at home is going, discuss any new concerns, remind parents that they are not explicitly part of next few sessions and will be reintegrated in the final session.

CONCLUSION

Three evidence-based interventions were briefly described. These interventions, although developed independently, share common components. It is not yet possible to determine whether these shared components account for treatment efficacy or if something unique about each one results in each approach's respective effectiveness. All three interventions are highly structured, teach participants new skills, and provide opportunities for application through structured homework assignments. Notably, all three also involve parents in some capacity. At the core of the three interventions is goal setting and self-monitoring of improvement in mood, which often occurs as a result of BA. Within both the ACTION program and BA for depression, improved mood is accomplished during the early sessions when BA is taught as a coping strategy and engagement in pleasant activities is experienced in session and then increased through activity scheduling. Within the initial phase of IPT-A, BA is also one of the primary objectives and is accomplished through activity scheduling. Both ACTION and BA for depression include training in a broad array of coping skills in which the participants are taught to apply the skill when they face a stressor that is outside of their control. In all three treatment programs, problem solving is directly taught as a way to eliminate or manage stressors that are within the child's control. Finally, improving interpersonal relationships and communication are addressed in multiple interventions. This is a direct focus of treatment in IPT-A, and a frequent topic of discussion within ACTION. In fact, the majority of stressful situations and problems that ACTION participants bring to treatment are interpersonal in nature. In addition, even BA for depression treatment highlights the importance of identifying and making use of supportive others. All three interventions presented have been shown empirically to be useful in reducing symptoms of depression in youth.

UNIVERSAL TECHNIQUES FOR WORKING WITH DEPRESSED YOUTH

No matter which evidence-based treatment therapists employ with depressed clients, there are several universal techniques that augment therapy. Some of these are outlined in the following sections.

Mood and Energy Ratings

It is important to be constantly aware of a depressed child's changing mood and energy level throughout each session. Not only does this information inform how to proceed, but also it aids the child in developing self-reflection skills that are useful outside of the therapy office. Sometimes patients do not believe they have the energy to use the tools the therapist is teaching them. This often mirrors their experience of lacking energy to complete homework or other tasks outside session. Fatigue should be conceptualized as a problem to be solved and treated with coping strategies that boost mood and energy. Similarly, some depressed children demonstrate irritability as their primary mood disturbance. If a depressed child appears angry during the session, the therapist must intervene before the child is overcome by negative affect. Intervention could include initiating a coping activity or restructuring the child's perception of the interaction that triggered the anger. By asking children to rate (and track) their energy level and feelings throughout the session, the therapist and child can identify techniques that elevate the child's mood and bring awareness to the improvements that accrue from effective techniques.

Coping

Coping skill training is another universal strategy for treating children with depression. Coping is used when there are no alternative solutions; it moderates the effects of uncontrollable events and resulting negative mood changes. Among the most common coping skills are: (a) doing something (e.g., engaging in activities that are relaxing, distracting, or expend energy), (b) talking to someone (e.g., about the situation), and (c) changing thoughts (e.g., constructing more realistic thoughts about the uncontrollable event and what might happen next). Ensuring that children master coping skills is important because it increases the probability they will use other strategies taught in treatment. A child who is overwhelmed or dysphoric may not try strategies he or she has learned, and may instead use excuses, such as "I didn't feel good enough to try it," "I didn't feel like doing anything," or "I didn't have the energy to try to solve the problem." Children have to raise their mood to have the energy and affective state necessary for trying to use new therapeutic strategies. Effective use of coping skills and a developing mastery over mood can be highlighted as evidence to reinforce beliefs about a positive self and future.

Problem Solving

Because depressed children in treatment are typically ineffective at changing their circumstances, and because some of the undesirable things that happen are actually controllable, all depressed children should be taught how to solve problems. Problem solving is a strategy for changing situations within the child's control but that produce stress, unwanted outcomes, or undesirable affect. Changing undesirable situations can lead to a permanent improvement in the child's life and increase his or her sense of personal efficacy. Teaching problem-solving strategies should include collaboratively creating a list of potential solutions to identified problems, evaluating the potential solutions, and then concluding which is the best plan to try.

It is important to note that therapists must recognize that children will not problem solve effectively if they are experiencing overwhelming negative affect or do not believe that any problem-solving approach will be effective. Consequently, the child's mood must be elevated, and collaborative problem solving must continually involve identifying and restructuring negative, interfering thoughts. As the child may be "stuck" in his or her perceptions, it is often useful to have the child rate how much he or she believes a chosen plan will work and how likely the child is to implement the plan. It is helpful to rehearse the plan through imagery and have the child envision the desired outcome and the rewarding emotion that accompanies it. The therapist should also help the child implement as much of the plan during the session as possible to enhance the likelihood that the plan will be finished outside of the meeting. In addition, the therapist should involve parents or technology (such as taking a cell phone photo of the plan or setting cell phone reminder alarms) to help coach the child through the completion of the plan. Finally, therapists should ensure the final step of the problem-solving procedure involves a self-reward (or in certain cases, parent-supplied reward) to reinforce the child's efforts and thereby increase the probability that the child will attempt the strategy in the future.

SELECT BIBLIOGRAPHY

Chorpita, B. F., & Weisz, J. R. (2009). *MATCH-ADTC: Modular approach to therapy for children with anxiety, depression, trauma, or conduct problems.* Satellite Beach, FL: PracticeWise. *This program is an evidence-based modular approach to treatment. The treatment provider is able to individualize treatment based on a child's presenting concerns using flowcharts that direct the provider through 33 different evidence-based procedures. The provider can choose from using an online format or a book format.*

Effective Child Therapy. (2013). Retrieved from http://effectivechildtherapy.com/content/depression *The Effective Child Therapy website is a resource developed through a partnership between the Association for Behavioral and Cognitive Therapies and the Society of Clinical Child and Adolescent Psychology. It gives an overview of types of evidence-based treatment for depression and other disorders. Based on research data evaluating different approaches, each type of therapy is defined as a well-established, probably efficacious, possibly efficacious, experimental, or ineffective treatment. Different approaches are also divided and categorized in terms of efficacy with children and with adolescents.*

Kendall, P. C., Stark, K., Martinsen, K., Rodriguez, K., & Arora, P. (2013). *Group leader manual for EMOTION: "Coping kids" managing anxiety and depression.* Ardmore, PA: Workbook. *The EMOTION program is a manualized cognitive behavioral approach to group treatment used with youth suffering from symptoms of both depression and anxiety. This treatment includes both a child group and a parent group. Several resources are available, including parent and child workbooks and therapist manuals for leading the child group and for leading the parent group.*

PsyberGuide. Retrieved from http://psyberguide.org/product-listing/ *Psyberguide is a nonprofit website seeking to facilitate responsible and informed decision*

making about software and apps designed for mental health purposes. The website helps users choose apps for specific disorders or types of treatment. It also provides a list of citations of research examining the effectiveness of technology-assisted therapies.

REFERENCES

American Psychiatric Association (APA). (2013). *Diagnostic and statistical manual of mental disorders* (5th ed.). Arlington, VA: American Psychiatric Publishing.

Andersen, S. L., & Teicher, M. H. (2008). Stress, sensitive periods and maturational events in adolescent depression. *Trends in Neurosciences, 31*(4), 183–191.

Beck, A. T. (1967). *Depression: Clinical, experimental, and theoretical aspects.* New York, NY: Harper & Row.

Costello, E. J., Erklani, A., & Angold, A. (2006). Is there an epidemic of child or adolescent depression? *Journal of Child Psychology and Psychiatry, 41*(12), 1263–1271.

Davey, C. G., Yücel, M., & Allen, N. B. (2008). The emergence of depression in adolescence: Development of the prefrontal cortex and the representation of reward. *Neuroscience and Biobehavioral Reviews, 32*(1), 1–19.

Dimidjian, S., Hollon, S. D., Dobson, K. S., Schmaling, K. B., Kohlenberg, R. J., Addis, M. E., . . . Jacobson, N. S. (2006). Randomized trial of behavioral activation, cognitive therapy, and antidepressant medication in the acute treatment of adults with major depression. *Journal of Consulting and Clinical Psychology, 74*(4), 658–670.

Garber, J., & Horowitz, J. L. (2002). Depression in children. In I. H. Gotlib & C. L. Hammen (Eds.), *Handbook of depression* (pp. 510–540). New York, NY: Guilford Press.

Jacobson, N. S., Dobson, K. S., Truax, P. A., Addis, M. E., Koerner, K., Gollan, J. K., . . . Prince, S. E. (1996). A component analysis of cognitive-behavioral treatment for depression. *Journal of Consulting and Clinical Psychology, 64*(2), 295–304.

Kaufman, J., Birmaher, B., Brent, D., Rao, U., Flynn, C., Moreci, P., & Ryan, N. (1997). Schedule for affective disorders and schizophrenia for school-age children-present and lifetime version (K-SADS-PL): Initial reliability and validity data. *Journal of the American Academy of Child & Adolescent Psychiatry, 36,* 980–988.

Kazdin, A. E., & Marciano, P. L. (1998). Childhood and adolescent depression. In E. J. Mash & R. A. Barkely (Eds.), *Treatment of childhood disorders* (pp. 211–248). New York, NY: Guilford Press.

Keller, M. B. (2003). Past, present, and future directions for defining optimal treatment outcome in depression: Remission and beyond. *Journal of American Medical Association, 289*(23), 3152–3160.

McCauley, E., Gudmundsen, G., Schloredt, K., Martell, C., Rhew, I., Hubley, S., & Dimidjian, S. (2016). The adolescent behavioral activation program: Adapting behavioral activation as a treatment for depression in adolescence. *Journal of Clinical Child & Adolescent Psychology, 45*(3), 291–304.

McCauley, E., Schloredt, K., Gudmundsen, G., Martell, C., & Dimidjian, S. (2011). *Adolescents Taking Action: Behavioral activation treatment for depressed adolescents.* Seattle Children's Hospital and University of Washington, Seattle, Washington.

Mufson, L., Dorta, K. P., Moreau, D., & Weissman, M. W. (2004). *Interpersonal psychotherapy for depressed adolescents* (2nd ed.). New York, NY: Guilford Press.

Mufson, L., Dorta, K. P., Olfson, M., Weissman, M. M., & Hoagwood, K. (2004). Effectiveness research: Transporting interpersonal psychotherapy for depressed adolescents (IPT-A) from the lab to school-based health clinics. *Clinical Child and Family Psychology Review, 7*(4), 251–261.

Mufson, L., Dorta, K. P., Wickramaratne, P., Nomura, Y., Olfson, M., & Weissman,

M. M. (2004). A randomized effectiveness trial of interpersonal psychotherapy for depressed adolescents. *Archives of General Psychiatry, 61*(6), 577–584.

Mufson, L., Weissman, M. M., Moreau, D., & Garfinkel, R. (1999). Efficacy of interpersonal psychotherapy for depressed adolescents. *Archives of General Psychiatry, 56*(6), 573–579.

Rosselló, J., & Bernal, G. (1999). The efficacy of cognitive-behavioral and interpersonal treatments for depression in Puerto Rican adolescents. *Journal of Consulting and Clinical Psychology, 67*(5), 734–745.

Stark, K. D., Simpson, J., Schnoebelen, S., Hargrave, J., Molnar, J., & Glen, R. (2007). "ACTION" *Workbook: Cognitive-behavioral therapy for treating depressed girls.* Ardmore, PA: Workbook Publishing.

Stark, K. D., Schnoebelen, S., Simpson, J., Hargrave, J., Molnar, J. & Glen, R. (2007). *Treating depressed youth: Therapist's manual for 'ACTION'.* Ardmore, PA: Workbook Publishing.

Stuss, D. T., Gow, C. A., & Hetherington, C. R. (1992). "No longer Gage": Frontal lobe dysfunction and emotional changes. *Journal of Consulting and Clinical Psychology, 60*(3), 349–359.

Substance Abuse and Mental Health Services Administration (SAMHSA). (2009). *Results from the 2008 National Survey on Drug Use and Health: National Findings* (Office of Applied Studies, NSDUH Series H-36, HHS Publication No. SMA 09–4434). Rockville, MD: SAMHSA.

Sullivan, P. F., Neale, M. C., & Kendler, K. S. (2000). Genetic epidemiology of major depression: Review and meta-analysis. *The American Journal of Psychiatry, 157*(10), 1552–1562.

Evidence-Based Interventions for Persistent Depressive Disorder in Children and Adolescents

Ralph E. Cash, Sarah Valley-Gray, Shannon Worton, and Alyssa Newman

OVERVIEW

Historically, depression has been considered a diagnosis reserved only for adults, because children and adolescents were not presumed to have a well-internalized superego (Bracken & Howell, 2004). Rather, it was believed that symptoms of depression among children were transitory in nature and would dissipate over time (Depression in Children, 2002). Over the last few decades, however, researchers and clinicians have begun to view depression as a disorder occurring in childhood or adolescence with subtle, but important, differences in clinical presentation (Dinya, Csorba, & Grósz, 2012; Hammen & Rudolph, 2002). Although the diagnostic criteria for child and adolescent onset depression are included within the adult depression criteria and share many commonalities, some depressive symptoms manifest differently in children and adolescents based on developmental stages. For example, for children younger than 2 years, depression may be characterized by feeding problems, lack of playfulness, tantrums, or overall decreased expression of positive feelings (Cash, 2010b). For children between the ages of 3 and 5 years, depression may be expressed as a regression in developmental milestones, or the child may apologize excessively for minor mistakes (Cash, 2010b). Children 6 to 8 years of age may be overly aggressive, cling excessively to their parents, or avoid new people (Cash, 2010b), whereas children in the 9- to 12-year age group may exhibit worries about schoolwork, have difficulty sleeping, engage in self-blame, or have morbid thoughts (Cash, 2010b).

Depressed adolescents are likely to appear oppositional or defiant, experience behavioral problems in school, demonstrate poor concentration, exhibit truancy from classes or generally withdraw from others and from activities in which they previously engaged, have fights with people close to them, or evidence a decline in grades (Cash, 2010a). In addition, adolescents demonstrate depression through sexual promiscuity, substance use, anxiety, learning problems, or self-injury (Cash, 2010a). The presence of the aforementioned symptoms in adolescents differs from youth without depression, in that these behaviors are more intense, persist, and cause more dysfunction than the typical moodiness frequently evidenced during the teenage years (Cash, 2010a).

Traditionally, depression has been diagnosed using two primary categories—major depressive disorder (MDD) or dysthymic disorder (DD; First & Tasman, 2004). With the publication of the *Diagnostic and Statistical Manual of Mental Disorders* (5th ed.; *DSM-5*; American Psychiatric Association, 2013), however, a new depressive disorder, persistent depressive disorder (PDD), has replaced DD and overlaps somewhat with MDD, which remains in the *DSM-5*. In fact, PDD is defined as a combination of *DSM-IV-TR's* (4th ed., text rev.; American Psychiatric Association, 2000) DD and MDD. The APA estimates that PDD affects approximately 0.5% of the general population (Blanco et al., 2010). Although little is yet known about PDD's prevalence among children and adolescents, in a sample of 10,123 adolescents 13 to 18 years of age who completed the National Comorbidity Survey Replication (NCS-R), 11.7% met criteria for MDD or DD (Merikangas et al., 2010). Youth meeting the diagnostic criteria for PDD frequently exhibit irritability and/or depressed mood for at least 1 year, with additional symptoms of insomnia or hypersomnia, overeating or loss of appetite, decreased energy, diminished self-esteem, poor concentration, and/or feelings of hopelessness (American Psychiatric Association, 2013). In addition, children and adolescents must meet the following criteria as outlined by *DSM-5*:

- Exhibit the aforementioned symptoms continuously for at least 1 year, within which the child or adolescent experienced no more than 2 months without depressive symptoms.
- Have no history of hypomanic or manic episodes.
- That the symptoms are not better explained by schizophrenia or another psychotic disorder, a medical condition, or substance use.
- Experience impairment in functioning that affects the child/adolescent's life (American Psychiatric Association, 2013).

There are also a number of specifiers that a child or adolescent may receive in conjunction with a PDD diagnosis. The specifiers include the following: with anxious distress, mixed features, melancholic features, atypical features, mood-congruent psychotic features, or mood-incongruent psychotic features; peripartum onset, early onset or late onset; with pure dysthymic syndrome, persistent major depressive episode, intermittent major depressive episodes with current episode, or intermittent major depressive episodes without current episode; and mild, moderate, or severe severity (American Psychiatric Association, 2013). It should be noted that if the symptoms required for a diagnosis of major depressive episode (MDE) are met, then the youth will not meet the criteria necessary for a PDD diagnosis, despite having depressive symptoms for a year or more (American Psychiatric Association, 2013).

Given that DD frequently presents among children 11 to 12 years of age and that MDD has an average onset at 14 years of age, research suggests that PDD would also have an early onset, in addition to having a chronic course (e.g., Dinya et al., 2012; Hammen & Rudolph, 2002). It is important to note that the length of depression experienced among youth has been found to be predictive of an overall prognosis rather than the number of symptoms present (Jonsson et al., 2011). In addition, high levels of negative affectivity (e.g., sadness and hopelessness) indicate a poorer prognosis (American Psychiatric Association, 2013).

ETIOLOGY AND FACTORS CONTRIBUTING TO PDD IN CHILDREN AND ADOLESCENTS

Although a diagnosis of PDD can occur at any age, certain risk factors may increase the likelihood of a PDD diagnosis in children and adolescents. Given PDD's relatively new diagnostic formulation and the restricted manner in which research with DD has been conducted, limited information is available for PDD or DD alone and, instead, has been combined with other depressive disorders such as MDD. This lack of differentiation in the research has resulted in little being known about the genetic underpinnings of different depressive conditions (Rhebergen & Graham, 2014). However, it is likely that children and adolescents with PDD have more first-degree relatives with PDD than children and adolescents with other depressive disorders, based on extrapolations from previous research (American Psychiatric Association, 2013).

Other factors that increase the risk of the development of a depressive disorder include childhood loss or separation, frequent conflicts with family or friends, low socioeconomic status, low self-esteem, poor academic functioning, poor physical health, substance use, and maladaptive coping skills (American Psychiatric Association, 2013; Cash, 2010a). Furthermore, in a compilation of mental health surveys from the World Health Organization (Gureje, 2011), it was found that increased rates of DD existed more frequently in high-income countries when compared with low- or middle-income countries. Research has shown that individuals with suicide risk behaviors (SRB) have higher family dysfunction, a greater sense of hopelessness, and greater severity of depressive symptoms (Hetrick, Parker, Robinson, Hall, & Vance, 2012). In addition, depressive diagnoses are more common among girls than boys during adolescence, making gender another possible risk factor for PDD (Hammen & Rudolph, 2002).

When compared with youth diagnosed with MDD, children and adolescents with PDD are at increased risk for having a comorbid psychiatric disorder (American Psychiatric Association, 2013). Research has shown that approximately 70% of children diagnosed with DD later go on to meet diagnostic criteria for MDD, lending credence to *DSM-5*'s PDD diagnostic criteria (Hammen & Rudolph, 2002). Comorbid conditions associated with PDD include anxiety disorders, substance use disorders, attention deficit hyperactivity disorder (ADHD), oppositional defiant disorder (ODD), conduct disorder (CD), various psychotic disorders, and Cluster B (i.e., antisocial, borderline, histrionic, and narcissistic) and C (i.e., avoidant, dependent, and obsessive-compulsive) personality disorders (American Psychiatric Association, 2013; Chronis-Tuscano et al., 2010; Weiser et al., 2008). Moreover, girls diagnosed with ADHD are at a higher risk of developing depression and attempting suicide than boys with ADHD, although suicidal ideation between genders does not differ (Chronis-Tuscano et al., 2010). Another study examining male adolescents found that later hospitalization for a psychotic disorder was three times more likely for those diagnosed with DD than for those without, even after accounting for socioeconomic status and intelligence (Weiser et al., 2008). Based on these findings, Weiser et al. (2008) concluded that adolescents with DD in combination with other risk factors have an increased likelihood of being diagnosed with a psychotic disorder at some time in their lives.

EVIDENCE-BASED INTERVENTIONS AND EMPIRICAL SUPPORT FOR PDD IN CHILDREN AND ADOLESCENTS

Evidence-based interventions for the treatment of depression have been well established in the literature. The most common treatments include various forms of interpersonal psychotherapy (IPT), cognitive behavioral therapy (CBT), and psychotropic medication (Martinez, Zychinski, & Polo, 2012). It is important to note that medication, in conjunction with psychotherapy, is recommended for individuals experiencing moderate to severe depression (Emslie, Kennard, & Mayes, 2011). Moreover, selective-serotonin reuptake inhibitors (SSRIs) are one of the more common classes of medications prescribed (Grohol, 2008).

Several forms of psychotherapy have been demonstrated to be effective for the treatment of depression (David-Ferndon & Kaslow, 2008). IPT is a well-established, evidence-based intervention defined by the Task Force on Promotion and Dissemination of Psychological Procedures (David-Ferndon & Kaslow, 2008), and it has been adapted for use with adolescents. This adaptation, referred to as IPT for Depressed Adolescents (IPT-A) is a brief treatment used for the reduction of depressive symptoms (Mufson, Pollack Dorta, Moreau, & Weissman, 2004). The core components of IPT-A include psychoeducation (with both the adolescent and his or her caregiver), emphasis on a central problem area (e.g., grief, interpersonal disputes, role transitions, and interpersonal deficits), encouragement of affect (i.e., expressing, understanding, and managing emotions), communication analysis, decision analysis, and role-play of appropriate and useful behaviors (Mufson et al., 2004). IPT-A is most effectively applied in the case of adolescents who are experiencing an exacerbated depression caused by interpersonal difficulties, those who have not had severe interpersonal problems previously, and those who have experienced acute depressive symptoms (Mufson et al., 2004).

In addition to IPT-A, many applications of CBT have been empirically researched for use with children and adolescents. Two such applications, the Treatment for Adolescents with Depression Study (TADS) and the Penn Resiliency Project (PRP), have demonstrated their effectiveness in the treatment of childhood/adolescent-based depression (Brunwasser, Gillham, & Kim, 2009; TADS Team, 2009). The core components of TADS include psychoeducation with the individual adolescent and his or her parent or parents, goal setting, mood monitoring, behavioral activation, cognitive distortion identification, problem solving, development of social and communication skills as well as negotiation and compromise, and relapse prevention (Curry et al., 2005). In contrast, PRP is implemented in a group setting but also uses cognitive behavioral principles and the enhancement of social skills.

The specific treatment manual for each of the programs described earlier should be referred to for detailed information regarding how to implement each therapeutic approach (Curry et al., 2005; Mufson et al., 2004; University of Pennsylvania, 2009b). However, a brief step-by-step guide for each is outlined in the following section to guide clinicians in working with children and adolescents diagnosed with depression.

HOW TO: A GUIDE TO THE IMPLEMENTATION OF INTERVENTIONS FOR PDD IN CHILDREN AND ADOLESCENTS

IPT for Depressed Adolescents

A summary of the step-by-step implementation of IPT-A is provided in what follows. For more detailed information regarding the steps or troubleshooting, the reader is referred to the treatment manual (Mufson et al., 2004).

Initial Phase (Sessions 1–4)

1. Confirm diagnosis of PDD using *DSM-5* criteria.
2. Determine whether the adolescent is an appropriate candidate for IPT-A. Specific factors required for suitability of this intervention include being capable of verbally engaging in treatment; requiring no more than one session per week; and ascertaining that depression is the primary disorder when other comorbid symptoms are present.
3. Emphasize the opportunity to integrate various treatment approaches consistent with the implementation of the model, high rates of recovery using IPT-A, and the possibility to include medication as an adjunct to treatment.
4. Assign the adolescent to the "sick role," which encourages the youth to view himself or herself as having an illness that impacts performance quality and motivation and to think of himself or herself as being in treatment. By allowing the adolescent to have a "sick role," he or she can be relieved from the pressure of performing typical

social roles, though he or she should be encouraged to interact with others as much as possible.
   • Use examples of symptoms provided by the adolescent to illustrate the diagnosis of PDD. Focus on the treatability of the disorder and the impact of depression on activity level.
5. Involve caregivers during the initial session to discuss how they can assist with treatment, provide psychoeducation about PDD and the structure of treatment, and ensure that caregivers understand that reduced task completion is a symptom of the disorder.
6. Weekly, at the beginning of each session, ask the adolescent to rate his or her depressive symptoms and assess for suicidality on a scale from 1 to 10, with one representing the best the adolescent could feel and 10 representing the worst he or she could feel. The therapist should also evaluate whether or not the adolescent experienced a lower rating at any point during the week and, if so, the circumstances surrounding the low score(s).
7. Conduct an interpersonal inventory, an assessment of interpersonal symptoms that identifies individuals with whom the adolescent has a close connection, in either a positive or negative way. This provides a vehicle for greater exploration of relationships, including expectations, positive and negative interactions, and changes that he or she would like to make to the relationships (see Closeness Circle, Mufson et al., 2004). Some specific questions recommended to ask during the interpersonal inventory can be found in Mufson et al. (2004).
8. After completing the interpersonal inventory, provide the adolescent with a summary of how his or her depression relates to interpersonal difficulties. The four problem areas include interpersonal disputes, role transitions (e.g., changing schools, puberty, becoming sexually active, and illness of parent), grief as a result of death, or interpersonal deficits (e.g., communicating feelings to others and maintaining relationships).
9. Complete a client–therapist contract and include identification of a problem area, delineation of adolescent and therapist roles and expectations, general policies (e.g., session number and missing sessions), and the role of caregivers in treatment.

Middle Phase (Sessions 5–8)

1. Based on the therapist's interpersonal formulation of the adolescent, select one of the identified problem areas listed previously (e.g., interpersonal disputes, role transitions, grief, or interpersonal conflicts).
2. Shift responsibility from the therapist to the adolescent and allow the youth to direct the topics and flow of each session. The adolescent is expected to discuss events related to the selected problem area that occurred the previous week, to report how he or she felt about the situation, and to begin to apply skills learned in session to outside relationships.
3. Include family members as the therapist sees fit. Family members may be asked to attend one or two sessions depending on the adolescent's identified problem area.
4. Apply directive exploratory techniques (e.g., interpersonal inventory, clinical interview with a focus on PDD) to clarify clinical status, to confirm safety, or to acquire specific information using targeted questioning. Use nondirective exploratory techniques (e.g., receptive silence, extension of the adolescent's topic of discussion, and supportive acknowledgement) to obtain general information through the use of open-ended statements and questions.
5. Implement affect encouragement techniques (e.g., accepting painful emotions about different situations, encouraging the expression of emotions making interpersonal changes using emotional experience) to teach the adolescent how to cope with, understand, and feel comfortable expressing various mood states. Affect encouragement is critical to IPT-A, in that it emphasizes the connection between interpersonal difficulties and feelings.
6. Implement communication analysis techniques (i.e., breaking down and analyzing a conversation between the adolescent and another individual) through role-play, to help the adolescent learn to communicate more directly and to understand the impact of his or her communication on others. The reader is referred to pages 88 to 92 in the treatment manual for examples of how to apply communication analysis.
7. Implement behavioral change techniques. *Directive techniques* include modeling decision making,

expressing emotions and effective communication, limit setting, advising, and psychoeducation. *Decision analysis* involves seven steps, including (a) identifying what decisions are needed, (b) deciding on a goal, (c) creating alternative solutions, (d) describing decision-making patterns observed to the adolescent, (e) evaluating consequences of each solution, (f) applying the best option, and (g) evaluating the results and possibility for another solution. *Role-plays* offer a safe place for the practice of skills learned in treatment and the application of the skills before trying them outside of session.

Termination Phase (Sessions 9–12)

1. Two to four weeks before termination, the adolescent should be reminded of the termination date. Strategies and techniques learned in therapy should be reviewed and feelings regarding termination should be processed. Caregivers should be included in the termination process in a joint adolescent and caregiver session.

Treatment for Adolescents With Depression Study (TADS)

A summary of the step-by-step implementation of TADS is provided in the following. For additional detailed information regarding this intervention, the reader is referred to the treatment manual (Curry et al., 2005).

The TADS protocol is an evidence-based CBT intervention manual for use with children and adolescents presenting with depressive symptoms. TADS is delivered in three stages. Stage I focuses on acute treatment and is conducted in four phases. Phase I emphasizes a collaborative treatment approach to reduce depressive symptoms; phase II strengthens the skills (described in the following discussion) learned during phase I; phase III is designed to maintain the progress achieved during phases I and II while emphasizing relapse prevention; and phase IV prepares the child or adolescent for transition into stage II. Each phase of treatment in stage I has specific goals and strategies, with numerous worksheets provided in the manual. Select general strategies are described in the following to provide an outline for implementation (for more detailed information regarding each stage/phase, the reader is referred to the treatment manual). Each session within the stages follows a three-part structure. The first part of the session is spent reviewing the past week's homework, addressing the goals for the current session, and identifying any "incidents or issues." The second part of the session is focused on teaching/practicing specific skills (addressed in the following). Finally, the third part of the session sets the homework for the upcoming week, and addresses the incidents/issues identified at the beginning of the session, and works toward applying the newly learned skills to the incidents/issues.

Stage I

Phase I of Acute Treatment (Weeks 1 and 2)

Goals:

1. A collaborative therapeutic relationship is established, with both the therapist and the teen engaging as active participants. Principles of person-centered theory (e.g., genuineness and empathy) are used to strengthen the therapeutic relationship. The teen, his or her parent(s), and the therapist form a team with a shared goal: combating the teen's depression.
2. The teen and his or her parent(s) are provided with psychoeducation regarding the model's view of depression, etiology, symptomology, and treatment options.
3. The teen's level of motivation for change and feelings of hopelessness are assessed regularly through interviews. Select measures (e.g., affective disorder screening and mood monitoring) may be used as assessment tools. Suicidal ideation is evaluated and monitored, and a no-suicide contract is signed at the onset of treatment. An adjunct manual, *Procedures for Managing Suicidality in the NIMH Treatment of Adolescent Depression Study*, is used to guide clinicians in conducting an assessment of suicidality and hopelessness (this manual can be found at trialweb.dcri.duke.edu/tads/tad/manuals/TADS_CBT.pdf).
4. Goals for treatment are identified through collaboration with the teen and his or her parent(s).
5. An understanding of the teen's personal experience with depression, including his or her thoughts, feelings, and behaviors is explored. This understanding is initiated during the first session, in collaboration with the teen's parent(s). Identification of thoughts (the maladaptive beliefs that mediate depressive symptoms), feelings (the emotional responses triggered by the maladaptive thoughts), and behaviors in connection to the teen's depression is continued throughout the individual sessions.

General Strategies:

1. An initial feedback interview is conducted, during which the rationale for treatment is explored and treatment goals are established. The initial interview session is further used to establish goals based on input from both the teen and his or her parent(s).
2. Psychoeducation regarding the relationship among thoughts, feelings, and behaviors, and their implications for mood is provided, along with a review of the efficacy of the TADS treatment approach. It is emphasized that both the teen and his or her parent(s) are part of the team that responds to the youth's depression.
3. Therapeutic goals are established.
   - The goals established by the adolescent during the initial interview are reviewed.
   - Strategies that have been used, including what has been effective and what has not been effective, are discussed.
   - Goals are delineated into smaller, more concrete subgoals to make them less overwhelming and to increase the chances for attainment.
4. The teen is taught to monitor his or her mood and to assess the degree to which he or she experiences specific emotions daily, using the emotional thermometer provided in the TADS manual. Emotions are evaluated on a scale from 0 to 10, with 0 representing the worst emotions and 10 representing the best emotions. The teen is additionally taught to use the daily mood monitor (also provided in the TADS manual) to identify situations that make him or her feel happy or sad, as well as the thoughts that contribute to the specific emotion. The teen then rates the experienced emotion using the emotional thermometer.
   - Homework is assigned that involves practicing the use of mood monitoring. The teen is asked to record three situations each day using both the daily mood monitor and the emotions thermometer.

5. Socratic questioning (i.e., having the teen deeply examine his or her core beliefs) is used to explore the components of the teen's depression, including the thoughts, attributions, and behaviors that contribute to his or her mood. For example, one might ask: "When you make a mistake, what makes you think you are worthless?"; "Might another person view that differently?"; "What evidence do you have that this is true?"; and "What other explanation could there be for your mistake?"

Phase II of Acute Treatment (Weeks 3–6). Focuses on reinforcing skills learned during stage I and addresses relapse prevention:

Goals:

1. Implement behavioral activation to increase the teen's activity level.
2. Increase engagement in activities that are positively reinforcing.
3. Teach problem-solving skills, particularly as they relate to interpersonal relationships, through instruction, demonstrations, and role-playing (see the following for a step-by-step guide).
4. Identify negative automatic thoughts, beliefs, and attributions. Establish more balanced, thoughts, beliefs, and attributions.
5. Continually assess the teen's level of motivation for change, feelings of hopelessness, and suicidal ideation.
6. Identify factors within the teen's family that might have an impact on his or her depression.
7. Provide psychoeducation to the teen's parent(s) to ensure an understanding of the skills the child is learning.

General Strategies:

1. In order to identify pleasant activities, the therapist works with the adolescent to create a list of 8 to 10 pleasurable activities. Behaviors that involve social interaction and feelings of success are emphasized. The record form provided in the TADS manual is used to monitor engagement in pleasant activities.
2. For teens who have a difficult time identifying pleasant activities or are experiencing significant psychomotor retardation, an activity calendar is used to list the activities in which they will engage during the following week. For each activity completed, the teen rates his or her sense of accomplishment, as well as how much or little he or she enjoyed the activity on a 10-point Likert scale.
3. Problem-solving skills are taught using direct instruction, role-playing, and modeling. An example "problem" is offered to help the teen: (a) identify the problem, (b) brainstorm possible solutions, (c) evaluate the solutions by identifying the potential benefits and consequences, and (d) choose a solution for the problem. Psychoeducation regarding the impact of thoughts on the interpretation of and reaction to situations is provided to the teen. The mental health professional explains that, while he or she might not have control over every situation, he or she can develop mastery over thoughts and perceptions.
4. Cognitive distortions and negative self-talk are identified, and more balanced thoughts are developed through Socratic questioning and role-play.
5. Provision of psychoeducation is continued for the teen's parent(s).

Phase III of Acute Treatment (Weeks 7–11). Focuses primarily on relapse prevention and sessions occur every 6 weeks:

Goals:

1. Explore and strengthen social skills, address communication/listening skills, use role-play, and employ techniques for reaching a compromise (i.e., through the application of problem-solving strategies).
2. Identify and alter negative automatic thoughts, attributions, and beliefs.
3. Explore and strengthen compromise and negotiation skills.
4. Improve the relationship and communication between the teen and his or her parent(s), particularly as it is related to the teen's depression.
5. Address additional problems and concerns that are contributing factors to the teen's depression.

General Strategies:

1. Depending on the skill deficits of the adolescent, social skills training, assertiveness training, or communication skills are provided.

2. Techniques to challenge negative thoughts and maladaptive beliefs are taught.
3. Sessions involving the teen's parent(s) are used to facilitate treatment.
4. Opportunities to work with the family are used to enhance communication and to learn skills of negotiation and compromise.
5. As necessary, the therapist trains the teen in emotional regulation strategies, such as anxiety reduction, impulse control, and relaxation.

Phase IV of Acute Treatment (Week 12 Session)

Goals:

1. Prepare the teen for the transition to stage II.

General Strategies:

1. Progress the teen has made throughout stage I of treatment is reviewed.
2. The specific cognitive and behavioral skills the teen has developed are assessed.
3. Skills that have been beneficial for and helpful to the teen are identified.
4. Stage II is previewed.

Stages II and III

Following acute treatment (stage I), the teen transitions to stage II. Implementation of stage II is based on the teen's response to the acute treatment phase (i.e., Did the teen learn the necessary skills? Did the teen experience a reduction in his or her depressive symptoms?). For teens who responded fully to the Acute treatment, stage II focuses on maintenance of their progress, generalization of learned skills, and relapse prevention (using the TADS Relapse Prevention Plan). The developed Relapse Prevention Plan should include a discussion of how the teen and his or her parent(s) will continue to monitor his or her mood, identify the initial signs of his or her depression, explore the growth he or she has made, and identify "tools" (i.e., coping strategies) the teen will use to handle a "lapse" (i.e., recurrence of symptoms). No new skills are addressed during stage II for teens who responded fully. For teens who did not respond fully to the Acute Treatment Stage, stage II focuses on addressing remaining symptoms, enhancing learned skills, generalizing the learned skills, and preventing relapse (using the TADS Relapse Prevention Plan). Clinicians may introduce

new skills (appearing in the TADS manual) that were not covered in the acute treatment phase. The number of sessions for stage II is dependent on the teen's response to the acute treatment phase (i.e., three sessions for more than 6 weeks for those who responded fully, and six sessions for more than 6 weeks for those who responded partially). Parent(s) may also be involved in stage II, depending on the clinician's judgment and the needs of the teen. Stage III, the final stage of TADS, focuses on continuing to maintain progress, generalizing learned skills, and preventing relapse (using the developed Relapse Prevention Plan as a guide). Sessions are held once every 6 weeks for a total of three sessions.

The Penn Resiliency Project (PRP)

A summary of the step-by-step implementation of the PRP is provided in the following section. For more detailed information regarding each stage/phase, the reader is referred to the treatment manual (University of Pennsylvania, 2009a, 2009b, and www.ppc.sas.upenn.edu/prpsum.htm).

The PRP, investigated and codirected by Gillham et al. (2007) and based in part on the work of Aaron Beck, Albert Ellis, and Martin Seligman, is a manualized treatment program for use with late elementary to middle school students presenting with depressive symptoms. The PRP is delivered in a group format. Each session focuses on the implementation of cognitive behavioral techniques and problem-solving skills as they relate to interpersonal relationships.

Session 1. Rapport and group cohesion are established among the students and the group leader(s). Ellis's (1962) Adversity-Beliefs-Consequences (ABC) model is used to provide a framework as the concept of automatic thoughts is introduced. Students list problematic situations/events and practice describing corresponding automatic thoughts as well as identifying and exploring the resultant feelings.

Session 2. Optimism and pessimism are explored through acting out these thought styles in scripted skits. Stable thoughts that appear across multiple skits (as expressed by the characters within the skits) are identified, and the impact one's explanatory style has on the thoughts he or she experiences is discussed. Children then practice creating new, more balanced thoughts to replace the stable, negative, automatic thoughts. The skill of creating balanced thoughts is reinforced outside of session using homework assignments.

Session 3. Students learn to evaluate their automatic thoughts and core beliefs. A story (to be found in the manual) about two detectives, one of whom is good at looking at all the evidence, the other of whom is not, is used to demonstrate the importance of evaluating the evidence for and against one's automatic thoughts. A story of a fictional child is used as an example to explore with the students whether or not the child's automatic thoughts are accurate.

Session 4. Although previous sessions focused on identifying negative thoughts related to past events, focus now is on reducing negative automatic thoughts as they relate to future events, more specifically, catastrophizing. The story of "Chicken Little" is used to discuss "worst case," "best case," and "most likely" future consequences for Chicken Little. Children are then taught to apply the cognitive restructuring skills they have acquired in sessions one through four in the present moment.

Session 5. Skills learned during sessions 1 to 4 are reinforced. Attention is paid to modifying maladaptive beliefs and catastrophic thoughts.

Session 6. Focus of the sessions is shifted to interpersonal relationships. Interaction patterns, social skills, and problem solving are addressed in an effort to enhance relationships. An emphasis is placed on three interaction styles: aggressiveness, passivity, and assertiveness. Skits from the manual are used to highlight each style. Thoughts that maintain the specific styles, as well as the consequences of each, are discussed. Assertiveness skills are practiced via role-play exercises, and negotiation skills are taught.

Session 7. Children learn coping mechanisms to use when experiencing unpleasant emotions (e.g., breathing techniques and progressive muscle relaxation). Personalized visualizations are created to facilitate future guided imagery/mindfulness activities. Youth are also encouraged to build and/or to strengthen their social support systems.

Session 8. Procrastination is explored, and all-or-none thinking, a contributing factor toward procrastination, is addressed. Children are taught to break up larger tasks into smaller, more manageable ones in an effort to prevent procrastination. Skills learned during the first four sessions are then applied to projects and chores so as to combat negative thoughts.

Session 9. Children are presented with hypothetical examples from the manual to facilitate a review of the skills learned during sessions 6 to 8; behavioral techniques (relaxation and assertiveness) are then practiced. Indecisiveness is discussed, after which students are taught skills to promote effective decision making, including listing the pros and cons for each option to help decipher the best solution. Scenarios that the students have faced in their own lives are used to practice decision making.

Session 10. Problem solving (in the context of targeting negative and hostile attribution biases) is taught using a five-step model.

Session 11. Newly learned problem-solving skills are applied to social scenarios.

Session 12. Students review the program and participate in a party. Students are also encouraged to attend a maintenance session.

CONCLUSION

Depression in children and adolescents is a serious, potentially life-threatening problem. Many youth struggle with chronic, sometimes debilitating depression for extended periods of time, leading to underachievement, secondary substance abuse, school failure and drop-out, violent or self-harming behavior, and even death by suicide. Clearly, evidence-based psychotherapeutic interventions are needed. Unfortunately, PDD, a new disorder in *DSM-5* that combines features of MDD and DD, has not yet been extensively researched. However, the interventions reviewed in this chapter are backed by solid research documenting their efficacy in treating MDD and DD. As a result, they show great promise in ameliorating PDD.

SELECT BIBLIOGRAPHY

Cash, R. E. (2010a). Depression in teens: What parents can do. In A. Canter, L. Z. Page, & S. Shaw (Eds.), *Helping children at home and at school III: Handouts for families and educators.* Bethesda, MD: National Association of School Psychologists. *This article, written especially for parents of depressed teenagers, defines depression and differentiates it from sadness and the common moodiness of adolescence. It enumerates the signs and symptoms of clinical depression, lists risk factors, and provides specific ways in which parents can help their depressed teens.*

Cash, R. E. (2010b). Depression in young children. In A. Canter, L. Z. Page, & S. Shaw (Eds.), *Helping children at home and at school III: Handouts for families and educators.* Bethesda, MD: National Association of School Psychologists. *This article is directed specifically at parents who are concerned that their young child or preadolescent may be suffering from depression. It clarifies types of depression and co-occurring disorders, presents symptoms and risk factors, describes effective evaluation and treatment planning, and specifies what school personnel can do and how parents can help.*

Evans, D. L., & Andrews Wasmer, L. (2005). *If your adolescent has depression or bipolar disorder: An essential resource for parents.* New York, NY: Oxford University Press, Inc. *This book works toward establishing a greater understanding of depressive and bipolar disorders. Etiology, treatment, and psychopharmacological interventions are discussed, as the authors focus on providing guidance to parents on how best to help their teens. Effective coping skills are addressed, and the importance of preventing future depressive episodes is explored.*

REFERENCES

American Psychiatric Association. (2000). *Diagnostic and statistical manual of mental disorders* (4th ed., text rev.). Washington, DC: Author.

American Psychiatric Association. (2013). *Diagnostic and statistical manual of mental disorders* (5th ed.). Arlington, VA: American Psychiatric Publishing.

Blanco, C., Okuda, M., Markowitz, J. C., Liu, S. M., Grant, B. F., & Hasin, D. S. (2010). The epidemiology of chronic major depressive disorder and dysthymic disorder: Results from the National Epidemiologic Survey on Alcohol and Related Conditions. *Journal of Clinical Psychiatry, 71*(12), 1645–1656.

Bracken, B. A., & Howell, K. (2004). *Examiner's manual: Clinical assessment of depression.* Lutz, FL: Psychological Assessment Resources.

Brunwasser, S. M., Gillham, J. E., & Kim, E. S. (2009). A meta-analytic review of the Penn Resiliency Program's effect on depressive symptoms. *Journal of Consulting and Clinical Psychology, 77*(6), 1042–1054. doi:10.1037/a0017671

Cash, R. E. (2010a). Depression in teens: What parents can do. In A. Canter, L. Z. Page, & S. Shaw (Eds.), *Helping children at home and at school III: Handouts for families and educators.* Bethesda, MD: National Association of School Psychologists.

Cash, R. E. (2010b). Depression in young children. In A. Canter, L. Z. Page, & S. Shaw (Eds.), *Helping children at home and at school III: Handouts for families and educators.* Bethesda, MD: National Association of School Psychologists.

Chronis-Tuscano, A., Molina, B. S. G., Pelham, W. E., Applegate, B., Dahlke, A., Overmyer, M., & Lahey, B. B. (2010). Very early predictors of adolescent depression and suicide attempts in children with attention-deficit/hyperactivity disorder. *Archives of General Psychiatry, 67*(10), 1044–1051. doi:10.1001/archgenpsychiatry.2010.127

Curry, J. F., Wells, K. C., Brent, D. A., Clarke, G. N., Rohde, P., Albano, A. M., Kolker, J. (2005). *Cognitive behavior therapy manual.* Retrieved from https://trialweb.dcri.duke.edu/tads/manuals.html

David-Ferndon, C., & Kaslow, N. J. (2008). Evidence-based psychosocial treatments for child and adolescent depression. *Journal of Clinical Child & Adolescent Psychology, 37*, 62–104.

Depression in Children—Part 1. (2002, February). *Harvard mental health letter.* Retrieved from http://www.health.harvard.edu/newsweek/Depression_in_Children_Part_I.htm

Dinya, E., Csorba, J., & Grósz, Z. (2012). Are there temperament differences between major depression and dysthymic disorder in adolescent clinical outpatients? *Comprehensive Psychiatry, 53*(4), 350–354. doi:10.1016/j.comppsych.2011.05.013

Ellis, A. (1962). *Reason and emotion in psychotherapy.* New York, NY: Lyle Stewart.

Emslie, G. J., Kennard, B. D., & Mayes, T. L. (2011). Predictors of treatment response in adolescent depression. *Psychiatric Annals, 41*(4), 213–219. doi:10.3928/00485713–20110325-04

First, M. B., & Tasman, A. (2004). *DSM-IV-TR mental disorders™: Diagnosis, etiology, and treatment*. West Sussex, England: Wiley.

Gillham, J. E., Reivich, K. J., Freres, D. R., Chaplin, T. M., Shatté, A. J., Samuels, B.,…Seligman, M. E. P. (2007). School-based prevention of depressive symptoms: A randomized controlled study of the effectiveness and specificity of the Penn Resiliency Program. *Journal of Consulting and Clinical Psychology, 75,* 9–19.

Grohol, J. (2008). Dysthymia treatment. *Psych Central*. Retrieved from http://psychcentral.com/lib/dysthymia-treatment/0001522

Gureje, O. (2011). Dysthymia in a cross-cultural perspective. *Current Opinion in Psychiatry, 24*(1), 67–71. doi:10.1097/YCO.0b013e32834136a5

Hammen, C., & Rudolph, K. D. (2002). Childhood mood disorders. In E. J. Mash, & R. A. Barkley (Eds.), *Child psychopathology* (2nd ed., pp. 233–263). New York, NY: Guilford Press.

Hetrick, S. E., Parker, A. G., Robinson, J., Hall, N., & Vance, A. (2012). Predicting suicidal risk in a cohort of depressed children and adolescents. *Crisis: The Journal of Crisis Intervention and Suicide Prevention, 33*(1), 13–20. doi:10.1027/0227–5910/a000095

Jonsson, U., Bohman, H., von Knorring, L., Olsson, G., Paaren, A., & von Knorring, A. (2011). Mental health outcome of long-term and episodic adolescent depression: 15-year follow-up of a community sample. *Journal of Affective Disorders, 130*(3), 395–404. doi:10.1016/j.jad.2010.10.046

Martinez, W., Zychinski, K., & Polo, A. (2012). Depressive disorders in children and adolescents. In M. Hersen & P. Sturmey (Eds.), *Handbook of evidence-based practice in clinical psychology: Child and adolescent disorders* (Vol. 1, pp. 521–540). Hoboken, NJ: Wiley.

Merikangas, K. R., He, J., Burstein, M., Swanson, S. A., Avenevoli, S., Cui, L., & Swendsen, J. (2010). Lifetime prevalence of mental disorders in U.S. adolescents: Results from the National Comorbidity Study-Adolescent Supplement (NCS-A). *Journal of the American Academy of Child Adolescent Psychiatry, 49*(10), 980–989.

Mufson, L., Pollack Dorta, K., Moreau, D., & Weissman, M. M. (2004). *Interpersonal psychotherapy for depressed adolescents* (2nd ed.). New York, NY: The Guilford Press.

Rhebergen, D., & Graham, R. (2014). The re-labelling of dysthymic disorder to persistent depressive disorder in *DSM-5*: Old wine in new bottles? *Current Opinion in Psychiatry, 27*(1), 27–31. doi:10.1097/YCO.0000000000000022

TADS Team. (2009). The Treatment for Adolescents with Depression Study (TADS): Over 1 year of naturalistic follow-up. *The American Journal of Psychiatry, 166*(10), 1141–1149.

University of Pennsylvania. (2009a). *Description of PRP lessons*. Retrieved from https://ppc.sas.upenn.edu/sites/ppc.sas.upenn.edu/files/prplessons.pdf

University of Pennsylvania. (2009b). *Resilience research in children*. Retrieved from https://ppc.sas.upenn.edu/research/resilience-children

Weiser, M., Lubin, G., Caspi, A., Rabinowitz, J., Shmushkevitz, M., Yoffe, R., & Davidson, M. (2008). Dysthymia in male adolescents is associated with increased risk of later hospitalization for psychotic disorders: A historical-prospective cohort study. *Early Intervention in Psychiatry, 2*(2), 67–72. doi:10.1111/j.1751–7893.2008.00060.x

Evidence-Based Interventions for Pediatric Bipolar Disorder

Molly R. Meers and Mary A. Fristad

OVERVIEW

Pediatric bipolar disorder (PBD) has been associated with a number of negative behavioral, academic, and interpersonal outcomes for children and adolescents (Birmaher et al., 2009). The course of the disease is typically chronic, resulting in an elevated risk of hospitalizations, suicide attempts/completions, and substance use. A recent meta-analysis reported mean prevalence rates of PBD at 1.8% (Van Meter, Moreira, & Youngstrom, 2011). In addition, data from six urban community mental health centers found that 6% of all youth seen received a PBD diagnosis (Youngstrom, Youngstrom, & Starr, 2005). Research has also shown that as many as 34% of children and 26% of adolescents discharged from psychiatric inpatient units have a primary diagnosis of PBD (Blader & Carlson, 2007). This is likely because key phenomenological characteristics of the disorder (e.g., aggressive behavior, mood volatility), are often the presenting problem for inpatient psychiatric care.

Diagnosing PBD in youth involves a careful longitudinal assessment of key mood states. The depressed phase is manifest by dysphoric and/or irritable mood whereas the manic phase includes extreme irritability or euphoric/expansive mood accompanied by increased energy/activity. Associated depressive symptoms include: changes in sleep, appetite or energy, fatigue, loss of interest, decreased concentration, feelings of guilt or worthlessness, and suicidal or morbid ideation. Associated manic symptoms include: inflated self-esteem/grandiosity; decreased sleep and attention; increased speech, speed of thinking, and goal-directed activity or psychomotor agitation; and excessive involvement in activities that demonstrate poor judgment. As a detailed description of empirically supported assessment is beyond the scope of this chapter, please refer to Youngstrom, Jenkins, Jensen-Doss, and Youngstrom (2012) for a more comprehensive review. Youth may be diagnosed with bipolar I disorder, characterized by the presence of at least one manic episode (i.e., extremely irritable or euphoric/expansive mood and associated symptoms lasting 7 or more days or requiring hospitalization); bipolar II disorder, characterized by the presence of at least one hypomanic episode (i.e., extremely irritable or euphoric/expansive mood and associated symptoms lasting between 4 and 7 days) and one major depressive episode; cyclothymic disorder, diagnosed if prominent hypomanic and depressive symptoms are present for at least 1 year; and "Other Specified" (formerly bipolar disorder–not otherwise specified [BP-NOS]) if there are symptoms of mania present that are clearly impairing but criteria for the other bipolar spectrum disorders are not met (American Psychiatric Association [APA], 2013).

In addition to assessing for the presence of manic and depressive symptoms, diagnosis of PBD includes a central focus on episodic mood and energy levels. For example, amped up energy has been identified as a hallmark feature of manic irritability in youth (Blader & Carlson, 2007). In addition, youth diagnosed with PBD are more likely to present with mixed episodes (i.e., the presence of both mania and depressive mood states and symptoms) and greater rapid cycling between mood polarities than adults (Goldstein & Birmaher, 2012). In addition, it is common that children do not meet diagnosis for Bipolar I or II because duration criteria for the symptoms are not met (Axelson et al., 2006). However, research demonstrates that across bipolar spectrum disorder diagnoses (BP1, BP2, BP-NOS), youth do not differ in age of onset, severity of worst mood symptoms, comorbidities (except anxiety), family mental health history, suicidal ideation, or number of years they have experienced mood symptoms (Birmaher et al., 2009). Thus, it is inaccurate to assume that BP-NOS is a less severe bipolar spectrum disorder diagnosis in youth.

There are also important phenomenological characteristics specific to PBD. For children and adolescents, excessive involvement in activities with a potential for painful consequences may look different than in adults; that is, rather than going on a massive shopping spree, children may distribute their toys and/or belongings among all of the children in the neighborhood or on their school bus. In addition, salient symptoms of the disorder differ between adults and youth. For example, Kowach, Youngstrom, Danielyan, and Findling (2005) found that the most common symptoms of BD in youth include increased energy, distractibility, and pressured speech with at least 70% of youth also displaying threshold symptoms of irritable mood, grandiosity, elevated/euphoric mood, decreased need for sleep, and racing thoughts. The least-endorsed symptoms include flight of ideas, hypersexuality, and psychotic features, symptoms that are more frequent in adults.

Because of the clinical profile of PBD described earlier, the differential diagnosis between PBD and disruptive behavior disorder diagnoses can be a challenge for clinicians. Supporting this claim, archival data from six urban community health centers found that 80% of children diagnosed with PBD initially received a disruptive behavior disorder diagnosis (Youngstrom et al., 2005). As amped up energy is a hallmark characteristic of PBD, it is not surprising that, in combination with anger and/or irritability and behavioral disinhibition, differentiating these symptoms and characteristics between PBD and disruptive behavior disorders is difficult (Blader & Carlson, 2007). Adding to this difficulty is the finding that the three most common symptoms of PBD (i.e., increased energy, distractibility, pressured speech) overlap with symptoms of attention deficit hyperactive disorder (ADHD; Axelson et al., 2006).

Youngstrom and colleagues (2005) also found that children with BD have higher rates of ADHD and oppositional defiant disorder (ODD) than clinically referred children who do not have BD, further confounding differential diagnosis. Because of the high rates of comorbidity with ADHD and ODD (estimated at 69%–87% and 46%–86%, respectively; Axelson et al., 2006), some researchers have proposed that PBD may be a distinct form of BD, with an etiology and phenomenology more similar to the disruptive behavior disorders (Spencer et al., 2001; Todd, 2002). High rates of comorbid anxiety disorders have also been found in children with PBD (Wagner, 2006).

A number of associated symptoms of PBD also identify this disorder as a serious public health concern. For example, high rates of current and past suicidal ideation and acts are common in PBD (Algorta et al., 2011), in addition to nonsuicidal self-injury (Esposito-Smythers et al., 2010). Adolescents with elevated symptoms of mania are also much more likely to be sexually active and engage in risky sexual behaviors (e.g., multiple sexual partners, unprotected sex) than youth with other psychiatric diagnoses (Stewart et al., 2012). Furthermore, higher rates of substance-use disorders are found among BD adolescents compared with non-BD adolescents, with substance-use disorder among BD adolescents further predicting risky sexual behaviors, involvement with the police, and increased prevalence of suicide attempts (Goldstein et al., 2008).

PBD is also related to poorer psychosocial functioning and impairment in peer and family relationships compared with healthy controls and youth diagnosed with ADHD (Keenan-Miller & Miklowitz, 2011). Youth with BD have marked disruptions in both positive (e.g., elation) and negative affect (Walsh, Royal, Brown, Barrantes-Vidal, & Kwapil, 2012), resulting in disrupted emotional processing (Garrett et al., 2012; Pavuluri, Passarotti, Harral, & Sweeney, 2009) and greater levels of emotional reactivity in relationships. In addition, youth with BD display greater deficits in social skills, related to performance rather than knowledge, compared with controls without a psychiatric diagnosis (Goldstein, Miklowitz, & Mullen, 2006). Furthermore, families of youth with PBD show high levels of conflict, poor communication, low levels of warmth, and high levels of expressed emotion, contributing to the course and outcome of the disorder (Algorta et al., 2011; Coville, Miklowitz, Taylor, & Low, 2008; Du Rocher Schudlich, Youngstrom, Calabrese, & Findling, 2008).

PBD is also associated with cognitive and learning difficulties. Compared with healthy controls, youth with BD have large to moderate differences in executive functioning, attention, working memory, and visual and verbal long-term memory (Joseph, Frazier, Youngstrom, & Soares, 2008). In addition, reduced sleep and insomnia are common features of BD in youth, compounding the negative impact on course, symptom expression, and cognitive functioning (Harvey, 2009). A better understand of cognitive and learning abnormalities found in youth with BD is helpful for better understanding the underlying neurobiological etiology, and vice versa.

ETIOLOGY AND FACTORS CONTRIBUTING TO PBD IN CHILDREN AND ADOLESCENTS

Family, twin, and adoption studies have clearly documented a genetic etiology for PBD (Smoller & Finn, 2003). Concordance rates of BD among monozygotic and dizygotic twins indicate heritability rates ranging from 59% to 87% (Smoller & Finn, 2003). In addition, offspring studies have found a 14% to 50% incidence rate of BPSD among children of parents with BD (Chang, Steiner, & Ketter, 2000; Duffy, Alda, Kutcher, Fusee, & Grof, 1998). Furthermore, compared with controls, first-degree relatives of individuals with BD have an approximate 10-fold increased risk of having the

disorder (Smoller & Finn, 2003). There is also a strong link between early onset PBD and BD in first-degree relatives, more so than youth with other mental health diagnoses and normal controls (Pavuluri, Birmaher, & Naylor, 2005). Thus, there is clear evidence that BD runs in families and has a strong genetic component.

Structural and functional abnormalities in the areas of the brain responsible for emotional control have also been implicated in the development of BD (Garrett et al., 2012; Pavuluri, Passarotti, Harral, & Sweeney, 2009; Strakowski et al., 2012). The general consensus model of the neuroanatomy of PBD posits that disruption of neural connectivity in early development results in abnormal development of the structures and functions of the amygdala as well as regions of the prefrontal cortex that control the limbic system (Strakowski et al., 2012). Underactive prefrontal cortex areas and over active limbic system areas result in more intense emotional responses and decreased top-down control of emotional reactivity, contributing to the impairment seen in individuals with PBD (Garrett et al., 2012; Pavuluri et al., 2009). For example, consistent with adult BD studies, children with BD demonstrate greater amygdala activation when presented with facial expressions (Garrett et al., 2012). This leads BD youth to have greater difficulty processing the emotional facial expressions of others, often leading to the misinterpretation of emotions. In addition, heightened amygdala activation over time is thought to lead to poorer emotion regulation skills (Strakowski et al., 2012).

EVIDENCE-BASED INTERVENTIONS AND EMPIRICAL SUPPORT FOR PBD IN CHILDREN AND ADOLESCENTS

The American Academy of Child and Adolescent Psychiatry (AACAP, 2007) suggests combining medications and psychotherapeutic interventions to address both the symptoms and the associated psychosocial factors in youth with BD. First-line pharmacologic treatment for PBD involves monotherapy (i.e., treatment with one medication) with atypical antipsychotics (i.e., aripiprazole, quetiapine, risperidone, ziprasidone), with second-line pharmacological treatments, including a trial of a different first-line medication, olanzapine, or a mood stabilizer (i.e., lithium, valproate; Kowatch, Strawn, & Sorter, 2009). Additional augmentation/combination therapy may then be warranted if there is a lack of response or still room for improvement. It is unfortunate to note that mood stabilizers and atypical antipsychotics have a number of adverse side effects, including, but not limited to, weight gain, drowsiness, decreased motor activity, constipation, increased salivation, rigidity, and dystonia (Fleischhaker et al., 2006).

More recently, attention has turned to complementary and alternative medicines in the treatment of PBD, as they are associated with fewer side effects. For example, there is growing empirical support for the use of omega-3 fatty acids in the treatment of PBD (Clayton et al., 2009; Wozniak et al., 2007) and mood disorders more generally. Omega-3 has been shown to be more effective than placebo for depressive symptoms in adults and youth (Osher & Belmaker, 2009); it was also 5.6 times more effective than placebo in preventing psychosis in a 1-year clinical trial for high-risk adolescents (4.9% vs. 27.5%; Amminger et al., 2010). In addition, a recent open-label study of EMPowerplus™ (EMP⁺), a multinutrient supplement, demonstrated decreased depression and mania symptoms more than 8 weeks for children with bipolar spectrum disorders (Frazier, Fristad, & Arnold, 2012). Although these treatment effects are promising, they have yet to acquire the extent of empirical support available for the first-line pharmacotherapy interventions discussed earlier.

In addition to pharmacological interventions, psychotherapy is also recommended for the treatment PBD (Kowatch, Fristad, Findling, & Post, 2009; McClellan, Kowatch, Findling, & Issues, 2007). For example, family-focused psychoeducation plus skill building has been shown to decrease mood symptoms severity and increase family and global functioning in youth with BD (Fristad, 2006; Miklowitz, 2012). Indeed, a recent comprehensive review examining the evidence base of psychotherapeutic treatments for PBD found that psychoeducation plus skill building has been the most thoroughly examined psychotherapeutic intervention and is considered a probably efficacious treatment for PBD (Fristad & MacPherson, 2014). One such therapeutic intervention, for which there are multiple randomized clinical trials (RCT), is

psychoeducational psychotherapy (PEP; Fristad, 2006; Fristad, Goldberg-Arnold, & Gavazzi, 2002; Fristad, Verducci, Walters, & Young, 2009). PEP uses a biopsychosocial model and combines family therapy, psychoeducation, and cognitive behavioral therapy (CBT) techniques with the goal of helping families to better understand and manage the symptoms of PBD and coordinate more effective treatment (Fristad, Goldberg-Arnold, & Leffler, 2011). A description of PEP, including three key interventions of this therapeutic approach (Psychoeducation and Motto, Building a Tool Kit, Thinking–Feeling–Doing), will be the focus of the remainder of this chapter.

HOW TO: A GUIDE TO THE IMPLEMENTATION OF INTERVENTIONS FOR PBD

PEP is a manual-based treatment designed for youth with mood disorders and their caregivers, broken down into separate youth and caregiver sessions. Sessions focus primarily on psychoeducation and skills building (e.g., problem solving, communication) and are delivered in individual family (IF-PEP) and multiple family formats (MF-PEP). MF-PEP consists of eight 90-minute concurrent youth and caregiver sessions that begin and end together, whereas the bulk of each session is held separately for youth and caregivers. IF-PEP includes 20 content sessions (10 youth sessions and 10 caregiver sessions) and "in-the-bank" sessions as needed to address crises, repeat material that requires additional reinforcement, and so forth. IF-PEP also includes specific sessions focused on healthy habits (i.e., sleeping, eating, and exercise) and resolving sibling conflict, topics discussed more generally in MF-PEP. Both formats include brief weekly take-home projects meant to encourage families to practice skills between sessions.

Psychoeducation and Motto

The first key intervention in a psychoeducational approach to PBD is to emphasize that PBD is a "no-fault" illness, the symptoms of which can be controlled and managed (Fristad, Gavazzi, & Soldano, 1999). In PEP, psychoeducation involves providing information about pediatric mood disorders, symptoms of mania and depression, diagnostic criteria for PBD, the influence of genetics on PBD, brain differences of children with PBD, common co-occurring disorders and difficulties, as well as risk factors for suicidality. These subjects are covered in both youth and parental PEP sessions.

The initial step in providing psychoeducation on mood disorders to caregivers involves addressing common myths that may prevent children from getting treatment. Two common myths include, "It will go away (soon) on its own" and "Everybody gets this way" (Fristad et al., 2011, p. 89). Although it is true that everyone has normal variations in mood, it is important for parents to understand that normal variations in mood do not lead to the level of impairment in social, educational, or family functioning seen in the lives of children with PBD. In addition, normal variations in mood typically do not persist over the course of, for example, 6 months. Other myths to address may include the following: "You ought to just 'snap out of it.'"; "Getting treatment is a sign of weakness."; "Mood-impaired kids are bad or lazy."; and "Teenagers are 'just moody.'" Following a discussion of myths, it is helpful to provide parents with basic information about the prevalence of mood disorders in children, such as "Nearly 4% of children aged 8–15 have a mood disorder."

Psychoeducation then turns to a discussion of the etiology (i.e., genetic, biological) of PBD in order to lay the foundation for parental understanding of PBD as a "no-fault brain disorder." The genetic transmission of the disorder is described, highlighting the genetic risk among twins, offspring, and first-degree relatives. As this has the potential to evoke guilt in parents, it is important next to emphasize that parents cannot choose the genes they receive or the genes they pass on to their child; thus, they are not responsible for causing the disorder in their child. It is helpful to overtly state that mistakes in parenting, which all parents will make, do *not* cause PBD. Finally, this session summarizes for parents the research on brain differences in adolescents with BD. This involves describing general differences in the prefrontal cortex and limbic system that result in intense emotional responses that may feel like emergencies to youth with BD. These urgent messages occur at the expense of more rational/thought-out responses. Also important to describe are deficits in perceiving emotional stimuli

and the ability to take into account the point of view of others. Explaining these brain differences helps parents acknowledge that their children's trying behavior is not done purposefully to drive their parents crazy; rather, their child's brain works differently and, at times, this can lead to greater difficulty inhibiting immediate emotional responses and misperceived social interactions.

After clarifying the "how" and "why" of parents not *causing* their child's problem, it is equally important to emphasize that parents can play an important role in the *course* of the disorder. The information presented thus far lays the foundation for now introducing the PEP motto, "It's not your fault, but it's your challenge!" The remainder of the information presented and interventions recommended are then framed within the context of this motto.

The first challenge parents have is to better understand the criteria for diagnosing mood disorders with some brief acknowledgment of why diagnosing mood disorders in children can be difficult (e.g., distinguishing between ordinary and "clinical" ups and downs, distinguishing between mood symptoms and children's personality traits). Parents are given information on key mood states and associated symptoms required to diagnose the presence of manic and depressive episodes in addition to duration requirements for making different mood disorder diagnoses, with a reminder that symptoms must be severe enough to cause impairment for the youth or family.

The first session concludes with a discussion of warning signs and risk factors for suicide and a description of other common comorbid disorders (e.g., anxiety, ADHD, learning disorders). As access to guns is the most important risk factor for completed suicide, parents are strongly urged to remove guns from their home if their child is at risk for suicidal ideation and/or acts (this is clearly stated as a pro-safety rather than an antigun recommendation). This section ends with a discussion of additional treatments that may be required for co-occurring disorders. Parents are also provided with information on psychotic symptoms that may be present during mood episodes and told that these symptoms will most likely go away once mood is treated.

Psychoeducation and the motto are also addressed in the first youth session of PEP. To help children gain an increased awareness of their moods and associated triggers, this session and subsequent sessions begin with emotion identification and rating activity. Youth are instructed to identify how they are feeling by selecting from a set of pictures depicting various emotions. They are then instructed to rate the intensity of the emotion using a feelings thermometer, with anchors ranging from low to "danger zone," and encouraged to identify the trigger for this emotion. This leads to a teaching moment on how emotions in the "danger zone" place children at risk for losing control of their behaviors, laying the foundation for training children to use their Tool Kits when emotions are in the "danger zone," a skill discussed in greater detail in the following sections. To further model feeling identification for youth, the therapist may also demonstrate the use of the feeling thermometer, describing out loud their triggers and the intensity of their emotions (e.g., feelings of excitement of medium intensity because of starting therapy with a new family).

The next step is to gain additional information about what children already know about depression and mania. This begins with a discussion on what "symptoms" are, explaining to children that symptoms are feelings or behaviors that cluster together as part of a disorder. Using a cold as a metaphor, the therapist can prompt the youth to identify the different symptoms that cluster together as part of the illness. The youth then list known symptoms of mania and depression and the therapist provides information about additional symptoms using developmentally appropriate language. Child-specific symptoms are listed in separate columns for mania and depression, further providing foundational language for the youth to talk about their mood disorder. This leads to a discussion of the "ups and downs" of mania, explaining that some children may have symptoms of mania or depression for days whereas others have symptoms that change more frequently, including moods that may change as often as multiple times a day. Finally, the therapist then takes a few minutes to discuss symptoms of other comorbid conditions the youth might be experiencing (e.g., ADHD, anxiety).

This session concludes with a discussion of the PEP motto, "It's not your fault, but it's your challenge!" The youth is explicitly told, often for the first time, that his or her symptoms of depression, mania, and other comorbid disorders are not the youth's fault. Brief, developmentally appropriate descriptions of genetic and biological causes are provided. As with the parents, the message immediately following "It's not your fault" is "but it's your challenge!" It is important for youth to understand that mood symptoms can, unmanaged, wreak havoc with their social lives, in school and at home. Learning ways to lower their mood when they feel manic and raise their mood when they feel depressed is part of their challenge. Children then learn belly breathing, one of three breathing techniques they will be taught over the course of treatment, with instructions to practice at home as the first Tool Kit item for helping to cope with strong emotions.

Building a Tool Kit

A second key intervention in a psychoeducational and skills-building treatment approach for PBD is Building a Tool Kit. This is a collection of coping strategies for children to use when they are in a manic or depressive mood state. In the Tool Kit–building session of PEP, children are first encouraged to generate a list of triggers for sad, mad, or bad (i.e., anxious) feelings. Additional points to cover during this discussion include: how triggers may lead to different feelings depending on the day; people can have more than one feeling at a time; and feelings are not "good" or "bad" in and of themselves, rather, it is the thoughts and actions that feelings propel that can cause trouble. The goal is to increase children's awareness of the behavioral antecedents for intense emotions so that they can learn what to do in response to these situations. This conversation then leads to a discussion of the physiological signals of different emotions. Children are shown an outline of a body and instructed to indicate, with different colors, the physical sensations associated with feeling sad (blue), mad (red), and anxious (yellow). Depending on the youth's interoceptive awareness, the therapist may provide additional examples (e.g., face flushing, balled fists, tensed muscles, heart racing, tearfulness, tightness of throat, shaking muscles, butterflies in stomach) to assist the youth with this activity.

Children are encouraged to identify their typical responses (i.e., actions, behaviors) to feeling sad, mad, or bad. As children list responses, they are categorized as "helpful" if the answer is "no," and "hurtful" if the answer is "yes," to any of the following questions evaluating the outcome: (a) "Does it hurt me?"; (b) "Does it hurt someone or something else?"; and (c) "Does it get anyone in trouble?" If the youths are having difficulty generating examples of typical responses, the therapist can help prompt them by using previously discussed triggers as examples. This lesson is then tied back to the PEP motto by explaining that children cannot control how they *feel*, but they can control what they *do* in response to their feelings. Once the youths seem to understand the links between triggers, feelings, and responses, the therapist then moves to a discussion of how to build a Tool Kit.

The therapist then helps the youths generate several strategies they can use to raise or lower their mood. Youths are encouraged to identify tools they can use in different environments (e.g., school, home, at the park) and for different mood states and energy levels. For example, a youth who is feeling manic may need to identify relaxing activities, such as taking a hot bath or shower or listening to music in his or her room, whereas a youth who is feeling depressed and lethargic/tired may need to identify activating activities such as jumping on the trampoline or taking a walk. As youths come up with their list of items, they are sorted into four categories (creative, active, rest and relaxation, and social = CARS, which take you where you want to go). Creative tools are meant to require imagination that can allow for venting (e.g., drawing, journaling) or distracting (e.g., playing with Legos); active tools are meant to get a youth moving, which provides aerobic antidepressant benefits (e.g., play catch with the dog; jog); rest and relaxation tools help calm a youth (e.g., bubble bath, deep breaths); and social tools are meant to engage a youth with other people and/or pets (e.g., talk with friend, pet guinea pig) or, conversely, to engage in solitude if that is a better calming strategy (e.g., to temporarily withdraw from others). Once they have identified several tools for each category, they are encouraged to continue updating the lists over time.

Once the initial Tool Kit items are generated, allow the youths to choose whether they would like their Tool Kit to remain a list or whether they would like to create a physical Tool Kit, providing the youth with a shoebox to use if desired. In this box, they are instructed to place actual Tool Kit items (e.g., journal and pencil) or symbols of items from their list (e.g., a picture of a sunset to remind them to sit on the porch and take deep breaths). The Tool Kit should be kept in a place that is easily accessible to them and parents may be helpful in identifying additional items to add to it. As their take-home project, children are instructed to practice using their Tool Kit when they feel sad, mad, or worried. If car travel is a particularly difficult time for a child, building a second Tool Kit that can remain in the car can be very beneficial.

Thinking, Doing, and Feeling Activity

Another key intervention in a psychoeducational and skills-building treatment approach to treating PBD involves using classic CBT skills to highlight the connection between thoughts, feelings, and behaviors. Once children know what *to do* when feeling sad, mad, or bad, they are ready to learn to differentiate between "helpful" and "hurtful" thoughts. The therapist leads a discussion on the connection between thoughts, feelings, and behaviors, referring back to the PEP motto by explaining that, although children *do not* have control over how they feel ("not your fault"), they *do* have control over how they think and behave in response to those feelings ("your challenge"). Before introducing the role of helpful thoughts in managing unpleasant mood states, children must have a clear understanding of the difference between thoughts, feelings, and behaviors. Provide additional practice, modeling, and scaffolding as needed. Using a Thinking, Feeling, Doing handout (Fristad, Davidson, & Leffler, 2008) will help organize the following task instructions.

First, ask the youths to identify a time that they felt mad, sad, or bad. The trigger is then recorded on the appropriate section of the handout. Then the youths are encouraged to identify their initial "hurtful" feelings in the box denoted by a minus sign. Each youth then identifies any hurtful behaviors resulting from this trigger. Again, the youth is instructed to identify hurtful behaviors by asking himself or herself the following questions: (a) "Does it hurt me?"; (b) "Does it hurt anything or anyone else?"; and (c) "Does it get anyone in trouble?" The next step is to help the youths identify the hurtful thoughts that resulted from the trigger. Depending on the developmental level of the youths or their ability to distinguish between events and private self-talk, the therapist may need to provide additional assistance in helping the youths to articulate their thoughts. Questions that can be helpful for this purpose include: "What were you telling yourself?" and "What were you saying to yourself in your head?" These hurtful thoughts are then entered into the portion of the thought cloud with a minus sign. At this time, a general discussion on the bidirectional relationship between hurtful thoughts, feelings, and behaviors (as depicted by double-sided arrows) is facilitated using the examples provided by the youths.

After reviewing the hurtful Thinking–Feeling–Doing cycle, the youths are asked how they would rather feel in the situation provided (e.g., "How would you rather feel? Calm? Relaxed? Content?"). This more helpful feeling is recorded in the feeling heart with a plus sign. A discussion of how the youths can make choices about how they think and respond to hurtful feelings, referring back to the PEP motto, may proceed as follows.

We can't always keep from getting upset and we can't immediately change how we feel. Our feelings are not our fault. However, we do have control over how we think and act in response to triggers and feelings. The challenge is to come up with more helpful ways to think and act in response to these triggers to help us feel more calm and relaxed.

The therapist then prompts the youths to identify more helpful actions, referring back to previously identified Tool Kit items as needed. These more helpful actions are added to the portion of the "Doing" box with a plus sign. The final therapist questions then focus on helping children identify and list (in the "Thinking" box) more helpful thoughts. Depending on the children's developmental level, they may again need more or less assistance in doing so. Youths are then asked to predict the likely impact these helpful thoughts and actions will have on their feelings. These steps may be repeated with additional youth-generated triggers or by collaboratively "talking out loud" using provided examples. Overall, the goal is to help children learn that they may not have control over the initial feelings, but they do have control over how they think and act.

CONCLUSION

PBD in children and adolescents is a chronic disease with deleterious behavioral, academic, and interpersonal outcomes. Diagnosing PBD in youth involves a careful longitudinal assessment of key mood states. In addition to assessing for the presence of manic and depressive symptoms, diagnosis of PBD includes a central focus on episodic mood and energy levels. For example, amped up energy has been identified as a hallmark feature of manic irritability in youth. In addition, youth diagnosed with PBD are more likely to present with mixed episodes and greater rapid cycling between mood polarities than adults. The most common symptoms of BD in youth include increased energy, distractibility, and pressured speech with at least 70% of youth also displaying threshold symptoms of irritable mood, grandiosity, elevated/euphoric mood, decreased need for sleep, and racing thoughts. Research has established a genetic etiology as well as structural and functional abnormalities in the areas of the brain responsible for emotional control. There are several evidence-based interventions that may be employed for youth with PBD including medication, Psychoeducation and Motto, Building a Tool Kit, and the Thinking–Feeling–Doing game. These treatments are discussed in a step-by-step manner for mental health professionals to employ to facilitate and enhance overall quality of life for children with this disorder.

SELECT BIBLIOGRAPHY

Fristad, M. A., & Goldberg-Arnold, J. S. (2004). *Raising a moody child: How to cope with depression and bipolar disorder*. New York, NY: Guilford Press.
In this book, Drs. Fristad and Goldberg-Arnold provide practical information and support for parents and caretakers of children and adolescents with depression and BD. They provide information on how mood disorder diagnoses are made in children and adolescents and the multipronged approach to effective treatment (i.e., medication, therapy, coping skills). This book provides concrete advice on how parents can best advocate for their children with mood disorders and obtain optimal treatment.

Fristad, M. A., Goldberg-Arnold, J. S., & Leffler, J. M. (2011). *Psychotherapy for children with bipolar and depressive disorders*. New York, NY: Guilford Press.
This book provides step-by-step instructions for implementing individual and multifamily psychoeducational psychotherapy, an evidence-based psychotherapy model for children with mood disorders (i.e., depression or BD). The authors provide background information for the treatment in addition to rationales for each therapy component. Also included are multiple handouts for clinicians.

Fristad, M. A., & MacPherson, H. A. (2014). Evidence-based psychosocial treatments for child and adolescent bipolar spectrum disorders. *Journal of Clinical Child and Adolescent Psychology, 43*(3), 339–355.
This review article details a comprehensive literature search of psychosocial intervention trials on the treatment of PBD, evaluating each according to the Task Force on the Promotion and Dissemination of Psychological Procedures guidelines.

Depression and Bipolar Support Alliance. Retrieved from www.dbsalliance.org
The Depression and Bipolar Support Alliance (DBSA) website is a wellness-based resource created for and by individuals with depression and BD. It contains links to educational resources, wellness and treatment options, and peer support for individuals with mood disorders in addition to educational resources for friends, family members, and clinicians of individuals with mood disorders. It also includes links to research in the field as well as information on becoming involved in local alliance chapters.

Youngstrom, E. A., Jenkins, M. M., Jensen-Doss, A., & Youngstrom, J. K. (2012). Evidence-based assessment strategies for pediatric bipolar disorder. *The Israel Journal of Psychiatry and Related Sciences, 49*(1), 15–27.
This review article provides a description for why evidence-based assessment of PBD is needed, when assessment is warranted, new developments in the field, as well as when to use different techniques over the course of diagnosis and treatment. The authors also detail a decision-making framework to help guide assessment in addition to a discussion of the techniques that are most valid and applicable to community-based clinical settings.

REFERENCES

Algorta, G. P., Youngstrom, E. A., Frazier, T. W., Freeman, A. J., Youngstrom, J. K., & Findling, R. L. (2011). Suicidality in pediatric bipolar disorder: Predictor or outcome of family processes and mixed mood presentation? *Bipolar Disorders, 13*(1), 76–86.

American Academy of Child and Adolescent Psychiatry (AACAP). (2007). Practice parameters for the assessment and treatment of children and adolescents with bipolar disorder. *Journal of the American Academy of Child and Adolescent Psychiatry, 46*(1), 107–125.

American Psychiatric Association (APA). (2013). *Diagnostic and statistical manual of mental disorders* (5th ed.). Arlington, VA: American Psychiatric Publishing.

Amminger, G. P., Schäfer, M. R., Papageorgiou, K., Klier, C. M., Cotton, S. M., Harrigan, S. M.,...Berger, G. E. (2010). Long-chain omega-3 fatty acids for indicated prevention of psychotic disorders: A randomized, placebo-controlled trial. *Archives of General Psychiatry, 67*(2), 146–154.

Axelson, D., Birmaher, B., Strober, M., Gill, M. K., Valeri, S., Chiappetta, L.,...Keller, M. (2006). Phenomenology of children and adolescents with bipolar spectrum disorders. *Archives of General Psychiatry, 63*(10), 1139–1148.

Birmaher, B., Axelson, D., Goldstein, B., Strober, M., Gill, M. K., Hunt, J.,...Keller, M. (2009). Four-year longitudinal course of children and adolescents with bipolar spectrum disorders: The Course and Outcome of Bipolar Youth (COBY) study. *The American Journal of Psychiatry, 166*(7), 795–804.

Blader, J. C., & Carlson, G. A. (2007). Increased rates of bipolar disorder diagnoses among U.S. child, adolescent, and adult inpatients, 1996–2004. *Biological Psychiatry, 62*(2), 107–114.

Chang, K. D., Steiner, H., & Ketter, T. A. (2000). Psychiatric phenomenology of child and adolescent bipolar offspring. *Journal of the American Academy of Child and Adolescent Psychiatry, 39*(4), 453–460.

Clayton, E. H., Hanstock, T. L., Hirneth, S. J., Kable, C. J., Garg, M. L., & Hazell, P. L. (2009). Reduced mania and depression in juvenile bipolar disorder associated with long-chain omega-3 polyunsaturated fatty acid supplementation. *European Journal of Clinical Nutrition, 63*(8), 1037–1040.

Coville, A. L., Miklowitz, D. J., Taylor, D. O., & Low, K. G. (2008). Correlates of high expressed emotion attitudes among parents of bipolar adolescents. *Journal of Clinical Psychology, 64*(4), 438–449.

Duffy, A., Alda, M., Kutcher, S., Fusee, C., & Grof, P. (1998). Psychiatric symptoms and syndromes among adolescent children of parents with lithium-responsive or lithium-nonresponsive bipolar disorder. *The American Journal of Psychiatry, 155*(3), 431–433.

Du Rocher Schudlich, T. D., Youngstrom, E. A., Calabrese, J. R., & Findling, R. L. (2008). The role of family functioning in bipolar disorder in families. *Journal of Abnormal Child Psychology, 36*(6), 849–863.

Esposito-Smythers, C., Goldstein, T., Birmaher, B., Goldstein, B., Hunt, J., Ryan, N.,...Keller, M. (2010). Clinical and psychosocial correlates of non-suicidal self-injury within a sample of children and adolescents with bipolar disorder. *Journal of Affective Disorders, 125*(1–3), 89–97.

Fleischhaker, C., Heiser, P., Hennighausen, K., Herpertz-Dahlmann, B., Holtkamp, K., Mehler-Wex, C.,...Warnke, A. (2006). Clinical drug monitoring in child and adolescent psychiatry: Side effects of atypical neuroleptics. *Journal of Child and Adolescent Psychopharmacology, 16*(3), 308–316.

Frazier, E. A., Fristad, M. A., & Arnold, L. E. (2012). Feasibility of a nutritional supplement as treatment for pediatric bipolar spectrum disorders. *Journal of Alternative & Complementary Medicine, 18*(7), 678–685. doi:10.1089/acm.2011.0270

Fristad, M. A. (2006). Psychoeducational treatment for school-aged children with bipolar disorder. *Development and Psychopathology, 18*(4), 1289–1306.

Fristad, M. A., Davidson, K. H., & Leffler, J. M. (2008). Thinking–feeling–doing. *Journal of Family Psychotherapy, 18*(4), 81–103. doi:10.1300/J085v18n04_06

Fristad, M. A., Gavazzi, S. M., & Soldano, K. W. (1999). Naming the enemy. *Journal of Family Psychology, 10*(1), 81–88. doi:10.1300/J085v10n01_07

Fristad, M. A., Goldberg-Arnold, J. S., & Gavazzi, S. M. (2002). Multifamily psychoeducation groups (MFPG) for families of children with bipolar disorder. *Bipolar Disorders, 4*(4), 254–262.

Fristad, M. A., Goldberg-Arnold, J. S., & Leffler, J. M. (2011). *Psychotherapy for children with bipolar and depressive disorders*. New York, NY: Guilford Press.

Fristad, M. A., & MacPherson, H. A. (2014). Evidence-based psychosocial treatments for child and adolescent bipolar spectrum disorders. *Journal of Clinical Child and Adolescent Psychology, 43*(3), 339–355.

Fristad, M. A., Verducci, J. S., Walters, K., & Young, M. E. (2009). Impact of multifamily psychoeducational psychotherapy in treating children aged 8 to 12 years with mood disorders. *Archives of General Psychiatry, 66*(9), 1013–1021.

Garrett, A. S., Reiss, A. L., Howe, M. E., Kelley, R. G., Singh, M. K., Adleman, N. E.,...Chang, K. D. (2012). Abnormal amygdala and prefrontal cortex activation to facial expressions in pediatric bipolar disorder. *Journal of the American Academy of Child and Adolescent Psychiatry, 51*(8), 821–831.

Goldstein, B. I., & Birmaher, B. (2012). Prevalence, clinical presentation and differential diagnosis of pediatric bipolar disorder. *The Israel Journal of Psychiatry and Related Sciences, 49*(1), 3–14.

Goldstein, B. I., Strober, M. A., Birmaher, B., Axelson, D. A., Esposito-Smythers, C., Goldstein, T. R.,...Keller, M. B. (2008). Substance use disorders among adolescents with bipolar spectrum disorders. *Bipolar Disorders, 10*, 469–478.

Goldstein, T. R., Miklowitz, D. J., & Mullen, K. L. (2006). Social skills knowledge and performance among adolescents with bipolar disorder. *Bipolar Disorders, 8*(4), 350–361.

Harvey, A. G. (2009). The adverse consequences of sleep disturbance in pediatric bipolar disorder: Implications for intervention. *Child and Adolescent Psychiatric Clinics of North America, 18*(2), 321–38, viii.

Joseph, M. F., Frazier, T. W., Youngstrom, E. A., & Soares, J. C. (2008). A quantitative and qualitative review of neurocognitive performance in pediatric bipolar disorder. *Journal of Child and Adolescent Psychopharmacology, 18*(6), 595–605.

Keenan-Miller, D., & Miklowitz, D. J. (2011). Interpersonal functioning in pediatric bipolar disorder. *Clinical Psychology-Science and Practice, 18*(4), 342–356. doi:10.1111/j.1468-2850.2011.01266.x

Kowatch, R. A., Fristad, M. A., Findling, R. L., & Post, R. M. (2009). *Clinical manual for management of bipolar disorder in children and adolescents* (1st ed.). Washington, DC: American Psychiatric Publishing.

Kowatch, R. A., Strawn, J. R., & Sorter, M. T. (2009). Clinical trials supporting new algorithm for treating pediatric bipolar mania. *Current Psychiatry, 8*(11), 19–34.

Kowatch, R. A., Youngstrom, E. A., Danielyan, A., & Findling, R. L. (2005). Review and meta-analysis of the phenomenology and clinical characteristics of mania in children and adolescents. *Bipolar Disorders, 7*(6), 483–496.

McClellan, J., Kowatch, R., Findling, R. J., & The Work Group on Quality Issues (2007). Practice parameter for the assessment and treatment of children and adolescents with bipolar disorder. *Journal of the American Academy of Child and Adolescent Psychiatry, 46*(1), 107–125. doi:10.1097/01.chi.0000242240.69678.c4

Miklowitz, D. J. (2012). Family-focused treatment for children and adolescents with bipolar disorder. *The Israel Journal of Psychiatry and Related Sciences, 49*(2), 95–101.

Osher, Y., & Belmaker, R. H. (2009). Omega-3 fatty acids in depression: A review of three studies. *CNS Neuroscience & Therapeutics, 15*(2), 128–133.

Pavuluri, M. N., Birmaher, B., & Naylor, M. W. (2005). Pediatric bipolar disorder: A review of the past 10 years. *Journal of the American Academy of Child and Adolescent Psychiatry, 44*(9), 846–871.

Pavuluri, M. N., Passarotti, A. M., Harral, E. M., & Sweeney, J. A. (2009). An fMRI study of the neural correlates of incidental versus directed emotion processing in pediatric bipolar disorder. *Journal of the American Academy of Child and Adolescent Psychiatry, 48*(3), 308–319.

Smoller, J. W., & Finn, C. T. (2003). Family, twin, and adoption studies of bipolar disorder. *American Journal of Medical Genetics. Part C, Seminars in Medical Genetics, 123C*(1), 48–58.

Spencer, T. J., Biederman, J., Wozniak, J., Faraone, S. V., Wilens, T. E., & Mick, E. (2001). Parsing pediatric bipolar disorder from its associated comorbidity with the disruptive behavior disorders. *Biological Psychiatry, 49*(12), 1062–1070.

Stewart, A. J., Theodore-Oklota, C., Hadley, W., Brown, L. K., Donenberg, G., & DiClemente, R.; Project STYLE Study Group. (2012). Mania symptoms and HIV-risk behavior among adolescents in mental health treatment. *Journal of Clinical Child and Adolescent Psychology, 41*(6), 803–810.

Strakowski, S. M., Adler, C. M., Almeida, J., Altshuler, L. L., Blumberg, H. P., Chang, K. D., . . . Townsend, J. D. (2012). The functional neuroanatomy of bipolar disorder: A consensus model. *Bipolar Disorders, 14*(4), 313–325.

Todd, R. D. (2002). Genetics of early onset bipolar affective disorder: Are we making progress? *Current Psychiatry Reports, 4*(2), 141–145.

Van Meter, A. R., Moreira, A. L., & Youngstrom, E. A. (2011). Meta-analysis of epidemiologic studies of pediatric bipolar disorder. *The Journal of Clinical Psychiatry, 72*(9), 1250–1256.

Wagner, K. D. (2006). Bipolar disorder and comorbid anxiety disorders in children and adolescents. *Journal of Clinical Psychiatry, 67*, 16–20.

Walsh, M. A., Royal, A., Brown, L. H., Barrantes-Vidal, N., & Kwapil, T. R. (2012). Looking for bipolar spectrum psychopathology: Identification and expression in daily life. *Comprehensive Psychiatry, 53*(5), 409–421.

Wozniak, J., Biederman, J., Mick, E., Waxmonsky, J., Hantsoo, L., Best, C., Cluette-Brown, J. E., & Laposata, M. (2007). Omega-3 fatty acid monotherapy for pediatric bipolar disorder: A prospective open-label trial. *European Neuropsychopharmacology: The Journal of the European College of Neuropsychopharmacology, 17*(6–7), 440–447.

Youngstrom, E. A., Jenkins, M. M., Jensen-Doss, A., & Youngstrom, J. K. (2012). Evidence-based assessment strategies for pediatric bipolar disorder. *The Israel Journal of Psychiatry and Related Sciences, 49*(1), 15–27.

Youngstrom, E., Youngstrom, J. K., & Starr, M. (2005). Bipolar diagnoses in community mental health: Achenbach Child Behavior Checklist profiles and patterns of comorbidity. *Biological Psychiatry, 58*(7), 569–575.

Evidence-Based Interventions for Posttraumatic Stress Disorder in Children and Adolescents

Laurie J. Zandberg, Sandy Capaldi, and Edna B. Foa

OVERVIEW

Children and adolescents are at high risk of trauma exposure, with nearly 62% of adolescents experiencing a traumatic event in their lifetimes (McLaughlin et al., 2013). Because childhood and adolescence are critical developmental periods that include myriad physical, social, and emotional changes, traumatic events may result in significant long-term effects. Although trauma has wide-ranging implications, posttraumatic stress disorder (PTSD) is among the most severe and may develop immediately following a traumatic event, or many years later (*The Diagnostic and Statistical Manual of Mental Disorders*, 5th ed.; *DSM-5*; American Psychiatric Association, 2013). This chapter first presents a brief overview of PTSD in childhood and adolescence, including how symptoms may present and what factors are associated with risk of developing PTSD. Subsequently, a review of the research literature and a step-by-step guide for practice will be provided for two empirically validated treatments for youth PTSD.

Symptoms of PTSD in Children and Adolescents. When a child or adolescent experiences a traumatic event, negative reactions may appear shortly after the experience, and are considered to be common.

For this reason, PTSD is diagnosed only when the duration of symptoms is longer than 1 month. The symptoms of PTSD are grouped into four clusters: intrusion symptoms, avoidance symptoms, cognition and mood symptoms, and arousal and reactivity symptoms. In order to receive a diagnosis of PTSD, an older child or adolescent must express at least one intrusion symptom, one avoidance symptom, two cognition and mood symptoms, and two arousal and reactivity symptoms. For children younger than 6 years of age, avoidance and cognition/mood symptoms are grouped together and only one symptom is required.

Intrusion Symptoms. Intrusion symptoms of PTSD involve ways of reexperiencing the traumatic event. Older children and adolescents may reexperience the trauma through recurrent and intrusive distressing memories of the event, which are experienced as involuntary and upsetting. Conversely, younger children may not appear distressed and express symptomatology through play reenactment that is linked in some way to the trauma (e.g., playing firefighter) or through storylines in play that involve being helped or saved. Intrusion symptoms also occur in the form of distressing dreams. Older children and adolescents often report upsetting dreams that either replay the traumatic event or portions of it, or are related to upsetting traumatic themes, such as being threatened or chased. Young children may be unable to relay the content or themes of their distressing dreams. Flashbacks are also considered intrusion symptoms, in which the child feels as though the trauma is actually happening again for a period of anywhere from a few seconds to several hours. In more severe cases, flashbacks involve loss of contact with the present reality, while less severe cases may involve brief sensory disruptions related to the memory. For young children, these types of dissociative reactions may occur in play. Experiencing intense emotional distress when reminded of the trauma and physical responses (increased heart rate and sweating) to trauma reminders are also included in this symptom cluster.

Avoidance Symptoms. Avoidance symptoms of PTSD involve cognitive (avoiding thoughts and feelings related to the trauma) and behavioral avoidance (avoiding situations, places, or things that remind the adolescent of the trauma). For example, a child or adolescent with PTSD may refuse to speak about the trauma, or may make efforts to keep busy in order to avoid thinking about the memory. Behavioral avoidance includes avoiding reminders of the trauma, as well as situations previously considered safe that feel more dangerous following the trauma—even if these situations are not directly linked to the traumatic event. For example, an adolescent may avoid crowded public places after being raped or a child may avoid sleeping away from home after experiencing a school shooting. Adolescents may also avoid engaging in typical developmental opportunities such as dating or learning to drive. For younger children, preoccupation with trauma reminders may be present in addition to avoidance. For example, a young child who witnessed a gruesome murder may be persistently concerned that there will be ketchup on tables in restaurants, as it reminds them of blood.

Cognition and Mood Symptoms. Cognition and mood symptoms refer to alterations in thoughts and feelings following a traumatic event. The first two of these symptoms are assessed only in children older than 6 years and include (a) not being able to remember important parts of a traumatic event (even when head injury, alcohol, and drugs are not involved), and (b) having excessively negative thoughts about oneself, others, or the future. For adolescents in particular, believing that the trauma has irrevocably changed them is common, such that they may believe that others will not want to engage with them socially because they are "broken" or "defective" in some way. Enduring negative moods are also included in this cluster. These include feeling persistently angry, afraid, ashamed, sad, or confused. Children and adolescents may also express less interest in doing the things they used to do. Everyday and even preferred activities such as play may begin to feel boring or pointless. Feelings of not having anything in common with others may occur, resulting in estrangement or socially withdrawn behavior. Finally, children and adolescents may have difficulty experiencing and expressing positive emotions. For example, a child with PTSD may know that a positive emotion (e.g., joy) should be present when something good happens, yet feel unable to access and express that emotion.

Arousal and Reactivity Symptoms. Arousal and reactivity symptoms constitute the last cluster of PTSD symptoms. These include difficulty concentrating, sleep disturbance, exaggerated startle responses, and hypervigilance for potential sources of danger. Arousal and reactivity symptoms also include aggressive and risk-taking behaviors that were not present before the trauma. Children and adolescents may report throwing and slamming objects or engaging in physical fights with very little provocation. Extreme temper tantrums are common in children younger than 6 years. Older children and adolescents may engage in reckless and self-destructive behaviors, such as nonsuicidal self-harm, driving under the influence of alcohol, or unprotected sex.

ETIOLOGY AND FACTORS RELATED TO PTSD IN CHILDREN AND ADOLESCENTS

Estimates of prevalence rates of PTSD in childhood and adolescence vary from 5% (Merikangas et al., 2010) to 16% (Alisic et al., 2014). Approximately 75% of adolescents with PTSD will have another comorbid diagnosis, most commonly depressive disorder or substance use disorders (Kilpatrick et al., 2003). Younger children may experience developmental regression, in which attainment of some developmental milestones is lost. Loss of language skills and enuresis are common types of developmental regression. Prolonged and severe traumatic events in childhood can also result in emotion-regulation difficulties, difficulties in interpersonal relationships, or other dissociative symptoms or disorders. In adolescence, PTSD is associated with marked impairments in academic and social functioning (Bolton et al., 2004; McLean, Rosenbach, Capaldi, & Foa, 2013). In addition, adolescents with PTSD are up to three times more likely to make a suicide attempt compared with adolescents with no trauma or PTSD history (Nooner et al., 2012).

It is important to remember that not every exposure to traumatic events will result in PTSD, but research has shown individuals exposed to traumatic events that involve interpersonal violence such as sexual assault, kidnapping, and physical assault are more likely to develop PTSD (McLaughlin et al., 2013). Current prevalence rates of PTSD are higher for girls than for boys (8% vs. 2.3%; Merikangas et al., 2010). Other risk factors for development of PTSD include living with less than two biological parents, exposure to a traumatic event in adolescence as compared with childhood, and the presence of preexisting mental disorders (McLaughlin et al., 2013).

EVIDENCE-BASED INTERVENTIONS AND EMPIRICAL SUPPORT FOR PTSD IN CHILDREN AND ADOLESCENTS

Over the past several decades, many treatments have been developed for youth PTSD. To date, the treatments with the largest body of empirical support are variants of cognitive behavioral therapy (CBT; Dorsey, Briggs, & Woods, 2011; Silverman et al., 2008). These therapies share many core elements, most notably (a) psychoeducation regarding trauma and PTSD symptoms, which aim to normalize common reactions to traumatic events; (b) relaxation and anxiety management strategies, for managing emotional

distress; (c) reducing situational avoidance and re-engaging developmentally appropriate activities; (d) repeated exposure to trauma memories in a safe and supportive context, via in-session trauma narrations; and (e) exploration and modifications of problematic beliefs regarding the self, world, and others that developed as a result of the trauma. As with other CBT approaches, trauma-focused CBTs (TF-CBTs) are structured and time limited, and emphasize between-sessions-practice of skills (i.e., homework) to ensure generalization to the youth's natural environment. In the following discussion, a review of the research supporting TF-CBT (Cohen, Mannarino, & Deblinger, 2006), the most extensively studied trauma-focused treatment for school-aged children, and Prolonged Exposure for Adolescents (PE-A; Foa, Chrestman, & Gilboa-Schechtman, 2008), a PTSD treatment directly adapted from the most extensively validated adult PTSD intervention, is provided.

Trauma-Focused CBT

TF-CBT was initially developed to address trauma associated with child sexual abuse and has subsequently been adapted for use with children who have experienced other trauma types. Research indicates that TF-CBT is effective in treating PTSD, depression, and related behavioral problems in children exposed to traumatic events. To date, there are nine randomized controlled trials supporting the use of TF-CBT for children with PTSD. These studies have found that TF-CBT is superior to both waitlist and to alternative treatments such as supportive or client-centered therapies in reducing PTSD symptoms, depression, and behavioral difficulties. For example, in a sample of 229 children (aged 8–14 years) with PTSD, children treated with TF-CBT were 50% more likely to achieve diagnostic remission compared with client-centered supportive counseling; 79% of youths treated with TF-CBT no longer met criteria for PTSD at posttreatment (Cohen et al., 2004). Moreover, sustained treatment benefits have been demonstrated at 6-month, 1-year, and 2-year follow-ups. Based on this evidence, several reviews have deemed TF-CBT the treatment with the highest degree of empirical support for childhood PTSD (Dorsey, Briggs, & Woods, 2011; Silverman et al., 2008).

Prolonged Exposure for Adolescents

Prolonged exposure therapy has demonstrated efficacy in 29 randomized controlled trials with adult PTSD. Recently, this treatment has been adapted for use with adolescents, and the results of two randomized controlled trials demonstrate comparable effectiveness with youth samples. The first investigation compared PE-A with time-limited dynamic psychotherapy (TLDP) in a sample of adolescents (aged 12–18 years) who had experienced a single-event trauma (Gilboa-Schechtman et al., 2010). Adolescents completing PE-A showed greater improvement in PTSD, depression, and global functioning than TLDP, and 68% (compared with 37% in TLDP) achieved diagnostic remission. Gains were maintained at 17-month follow-up. A second investigation compared PE-A with client-centered therapy, delivered in a rape crisis center, with treatment provided by community clinicians previously unfamiliar with PE (Foa, McLean, Capaldi, & Rosenfield, 2013). Participants were adolescent females (aged 13–18 years) with sexual abuse–related PTSD. The PE-A group showed greater improvement in PTSD symptoms and all secondary outcomes (i.e., depression and functioning), and treatment differences were maintained through 12-month follow-up. Moreover, 83% of PE-A participants no longer met criteria for PTSD after treatment. Taken together, these studies show strong preliminary support for the efficacy and effectiveness of PE-A, in both research and naturalistic settings.

HOW TO: A GUIDE TO THE IMPLEMENTATION OF INTERVENTIONS FOR PTSD IN CHILDREN AND ADOLESCENTS

The following sections provide a step-by-step breakdown of TF-CBT and PE-A interventions, including descriptions of core components and standard implementation practices. Both treatments involve exercises designed to help the individual with PTSD repeatedly approach and process the traumatic memory, rather than avoiding it, as well as exercises designed to help the child or adolescent reduce situational avoidance that otherwise prevents new learning about what is and is not safe in the aftermath of a trauma.

Trauma-Focused CBT

Treatment Overview. TF-CBT is designed to be approximately 12 to 18 weekly sessions. The treatment follows a component-based model, in which a set of inter-related skills are presented to the child progressively. The acronym PRACTICE is used to represent the ten core components of TF-CBT and the typical sequence in which they are presented (see the following discussion). When following the standard program, the child works through several skills designed to help identify and effectively manage difficult emotions before talking specifically about his or her trauma. Rather than following a strict, session-by-session protocol, therapist discretion is used to determine component sequencing and how many sessions are dedicated to each component.

Parental involvement, whenever possible, is considered a critical part of treatment that helps to promote long-term maintenance of treatment gains. Indeed, improving the parent–child relationship and enhancing both parties' ability to talk with each other about the traumatic experience is an explicit aim of treatment. To this end, most TF-CBT sessions include individual meeting time with the child, followed by individual meeting time with the parent(s). Parent meetings serve two main goals: (a) to educate the parent(s) about the content covered in the child session and (b) to encourage the parent(s) to reinforce this material with the child between sessions. Parent sessions typically begin by asking about successes the parent(s) noticed between appointments in the child's use of skills, and then move to a summary of what was presented to the child. Later in treatment, conjoint parent–child sessions are implemented as a core component, but combined meetings can be used at any point if deemed appropriate.

Component 1: Psychoeducation. Psychoeducation serves the primary aim of normalizing both the child's and parent's response to traumatic events and providing corrective information about the trauma. Information sheets have been developed to provide general information about the specific type of traumatic event experienced by the child. For example, in the event of sexual abuse, the mental health professional may share information about types of sexual abuse, how often it happens, and why many kids do not tell others about the abuse. Thus, TF-CBT aims to disabuse misperceptions about the trauma that the child may hold (e.g., that sexual abuse happened because of something the child said/did). In addition, the therapist provides information about common emotional and behavioral reactions to trauma, and how treatment helps to improve these reactions over time. In the parallel parental session, the therapist orients the parent(s) more formally to the TF-CBT model and its components. In particular, the therapist explains to the parent(s) that treatment will involve talking about the trauma in detail, but in a gradual way and after skills for managing distress are practiced.

Component 2: Parenting Skills. Parenting skills are typically presented in the first few sessions and are especially relevant for children exhibiting behavioral problems. TF-CBT parenting skills include the use of praise, selective attention, time-out procedures, and contingency reinforcement schedules to reduce unwanted behaviors and increase desired behaviors. Praise and selective attention is based on the idea that kids want focused attention from their parents and they will behave in ways that capture this attention, even if it takes a negative form (e.g., yelling). The TF-CBT therapist teaches parents to reward behaviors they want to encourage with attention, and to selectively ignore most negative behaviors. Parents are trained to notice and praise positive behaviors (referred to as "catching your child being good") as close to the time of action as possible, and to use specific rather than vague, global feedback (e.g., "I love how you picked up your room when I asked you to." vs. "You're such a good girl."). In session, this is accomplished using a combination of didactic discussion and role-play, where the therapist plays the child and the parent puts his or her new skills to use. When the child exhibits negative behaviors, selective attention, also known as "planned ignoring," is used. Parents are coached to respond to negative behaviors by calmingly walking away, and shifting attention to another activity. It is important to warn parents that planned ignoring can lead initially to escalation of problem behaviors (referring to as an "extinction burst"), and that if they the course without providing attention, negative behaviors will very likely end. It is extremely important that parents do

not give in during the extinction burst, because this will inadvertently reward the escalated behavior. As soon as the child behaves well, parents should provide specific, positive praise. Other approaches to negative behavior include judicious use of time-out procedures. TF-CBT advises that 1 minute of time-out be used for every year of age (i.e., a 5-year-old should have a 5-minute time-out). More persistent behavioral problems are addressed with contingency reinforcement or behavior charts. This approach uses a token economy to reward positive behavior. Behavior charts make very explicit to the child how he or she can earn points, and for what those points can be cashed in at the end of a reward period (typically 1 week). A successful behavior chart will start with modest goals that the child has a high likelihood of achieving, and progressively increase the demand required to receive a reward.

Component 3: Relaxation. Relaxation skills are presented before trauma-focused components to help the child understand the body's reactions to stress and to teach techniques that can be used to gain control over anxious feelings. Two main relaxation strategies are recommended: deep breathing and progressive muscle relaxation. For each, the therapist demonstrates a relaxation technique and then guides the child through in-session practice. Deep breathing is practiced by placing one hand on the belly and one hand on the chest, and breathing so that the belly rises and falls with each breath and the chest stays relatively still. This can also be demonstrated by lying down on the floor with a toy or book on the belly, watching it move up and down with each breath. Next, the child works on breathing more slowly on the exhalations than the inhalation. This can be accomplished by counting to a certain number, or simply by focusing on breathing out slowly. The therapist praises the child's practice attempts, and then has the child select a calming word to say to himself or herself while he or she exhales (e.g., "relax," "calm"). If other, distracting, thoughts come into the mind, the therapist might suggest that the child picture them floating away.

In progressive muscle relaxation, the therapist instructs the child to tense and then relax one set of muscles at a time. The mental health professional explains that when we are stressed, we often tense our muscles. The distinction between tense and relaxed muscles can be demonstrated by having the child practice acting like a robot (tense and rigid), and then a rag doll (loose and relaxed). Relaxing muscles is one way to manage anxious feelings. The therapist and child practice tensing (e.g., "Make a tight fist like you are squeezing a lemon!") and releasing ("And let go…let your hands go limp.") one muscle group at a time. It should be noted that if a child is not comfortable with these relaxation exercises, or is unwilling to practice, the practitioner can be creative in generating and practicing alternative relaxing activities (e.g., listening to music, stretching, or playing a game). When the parent joins the session, the child can take the lead in teaching him or her how to relax. This allows for additional opportunities to reinforce the child's mastery of these skills, and provides a new skill for both child and parent to practice at home when strong emotions are present.

Component 4: Affective Modulation. The aim of this module is to teach the child how to (a) identify and (b) appropriately express a wide range of emotions. As with many of the TF-CBT skills, this can be accomplished using a combination of role-play, games, and drawings. To start, the therapist assesses how many emotions the child knows, and then encourages a discussion of how we know when we are feeling a given emotion. This can be done by generating a list or making a drawing together with the child. When the child runs out of ideas, the mental health professional presents hypothetical situations that pull for additional emotions (e.g., embarrassment) and asks the child what he or she might feel in that scenario. In these discussions, attention is drawn to bodily sensations that are associated with various emotional states. The therapist and child can play a game of "feelings charades" in which each takes a turn picking a "feeling" (written on a piece of paper) out of a box, acts out the emotion, and has the other person guess the feeling that was selected. Then, the practitioner wants to present the idea of rating the intensity of an emotion (e.g., what it feels like to be a *little* excited vs. *very* excited). The emotions thermometer can be used to rate the intensity of an emotion on a scale from 0 to 10. For homework, the therapist may ask the child to practice feelings identification and ratings in real life.

After the child has expanded his or her feelings vocabulary (in the same session or subsequent session), the therapist turns to feeling expression and how to appropriately communicate emotions to others. The therapist might present specific examples when he or she felt a strong emotion and shared it with someone else, and then ask the child to share examples of his or her own. Role-plays present a good way to demonstrate ways the therapist and child have expressed feelings in real-life situations. Following the role-play, therapist and child review how the feeling was expressed and discuss more effective ways to express feelings if necessary (e.g., with words rather than actions; using "I" statements). The therapist should present the idea that expressing feelings, rather than holding them in, can help the child feel better. Feelings can be expressed in various ways, such as talking to trusted friends or family members, drawing, writing, and so forth.

In parental sessions, the mental health professional explains the concepts covered with the child (labeling emotions and how to share them), and discusses any difficulties their child is having in expressing his or her feelings. Parents are coached in how they can help their child identify and express emotions; for example, asking the child to label the feelings when he or she seems upset. In addition, the therapist should remind parents to praise their child whenever he or she effectively manages difficult emotions or communicates them appropriately.

Component 5: Cognitive Coping. Cognitive coping (CC) encompasses a set of interventions derived from cognitive therapy (Beck, 1995) aimed at exploring and challenging cognitions that are unhelpful or inaccurate. In TF-CBT, CC skills are first presented as a stand-alone skill and applied to nontrauma-related content, and are then later revisited to enhance trauma-focused work. CC begins by explaining that we all talk to ourselves in ways that impact our feelings. The therapist can use various examples or games (e.g., drawing cartoons and writing out the characters' thoughts in bubbles) to illustrate the link between thoughts and feelings to the child. The idea is then presented that sometimes we have thoughts that are inaccurate or unhelpful. The therapist provides practice scenarios where the child guesses both the thought that might go through his or her mind and the feeling that would result from that thought. The manual presents the following example: *Situation: Your mother blames you for something your little brother did. Thought: "She's not being fair." Feeling: "mad."* Once this link has been mastered, the therapist encourages the child to think of alternative ways of thinking about the same scenario that lead to a different feeling. This may be referred to as "changing the channel" or "putting on different-colored sunglasses." The therapist may suggest, "Can we come up with something else you could say to yourself that might help you feel better?" Finally, the therapist guides the child to think of how different thoughts lead to different behaviors and outcomes. For example, the thought "mom's not being fair" leads to "feeling mad," which leads to "saying 'I hate you!' and running to my room" which ultimately leads to being punished. Whereas the alternative thought "mom won't be mad once I tell her the truth" leads to feeling hopeful, and "explaining to mom I didn't do it," and as a result mom apologizes for blaming you. Examples of common thinking traps can be presented in kid-friendly language and using examples of "other kids" and things they might think in various scenarios.

Component 6: Trauma Narrative. In building the trauma narrative, the therapist uses gradual procedures to encourage the child to describe more and more detail about what happened before, during, and after the traumatic event. This component is designed to take place over several sessions, with the mental health professional guiding the child to discuss increasingly upsetting aspects of the trauma. Although several creative options are available to the therapist (e.g., pictures, songs, and poems), the trauma narrative process is usually conducted by having the child create a book that tells his or her personal story.

Before any work is done on the trauma, the rationale for talking about the trauma is presented. This can be accomplished with the metaphor of falling off a bike and skinning a knee. The therapist can explain to the child that in this situation we really have two choices: (a) we can ignore it—not wash it off nor put medicine on it; sometimes this works out fine, but other times, the wound gets infected and over time gets worse and worse—or (b) we can

wash out the wound very carefully, getting all the dirt and germs out. This is painful and stings! But then the pain goes away and the wound can heal once and for all. Overall, this hurts much less than if the wound gets infected. The mental health professional explains to the child that telling the story of what happened is like cleaning out the wound. Emphasis is placed on doing this carefully "at just the right pace so that it never hurts more than a little bit" (Cohen, Mannarino, & Deblinger, 2006). When starting the trauma narrative, the therapist begins by having the child write a chapter about a favorite activity or event, thus easing the child into the process of writing about himself or herself. The child is then asked to write about what happened on the day of the trauma. It is not uncommon for a child to describe very little, and it becomes the task of the therapist to elicit more and more detail over multiple sessions. For example, the therapist may ask the child to verbally describe what he or she was doing before the trauma, and what happened next, and after that, and so on. Once verbalized, the therapist can suggest that the child write down what he or she described, or can provide the option of acting as the "secretary," writing while the child narrates. Following each segment of writing, the therapist asks the child to read what he or she has written so far. This produces repetition of narrating the traumatic experience and increased tolerance in recounting the trauma narrative. Throughout, the therapist offers encouragement and ample praise to the child for his or her bravery in telling the story. At the conclusion of the session, the therapist may reward the child's efforts by playing a short game or providing a small prize, like a sticker.

At this stage of treatment, parent-meeting time focuses on sharing the child's narrative with the parent(s) and discussing their reactions. The goals of these parent sessions are multifaceted: (a) to ameliorate parental distress about the trauma through repeated exposure; (b) to reduce parental avoidance of the topic so that, as with all TF-CBT skills, the parent(s) can be coached to reinforce the child's being open about these memories; (c) to provide opportunities for the parent(s) to understand the mistaken beliefs the child may hold about the trauma; and (d) to provide feedback that might reduce the child's guilt or shame about the trauma. In the first trauma narrative session, the therapist asks the parent(s) to describe his or her own experience of the trauma before hearing the child's. Then, the mental health professional should reread the child's trauma narrative aloud to the parent(s) each session. The child should be told that the narrative will be shared with his or her parent(s), and for adolescents in particular, that things the child/adolescent does not want shared will be kept confidential. It is very important to allow time for the parent(s) to regain composure before the session is ended, as it can be counterproductive for the child to see his or her parent(s) upset. Indeed, this may be an explicit reason that the child does not otherwise talk about the trauma. The therapist should emphasize the child's competence by praising his or her ability to the parent(s). In addition, the therapist praises the parent(s) for supporting and encouraging the child to attend therapy and for sharing these memories, even though it is difficult.

In subsequent sessions, the therapist aims to deepen the trauma narrative by asking the child to describe what he or she was thinking to himself or herself and feeling at the time of the trauma and to include this in the narrative. This procedure culminates in asking the child to describe the absolute worst parts of the memory. If at any point the child exhibits high distress, TF-CBT encourages coaching of previously learned relaxation skills in session, and, for some children, the use of brief distraction exercises (e.g., talking about something unrelated) may be employed to de-escalate intense emotions. When a young child is having difficulty verbalizing emotions and thoughts, puppets may be used to act out scenes in the third person ("What is the bear feeling now?"), which can then be integrated into the story narrative and discussed more directly. Each session, a new section is completed and the child re-reads what he or she has created. When the full narrative has been completed, the therapist begins to use cognitive-processing skills in order to explore and modify mistaken or unhelpful beliefs about the trauma (see the next component). These lessons can then be added to the text of the story. A final section is then written that includes ways the child has changed since the trauma and since the beginning of treatment, as well as what he or she has learned, how he or she has grown, and any advice he or she might give to other children in his or her position.

Component 7: CC and Processing. Once the trauma narrative has been generated, the TF-CBT therapist begins to incorporate CC skills to explore and gently challenge unhelpful or inaccurate thoughts related to the trauma in an empathic manner. As noted previously, before the narrative is finalized, the therapist helps the child to elicit his or her thoughts at various turning points in the trauma narrative. As the child or therapist re-reads a given section of the narrative, attention is drawn to these thoughts. Socratic questioning is used to explore and challenge the accuracy of inaccurate or extreme negative thoughts about the child or the trauma experience. For example, to the rape survivor who thinks she is responsible for the rape because she was intoxicated, the therapist might say, "Help me understand this. So every girl who gets drunk is raped? Is that right?" Thoughts can be gently challenged by asking the child to help you understand his or her thinking, and then making statements that take the unhelpful thought to its logical extension in a way that will prompt the child to disagree. To the child who thinks "Scary things happen at school. It's dangerous there," the therapist may say, "Huh, so school is always a dangerous, scary place, cause every single day, something bad happens there?" Helping the child to identify "exceptions" to the thought provides a starting point for developing and practicing more helpful alternative thoughts (e.g., "Sometimes bad things happen at school, but not always."). As blame is a common issue in processing trauma, it can be useful for therapists to explain the concept of accidents (some things just happen and no one is at fault). The manual suggests asking the child "Why do you think people invented the word 'accident'? Was it just another word for someone's fault?"

In this component, when working with the parent(s), the therapist should ask the parent(s) if he or she had any troubling feelings or thoughts over the past week about the trauma and apply the same procedure: identifying unhelpful thoughts, reflecting and gently challenging these cognitions, and practicing more realistic, helpful ways of thinking. Often these thoughts may apply to the child (e.g., "My child will never be happy again.").

Component 8: In Vivo Mastery of Trauma—Reminders. In vivo mastery involves gradual exposure to trauma-related cues that are objectively safe but that the child is currently avoiding because of fear of the trauma recurring, or fear of being reminded of the trauma. The first step for the therapist in this component is to get as much information as possible about feared situations and why they are feared. Avoidance behaviors that have developed since the trauma and have the potential to disrupt the child's developmental trajectory are given priority. Next, the therapist works to progressively expose the child, in a step-by-step manner, to the avoided cues. For example, a child may fear going to school following a traumatic event. In this case, the goal will be to progressively increase time at school, little by little, creating a step-by-step in vivo exposure plan. For younger children, in vivo plans can incorporate rewards to increase child motivation, and all successful experiences should be reinforced with parental praise.

Component 9: Conjoint Sessions. As the trauma narrative and processing component near an end, the groundwork is laid in both child and parental trauma-processing sessions to prepare clients for conjoint sessions. The objective of the conjoint sessions is for the child to share his or her completed trauma narrative with the parent(s). In parent meetings, the therapist role-plays the child reading the trauma narrative out loud and coaches the parent(s) to listen actively and make supportive, helpful statements. In child sessions, the therapist suggests to the child that he or she is ready to share the narrative with his or her parent(s), and helps the child develop a list of questions or ideas he or she would like to bring up with his or her parent(s).

For a conjoint session, the therapist first prepares the child alone (15 minutes) and then the parent(s) alone (15 minutes) before bringing them together for a combined session (30 minutes). Of note, by this stage, the child should feel comfortable reading the narrative to the therapist and should be willing to share it with the parent(s). Likewise, the parent(s), via parallel trauma narrative sessions, should have heard the full narrative and demonstrated the ability to maintain emotional control and to make supportive statements (practiced during parent sessions). Directly before the combined session, the parent(s) is prepared by once more reading the trauma narrative

and reviewing the child's questions to help him or her consider ways of responding. If the parent(s) has questions for the child, the therapist helps the parent(s) to phrase these in ways the child is likely to find supportive and nonjudgmental.

In the combined session (30 minutes), the child reads the trauma narrative, receives praise from therapist and parent(s), and works through each of his or her questions or comments. The therapist helps the child and parent(s) communicate directly to each other, intervening only where necessary (e.g., if an unhelpful cognition is raised without being challenged). If conflicts or tensions emerge, the mental health professional will encourage another joint session to facilitate greater ease in talking about the trauma together. The idea is to bring concerns related to the trauma and its impact (e.g., healthy sexuality, safety planning, and picking appropriate romantic partners) into the open for discussion. The therapist ends the session by encouraging the parent(s) and child to praise each other for one thing they did in session or during the past week that was appreciated. If the parent(s) is overtly critical or expresses unproductive remarks, the therapist attempts to model more helpful responses. If the parent(s) is unable to conduct himself or herself appropriately, this part of the session should be ended, and the therapist should meet independently with the parent(s) to discuss what went wrong.

Component 10: Enhancing Future Safety and Development. This component is designed to address *realistic* safety concerns following a trauma, to increase feelings of preparedness should a similar situation arise in the future, and to reduce the risk of future victimization. The therapist should start by recognizing and praising positive elements of the child's natural response to the trauma, including having the courage to tell someone about their victimization. Enhancing safety skills are then presented as things most kids never learn about: "So what you did when (the trauma happened) was the best way you knew how to respond at that time!" Relevant education is provided and safety skills are practiced in-session using experiential exercises and role-plays. TF-CBT safety skills fall into six categories: (a) communicating feelings clearly and openly, (b) paying attention to "gut" feelings, (c) identifying people and places that are safe (e.g., making a list of safe places and trustworthy people; practicing calling 911 with the phone unplugged), (d) learning body ownership and rules about "ok" and "not ok" touches, (e) learning the difference between surprises and "scary" secrets that should not be kept (i.e., secrets that kids are asked to keep from their parents or never tell anyone), and (f) asking for help until someone provides the help needed. The TF-CBT manual offers numerous resources for teaching personal safety, including workbooks by the treatment developers (e.g., Stauffer & Deblinger, 2003, 2004).

Prolonged Exposure for Adolescents

Treatment Overview. PE-A comprises 10 to 15 weekly sessions that are 60 or 90 minutes in length, depending on the child's developmental level. The program consists of an optional pretreatment preparation phase and three required treatment phases that are designed to be completed sequentially, including treatment planning and preparation, exposures, and relapse prevention. Each of the four phases includes several modules that focus on a specific therapeutic task and/or goal. Modules are designed to be flexible and completed in as much time as is needed to reach the goal of the module. Depending on the population being served, parental involvement in sessions will occur to varying degrees and is not considered a core component of PE-A. However, if parents are available, they are typically included in the last portion of the session to review session content and answer any questions they may have, except as noted in what follows. PE-A sessions are audio-recorded for the adolescent's use between sessions.

Phase 1: Pretreatment Preparation
Motivational Interview. The Motivational Interview module assesses the adolescent's motivation for treatment and aims to increase motivation if it is lacking. This module is typically completed in one session or less. The adolescent is asked to describe why he or she is seeking treatment now, how he or she feels about beginning treatment, and to rate his or her level of motivation for treatment on a scale from 0 to 10, with 0 being no motivation at all and 10 being extremely motivated. Once level of motivation is established, the therapist uses motivational interviewing techniques to enhance the adolescent's commitment to change. For example, if the adolescent rates his or her motivation at 8, the therapist may ask, "Why an 8 and not a 5?" to further elicit change talk and reasons for working in treatment.

Case Management. The Case Management module is designed to address potential obstacles to treatment. This module is usually completed in one to two sessions. Issues that predated the trauma should be discussed to ensure that PTSD is the current primary problem. The mental health professional and adolescent discuss how involved his or her parent(s) will be, the limits of confidentiality, and any risky or dangerous behaviors occurring. A crisis-coping plan is developed if risk factors are present (e.g., self-harm, running away behaviors, or substance use). If a parental figure is available, the practitioner then meets alone with the parent to identify other problems that may be affecting the adolescent and to review the limits of confidentiality. The module concludes by meeting together with the adolescent and parent to discuss the amount of information that will be shared with the parent, to review the crisis-coping plan (if necessary), and to discuss possible barriers to treatment.

Phase 2: Psychoeducation and Treatment Planning
Module 1: Treatment Rationale. In this module, the therapist describes the structure of the treatment (10–15 weekly 60- to 90-minute sessions) and presents the rationale for treatment. The mental health professional explains the two major reasons that PTSD symptoms persist: (a) avoidance of thoughts, feelings, and situations related to the trauma, and (b) the presence of unhelpful thoughts and beliefs about the trauma. In this discussion, it is important to let the adolescent know that many people have difficulties following a trauma, and these difficulties get better for some, whereas others continue to suffer for a much longer time. Those who continue to suffer tend to be the adolescents who are better at avoiding thoughts, feelings, and reminders of the trauma. Interactive discussion can be initiated here by asking the adolescent what his or her experience of trying not to be reminded of the trauma has been. The therapist continues by explaining that, while avoidance is understandable, it works only in the short run. By avoiding,

the adolescent does not give himself or herself the chance to learn that the memory itself is not harmful and that avoided situations may be safe. Thus, in the long run, avoidance makes it more difficult to get past posttrauma reactions. The practitioner then explains the techniques that will be used during treatment: recounting the memory, which requires the adolescent to repeatedly remember and talk about the trauma in sessions; and real-life experiments, where the adolescent will be encouraged to face avoided situations. The therapist also explains that many people notice changes in their beliefs about the world and about themselves after a trauma, and that some of these thoughts help to keep PTSD symptoms alive. During treatment, the adolescent and therapist will work together to identify and modify these beliefs.

Before ending Module 1, the practitioner introduces breathing retraining, an exercise designed to help the adolescent manage anxious feelings. The adolescent is asked to take a normal breath through the nose, and then to exhale very slowly while thinking the word "calm" or "relax.". After exhaling, the adolescent is instructed to count to 4 before inhaling again. The therapist talks the adolescent through repetitions of this cycle for 3 or 4 minutes, while audio recording so that the adolescent can practice at home. *Homework assigned for Module 1:* Listening to the recording of the session and practicing breathing retraining daily.

Module 2: Gathering Information. The Trauma Interview is a structured interview tool that allows the therapist and adolescent to choose the trauma that will be the focus of treatment, decide on the start and end points of that trauma, and identify unhelpful beliefs about the trauma. It begins with the therapist asking the adolescent to briefly describe the trauma memory that is currently the most bothersome to him or her. If the adolescent is having difficulty identifying this index trauma, the mental health professional can assist by listing the traumas the adolescent has experienced and discussing the ways in which each trauma currently affects him or her. It is helpful to focus on reexperiencing symptoms of PTSD here, as the trauma most related to the adolescent's current reexperiencing symptoms is typically the most appropriate index trauma. Next, the practitioner

works to identify the start and end points of the index trauma. The start point is typically a few minutes before the adolescent feels he or she is in danger. The end point occurs when the adolescent reaches relative safety. After agreeing on the index trauma and start and end points, the therapist continues the interview by asking about the adolescent's feelings during the trauma, inquiring about feelings of blame and shame, and asking about any injuries that resulted from the trauma.

After completing the Trauma Interview, the therapist has the option of completing the Secret Weapons worksheet, which aims to highlight for the adolescent that he or she has the strength and support to overcome PTSD symptoms. Using the worksheet, the therapist helps the adolescent identify and list strengths in three main categories: Skills and Talents, Experiences and Accomplishments, and Allies and Assets. Skills and Talents includes anything the adolescent can do well that shows his or her ability to learn new things and can include activities such as singing or dancing, riding a bike, or skateboarding. Experiences and Accomplishments should include life events that demonstrate hard work the adolescent has done, even if it was difficult or unpleasant (e.g., healing from an illness and getting a good grade in a difficult class). Allies and Assets includes people, places, and things that the adolescent feels helps him or her to feel supported. This category might include parents, teachers, friends, and sentimental objects. *Homework assigned for Module 2:* Listening to the recording of the session, reviewing the Secret Weapons worksheet, and practicing breathing retraining daily.

Module 3: Common Reactions to Trauma. The goal of this module is to discuss the reactions commonly seen among trauma survivors in an effort to normalize the reactions the adolescent is experiencing. Common reactions to trauma include such things as: increased fear and anxiety; feeling on edge; reexperiencing intrusive thoughts, nightmares, and flashbacks; avoidance of trauma-related thoughts and situations; emotional numbness, anger, guilt or shame; feelings of losing control; changes in perceptions of self and the world; and hopelessness. Reactions should be normalized by explaining how it makes sense for the adolescent to experience that particular reaction or how commonly it occurs. *Homework assigned for Module 3:* Listening to the recording of the session, reviewing the Common Reactions worksheet, and practicing the breathing retraining exercise daily.

Phase 3: Exposures

Module 4: Real Life Experiments. After reviewing the homework from the previous module, this module begins with the therapist discussing the rationale for real-life experiments. The therapist explains that it is natural to want to avoid situations or reminders of the trauma because these situations are uncomfortable and avoidance typically brings about some relief. Although avoiding trauma reminders feels better temporarily, it also keeps fears about those reminders alive, and prevents the adolescent from doing things he or she might otherwise want to do. As avoiding reminders makes things worse in the long-term, this program is designed to help stop avoidance and to instead confront fears so that the adolescent can learn that the situation is not as dangerous as it may seem.

The therapist then introduces real-life experiments that involve repeatedly approaching avoided situations to test out what will happen. This allows the adolescent to experience the situation, gather evidence like a scientist, and see how safe the situation really is. The adolescent is informed that the mental health professional will not ask the adolescent to approach a situation that is actually dangerous, but rather, that the work will be to approach situations that currently *feel* dangerous because of the trauma they experienced. The therapist also explains the ways that real-life experiments will help reduce the adolescent's symptoms: (a) by breaking the habit of reducing distress by avoiding, (b) by helping the adolescent to get used to the situation so that it becomes less upsetting over time, (c) by letting the adolescent learn that the situation he or she is avoiding is actually safe, (d) by proving to the adolescent that distressing feelings do not last forever, and (e) by helping the adolescent to feel more in control and to feel better about himself or herself.

The therapist and adolescent discuss a way to measure anxiety or other upsetting feelings by using a "stress thermometer" that goes from 0 to 10, with 0 being not feeling upset at all and 10 being the most upset the adolescent has ever been. It is helpful to get examples of situations that constitute a 0, 5, and 10 with the adolescent to ensure understanding of the stress thermometer. The therapist and adolescent then begin to build the real-life experiment hierarchy together (i.e., a list of avoided but safe situations ranging from moderately challenging to very challenging). Once a list of 10 to 15 items has been generated, the therapist asks the adolescent to rate the degree of distress each of the situations would cause using the stress thermometer. Initial targets for practice should have ratings of about 4 or 5 in order to ensure that the activity is challenging but manageable. If a real-life experiment has been identified that is easily conducted in or around the office, it can be helpful to complete the first exercise with the adolescent, where feasible, to observe the adolescent's reactions and to provide immediate support.

The final part of this module focuses on assignment of homework: Two real-life experiments in the 4 to 5 range on the stress thermometer are identified with the adolescent and assigned for practice. The therapist should explain to the adolescent that the goal is to stay in the situation for a period of time (30–45 minutes) without escaping. The mental health professional also explains that it is important to work on these experiments step by step, and to discourage jumping ahead on the list. *Homework assigned for Module 4:* Listening to the recording of the session, practicing assigned real-life experiments each day and recording stress thermometer ratings, and practicing breathing retraining as needed.

Module 5: Recounting the Memory. After reviewing the homework from the previous module, Module 5 begins with the therapist discussing the rationale for recounting the trauma memory. The therapist normalizes the adolescent's urges to avoid thinking about the trauma while at the same time pointing out that trying not to think about it has not made the trauma any easier to deal with. The mental health professional explains that the purpose of recounting the memory is to allow the adolescent to organize and digest what happened so that it will not feel so overwhelming or confusing. Although talking about what happened can be difficult, recounting the memory will allow the adolescent to see that thinking about the trauma and having actually experienced it are two very different things. Recounting the memory will also allow the adolescent to see that he or she will not fall apart while talking about it and thus to learn about his or her own competency and strength.

Recounting the memory is most often accomplished through imaginal exposure to the memory of the traumatic event. If the adolescent is unable or unwilling to verbally recount the memory, other options include writing the memory, drawing it, or recounting through stories. In this module, the adolescent is typically asked to close his or her eyes and tell his or her story of the trauma from the beginning of the event to end. This should occur for approximately 30 minutes, with the adolescent repeating the story until the 30 minutes are up. The adolescent is asked to recount the memory in the present tense and to include as many details as possible, including thoughts, feelings, and sensations during the trauma. Finally, the adolescent is told that the therapist will check in on his or her stress thermometer ratings every 5 minutes. During memory talk, the mental health professional should encourage the adolescent with short remarks (e.g., "You're doing a great job!") between repetitions of the memory.

After 20 to 30 minutes of recounting the memory, time is devoted to processing the trauma through discussion with the therapist. This involves discussing the experience of recounting the memory, as well as discussing the adolescent's thoughts and beliefs related to the trauma and its aftermath. Processing in early sessions often focuses on the process of doing the recounting (e.g., "What was it like for you to tell the story today?" "What did you notice about your stress levels today compared to last week?"). Later, processing begins to address themes of guilt, anger, and shame, and aims to help the adolescent get a new perspective on what happened. For example, the therapist may ask the adolescent how certain details of the trauma affect his or her understanding of what happened, or how they influence the adolescent's belief about himself or herself. The therapist poses questions that help the adolescent to reevaluate unhelpful beliefs, and to put his or her own behavior into context given the specific details described in the recounting. This module is repeated for several sessions until recounting of the trauma memory elicits only minimal distress.

Homework assigned for Module 5: Listening to a recording of the recounting exercise and practicing assigned real-life experiments daily.

Module 6: Worst Moments. As recounting the trauma memory becomes easier, the therapist will help the adolescent to selectively recount the most distressing parts of the memory (referred to as "worst moments"). This module will be repeated for the remainder of Phase 3. After reviewing the homework from the previous module, this module begins with the therapist and adolescent choosing the worst moments of the trauma memory and discussing the fact that recounting these worst moments in greater detail will help the adolescent to get past even the most distressing parts of his or her trauma. Recounting the memory continues as in previous sessions with focus on just one worst moment at a time, so that the adolescent gets to repeat the recounting as many as six or seven times in a session. As in previous sessions, time is devoted to processing the trauma memory after recounting is completed. *Homework assigned for Module 6*: Listening to the recording of the recounting of the memory and practicing assigned real-life experiments daily.

Phase 4: Relapse Prevention and Treatment Termination

Module 7: Relapse Prevention. As the adolescent finds that recounting the worst moments is easier and that PTSD symptoms are waning, the program focuses on identifying potential future triggers and tools the adolescent has learned to deal with stressors. The therapist and adolescent discuss possible triggers, such as additional traumatic events or high stress experiences, and list possible ways of coping. Skills learned in treatment (e.g., facing fears and breathing retraining) are highlighted. This module also includes an optional Final Project in which the adolescent is invited to create something that can show how far he or she has come and what he or she has learned. This project can include creative exercises like writing the story of the trauma, making a self-portrait of how he or she feels now, or writing about how he or she felt after the trauma occurred. Plans for the final session are also made in this module and can include fun activities the adolescent likes to do, a preferred snack, or favorite music to be played. *Homework assigned for*

Module 7: Completing Final Project activities, continuing to listen to the recording of the recounting of the memory and continuing to practice assigned real-life experiments daily.

Module 8: Final Session. In this module, the tone is congratulatory and the adolescent's successes should be highlighted. The module begins with the adolescent completing a round of recounting the memory with the entire trauma memory. During processing, the therapist asks how the adolescent feels now compared with the start of treatment. Items from the real-life experiment hierarchy are then re-rated by the adolescent. The therapist and adolescent discuss how these ratings have changed, as well as what the adolescent feels has helped the most and least during the treatment. Finally, the plans made in the previous module are put into place, and the adolescent and therapist celebrate the adolescent's accomplishments together.

CONCLUSION

PTSD impacts between 5% and 16% of youth and is associated with marked impairment in functioning during critical windows of development. Short term CBTs for PTSD in childhood and adolescence have been the most extensively studied interventions for youth PTSD, and the evidence strongly supports use of these treatments when treating the disorder in clinical practice. TF-CBT and PE-A both address the core features thought to maintain PTSD: namely, avoidance of trauma memories and reminders that are objectively safe but are perceived as dangerous following the traumatic experience(s). By giving adolescents and children an opportunity to talk through their traumatic experiences in a supportive environment, both therapies afford youth the chance to reevaluate unhelpful beliefs about themselves and the traumatic event that provoke negative emotions in the aftermath of trauma.

SELECT BIBLIOGRAPHY

Chrestman, K. R., Gilboa-Schechtman, E., & Foa, E. B. (2008). *Prolonged exposure therapy for PTSD*

teen workbook. New York, NY: Oxford University Press.
This is the PE-A companion workbook for teens. This resource is designed for use by the adolescent receiving or considering PE-A therapy for PTSD. Chapters present the main treatment components and the rationale for their use in language appropriate for teens.

Cohen, J. A., Mannarino, A. P., & Deblinger, E. (2006). *Treating trauma and traumatic grief in children and adolescents.* New York, NY: The Guilford Press.
This is the TF-CBT treatment manual for professionals. This resource provides in-depth explanations of all TF-CBT components, and includes chapters on special issues that may present when working with children with PTSD and their families.

Foa, E. B., Chrestman K., & Gilboa-Schechtman, E. (2008). *Prolonged exposure manual for children and adolescents suffering from PTSD.* New York, NY: Oxford University Press.
This is the PE-A treatment manual for professionals. This resource provides detailed information on the theory and practice of Prolonged Exposure with adolescents.

Trauma-Focused Cognitive Behavioral Therapy. Retrieved from http://tfcbt.musc.edu
This is a web-based training program for therapists interested in learning more about the components of TF-CBT. This resource includes instructional videos demonstrating treatment techniques with children of various ages.

REFERENCES

Alisic, E., Zalta, A. K., van Wesel, F., Larsen, S. E., Hafstad, G. S., Hassanpour, K., & Smid, G. E. (2014). Rates of post-traumatic stress disorder in trauma-exposed children and adolescents: Meta-analysis. *The British Journal of Psychiatry, 204,* 335–340.

American Psychiatric Association. (2013). *Diagnostic and statistical manual of mental disorders* (5th ed.). Arlington, VA: American Psychiatric Publishing.

Beck, J. S. (1995). *Cognitive therapy: Basics and beyond.* New York, NY: The Guilford Press.

Bolton, D., Hill, J., O'Ryan, D., Udwin, O., Boyle, S., & Yule, W. (2004). Long-term effects of psychological trauma on psychosocial functioning. *Journal of Child Psychology & Psychiatry, 45,* 1007–1014.

Cohen, J. A., Deblinger, E., Mannarino, A. P., & Steer, R. (2004). A multisite randomized controlled trial for multiple traumatized children with sexual abuse-related PTSD. *Journal of the American Academy of Child and Adolescent Psychiatry, 29*, 747–752.

Cohen, J.A., Mannarino, A.P., & Deblinger, E. (2006). *Treating trauma and traumatic grief in children and adolescents.* New York, NY: The Guilford Press.

Dorsey, S., Briggs, E. C., & Woods, B. A. (2011). Cognitive behavioral treatment for posttraumatic stress disorder in children and adolescents. *Child Adolescent Psychiatric Clinics of North America, 20*, 255–269.

Foa, E. B., Chrestman, K., & Gilboa-Schechtman, E. (2008). *Prolonged exposure manual for children and adolescents suffering from PTSD.* New York, NY: Oxford University Press.

Foa, E. B., McLean, C. P., Capaldi, S., & Rosenfield, D. (2013). Prolonged exposure vs. supportive counseling for sexual abuse–related PTSD in adolescent girls. *Journal of the American Medical Association, 310*, 2650–2657.

Gilboa-Schechtman, E., Foa, E. B., Shafran, N., Aderka, I. M., Powers, M. B., Rachamim, L.,…Apter, A. (2010). Prolonged exposure versus dynamic therapy for adolescent PTSD: A pilot randomized controlled trial. *Journal of the American Academy of Child and Adolescent Psychiatry, 49*(10), 1034–1042.

Kilpatrick, D. G., Ruggiero, K. J., Acierno, R., Saunders, B. E., Resnick, H. S., & Best, C. L. (2003). Violence and risk of PTSD, major depression, substance use/dependence, and comorbidity: Results from the National Survey of Adolescents. *Journal of Consulting and Clinical Psychology, 71*, 692–700.

McLaughlin, K. A., Koenan, K. C., Hill, E. D., Petukhova, M., Sampson, N. A., Zaslavsky, A. M., & Kessler, R. C. (2013). Trauma exposure and posttraumatic stress disorder in a national sample of adolescents. *Journal of the American Academy of Child and Adolescent Psychiatry, 52*, 815–830.

McLean, C. P., Rosenbach, S. B., Capaldi, S., & Foa, E. B. (2013). Social and academic functioning in adolescents with child sexual abuse–related PTSD. *Child Abuse & Neglect, 37*, 675–678.

Merikangas, K. R., He, J., Burstein, M., Swanson, S. A., Avenevoli, S., Cui, L.,…Swendsen, J. (2010). Lifetime prevalence of mental disorders in U.S. adolescents: Results from the National Comorbidity Study-Adolescent Supplement (NCS-A). *Journal of the American Academy of Child and Adolescent Psychiatry, 49*, 980–989.

Nooner, K. B., Linares, L. O., Batinjane, J., Kramer, R. A., Silver, R., & Cloitre, M. (2012). Factors related to posttraumatic stress disorder in adolescence. *Trauma, Violence, & Abuse, 13*, 153–166.

Silverman, W. K., Ortiz, C. D., Viswesvaran, C., Burns, B. J., Kolko, D. J., Putnam, F. W., & Amaya-Jackson, L. (2008). Evidence-based psychosocial treatments for children and adolescents exposed to traumatic events. *Journal of Clinical Child and Adolescent Psychology, 37*(1), 156–183.

Stauffer, L., & Deblinger, E. (2003). *Let's talk about taking care of you: An educational book about body safety.* Hatfield, PA: Hope for Families, Inc.

Stauffer, L., & Deblinger, E. (2004). *Let's talk about taking care of you: An educational book about body safety for young children.* Hatfield, PA: Hope for Families, Inc.

Psychosocial Adjustment

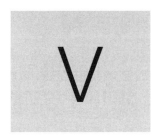

Evidence-Based Interventions for Stress in Children and Adolescents

Robyn S. Hess, Casey R. Shannon, and Ronald P. Glazier

OVERVIEW

Stress is a ubiquitous experience in the lives of children and adolescents, regardless of the schools they attend, their families' income, or the neighborhood in which they live. Over years of research, two different ways of conceptualizing stress have emerged. Early definitions simply considered the occurrence of an event that resulted in a significant change in the individual's environment. Later models proposed a more transactional approach in which the individual's appraisal of the change (e.g., threatening, challenging) was considered important to the experience of stress. From a developmental perspective, it is known that very young children feel stress, yet their cognitive appraisal of the environmental event may not play the same role as it does for adults. Therefore, Grant et al. (2003) defined stress as "environmental events or chronic conditions that objectively threaten the physical and/or psychological health or well-being of individuals of a particular age in a particular society" (p. 449). In other words, stress is a biological and psychological response to the demands made on individuals by their environment, perceptions, and relationships.

It is helpful to understand the distinction between the terms "stressor" and "stress," which are commonly found in the research. A *stressor* is considered an environmental event that a person encounters whereas *stress* represents an umbrella term that includes stressors, as well as associated biological and psychological events that occur when stressors are encountered (Grant et al., 2003). Individuals respond in different ways and to varying degrees depending on how the stressor is perceived (Grant, McMahon, Duffy, Taylor, & Compas, 2011). Furthermore, stress can be conceptualized as both normative and non-normative (Ryan-Wenger, Wilson, & Broussard, 2012). For example, the stress associated with everyday life, such as having a disagreement with a friend or receiving a bad grade on a test is considered normative. Conversely, non-normative stressors tend to be associated with serious or traumatic experiences such as a natural disaster or child abuse. Stressors vary in both intensity and duration and occur in the form of acute traumatic events, chronic strain and adversity, and accumulated stressful life events and daily hassles (Haggerty, Sherrod, Garmezy, & Rutter, 1994).

ETIOLOGY AND FACTORS CONTRIBUTING TO STRESS IN CHILDREN AND ADOLESCENTS

Although all children and adolescents face stressors at various times throughout their lives, those living in poverty may be subjected to more environmental stressors and multiple events that are damaging in the long term (Evans & Kim, 2013). For example, children living in poverty commonly experience familial environments characterized by chaos, discord, violence, dissolution, parental psychopathology, and poor parenting (Evans & Kim, 2013). Furthermore, impoverished neighborhoods are more likely to experience higher crime rates, more noise and pollutants, overcrowded conditions, and fewer play areas (Evans, 2004).

There is clear evidence correlating low socioeconomic status (SES) with increases in exposure to violence and other traumatic and stressful experiences (Hatch & Dohrenwend, 2007). Because low SES is associated with access to fewer community resources and opportunities, this environment creates a vulnerability to negative life experiences such as exposure to violence. Low SES has also been linked to increases in parental distress, which can lead to decreased parental involvement and parent–child interactions that are less supportive and warm (Grant et al., 2003). When parents are emotionally unresponsive and consistently unavailable, children may develop an insecure attachment, and subsequently lack a model for how to effectively cope with stress. When children develop secure caregiver attachments, it is easier for them to effectively regulate stress by seeking closer proximity to the caregiver or relying on schema from previous experiences during which stress was successfully navigated (Nolte, Guiney, Fonagy, Mayes, & Luyten, 2011).

Consistent with the findings related to SES, youth of color living in urban areas experience high rates of stressful events. For example, in a community sample of 1,093 high school seniors, Schilling, Aseltine, and Gore (2007) found that some of the most commonly reported stressful childhood experiences were parental separation, parental unemployment, parental substance abuse, and witnessing serious injury or murder. Important ethnic differences emerged with Black and Hispanic high school seniors witnessing serious violence at a rate twice that of White adolescents. Immigrant Latino youth may be especially vulnerable to the effects of stress because of exposure to violence and undocumented status (Jaycox et al., 2002).

Gender and age also are important factors to consider as related to the amount and type of stress experienced by youth (Hatch & Dohrenwend, 2007). Males are more likely to report experiencing traumatic events than females, but there are inconsistent findings related to gender differences for stressful, nontraumatic events. Adolescents and young adults report experiencing traumatic and other stressful events, including being the victim of physical and sexual assault, more often than adults do. As individuals transition into adulthood, they continue to encounter high levels of nontraumatic stress such as beginning their careers, moving to a new area, and starting their own families.

Physiological Responses to Stressors

When individuals encounter psychosocial stressors, whether they are of short (acute) or long (chronic) duration, a complex physiological response ensues that includes the release of hormones and neurotransmitters, including epinephrine and cortisol, as well as changes at a cellular level when exposed to chronic stress. The perceived stressor, or change in environment, initiates a physiological reaction to which an individual's body attempts to regulate internal systems to maintain stability, or allostasis (Danese & McEwen, 2012). The three main allostatic systems involved in physiologic reactions to stress include the nervous system, the endocrine system, and the immune system. It is beyond the scope of this chapter to discuss these systems in depth; however, there are two key components important to understanding biological responses to stress. The first, known as the "fight-or-flight" response, is an adaptive biological response of the nervous system that activates an individual's heightened alertness and hyper-focus to the environment (Danese & McEwen, 2012). It occurs because of the release of the neurotransmitter epinephrine (adrenaline) that is discharged in varying amounts (Wong et al., 2012). The fight-or-flight response is so named because, when individuals encounter stressful situations, their reactions are conceptualized as either staying put and resisting the stressor or running away to avoid the perceived threat. Regardless of the response to the encountered stressor, there is an established link between high levels and prolonged exposure to epinephrine and cardiovascular disease, posttraumatic stress disorder (PTSD), depression, and acceleration of cancer in adults (Wong et al., 2012).

The second key component is a neuroendocrine response to stress, the hypothalamic–pituitary–adrenal (HPA) axis (Dickerson & Kemeny, 2004), which is responsible for the release of the hormone cortisol (a glucocorticoid) (Hanson & Chen, 2010). High levels of cortisol production are associated with negative physiological and psychological outcomes (Laurent, Gilliam, Bruce, & Fisher, 2014). For example, children who are in high-risk living conditions and who have high and unstable levels of cortisol production experience more internalizing symptoms (e.g., anxiety, depression) than children with lower or stable cortisol levels (Laurent et al., 2014). According to Danese and McEwen (2012), persistent exposure to stressors leads to detrimental physiological changes that occur because of a "cumulative wear and tear" (p. 30) effect known as "allostatic load."

In addition to the allostatic responses to stressors, there is emerging evidence that individuals may undergo changes at the cellular level, which are associated with deleterious psychological and biological outcomes that can have a cumulative effect on the body and lead to the onset of disease (Hanson & Chen, 2010). Recent research has focused on the connection between early childhood stress and the erosion of telomere length (Price, Kao, Burgers, Carpenter, & Tyrka, 2013). A telomere is a complex mass of DNA protein and each time a cell replicates the telomere shortens, resulting in a gradual deterioration of the cell (Price et al., 2013). This process, referred to as "senescence," happens to cells naturally but is exacerbated by chronic exposure to stress. There is an increasing amount of evidence indicating a relationship between short telomeres and major medical and mental disorders such as depression (Shalev et al., 2013).

This finding is consistent with a diathesis-stress model that connects vulnerability and stress to negative mental health outcomes. That is, early experiences of significant stress may cause physiological and psychological changes for children, increasing vulnerability to subsequent stressors. Shapero et al. (2014) explored the negative impact of childhood emotional abuse with 281 individuals ranging in age from 16 to 24 to determine whether emotional abuse had a moderating effect on how individuals dealt with current stressful life events. They found that all types of early life stress predicted, exacerbated, increased, or sustained a variety of psychiatric diagnoses in adulthood (Shapero et al., 2014).

Developmental Aspects of Stress

There are certain periods during which vulnerability to stress fluctuates. Early childhood is a time during which both genders are especially sensitive to stress. Another period of vulnerability is during early adolescence; however, this finding appears greater for females than males (Laceulle et al., 2014). Although much of the research has focused on children's experience of stress from their environments in a unidirectional manner, for some children and adolescents this effect is bidirectional. That is, children are active agents in creating their environments. They may have psychological difficulties that manifest as disruptive behaviors, irritability, or depressive symptoms that negatively affect family functioning or peer relationships, and result in more stressful situations (Laceulle et al., 2014).

Across the life span, individuals are most affected by chronic stress, but minor, frequent stressors, referred to as "daily hassles," are also distressing (Bridley & Jordan, 2012; Haggerty et al., 1994). For youth, these types of stressors often include social demands and school problems and they appear to exacerbate the symptoms of existing physical and psychological disorders. As with major stressors, certain familial and individual characteristics can serve as moderators for this type of stress. For example, family and child routines can help buffer against the negative effects of everyday stressors (Bridley & Jordan, 2012).

Entry into adolescence represents a particularly vulnerable time for youth; individuals who encounter multiple simultaneous stressful life changes are more likely to experience emotional and behavioral disturbances (Grant et al., 2003). Support from significant adults and feelings of worth appear to provide an important foundation for effective coping at this developmental stage (DuBois et al., 2002). As adolescents progress through subsequent developmental stages, they develop increasing capacities for abstract thought and self-reflection. These changes allow adolescents to exert greater control over their perceptions of stress and to regulate their subsequent actions, allowing for a broader range of coping strategies directed toward problem solving.

It is impossible to fully understand stress without also considering the efforts used by individuals to cope with and manage their stress. Although the relationship between significant stressors and psychopathology is robust, it is not absolute. Various moderators both internal to the child (e.g., age, gender, ethnicity) and those present in his or her environment (e.g., SES) can work as protective factors by reducing the likelihood of negative outcomes. For example, social competence may serve to decrease the likelihood of negative effects from stress because children with high social competence more often employ the use of social supports and other active coping strategies than those with low social competence (Zimmer-Gembeck, Lees, & Skinner, 2011).

Practitioners are limited in their ability to decrease or change the number or types of stressors experienced by children and adolescents or the moderators that are already present. However, the actions that youth take in response to stressors can mediate the potential negative effects of the situation. Therefore, focus should be directed toward providing supports that enhance the individual's coping capacity and ability to manage stress using evidence-based interventions.

EVIDENCE-BASED INTERVENTIONS AND EMPIRICAL SUPPORT FOR STRESS IN CHILDREN AND ADOLESCENTS

Early conceptualizations for intervening with stress focused on the importance of effective coping. As maladaptive coping is associated with negative outcomes (e.g., Grant et al., 2011), many prevention programs have been developed to help children and adolescents identify and use appropriate coping strategies to address both acute and chronic stressors. These types of primary prevention programs are effective in reducing stress and enhancing coping skills (Kraag et al., 2006). In the schools, these programs can be implemented universally; they serve as a prevention strategy for students with adequate coping skills and as early intervention for those who are struggling.

Given the diversity of stressors that impact individuals and the need for interventions that can be implemented at tiered levels within a school setting, promising primary and secondary interventions for stress include training in coping skills, stress reduction, and mindfulness. Three programs are introduced that focus on different approaches and aspects of managing stress. The first, Zippy's Friends, focuses on changing cognitions and building coping skills for managing stressful experiences. Zippy's Friends was recently reviewed (February 2012) and identified as an evidence-based program by the Substance Abuse and Mental Health Services Administration's (SAMHSA) National Registry of Evidence-Based Programs and Practices (NREPP; SAMHSA, n.d.). This designation was based on numerous studies supporting its use. For example, Mishara and Ystgaard (2006) found that the students who completed Zippy's Friends experienced a significant increase in coping skills and decrease in problem behaviors such as hyperactivity and other externalizing behaviors.

Another early intervention approach for stress reduction focuses on the self-regulation aspect of managing stress. There is a growing body of research supporting the use of relaxation training and imagery to increase well-being in children and adolescents (e.g., Goldbeck & Schmid, 2003). This type of stress management technique (SMT) has diverse applications including stress reduction in children with asthma (Long et al., 2011), and the reduction of internalizing symptoms among children with emotional problems (Goldbeck & Schmid, 2003). Only recently has this approach been modified for use with larger groups in a classroom setting (Bothe, Grignon, & Olness, 2014).

The third type of intervention, which offers an alternative to training in coping and stress reduction, is mindfulness. Mindfulness activities result in a wide range of positive outcomes for children and adolescents, including lower rates of stress and anxiety, as well as increased ability to sustain attention (e.g., Burke, 2010). This approach has emerged as a promising strategy to address stress in youth, and several school-based programs have demonstrated positive effects (e.g., Felver, Doerner, Jones, Kaye, & Merrell, 2013). One such program, Learning to BREATHE (Broderick & Metz, 2009), resulted in lower levels of perceived stress and psychosomatic complaints as well as increased emotional regulation among 216 high school students after six 15- to 25-minute sessions of the program (Metz et al., 2013). In a community-based, randomized clinical trial, the efficacy of Stressed Teens, a Mindfulness-Based Stressed Reduction (MBSR) curriculum for adolescents, was evaluated with youth who were receiving outpatient treatment. Findings indicated reduced perceptions of stress as well as decreased obsessive symptoms and interpersonal difficulties. In addition, MBSR participants demonstrated improved mental health and increased overall functioning (Biegel, Brown, Shapiro, & Schubert, 2009), with continued positive effects evidenced at a 3-month follow-up.

HOW TO: A GUIDE TO THE IMPLEMENTATION OF INTERVENTIONS FOR STRESS IN CHILDREN AND ADOLESCENTS

Overview of Zippy's Friends

"Zippy's Friends" is a school-based mental health promotion and intervention program for younger students in Kindergarten through first grade. This program helps children cope with adversity by encouraging them to recognize and express their feelings in positive ways, showing them how to communicate with others effectively, assisting them in making friends, dealing with bullies and bullying situations, and coping with loss (Mishara & Ystgaard, 2006). The Zippy's Friends program encourages students to understand their feelings and behavior that facilitates self-reliance and self-confidence. According to Gfroerer, Nelson, and Kern (2013), encouragement is a powerful tool that has been shown to diminish school-related stress through the development of positive coping skills.

Originally developed by Befrienders International, the program is distributed through the nonprofit organization Partnership for Children (www.part-nershipforchildren.org.uk). This organization has an established partnership with Montclair State University, which is currently the sole licensed provider of this program in the United States. Zippy's Friends is presently implemented in more than 30 countries across five continents. As such, most of the supporting evidence for this program has been established with international populations.

Implementation. Zippy's Friends is a curriculum-based program with explicit instructions to guide

classroom teachers and other trained educators in its implementation. It comprises 24 lessons (six modules; four lessons per module) that are led on a weekly basis (see Table 28.1 for a list of modules).

Zippy, a stuffed animal stick insect, and his group of friends are the main characters. The program is composed of six 45-minute stories in which Zippy and his friends confront common problems encountered by most young children relating to friendship, communication, feeling lonely, bullying, dealing with loss and change, and making a new start. Each lesson begins with the teacher reading a story to the class followed by students engaging in activities, discussions, and games related to the theme of the story. The components are designed to assist children in exploring their feelings and better understanding their behavior (Partnership for Children, n.d.). When children understand how to manage their feelings and learn positive ways of dealing with adverse situations, it helps them to cope more effectively with stress by developing an internal locus of control (Gfroerer et al., 2013).

Overview of the SMT. The daily SMT is a 10-minute activity that can be led by a teacher or other educational personnel (Bothe et al., 2014). It is designed to be delivered daily in a classroom setting and incorporates relaxation, movement, and imagery into the instruction. Because this specific technique is relatively new to the school setting, there is limited information on the effects for the length of intervention (both in terms of daily administration and over the course of the school year), time of delivery, and differential effects based on age, gender, and other demographic variables.

Implementation. The SMT is introduced using a detailed outline available from Bothe et al. (2014) with two 30-minute teaching sessions. The first of these two sessions focuses on teaching the concepts of stress and relaxation, as well as ways that the body responds to these. The second session teaches the actual SMTs that children and adolescents will use during their 10-minute daily session. Each child is instructed in the use of diaphragmatic breathing. This technique, also known as "belly breathing" or "deep breathing," involves contracting the diaphragm. During diaphragmatic breathing, students inhale deeply through the nose expanding their stomachs while

TABLE 28.1

ZIPPY'S FRIENDS PROGRAM MODULES		
Module	**Goal**	**Sessions**
1. Feelings	To improve children's abilities to recognize difficult feelings and to identify coping strategies to deal with those feelings	1. Feeling sad—feeling happy 2. Feeling angry or annoyed 3. Feeling jealous 4. Feeling nervous
2. Communication	To improve children's abilities to communicate their feelings	1. Improving communication 2. Listening 3. Who can help us? 4. Saying what you want to say
3. Making and breaking relationships	To improve children's abilities to make friends and to cope with rejection and loneliness	1. How to keep a friend 2. Dealing with loneliness and rejection 3. How to resolve conflicts with friends 4. How to make friends
4. Conflict resolution	To improve children's abilities to resolve conflicts	1. How to recognize good solutions 2. Bullying 3. Solving problems 4. Helping others resolve conflicts
5. Dealing with change and loss	To improve children's abilities to deal with change	1. Change and loss are part of life 2. Coping with death 3. Visit to a graveyard 4. Learning from change and loss
6. We cope	To improve children's abilities to use a variety of coping strategies	1. Different ways to cope 2. How to help others 3. Adapting to new situations 4. Celebrating together

Recreated with permission from http://www.partnershipforchildren.org.uk

keeping their chests still. Emphasis is placed on exhaling fully and waiting a few seconds before taking the next breath.

Once daily practice begins, youths may either stand or sit as they complete the three parts to each session. The first component is deep breathing (described earlier), followed by movement, and then guided imagery. Students engage in about 1 minute of diaphragmatic breathing, 4 minutes of gentle stretching movements (e.g., growing like a flower, standing like a mountain focusing on one spot), another minute of deep breathing, and 4 minutes of guided imagery. Details describing the movements and the scripts for the guided imagery, which include directions for muscle relaxation and imaging a favorite location, are available

from Bothe et al. (2014). This pilot study featured a rigorous research protocol; however, it is likely that, as long as these three elements are generally used as described, the gentle stretching movements and imagery scripts could vary from those specifically used in this study. If employed in schools, the teacher should integrate the practice into the daily classroom routine by offering the session after the midday lunch/recess period as this is often a time when students need to refocus.

Overview of Mindfulness-Based Stress Reduction. Mindfulness-based techniques enable adults to cope with a wide range of psychological and medical disorders (Baer, 2003). As research has demonstrated the beneficial effects of mindfulness in adults, there is a growing interest in applying mindfulness strategies as interventions for use with children and adolescents (Felver et al., 2013). The foremost therapeutic approaches that incorporate mindfulness techniques include acceptance and commitment therapy (ACT), dialectical behavior therapy (DBT), mindfulness-based cognitive therapy (MBCT), and MBSR. Among these, MBCT and MBSR include "mindfulness meditative practices" as a core component (Burke, 2010, p. 133). Mindfulness has been defined as "the awareness that emerges through paying attention on purpose, in the present moment, and non-judgmentally to the unfolding of experience moment by moment" (Kabat-Zinn, 2003, p. 145). Although rooted in Buddhist traditions, a secular application of mindfulness is more common in Western psychological interventions.

Practicing mindfulness involves present-centered awareness and emphasizes acceptance of thoughts and experiences, in contrast to the traditional focus of cognitive behavioral models on changing dysfunctional thought patterns or perceptions. Conceptualizations of mindfulness continue to evolve along with a growing understanding of mindfulness as a construct (see Shapiro, Carlson, Astin, & Freedman, 2006). One operational definition, constructed through consensus among several prominent mindfulness scholars, defines mindfulness as a metacognitive skill involving the self-regulation of attention in the present moment and an attitude toward that experience that is characterized by curiosity, acceptance, and openness or receptiveness to whatever occurs (Bishop et al., 2004).

A number of mindfulness programs have been developed for implementation in both school and community-based settings with a focus on younger participants. Some programs also involve parents and/or educators; therefore, approaches for adult inclusion are one element of potential variation across programs. Although most feature a set curriculum that represents a child-friendly adaptation of the original 8-week MBSR curriculum developed for adults (Kabat-Zinn, 1990), the unique characteristics of instructors, participants, and what arises in each session contribute to the flow and fluidity of the group itself; programs are adapted to reflect group needs and goals. Furthermore, variation exists in the frequency and duration of sessions and the specific practices used. A specific curriculum, Still Quiet Place, is discussed in the following sections to highlight the core elements and implementation approaches of a mindfulness-based program.

Implementation. Still Quiet Place (Saltzman, 2014) is an 8-week curriculum for children and adolescents founded in the practices of MBSR. A detailed description and implementation guide are provided in text (Saltzman, 2014) with detailed practice scripts available on a CD (Saltzman, 2004). Instructors who lead mindfulness programs are encouraged to first be familiar with and regularly practice mindfulness in their own lives (Kabat-Zinn, 2003; Saltzman & Goldin, 2008). Setting the stage for success is important; the amount of time initially spent engaged in mindful activities should be brief and aligned with the developmental abilities of the participant(s). Saltzman and Goldin (2008) suggest that most children of 9 years and older are capable of using mindfulness similar to adults, whereas younger children are generally capable of engaging in 1 minute of practice per years of age.

Still Quiet Place sessions last 45 to 60 minutes each, with variation attributed to setting and number of participants. The sessions can be provided to eight to thirty children. During sessions, guided practices last between 5 and 12 minutes, considering the developmental needs of younger participants. The course involves in-class exercises and training in both formal and informal mindfulness practices, as well as home-based practice between sessions. Formal practice refers to the intentional and regular engagement in mindfulness for a sustained time period, and informal practice represents the generalization of mindful awareness throughout daily activities (Kabat-Zinn, 2003). Participants each receive a workbook, a CD of 12 distinct short guided practices (Saltzman, 2004), and worksheets to monitor practice outside of sessions. Although these elements are designed to increase adherence to the program, instructors have flexibility in how lessons are presented and the length of lessons, whereas participants determine the amount of practice that occurs between lessons.

Before starting the course, Saltzman (2014) recommends an introductory meeting with parents during which a review of mindfulness and its research base are provided and relevant psychoeducational aspects of the course are discussed. If parental participation is limited, alternative approaches to communicating this information are encouraged. Certain guiding principles such as creating a safe space, encouraging the continued use of mindfulness when transitioning between group activities, use of nonverbal signals when it is necessary to refocus group members (e.g., intentional instructor silence, sounding a chime, raising one hand), and the use of "languaging" and "do-overs" are recommended to facilitate mindfulness instruction (Saltzman, 2014). Languaging refers to the purposeful word choices of instructors to invite engagement in an activity ("Now breathing in"), in contrast to dictating ("Now breathe in") such participation (Saltzman & Goldin, 2008, p. 50). The inclusion of do-overs as a natural element of instruction serves a model that things need not be perfect.

To establish routine and signify the commencement of mindfulness practice, each session begins and ends with Mindful Listening practice. Participants are first invited to quiet their bodies and be still. Speaking slowly, the group facilitator guides the group through the practice of Mindful Listening. The following excerpt provides an example of how this may be done, with the ellipses representing long pauses in the narrative.

> In a moment I will ring this tone bar, and you will hear a sound. See if you can listen to the sound with all of your attention—with your ears, your mind, your heart, and your body. When the sound fades and you can't hear it anymore, quietly raise your hand. Please keep your eyes closed and your hand raised. Okay, please close your eyes…(Ring the tone bar or similar, then wait until the sound has faded and everyone's hand is raised). Now before you open your eyes, take a moment to listen to the quiet underneath the sound…And now, notice how your body, mind, and heart feel after listening in this way…When you are ready you may open your eyes and we will continue, doing our best to listen to each other with our full attention, just like we listened to the sound. (Saltzman, 2014, p. 59)

After the Mindful Listening practice, a review of the home-based practice occurs. The majority of sessions are focused on mindful practices or exercises, with group discussion following each. Chosen practices build on previously learned skills and include the introduction of new techniques. The weekly topics are outlined by Saltzman (2014) and generally align with the topics presented in the original program Kabat-Zinn (1990). Some changes have been made in the presentation order of the topics. For example, body scan practice occurs later in the series (e.g., session 6 rather than session 1), because youth require more practice with remaining still and quiet before attempting this activity (Saltzman, 2014). Even in their briefest form, body scans can last 12 minutes. The body scan is a guided practice during which participants lie on the floor or sit in a chair. They are invited to focus attention and awareness on their bodies beginning with their toes, moving slowly up through the entire body, and concluding with breathing, sensing, and attending to the whole body. (A script can be downloaded from the website that accompanies the text or from other resources.)

Different types of exercises allow for further exploration of thinking habits and several example exercises are provided throughout the curriculum (e.g., Pleasant Experiences exercise, Unpleasant Events exercise, Brief Go-Round exercise, Emotion Improve exercise). "Nine dots" is one such common exercise during which participants are asked to complete a puzzle using specific instructions. Throughout the process, group members are encouraged to be mindful of their reaction to the task, the thoughts that emerge, and their self-talk while attempting to solve the puzzle. Saltzman (2014) recommends that participant comments guide the follow-up discussions about exercises; therefore, discussions are likely to vary from group to group. Sessions conclude with an overview of the home practice for the upcoming week, followed again with Mindful Listening practice.

A number of practices are taught throughout the curriculum, many of which emulate those taught to adults. Traditional formal meditative practices include body scan, sitting meditation, and movement (e.g., yoga). Saltzman (2014) uses adapted youth-friendly approaches such as Jewel, a breath-based technique, to cultivate the practice of returning one's attention after wandering thoughts. With this technique, children and adolescents are invited to choose a stone or jewel and subsequently place it on their belly buttons while sitting or lying down. The item is used as a focal point to gain awareness of one's breath by observing the jewel rise and fall while inhaling and exhaling. Although an instructor may use the exact curriculum as presented by Saltzman (2014), practitioners are encouraged to adapt their sessions based on the needs of their students.

CONCLUSION

Children and adolescents encounter a variety of stressors on a daily basis. The sources of stress vary greatly, and school personnel often may not know when a student is experiencing stress. Therefore, preventive practices that teach students the tools they will need to manage their stress will likely have the greatest impact. The three strategies of coping skill training, stress management, and mindfulness all show promise for very young children to high school students. Through these evidence-based interventions, mental health professionals may help students effectively manage the stress in their lives and enhance their overall well-being.

SELECT BIBLIOGRAPHY

Biegel, G. (2009). *The stress reduction workbook for teens: Mindfulness skills to help you deal with stress.* Oakland, CA: Instant Help Books.
This workbook provides 37 mindfulness activities for adolescents intended to support stress reduction. Additional information including articles and supporting materials (CD and a telephone app) can be found at www.stressedteens.com.

Bothe, D. A., Grignon, J. B., & Olness, K. N. (2014). The effects of a stress management intervention in elementary school children. *Journal of Developmental & Behavioral Pediatrics, 35,* 62–67.
This article provides an overview of the SMT as delivered in a classroom setting. Directions for classroom training and guided imagery scripts are available from the authors.

Broderick, P. C. (2013). *Learning to BREATHE: A mindfulness curriculum for adolescents.* Oakland, CA: New Harbinger.

This book provides detailed information about an evidence-based mindfulness curriculum for use with adolescents in a variety of settings, including schools. Additional information is available on the author's website www.learning2breathe.org.

Zippy's Friends. Retrieved from http://www.montclair .edu/cehs/academics/centers-and-institutes/autism/ zippys-friends/
Information on how to become a trainer using Zippy's Friends is available at this website as well as a brief video clip showing the Zippy's Friends program in action at www.mybuddytodd.org.

REFERENCES

Baer, R. A. (2003). Mindfulness training as a clinical intervention: A conceptual and empirical review. *Clinical Psychology: Science and Practice, 10*(2), 125–143. doi:10.1093/clipsy.bpg015

Biegel, G. M., Brown, K. W., Shapiro, S. L., & Schubert, C. M. (2009). Mindfulness-based stress reduction for the treatment of adolescent psychiatric outpatients: A randomized clinical trial. *Journal of Consulting and Clinical Psychology, 77,* 855–866. Retrieved from http://dx.doi.org/10.1037/ a0016241

Bishop, S. R., Lau, M., Shapiro, S., Carlson, L., Anderson, N. D., Carmody, J.,...Devins, G. (2004). Mindfulness: A proposed operational definition. *Clinical Psychology: Science and Practice, 11*(3), 230–241. doi:10.1093/clipsy.bph077

Bothe, D. A., Grignon, J. B., & Olness, K. N. (2014). The effects of a stress management intervention in elementary school children. *Journal of Developmental and Behavioral Pediatrics, 35*(1), 62–67.

Bridley, A., & Jordan, S. S. (2012). Child routines moderate daily hassles and children's psychological adjustment. *Children's Health Care, 41,* 129–144. doi:10.1080/02739615.2012.657040

Broderick, P. C., & Metz, S. (2009). Learning to BREATHE: A pilot trial of a mindfulness curriculum for adolescents. *Advances in School Mental Health Promotion, 2*(1), 35–46. doi:10.1080/17547 30X.2009.9715696

Burke, C. A. (2010). Mindfulness-based approaches with children and adolescents: A preliminary review of current research in an emergent field. *Journal of Child and Family Studies, 19,* 133–144. doi:10.1007/s10826-009-9282-x

Danese, A., & McEwen, B. (2012). Adverse childhood experiences, allostatis, allostatic load, and age-related disease. *Physiology & Behavior, 106*, 29–39. doi:10.1016/j.physbeh.2011.08.019

Dickerson, S. S., & Kemeny, M. E. (2004). Acute stressors and cortisol responses: A theoretical integration and synthesis of laboratory research. *Psychological Bulletin, 130*(3), 355–391.

DuBois, D. L., Burk-Braxton, C., Swenson, L. P., Tevendale, H. D., Lockerd, E. M., & Moran, B. L. (2002). Getting by with a little help from self and others: Self-esteem and social support as resources during early adolescence. *Developmental Psychology, 38*, 822–839. Retrieved from http://dx.doi.org/10.1037/0012–1649.38.5.822

Evans, G. W. (2004). The environment of childhood poverty. *American Psychologist, 59*, 77–92. Retrieved from http://dx.doi.org/10.1037/0003–066X.59.2.77

Evans, G. W., & Kim, P. (2013). Childhood poverty, chronic stress, self-regulation, and coping. *Childhood Development Perspectives, 7*, 43–48. doi:10.1111/cdep.12013

Felver, J. C., Doerner, E., Jones, J., Kaye, N. C., & Merrell, K. W. (2013). Mindfulness in school psychology: Applications for intervention and professional practice. *Psychology in the Schools, 50*, 531–547. doi:10.1002/pits.21695

Gfroerer, K., Nelsen, J., & Kern, R. M. (2013). Positive discipline: Helping children develop belonging and coping resources using individual psychology. *Journal of Individual Psychology, 69*, 294–304.

Goldbeck, L., & Schmid, K. (2003). Effectiveness of autogenic relaxation training on children and adolescents with behavioral and emotional problems. *Journal of the American Academy of Child and Adolescent Psychiatry, 42*(9), 1046–1054.

Grant, K. E., Compas, B. E., Stuhlmacher, A. F., Thurm, A. E., McMahon, S., & Halpert, J. A. (2003). Stressors and child and adolescent psychopathology: Moving from markers to mechanisms of risk. *Psychological Bulletin, 129*, 447–466. Retrieved from http://dx.doi.org/10.1037/0033–2909.129.3.447

Grant, K. E., McMahon, S. D., Duffy, S. N., Taylor, J. J., & Compas, B. E. (2011). Stressors and mental health problems in childhood and adolescence. In R. J. Contrada & A. Baum (Eds.), *The handbook of stress science: Biology, psychology, and health*

(pp. 359–372). New York, NY: Springer Publishing Company.

Haggerty, R. J., Sherrod, L. R., Garmezy, N., & Rutter, M. (Eds.). (1994). *Stress, risk, and resilience in children and adolescents: Processes, mechanisms, and interventions*. New York, NY: Cambridge University Press.

Hanson, M. D., & Chen, E. (2010). Daily stress, cortisol, and sleep: The moderating role of childhood psychosocial environments. *Health Psychology, 29*(4), 394–402.

Hatch, S. L., & Dohrenwend, B. P. (2007). Distribution of traumatic and other stressful life events by race/ethnicity, gender, SES and age: A review of the research. *American Journal of Community Psychology, 40*(3–4), 313–332.

Jaycox, L. H., Stein, B. D., Kataoka, S. H., Wong, M., Fink, A., Escudero, P., & Zaragoza, C. (2002). Violence exposure, posttraumatic stress disorder, and depressive symptoms among recent immigrant schoolchildren. *Journal of the American Academy of Child and Adolescent Psychiatry, 41*(9), 1104–1110.

Kabat-Zinn, J. (1990). *Full catastrophe living: Using the wisdom of your body and mind to face stress, pain, and illness*. New York, NY: Bantam Dell.

Kabat-Zinn, J. (2003). Mindfulness-based interventions in context: Past, present, and future. *Clinical Psychology: Science and Practice, 10*, 144–156. doi:10.1093/clipsy.bpg016

Kraag, G., Zeegers, M. P., Kok, G., Hosman, C., & Abu-Saad, H. H. (2006). School programs targeting stress management in children and adolescents: A meta-analysis. *Journal of School Psychology, 44*, 449–472. doi:10.1016/j.jsp.2006.07.001

Laceulle, O. M., O'Donnell, K., Glover, V., O'Connor, T. G., Ormel, J., van Aken, M. A., & Nederhof, E. (2014). Stressful events and psychological difficulties: Testing alternative candidates for sensitivity. *European Child & Adolescent Psychiatry, 23*(2), 103–113.

Laurent, A. K., Gilliam, K. S., Bruce, J., & Fisher, P. A. (2014). HPA stability for children in foster care: Mental health implications and moderation by early intervention. *Developmental Psychobiology*, 1–10. doi:10.1002/dev.21226

Long, K. A., Ewing, L. J., Cohen, S., Skoner, D., Gentile, D., Koehrsen, J.,…Marsland, A. L. (2011). Preliminary evidence for the feasibility of a stress management intervention for 7- to 12-year-olds with asthma. *The Journal of Asthma, 48*(2), 162–170.

Metz, S. M., Frank, J. L., Reibel, D., Cantrell, T., Sanders, R., & Broderick, P. C. (2013). The effectiveness of the Learning to BREATHE program on adolescent emotion regulation. *Research in Human in Human Development, 10*(3), 252–272. doi:10.1080/15427609.2013.818488

Mishara, B. L., & Ystgaard, M. (2006). Effectiveness of a mental health promotion program to improve coping skills in young children: Zippy's Friends. *Early Childhood Research Quarterly, 21*, 110–123. doi:10.1016/j.ecresq.2006.01.002

Nolte, T., Guiney, J., Fonagy, P., Mayes, L. C., & Luyten, P. (2011). Interpersonal stress regulation and the development of anxiety disorders: An attachment-based developmental framework. *Frontiers of Behavioral Neuroscience, 5*(55), 1–21. doi:10.3389/fnbeh.2011.00055

Partnership for Children. (n.d.). *Teaching Zippy's Friends*. Retrieved from http://www.partnershipforchildren.org.uk/teachers/zippy-s-friends-teachers/programmecontent.html

Price, L. H., Kao, H. T., Burgers, D. E., Carpenter, L. L., & Tyrka, A. R. (2013). Telomeres and early-life stress: An overview. *Biological Psychiatry, 73*(1), 15–23.

Ryan-Wenger, N. A., Wilson, V. L., & Broussard, A. G. (2012). Stress, coping, and health in children. In V. Hill Rice (Ed.), *Handbook of stress, coping, and health: Implications for nursing research, theory, and practice* (2nd ed., pp. 226–253). Los Angeles, CA: Sage.

Saltzman, A. (2004). *Still quiet place: Mindfulness for young children* [CD]. Retrieved from http://www.stillquietplace.com

Saltzman, A. (2014). *A still quiet place: A mindfulness program for teaching children and adolescents to ease stress and difficult emotions*. Oakland, CA: New Harbinger.

Saltzman, A., & Goldin, P. (2008). Mindfulness-based stress reduction for school-age children. In L. A. Greco & S. C. Hayes (Eds.), *Acceptance and mindfulness treatments for children and adolescents: A practitioner's guide* (pp. 139–161). Oakland, CA: New Harbinger.

Schilling, E. A., Aseltine, R. H., & Gore, S. (2007). Adverse childhood experiences and mental health in young adults: A longitudinal survey. *BMC Public Health, 7*, 30.

Shalev, I., Entringer, S., Wadhwa, P. D., Wolkowitz, O. M., Puterman, E., Lin, J., & Epel, E. S. (2013). Stress and telomere biology: A lifespan perspective. *Psychoneuroendocrinology, 38*(9), 1835–1842.

Shapero, B. G., Black, S. K., Liu, R. T., Klugman, J., Bender, R. E., Abramson, L. Y., & Alloy, L. B. (2014). Stressful life events and depression symptoms: The effect of childhood emotional abuse on stress reactivity. *Journal of Clinical Psychology, 70*(3), 209–223.

Shapiro, S. L., Carlson, L. E., Astin, J. A., & Freedman, B. (2006). Mechanisms of mindfulness. *Journal of Clinical Psychology, 62*(3), 373–386.

Substance Abuse and Mental Health Services Administration (SAMHSA). (n.d.). *National registry for programs and practices database*. Retrieved from www.nrepp.samhsa.gov

Wong, D. L., Tai, T. C., Wong-Faull, D. C., Claycomb, R., Meloni, E. G., Myers, K. M., . . . Kvetnansky, R. (2012). Epinephrine: A short- and long-term regulator of stress and development of illness: A potential new role for epinephrine in stress. *Cellular and Molecular Neurobiology, 32*(5), 737–748.

Zimmer-Gembeck, M. J., Lees, D., & Skinner, E. A. (2011). Children's emotions and coping with interpersonal stress as correlated of social competence. *Australian Journal of Psychology, 63*, 131–141. doi:10.1111/j.1742-9536.2011.00019.x

Evidence-Based Interventions for Children and Adolescents of Divorced Parents

John E. Desrochers

OVERVIEW

Divorce is a lengthy developmental process and, in the case of children and adolescents, one that can encompass most of their young lives. Long before the actual divorce, the family usually endures a lengthy period of increasing marital estrangement and conflict, with the divorce decree marking the culmination of that part of the process and the beginning of a stage of postdivorce adjustment that involves custody, visitation, stepfamilies, and changes in situations that can affect all areas of the family's life. This does not mean that outcomes are all negative; there are often beneficial outcomes to divorce, and most youth emerge from the process becoming healthy and happy adults. Divorce is not a disorder, but it is a significant risk factor in the lives of a great many children and adolescents. In fact, it is safe to say that it is a rare mental health professional—whether working with children, adolescents, or adults—who does not confront issues of divorce in daily practice. This chapter explores the experience of divorce from the perspective of the children, reviews the evidence base and empirical support for interventions, and provides examples of three evidence-based intervention programs (*Children in Between*, Children of Divorce Intervention Program, and *New Beginnings*) appropriate for use with children, adolescents, and their parents.

Nearly half of first marriages of men and women between the ages of 15 and 44 years (the ages of the parents when 99.7% of births occur) end in divorce (Copen, Daniels, Vespa, & Mosher, 2012); divorce rates for subsequent remarriages are even higher. An estimated 30% to 40% of children and adolescents in the United States will experience their parents' divorce (National Center for Health Statistics, 2008); some will even undergo a second divorce process.

ETIOLOGY AND FACTORS CONTRIBUTING TO POSTDIVORCE ADJUSTMENT

Although divorce is no longer considered unusual in our society (Gladstone, Beardslee, & O'Connor, 2011), it remains a significantly stressful disruption in a child's life (Pedro-Carroll, 2005). The most difficult time for most children (and parents) is immediately following the divorce, which is accompanied by the most dramatic changes in family life. By the beginning of the second year after divorce, most families have reached a new form of stability and the most immediate stressors have abated. Divorce is best thought of as a process in which children feel the effects from the initial conflicts through the aftermath, with the entire process potentially taking several years.

Children and adolescents typically mention several core issues when talking about how divorce affects them, including:

- Asking factual questions about what divorce actually is, the role of the court, and how decisions will be made about their future;
- Questioning custody and visitation issues, such as with whom and where they will live, how often they will see the noncustodial parent, and whether they will be separated from their siblings;
- Worrying about financial issues such as whether there will be enough to eat, being able to stay in their current home and school, and being able to attend college;
- Expressing social concerns, such as believing they are the only ones whose parents are divorced, wondering which parent will go to their school and extracurricular events and how to handle those situations, and explaining their new family situation to their peers;
- Voicing concern regarding how much their parents are suffering psychologically; and harboring feelings of shame, guilt and self-blame (e.g., is the divorce my fault?), anger, sadness, anxiety, conflicting loyalties, hope for a parental reconciliation, and fear (e.g., that they will be abandoned or unloved).

Research has established that the quality of parenting that children experience from both parents significantly affects their postdivorce outcomes (Sandler, Braver, & Wheeler, 2013). The divorce process, however, is a period when parents are under a great deal of stress, which in turn affects their ability to provide optimal parenting to their children. Stressors are often contextual and can include the experiences of reduced financial and emotional supports, changes in residence, changes in family routines, isolation from friends and family, and interparental conflict. Anger, depression, and anxiety can also impact their availability for parenting.

Given the essential, even existential nature of these issues for a young person, it is no surprise that some children and adolescents have more difficulty negotiating their parents' divorce than do others. Most young people do not experience long-term mental, emotional, or behavioral problems

as a result of their parents' divorce (e.g., Amato, 2001), but they are at increased risk and have lower overall success in meeting developmental tasks than their peers from two-parent families. For some children, these difficulties can extend through adulthood (National Research Council and Institute of Medicine [NRC & IOM], 2009) and result in increased substance abuse, mental and physical health disorders, and relationship difficulties.

EVIDENCE-BASED INTERVENTIONS FOR CHILDREN AND ADOLESCENTS OF DIVORCED PARENTS

Promoting protective factors and limiting risk factors during childhood and adolescence can prevent many mental, emotional, and behavioral problems and disorders during those years and into adulthood. Focusing on the promotion of protective factors and the reduction of risk factors for young people is critical because the vast majority of mental, emotional, and behavioral problems begin during the school-aged years and most mental disorders are diagnosed in young adulthood (NRC & IOM, 2009).

A number of studies have documented the positive effects of divorce prevention programs designed for children (e.g., Pedro-Carroll, Sutton, & Wyman, 1999) and for parents (e.g., Wolchik et al., 2013). Because a child or adolescent's adjustment to divorce is a function of contextual and intrachild protective and risk factors, different programs focus on one or the other but all operate from the premise that building protective factors and reducing risk factors produce better outcomes. There are a number of programs available for children of divorce, but few have been well researched. However, those that have been extensively evaluated have been shown to improve a variety of children's and adolescents' mental health, emotional, behavioral, and academic outcomes practice (Desrochers & Houck, 2013).

Programs listed on the National Registry of Evidence-Based Programs and Practice related to divorce are listed in Table 29.1. All of these programs use psychoeducation and cognitive behavioral techniques to build skills. *Two Families*

TABLE 29.1

DIVORCE INTERVENTIONS LISTED WITH THE NATIONAL REGISTRY OF EVIDENCE-BASED PROGRAMS AND PRACTICES		
Program Name	**Description**	**Access**
Children in Between	Focus on parents; parenting skills, interparental conflict reduction	http://www.divorce-education.com
Children of Divorce Intervention Program	Focus on children, grades K–8; feelings, coping skills, emotion regulation	http://www.childrensinstitute.net
New Beginnings Program	Focus on parents; interparental conflict, parent–child communication and relationship, discipline	https://asupreventionresearch.com/referral-agents/research
Parenting Through Change	Focus on parents; parenting, discipline	Marion S. Forgatch, PhD Executive Director Implementation Sciences International, Inc. 2852 Willamette Street, #172 Eugene, Oregon 97405
Two Families Now: Effective Parenting Through Separation and Divorce	Online program; focus on parents; co-parenting, self-care, parenting	http://www.twofamiliesnow.com

Now is an Internet-based program, and Children in Between has an Internet version; the other programs are based on skill building and small-group process. Some focus on working with parents and others are implemented directly with children. Contrary to expectations, there is evidence indicating that a dual-component (i.e., concurrent mother and child) intervention may not yield an additive benefit over a single-component (i.e., child-only or parent-only) program (Wolchik et al., 2013).

More research is needed to assess long-term effects of child-only prevention programs and programs for noncustodial parents, determine the "real-world" effectiveness (and cost-effectiveness) of various programs employed with children and adolescents across a wide variety of demographic characteristics, and identify the components of programs that are specifically responsible for successful outcomes (Wolchik et al., 2013).

HOW TO: A GUIDE TO THE IMPLEMENTATION OF INTERVENTIONS FOR CHILDREN AND ADOLESCENTS OF DIVORCE

In this section, three interventions chosen from the National Registry of Evidence-Based Programs and Practices are described. The Children in Between program is the shortest in duration, the least expensive, and has an Internet version. This intervention is designed to be used with parent groups; the *Children of Divorce Intervention Program* is a 12- to 15-session intervention designed to be implemented with groups of children; and the New Beginnings program is a 10-session intervention for parents.

Children in Between

In recognition that the exposure of children to postdivorce conflict between ex-spouses is one of the major risk factors for developing mental, emotional, and behavioral problems, the Children in Between program (formerly known as *Children in the Middle*) improves the communication skills of divorced parents and avoids placing their children in the middle of interparental conflict. Children in Between was originally designed for use in court-mandated programs for divorcing parents, and is shorter in duration and less expensive than many other evidence-based programs.

The Children in Between program is listed on the Substance Abuse and Mental Health Services Administration (SAMHSA) National Registry of

Evidence-Based Programs and Practices. Positive program outcomes have been documented for improvements in parents' awareness of how children feel about their divorced parents (Arbuthnot & Gordon, 1996), reducing legal actions by parents (Arbuthnot, Kramer, & Gordon, 1997), and enhancing parental communication (Arbuthnot, Poole, & Gordon, 1996; Kramer, Arbuthnot, Gordon, Rousis, & Hoza, 1998).

The program is delivered to groups of 6 to 12 participants. Most groups participate in a single session, lasting 2 to 3 hours; a two-session variant is also available, taking a total of 4 or more hours to complete. An online version of the course is available for self-study, which may also be used as a presession introduction to the group course. Print materials are available in both English and Spanish, and a parallel version of the program is available for children (*Children in Between: Children's Version*). This latter version may be implemented concurrently with the parental version or conducted at another time. The children's version uses a DVD format similar to that used in the parents' version, along with discussion and workbook activities. The children's version covers reasons why parents divorce, myths about divorce, and feelings that accompany divorce. The program also teaches specific coping skills to address these issues. For children aged 3 to 8 years, a special *Family Circus* booklet provides activities involving cartoons, puppets, and coloring. See the Center for Divorce Education website (www.divorce-education.com) for more information.

The cost for program materials is approximately $375 for the parents' version ($40 for the online version) and $275 for the children's version, with quantity discounts offered for additional materials. The program does not require special training or supervision for group leaders. Although they are considered helpful, training and experience in mental health are not considered necessary; adept paraprofessionals may deliver this program successfully (Arbuthnot & Gordon, 2012).

The Children in Between program uses lectures, skill training, and discussions anchored by a series of five vignettes presented on DVD. The manual highlights the main teaching points and provides specific discussion questions for each vignette. The topics that follow may be covered in a 2- to 4-hour session.

- An introduction covering divorce statistics, family transition issues, and how to discriminate between marital and parental issues
- An explanation of children's reactions to divorce
- A discussion of the factors that influence outcomes for children (e.g., child involvement in parental conflict, access to both parents, geographic and financial stability, cooperative conflict resolution, and parental self-care)
- Skills training (e.g., how to avoid putting children in the middle of parental conflict, improving communication skills with one's ex-partner, and conflict reduction skills)

Longer or multiple sessions allow for more extensive skill training or coverage of additional topics, such as stepfamily relationships, domestic violence, and lesbian, gay, bisexual, and transgender (LGBT) issues, among others.

The topics covered by each DVD vignette are:

- Using children to carry messages between ex-partners
- Parents using put-downs of the other parent
- Handling money issues
- Parents asking children to report on the other parent's life
- Visitation issues

Five other scenarios are presented for discussion but are not depicted on the DVD. These scenarios include parents playing one sibling against another, handling events that both parents attend (e.g., school events and sports events), causing children to feel guilty over a parent's loneliness, and custodial parents making threats to limit the noncustodial parent's access to the children.

Children of Divorce Intervention Program

The *Children of Divorce Intervention Program* (CODIP) is a small-group intervention (Pedro-Carroll, 2005) designed to:

- Create a supportive group experience
- Help children accept their feelings about their parents' divorce
- Present facts about divorce and dispel misconceptions
- Teach coping and problem-solving skills

- Help children develop positive feelings about themselves and their families

Ultimately, the goal of the program is to prevent children's mental, emotional, and behavioral problems by increasing their resiliency and coping abilities.

The CODIP is listed on the SAMHSA National Registry of Evidence-Based Programs and Practices. Six controlled studies and a 2-year longitudinal study have demonstrated positive outcomes of the program for children (Pedro-Carroll, 2005; Pedro-Carroll et al., 1999).

Programs are available for four age ranges: kindergarten and first grade, second and third grades, fourth through sixth grades, and grades seven and eight. Each program has its own manual featuring activities and materials appropriate for the developmental level of the participants.

Groups are led by mental health professionals or by paraprofessionals under the supervision of a mental health professional. A single leader can conduct the program, but groups co-led by a male and female leader are considered ideal. Training and supervision is optional and available through the program developers. The cost of each of the leaders' manuals is approximately $125. Training is available for approximately $2,500 per day and consultation/supervision is approximately $1,000 per day.

Depending on the age of the children, programs consist of 12 to 15 sessions lasting 40 to 60 minutes each and involve games, role-playing, skits, and discussion. As an example, the program for kindergarten and first grade consists of the 12 45-minute sessions outlined in the following. More complete descriptions of the program may be found in Pedro-Carroll (2008) and in the four program manuals for the different age groups (available along with other resources at the Children's Institute website: www.childrensinstitute.net).

- Session 1 begins the process of creating a supportive group environment with a series of activities designed to introduce the children in the group to each other and to orient them to the purpose of the group. Activities such as the *Getting to Know You Game*, along with stickers, personal folders, and a group puppet are used to engage young children in a developmentally appropriate

way. All activities are scripted in the manual, but leaders are encouraged to be creative within the general outline of the session.
- Session 2 helps children to recognize and communicate feelings. The group puppet introduces the topic and a feelings vocabulary is developed through activities such as the *Feelings Grab Bag Game*, reading a book about feelings, and using a feelings poster. A letter (sample provided in the manual) is sent to parents and teachers describing what is happening in the group and soliciting parents' help in reinforcing what their children are learning.
- Session 3 builds on the first session to teach children about recognizing, accepting, and communicating feelings. Leaders engage children with the group puppet, the *I Feel Game*, and the feelings poster and each child creates a *Feeling Telegram* to give to a parent or teacher.
- Session 4 is the first of three sessions designed to teach children about divorce and how their families are changing. The work on communication of feelings continues throughout the program. In this session, the group puppet introduces a discussion of the commonalities and unique features of different families. Children draw pictures of their families and share family experiences.
- In session 5, the concept of divorce and the feelings surrounding the experience are discussed. Leaders read and lead a discussion about a book about divorce. During this week, another letter is sent to parents and teachers describing what the children have been learning in the first four sessions and what will be covered next. A handout on ways to help children cope with divorce accompanies the letter.
- In session 6, leaders start by reading a book about divorcing families and, with the help of the group puppet and the *Ask the Dinosaur* game, teach children how to ask adults for help or information. Further work with emotions focuses on what children can do when they feel upset about something.
- Sessions 7 through 9 focus on teaching coping and problem-solving skills. In session 7, leaders introduce a basic problem-solving method, exploring the idea that there are many possible ways to solve a problem. Activities include the use of a three-step problem-solving cartoon, the *What Can I Do?* game, and puppet-facilitated

discussion. Children are encouraged to use what they have learned about solving problems in the upcoming week. A third letter is sent to parents and teachers telling them about the problem-solving method that their children will be using.

- Session 8 continues the teaching of a problem-solving method with attention turned to generating alternative solutions and choosing the best among them. Puppets and the *What Can You Do If...?* game are used to teach these skills as applied to problems commonly faced by children experiencing divorce.

- Session 9 teaches children to tell the difference between divorce-related problems that they can and cannot solve. Using puppets, the three-part problem-solving model, and the *Red-Light Green-Light* game, leaders work with children to generate alternative solutions and their consequences as a way toward illustrating that some problems cannot be solved. They are then taught to engage in positive activities when solving the problem is not within their capabilities. Children are guided through the entire problem-solving process with a number of common divorce-related situations.

- The last three sessions of the program review concepts taught earlier in the course, building self-esteem, and teaching children how to access support once the program ends. Session 10 begins this process with the children describing how they used the problem-solving method since the last session. They play the *Daring Dinosaurs* game as a way to review the skills taught in the program. The idea of program termination is introduced and repeated in subsequent sessions.

- Self-esteem is the focus of session 11. Leaders help children work on an *I Am Special* book that summarizes their individual strengths and the strengths of their families.

- Session 12 is the final session and the focus is on reviewing group experiences, saying goodbye, and reiterating that children can communicate with adults about their feelings and concerns. Children are given their *All About Me* folders and a certificate in the context of a celebration. The final letter, sent to parents and teachers, summarizes topics covered in the last few sessions, thanks them for their support, and tells them that the group leader will contact them by phone to answer any questions they may have about their child's progress within the program.

New Beginnings

The New Beginnings program is designed to assist divorced or separated mothers and fathers by teaching them how to improve relationships with their children, develop effective listening skills, protect their children from interparental conflict and improve children's relationships with the noncustodial parent, better manage their children's behavior, and maintain changes they have accomplished through the program. The program ultimately aims to reduce the occurrence of mental, emotional, and behavioral problems in children by teaching their parents the skills needed to reduce the risk factors their children are exposed to as a result of their family circumstances and to increase children's exposure to protective factors that build resiliency and competency.

The New Beginnings program is listed on the SAMHSA National Registry of Evidence-Based Programs and Practices. Positive program outcomes have been demonstrated for reduced mental, emotional, and behavioral problems and increased self-esteem and school performance (Sigal, Wolchik, Tein, & Sandler, 2012). A recent 15-year follow-up of a randomized trial of the New Beginnings program found significant positive long-term effects on preventing mental disorders during young adulthood for all children in the study and on reducing substance abuse in males (Wolchik et al., 2013). The longitudinal research was conducted with 10-session mothers-only groups, but for the past several years, the program has been offered to fathers as well. Studies are currently underway examining the effectiveness of a two-session version as compared with the 10-session version (see https://asupreventionresearch.com/referral-agents/study).

Master's-level clinicians typically serve as group leaders for this intervention. The program recommends a 3-day initial training session followed by several hours of training and supervision for first-time leaders, and additional supervision for full certification as leaders of the New Beginnings Program. The approximate costs of the program are listed in Table 29.2; consult the program developer for current costs.

TABLE 29.2

COSTS ASSOCIATED WITH THE NEW BEGINNINGS PROGRAM	
Item	Cost
Mother and father program DVD sets	$120 per set
Parental handbooks	$30 per set per parent
Group leader manuals	$150 each
30-hour initial group leader training at Arizona State University (Tempe)	$5,000 for up to six participants, plus travel expenses
20-hour supervision and continued training	$2,000 per participant
Online quality assurance monitoring tool	$500

Source: SAMSHA National Registry of Evidence-Based Programs and Practices. Retrieved from http://legacy.nreppadmin.net/ViewIntervention.aspx?id=27

The program consists of 10 sessions, each of approximately 1.75 hours duration. As the program for mothers was the focus of the longitudinal studies, program components for that program are outlined as follows. The program for fathers is very similar to the program for mothers. More comprehensive descriptions of the program may be found in Wolchik, Sandler, Weiss, and Winslow (2007) and in the program materials themselves (see New Beginnings website: https://asupreventionresearch.com/referral-agents/research).

- Session 1 provides an orientation to the program, an introduction to the group leaders and fellow participants, and provides an opportunity to set goals for change within each family. Throughout all activities and sessions, the leaders work to normalize the common issues following divorce and to establish trust and a sense of connectedness within the group. *Family fun time* is introduced as a skill that involves improving mothers' relationships with their children through the scheduling of weekly activities, such as games or family excursions. Parents role-play introducing the activity to their children and are shown how to complete weekly diaries of these activities, which group

leaders read and comment on throughout the program.

- Session 2 begins with a review of the previous week's family fun time and moves to a discussion of how to change escalating patterns of negative interactions between mothers and their children by focusing on appropriate behaviors, ignoring inappropriate behaviors, and providing positive attention. Parents are taught the *catch 'em being good* skill, which involves giving praise and positive attention for appropriate behavior, through video modeling and role-play activities within the group. Group members are also taught, through a video, role-playing, and discussion, how to provide 15 minutes per week of *one-on-one time* with each of their children. Both activities are assigned as weekly homework.
- Session 3 introduces developing effective listening skills with two videos that explain the difference between effective and ineffective listening and describes the characteristics of effective listening. Leaders model and mothers role-play skills such as paying close attention to what their children are saying and using open-ended questions. This session is followed by sessions with individual group members reviewing and sharpening the skills learned during earlier group sessions.
- Session 4 expands on the work of the previous session by adding the skills of *think before you respond* (i.e., resisting the urge to give immediate advice and, instead, paying attention to and thinking about what the child has said before responding) and using *summary responses* (i.e., summarizing the child's message and checking for accuracy before responding).
- Session 5 uses video and role-play to teach parents how to respond to emotional messages from their children. Parents are taught how to reflect their children's feelings and ask whether they reflected accurately. In small groups, parents practice using all of the listening skills they have been taught and are introduced to a problem-solving process to help children decide on appropriate actions.
- Through video and discussion, session 6 teaches mothers how it feels to their children to be placed in the middle of interparental conflicts. The mothers are taught to become aware of their anger toward their ex-spouse

and to use self-statements and other strategies to manage their anger in front of their children and in interactions with their ex-spouses. This session is followed by sessions with individual group members where they discuss how to reduce visitation barriers and how to support their child's paternal relationship.

- Session 7 begins with a discussion of maintaining child discipline as a single parent. Leaders help parents identify their disciplinary style and evaluate whether expectations they have for their children's behavior are realistic and clear. The parents identify a problem behavior that they wish to change and are taught to record baseline frequency of that behavior over the coming week.
- In session 8, parents develop a behavioral change plan for the problem behavior they identified and monitored the previous week. Group leaders show videos of effective and ineffective methods of behavior management, and through the use of videos, discussion, and role-play, teach parents how to effectively use several kinds of positive and negative consequences. Leaders follow up with a phone call to parents later in the week inquiring about progress and troubleshooting problems the parent might be having in carrying out the behavioral plan.
- Session 9 begins with a discussion of how to evaluate and modify the behavior change plan. Parents then develop a change plan for another problem behavior and an additional one focusing on a positive behavior they would like their children to exhibit more often.
- Session 10 reviews skills learned throughout the program, activities designed to encourage mothers to appreciate the improvements they have created in their families, and plans for continued improvement. Parents are taught to record their continued use of the skills learned in the program.

CONCLUSION

Although divorce affects an estimated 30% to 40% of children and adolescents in the United States, most children do not experience long-term mental, emotional, or behavioral problems as a result, but some do, and all experience significant stress. Divorce is a significant risk factor for the development of a variety of psychosocial difficulties, including substance abuse; mental, emotional, and behavioral disorders; relationship problems; and lack of success in a number of developmental tasks extending through adulthood. Fortunately, evidence-based interventions that can prevent many of these problems are readily available for school and community implementation.

SELECT BIBLIOGRAPHY

Emery, R. E. (2012). *Renegotiating family relationships* (2nd ed.). New York, NY: Guilford Press. *This book, written primarily for professionals, covers the psychological dynamics of divorce, conflict resolution, mediation, and an overview of divorce and custody law.*

Justice Education Society of British Columbia. *Families change.* Retrieved from http://www .familieschange.ca *This website with separate sections for parents, children, and adolescents provides information about dealing with the changes brought on by divorce and answers questions in developmentally appropriate ways using print, video, and games.*

Pedro-Carroll, J. (2010). *Putting children first: Proven parenting strategies for helping children thrive through divorce.* New York, NY: Penguin. *This book, written for parents but a good introduction for professionals as well, covers children's experience of divorce and provides parents strategies for reducing conflict and improving parenting skills.*

REFERENCES

Amato, P. R. (2001). Children of divorce in the 1990s: An update of the Amato and Keith (1991) meta-analysis. *Journal of Family Psychology, 15,* 355–370. doi:10.1037/0893–3200.15.3.355

Arbuthnot, J., & Gordon, D. A. (1996). Does mandatory divorce education for parents work? A six-month outcome evaluation. *Family and Conciliation Courts Review, 34*(1), 60–81.

Arbuthnot, J., & Gordon, D. A. (2012). *Programs for divorcing parents: A service provider's handbook.* Athens, OH: The Center for Divorce Education.

Arbuthnot, J., Kramer, K. M., & Gordon, D. A. (1997). Patterns of re-litigation following divorce education. *Family and Conciliation Courts Review, 35*(3), 269–279.

Arbuthnot, J., Poole, C. J., & Gordon, D. A. (1996). Use of educational materials to modify stressful behaviors in post-divorce parenting. *Journal of Divorce and Remarriage, 25*(1–2), 117–137.

Copen, C. E., Daniels, K., Vespa, J., & Mosher, W. D. (2012). *First marriages in the United States: Data from the 2006–2010 National Survey of Family Growth. National health statistics reports,* #49. Hyattsville, MD: National Center for Health Statistics.

Desrochers, J. E., & Houck, G. M. (2013). *Depression in children and adolescents: Guidelines for school practice.* Silver Spring, MD: National Association of School Nurses (a joint publication with the National Association of School Psychologists).

Gladstone, T. R. C., Beardslee, W. R., & O'Connor, E. E. (2011). The prevention of adolescent depression. *Psychiatric Clinics of North America, 34,* 35–52.

Kramer, K. M., Arbuthnot, J., Gordon, D. A., Rousis, N. J., & Hoza, J. (1998). Effects of skill-based versus information-based divorce education programs on domestic violence and parental communication. *Family and Conciliation Courts Review, 36*(1), 9–31.

National Center for Health Statistics. (2008). *Marriage and divorce.* Retrieved from http://www.cdc.gov/nchs/fastats/divorce.him

National Research Council and Institute of Medicine (NRC & IOM). (2009). *Preventing mental, emotional, and behavioral disorders among young people: Progress and possibilities.* Washington, DC: National Academies Press. Retrieved from http://www.nap.edu/catalog.php?record_id=12480

Pedro-Carroll, J. L. (2005). Fostering resilience in the aftermath of divorce: The role of evidence-based programs for children. *Family Court Review, 43,* 52–64.

Pedro-Carroll, J. L. (2008). The Children of Divorce Intervention Program: Fostering children's resilience through group support and skill building—Procedures for facilitating a supportive group intervention with second and third grade children. In C. W. LeCroy (Ed.), *Handbook of evidence-based treatment manuals* (2nd ed., pp. 314–359). New York, NY: Oxford University Press.

Pedro-Carroll, J. L., Sutton, S. E., & Wyman, P. A. (1999). A two-year follow-up evaluation of a preventive intervention for young children of divorce. *School Psychology Review, 28,* 467–476.

SAMSHA National Registry of Evidence-Based Programs and Practices. (2016). Retrieved from http://legacy.nreppadmin.net/ViewIntervention.aspx?id=27

Sandler, I. N., Braver, S. L., & Wheeler, L. A. (2013). Relations of parenting quality, inter-parental conflict, and overnights with mental health problems of children in divorcing families with high legal conflict. *Journal of Family Psychology, 27,* 915–924.

Sigal, A. B., Wolchik, S. A., Tein, J. Y., & Sandler, I. N. (2012). Enhancing youth outcomes following parental divorce: A longitudinal study of the effects of the New Beginnings Program on educational and occupational goals. *Journal of Clinical Child and Adolescent Psychology, 41*(2), 150–165. doi:10.1080/15374416.2012.651992

Wolchik, S. A., Sandler, I. N., Tein, J. Y., Mahrer, N. E., Millsap, R. E., Winslow, E.,…Reed, A. (2013). Fifteen-year follow-up of a randomized trial of a preventive intervention for divorced families: Effects on mental health and substance use outcomes in young adulthood. *Journal of Consulting and Clinical Psychology, 81,* 660–673. doi:10.1037/a0033235

Wolchik, S. A., Sandler, I., Weiss, L., & Winslow, E. B. (2007). New beginnings: An empirically based program to help divorced mothers promote resilience in their children. In J. M. Briesmeister & C. E. Shaefer (Eds.), *Handbook of parent training: Helping parents prevent and solve problem behaviors* (pp. 25–62). New York, NY: Wiley.

Evidence-Based Interventions for Social Skill Deficits in Children and Adolescents

Frank M. Gresham

OVERVIEW

Children and youth with serious emotional, behavioral, and social difficulties present challenges for teachers, parents, and peers. These challenges cut across disciplinary, instructional, and interpersonal domains and frequently create chaotic home, school, and classroom environments. Children with or who are at risk of emotional and behavioral disorders (EBD) often overwhelm the capacity of schools to effectively accommodate their instructional and disciplinary needs (Walker, Ramsay, & Gresham, 2004). Schools are charged with teaching an increasingly diverse student population in terms of prevailing attitudes, beliefs, behavioral styles, and racial-ethnic and language backgrounds. In addition, pressures for higher academic standards and outcomes for all students are reaching nearly unattainable levels for students with severe behavioral challenges.

An important distinction in the theoretical conceptualization of social behavior is the distinction among the concepts of "social skills," "social tasks," and "social competence." Social skills are a specific class of behaviors that are needed to successfully complete a social task. Social tasks might include such things as peer group entry, having a conversation, making friends, or playing a game with peers.

Social competence, in contrast, is an evaluative term based on *judgments* (given certain criteria) that an individual has performed a social task adequately. Social agents make these judgments based on the student's social interactions within natural environments (e.g., home, school, community). Given this conceptualization, social skills are behaviors exhibited in specific situations that lead others to judge that the behaviors are competent or incompetent in accomplishing social tasks (Gresham, 2010).

Social Skills as Academic Enablers. Researchers have documented meaningful and predictive relationships between children's social behaviors and their long-term academic achievement (DiPerna & Elliott, 2002; Malecki & Elliott, 2002; Wentzel, 2009). Children who have positive interactions and relationships with their peers tend to be more academically engaged and have higher levels of academic achievement than peers with less positive peer interactions and relationships (see Wentzel, 2009 for a review).

Researchers often make a distinction between academic skills and academic enabling behaviors (i.e., academic enablers). Academic skills are basic and complex skills that are the focus of academic instruction. In contrast, academic enablers are the attitudes and behaviors that facilitate students' participation in and ultimate benefit from academic instruction in the classroom. Research using the Academic Competence Evaluation Scales (ACES; DiPerna & Elliott, 2002) showed that academic enablers were moderately related to students' academic achievement as measured by standardized achievement tests (Mdn r = 0.50). In a longitudinal study, Caprara, Barbaranelli, Pastorelli, Bandura, and Zimbardo (2000) found that teacher ratings of children's prosocial behavior in third grade predicted the students' eighth-grade academic achievement better than their third-grade academic achievement (Caprara et al., 2000).

Most researchers conclude that positive peer interactions promote competent social behavior, which in turn promotes successful academic performance. Behaviors such as cooperation, following rules, and getting along with others contribute to efficient classrooms and allow students to benefit from academic instruction (Gresham & Elliott, 2008; Walker, Irvin, Noell, & Singer, 1992). Displays of prosocial behavior and restraint from disruptive and antisocial behavior have been consistently and positively related to peer acceptance, achievement motivation, and academic success (Wentzel, 2009). Socially competent behavior provides the conditions for learning that permit students to benefit from classroom instruction (DiPerna & Elliott, 2002; Elliott & Gresham, 2007; Wentzel & Looney, 2007).

Problem Behaviors as Academic Disablers. Although social skills or prosocial behaviors function as academic enablers, problem behaviors, particularly externalizing behavior patterns, interfere or compete with the acquisition of social and academic skills (Gresham, 2010; Gresham & Elliott, 2008; Walker et al., 1992). These competing problem behaviors function as *academic disablers* in that they are associated with delayed academic performance. Children with externalizing behaviors, such as aggression, noncompliance, and/or teacher defiance, often have moderate to severe academic skill deficits (Hinshaw, 1992; Offord, Boyle, & Racine, 1989; Reid, 1993). It is unclear whether these academic problems are primarily the correlates (moderators), causes (mediators), or consequences of problem behaviors; however, there is little doubt that academic delays are associated with problem behaviors. Moreover, as children with problem behaviors progress through their school careers, their academic deficits and achievement problems generally become more severe (Walker et al., 2004).

ETIOLOGY AND FACTORS CONTRIBUTING TO SOCIAL SKILL DEFICITS IN CHILDREN AND ADOLESCENTS

An important conceptual consideration in designing and delivering social skills interventions (SSIs) is distinguishing between different types of social skills deficits. Gresham (1981) was the first to distinguish between social skill *acquisition deficits* and *performance deficits*. Since then, other researchers in the social skills area have supported this distinction (Elliott & Gresham, 2008; Gumpel, 2007; Maag, 2005; Walker et al., 2004). This distinction is important because different intervention approaches in remediating social skills deficits are indicated and different settings (e.g., general education classrooms versus pullout groups) are required for selected interventions. Children who cannot perform given social skills would most benefit from a skill-building intervention. Children who are not motivated to perform given social skills would most benefit from an intervention that arranges contingencies to maximize the probability of adequate social skill performances.

Acquisition deficits result from a lack of knowledge about how to perform a given social skill, an inability to fluently enact a sequence of social behaviors, or difficulty in knowing which social skills are appropriate in specific situations (Gresham, 2002, 2010). Social skills acquisition deficits can be clarified by using an academic example. A child who does not know the meaning of the "+" operation sign has an acquisition deficit in that the child does not know what behavior to exhibit when seeing the operation sign for addition. Similarly, a child can know the meaning of the "+" operation sign, but not know how to regroup numbers when confronted with a problem (e.g., 32 + 19 =___). A practical barometer for determining whether an individual has an acquisition deficit is the individual's *knowledge* or *past performance* of the skill. That is, if the individual does not know how to perform the skill or has never been observed to perform the skill, the social skills deficit is likely to be caused by a lack of acquisition.

Based on this conceptualization, acquisition deficits can result from deficits in social cognitive abilities, difficulties integrating fluent behavior patterns, and/or deficits in appropriate discrimination of social situations. Acquisition deficits can be characterized as being more of a "can't do" problem because the child has difficulty performing a given social skill given optimal motivation. Remediation of acquisition deficits requires direct instruction of social skills in settings that promote the attainment of socially skilled behaviors.

Performance deficits may be conceptualized as the failure to perform a given social skill at an acceptable level even though the child knows how to perform the social skill. These types of social skills deficits can be thought of as more of a "won't do" problem because the child knows what to do, but chooses not to perform a particular social skill. Performance deficits can best be thought of as a *motivational* or functioning problem rather than a learning or acquisition problem. As such, remediation of these types of deficits often requires manipulation of antecedents and consequences in naturalistic settings to increase the frequency of the appropriate behaviors.

Additional evidence for this distinction comes from the academic intervention literature. VanDerHeyden and Witt (2008) traced the distinction back to Bandura (1969), in which he integrated performance and skill deficits into his social learning theory. Noell et al. (2000) revealed that some children benefited from contingent rewards for better performances, suggesting a performance deficit, whereas other children did not benefit from contingent rewards, suggesting an acquisition deficit. Other researchers have replicated this finding across academic areas (Duhon et al. 2004; VanDerHeyden & Witt, 2005) with similar results.

EVIDENCE-BASED INTERVENTIONS AND EMPIRICAL SUPPORT FOR SOCIAL SKILL DEFICITS IN CHILDREN AND ADOLESCENTS

Research Evidence

Evidence-based practices are employed with the goal of preventing or ameliorating the effects of disruptive behavior disorders (DBDs) in children and youth. Multiple types of research evidence are used to support evidence-based practices, including: (a) efficacy studies, (b) effectiveness studies, (c) cost-benefit/cost-effectiveness studies, and (d) epidemiological studies. Various types of research designs are better suited to answer certain questions than others.

- Observation of DBDs within target settings, including case studies, can be a valuable source of hypotheses concerning behavioral problems of children and youths.
- Qualitative research can be used to describe the subjective or "real-world" experiences of individuals undergoing a given intervention procedure.
- Single-case experimental designs are useful in drawing causal inferences about the effectiveness of interventions for individuals in a controlled manner.
- Epidemiological research can be used to track the availability, utilization, and acceptance of various intervention procedures.
- Moderator/mediator studies can be used to identify correlates of intervention outcomes and to establish the mechanisms of change in specific intervention procedures.
- Randomized controlled trials (RCTs) or efficacy studies can be used to provide the strongest types of research evidence that protects against most threats to the internal validity of a study.
- Effectiveness studies can be used to assess the outcomes of interventions in less-controlled, real-world settings and to determine if causal relationships maintain across individuals, treatment agents, settings, and/or participants.
- Meta-analyses are employed if the research literature provides a quantitative metric or index concerning the effects of multiple studies across various populations, age groups, genders, and/or settings.

The importance of social competence for children with or who are at risk of serious social-behavioral difficulties has been translated into various service delivery and instructional approaches to remediate deficits in social skills functioning. SSIs are designed to remediate children's acquisition and performance deficits and to reduce or eliminate competing problem behaviors (Elliott & Gresham, 2008; Gresham, Sugai, & Horner, 2001; Gresham & Elliott, 2008). Between the late 1970s to early 1980s, SSIs were linked to the developmental literature and targeted poorly accepted or rejected children and the longitudinal course of poor peer relations (Bierman & Powers, 2009; Parker & Asher, 1987). By the early 1990s, SSIs were incorporated into epidemiologically based, long-term, multicomponent interventions targeting children with significant behavioral problems such as conduct disorders and attention deficit hyperactivity disorder (ADHD; Conduct Problems Prevention Research Group, 1992; Multimodal Treatment Study of Children with ADHD [MTA] Cooperative Group, 1999). From 2000 to the present, SSI research has focused primarily on promoting behavior change in special needs populations and has often been embedded in disorder-specific, multicomponent intervention models. Despite these advances, a comprehensive framework that facilitates the identification of theoretical and methodological common ground across SSI studies is currently lacking, thereby creating a disparate empirical literature on SSIs (Bierman & Powers, 2009).

Summary of Social Skills Research

Both narrative and meta-analytic reviews over the past 30 years suggest that SSIs are efficacious for children and youth with social-behavioral difficulties. All of these SSIs can be considered Tier 2 selected interventions (see Cook et al., 2008; Gresham, Cook, Crews, & Kern, 2004 for comprehensive reviews).

One recent study, however, by DiPerna, Lei, Bellinger, and Cheng was a cluster randomized trial (CRT) of a Tier 1 or universal SSI (DiPerna et al., 2015). This CRT involved 39 second-grade classrooms and 432 children. A total of 228 children (*n* = 20 classrooms) were randomly assigned to the SSI condition and 204 students were randomized to the control condition (*N* = 19 classrooms). The SSI was the Classwide Intervention Program (CIP; Elliott & Gresham, 2007) and involved 10 instructional units focusing on 10 social skills that had been identified by teachers as being important to classroom success (e.g., listening to others, following directions, following classroom rules, ignoring

peer distractions). Based on teacher ratings of social skills using the *Social Skills Improvement System–Rating Scales* (SSIS-RS, Gresham & Elliott, 2008), children in the CIP condition demonstrated overall improvement in social skills relative to children in the control condition. Children in the CIP condition also demonstrated improvements in teacher ratings of communication, cooperation, responsibility, empathy, and social engagement. These children also showed decreases in internalizing problem behaviors but not externalizing problem behaviors.

Quantitative reviews of the SSI literature suggest that approximately two thirds of children receiving SST improved compared with only one third of children in control groups. This figure is significantly higher in randomized SSI studies than in nonrandomized or quasi-experimental studies. Depending on the degree of internal validity, SSI studies produce medium to large effect size estimates using conventional standards for interpreting effect sizes. Despite these positive findings, several important methodological and conceptual issues have not been addressed in the SSI literature.

HOW TO: A GUIDE TO THE IMPLEMENTATION OF SSI FOR CHILDREN AND ADOLESCENTS

The purpose of this section is to provide step-by-step descriptions of three evidence-based SSIs. To accomplish this, the following is descibed a Tier 1 or universal intervention (the Social Skills Improvement System–CIP [SSIS-CIP]; Elliott & Gresham, 2008); a Tier 2 or selected intervention (the SSIS–Intervention Guide [SSIS-IG]); and a Tier 3 or intensive SSIs (replacement behavior training [RBT] based on a functional behavioral assessment).

Social Skills Improvement System–Classwide Intervention Program

The SSIS-CIP is a curriculum that focuses on the development of those social skills most highly valued by educators. The program uses well-established and effective teaching models, including situated learning, positive peer models, and systematic, direct instruction. The program teaches the "Top 10" social skills that were selected in a survey asking more than 600 teachers to rate the 100 social skills based on how important they considered each skill for classroom success. The highest-rated social skills were: (a) listening to others, (b) following directions, (c) following the rules, (d) paying attention to school work, (e) asking for help, (f) taking turns when engaged in a conversation, (g) getting along with others, (h) staying calm with others, (i) doing the right thing, and (j) doing nice things for others.

The instructional format of the SSIS-CIP follows a six-step sequence that includes: (a) *Tell* (coaching) whereby the teacher presents and defines the social skill and key words, discusses the importance of the skill, and outlines steps to perform the targeted social behavior; (b) *Show* (modeling) whereby the teacher presents models of positive and negative social behavior using pictures, video clips, and role-play and then leads a discussion of alternatives to accomplish the social behavioral objective; (c) *Do* (role-playing) in which students review the definition, importance, and skill steps, then participate in additional role-plays with opportunities to give and receive feedback; (d) *Practice* (behavioral rehearsal) in which students review and practice their skills in class and the teacher encourages students to use skills beyond the social skills lessons; (e) *Monitor Progress* (progress monitoring) in which students reflect on their own progress and the teacher encourages this reflection using the student booklet activity and progress charts; and (f) *Generalize* (generalization across settings and situations) whereby the students apply their skills in a variety of situations and the teacher encourages students to practice by assigning homework.

Social Skill Improvement System– Intervention Guide

The SSIS-IG (Elliott & Gresham, 2008) is a *selected* intervention intended for students who do not respond or who respond poorly to a universal intervention (e.g., the SSIS-CIP). These students are at risk for more serious academic and social-behavioral difficulties and therefore require more intensive small-group interventions. The SSIS-IG provides students direct instruction, modeling, and practice in social skills until the students can generalize the appropriate application of these skills in other settings and situations.

The SSIS-IG is delivered in a small-group setting with four to six students conducted by an experienced group leader, such as a school psychologist, guidance counselor, or social worker. Each unit is implemented in two sessions per week for 45 minutes per session (90 minutes weekly) over a period of about 10 weeks (approximately 22.5 hours of intervention).

The SSIS-IG centers on 20 instructional units that deal with social skills across seven domains: communication, cooperation, assertion, responsibility, empathy, engagement, and self-control. These domains are derived from subscales of the SSIS-RS (Gresham & Elliott, 2008). These 20 social skills were selected because they are likely to function as *keystone behaviors*; that is, behaviors that, when changed, are likely to lead to changes in other behaviors not targeted for intervention.

Instructional strategies in the SSIS-IG are based on principles derived from social learning theory and cognitive behavioral therapy (CBT). Specifically, instructional strategies rely on modeling, coaching, behavioral rehearsal, performance feedback, and social problem solving. The theory of change for these intervention procedures and how they impact intervention outcomes is presented in Figure 30.1.

The theory of change model is derived from social learning theory (Bandura, 1977, 1986) and uses the concept of vicarious learning and cognitive-mediational processes in determining which environmental events are attended to, retained, and subsequently performed. Social learning theory is based on reciprocal determinism, which describes the role an individual's behavior has on changing the environment and vice versa. The model utilizes strategies from social learning theory including modeling (vicarious learning), coaching (verbal instruction), behavioral rehearsal (practice) to enhance fluency of instructed social skills, and feedback/generalization programming strategies to facilitate transfer of taught social skills to naturalistic environments and situations outside of the group instructional setting.

Social skills are taught in this theory of change model using a six-step instructional sequence: *Tell* (coaching), *Show* (modeling), *Do* (role-playing), *Practice* (behavioral rehearsal), *Monitor Progress* (feedback and self-assessment), and *Generalize* (generalization programming). It is important to

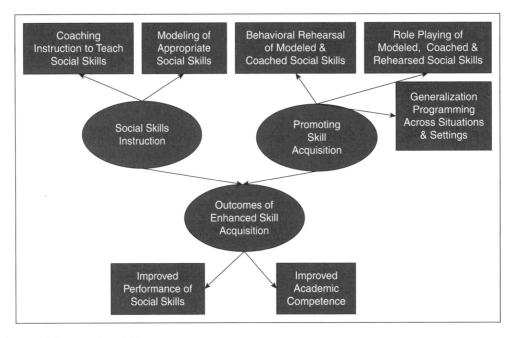

FIGURE 30.1 Theory of change: Acquisition.

note that, in each phase, while one strategy provides the basis for instruction, other strategies may be concurrently used to augment learning. For example, in the *Tell* phase, while coaching is the focal point of the lesson, elements of modeling may be used to illustrate examples of the featured skill, and social problem solving can help students to discuss and understand the importance of learning the skill.

The outcomes of this six-step instructional model lead to improved acquisition and performance of social skills and their generalization to other settings and social situations. In addition, based on the earlier discussion of social skills as *academic enablers*, improved social skill performance is expected to lead to improved academic performance because it enables students to benefit from academic instruction.

Intensive SSIs

One of the most conceptually powerful learning principles is known as the "Matching Law," which states that the relative rates of any behavior will match the relative rate of reinforcement for that behavior (Herrnstein, 1961). Matching is studied experimentally in what are known as "concurrent schedules of reinforcement," which

is an experimental arrangement involving two or more behaviors being reinforced according to two or more schedules of reinforcement that are available concurrently. In other words, the individual has the "choice" of which schedule of reinforcement he or she will respond to more frequently. The concept of matching predicts that the behavior that is reinforced more frequently will be performed at a higher rate. For example, if arguing with teachers or parents is reinforced every five times it occurs and staying calm when disagreeing with teachers or parents is reinforced every 20 times it occurs, then arguing will be performed *four times* more frequently than staying calm in disagreements.

Many children and youth who are poor responders to universal and intensive SSIs have a choice between engaging in behaviors that coerce or harm others and engaging in prosocial forms of behavior. This "choice" depends directly on the relative rate of reinforcement that is concurrently available for each behavior. Based on the learning histories of many of these children, coercive, defiant behaviors typically receive reinforcement more frequently than prosocial behaviors and therefore these behaviors will occur more frequently (Snyder & Stoolmiller, 2002).

Maag (2005) suggested that a potentially effective way of decreasing competing problem behaviors is to teach *positive replacement behaviors* or what has been called "RBT." RBT is based on the Matching Law described earlier. The goal of RBT is to identify a prosocial behavior that will result in more frequent reinforcement relative to a competing problem behavior. Conceptually, RBT depends on identifying *functionally equivalent behaviors*. Behaviors are considered to be functionally equivalent if they produce similar or greater amounts of reinforcement from the environment (Horner & Billingsley, 1988). In addition, functional equivalence of behavior is based on the notion of *differential reinforcement of incompatible behaviors* or "DRI." DRI is a procedure in which a behavior that is incompatible with the problem behavior is reinforced. Behaviors are considered incompatible if they *cannot* occur simultaneously. For example, arguing and calmly resolving conflicts cannot occur at the same time. A practitioner using DRI would increase the rate of reinforcement for a prosocial, incompatible behavior and decrease the rate of reinforcement (i.e., adult negative attention) for the disruptive behavior alternative (Cooper, Heron, & Heward, 2007).

DRI. As noted earlier, DRI refers to the reinforcement of behaviors that are incompatible with problem behaviors and the withholding of reinforcement for problem behaviors. The following table shows problem behaviors and incompatible socially skilled replacement behaviors:

Problem Behavior	Replacement Behavior
Often bullies, threatens, or intimidates others	Acts responsibly when with others
Often initiates physical fights	Resolves disagreements calmly
Often loses temper	Makes a compromise during conflict
Argues with adults (parents and teachers)	Speaks in an appropriate tone of voice

The following guidelines can greatly improve the effectiveness of DRI in teaching positive replacement behaviors.

First, select prosocial behaviors that are incompatible with the problem behavior. These behaviors should: (a) already be in the individual's repertoire, (b) require equal or preferably less response effort to perform than the problem behavior, (c) be emitted at a rate before the DRI intervention that will provide sufficient opportunities for reinforcement, and (d) be likely to be reinforced in the student's natural environment after the intervention is terminated.

Second, select reinforcers that are powerful and can be delivered consistently. The magnitude of the reinforcer used in DRI is most likely less important that its *consistent delivery* and *control*.

Third, reinforce incompatible behaviors immediately and consistently. Initially, practitioners should use a continuous reinforcement schedule (CRS) for the incompatible behavior whereby each occurrence of the incompatible behavior receives reinforcement. After establishing the incompatible behavior, the reinforcement schedule should be thinned to an intermittent schedule of reinforcement.

Fourth, withhold reinforcement for the competing problem behavior. The success of DRI depends entirely on the incompatible behavior being reinforced at a higher rate than the competing problem behavior (recall the Matching Law described earlier).

CASE STUDY: LUKAS

Lukas, an 8-year-old third-grade student, was referred for intervention because of aggressive and disruptive behavior in the classroom and on the playground. According to his teacher, Lukas often bullied others, got angry, and frequently refused to comply with requests and instructions. Lukas's parents also observed frequent noncompliant behavior, problems controlling his temper, and some aggressive social interactions with children in the neighborhood. In addition to his social-behavioral problems, Lukas was having difficulties in math and reading.

Lukas's teacher and parents were concerned about his poor self-control when interacting with peers and adults. They also complained that he did not follow their directions and reacted angrily when given feedback about his disruptive and noncompliant behavior. The teacher and Lukas's parents were eager for him to participate in a social skills group to improve his social skills. The school counselor, however, noted that Lukas had participated in the CIP in first grade with minimal success and had received the SSIS-IG in the second grade with similar poor results. Given that Lukas had been unsuccessful in both universal and more intensive SSI programs, it was decided that he needed a Tier 3 intensive SSI program.

Step 1: Conduct Assessment of Lukas.
To facilitate an understanding of Lukas's strengths and weaknesses in social behavior, Lukas's teacher, his mother, and Lukas himself completed the SSIS-RS. On the Social Skills scale, the ratings from Lukas's teacher resulted in a standard score of 84 that corresponded to the 15th percentile (below average). Ratings from Lukas's mother resulted in a standard score of 84 placing him at the 13th percentile (below average). Lukas's self-ratings resulted in a standard score of 92 that corresponded to the 31st percentile that was in the average range.

On the Problem Behaviors scale, Lukas received a standard score of 116 from his teacher, 117 from his mother, and 106 from himself that corresponded to the 83rd (above average), 87th (above average), and 69th (average) percentiles, respectively. On the Academic Competence scale, Lukas's teacher rated him as functioning at the 58th percentile (average) with a standard score of 103.

Step 2: Select Replacement Behaviors for Problem Behaviors.
A detailed analysis using the SSIS-RS identified the following problem behaviors and replacement behaviors given in the following table:

Problem Behavior	Replacement Behavior
Bullies, threatens, or intimidates other	Doing nice things for others
Often loses temper	Makes compromise during conflict
Often blames others for mistakes	Takes responsibility for own mistakes
Is often angry and resentful	Interacts well with others
Argues with adults	Speaks in appropriate tone of voice

The problem behaviors received an SSIS-RS rating of 2 (often exhibits the behavior) and a social skills rating of 1 (seldom exhibits the behavior). To corroborate these ratings, the school psychologist conducted a systematic direct observation using frequency recording over a period of 5 days during various instructional and noninstructional activities. This observation revealed that Lukas engaged in the five problem behaviors a total of 20 times over the observation period and never exhibited any of the replacement behaviors.

Step 3: Implement the Intervention for Lukas.
Based on Lukas's problem behaviors, DRI was chosen as the intervention. Before the DRI intervention, however, the school psychologist conducted *precorrection sessions* each day for 5 days. Precorrection involves identifying a problem behavior and then providing a prompt for an appropriate social behavior alternative. For example, the school psychologist would tell Lukas that he sometimes bullies, threatens, or intimidates others and that Lukas should do nice things for others instead (e.g., helping them out, giving a

compliment, sharing things). Precorrection involves the following steps:

- Specify the context for the expected behaviors. This context can be any situation, circumstance, setting, or occasion in which the target behavior is expected to occur.
- Specify the expected behavior to Lukas. The expected behavior is incompatible with the problem behavior (bullying vs. doing nice things for others).
- Modify the situation in which a problem behavior is more likely to occur. For example, if Lukas and another student are arguing with each other in class, the teacher might move them away from each other in the classroom. This would make arguing less likely to occur.
- Practice behavioral rehearsal of the expected target behavior. For example, if the expected behavior is interacting well with others, role-play this skill with Lukas to ensure that he knows what to do.
- Reinforce Lukas's appropriate performance of the appropriate target behavior throughout the day.
- Prompt the expected behavior throughout the day.
- Monitor Lukas's performance of the expected behavior using teacher reports, self-monitoring, or peer reporting.

After the precorrection sessions, the DRI intervention was implemented in the classroom using the classroom teacher as the primary interventionist. The teacher was instructed to verbally reinforce each occurrence of the positive replacement behavior and to not reinforce any occurrence of the competing problem behavior. The teacher was also told that, in addition to verbal reinforcement, she could reward Lukas for engaging in the replacement behaviors with activity reinforcers (e.g., free time, computer time, extra recess) and special privileges. The school psychologist who spot-checked the integrity with the teacher was implementing the DRI intervention for a period of 3 weeks. If integrity fell below 70%, then the school psychologist gave the teacher specific performance feedback to increase the integrity of the DRI intervention. Over the 3-week period, treatment integrity of the DRI intervention was 90%.

Step 4: Evaluate the Intervention for Lukas. The fourth step focused on evaluating the effects of the DRI intervention on Lukas's problem behaviors and replacement behaviors. After a period of 5 weeks of the DRI intervention, Lukas's teacher and his mother completed the SSIS-RS. Teacher rating of social skills showed that Lukas's social skills increased 12 points from 84 (below average) to 96 (average). Teacher ratings of problem behaviors decreased by 8 points from 116 (above average) to 108 (average). The school psychologist conducted systematic direct observations of Lukas's problem behaviors and replacement behaviors using frequency recording over a period of 5 days. The frequency of problem behaviors decreased from a baseline level of 20 occurrences to a postintervention level of five occurrences. Replacement behaviors increased from a baseline level of 0 to a postintervention level of 10 occurrences. Given these findings, the DRI intervention was deemed successful and Lukas's participation in the intervention was discontinued.

CONCLUSION

Children who exhibit challenging social, emotional, and behavioral problems present significant challenges to schools, teachers, parents, and peers. Youth who are at risk for EBD are particularly vulnerable in the areas of peer and adult social relationships. The emphasis on meeting academic standards and outcomes for children and youth in schools has unfortunately pushed the topic of social-emotional development to the proverbial back burner. This chapter emphasizes that social skills might be considered *academic enablers* because these positive social behaviors predict short-term and long-term academic achievement. Academic enablers are the attitudes and behaviors that allow students to participate in and benefit from academic instruction. Behaviors, such as following rules, getting along with others, and cooperation create efficient classrooms and higher levels of academic performance for all students. In contrast, problem behaviors (particularly externalizing behaviors) might be considered *academic disablers*. Behaviors such as aggression, noncompliance, and defiance are associated with decreases in academic performance.

An important distinction in designing and delivering SSIs is differentiating between different types of social skills deficits. Social skills deficits may be either *acquisition deficits* or *performance deficits*. Acquisition deficits stem from either the lack of knowledge about how to perform a given social skill, an inability to fluently enact a sequence social behavior, or difficulty in knowing which social skills are appropriate in specific situations. Performance deficits can be thought of as the failure to perform a given social skill at an acceptable level even though the individual knows how to perform the social skill. These types of social skills problems can be conceptualized as motivational or performance problems rather than learning or acquisition problems.

SELECT BIBLIOGRAPHY

DiPerna, J. C., Lei, P., Bellinger, J., & Cheng, W. (2015). Efficacy of the Social Skills Improvement System Classwide Intervention Program (SSIS-CIP) primary version. *School Psychology Quarterly*, 30(1), 123–141.
A multisite cluster randomized trial was conducted to examine the effect of the SSIS-CIP (Elliott & Gresham, 2007) on students' classroom social behavior. Results indicated that the SSIS-CIP demonstrated positive effects on teacher ratings of participants' social skills and internalizing behaviors, with the greatest changes occurring in classrooms with students who exhibited lower social skill proficiency before implementation.

Gresham, F. M., Elliott, S. N., Cook, C. R., Vance, M. J., & Kettler, R. (2010). Cross-informant agreement for ratings for social skill and problem behavior ratings: An investigation of the Social Skills Improvement System-Rating Scales. *Psychological Assessment*, 22(1), 157–166.
This article presents systematically explored patterns of agreement among teacher, parents/caregivers, and students in domains of social skills and problem behaviors using the SSIS-RS (Gresham & Elliott, 2008). Results showed that convergent validity coefficients were consistently stronger than the discriminant validity correlations. Implications for assessment practices and future research are discussed.

Gresham, F. M., Elliott, S. N., & Kettler, R. J. (2010). Base rates of social skills acquisition/performance deficits, strengths, and problem behaviors: An analysis of the Social Skills Improvement System–Rating Scales. *Psychological Assessment*, 22(4), 809–815.
This study empirically determined the base rates of social skills acquisition and performance deficits, social skills strengths, and problem behaviors using a nationally representative sample of children and adolescents ages 3 to 18 years. Base rates for social skills performance deficits and social skills strengths were considerably higher, with students in the 5- to 12-year-old age group reporting fewer performance deficits and more social skills strengths than older children (13–18 years of age). Teachers and parents reported more performance deficits and fewer social skills strengths across all age groups than students in the 5- to 12-year-old age group. These results are discussed in terms of the utility of base rate information in clinical decision making.

Gresham, F. M., Elliott, S. N., Vance, M. J., & Cook, C. R. (2011). Comparability of the Social Skills Rating System to the Social Skills Improvement System and psychometric comparisons across elementary and secondary age levels. *School Psychology Quarterly*, 26, 27–44.
This study compared the SSIS (Gresham & Elliott, 1990) with the revision of the SSRS, now called the SSIS-RS (Gresham & Elliott, 2008) across three raters (teacher, parent, and student) for elementary- and secondary-aged students. The authors concluded that the SSIS-RS offers researchers and practitioners assessing social behavior of children and youth a broader conceptualization of key social behaviors and psychometrically superior assessment results when using the SSIS-RS over the SSRS.

REFERENCES

Bandura, A. (1969). *Principles of behavior modification*. Englewood Cliffs, NJ: Prentice-Hall.

Bandura, A. (1977). *Social learning theory*. Englewood Cliffs, NJ: Prentice-Hall.

Bandura, A. (1986). *Social foundations of thought and action: A social cognitive theory.* Englewood Cliffs, NJ: Prentice-Hall.

Bierman, K. L., & Powers, C. J. (2009). Social skills training to improve peer relations. In K. Rubin, W. Bukowski, & B. Laursen (Eds.), *Handbook of peer interactions, relationships, and groups* (pp. 603–621). New York, NY: Guilford.

Caprara, G. V., Barbaranelli, C., Pastorelli, C., Bandura, A., & Zimbardo, P. G. (2000). Prosocial foundations of children's academic achievement. *Psychological Science, 11*(4), 302–306.

Conduct Problems Prevention Research Group. (1992). A developmental and clinical model for the prevention of conduct disorders: The Fast Track Program. *Development & Psychopathology, 4,* 505–527.

Cook, C. R., Gresham, F. M., Kern, L., Barreras, R. B., Thornton, S., & Crews, S. D. (2008). Social skills training with secondary EBD students: A review and analysis of the meta-analytic literature. *Journal of Emotional and Behavioral Disorders, 16,* 131–144. doi:10.1177/1063426608314541

Cooper, J., Heron, T., & Heward, W. (2007). *Applied behavior analysis* (2nd ed.). Upper Saddle River, NJ: Prentice-Hall.

DiPerna, J., & Elliott, S. N. (2002). Promoting academic enablers to improve student achievement. *School Psychology Review, 31,* 293–298. Retrieved from www.nasponline.org/publications, spr/sprmain.aspx

DiPerna, J., Lei, P., Bellinger, J., & Cheng, W. (2015). Efficacy of the Social Skills Improvement System Classwide Intervention Program (SSIS-CIP) primary version. *School Psychology Quarterly, 30,* 123–141. Retrieved from http://dx.doi.org/10.1037/spq0000079

Duhon, G. J., Noell, G. H., Witt, J. C., Freeland, J. T., Dufrene, B. A., & Gilbertson, D. N. (2004). Identifying academic skill and performance deficits: The experimental analysis of brief assessments of academic skills. *School Psychology Review, 33,* 429–433.

Elliott, S. N., & Gresham, F. M. (2007). *Social skills improvement system: Classwide intervention program teacher's guide.* Minneapolis, MN: Pearson Assessments.

Elliott, S. N., & Gresham, F. M. (2008). *Social skills improvement system: Intervention guide.* Minneapolis, MN: Pearson Assessments.

Gresham, F. M. (1981). Assessment of children's social skills. *Journal of School Psychology, 19,* 120–134. Retrieved from http://dx.doi.org.proxy.wm.edu/10.1016/0022–4405(81)90054–6

Gresham, F. M. (2002). Teaching social skills to high-risk children and youth: Preventive and remedial strategies. In M. Shinn, H. Walker, & G. Stoner (Eds.), *Interventions for academic and behavior problems: Preventive and remedial approaches* (2nd ed., pp. 403–432). Bethesda, MD: National Association of School Psychologists.

Gresham, F. M. (2010). Evidence-based social skills interventions: Empirical foundations for instructional approaches. In M. Shinn & H. Walker (Eds.), *Interventions for achievement and behavior problems in a three-tier model including RTI* (pp. 337–362). Bethesda, MD: National Association of School Psychologists.

Gresham, F. M., Cook, C. R., Crews, S. D., & Kern, L. (2004). Social skills training for children and youth with emotional and behavioral disorders: Validity considerations and future directions. *Behavioral Disorders, 30,* 19–33.

Gresham, F. M., & Elliott, S. N. (2008). *Social skills improvement system: Rating scales manual.* Minneapolis, MN: Pearson Assessments.

Gresham, F. M., Sugai, G., & Horner, R. (2001). Interpreting outcomes of social skills training for students with high-incidence disabilities. *Exceptional Children, 67,* 331–344.

Gumpel, T. P. (2007). Are social competence difficulties caused by performance or acquisition deficits? The importance of self-regulatory mechanisms. *Psychology in the Schools, 44,* 351–372. Retrieved from http://dx.doi.org.proxy.wm.edu/10.1002/pits.20229

Herrnstein, R. J. (1961). Relative and absolute strength of response as a function of frequency of reinforcement. *Journal of Experimental Analysis of Behavior, 4,* 267–272.

Hinshaw, S. (1992). Externalizing behavior problems and academic underachievement in childhood and adolescence: Causal relationships and underlying mechanisms. *Psychological Bulletin, 111,* 127–155. Retrieved from http://dx.doi.org.proxy.wm.edu/10.1037/0033–2909.111.1.127

Horner, R., & Billingsley, F. (1988). The effects of competing behavior on the generalization and maintenance of adaptive behavior in applied settings. In R. Horner, G. Dunlap, & R. Koegel (Eds.), *Generalization and maintenance: Lifestyle changes in applied settings* (pp. 197–220). Baltimore, MD: Brookes.

Maag, J. W. (2005). Social skills training for youth with emotional and behavioral disorders and learning disabilities: Problems, conclusions, and suggestions. *Exceptionality, 13*, 155–172. Retrieved from http://dx.doi.org.proxy.wm.edu/10.1207/s15327035ex1303_2

Malecki, C. M., & Elliott, S. N. (2002). Children's social behaviors as predictors of academic achievement: A longitudinal analysis. *School Psychology Quarterly, 17*, 1–23. Retrieved from http://dx.doi.org.proxy.wm.edu/10.1521/scpq.17.1.1.19902

Multimodal Treatment Study of Children With ADHD (MTA) Cooperative Group. (1999). A 14-month randomized clinical trial of treatment strategies for attention-deficit/hyperactivity disorder. *Archives of General Psychiatry, 56*, 1073–1086.

Noell, G. H., Witt, J. C., LaFleur, L. H., Mortenson, B. P., Ranier, D. D., & LeVelle, J. (2000). Increasing intervention implementation in general education following consultation: A comparison of two follow-up strategies. *Journal of Applied Behavior Analysis, 33*(3), 271–284. doi:10.1901/jaba.2000.33.33-271

Offord, D., Boyle, M., & Racine, Y. (1989). Ontario Child Health Study: Correlates of disorder. *Journal of the American Academy of Child and Adolescent Psychiatry, 28*, 856–860. Retrieved from http://dx.doi.org/10.1097/00004583-198911000-00008

Parker, J., & Asher, S. (1987). Peer relations and later personal adjustment: Are low-accepted children at risk? *Psychological Bulletin, 102*, 357–389. Retrieved from http://dx.doi.org/10.1037/0033-2909.102.3.357

Reid, J. (1993). Prevention of conduct disorder before and after school entry: Relating interventions to developmental findings. *Development &*

Psychopathology, 5, 311–319. Retrieved from http://dx.doi.org/10.1017/S0954579400004375

Snyder, J., & Stoolmiller, M. (2002). Reinforcement and coercion mechanisms in the development of antisocial behavior: The family. In J. Reid, G. Patterson, & J. Snyder (Eds.), *Antisocial behavior in children and adolescents: A developmental analysis and model for intervention* (pp. 65–100). Washington, DC: American Psychological Association.

VanDerHeyden, A., & Witt, J. C. (2008). Best practices in can't do/won't do assessment. In A. Thomas & J. Grimes (Eds.), *Best practices in school psychology V* (pp. 131–139). Bethesda, MD: National Association of School Psychologists.

VanDeryHeyden, A. M., & Witt, J. C. (2005). Quantifying context in assessment: Capturing the effect of base rates on teacher referral and a problem-solving model of identification. *School Psychology Review, 34*, 161–183.

Walker, H. M., Irvin, L., Noell, J. & Singer, G. (1992). A construct score approach to the assessment of social competence: Rational, technological considerations, and anticipated outcomes. *Behavior Modification, 16*, 448–474. Retrieved from http://dx.doi.org/10.1177/01454455920164002

Walker, H. M., Ramsay, E., & Gresham, F. M. (2004). *Antisocial behavior at school: Evidence-based practices.* Belmont, CA: Wadsworth/Thomson Learning.

Wentzel, K. R. (2009). Peers and academic functioning at school. In K. H. Rubin, W. M. Bukowski, & B. Laursen (Eds.), *Handbook of peer interactions, relationships, and groups* (pp. 531–547). New York, NY: Guilford Press.

Wentzel, K. R., & Looney, I. (2007). Socialization in school settings. In J. E. Grusec & P. D. Hastings (Eds.), *Handbook of socialization: Theory and research* (pp. 382–403). New York, NY: Guilford Press.

Evidence-Based Interventions for Self-Concept in Children and Adolescents

Bruce A. Bracken

OVERVIEW

The importance of self-concept as a psychological construct has been accepted since the work of the earliest American psychologists (e.g., Cooley, 1902; James, 1890/1983). The degree of emphasis placed on the construct has changed little over the past century, leading Bracken and Lamprecht (2003) to conclude that "It might be only a slight exaggeration to suggest that fostering healthy, positive self-concepts, self-esteem, or self-images in children and adolescents has become a national preoccupation among parents, teachers, psychologists, and educational policy makers" (p. 103). Others have expressed similar conclusions. Sheldon, Elliot, Kim, and Kasser (2001), for example, asserted, "It is interesting that if one were to pick a single need that is most important to satisfy in the United States, the current data suggest it would be self-esteem" (p. 336). The rationale for a societal emphasis on self-concept is easily understood; people with positive self-views tend to be happier (Swann, 1990), better adjusted (Dumont & Provost, 2001), more popular (Jackson & Bracken,1998), have a better subjective sense of well-being (DeNeve & Cooper, 1998; McCullough, Huebner, & Laughlin, 2000), possess better learning strategies (Ganjie & Soufi, 2015) and academic achievement (Huang, 2011;

Marsh & Martin, 2011), profess greater life satisfaction (Diener, 1984; Diener & Diener, 1995; Huebner, 1994; Huebner, Gilman, & Laughlin, 1999; Terry & Huebner, 1995), have a greater likelihood of coming from intact families (Sweeney & Bracken, 2000), and are less likely to run away from home (Swaim & Bracken, 1997) than individuals who have negative self-views.

A consensus among professionals and the general population holds that helping children develop healthy self-concepts is a worthwhile goal. This chapter describes how healthy self-concepts are developed naturally and remediated through evidence-based interventions. Interventions for enhancing self-concept require a sound working theory, receptive and informed participants, thoughtful planning, and treatment fidelity. This chapter provides the reader with the theory and methodology to develop positive self-concepts in children and adolescents.

ETIOLOGY AND FACTORS CONTRIBUTING TO SELF-CONCEPT DEFICITS IN CHILDREN AND ADOLESCENTS

There are a number of factors and models of self-concept that describe different factors contributing to self-concept development. The prominent models include cognitive and behavioral orientations, each with related contributing factors.

Cognitive Models. The "self" has been a fertile psychological construct with a history dating back to the early writings of William James (1890/1983). James conceived of self-esteem as a ratio between a person's true skills and abilities and his or her perception of those attributes. Although James's conception is illustrative in a broad sense, it does not take into account the interactive influence of environmental factors on a person's perceptions and developing abilities. By placing emphasis solely on the individual rather than the interaction of the individual and the external environment, James set the stage for a cognitive-affective system that emphasized the "self" as an important and authentic entity, which eventually spawned a host of related "self" attributes (e.g., self-actualization, self-control, self-confidence, self-discipline, self-esteem, and self-regulation).

Behavioral Model. One of the shortcomings of various cognitively oriented self-concept models is lack of a clear explanation for how self-concept is acquired or modified. Bracken's (1992) model incorporates behavioral learning theory to explain how children acquire self-concepts as a function of direct and indirect interactions with their environment and others within that environment. This model is relevant not only for self-concept acquisition, but self-concept interventions as well.

As individuals interact, they achieve successes (i.e., contingent reinforcements) and experience failures (i.e., punishing experiences) to varying degrees in specific ecological contexts. People receive environmental feedback on their behavior or attributes from two feedback modes or perspectives—directly from their personal experiences (i.e., *personal perspective*) and indirectly from other individuals within their environment (i.e., *other perspective*). The feedback individuals receive can be evaluated according to four standards (e.g., *absolute, comparative, ipsative, and ideal*). A detailed explanation of each of the two perspectives and the four standards follow.

Perspectives

James's early writings characterized self-concept development as an internal event, with little emphasis on external contributors. James recognized the value of the individual's self-perspective. On the other hand, Cooley (1902), as a contemporary of James, emphasized the external perspective on which an individual's self-concepts are based. Cooley coined the term "looking glass self," suggesting that we tend to see ourselves as others reflect our actions and characteristics back to us. That is, our self-perceptions are directly affected by how others in our environment act toward us and respond to our actions and attributes. Bracken's (1992, 2006) model acknowledges and incorporates both of these behavioral perspectives (i.e., *personal* and *other*).

Standards

After we directly (*personal perspective*) or indirectly (*other perspective*) receive feedback from our environment about our performance or our characteristics, we evaluate that information according to four evaluation standards, separately and in combination. The four identified standards of evaluation include the absolute, comparative, ipsative, and ideal. Each of the four standards is contrasted in the following in an example that uses the same behavioral event (i.e., the standing long jump).

Absolute Standard. An absolute standard reflects an objective personal evaluation based on observable outcomes. A child who jumps forward from a standing position for a distance of 4 feet sees the distance covered and evaluates the accomplishment directly. The accomplishment, whether evaluated privately (i.e., *personal perspective*) or by others (i.e., *other perspective*), is based on an absolute, direct, and objective outcome.

Comparative Standard. The comparative standard comes into play when an individual's behaviors or characteristics are contrasted with the behaviors or characteristics of another person or a reference group. Standing long jump can be appreciated as either a solitary or group comparison activity; friendly competitions among peers may develop in such group activities, with students trying to best others. With each standing long jump, students receive absolute affirmation of their abilities (i.e., absolute standard) and their prowess can be compared with others (i.e., comparative standard). As with the other standards, the comparative standard can be evaluated personally (i.e., *personal perspective*) or by others (i.e., *other perspective*).

Ipsative Standard.

Ipsative standards represent the evaluation of one's prowess in light of other skills or characteristics possessed by the child (Bracken, 1992; Crain, 1996; Crain & Bracken, 1994). Bracken's ipsative standard is similar to Marx and Winne's (1980) concept of "compensatory self-concept" in which a student might balance negative self-evaluations in one area of functioning with positive self-evaluations in other domains. A child who is not an especially strong distance jumper might still exhibit a positive self-concept in other domains by accepting that his or her well-developed skills lie in other physical (e.g., appearance) or nonphysical areas (e.g., social and academic).

Ideal Standard.

Ideal standards are employed when an ideal level of accomplishment is used as the standard of comparison by either the child (*personal perspective*) or by others (*other perspective*). Ideal goals seldom reflect realistic expectations, but may be used in a healthy manner to motivate children and adolescents to maximize their improvement. As such, the goal of being the person who can jump the farthest might be realistic for only a few students, but for most students the goal of being the best is unrealistic. As a realistic goal, students might strive to be the best of all other jumpers or, importantly, to be the best standing long jumper he or she can possibly be. As an unrealistic goal, jumpers will continually fail to meet their respective goals and experience disappointment and frustration as a result. In contrast to an unrealistic goal pursuit, Sheldon and Houser-Marko (2000) present the folk wisdom that "it is possible to be happier through one's striving pursuits, if one picks the right goals and does well at them" (p. 160). To develop healthy self-concepts, it is important for parents and teachers to help students identify reasonable, attainable goals to work toward as their ideal, and to work toward being the best they can possibly be.

Global Versus Multidimensional Models.

Current cognitive and behavioral self-concept theorists recognize that self-concept has evolved since its early conceptions. James's formula for self-esteem not only led the field toward a cognitively oriented self-system, it also set the stage for the view of self-esteem as a unitary human characteristic; that is, there is only one "self" within an individual; ergo a person must have only one self-concept. As such, self-concept was long viewed as a global construct that included all aspects of self-evaluation collectively. Cooley (1902), like James, was an early proponent of a "generalized" or global self-concept. As a global entity, self-concept was seen as all-encompassing and generalizable to all aspects of a person's life, much like general intelligence. Although most self-concept theorists eventually accepted self-concept as a multidimensional construct, the media, public, and the "occasional" self-concept researcher continue to focus on global self-concept rather than its various subdomains.

Since the late 20th century and the seminal work of Shavelson, Hubner, and Stanton (1976), psychologists have recognized that there are in fact multiple important self-concepts to be considered when referring to a person's adjustment (e.g., Bear, Minke, Griffin, & Deemer, 1997; Bracken, 1992; Byrne, 1996; Harter, 1983; Hattie, 1992; L'Ecuyer, 1981; Marsh, 1990; Marsh & Holmes, 1990; Minton, 1979; Piers, 1984; Rosenberg, 1979). The context-dependent self-concept domains proposed by Bracken (1992, 2006)— *academic, affect, competence, family, physical, and social*—were culled from the literature and have not only gained common acceptance as foundational domain-specific self-concepts, the universality of the six context-dependent self-concept domains have been supported empirically (Bracken, Bunch, Keith, & Keith, 2000) through a multiple instrument factor analysis. It is important to note that multiple meta-analyses of self-concept intervention efficacy consistently show that targeting specific dimensions of self-concept results in larger effect sizes than when global self-concept is targeted (e.g., Hattie, 1992; O'Mara, Marsh, Craven, & Debus, 2006).

In addition to being considered multidimensional and context-dependent, self-concept is now generally accepted as hierarchically structured. Such a theoretical organization presents global self-concept as embodying all domains together, as in an intellectual *g*-factor, with various intercorrelated foundational dimensions comprising secondary levels of self-concepts (e.g., Bracken, 1992, 1996; Epstein, 1973; Shavelson et al., 1976).

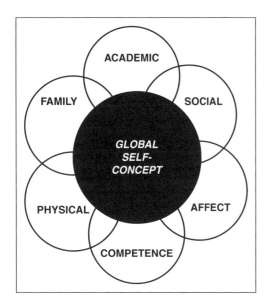

FIGURE 31.1 Multidimensional self-concept.

Figure 31.1 depicts Bracken's (1992) hierarchical, multidimensional model of self-concept, with global self-concept depicted at the center and six context-dependent domains overlapping the core, thereby contributing shared variance with global self-concept and yet having sufficient specific variance to remain independent. A brief definition of each context-dependent domain follows:

Academic self-concept represents how a person evaluates himself or herself within an academic setting (e.g., classroom) or in relation to his or her academic progress (e.g., grades).

Affect self-concept is a self-evaluative awareness of one's affective state and the issues or conditions that contribute to different affective states experienced by the individual. Affect self-concept could be considered as "how a person feels about how he or she feels." That is, an awareness and self-evaluation of how people's emotions affect their self-evaluation.

Competence self-concept is defined as a person's self-judgment of his or her ability to get basic needs met. Competence begins to develop in infancy and continues to evolve throughout the life span.

Family self-concept represents children and adolescents' evaluations of themselves as members of a family, functioning within a family milieu, and their sense of relative importance within the family constellation.

Physical self-concept is essentially how a person regards himself or herself as a physical being, including one's physical appearance (e.g., size, attractiveness, hair or skin color), health and physical limitations (e.g., chronic health limitations, disabilities, robust health), and prowess (e.g., stamina, agility, and athletic ability).

Social self-concept reflects how a person evaluates his or her ability to interact with others, participate socially, and be accepted within social settings. As with any specific domain, there may be subareas of social self-concept that can be acquired, depending on individual successes and failures (e.g., same-sex peer relations; opposite-sex peer relations; same-sex adult relations; opposite-sex adult relations). It is important to note that social interactions and interpersonal relations are fundamental to healthy mental development (Bracken, 2006).

EVIDENCE-BASED INTERVENTIONS AND EMPIRICAL SUPPORT FOR SELF-CONCEPT IMPROVEMENT IN CHILDREN AND ADOLESCENTS

By systematically using the Bracken (1992) model for developing, maintaining, and remediating children's self-concepts, more consistent and favorable results will emerge than when less systematic or theoretically sound procedures are employed. Meta-analyses of self-concept intervention effectiveness make several salient points regarding which types of interventions have empirical support and which do not. In summary, those interventions that work best (i.e., greatest effect sizes) include the following: (a) remediating extant weaknesses rather than providing prophylactic protection; (b) focusing on specific domains of self-concept rather than global self-concept; (c) combining contingent reinforcement (e.g., praise) and encouragement with task improvement; (d) focusing on direct as opposed to indirect self-concept enhancement; and (e) when implementing done by teachers in the classroom as opposed to counselors or psychologists outside the natural environment (Hattie, 1992; O'Mara et al., 2006).

Individuals interested in improving their own or others' self-concepts must be cognizant of several important issues. First, interventionists must recognize that self-concepts are multidimensional and it is much easier to target one or more specific context-specific domains for change than it is to attempt to improve a person's global or overall self-concept. The more refined, focused, and intense the intervention, the more likely it will succeed.

Second, interventionists must understand that self-concept is a barometer of internalized evaluations (by oneself and others) of one's successes and failures. To improve a person's domain-specific self-concept, interventionists must reinforce participants' efforts and skill growth and help individuals become or perceive themselves as becoming more successful than they were previously.

Third, the behavioral extension of Cooley's (1902) concept of the "looking glass self" is important to incorporate in self-concept interventions. Children and adolescents often accept and adopt the embarrassment, humiliation, disappointment, and shame, or conversely the pride, confidence, and happiness that they see reflected in the eyes of others who are watching and judging them. If parents, teachers, and therapists wish to improve the self-concepts of children and adolescents, they must first become more supportive, accepting, and encouraging. That is, interventionists must project the honest hope, confidence, and belief in the child that they want children to project about themselves. It is important that interventionists realize that the child sees himself or herself in part in the expressions of and as an extension of the viewer. Therefore, it is important that the viewer express praise, encouragement, and unconditional acceptance.

Fourth, interventionists must understand that the child may not have an accurate self-perception and his or her negative self-appraisal would not seem warranted by any objective standard. In instances of overly critical self-perceptions (e.g., perfectionistic students), interventionists should employ cognitive behavioral approaches to help "reframe" or adjust the student's personal expectations, perceptions, or beliefs. Talking openly and encouragingly about the student's feelings and helping him or her to accept a less self-critical and more accurate self-perception will facilitate the child's adoption of more realistic self-expectations and positive self-concepts.

Fifth, interventionists must create an environment that is rich with successful opportunities, and allow for successive approximations leading toward the end goal, with ample praise for successful approximations of the desired skill or ability. As students acquire confidence that they can successfully complete the range of individual steps leading to the end goal, the more confident they will feel.

Sixth, interventionists should carefully employ each of the four standards of evaluation, helping the child or adolescent and others to create a healthy environment for acquiring positive self-concepts. As children and adolescents improve in their "absolute" performance (i.e., absolute standard), the more favorably they will compare with their peers (i.e., comparative standard), the less their targeted behavior will stand out as an intrachild weakness (i.e., ipsative standard), and the closer they will approach their ideal behavior (i.e., ideal standard). Moreover, as children and adolescents improve in their respective abilities, the more they will take note of the improvement (i.e., self-perspective), as will others in their environment (i.e., *other perspective*).

HOW TO: A GUIDE TO THE IMPLEMENTATION OF INTERVENTIONS FOR SELF-CONCEPT

Methods for remediating self-concept deficiencies are straightforward and follow time-proven behavioral and social-contextual approaches put forth by such notable researchers as Bandura (2004) and Skinner (1990), but also reflect the contributions of cognitive theorists such as James (e.g., contrast between perceived and objective conditions), Cooley (e.g., looking glass self), and selecting the right goals toward which to strive (Anthony & Houser-Marko, 2000). Importantly, successful self-concept intervention requires identifying and attending to specific domain-specific self-concepts, rather than global self-concepts (e.g., Bracken, 1996; Haney & Durlak, 1998; Hattie, 1992; O'Mara et al., 2006). The following five steps can be used to guide successful self-concept interventions.

Step 1: Identify. The *Multidimensional Self-Concept Scale* (Bracken, 1992) or other multidimensional self-concept scales (e.g., Bracken et al., 2000; Bracken & Mills, 1994; Davis-Kean & Sandler, 2001; Keith & Bracken, 1996) should be administered to identify the child's normative strengths and weaknesses (i.e., comparative standard) and ipsative strengths and weaknesses (i.e., ipsative standard) across each of the six previously cited domains. Context-based observations and clinical interviews with the child or adolescent and his or her parents and teachers will permit examination of absolute and ideal standards held by the child and others (i.e., self and *other perspectives*). Triangulation of information from self-reports and views of other important figures in the child's or adolescent's life will help identify domains of strength and weakness; standards of evaluation that may be helpful in remediation or those that contribute to the child's or adolescent's poor self-concept (i.e., absolute, comparative, ipsative, and ideal); and, how differing perspectives (i.e., self or other) may be problematic or helpful.

Step 2: Collaborate. Meet with the child, child's teacher, and parents to explain the nature of the child's self-concept deficit. For example, identify the domain-specific self-concepts that are in need of intervention (e.g., social self-concept) and highlight the stronger self-concept domains that may be employed to facilitate the child's self-concept improvement (e.g., academic and physical self-concept). Identify specific standards of evaluation that might be faulty (e.g., self-evaluation does not appear to match objective criteria) and plan approaches to address the child's or other's faulty perceptions. Plan an approach for improving real and perceived behavioral deficits by addressing specific behaviors (e.g., social skills), employing standards of evaluation in a meaningful way, and ensuring that self and other's perceptions are consistent and positive (i.e., employ opportunities for success and abundant reinforcement). The agreed-upon plan should identify specific roles, expectations, and behaviors for each participant and be set to occur for a predetermined amount of time.

Step 3: Implement. Using the plan developed in conjunction with the child and the child's parents and teachers, implement the activities, ensuring that everyone follows the plan as agreed upon (i.e., treatment fidelity). It is important that the plan be implemented in the natural contexts in which the child's self-concepts are developing.

Step 4: Observe and Modify. Once the plan is activated, observe its implementation when possible (e.g., in the school) or schedule regular sessions with the participants to determine whether the plan is being implemented faithfully and, importantly, whether the participants believe it is working. Modify the plan as needed to enhance the likelihood of success, address issues that arise, and continue to correct faulty perceptions and improve participants' perceptions through praise and other contingent reinforcers.

Step 5: Evaluate. Reassess the child's domain-specific self-concepts using the same instrument as was used during the identification process (i.e., Step 1). Both normative and ipsative gains across all domains can be considered and self-concept growth can be plotted and evaluated using standard effect size calculations (e.g., pretest score—posttest score/population standard deviation). If the domain-specific intervention was beneficial, the resulting effect size should be moderate to large and greater than the effect sizes generated for the nontargeted self-concept domains. Based on the results of the evaluation, the intervention can be continued as is (i.e., for additional improvement), modified (i.e., to enhance the treatment power), or discontinued (i.e., if desired goals have been met).

Working Example

Anthony, a 10-year-old fifth-grade student, was referred by his teacher because she perceived that the young man had poor social interactions with his peers and consistently shied away from his age peers of both genders. Although he was accepted by his classmates as one of the smartest students in the class, he appeared to have little in common with most of his classmates and shared few of their interests. Anthony was administered the *Multidimensional Self-Concept Scale* to assess his self-reported self-concepts in six important life domains. Normatively, his academic and competence domain-specific self-concepts were in the high average range; his affect and physical self-concepts were in the average range; his social and family self-concepts were classified as low average. Ipsatively, Anthony's Social and Family self-concepts were classified as weaknesses; Physical and Affect were average, and Competence and Academic self-concept domains were classified as relative strengths. Anthony's parents and teacher concurred that the self-concept scale portrayed accurately what they perceived as the student's self-concept strengths and weaknesses, both as compared to his age peers and his own domain-specific self-concepts domains.

Anthony, his parents, and his teacher and school counselor met with the school psychologist to develop a plan to help Anthony improve his social skills and enhance his social self-concept. It was agreed that much of the feedback Anthony had received about his social interactions were negatively portrayed by his parents and teacher (i.e., *other perspective*), based on their comparative and ideal expectations and standards of evaluation. That is, his parents and teacher believed that Anthony's social interactions and self-concept were not commensurate with his overall intelligence and achievement, or even the social skills of his peers. They voiced and showed their displeasure or disappointment in sometimes subtle and other times not so subtle ways.

A contingency reinforcement plan was developed for his parents and teacher to consistently and enthusiastically praise and show appreciation of all of Anthony's social contact efforts. Moreover, Anthony's teacher agreed to arrange opportunities within the classroom for Anthony to succeed socially, allowing him to serve as a reading peer tutor and to be a group leader on a project working with four generally accepting students (i.e., two male peers and two female peers). Anthony's parents arranged for reciprocal sleepovers with a couple of his first cousins, with planned social outings as part of the sleepover. The school psychologist created a social skills and social self-concept group, which included Anthony and four other fifth-grade students. The school counselor added Anthony to her "Lunch Buddies" group in which students with social self-concept deficits were invited to eat lunch with her and talk openly about whatever topic they chose on a daily basis. The counselor guided the conversation to ensure that appropriate social interactions occurred and she praised students for their reflective listening and responding (e.g., "That was a thoughtful idea, Anthony."), but otherwise let the students do the talking.

At the end of the 9-week grading period, the school psychologist readministered the MSCS and calculated gain scores and subsequent effect sizes for each scale to determine whether the program was bringing about the desired effects. Not only did the Social and Family scales improve more so than did the remaining four scales, the self-concept growth in both targeted domains increased with corresponding moderate to large effect sizes. After

meeting with the parents, teacher, and counselor to discuss what seemed to be working well and what was not working as well, the team decided to continue the program for another 9 weeks with new supervised social experiences at home with direct linkages to the classroom (e.g., home sleepovers, skating outings, and sports events including select classmates). In school, Anthony's teacher continued to arrange for successful in-class social opportunities; his counselor discontinued Anthony from the Lunch Buddies group because he now had two male friends with whom he wanted to join at the lunch table; the school psychologist continued Anthony in the social skills and social self-concept group.

CONCLUSION

A consensus exists among professionals and the general population that helping children and adolescents develop healthy self-concepts is a worthwhile goal. This chapter described how healthy self-concepts are developed naturally and remediated through evidence-based interventions. Research on self-concept intervention effectiveness highlights the findings that interventions work best when they remediate extant weaknesses rather than provide prophylactic protection; focus on specific domains of self-concept rather than global self-concept; combine contingent reinforcement and encouragement with task improvement; focus on direct as opposed to indirect self-concept enhancement; and are implemented by teachers in the classroom and at home. Combining these principles with a sound theory of self-concept acquisition suggests that interventionists should focus on specific self-concept domain deficits, consider both the child's or adolescent's self-view, as well as significant others' vantage, and determine which of four evaluation standards are contributing most to the child's or adolescent's negative self-evaluation.

SELECT BIBLIOGRAPHY

Bracken, B. A. (Ed.). (1996). *Handbook of self-concept: Developmental, social, and clinical considerations.* New York, NY: Wiley.
This book considers the theoretical and applied aspects of self-concept development and

intervention across multiple context-dependent domains. The chapters address educational, social, clinical, and behavioral aspects of self-concept and provide recommendations for self-concept remediation.

Byrne, B. M. (1996). *Measuring self-concept across the life span: Issues and instrumentation.* Washington, DC: American Psychological Association.
This book is a useful guide for assessing the quality and methodology of self-concept measurements. Given that the field of self-concept has multiple measures, many of which are first generation scales that focus primarily on global self-concept or lack nationally representative standardization samples, this book provides a solid foundation on which to evaluate tests published before and after the book's appearance in 1996.

O'Mara, A. J., Marsh, H. W., Craven, R. G., & Debus, R. L. (2006). Do self-concept interventions make a difference? A synergistic blend of construct validation and meta-analysis. *Educational Psychologist, 41*(3), 181–206.
This article is the most recent and complete evaluation of evidence-based interventions for self-concept—what works and what does not. The meta-analytic study included 145 studies with 200 interventions employed, and provided a systematic and detailed description of procedures, methodology, and outcomes.

REFERENCES

Bandura, A. (2004). Swimming against the mainstream: The early years from chilly tributary to transformative mainstream. *Behavior Research and Therapy, 42*(6), 613–630. doi:10.1016/j.brat.2004.02.001

Bear, G. G., Minke, K. M., Griffin, S. M., & Deemer, S. A. (1997). Self-concept. In G. Bear, K. Minke, & A. Thomas (Eds.), *Children's needs II: Development, problems, and alternatives* (pp. 257–269). Bethesda, MD: National Association of School Psychologists.

Bracken, B. A. (1992). *Examiner's manual for the Multidimensional Self-Esteem scale.* Austin, TX: Pro-Ed.

Bracken, B. A. (1996). Clinical applications of a context-dependent, multidimensional model of self-concept. In B. A. Bracken (Ed.), *Handbook of self-concept: Developmental, social, and clinical considerations* (pp. 463–504). New York, NY: Wiley.

Bracken, B. A. (2006). *Examiner's manual for the clinical assessment of interpersonal relations.* Odessa, FL: Psychological Assessment Resources.

Bracken, B. A., Bunch, S., Keith, T. Z., & Keith, P. B. (2000). Child and adolescent multidimensional self-concept: A five-instrument factor analysis. *Psychology in the Schools, 37,* 483–493. doi:10.1002/1520–6807(200011)37:6<483::AID-PITS1>3.0.CO;2-R

Bracken, B. A., & Lamprecht, M. S. (2003). Self-concept: An equal opportunity construct. *School Psychology Quarterly, 18,* 103–121. doi:10.1521/scpq.18.2.103.21859

Bracken, B. A., & Mills, B. C. (1994). School counselors' assessment of self-esteem: A comprehensive review of ten instruments. *The School Counselor, 42,* 14–31.

Byrne, B. M. (1996). *Measuring self-concept across the life span: Issues and instrumentation.* Washington, DC: American Psychological Association. doi:10.1037/10197–000

Cooley, C. H. (1902). *Human nature and the social order.* New York, NY: Scribner's.

Crain, R. M. (1996). The influence of age, race, and gender on child and adolescent multidimensional self-concept. In B. A. Bracken (Ed.), *Handbook of self-concept: Developmental, social, and clinical considerations* (pp. 395–420). New York, NY: Wiley.

Crain, R. M., & Bracken, B. A. (1994). Age, race, and gender differences in child and adolescent self-concept: Evidence from a behavioral acquisition, context-dependent model. *School Psychology Review, 23,* 496–511.

Davis-Kean, P. E., & Sandler, H. M. (2001). A meta-analysis of measures of self-esteem for young children: A framework for future measures. *Child Development, 72,* 887–906. doi:10.1111/1467–8624.00322

DeNeve, K. M., & Cooper, H. (1998). The happy personality: A meta-analysis of 137 personality traits and subjective well-being. *Psychological Bulletin, 124,* 197–229. doi:10.1037/0033–2909.124.2.197

Diener, E. (1984). Subjective well-being. *Psychological Bulletin, 95,* 542–575. doi:10.1037/0033–2909.95.3.542

Diener, E., & Diener, M. (1995). Cross-cultural correlates of life satisfaction and self-esteem. *Journal of Personality and Social Psychology, 69,* 120–129. doi:10.1007/978–90–481–2352–0_4

Dumont, M., & Provost, M. A. (2001). Resilience in adolescents: Protective role of social support, coping strategies, self-esteem, and social activities on experience of stress and depression. *Journal of Youth and Adolescence, 28,* 343–363. doi:10.1023/A:1021637011732

Epstein, S. (1973). The self-concept revisited or a theory of a theory. *American Psychologist, 28,* 405–416. doi:10.1037/h0034679

Ganjie, H., & Soufi, S. (2015), Contribution of self-concept, learning strategies, and self-determination motivation, and global self-esteem in academic achievement. *Psychological Research, 17*(2), 11–29.

Harter, S. (1983). Developmental perspectives on the self-system. In P. H. Mussen (Ed.) & E. M. Hetherington (Series Ed.), *Handbook of child psychology: Vol. 4. Socialization, personality and social development* (pp. 275–385). New York, NY: Wiley.

Hattie, J. (1992). *Self-concept.* Hillsdale, NJ: Erlbaum.

Huang, C. (2011). Self-concept and academic achievement: A meta-analysis of longitudinal relations. *Journal of School Psychology, 49*(5), 505–528. doi:10.1016/j.jsp.2011.07.001

Huebner, E. S. (1994). Conjoint analyses of the Student's Life Satisfaction Scale and the Piers–Harris Self-Concept Scale. *Psychology in the Schools, 31,* 273–277.

Huebner, E. S., Gilman, R., & Laughlin, J. E. (1999). A multimethod investigation of the multidimensionality of children's well-being reports: Discriminant validity of life satisfaction and self-esteem. *Social Indicators Research, 46,* 1–22. doi:10.1023/A:1006821510832

Jackson, L. D., & Bracken, B. A. (1998). Relationship between students' social-status and global and domain-specific self-concepts. *Journal of School Psychology, 36,* 233–245. doi:10.1016/S0022–4405(97)00052–6

James, W. (1983). *The principles of psychology.* Cambridge, MA: Harvard University Press. (Originally published in 1890). doi:10.1016/S0022–4405(97)00052–6

Keith, L. K., & Bracken, B. A. (1996). Self-concept instrumentation: A historical and evaluative review. In B. A. Bracken (Ed.), *Handbook of self-concept: Developmental, social, and clinical considerations* (pp. 91–170). New York, NY: Wiley.

L'Ecuyer, R. (1981). The development of the self-concept through the life-span. In M. D. Lynch, A. A. Norem-Hebeisen, & K. Gergen (Eds.), *Self-concept: Advances in theory and research.* Cambridge, MA: Ballinger.

Marsh, H. W. (1990). A multidimensional, hierarchical model of self-concept: Theoretical and empirical justification. *Educational Psychology Review, 2,* 77–172.

Marsh, H. W., & Holmes, I. W. (1990). Multidimensional self-concepts: Construct validation of responses by children. *American Educational Research Journal, 27,* 89–117. doi:10.2307/1163070

Marsh, H. W., & Martin, A. J. (2011). Academic self-concept and academic achievement: Relations and causal ordering. *British Journal of Educational Psychology, 81*(1), 59–77. doi:10.1348/000709910X503501

Marx, R. W., & Winne, P. H. (1980). Self-concept research: Some current complexities. *Measurement and Evaluation in Guidance, 13*(2), 72–82.

McCullough, G., Huebner, E. S., Laughlin, J. E. (2000). Life events, self-concept, and adolescents' positive subjective well-being. *Psychology in the Schools, 37,* 281–290. doi:10.1002/(SICI)1520–6807(200005)37:3<281::AID-PITS8>3.0.CO;2–2

Minton, B. (1979). *Dimensions of information underlying children's judgments of their competence.* Unpublished master's thesis, University of Denver, Denver, CO.

O'Mara, A. J., Marsh, H. W., Craven, R. G., & Debus, R. L. (2006). Do self-concept interventions make a difference? A synergistic blend of construct validation and meta-analysis. *Educational Psychologist, 41*(3), 181–206. doi:10.1207/s15326985ep4103_4

Piers, E. V. (1984). *Piers–Harris Children's Self-Concept Scale: Revised manual.* Los Angeles: Western Psychological Services.

Rosenberg, M. (1979). *Conceiving the self.* New York, NY: Basic Books.

Shavelson, R. J., Hubner, J. J., & Stanton, G. C. (1976). Self-concept: Validation of construct interpretations. *Review of Educational Research, 46,* 407–441. doi:10.2307/1170010

Sheldon, K. M., Elliot, A. J., Kim, Y., & Kasser, T. (2001). What is satisfying about satisfying events? Testing 10 candidate psychological needs. *Journal of Personality and Social Psychology, 80,* 325–339. doi:10.1037/0022–3514.80.2.325

Sheldon, K. M., & Houser-Marko, L. (2000). Self-concordance, goal attainment, and the pursuit of happiness: Can there be an upward spiral. *Journal of Personality & Social Psychology, 80,* 152–165. doi:10.1037/0022–3514.80.1.152

Skinner, B. F. (1990). Can psychology be a science of mind? *American Psychologist, 45,* 1206–1210. doi:10.1037/0003–066X.45.11.1206

Swaim, K. F., & Bracken, B. A. (1997). Global and domain-specific self-concepts of a matched sample of adolescent runaways and nonrunaways. *Journal of Clinical Child Psychology, 26,* 397–403. doi:10.1207/s15374424jccp2604_8

Swann, W. B. (1990). To be adored or to be known: The interplay of self-enhancement and self-verification. In R. M. Sorrentino, & E. T. Higgins (Eds.), *Motivation and cognition* (Vol. 2, pp. 408–448). New York, NY: Guilford.

Sweeney, R. B., & Bracken, B. A. (2000). Influence of family structure on children's self-concept development. *Canadian Journal of School Psychology, 16,* 39–52. doi:10.1177/082957350001600103

Terry, T., & Huebner, E. S. (1995). The relationship between self-concept and life satisfaction in children. *Social Indicators Research, 35,* 39–52. doi:10.1007/BF01079237

Evidence-Based Interventions for Promoting Subjective Well-Being in Children and Adolescents

Aileen Fullchange, Michael James Furlong, Rich Gilman, and E. Scott Huebner

OVERVIEW

Perceived quality of life is shaped by internal beliefs and social interactions (Veenhoven, 2013). These experiences elicit a range of positive and negative reactions that prompt individuals to make sense of, organize, and incorporate into emerging self-schemas. Intuitively, a low ratio of positive-to-negative emotional reactions would be akin to poor life quality, whereas the reverse would be considered to contribute to high life quality. There is empirical support for the dual nature of emotions in mental health, both among adults (e.g., Conway, Tugade, Catalino, & Frederickson, 2013) and youth (Fussner, Luebbe, & Bell, 2014). Nevertheless, empirical evidence has shown that life quality is more than distinguishing positive from negative emotional experiences. Cognitive evaluations about one's life direction, which include personal goals, aspirations, meaning and contributions to society, are also significant predictors of the fundamental question: How is my life going thus far? Whether specific to a domain (e.g., peer relationships) or for life in general, both emotional and cognitive factors are necessary components when evaluating "happiness"—or "subjective well-being" (SWB), as the term is commonly used among researchers (Kim-Prieto, Diener, Tamir, Scollon, & Diener, 2005).

Although many well-being studies have focused on adults, research over the past two decades has examined SWB in school-aged youth. This emphasis has been made for two reasons. First, helping professionals have long sought to identify individuals' "problems" (e.g., psychological symptoms) and develop interventions to decrease or eliminate them. In spite of the amount of resources and effort spent toward attaining these goals, only modest progress has been made (Houtrow & Okumura, 2011). Relatedly, most efforts to this end have focused on youth with the most pressing mental health needs, ignoring the larger numbers of youth who do not report significant life distress, yet experience boredom and discontent; of "being trapped in the present, waiting for someone to prove to them that life is worth living" (Larson, 2000, p. 170). These students would appear psychologically "healthy" (on most rating scales assessing severity of distress), even though their well-being reports would indicate otherwise (Suldo & Shaffer, 2008). Second, the foremost goal of most parents is not to prevent psychopathology in their child but to instill and promote skills and values that contribute to a meaningful and productive life. Indeed, research has shown that numerous psychological, social, and academic benefits are afforded to those individuals who maintain incrementally higher levels of well-being (see Gilman, Huebner, & Furlong, 2014 for a recent review). For these reasons, proponents such as Keyes and Haidt (2003) have argued for a more ambitious agenda to foster optimal SWB levels within youth, their social affiliations, and the larger systems within which they are embedded. Hence, the past decade has seen the emergence of efforts to increase SWB among youth, incorporating attention to both major internal personal assets and external environmental resources.

Although remaining in its emergent stage, there are empirically validated SWB promotion strategies that warrant attention. The aim of this chapter is to provide an overview of a number of these programs and strategies that have been used to foster youths' positive SWB, with a particular focus on school-based practices. This chapter is divided into four sections. First, the benefits of SWB among youth are summarized. Second, specific domains that have been addressed vis-à-vis SWB promotion strategies are described. Third, the chapter summarizes multicomponent programs and narrowband strategies that have been shown to promote SWB levels. Finally, the chapter concludes with a description of the factors to consider when implementing efforts to foster SWB and provides some key resources to support these efforts.

BENEFITS OF SWB

As with adults, higher levels of SWB facilitate a number of positive outcomes in children and adolescents, including higher levels of school engagement and parental support and less peer victimization and maladaptive behavior (for reviews see Huebner, Hills, Siddall, & Gilman, 2014; Proctor, Linley, & Maltby, 2009). Although some studies have focused on U.S. samples, burgeoning lines of research parallel these findings with respect to youth representing both Western and Eastern cultures. Economic constraints may interfere with the attainment of basic needs, which themselves are partial predictors of well-being. Nevertheless, after controlling for gross national income, regardless of nationality, it is of universal importance to examine the effects of optimal SWB levels on psychological, social, and academic outcomes (Land, Lamb, &

Zheng, 2011). These findings also extend to gender and household income (Gilman & Huebner, 2006). Several studies also reveal that SWB serves both as a mediator and moderator function in positive youth adaptation. For example, McKnight, Huebner, and Suldo (2002) demonstrated that life satisfaction self-reports mediated the association between stressful life events and adolescents' behavioral problems (see also Lewis et al., 2013 for similar findings with respect to emotions). Adolescents' SWB reports also appear to moderate the relation between the experience of stressful life events and adolescents' behavioral problems. Specifically, adolescents who reported positive, global life satisfaction (vs. those who reported global dissatisfaction) had more resilience; that is, they were less likely to show externalizing problem behaviors in response to the occurrence of stressful life events (Suldo & Huebner, 2004).

Etiology and Factors Contributing to SWB in Children and Adolescents

There are many possible reasons for why maintaining optimal SWB levels confer developmental benefits. Perhaps the most intriguing is the notion of a homeostatic SWB "set point," in which an established SWB level—determined by evolutionary standards—is set for most individuals above a neutral point (Tomyn & Cummins, 2011). Having a positive set point creates a background against which negative emotional or cognitive experiences are perceived and addressed quickly. In this manner, a decline in SWB would signal an existential threat, thus prompting the individual to adapt in order to maintain homeostasis (see Gilman, Huebner, & Carboni, in press). Maintaining a positive SWB set point thus facilitates individuals' efforts to secure whatever basic (e.g., food, shelter) and secondary (e.g., autonomy, relatedness) needs that are necessary for optimal functioning. Nevertheless, that SWB reports can change in response to life experiences also suggests that the set point is amenable to interventions. For example, youths' SWB reports youths vary in response to significant fluctuations in perceived quality of friendships and family relationships, the amount of time spent in productive activities, and the types of goals that youths pursue. Even considering set points, there is evidence that SWB declines from early to mid adolescence

(Tomyn, Cummins, & Norrish, 2014). Thus, SWB appears to be sensitive to life circumstances, and that various intrapersonal (e.g., coping styles, personality characteristics) and interpersonal (e.g., availability of social support) resources might moderate the extent of change and time needed for the individual's life satisfaction to return to baseline. Collectively, such findings suggest that interventions targeting SWB, particularly among youths with lower SWB (Tomyn, Norrish, & Cummins, 2013), can be enhanced if SWB fostering skills and activities are deliberately practiced (Lyubomirsky & Layous, 2013).

TARGETING SPECIFIC SWB DOMAINS FOR INTERVENTION

Although a number of domains may be considered for SWB interventions (see Tomyn & Cummins, 2011), most youth intervention efforts have focused on naturally occurring family, peer, and school experiences (Huebner & Gilman, 2006; Lambert et al., 2014; Van De Wetering, Van Exel, & Brouwer, 2010). The existing literature has been summarized in several publications (e.g., Bird & Markle, 2012; Huebner, Gilman, & Ma, 2012; Proctor et al., 2009), but a more recent summary is provided in the following section.

Within-individual strategies have typically focused on cognitive, affective, and motivational factors that are under volitional control. Examples of such factors include attributional style (Seligman, Reivich, Jaycox, Gillham, & Kidman, 1995), gratitude (Froh et al., 2014; Froh, Kashdan, Ozimkowski, & Miller, 2009), emotion regulation (Furlong, Renshaw, You, Smith, & O'Malley, 2013), and hope (Marques, Lopez, & Pais-Ribiero, 2011). A useful heuristic framework labeled "Values in Action" (Peterson & Seligman, 2004) outlines how several virtues (e.g., wisdom, courage) and character strengths (curiosity, perseverance, modesty) can be amenable to interventions that promote positive SWB in youth (Gillham et al., 2011).

Although much less of a focus, SWB reports are largely influenced by contextual factors, which may be targeted through multisystemic interventions. Indeed, emotional support from social agents, such as parents, peers, teachers, and community members appears crucial to children's and adolescents' SWB (Carboni & Gilman, 2012; Huebner et al., 2012). Critical elements of trust, openness, constructive communication, and accountability for one's actions are key toward adolescents' perceptions of themselves and their value to society (Armezzani & Paduanello, 2013; Siddall, Huebner, & Jiang, 2013). Not surprisingly, conflicts within any one of these elements can significantly reduce SWB levels (Martin & Huebner, 2007).

Although the aforementioned variables appear to be most relevant to SWB interventions, it must be noted that prognosis is explained, in part, by other variables that might be less amenable to change. For example, Ng and Diener (2009) found that the personality trait of neuroticism influenced college students' response to a cognitive reappraisal intervention, such that students who were high on neuroticism were less able to decrease negative emotions than students who were low on neuroticism. As another example, the level of psychological distress present within the individual before intervention, regardless of environmental support, might also attenuate efficacy (Bolier et al., 2013). Nonetheless, much more research is needed to know which youth variables influence response to SWB-fostering strategies. Thus, as with all interventions, professionals need to carefully evaluate the potential efficacy of SWB interventions as applied to youths who have specific intra- and interpersonal challenges (Farrell, Henry, & Bettencourt, 2013).

EVIDENCE-BASED INTERVENTIONS AND EMPIRICAL SUPPORT FOR PROMOTING SWB IN CHILDREN AND ADOLESCENTS

The notion of improving SWB for its own benefit extends back to the 1970s with Michael Fordyce's intervention to improve "happiness" among a general sample of college students (Fordyce, 1977, 1983). Since then, several programs have been designed to promote specific attributes that contribute to SWB, although few interventions have been designed specifically to promote SWB as a whole. However, this is not to state that the benefits of SWB interventions are unknown. For example, a series of meta-analyses examining the efficacy of

SWB interventions reported effect sizes in the small to moderate range (Bolier et al., 2013). As mentioned previously, most SWB interventions focused on adults, with much more research needed with children and adolescents.

Despite the concerns stated earlier, there does appear to be empirical support for youth-focused SWB interventions. Many of these interventions acknowledge the multidimensional and integrative nature of SWB and address one or more of the numerous components that contribute to its development. Such programs include but are not limited to the Penn Resiliency Program (Gillham et al., 2007), the character educational program being piloted in KIPP Foundation charter schools (KIPP Foundation, 2014), well-being therapy (Belaise et al., 2010; Ruini et al., 2009), interventions based on Seligman's Positive emotion, Engagement, positive Relationships, Meaning, Accomplishment/achievement (PERMA) model (Shoshani & Steinmetz, 2014), 40 developmental assets (Search Institute, 2014), and 4-H programs (Lerner et al., 2005). Our review in the following section summarizes interventions and strategies that explicitly aim to boost SWB and/or related constructs such as positive affect and life satisfaction. Put simply, our summary describes interventions that have a primary goal of making youths happier.

Comprehensive Programs

Programs in this category are comprehensive, have multiple components, and are suitable for school-wide use. The universal program currently with the most empirical support, You Can Do It!, is a social-emotional program with scripted lessons that are aimed at building students' social, emotional, and motivational capacity and strengths. The program centers around developing a youth's confidence, persistence, organization, getting along, and resilience in order to eliminate the five negative habits of mind that are barriers to learning and well-being: feeling worried, feeling down, procrastination, lack of attention, and feeling angry (You Can Do It!, n.d.). Although the program is designed for K–12 students, studies conducted thus far have focused on primary grade students with results indicating that students improved in their overall satisfaction with school (a dimension of life satisfaction) as well as their overall social-emotional well-being (Ashdown & Bernard, 2012; Bernard & Walton, 2011).

Other interventions that have been shown to be effective include: (a) a school-based intervention based on Seligman's positive psychology framework, which focuses on gratitude, acts of kindness, development of character strengths, optimistic thinking, and hope (Suldo, Savage, & Mercer, 2013); (b) Positive Action, a social-emotional learning program based on the belief that positive actions lead to positive feelings and thoughts, which is aimed at maximizing positive actions among youth (Lewis et al., 2013); and (c) Strengths Gym, a U.K.-based program that helps students build existing strengths, learn new ones, and recognize strengths in others (Proctor et al., 2011). Two other programs were also effective at increasing well-being–related constructs; first, Building Hope for the Future is a 5-week intervention designed to increase hope, life satisfaction, self-worth, mental health, and academic achievement (Marques et al., 2011). Second, Promotion of Positive Experiences—Children and Youth aims to develop six life skills: stress management, motivation, time management, problem solving, communication, and team work (Gomes & Marques, 2013).

Several other programs have aimed to increase well-being in youths by using evidence-based approaches and activities. For example, the Bounce Back program is a school-wide social-emotional curriculum that uses cooperative learning and educational games to build positive relationships, positive emotions, and teach social-emotional skills (Noble & McGrath, n.d.). Another program, Project Happiness, which encompasses all grade levels and has been implemented by over 100 schools and nongovernmental organizations nationally and 50 internationally, focuses on mindfulness, forgiveness, generosity, and gratitude. In the upper grades, additional components focus on exploring the science of happiness, learning practical tools to cultivate happiness, and engaging in discussions that increase empathy (Project Happiness, 2012). Given the widespread use of these programs and their strong research-based underpinnings, researchers have the opportunity to further examine their effectiveness.

Specific Strategies

A number of stand-alone activities also have support as effective interventions that increase SWB among children and/or adolescents. The activities with the strongest research evidence to support their effectiveness as interventions are mindfulness, gratitude, and acts of kindness. Mindfulness can take many forms, including formal meditations, informal mindfulness-based activities, and mindfulness in therapy settings. Overall, studies to date using adolescent populations indicate positive effects for SWB and positive affect (Huppert & Johnson, 2010; Kuyken et al., 2013; Lau & Hue, 2011; Schonert-Reichl & Lawlor, 2010). Gratitude has been researched in school-based interventions because of the known high correlation between youth self-reported gratitude and general life satisfaction. Specific strategies used to foster youth gratitude have included: (a) counting blessings exercises (Froh et al., 2009), (b) daily journal gratitude reflections (Froh et al., 2009; Owens & Patterson, 2013), and (c) a psychoeducational curriculum to teach children benefit appraisal (Froh et al., 2014; Froh & Bono, 2014). The literature on gratitude interventions among adolescents has indicated that higher levels of gratitude are associated with increased life satisfaction and positive affect, both components of SWB, when compared with control groups. It has been hypothesized that the experience of gratitude evokes a positive development spiral in which gratitude enhances life satisfaction, which builds social integration and ultimately results in greater levels of gratitude (Froh et al., 2009). Consequently, gratitude can be seen as an emotion that acts to instill a sense of bonding among people and communities, a key component of building a positive school climate. Finally, one study found that students who perform acts of altruistic kindness exhibit increased life satisfaction and positive affect on pre- and postcomparisons (Layous, Nelson, Oberle, Schonert-Reichl, & Lyubomirsky, 2012).

HOW TO: A GUIDE TO THE IMPLEMENTATION OF INTERVENTIONS FOR SWB IN CHILDREN AND ADOLESCENTS

Just as SWB represents the complex formation and evolution of a core personal psychological disposition or self-schema, efforts to foster its development will also need to emphasize the implementation of broader programs (e.g., Strengths Gym) and more focused strategies (e.g., fostering gratitude) within each child's development across time and across transactional-ecological domains (e.g., family, school, peer). It is likely that efforts to foster high levels of SWB will need to be sustained from childhood through adolescence, which is why school-based programs are a core consideration, and should address these central considerations.

1. *Determine the model of SWB to be used and select an intervention in concert with the model.* Examples of existing frameworks beyond that of Kim-Prieto et al. (2005) include: (a) Ryff's model of psychological well-being: autonomy, environmental mastery, personal growth, positive relations with others, purpose in life, and self-acceptance (Ryff & Keyes, 1995); (b) the 4-H model of positive youth development (PYD; Lerner et al., 2005), which centers on the "5 Cs": competence, confidence, character, connection, and caring or compassion; (c) the positive educational practices (PEP) framework, which consists of: social and emotional competence, positive emotions, positive relationships, engagement through strengths, and a sense of meaning and purpose in life (Noble & McGrath, 2008); and (d) the PERMA model of SWB—positive emotions, engagement, relationships, meaning, and achievement (Seligman, 2012).

2. *Use valid assessment instruments that are aligned with the chosen model for screening, progress monitoring, and assessment of outcomes.* The choice of assessment measure will depend on the scope of the program (e.g., school wide vs. high-need targeted youths and screening vs. diagnosis). Information about validated tools for measuring SWB and its related constructs is provided in the Select Bibliography section of this chapter.

3. *Decide on a whole school prevention approach or one for students with low SWB.* Because of the variety of available programs, practitioners need to consider whether the desired aim is to have a universal and comprehensive program of prevention and intervention or if the scope of the program is more targeted. School-wide programs may have the benefit of boosting the overall average SWB of students and staff, which would have synergistic effects, although they will also require more staff buy-in, resources,

and planning time in order to execute them effectively (Visani, Albieri, & Ruini, 2014).

4. *Examine the current evidence of program effectiveness.* Currently, the most thoroughly researched program is *You Can Do It!* (Ashdown & Bernard, 2012; Bernard & Walton, 2011). The intervention spans grades 1 to 2 and consists of five units. The first unit introduces students to success, well-being, negative habits of mind, and positive habits of mind. The second unit teaches confidence, the third teaches persistence, the fourth teaches organization, and the fifth teaches getting along with others. In addition to the classroom-based social-emotional learning component, there are parental education components as well as a program targeted for students with behavioral, social, emotional and/or learning difficulties (You Can Do It!, n.d.; see www.youcandoiteducation.com/whatis.html for a complete program description).

On the other hand, schools may choose to use stand-alone strategies either for the whole school or for students of concern who may have diminished SWB. The most effective strategy seems to be mindfulness, which involves focused attention on the present moment without judgment. Recent years have seen an increase in mindfulness-based intervention strategies in order to foster the well-being of individuals across all age spans. Among youth, meditation seems to be gaining traction. Mindfulness involves an intentional directing of attention and an orientation toward one's experiences in the present moment (Bishop et al., 2004). A common mindfulness activity involves awareness of one's breath. For example, participants may be prompted in this way, "Practice paying attention to the tip of your nose or your abdomen. If your attention wanders, gently bring it back to either the tip of your nose or the abdomen. Feel the breath pass through your nose or feel the breath settle in your abdomen. Pay attention only to your breathing" (Britton et al., 2014, p. 268).

Attention can also be directed toward one's thoughts and feelings, with prompts such as "Label thoughts, feelings, and sensations. Thoughts are things in your mind, like, 'I wonder if I did my history homework,' or 'Do you think we'll have a pop quiz?' Feelings are things you feel in your body like hunger or boredom"

(Britton et al., 2014, p. 268). Attention can be directed toward bodily sensations as well, as in body sweeps, where participants are prompted to "sweep" their attention across different parts of the body in successive order (Britton et al., 2014). Participants may also simply be asked to pay attention to any sensations they experience in their bodies, label them, and return to breathing (Britton et al., 2014). Attention can also be directed toward their environment, when participants are asked to become aware of sounds (Huppert & Johnson, 2010).

Mindfulness-based interventions also can go beyond these activities and incorporate additional components such as psychoeducational formats (Britton et al., 2014; Broderick & Metz, 2009; Huppert & Johnson, 2010) and group discussions (Broderick & Metz, 2009). Body-and-breath awareness among sixth graders showed that meditation activities increased positive affect and decreased negative effect more so than an active control group that participated in experiential activities. Quasi-experimental designs have given support to mindfulness based stress reduction (MBSR; Huppert & Johnson, 2010), which incorporates awareness of breathing, sounds, and thoughts as well as a walking meditation; the Mindfulness in Schools Program, which incorporates activities from MBSR and mindfulness based cognitive behavioral therapy (MBCBT; Kuyken et al., 2013); and the Learning to BREATHE program, which includes activities pertaining to awareness of one's body, thoughts, and feelings (Broderick & Metz, 2009). There is also some evidence from a quasi-experimental design that mindfulness training, which incorporates parents as well, has a positive impact on SWB (Bögels, Hoogstad, van Dun, de Schutter, & Restifo, 2008). Burke's (2010) meta-analysis of mindfulness-based interventions for youths indicated promising results for the feasibility of mindfulness meditation practices among children and adolescents but also illuminated the need for more research that addresses positive aspects of psychosocial functioning in addition to negative ones. The Center for Greater Good provides resources about how to implement mindfulness strategies in school (see http://greatergood.berkeley.edu/article/item/eight_tips_for_teaching_mindfulness_in_high_school).

5. *Monitor implementation*. The fidelity of implementation of any program is key in effecting positive change, and, hence, a system for monitoring this should be in place concurrently with intervention implementation. Although some interventions offer scripted lessons that make it easier to check for compliance to the curriculum, other interventions are stand-alone activities that may require more nuanced ways of confirming fidelity of implementation.

CONCLUSION

We are clearly at the infancy stage of this subfield of positive psychology, which means that interested researchers and practitioners have ample opportunities to expand on the existing literature. Ultimately, adults who are motivated to foster positive SWB in youths will need to consider and reconsider what it is that makes children and adolescents happy (Weissbourd, Jones, Anderson, Kahn, & Russel, 2014). Specifically, programs will need to evaluate different pathways that help youths increase the ratio of pleasant to unpleasant affective experiences; that is, assist them experience life with more zest. For example, more information is needed about which practical day-to-day activities, from youths' perspectives, are associated with higher levels of SWB, such as self-determined music listening (e.g., Morinville, Miranda, & Gaudreau, 2013), social video gaming, and social network communications. At the same time, a greater challenge is to help each youth believe that his or her life has meaning and purpose and to support and address the question: "Am I generally satisfied with my life as it has been and do I see a future with purpose linked to personally meaningful goals?" Meaning-making is not a "social skill" that can be just taught. It must emerge out of real-life experiences that coalesce as a self-schema in which the youth sees herself or himself as making a difference in the world now and into the future. With continued efforts at developing programs that increase youths' SWB and more rigorous and numerous studies that assess the effectiveness of such interventions, it is quite possible that in the coming decades we will see a prioritization

of "engendering the positive" in youths (Fava & Ruini, 2003).

Although most of the interventions examined are grounded in a theoretical framework, a majority of them give less attention to the hedonic component of SWB and instead focus on the eudaimonic components that contribute to meaning and purpose in life. This is perhaps why nonpackaged activities, such as those that promote mindfulness, have a greater impact on SWB. In other words, these strategies appear to build the capacity to consider the meaning of life while still enjoying it (Gillham et al., 2011). However, as Reed Larson (2000) and others (e.g., Eryilmaz, 2012) have demonstrated, it is the combination of both enjoyable life experiences and meaningfulness that is the most impactful in predicting overall SWB. The Broaden-and-Build theory (Fredrickson, 2001) postulates that individuals who experience positive emotions are more likely to expand their cognitive and behavioral repertoires. It is this openness to new experiences that allows individuals to be more open to finding happiness and meaning in life. That is, hedonic and eudaimonic openness could be complementary and synergistic. It follows that the most effective programs are likely to be those that balance activities that target increases in both positive affect and meaningful living.

SELECT BIBLIOGRAPHY

Ben-Arieh, A., Casas, F., Frønes, I., & Korbin, J. E. (Eds.). (2014). *Handbook of child well-being: Theories, methods, and policies in global perspective*. Dordrecht, Netherlands: Springer Publishing Company.
This handbook offers a breadth of topics related to child and adolescent well-being.

Center for Greater Good Education. Retrieved from http://greatergood.berkeley.edu/education
This website provides current information and practical applied information about current research, strategies, and comprehensive school-wide programs that foster well-being and positive youth development. This center also offers a summer course for educators to learn how to integrate these strategies into the daily school routine.

Life Satisfaction Rating Scales. Retrieved from www.psych.sc.edu/faculty/Scott_Huebner

Personal Well-Being Index–Children. Retrieved from www.acqol.com.au/iwbg/wellbeing-index/index.php

Social Emotional Health Survey System. Retrieved from www.michaelfurlong.info/research/covitality.html
These sites provide access to measures that can be used to assess aspects of youth SWB.

REFERENCES

Armezzani, M., & Paduanello, M. (2013). Subjective well-being among youth: A study employing the pyramid procedure. *Journal of Constructivist Psychology, 26,* 37–49. doi:10.1080/10720537.2013.732533

Ashdown, D. M., & Bernard, M. E. (2012). Can explicit instruction in social and emotional learning skills benefit the social-emotional development, well-being, and academic achievement of young children? *Early Childhood Education Journal, 39,* 397–405. doi:10.1007/s10643–011-0481-x

Belaise, C., Tomba, E., Offidani, E., Visani, D., Ottolini, F., Bravi, A.,…Fava, G. A. (2010). [What are the differences between well-being therapy and anxiety management in the school setting?]. *Rivista di psichiatria, 45*(5), 290–301.

Bernard, M. E., & Walton, K. (2011). The effect of You Can Do It! Education in six schools on student perceptions of well-being, teaching-learning and relationships. *The Journal of Student Wellbeing, 5,* 22–37. Retrieved from www.ojs.unisa.edu.au/index.php/JSW/article/download/679/560

Bird, J. M., & Markle, R. S. (2012). Subjective well-being in school environments: Promoting positive youth development through evidence-based assessment and intervention. *The American Journal of Orthopsychiatry, 82*(1), 61–66.

Bishop, S. R., Lau, M., Shapiro, S., Carlson, L., Anderson, N. D., Carmody, J.,…Devins, G. (2004). Mindfulness: A proposed operational definition. *Clinical Psychology: Science and Practice, 11,* 230–241. doi:10.1093/clipsy.bph077

Bögels, S., Hoogstad, B., van Dun, L., de Schutter, S., & Restifo, K. (2008). Mindfulness training for adolescents with externalizing disorder and their parents. *Behavioural and Cognitive Psychotherapy, 36,* 193–209. doi:10.1017/S1352465808004190

Bolier, L., Haverman, M., Westerhof, G. J., Riper, H., Smit, F., & Bohlmeijer, E. (2013). Positive psychology interventions: A meta-analysis of randomized controlled studies. *BMC Public Health, 13,* 119.

Britton, W. B., Lepp, N. E., Niles, H. F., Rocha, T., Fisher, N. E., & Gold, J. S. (2014). A randomized controlled pilot trial of classroom-based mindfulness meditation compared to an active control condition in sixth-grade children. *Journal of School Psychology, 52*(3), 263–278.

Broderick, P. C., & Metz, S. (2009). Learning to BREATHE: A pilot trial of a mindfulness curriculum for adolescents. *Advances in School Mental Health Promotion, 2*(1), 35–46.

Burke, C. A. (2010). Mindfulness-based approaches with children and adolescents: A preliminary review of current research in an emergent field. *Journal of Child and Family Studies, 19,* 133–144. doi:10.1007/s10826-009-9282-x.

Carboni, I., & Gilman, R. (2012). Brokers at risk: Gender differences in the effects of structural position on social stress and life satisfaction. *Group dynamics: Theory, research, and practice, 16,* 218–230. doi:10.1037/a0028753

Conway, A. M., Tugade, M. M., Catalino, L. I., & Frederickson, B. L. (2013). The broaden-and-build theory of positive emotions: Form, function, and mechanisms. In S. A. David, I. Boniwell, & A. Conley Ayers (Eds.), *The Oxford handbook of happiness* (pp. 17–34). Oxford, UK: Oxford University Press.

Eryilmaz, A. (2012). A model for subjective well-being in adolescence: Need satisfaction and reasons for living. *Social Indicators Research, 107,* 561–574. doi:10.1007/s11205–011-9863–0

Farrell, A. D., Henry, D. B., & Bettencourt, A. (2013). Methodological challenges examining subgroup differences: Examples from universal school-based youth violence prevention trials. *Prevention Science, 14*(2), 121–133.

Fava, G. A., & Ruini, C. (2003). Development and characteristics of a well-being enhancing psychotherapeutic strategy: Well-being therapy. *Journal of Behavior Therapy and Experimental Psychiatry, 34*(1), 45–63.

Fordyce, M. W. (1977). Development of a program to increase personal happiness. *Journal of Counseling Psychology, 24,* 511–521. doi:10.1037/0022–0167.24.6.511

Fordyce, M. W. (1983). A program to increase happiness: Further studies. *Journal of Counseling*

Psychology, 30, 483–498. doi:10.1037/0022–0167.30.4.483

Fredrickson, B. L. (2001). The role of positive emotions in positive psychology. The broaden-and-build theory of positive emotions. *The American Psychologist, 56*(3), 218–226.

Froh, J. J., & Bono, G. (2014). *Making grateful kids.* West Conshohocken, PA: Templeton Press.

Froh, J. J., Bono, G., Fan, J., Emmons, R. A., Henderson, K., Harris, C.,…Wood, A. M. (2014). Nice thinking! An educational intervention that teaches children to think gratefully. *School Psychology Review, 43*, 132–152.

Froh, J. J., Kashdan, T. B., Ozimkowski, K. M., & Miller, N. (2009). Who benefits the most from a gratitude intervention in children and adolescents? Examining positive affect as a moderator. *The Journal of Positive Psychology, 4*, 408–422. doi:10.1080/17439760902992464

Furlong, M. J., You, S., Renshaw, T. L., Smith, D. C., & O'Malley, M. D. (2013). Preliminary development and validation of the Social and Emotional Health Survey for secondary students. *Social Indicators Research, 117*, 1011–1032. doi:10.1007/s11205–013-0373–0

Fussner, L. M., Leubbe, A. M., & Bell, D. J. (2015). Dynamics of positive emotion regulation: Associations with youth depressive symptoms. *Journal of Abnormal Child Psychology, 43*(3), 475–488. doi:10.1007/s10802–014-9916–3

Gillham, J. E., Reivich, K. J., Freres, D. R., Chaplin, T. M., Shatté, A. J., Samuels, B.,…Seligman, M. E. (2007). School-based prevention of depressive symptoms: A randomized controlled study of the effectiveness and specificity of the Penn Resiliency Program. *Journal of Consulting and Clinical Psychology, 75*(1), 9–19.

Gillham, J., Adams-Deutsch, Z., Werner, J., Reivich, K., Coulter-Heindl, V., Linkins, M.,…Seligman, M. E. P. (2011). Character strengths predict subjective well-being during adolescence. *The Journal of Positive Psychology, 6*, 31–44. doi:10.1080/17439760.2010.536773

Gilman, R., & Huebner, E. S. (2006). Characteristics of adolescents who report very high life satisfaction. *Journal of Youth and Adolescence, 35*, 311–319. doi:10.1007/s10964–006-9036–7

Gilman, R., & Huebner, E. S., & Carboni, I. (2015). Life satisfaction. In S. J. Lopez (Ed.), *The encyclopedia of positive psychology* (2nd ed.). New York, NY: Wiley-Blackwell.

Gilman, R., Huebner, E. S., & Furlong, M. J. (2014). Toward a science and practice of positive psychology in the schools: A conceptual model. In M. J., Furlong, R. Gilman, & E. S. Huebner (Eds.), *Handbook of positive psychology in schools* (2nd ed., pp. 3–11). New York, NY: Routledge/Taylor & Francis.

Gomes, A. R., & Marques, B. (2013). Life skills in educational contexts: Testing the effects of an intervention program. *Educational Studies, 39*, 156–166. doi:10.1080/03055698.2012.689813

Houtrow, A. J., & Okumura, M. J. (2011). Pediatric mental health problems and associated burden on families. *Vulnerable Children and Youth Studies, 6*(3), 222–233.

Huebner, E. S., & Gilman, R. (2006). Students who like and dislike school. *Applied Research in Quality of Life, 2*, 139–150. doi:10.1007/s11482–006-9001–3.

Huebner, E. S., Gilman, R., & Ma, C. (2012). Perceived quality of life of children and youth. In K. C. Land, A. C. Michalos, & M. J. Sirgy (Eds.), *Handbook of social indicators and quality of life research* (pp. 355–372). Berlin, Germany: Springer Publishing Company. doi:10.1007/978–94-007-2421-1_16.

Huebner, E. S., Hills, K. J., Siddall, J., & Gilman, R. (2014). Life satisfaction and schooling. In M. J. Furlong, R. Gilman, & E. S. Huebner (Eds.), *Handbook of positive psychology in the schools* (2nd ed., pp. 192–208). New York, NY: Routledge.

Huppert, F. A., & Johnson, D. M. (2010). A controlled trial of mindfulness training in schools: The importance of practice for an impact on well-being. *The Journal of Positive Psychology, 5*, 264–274. doi:10.1080/17439761003794148

Keyes, C. L. M., & Haidt, J. (2003). Introduction: Human flourishing. In C. L. M. Keyes & J. Haidt (Eds.), *Flourishing: Positive psychology and the life well-lived* (pp. 3–12). Washington, DC: American Psychological Association.

Kim-Prieto, C., Diener, E., Tamir, M., Scollon, C. N., & Diener, M. (2005). Integrating the diverse definitions of happiness: A time-sequential framework of subjective well-being. *Journal of Happiness Studies: An Interdisciplinary Periodical on Subjective Well-Being, 6*, 261–300. doi:10.1007/s10902–005-7226–8

KIPP Foundation. (2014). *Character at KIPP.* Retrieved from www.kipp.org/our-approach/character

Kuyken, W., Weare, K., Ukoumunne, O. C., Vicary, R., Motton, N., Burnett, R.,…Huppert, F.

(2013). Effectiveness of the mindfulness in schools programme: Non-randomised controlled feasibility study. *The British Journal of Psychiatry, 203*(2), 126–131.

Lambert, M., Fleming, T., Ameratunga, S., Robinson, E., Crengle, S., Sheridan, J.,...Merry, S. (2014). Looking on the bright side: An assessment of factors associated with adolescents' happiness. *Advances in Mental Health*. Advanced online publication. doi:10.5172/jamh.2013.4289

Land, K. C., Lamb, V. L., & Zheng, H. (2011). How are the kids doing? How do we know? *Social Indicators Research, 100*, 463–477. doi:10.1007/s11205–010-9624–5

Larson, R. W. (2000). Toward a psychology of positive youth development. *The American Psychologist, 55*(1), 170–183.

Lau, N. S., & Hue, M. T. (2011). Preliminary outcomes of a mindfulness-based program for Hong Kong adolescents in schools: Well-being, stress and depressive symptoms. *International Journal of Children's Spirituality, 16*, 315–330. doi:10.1080/1364436X.2011.639747

Layous, K., Nelson, S. K., Oberle, E., Schonert-Reichl, K. A., & Lyubomirsky, S. (2012). Kindness counts: Prompting prosocial behavior in preadolescents boosts peer acceptance and well-being. *PloS One, 7*(12), e51380.

Lerner, R. M., Lerner, J. V., Almerigi, J. B., Theokas, C., Phelps, E., Gestsdottir, S.,...von Eye, A. (2005). Positive youth development, participation in community youth development programs, and community contributions of fifth-grade adolescents findings from the first wave of the 4-H study of Positive Youth Development. *The Journal of Early Adolescence, 25*, 17–71. doi:10.1177/0272431604272461

Lewis, K. M., DuBois, D. L., Bavarian, N., Acock, A., Silverthorn, N., Day, J.,...Flay, B. R. (2013). Effects of positive action on the emotional health of urban youth: A cluster-randomized trial. *The Journal of Adolescent Health, 53*(6), 706–711.

Lyubomirsky, S., & Layous, K. (2013). How do simple positive activities increase well-being? *Current Directions in Psychological Science, 22*, 57–62. doi:10.1177/0963721412469809.

Marques, S. C., Lopez, S. J., & Pais-Ribeiro, J. L. (2011). Building hope for the future: A program to foster strengths in middle school students. *Journal of Happiness Studies, 12*, 139–152. doi:10.1007/s10902–009-9180–3

Martin, K. M., & Huebner, E. S. (2007). Peer victimization and prosocial experiences and emotional well-being of middle school students. *Psychology in the Schools, 44*, 199–208.

McKnight, C. G., Huebner, E. S., & Suldo, S. (2002). Relationships among stressful life events, temperament, problem behavior, and global life satisfaction in adolescents. *Psychology in the Schools, 39*, 677–687. doi:10.1002/pits.10062

Morinville, A., Miranda, D., & Gaudreau, P. (2013). Music listening motivation is associated with global happiness in Canadian late adolescents. *Psychology of Aesthetics, Creativity, and the Arts, 7*, 384–390. doi:10.1037/a0034495

Ng, W., & Diener, E. (2009). Personality differences in emotions: Does emotion regulation play a role? *Journal of Individual Differences, 30*, 100–106. doi:10.1027/1614–0001.30.2.100

Noble, T., & McGrath, H. (2008). The positive educational practices framework: A tool for facilitating the work of educational psychologists in promoting pupil well-being. *Educational and Child Psychology, 25*, 119–134. Retrieved from http://hdl.handle.net/10536/DRO/DU:30018015

Noble, T., & McGrath, H. (n.d.). *Bounce back!* Retrieved from www.bounceback.com.au/

Owens, R. L., & Patterson, M. M. (2013). Positive psychological interventions for children: A comparison of gratitude and best possible selves approaches. *The Journal of Genetic Psychology, 174*(4), 403–428.

Peterson, C., & Seligman, M. E. P. (2004). *Character strengths and virtues: A handbook and classification*. Washington, DC: APA Press and Oxford University Press.

Proctor, C. L., Linley, P. A., & Maltby, J. (2009). Youth life satisfaction: A review of the literature. *Journal of Happiness Studies, 10*, 583–630. doi:10.1007/s10902–008-9110–9

Proctor, C., Tsukayama, E., Wood, A. M., Maltby, J., Eades, J. F., & Linley, P. A. (2011). Strengths Gym: The impact of a character strengths-based intervention on the life satisfaction and well-being of adolescents. *The Journal of Positive Psychology, 6*, 377–388. doi:10.1080/17439760.2011.594079

Project Happiness. (2012). *Project happiness*. Retrieved from http://projecthappiness.org/

Ruini, C., Ottolini, F., Tomba, E., Belaise, C., Albieri, E., Visani, D.,...Fava, G. A. (2009). School intervention for promoting psychological well-being in adolescence. *Journal of Behavior Therapy and Experimental Psychiatry, 40*(4), 522–532.

Ryff, C. D., & Keyes, C. L. (1995). The structure of psychological well-being revisited. *Journal of Personality and Social Psychology, 69*(4), 719–727.

Schonert-Reichl, K. A., & Lawlor, M. S. (2010). The effects of a mindfulness-based education program on pre-and early adolescents' well-being and social and emotional competence *Mindfulness, 1*, 137–151. doi:10.1007/s12671–010-0011–8

Search Institute. (2014). *40 developmental assets for adolescents*. Retrieved from http://www.search-institute.org/content/40-developmental-assets-adolescents-ages-12-18

Seligman, M. E. P. (2012). *Flourish: A visionary new understanding of happiness and well-being*. New York, NY: Free Press.

Seligman, M. E. P., Reivich, K., Jaycox, L., Gillham, J., & Kidman, A. D. (1995). *The optimistic child*. New York, NY: Houghton Mifflin.

Shoshani, A., & Steinmetz, S. (2014). Positive psychology at school: A school-based intervention to promote adolescents' mental health and well-being. *Journal of Happiness Studies, 15*, 1289–1311. doi:10.1007/s10902–013-9476–1

Siddall, J., Huebner, E. S., & Jiang, X. (2013). A prospective study of differential sources of school-related social support and adolescent global life satisfaction. *The American Journal of Orthopsychiatry, 83*(1), 107–114.

Suldo, S. M., & Huebner, E. S. (2004). Does life satisfaction moderate the effects of stressful life events on psychopathological behavior during adolescence? *School Psychology Quarterly, 19*, 93–105. doi:10.1521/scpq.19.2.93.33313

Suldo, S. M., Savage, J. A., & Mercer, S. H. (2013). Increasing middle school students' life satisfaction: Efficacy of a positive psychology group intervention. *Journal of Happiness Studies, 15*, 19–42. doi:10.1007/s10902–013-9414–2

Suldo, S. M., & Shaffer, E. J. (2008). Looking beyond psychopathology: The dual-factor model of mental health in youth. *School Psychology Review, 37*, 52–68.

Tomyn, A. J., & Cummins, R. A. (2011). Subjective wellbeing and homeostatically protected mood:

Theory validation with adolescents, *Journal of Happiness Studies, 12*, 897–914. doi:10.1007/s10902–010-9235–5

Tomyn, A. J., Cummins, R. A., & Norrish, J. M. (2014). The subjective wellbeing of "at-risk" indigenous and non-indigenous Australian adolescents. *Journal of Happiness Studies*, Advanced online publication. doi:10.1007/s10902–014-9535–2

Tomyn, A. J., Norrish, J. M., & Cummins, R. A. (2013). The subjective wellbeing of indigenous Australian adolescents: Validating the personal wellbeing index-school children. *Social Indicators Research, 110*, 1013–1031. doi:10.1007/s11205–011-9970-y

Van De Wetering, E. J., Van Exel, N. J. A., & Brouwer, W. B. (2010). Piecing the jigsaw puzzle of adolescent happiness. *Journal of Economic Psychology, 31*, 923–935. doi:10.1016/j.joep.2010.08.004

Veenhoven, R. (2013). The four qualities of life ordering concepts and measures of the good life. In A. Della Fave (Ed.), *The exploration of happiness: Present and future perspectives* (pp. 195–226). Dordrecht, Netherlands: Springer Publishing Company. doi:10.1007/978–94-007–5702-8_11

Visani, D., Albieri, E., & Ruini, C. (2014). School programs for the prevention of mental health problems and the promotion of psychological well-being in children. In A. Delle Fave (series Ed.), *Cross-cultural advances in positive psychology*, G. A. Fava & C. Ruini, C. (volume 8 Eds.), *Increasing psychological well-being in clinical and educational settings* (pp. 177–185). Dordrecht, Netherlands: Springer Publishing Company. doi:10.1007/978–94-017–8669-0_11

Weissbournd, R., & Jones, S., with Anderson, T. R., Kahn, J., & Russel, M., (2014). *The children we mean to raise: The real message adults are sending about values*. Cambridge, MA: Making Caring Common Project, Harvard Graduate school of Education. Retrieved from http://sites.gse.harvard.edu/sites/default/files/making-caring-common/files/mcc_report_7.2.14.pdf

You Can Do It! (n.d.). *You Can Do It! Education: A new generation of resources for improving student outcomes*. Retrieved from http://www.youcandoiteducation.com/pdf/Brochure-US-3-08.pdf

PART

Physical Conditions and Health-Related Disorders

Evidence-Based Interventions for Eating Disorders in Children and Adolescents

Catherine Cook-Cottone and Rebecca K. Vujnovic

OVERVIEW

Eating disorders (EDs) are a complex and comparatively dangerous set of mental disorders that deeply affect the quality of life and well-being of the child or adolescent who is struggling with this problem as well as those who love and care for him or her (Cook-Cottone, 2006). The three major EDs (i.e., anorexia nervosa [AN], bulimia nervosa [BN], and binge ED [BED]) share a core characteristic: difficulty with self-regulation that manifests primarily as a persistent disturbance of eating behavior and difficulties with how one experiences the embodied self, or the self that one chooses to be and one's relationship with his or her world (Cook-Cottone, Tribole, & Tylka, 2013). Of particular concern is the increase in the prevalence and incidence of EDs among children and adolescents at progressively younger ages, with an estimated 119% increase in the rates of hospitalizations of children and adolescents with AN, BN, and BED between 1999 and 2006 (Agency for Healthcare Research and Quality [AHRQ], 2009; Hudson, Hiripi, Pope, & Kessler, 2007). It is estimated that approximately 0.3% to 0.5% of adolescent girls in the United States have AN, approximately 0.9% to 2% meet diagnostic criteria for BN, 1.6% meet criteria for BED, and that up to 5% to 10% of all

cases of EDs occur in males (Hoek & van Hoeken, 2003; Rosen, 2010; Swanson, Crow, Le Grange, Swendsen, & Merikangas, 2011). However, actual prevalence rates may be difficult to estimate because of the low prevalence rates for EDs in the general population and the secrecy associated with eating disordered behaviors amongst those who struggle with these disorders (Hoek & van Hoeken, 2003). Furthermore, actual prevalence rates of children and adolescents meeting full diagnostic criteria do not account for children and adolescents with subthreshold EDs, or those who engage in eating disordered behaviors but do not meet the stringent diagnostic criteria. Such prevalence rates have been estimated at 0.8% to 4.6% (Stice, Marti, Shaw, & Jaconis, 2009; Swanson et al., 2011).

The *Diagnostic and Statistical Manual of Mental Disorders* (5th ed.; *DSM-5*; American Psychiatric Association [APA], 2013) outlines specific criteria for the diagnosis of AN, BN, BED, and other specified feeding or ED. According to the *DSM-5*, AN is characterized by three critical features: (a) the refusal to maintain a healthy body weight through the restriction of caloric intake; (b) an intense fear of gaining weight; and (c) a disturbance in body image (APA, 2013). BN is another type of ED, characterized by (a) episodes of binge eating (eating a significantly large quantity of food in combination with a sense of lack of control over eating);

(b) followed by engagement in compensatory behaviors intended to prevent weight gain (i.e., vomiting, use of laxatives, diuretics, and excessive exercise), with both binging and compensatory behaviors occurring at least once a week for a period of at least 3 months (APA, 2013). The *DSM-5* characterizes BED by the engagement in compulsive eating (eating a significantly large quantity of food in combination with a sense of lack of control over eating), with marked feelings of distress during or after binging behaviors. Unlike BN, individuals with BED do not engage in compensatory behaviors to compensate for the binge (APA, 2013). The median age of onset for AN, BN, and BED is 12 to 13 years of age (Swanson et al., 2011). However, concerns related to body shape and weight have been evident among girls as young as 6 years of age, with 40% to 60% of elementary school-aged girls reporting weight-related concerns (Smolak, 2011).

According to the *DSM-5*, bipolar depression and anxiety disorders are commonly comorbid with diagnoses of AN and BED (APA, 2013). Many individuals with EDs report a diagnosis of an anxiety disorder or symptoms of anxiety before the onset of ED (APA, 2013). Similarly, co-occurring disorders among individuals with BN include depressive and other mood disorders, anxiety disorders, substance use disorders (SUDs), and associated personality disorders (APA, 2013). Finally, BED is also associated with anxiety, mood, and bipolar disorders (APA, 2013). More alarming than these comorbidities is the fact that EDs are associated with elevated rates of mortality, with AN known to have the highest documented rates of mortality among all other EDs and other mental health disorders (Arcelus, Mitchell, Wales, & Nielsen, 2011; Crisp, Callender, Halek, & Hsu, 1992; Crow et al., 2009).

ETIOLOGY AND FACTORS CONTRIBUTING TO EDS IN CHILDREN AND ADOLESCENTS

Negative body image, internalization of societal appearance, body surveillance, body comparison, and poor introspective awareness have been identified as ED risk factors related to maladaptive outcomes, including increased substance use, suicide, mortality, decreased social adjustment, and impaired interpersonal relationships (Cook-Cottone et al., 2013). Thus, individual and ecological factors

may contribute to maladaptive eating behaviors. The Attuned Representation Model of Self (ARMS; Cook-Cottone, 2006) defines the internal system (i.e., cognitive, emotional, and physiological) and the external system (i.e., family, community, and cultural) as two interdependent schemas interconnected by "attunement," or the ability to appropriately listen and to engage in adaptive behaviors to respond appropriately to the physical sensations of the body (Cook-Cottone et al., 2013). Attunement is the foundation of intuitive eating, allowing the individual to implement principles of healthy eating and external ideals, while honoring the individual's internal dynamics and physical sensations of the body (e.g., fullness, hunger, and taste). The representational self represents an attunement between the self and cultural systems (Cook-Cottone et al., 2013). The ARMS model of self acknowledges biological, psychological, and sociocultural factors and highlights the interactions among such factors that contribute to maladaptive eating behaviors (Cook-Cottone et al., 2013; Tylka & Kroon Van Diest, in press). Thus, symptoms of EDs emerge when the influences from the self and cultural systems lack attunement, thus creating risk (Cook-Cottone et al., 2013). For example, media pressure to be thin may drive a child or adolescent to internalize the thin ideal, resulting in the acknowledgement of hunger cues and restricting food intake. This results in the failure to experience attunement between the self and cultural systems, whereas the healthy self (the authentic or attuned self) effectively negotiates thoughts, feelings, and physical needs while navigating external systems in the family, community, and culture (Cook-Cottone et al., 2013). Thus, eating disordered behaviors fill the void between internal and external systems in a child or adolescent without the experience of attunement, creating a self-reinforcing disorder, as the child becomes increasingly more attuned to the maladaptive behaviors.

EVIDENCE-BASED INTERVENTIONS AND EMPIRICAL SUPPORT FOR EDS IN CHILDREN AND ADOLESCENTS

In reviewing evidence-based interventions for EDs, it is important to note that most of the research in this area has been conducted on young, adult females with more research needed on children, younger adolescents, males, and older individuals of both genders. However, overall, treatment of eating disordered behavior typically involves a three-facet approach: (a) medical assessment and monitoring, (b) nutritional counseling, and (c) psychological and behavioral treatment. Ideally, the three arms of treatment work together to bring the client toward a healthier and more intuitive relationship with eating and nutrition, to develop a practice of healthy physical activity, and to cultivate self-care and emotion-regulation practices (Cook-Cottone et al., 2013). Furthermore, client-specific and disorder-specific goals for treatment may be integrated (e.g., assertiveness training, and communications skills). Some treatments described in the following discussion address all three facets of ED treatment (i.e., medical, nutritional, and psychological), whereas others address only the psychological and behavioral components as these interventions address only the psychological aspects of the disorder. For example, cognitive behavioral therapy (CBT) addresses the distorted thinking patterns and behaviors associated with eating-disordered behaviors. However, the protocol does not integrate ongoing medical assessment and nutritional education and meal planning. A psychologist working with CBT would support the patient as he or she works with a medical doctor and a nutritionist on those aspects of treatment. Beyond the psychological intervention chosen, all three facets must be addressed.

Anorexia Nervosa

Because of the low incidence of AN, the challenges inherent in researching this population (i.e., treatment resistance, individuals who are at various stages of treatment or recovery, suffer from a variety of physical limitations, or are on a variety of medications), result in insufficient power to show effects (Grilo, 2006; Hartmann, Weber, Herpertz, Zeeck, & the German Treatment Guideline Group for Anorexia Nervosa, 2011; Smith & Cook-Cottone, 2011). Accordingly, more high-quality research is needed in this area. Currently, practitioners use the current available research, case studies, and a long history of clinical work with patients with AN to guide their efforts. There is no evidence to support the use of atypical antipsychotic medications or any other medication for

the treatment of AN (Kishi, Kafantaris, Sunday, Sheridan, & Correll, 2012; Lebow, Sim, Erwin, & Murad, 2013).

A critical aspect of treatment for children and adolescents with AN is weight restoration and nutritional rehabilitation (Grilo, 2006). This aspect of treatment is often the charge of the nutritionist and the medical doctor on the treatment team. For those in outpatient care, the nutritionist and/or medical doctor work with the client to create a meal plan. Regular nutrition/medical sessions are conducted to ensure compliance and progress. Starvation is believed to exacerbate a variety of possibly pre-existing neuropsychological and mental health challenges, such as rigidity in thinking, excessive focus on detail, anxiety, depression, and difficulty with problem solving (Cook-Cottone et al., 2013; Lock et al., 2013; Smith & Cook-Cottone, 2011). As weight is restored and nutritional status stabilized, youths may experience improvement in psychological adjustment (Grilo, 2006). Weight restoration and nutritional aspects of interventions are done either as the first phase of treatment or as a parallel treatment with psychological interventions (Hartmann et al., 2011). Parental psychoeducation is helpful as they learn not only about the disorder properly, but how to help their child (Holtkamp, Herpertz-Dahlmann, Vloet, & Hagenah, 2005).

Within the past 20 years, family-based interventions have been developed that address these issues within the home and family context. The Maudsley Method is an intensive outpatient, family-based intervention for AN that addresses refeeding within the home setting (Minuchin, Rosman, & Baker, 1978; Smith & Cook-Cottone, 2011). Refeeding is a process of increasing calorie intake and nutritional value of food with a goal of helping the patient increase weight and regain a stable health status (Kohn, Madden, & Clarke, 2011). Overall, this intervention is aligned with strategic family therapy and holds the family as central to recovery; therapists work to empower the family giving them tools to support refeeding and nutritional rehabilitation (Smith & Cook-Cottone, 2011). The treatment goals include: (a) restoration of weight to normal levels, (b) client control over eating, and (c) return to normal adolescent developmental challenges (for a review see Smith & Cook-Cottone, 2011). The first two goals were designed to replicate the initial stage of treatment conducted in inpatient sessions (Smith & Cook-Cottone, 2011). Thus, the therapist works with the youth's parents, teaching them to support meal plan compliance, observing the family's eating patterns, and facilitating parental development of the most effective ways to support eating (Smith & Cook-Cottone, 2011). Once the client makes solid weight gain (i.e., 90% of expected body weight for height), the parents then gradually decrease their engagement in and monitoring of food intake, releasing responsibility and control to the client.

CBT and interpersonal psychotherapy (IPT) are also evidence-based approaches to treatment for AN (Lock et al., 2013). Typically, CBT interventions explore cues and triggers, cognitions, emotions, and associated behaviors within the context of the near and longer-term consequences. Short-term consequences include the discomfort involved in eating and feeling full. Longer-term consequences include ongoing weight loss, possible inpatient placement, and need for devices such as feeding tubes. Frequently addressed cognitive distortions include conceptualizing foods as safe and not safe (i.e., good and bad), as well as the irrational fear of weight gain and loss of control. Modifications to traditional CBT for use with the AN populations and IPT treatment often address issues such as perfectionism, body image disturbance, internalization of excessively thin media ideals, poor distress tolerance, difficulties with feelings identification and emotional problem solving, low self-esteem, and interpersonal problems (Cook-Cottone et al., 2013; Hartmann et al., 2011).

In addition, more recent research has explored cognitive remediation therapy (CRT), which addresses the problematic cognitive style often experienced by patients with AN (e.g., inflexibility, excessive detail orientation, and weak central coherence; Lock et al., 2013). It is believed that by improving the cognitive processes, other related behavioral and psychosocial problems will also be improved (Lock et al., 2013). This intervention integrates practical cognitive exercises and discussions about the relevance of how ways of thinking and processing information can affect a patient's everyday life.

Specifically, this intervention addresses the *process* rather than the content of thinking. The intervention is designed to help patients develop a metacognitive awareness of their own thinking patterns and habits. The treatment provider helps the patient to identify and then focus on his or her unique cognitive impairments. Next, the provider helps bring awareness to current thinking processes and explore alternative strategies. By becoming aware of problematic cognitive patterns, the patient can reflect on how these affect everyday life. For example, patients with AN frequently present rigid and inflexible thinking patterns. Bringing awareness to this tendency and encouraging a more flexible, open, and accepting approach to problem solving provide a cognitive framework for more adaptive functioning.

As currently implemented, there is no direct focus on weight, eating, or eating-related psychopathology. CRT provides manualized, remediation exercises; initial sessions introduce and teach various cognitive exercises and further sessions encourage the client to reflect on his or her performance on the cognitive tasks and behaviors he or she is manifesting in real life (Tchanturia & Hambrook, 2009). Sessions include discussion, development of cognitive skills, and exploration of how the exercises might be helpful in life (Lock et al., 2013). Similar to CBT, later sessions require a youth to engage in explicit behavioral tasks in his or her real environment and process these experiences in session. The intervention is typically eight sessions in length with each session lasting for about 45 to 60 minutes. The manualized sessions include 8 to 10 processing tasks followed by conversations associated with the tasks.

Medical treatment and monitoring are critical to assess need for inpatient care at the commencement of treatment, addressing weight restoration and providing nutritional rehabilitation. Currently, the Maudsley Method, modified CBT and IPT, as well as other emerging interventions (i.e., CRT) are the current standard of practice.

Bulimia Nervosa

IPT and CBT are considered the treatments of choice for BN, with dialectical behavior therapy (DBT) emerging as a promising intervention (Erford et al., 2013; Grilo, 2006; Lavender et al., 2012; McIntosh, Carter, Bulik, Frampton, & Joyce, 2010). First, IPT addresses interpersonal concerns and problems that can be associated with low self-esteem and emotional distress. This model posits that eating behaviors and food are used to help the client cope with negative feelings and distress and that purging is compensatory for bingeing (Grilo, 2006). IPT helps the client to improve interpersonal functioning, decrease emotional distress, and improve self-esteem thereby removing the driving forces underlying bingeing and purging behaviors. Thus, if treatment is progressing well, the patient binges and purges less and experiences a more positive attitude regarding the importance of weight and shape (Grilo, 2006). There is some evidence to support the use of IPT; however, CBT, modified DBT (i.e., DBT with ED-specific content added), and other innovations (see what follows) have comparatively stronger outcomes (Grilo, 2006; McIntosh et al., 2010).

CBT is a multicomponent treatment including the normalization of eating; pscyhoeducation; identifying and consequently challenging overvalued cognitions about food, eating, weight, and shape; identifying cues for bulimic behaviors; use of strategies to decrease bulimic behaviors; and relapse prevention (Grilo, 2006; McIntosh et al., 2010). These strategies include the management of triggers or cues, exposure and response prevention (ERP), and relapse prevention (McIntosh et al., 2010). It is important to note that some forms of CBT for the treatment of BN do not include ERP. Furthermore, ERP can be implemented differently, either by (a) exposure to prepurge cues in which foods high risk for purging are eaten (P-ERP) or by (b) prebinge cue exposure in which cues for bingeing such as the sight and smell of foods are presented, but no food is eaten (B-ERP; McIntosh et al., 2010).

A review of literature suggests overall large effect sizes for the employment of CBT for bulimic behaviors (i.e., bingeing, AN, and purging) and psychological features of BN (McIntosh et al., 2010). As CBT interventions involve various components, researchers are working to identify the exact effective mechanism within CBT interventions. Modest, but superior effects have been found for CBT with B-ERP (i.e., prebinge cue exposure in which cues for bingeing such as the sight and smell of foods are presented, but no food is eaten), but not P-ERP (i.e., exposure to prepurge cues in which foods high risk for purging are eaten), when used for reduced cue reactivity, food restriction, body dissatisfaction, and depression (McIntosh, et al., 2010). Moreover, research shows a maintenance in long-term abstinence from binge eating and B-ERP and P-ERP had lower rates of purging (McIntosh et al., 2010).

Overall, the effects of CBT have been found to be superior to other treatment modalities (e.g., behavioral therapy, short-term psychotherapy, family therapy, and pharmacotherapy; Erford et al., 2013). The success of CBT with BN is believed to be due, in part, to the remediation of cognitive distortions regarding body shape and size (Erford et al., 2013). Furthermore, the effects of CBT may also be associated with additional therapeutic components that address training in assertiveness, communication skills, problem solving, and social skills (Erford et al., 2013). Of note, there is some evidence that shorter, group-based CBT interventions may be effective (e.g., Jones & Clausen, 2013).

According to the American Psychological Association's statement on evidence-based practices, research, clinical expertise, and patient characteristics are all relevant to beneficial outcomes (Levant & Hasan, 2008). Treatments must be individualized to address each patient's specific area of struggle. For example, if a patient understands the interpersonal dynamics and history of the manifestation of his or her eating problems, has developed a solid set of coping skills and a support network, yet continues to struggle with the behavioral aspects of the disorder, ERP may be a good approach. Conversely, a patient who is continually triggered by interpersonal stressors, has little insight into his or her coping, and does not yet have a set of strategies to negotiate stress, interpersonal therapy may be most effective.

DBT, considered a mindfulness-based therapy intended to increase an individual's ability to experience the present moment with openness and purposes (Musada & Hill, 2013), is considered a comprehensive and empirically validated treatment for affect regulation, addressing four areas of functioning: emotional regulation, distress tolerance, mindfulness, and interpersonal effectiveness (Musada & Hill, 2013; Safer, Telch, & Agras, 2001). Dysregulation is posited to evolve from the dynamic between emotional sensitivity and subjection to an invalidating environment (Bankoff,

Karpel, Forbes, & Pantalone, 2012). Modifications to DBT for clients with BN have included the removal of the interpersonal effectiveness module, individual sessions, group sessions, and the addition of ED-specific content (Bankoff et al., 2012). ED-specific content added to DBT includes mindful eating and self-monitoring of eating behaviors and urges (Bankoff et al., 2012). Effective ways to modify DBT interventions for EDs are being developed, such as integration into family therapy (Astrachan-Fletcher, 2013). Specifically, family-based DBT involves teaching the family members the skills of mindfulness, distress tolerance, emotional regulation, and interpersonal effectiveness, along with the client, so that family members can help each other with skill acquisition. Overall, DBT as a treatment for BN may help reduce binge/purge behaviors, improve mood and affect, and increase patient retention in treatment (Bankoff et al., 2012; Safer et al., 2001).

Researchers have recently provided exploratory data on the use of mindfulness and yoga approaches to recovery of BN (e.g., Carei, Fyfe-Johnson, Breuner, & Brown, 2010; Cook-Cottone, Beck, & Kane, 2008; Klein & Cook-Cottone, 2013). The integration of mind and body and increased internal awareness are viewed as key mechanisms of change (Carei et al., 2010; Cook-Cottone, 2006; Cook-Cottone et al., 2008). When participating in mindfulness and yoga interventions, clients learn how to manage their breathing and develop self-awareness. There has been a range of interventions that includes a variety of mindfulness and yoga techniques. For example, Carei et al. (2010) used an individual approach focusing on yoga practice, whereas Cook-Cottone et al. (2008) integrated yoga practice with modified DBT sessions designed to address body image, media literacy, emotional regulation, and interpersonal effectiveness. Studies found decreases in ED symptoms and decreases in food preoccupation after sessions (Carei et al., 2010) and reduced drive for thinness and body dissatisfaction (Cook-Cottone et al., 2008).

More recently, researchers have been exploring the effectiveness of guided self-help in the treatment of BN (e.g., Beintner, Jacobi, & Schmidt, 2014; Erford et al., 2013). Erford and colleagues (2013) define self-help as interventions that are performed primarily by an individual with or without guidance from a mental health practitioner,

whereas Beintner and colleagues (2014) restricted the definition of self-help interventions to those that provided a manualized intervention book, a CD-ROM or an Internet program with subsequent sessions and preassigned content. In an extensive meta-analysis using a random-effects model, Erford et al. (2013) reviewed studies over a 30-year period, finding that both counseling/psychotherapy and guided self-help approaches appear to result in clinically significant reductions in bingeing, purging, laxative use, self-reported bulimia ratings, and body dissatisfaction ratings. Self-help interventions show promise for longer-term effects than those of counseling/psychotherapy (Erford et al., 2013).

Finally, there is some evidence that medication may improve outcomes (Shapiro et al., 2007). In an extensive systematic review of randomized controlled trials, Shapiro et al., (2007) found promise for several medications and good evidence that fluoxetine (at a dose of 60 mg/d) reduced short-term core bulimic symptoms (i.e., bingeing and purging) and associated psychological features. Research examining the additive effects of medication on psychological interventions (i.e., CBT, IPT, and DBT) suggests that combined drugs and behavioral interventions offered preliminary and weak evidence for incremental efficacy (Shapiro et al., 2007).

Overall, it is difficult to recommend one clearly supported pathway for the most effective treatment of BN. First, IPT presents with some empirical support. Next, CBT shows efficacy with more research needed to further specify the best treatment modality (e.g., individual, group, or self-help) and the exact mechanisms of change. Finally, DBT has emerged as a compelling intervention with many modifications at this point, little replication, and a need for comparative research.

Binge Eating Disorder

New to the *DSM-5* as a distinct ED, BED has a comparatively smaller body of research. In a meta-analysis of the effectiveness of psychological and pharmacological treatments for BED, Vocks and colleagues (2010) found large effect sizes for psychological therapy (e.g., CBT and IPT) for the reduction of binge eating. Furthermore, the most effective treatment strategies are those that directly address disturbed eating patterns and their antecedents in the reduction of binge eating. Antecedents vary from person to person and can include meal skipping, poor meal planning, fatigue, interpersonal and daily stressors, mood dysregulation, intense or seemingly intolerable feelings, and boredom. Other effects of therapy include the reduction of overconcern with eating, weight, and shape and improving eating and body-related cognitions (Vocks et al., 2010). DBT also shows promise for those diagnosed with BED (Klein et al., 2013; Musada & Hill, 2013). Most DBT approaches for BED have been adapted in some way to address eating issues and to make participation more manageable for clients. Specifically, DBT for BED (DBT-BED) aims to reduce binge eating by improving emotion-regulation skills (Safer, Robinson, & Jo, 2010). The mechanism of change is believed to be the link between the youth's attempts to influence, change, or control painful emotional states via binge eating behaviors (Safer et al., 2010). Evidence suggests that modified DBT may be as effective as other forms of therapy (Safer et al., 2010). Musada and Hill (2013) note that DBT may be especially helpful for children and adolescents with comorbid psychiatric conditions such as borderline personality disorder (BPD) and SUD (Musada & Hill, 2013). Outcomes include lower dropout rates, reductions in behavioral and attitudinal features of disordered eating, reduction in substance use, and improved mood regulation (Klein et al., 2013; Musada & Hill, 2013). Furthermore, self-help has been found to be effective in reducing binge-eating frequency as well as associated cognitive symptoms such as concerned with eating, weight, and shape (Beintner et al., 2014; Vocks et al., 2010).

Recent promise has been found for the integration of mindfulness-based techniques into more conventional protocols, including mindfulness-based eating-awareness training (MB-EAT; Musada & Hill, 2013). Specifically designed for individuals with BED, this intervention is an integration of mindfulness and meditation exercises designed to enhance overall awareness (e.g., breath and body cognizance) and eating-specific mindfulness (e.g., mindful eating; Musada & Hill, 2013). Furthermore, the MB-EAT helps those with BED develop and practice nonjudgmental awareness and acceptance of thoughts, feelings, and physical sensations (Musada & Hill, 2013). The MB-EAT research demonstrates that this treatment reduces the frequency of binge days, compulsive overeating,

and decreases depressive symptoms (Musada & Hill, 2013).

Overall, therapy has been found to help reduce BED behaviors and enhance psychological outcomes. This includes CBT, IPT, and modified DBT. Structured self-help interventions are also helpful with more research needed to investigate the level of support required for effective change.

HOW TO: A GUIDE TO THE IMPLEMENTATION OF INTERVENTIONS FOR EDs IN CHILDREN AND ADOLESCENTS

For each ED, there are shared treatment components that are particularly salient at the commencement of treatment. These include:

- In the outpatient setting, establish a treatment team with expertise in working with clients with EDs that includes a medical doctor, nutritionist, and a mental health professional (e.g., psychologist, mental health counselor, or social worker).
  - Ensure that your client completes all necessary release of information forms to ensure ease of treatment team communication.
  - Verify that the youth continues to be regularly monitored by a nutritionist trained in the treatment of EDs to adjust meal plans as needed.
- Complete a full medical evaluation. ED-specific medical evaluation addresses the following: amenorrhea, presence of lanugo hair, erosion of tooth enamel from vomiting, partoid gland swelling, gastroesophageal reflux, arrhythmias, refeeding syndrome, osteoporosis, and electrolyte abnormalities such as hypokalemia. Providers must also remain alert for disordered eating in female athletes (the female athlete triad) and disordered eating in diabetics (Walsh, Wheat, & Freund, 2000). It is at this point that an assessment regarding inpatient versus outpatient care is conducted. Inpatient care is typically recommended for those patients who are medically fragile and are not responding to outpatient treatment. Current height and weight ratio, rate of weight loss, frequency of binge/purge behaviors, cardiac symptoms, electrolyte status, outpatient treatment compliance, and suicidality are all key considerations when determining if inpatient care is appropriate. If the patient is to

engage in outpatient care, routine follow-up and monitoring are conducted.

- Provide psychoeducation to the client and the family regarding the disorder. Psychoeducation provides the youth with motivation as risks and mortality rates are reviewed. Furthermore, psychoeducation regarding the benefits and challenges of treatment can be very helpful for the client and family members as they negotiate the sometimes, lengthy recovery process. See Select Bibliography for suggested materials.

- Review of the child's or adolescent's background and the emergence of the ED behaviors (e.g., dieting behaviors, family history of dieting and EDs, family attitudes toward appearance and weight, involvement in activities known to increase ED risk [e.g., esthetically oriented sports and modeling], date of first symptoms, frequency of symptoms, and rate of weight loss), the perceived role of the behaviors in his or her life, and the sense of remaining for change and perceived ability to control or manage behaviors.

- Conduct a functional analysis of the role of the disordered eating in the youth's life (e.g., regulate emotions, avoid distress or uncomfortable mood states; Cook-Cottone et al., 2013).
  - Evaluate triggers:
    - Evaluate situational triggers (e.g., meals, family dinners, buffets, trying on clothes at the mall, home, school, dining hall, peer social outings, and time alone in the house).
    - Review emotional triggers (e.g., boredom, intolerable mood states, loneliness, fear, shame, anger, and feeling overwhelmed).
    - Explore cognitive triggers (e.g., feeling fat, idealization of media models, perfectionism associated with appearance as well as interpersonal relationships, beliefs about achievement and appearance, food categorization as good or bad, and thoughts about internal and external control in situations).
  - Review the associated emotional experience (i.e., intensity, form, and perceived ability to cope):
    - Patient rates intensity of emotion experienced before symptom expression on a scale from 1 (i.e., mild) to 10 (overwhelmingly intense).
    - Investigate the emotion. The treatment provider can provide a list of emotions, have the patient identify and describe the emotion in the body, or encourage the patient to describe the emotion.
    - Patient rates his or her perceived ability to negotiate or cope with the emotion from 1 (having no option for coping) to 10 (having many options for coping).
  - Record the antecedents, ED behaviors, and consequences. Detail consequences that tend to reinforce the ED (e.g., relief from feeling too full) as well as those that are troublesome to the client (e.g., mother catching client purging in the bathroom and embarrassment).
  - Review beliefs about how the symptoms addressed triggers and emotional challenges (the functions of the symptoms) and what consequences follow the symptoms that may provide clues to the symptoms' functions. For example, boredom and loneliness may lead to bingeing and purging, which function as a distraction. Some symptoms may provide a sense of control (e.g., when restricting food intake) or a sense of relief (e.g., when purging unwanted food) for those who are feeling emotionally overwhelmed.
  - Match strategy and skill development to core need or function; for example: for those who struggle with emotional regulation—distress tolerance; those who are lonely and bored—distraction and support techniques; and for those who are triggered by body image thoughts and beliefs—body image work and self-care.

- Conduct an assessment of eating behavior and associated psychological constructs.
  - Cook-Cottone and colleagues (2013) provide an overview for the screening and assessment of children and adolescents for eating disordered behavior (see Chapter 8). Investigate disordered eating symptomatology, including eating in the absence of hunger, intuitive eating, body image, body appreciation, internalization of media ideals, as well as mood, anxiety, and other signs of dysregulation (e.g., substance use, excessive exercise, or compulsive shopping; Cook-Cottone et al., 2013).

- Assess the child's or adolescent's motivation to engage in treatment. Low motivation to recover can be an obstacle to treatment (inpatient and outpatient care).

- Commence the empirically supported and/or clinically appropriate treatment for the presenting problems (see specific EDs in the following).
  - Implement inventions that enhance social skills, interpersonal effectiveness, and ability to communicate needs effectively within relationships.
- Help the youth conceptualize self-regulation (i.e., emotions, cognitions, and behavior) as part of healthy eating.
- View mindfulness and awareness of the body as a process of careful discernment of physiological experiences, emotions, and thoughts, as well as a pathway to more mindful, intuitive eating that is based on authentic hunger cues and the body's needs (Cook-Cottone et al., 2013).
- Address physical exercise as one would address eating. That is, in order to develop a healthy relationship with his or her body, the youth will need to maintain a healthy relationship with daily exercise. Yoga and other mindfulness-based activities (e.g., tai chi, Tai Kwon Do) are often safe ways for patients to engage in physical activity with less risk of excessive exercise. Overall, moderation is key (Cook-Cottone et al., 2013).

Anorexia Nervosa

- Begin with the motivation phase of treatment in which motivation is assessed as weight restoration and nutritional rehabilitation begin. See Hoetzel, von Brachel, Schlossmacher, and Vocks's (2013) "Assessing Motivation to Change in Eating Disorders: A Systematic Review." For adolescents, consider integrating the Maudsley Method (www.thenewmaudsleyapproach.co.uk).
- Work with the youth to develop goals that increase interpersonal communication skills and socialization using DBT methodologies to increase interpersonal effectiveness.
- Support, encourage, and assess the client compliance with meal plans and explore food restriction as an effort to manage emotions, control feelings, or manage stressors through a CBT framework. Compliance can be difficult to assess as patients often strive to keep their symptoms a secret and feel pressure to present as good patients. It can be helpful to ask patients about their efforts to comply and how challenging compliance was between visits. In this way, they can talk about the challenge of compliance reducing the likelihood of false reporting. A solid team approach is helpful as the medical doctor monitors medical status, which provides physiological markers of patient treatment compliance.
- Explore perfectionism, idealization of the thin ideal, and address body image issues (see Thomas Cash's *Body Image* workbook; see Select Bibliography).
- Address any comorbid depression or anxiety by encouraging active cognitive behavioral exercises between sessions, DBT emotion-regulation techniques (e.g., distress tolerance, distraction, and self-soothing), and mindfulness and relaxation techniques (see Select Bibliography for suggestions).
- Gradually shift responsibility of weight monitoring, healthy eating, and self-regulation to the client.

Bulimia Nervosa and BED

With respect to the treatment of BN and BED, it might be helpful to think of intervention as a reduction in binge-eating behavior and an increase in healthy, more hunger cue–based eating (e.g., intuitive eating). Specific to BN, recall that attempting to stop the behavior once an individual has binged and is triggered to purge, is difficult and research suggests that it is not beneficial (e.g., McIntosh et al., 2010). Therefore, the most effective target for intervention for BN is the reduction of binges and the enhancement of healthy coping behavior.

- Establish a baseline of behavior regarding when the child or adolescent binges and purges (for BN), the context, time of day, foods eaten, and other relevant daily events. Use this baseline data to target key times of day, food, and situations that appear to be associated with the highest frequency of behavior.
  - Explore persistent triggers and cues for recent binge and purge (for BN) episodes and begin attempts at abstinence from bingeing. It can be helpful to work closely with the nutritionist at this point, perhaps removing high trigger foods, or addressing nutritional deficits (e.g., lack of protein, need for snacks) within the child's or adolescent's meal plan as he or she gains a sense of competency.
- Teach emotion-regulation skills and give tools for emotional control, self-soothing, and distress tolerance. Target high-risk times of day, foods, and situations for problem solving in this area.

See Cook-Cottone et al. (2008) for a functional analysis worksheet that can be used with children and adolescents.
- See aforementioned points that address interpersonal effectiveness and exercise.
- Work toward less mechanical eating (i.e., meal plan and food tracking) and toward a healthy physiological cue-based eating (i.e., intuitive eating; Cook-Cottone et al., 2013).

CONCLUSION

The treatment of EDs should be viewed as a team effort that integrates medical, nutritional, and mental health service providers. The first steps in treatment are to establish current health status and develop a plan to secure and maintain physiological safety. Next, treatment focuses on the normalization of eating and exercise while simultaneously addressing the unique features that the particular ED manifests (e.g., bingeing for BN and BED, restricting for AN). Successful treatment involves viewing symptoms as serving functions in the child's or adolescent's life. Understanding these purposes and helping the child or adolescent develop effective, healthier tools for functioning are key to successful treatment. Every child or adolescent who presents for treatment will bring a unique set of intra- and interpersonal challenges and strengths. Addressing specific strengths and challenges in an effort to empower effective and normal functioning is critical to long-term maintenance of recovery. Research continues to move toward more effective treatments.

SELECT BIBLIOGRAPHY

Academy for Eating Disorders (AED). Retrieved from http://www.aedweb.org
The academy provides information related to eating disorders, consequences of EDs, treatment guides for EDs, and resources for families.

F.E.A.S.T. Retrieved from https://feast-ed.site-ym.com
This organization of parents/caregivers provides support for other parents/caregivers of loved ones recovering from ED by providing information, promoting evidence-based treatment, and advocating for research and education.

Lock, J., & Le Grange, D. (2005). *Helping your teenager beat an eating disorder.* New York, NY: Guilford Press.
This book offers practical advice for parents and provides information on cause, therapy and treatment options, and concerns about comorbid conditions. The book provides suggestions on how to work with the professionals involved in the child's care.

National Eating Disorders Association (NEDA). Retrieved from http://www.nationaleatingdisorders.org
This association provides support and information for individuals and families affected by eating disorders and serves as a catalyst for prevention, treatment, and access to quality care.

REFERENCES

Agency for Healthcare Research and Quality (AHRQ). (2009, April 1). *Eating disorders sending more Americans to the hospital.* AHRQ News and Numbers. Retrieved from http://archive.ahrq.gov/news/newsroom/news-and-numbers/040109.html

American Psychiatric Association (APA). (2013). *Diagnostic and statistical manual of mental disorders* (5th ed.). Arlington, VA: American Psychiatric Publishing.

Arcelus, J., Mitchell, A. J., Wales, J., & Nielsen, A. (2011). Mortality rates in patients with anorexia nervosa and other eating disorders: A meta-analysis of 36 studies. *Archives of General Psychology, 68,* 724–731. doi:10.1001/archgenpsychiatry.2011.74

Astrachan-Fletcher, E. (2013). *Food family, and (dys) function: Family-based DBT for adolescent bulimia.* A symposium presented at the International Association of Eating Disorder Professionals Foundation's Annual Conference, Henderson, Nevada.

Bankoff, S. M., Karpel, M. G., Forbes, H. E., & Pantalone, D. W. (2012). A systematic review of dialectic behavioral therapy in the treatment of eating disorders. *Eating disorders: The Journal of Treatment and Prevention, 20,* 196–215.

Beintner, I., Jacobi, C., & Schmidt, U. H. (2014). Participation and outcome in manualized self-help for bulimia nervosa and binge-eating disorder: A systematic review and metaregression analysis. *Clinical Psychology Review, 34,* 158–176.

Carei, T. R., Fyfe-Johnson, A. L., Beuner, C. C., & Brown, M. A. (2010). Randomized controlled clinical trial of yoga in the treatment of eating disorders. *Journal of Adolescent Health, 46*, 346–351.

Cook-Cottone, C. P. (2006). The attuned representational model for the primary prevention of eating disorders: An overview for school psychologists. *Psychology in the Schools, 43*, 223–230.

Cook-Cottone, C. P., Beck, M., & Kane, L. (2008). Manualized-group treatment of eating disorders: Attunement in mind, body, and relationship (AMBR). *The Journal of Specialists in Group Work, 33*, 61–83.

Cook-Cottone, C. P., Tribole, E., & Tylka, T. (2013). *Healthy eating in schools: Evidenced-based interventions to help kids thrive.* Washington, DC: American Psychological Association.

Crisp, A. H., Callender, J. S., Halek, C., & Hsu, L. K., (1992). Long-term mortality in anorexia nervosa. A 20-year follow-up of the St George's and Aberdeen cohorts. *The British Journal of Psychiatry, 161*, 104–107. doi:10.1192/bjp.161.1.104

Crow, S. J., Peterson, C. B., Swanson, S. A., Raymond, N. C., Specker, S., Eckert, E. D., & Mitchell, J. E. (2009). Increased mortality in bulimia nervosa and other eating disorders. *The American Journal of Psychiatry, 166*, 1342–1346. doi:10.1176/appi.ajp.2009.09020247

Erford, B. T., Richards, T., Peacock, E., Voith, K., McGain, H., Muller, B., … Grilo, C. M. (2006). *Eating and weight disorders.* New York, NY: Psychology Press of Taylor & Francis Group.

Grilo, C. (2006). *Eating and weight disorders.* New York, NY: Psychology Press.

Hartmann, A., Weber, S., Herpertz, S., Zeeck, A., & the German Treatment Guideline Group for Anorexia Nervosa. (2011). Psychological treatment for anorexia nervosa: A meta-analysis of standardized mean change. *Psychotherapy and Psychosomatics, 80*, 216–226. doi:10.1159/000322360

Hoek, H. W., & van Hoeken, D. (2003). Review of the prevalence and incidence of eating disorders. *International Journal of Eating Disorders, 24*, 282–296. doi:10.1002/eat.10222

Hoetzel, K., von Brachel, R., Schlossmacher, L., & Vocks, S. (2013). Assessing motivation to change in eating disorders: A systematic review. *Journal of Eating Disorders, 1*, 38–39.

Holtkamp, K., Herpertz-Dahlmann, B., Vloet, T., & Hagenah, U. (2005). Group psychoeducation for parents of adolescents with eating disorders: The Aachen Program. *Eating Disorders, 13*, 381–390.

Hudson, J. I., Hiripi, E., Pope, H. G., Jr., & Kessler, R. C. (2007). The prevalence and correlates of eating disorders in the National Comorbidity Survey Replication. *Biological Psychiatry, 61*, 348–358. doi:10.1016/j.biopsych.2006.03.040

Jones, A., & Clausen, L. (2013). The efficacy of a brief group CBT program in treating patients diagnosed with bulimia nervosa: A brief report. *International Journal of Eating Disorders, 46*, 560–562.

Kishi, T., Kafantaris, V., Sunday, S., Sheridan, E. M., & Correll, C. U. (2012). Are antipsychotics effective for the treatment of anorexia nervosa? Results for a systemic review and meta-analysis. *Journal of Clinical Psychiatry, 73*, e757–e766.

Klein, J., & Cook-Cottone, C. P. (2013). The effects of yoga on eating disorder symptoms and correlates: A review. *Internal Journal of Yoga Therapy, 23*, 41–50.

Klein, J. S., Skinner, J. B., & Hawley, K. M. (2013). Targeting binge eating through components of dialect behavioral therapy: Preliminary outcomes for individually supported diary card self-monitoring versus group-based DBT. *Psychotherapy, 50*, 543–552.

Kohn, M. R., Madden, S., & Clarke, S. D. (2011). Refeeding in anorexia nervosa: Increased safety and efficiency through understanding the pathophysiology of protein calorie malnutrition. *Current Opinion in Pediatrics, 23*, 390–394.

Lavender, A., Startup, H., Naumann, U., Samarawickrema,N., DeJong, H., Kenyon, M., … Schmidt, U. (2012).Emotional and social mind training:A randomised controlled trial of a new group-based treatment for bulimia nervosa. *PLoS One, 7*(10), e46047.

Lebow, J., Sim, L. A., Erwin, P. J., & Murad, M. H. (2013). The effect of atypical antipsychotic medications in individuals with anorexia nervosa: A systemic review and meta-analysis. *International Journal of Eating Disorders, 46*, 332–339.

Levant, R. F., & Hasan, N. T. (2008). Evidence-based practice in psychology. *Professional Psychology: Research and Practice, 39*, 658.

Lock, J., Agras, W. S., Fitzpatrick, K. K., Bryson, S. W., Booil J., & Tchanturia, K. (2013). Is outpatient cognitive remediation therapy feasible to use in randomized clinical trials for anorexia nervosa? *International Journal of Eating Disorders, 46*, 567–575.

McIntosh, V. V. W., Carter, F. A., Bulik, C. M., Frampton, C. M. A., & Joyce, P. R. (2010). Five-year outcome of cognitive behavioral therapy and exposure with response prevention for bulimia nervosa. *Psychological Medicine, 41,* 1061–1071.

Minuchin, S., Rosman, B. L., & Baker, L. (1978). *Psychosomatic families: Anorexia nervosa in context.* Cambridge, MA: Harvard University Press.

Musada, A., & Hill, M. L. (2013). Mindfulness therapy for disordered eating: A systematic review. *Neuropsychiatry, 3,* 433–452.

Polnay, A., James, V. A. W., Hodges, L., Murray, G. D., Munro, C., & Lawrie, S. M. (2013). Group therapy for people with bulimia nervosa: Systematic review and meta-analysis. *Psychological Medicine, 44,* 2241–2254. doi:10.1017/S0033291713002791

Rosen, D. S., & the American Academy of Pediatrics Committee on Adolescence. (2010). Identification and management of eating disorders in children and adolescents. *Pediatrics, 126,* 1240–1253. doi:10.1542/peds.2010–2821

Safer, D., Robinson, A. H., & Jo, B. (2010). Outcome from a randomized controlled trial of group therapy for binge-eating disorder: Comparing dialectic behavior therapy adapted for binge eating to an active comparison group therapy. *Behavior Therapy, 41,* 106–120.

Safer, D. L., Telch, C. F., & Agras, W. S. (2001). Dialectic behavioral therapy for bulimia nervosa. *American Journal of Psychiatry, 158,* 632–634.

Shapiro, J. R., Berkman, N. D., Brownley, K. A., Sedway, J. A., Lohr, K. N., & Bulik, C. M. (2007). Bulimia nervosa treatment: A systematic review of randomized controlled trials. *International Journal of Eating Disorders, 40,* 321–336.

Smith, A., & Cook-Cottone, C. P. (2011). A review of the theoretical and empirical facets of family therapy as an effective intervention for anorexia nervosa

in adolescents. *Journal of Clinical Psychology in Medical Settings, 18,* 323–334.

Smolak, L. (2011). Body image development in childhood. In T. Cash & L. Smolak (Eds.), *Body image: A handbook of science, practice, and prevention* (2nd ed.). New York, NY: Guilford Press.

Stice, E., Marti, C. N., Shaw, H., & Jaconis, M. (2009). An 8-year longitudinal study of the natural history of threshold, subthreshold, and partial eating disorders from a community sample of adolescents. *Journal of Abnormal Psychology, 118,* 587–597. doi:10.1037/a0016481

Swanson, S., Crow, S., Le Grange, D., Swendsen, J., & Merikangas, K. (2011). Prevalence and correlates of eating disorders in adolescents. *Archives of General Psychiatry, 68,* 714–723. doi:10.1001/archgenpsychiatry.2011.22

Tchanturia, K., & Hambrook, D. (2009). Cognitive remediation. In C. Grilo & J. Mitchel (Eds.), *The treatment of eating disorders: Clinical handbook.* New York, NY: Guilford Press.

Tylka, T. L., & Kroon Van Diest, A. M. (2015). Protective factors in the development of eating disorders. In M. P. Levine & L. Smolak (Eds.), *The Wiley-Blackwell handbook of eating disorders.* New York, NY: Wiley.

Vocks, S., Tuschen-Caffier, B., Pietrowsky, R., Rustenback, S. J., Kersting, A., & Herpertz, S. (2010). Meta-analysis of the effectiveness of psychological and pharmacological treatments for binge-eating disorder. *International Journal of Eating Disorders, 43,* 205–217.

Walsh, J. M., Wheat, M. E., & Freund, K. (2000). Detection, evaluation, and treatment of eating disorders. *Journal of General Internal Medicine, 15,* 577–590.

Evidence-Based Interventions for Childhood Obesity

Lisa Ranzenhofer, Mary Beth McCullough, and Elissa Jelalian

OVERVIEW

Prevalence. Childhood and adolescent obesity is widely recognized as a significant public health concern in the United States. Obesity has been identified as the most common physical health problem among youth and the leading cause of preventable deaths (Ogden, Carroll, Kit, & Flegal, 2014). In children and adolescents, weight status is categorized using age- and sex-specific percentiles for body mass index (BMI, kg/m^2) with BMI percentiles greater than or equal to the 85th and 95th percentile respectively indicating overweight and obesity (Barlow, 2007). Although the acceleration in obesity prevalence has slowed, data from the most recent National Health and Nutrition Examination Survey (NHANES) indicate that absolute rates remain high. Among children and adolescents aged 2 to 19 years, 31% of youth are overweight and 17% are obese (Ogden et al., 2014). Notably, there is a substantial health disparity in obesity prevalence, with obesity disproportionately affecting racial and ethnic minority youth. Compared with non-Hispanic White youth (14.1%), obesity prevalence is higher among Hispanic (22.4%) and non-Hispanic Black youth (20.2%; Ogden et al., 2014).

Comorbidity. Overweight and obesity in childhood may result in a wide range of negative physical health problems as well as psychosocial concerns across the life course. Compared with children and adolescents of healthy weight, overweight youth are at a heightened risk for deleterious physical health outcomes such as orthopedic complications, type 2 diabetes, asthma, and sleep apnea (Daniels, 2009; Lazorick et al., 2011; Pulgarón, 2013). Moreover, pediatric obesity is associated with risk factors for cardiovascular disease, including hypertension and atherosclerosis (Daniels, 2009; Farpour-Lambert et al., 2009), as well as obesity during adulthood (Freedman et al., 2005; Magarey, Daniels, Boulton, & Cockington, 2003). A number of negative psychosocial concerns, including lower health-related quality of life, decreased physical self-worth, higher body dissatisfaction, and more weight-related teasing by peers and family members also accompany pediatric obesity (Schwimmer, Burwinkle, & Varni, 2003; Wardle & Cooke, 2005). Findings regarding psychological distress vary depending on the population sampled. In clinical samples, obese youth demonstrate higher rates of psychiatric disorders, such as mood and anxiety disorders, compared with healthy weight peers (Erermis et al., 2004), whereas findings are inconclusive among nonclinical samples (Crow, Eisenberg, Story, & Neumark-Sztainer, 2006; Tanofsky-Kraff et al., 2004).

ETIOLOGY AND FACTORS CONTRIBUTING TO CHILDHOOD OBESITY

At the core of obesity's etiology is the energy balance model. The energy balance model posits that weight change ensues when there is an imbalance between energy intake (calories in) and energy output (calories out). Although the energy balance model explains *how* energy intake and expenditure interact to produce obesity, an evolutionary perspective proposes *why* obesity's prevalence has risen dramatically within the past several decades. An evolutionary perspective proposes that humans are endowed with multiple genetic variants promoting energy conservation, attributable to the selective advantage of conserving energy in order to survive periods of starvation throughout evolutionary history (Crocker & Yanovski, 2011). Modern environmental conditions differ markedly from those characterizing evolutionary history in terms of food availability and requirements for physical activity. As a result, genes that formerly promoted survival by increasing fat storage, decreasing metabolism, and promoting eating in the absence of hunger and sedentary behavior may now confer risk for excess weight gain and obesity.

Although body weight directly relates to energy balance, a myriad of interacting individual-, family-, and societal-level factors impact both sides of the energy balance equation. Effective interventions for obesity consider intake and expenditure not in isolation but in the context of these factors.

Individual Level

Twin studies suggest that the heritability of obesity is approximately 70% (Dubois et al., 2012; Maes, Neale, & Eaves, 1997), with varying estimates across age, sex, population, and study design (Elks et al., 2012). Although molecular genetic studies have implicated the genes for melanocortin 4 receptor (MC4R) and fat mass and obesity-associated protein (FTO), as well as hundreds of additional genetic variants in the etiology of obesity, only a few have known functions and collectively they explain little variability in body weight (Hebebrand, Volckmar, Knoll, & Hinney, 2010). One mechanism by which genetic factors may confer obesity risk is by influencing weight-related behaviors. A range of such behaviors have been linked to genetic underpinnings such as binge eating (Bulik, Sullivan, & Kendler, 1998) and physical activity level (Carlsson, Andersson, Lichtenstein, Michaëlsson, & Ahlbom, 2006). Novel studies have also implicated a range of cognitive factors, such as impulsivity and attention bias to food cues, and psychological factors, such as depression, in the etiology of obesity.

Familial Level

Reflecting both genetic and environmental influences on children's weight outcomes, familial factors play an important role in children's eating and activity behaviors and weight status. There is evidence to suggest that specific parenting practices are associated with improved health behaviors and lower BMI, such as an authoritative parenting style (e.g., setting limits, high-parental warmth; Rhee, Lumeng, Appugliese, Kaciroti, & Bradley, 2006; Sleddens, Gerards, Thijs, de Vries, & Kremers, 2011), parental acceptance (Stein, Epstein, Raynor, Kilanowski, & Paluch, 2005), and modeling of physical activity and healthful eating practices (Pugliese & Tinsley, 2007). Beyond parental behaviors, the structure of the home environment may influence the child's eating behavior and physical activity through the foods and activities that are available. For instance, among preschool children, the availability of outdoor play equipment, computer gaming stations, fruits and vegetables, and sweetened beverages impacted children's eating and physical activity behaviors (Spurrier, Magarey, Golley, Curnow, & Sawyer, 2008).

Societal/Community Level

Characteristics of many Western societies, including widespread availability of highly palatable processed foods and excessive portion sizes, alongside concurrent decreases in daily physical activity requirements and increases in sedentary activities, promote increases in obesity at the societal level. Nationally representative data from 2013 indicate that more than 40% of teens spend more than 3 hours per day playing video games or using computers for nonschool-related activities, 32.5% watch television for over 3 hours per day, and the majority (52.7%) do not meet current physical activity recommendations (Kann et al., 2014). The quality of youths' diets has simultaneously declined, with the majority of youth failing to meet current dietary recommendations for fruits, vegetables, and fat intake (Kann et al., 2014; Sanchez et al., 2007). Taken together, a host of factors ranging from genetics to the broader cultural context contribute to the development of obesity. Interventions may include attention to all of these dimensions, but we focus here on treatments targeting the individual and family.

EVIDENCE-BASED INTERVENTIONS

The energy balance model, which focuses on achieving an energy deficient state in order to produce weight loss, forms the basis of nearly all weight-loss interventions. Noninvasive interventions, termed "lifestyle" interventions, involve three key components: (a) dietary prescription; (b) modification of physical activity and sedentary behavior; and (c) behavioral strategies such as goal-setting, self-monitoring, and positive reinforcement (Delamater, Jent, Moine, & Rios, 2008). Such approaches were initially found to be effective several decades ago (Epstein, Valoski, Wing, & McCurley, 1990, 1994) and continue to be at the center of efficacious approaches (Janicke et al., 2014; Whitlock, O'Connor, Williams, Beil, & Lutz, 2010).

Pediatric behavioral weight management interventions exist in many permutations and typically include some combination of contact with the child patient and adult caregiver. For children, there is considerable evidence to suggest that interventions involving at least one parent in addition to the child are superior to interventions delivered to children only based on greater weight loss and less weight regain (e.g., Epstein et al., 1990). Furthermore, there are now a number of studies to suggest that treatments involving parents only are equally or more efficacious compared with those including the child and the parent (Boutelle, Cafri, & Crow, 2011; Janicke et al., 2008) and more efficacious compared with those involving the child only (Golan & Crow, 2004). Targeting parents only in pediatric weight management interventions offers some benefits over traditional models including improved cost-effectiveness and ease

of dissemination as well as minimizing the potential for stigmatization or resistance in the child (Janicke, 2013).

For adolescents, there is mixed evidence regarding the benefits of parental involvement (e.g., parent and adolescent, adolescent only, and parent only) in weight control interventions (Delamater et al., 2008). Thus, for teens, the ideal treatment modality may depend on factors such as the teen's age, psychological maturity, motivation, willingness to engage in treatment, and the quality of the parent–child relationship. Interventions are often designed to be delivered in a group format, improving on the cost-effectiveness of treatment, but individual treatment delivery is also common in a clinical setting.

Depending on the age of the child and severity of obesity, other treatment approaches, such as immersion programs and bariatric surgery, may be appropriate. Immersion programs, typically delivered through therapeutic overnight camps or residential facilities over an extended time period, may be appropriate for youths with varying levels of obesity (Kirschenbaum, Kelly, & Germann, 2009), but they are more commonly prescribed for children with severe obesity (i.e., BMI greater than 99th percentile). Immersion programs include a controlled environment with regard to diet and physical activity, a focus on cognitive behavioral strategies, and social support from peers and counselors. A meta-analysis of immersion programs suggested favorable short-term efficacy compared with traditional lifestyle interventions (Kirschenbaum et al., 2009). Little research, however, has attended to patients' maintenance of weight loss following reentry into traditional environments.

Guidelines for bariatric surgery among pediatric populations recommend consideration of surgery for adolescents with a BMI exceeding 35 kg/m² in the presence of significant short-term comorbidities (e.g., type 2 diabetes, moderate to severe sleep apnea) or a BMI exceeding 40 kg/m² in the absence of short-term comorbidity (Pratt et al., 2009). A recent review of bariatric surgery outcomes in adolescents suggests that it is both efficacious and well tolerated (Thakkar & Michalsky, 2015). Notably, surgery and other intensive treatments are accompanied by guidelines and risks exceeding those of traditional behavioral approaches.

Psychological approaches targeting specific eating-related behaviors and cognitions are increasingly used in pediatric obesity treatments. Employing psychological approaches can be accomplished either by including psychological interventions in traditional weight management programs or by adapting traditional psychotherapies to target specific eating-related behaviors. For example, cognitive behavioral therapy (CBT) and interpersonal therapy, both with demonstrated efficacy for the treatment of binge-eating disorder in adults (Wilfley et al., 2002), have been adapted to target binge and loss of control eating among adolescent girls, with initial efficacy reported in pilot studies (Debar et al., 2013; Tanofsky-Kraff et al., 2010). A novel program targeting dysregulation in appetitive cues (e.g., eating when not hungry, eating in response to external cues) has also shown promise for eating when not hungry, external eating, and body weight measures (Boutelle et al., 2014).

HOW TO: A GUIDE TO THE IMPLEMENTATION OF INTERVENTIONS FOR CHILDHOOD OBESITY

As described earlier, the primary treatment modality used among children and adolescents seeking weight loss is behavioral, delivered to the child or adolescent patient and adult caregiver in either group or individual formats. In the following sections, the common components of weight control interventions are outlined followed by a description of three specific approaches. The first two treatments are behavioral in nature, with the first emphasizing the core structure of a behavioral treatment by detailing an adolescent, group-based intervention, and the second describing interventions for school-aged children, with a focus on parents. The final treatment places additional emphasis on the cognitive components of weight control.

Common Components of Behavioral Interventions

Components of standard behavioral interventions for childhood obesity include dietary and physical activity modifications, alongside concurrent behavioral strategies to support these changes. The dietary component of behavioral interventions is focused on reducing energy intake via establishing a hypocaloric diet (800–1,500/day) based on the child's age, weight, and activity level in consultation with a dietician, with recommended intake from specific food groups (Raynor, 2008). A well-reviewed approach to dietary intervention used among youths is the "Traffic-Light Diet," which distinguishes between foods that are low in fat/added sugars and high nutrient quality (green foods), foods that are moderate in fat/added sugars and average nutrient quality (yellow foods), and foods that are high in fat/added sugars and poor nutrient quality (red foods; Epstein, Valoski, Koeske, & Wing, 1986). The National Heart, Lung, and Blood Institute (NHLBI) recommends a similar diet: "Go, Slow, and Whoa!" foods, respectively describing foods that should be eaten anytime (Go foods), sometimes (Slow foods), and only once in a while (Whoa foods) (for more information, visit www.nhlbi.nih.gov/health/educational/wecan/eat-right/index.htm).

The second central component of successful behavioral weight-loss interventions among children is modification to their activity patterns, including increasing physical activity while concurrently decreasing sedentary activities (e.g., "screen time"; Raynor, 2008). Increasing physical activity can be accomplished by increasing both traditional exercise (e.g., playing on a sports team or going to the gym) as well as "lifestyle" physical activity (e.g., taking the stairs instead of the elevator, walking instead of driving; Epstein, Myers, Raynor, & Saelens, 1998). Finally, behavioral strategies are known to enhance individuals' abilities to carry out changes related to diet and exercise. Behavioral strategies are based on a range of principles including reinforcement, stimulus control, modeling, and self-monitoring. For an overview of pediatric behavioral weight management components, see "Evidence-Based Treatments for Childhood Obesity" in *Issues in Clinical Child Psychology: Handbook of Childhood and Adolescent Obesity* (Raynor, 2008, pp. 201–220).

Structure of an Adolescent, Group-Based Weight Management Intervention

Behavioral weight-loss interventions for adolescents typically begin with an individual assessment of the patient's anthropometrics (e.g., weight/height), eating and exercise patterns, motivation, and other relevant individual, family, and environmental factors that may enhance or interfere with weight management (e.g., psychiatric diagnoses, family mealtime, neighborhood safety, family economics, and access to healthy foods). The initial stage of traditional behavioral weight management approaches also include goal setting, in which the youth establishes realistic, measurable goals for weight loss and behavior, and motivational enhancement, in which the adolescent and interventionist clarify and strengthen the adolescent's motivation to engage in treatment.

Following the baseline assessment and goal-setting period, adolescents typically attend weekly sessions consisting of an individual check-in or meeting with a provider (nutritionist or mental health practitioner) and a group meeting. Although the majority of treatment encounters are typically conducted with adolescents only, parents are frequently involved in treatment in various capacities, such as attending an initial evaluation, attending sporadic treatment sessions, or encouraging parent–child communication regarding the adolescent's progress. The content of treatment sessions typically involves providing psychoeducation, monitoring adolescents' progress with regard to achieving specific behavioral targets and associated weight-loss goals, and facilitating discussion about strategies for implementing changes.

During initial group sessions, patients learn to self-monitor their dietary intake, a central component of behavioral weight-loss interventions. As underreporting of dietary intake is common, especially among overweight youth (Fisher, Johnson, Lindquist, Birch, & Goran, 2000), careful attention is paid to the importance of making complete, detailed recordings that include the type and amount of all foods consumed throughout the day. Some behavioral programs aim to enhance adolescents' compliance with self-monitoring by providing reinforcement (e.g., points or other prizes) for successfully completing dietary records. Electronic strategies, such as digitally tracking intake using cell phones or other personal devices, have demonstrated preliminary efficacy for increasing compliance with self-monitoring among adults (Glanz, Murphy, Moylan, Evensen, & Curb, 2006) and youth (Cushing, Jensen, & Steele, 2011). Also introduced early in treatment are the

dietary prescription—a hypocaloric, low-fat diet—and exercise prescription—typically 60 minutes per day, 5 days per week. Participants also learn basic nutritional concepts, such as portion control, and information regarding physical activity such as the value of "lifestyle" activity and reducing "screen time." Stimulus control, defined as modifying the environment in order to enhance the likelihood of engaging in dietary and exercise modifications, is often introduced at the beginning of treatment. Patients are encouraged to determine strategies for practicing stimulus control at home, at school, and with friends (e.g., bringing lunch from home).

Throughout treatment, adolescents continue to meet weekly to monitor progress, enhance motivation, and resolve treatment barriers via problem solving. As treatment progresses, the focus of treatment sessions tends to shift from providing basic nutritional and activity information to applying the information via identifying and rehearsing behavioral strategies (e.g., how to manage difficult situations like social gatherings centered around food). The final stage of treatment is typically focused on relapse prevention, during which adolescents plan for how they will maintain behavioral changes and/or weight loss following the conclusion of treatment. Providers and adolescents typically review the information presented throughout treatment, and the adolescent identifies strategies to promote continued progress, such as weighing oneself once per week, continuing to record food intake, or limiting eating out. Following the conclusion of treatment, many programs continue to offer less frequent (e.g., monthly) "booster" or "check-in" sessions to support the adolescent in maintaining progress.

Parent-Only Treatment

With young children, parents play a central role in determining what, when, where, and how much children eat. As a result, including parents in treatment is considered central to the success of weight management interventions with school-aged children. One of the first parent-only treatment models, developed by Golan and colleagues, is grounded in a systems approach, in which the child's weight is conceptualized as being related to the health behaviors of the entire family. Parent-only treatment frames parents as the family leaders and empowers parents to make environmental changes that facilitate weight loss (Golan & Weizman, 2001). The family, rather than the overweight child, is considered the agent of change (Golan, Weizman, Apter, & Fainaru, 1998), and the child is excluded from treatment in order to minimize treatment resistance and to avoid identification of the child as the "patient" (Golan et al., 1998).

Stimulus control is a central component of parent-only treatment, focusing on topics such as creating opportunities for physical activity, decreasing exposure to tempting foods, and decreasing the fat content of the family's diet (Golan & Weizman, 2001). Emphasis is placed on modifying the home environment, rather than relying on the child's ability to exert self-control within a tempting food environment. Specific strategies, such as consuming regular meals and snacks, engaging in leisure time activities that involve physical activity, and eliminating highly palatable foods from the home altogether, are discussed.

In addition to providing information, proposed agents of change in parent-only treatment include parental modeling of healthy behavior and employing positive parenting practices such as problem solving, self-efficacy and parent–child communication (Golan & Weizman, 2001). In treatment, parents learn to establish eating-related rules and routines, exert appropriate parental authority, and identify ways to help their children such as reinforcing specific behaviors (Golan & Weizman, 2001).

The parent-only model exemplified by the work of Golan and colleagues is supported through publicly available materials related to promotion of healthy diet and physical activity. NHLBI's "WE CAN!" (Ways to Enhance Children's Activity and Nutrition) website provides educational materials regarding topics such as energy balance, selecting appropriate foods and portion sizes, increasing children's physical activity, and reducing screen time (U.S. Department of Health and Human Services, 2013). For an example of a parent-based program focused on provision of information and tips, the reader is referred to www .nhlbi.nih.gov/health/educational/wecan/down-loads/leadersguide.pdf. Additional resources, including manuals and handouts for various programs targeting pediatric obesity, are also available at www.nhlbi.nih.gov/health/educational/wecan/tools-resources/curricula-toolkits .htm#parent-program

Inclusion of Psychological Components

There are a subset of children for whom psychological factors may play a role in weight-related behaviors through distorted cognitions and maladaptive behavioral patterns (Wilfley, Kolko, & Kass, 2011). For these children, programs that supplement behavioral approaches with cognitive behavioral treatment (CBT) techniques, such as cognitive restructuring, have been shown to improve treatment effectiveness (e.g., Herrera, Johnson, & Steele, 2004).

CBT for obesity consists of two phases, a treatment and a maintenance phase, which typically lasts from 20 to 24 sessions (Brennan, Walkley, Fraser, Greenway, & Wilks, 2008; Cooper, Fairburn, & Hawker, 2003). Although Cooper et al. (2003) outline the standard CBT model used for adults, the *Choose Health* CBT program described by Brennan et al. employs the same techniques while providing a model for using CBT with children and adolescents (Brennan et al., 2008). Therefore, the treatment from Brennan et al. (2008) will be used as a model for describing the integration of cognitive components into behavioral weight loss interventions.

According to Brennan et al. (2008) and Cooper et al. (2003), the first step in treatment involves assessing the child's weight problem from a cognitive behavioral standpoint. Information should be collected about social and cognitive factors that may be contributing to or maintaining weight-related behaviors, including barriers to treatment and motivation for weight loss. Refer to Cooper and colleagues (2003) for a comprehensive list of CBT-focused assessment questions.

During the initial treatment phase (sessions 1–13), the first several sessions (sessions 1–6) focus on the standard behavioral components explained in the previous section, including psychoeducation, self-monitoring of intake and activity patterns, stimulus control, changing eating and activity patterns, and reinforcement for behavioral change. The next phase of treatment (sessions 7–13) focus on cognitive behavioral strategies, such as cognitive restructuring, assertiveness training, and relapse-prevention techniques (Brennan et al., 2008).

Cognitive restructuring, or the process of identifying and changing negative cognitions, is a multistep process that is a fundamental aspect of CBT and covered over several sessions (sessions 7–9). The first step is to discuss the connections among a child's cognitions, emotions, and behaviors while highlighting the role that cognitive distortions or negative patterns of thinking (e.g., black and white thinking, missing the positive) play in influencing emotions and weight-related behaviors. The second step involves identifying the specific cognitive distortions that may be maintaining a child's negative pattern of weight-related behavior or body image concerns and subsequently guiding children in thinking about alternative viewpoints. For example, a child may report the thought "I'll *never* lose weight" and report feeling "worthless" in relation to not seeing any change in weight status. This negative thought and associated negative emotion may, in turn, contribute to the child not adhering to dietary and physical activity recommendations (Brennan et al., 2008). The next step in cognitive restructuring is for the therapist to use Socratic questioning to challenge these negative cognitions and help the child develop more accurate and helpful attitudes. For cognitive restructuring examples as well as monitoring forms for recording thoughts, emotions, and behaviors, refer to Cooper et al. (2003).

The final three sessions (sessions 10–13) focus on teaching assertive communication skills, problem solving around planning for meals and activities, and developing time-management skills. Relapse-prevention strategies, including identifying high-risk situations in the future (e.g., upcoming holidays, parties) and outlining coping strategies to use in those situations, are also discussed. Cognitive restructuring is often used during these sessions as well, in order to address thoughts and feelings that may interfere with maintaining weight loss. After the final treatment session, the maintenance phase begins (sessions 14–22). These brief sessions involve checking in on behavioral goals, reviewing coping plans, and identifying and planning for future high-risk situations (Brennan et al., 2008).

CONCLUSION

The prevalence of overweight and obesity among children and adolescents has increased tremendously over the past 30 years, particularly among adolescents and ethnic minority groups, underscoring the need for effective pediatric obesity prevention and intervention efforts. This chapter reviews factors contributing to obesity's etiology, including individual-, family-, and societal/community-level factors. Notably, although societal factors contribute substantially to obesity's etiology, the focus of this chapter is on psychological interventions, primarily targeting factors at the individual and family levels. Evidence-based treatments for obesity include behavioral strategies such as stimulus control, modification of physical and sedentary activities, as well as dietary prescriptions. The inclusion of cognitive components has also been shown to be effective among many youths and families. For younger children, including at least one parent in treatment appears to be the most effective format for intervention delivery, whereas the optimal format for older youth (adolescent-only, parent-adolescent, group-based) is less clear. Future research examining effective treatment modalities for adolescents, innovative methods for engaging children and adolescents in treatment, and methods for addressing interacting individual, family, community, and societal factors will improve efforts to address this significant public health concern.

SELECT BIBLIOGRAPHY

Brennan, L., Walkley, J., Fraser, S. F., Greenway, K., & Wilks, R. (2008). Motivational interviewing and cognitive behaviour therapy in the treatment of adolescent overweight and obesity: Study design and methodology. *Contemporary Clinical Trials, 29*(3), 359–375.
This article describes the structure of the Choose Health program, a CBT-based obesity intervention for adolescents, and provides a week-by-week description of how to implement the intervention.

Cooper, Z., Fairburn, C. G., & Hawker, D. M. (2003). *Cognitive-behavioral treatment of obesity: A clinician's guide.* New York, NY: Guilford Press. *This manual provides a comprehensive, step-by-step approach for integrating CBT into a standard behavioral obesity treatment. Although the treatment was developed for adults, the general concepts and structure can be applied to younger populations.*

Golan, M., & Weizman, A. (2001). Familial approach to the treatment of childhood obesity: A conceptual model. *Journal of Nutrition Education, 33*(2), 102–107.

This article describes the conceptual underpinnings and framework for a 14-session parent-only pediatric weight control program, but does not include a session-by-session description of the program.

Raynor, H. A. (2008). Evidence-based treatments for childhood obesity. In E. J. Jelalian & R. Steele (Eds.), *Issues in clinical child psychology: Handbook of childhood and adolescent obesity.* New York, NY: Springer Publishing Company.
This chapter provides an overview of pediatric weight management interventions by reviewing and compiling evidence from 13 RCTs. This chapter presents conclusions regarding best practices for diet, physical activity, sedentary behaviors, behavioral strategies, and structure of treatment.

U.S. Department of Health and Human Services. (2013). *We can! Energize our families: parent program: A leader's guide.* Retrieved from http://www.nhlbi.nih.gov/health/educational/wecan/downloads/leadersguide.pdf
This leader manual provides background and step-by-step guidelines for conducting "We Can! (Ways to Enhance Children's Activity and Nutrition)," a public education outreach program designed to promote healthy weight in 8- to 13-year-old children. The manual includes the four structured 90-minute sessions (including activities and discussions), pre- and postsession evaluations, and participant handouts.

REFERENCES

Barlow, S. E.; Expert Committee. (2007). Expert committee recommendations regarding the prevention, assessment, and treatment of child and adolescent overweight and obesity: Summary report. *Pediatrics, 120* (Suppl 4), S164–S192.

Boutelle, K. N., Cafri, G., & Crow, S. J. (2011). Parent-only treatment for childhood obesity: A randomized controlled trial. *Obesity, 19*(3), 574–580.

Boutelle, K. N., Zucker, N., Peterson, C. B., Rydell, S., Carlson, J., & Harnack, L. J. (2014). An intervention based on Schachter's externality theory for overweight children: The regulation of cues pilot. *Journal of Pediatric Psychology, 39*(4), 405–417.

Brennan, L., Walkley, J., Fraser, S. F., Greenway, K., & Wilks, R. (2008). Motivational interviewing and cognitive behaviour therapy in the treatment of adolescent overweight and obesity: Study design and methodology. *Contemporary Clinical Trials, 29*(3), 359–375.

Bulik, C. M., Sullivan, P. F., & Kendler, K. S. (1998). Heritability of binge-eating and broadly defined bulimia nervosa. *Biological Psychiatry, 44*(12), 1210–1218.

Carlsson, S., Andersson, T., Lichtenstein, P., Michaëlsson, K., & Ahlbom, A. (2006). Genetic effects on physical activity: Results from the Swedish Twin Registry. *Medicine and Science in Sports and Exercise, 38*(8), 1396–1401.

Cooper, Z., Fairburn, C., & Hawker, D. M. (2003). *Cognitive-behavioral treatment of obesity: A clinician's guide.* New York, NY: Guilford Press.

Crocker, M. K., & Yanovski, J. A. (2011). Pediatric obesity: Etiology and treatment. *Pediatric Clinics of North America, 58*(5), 1217–40, xi.

Crow, S., Eisenberg, M. E., Story, M., & Neumark-Sztainer, D. (2006). Psychosocial and behavioral correlates of dieting among overweight and non-overweight adolescents. *The Journal of Adolescent Health, 38*(5), 569–574.

Cushing, C. C., Jensen, C. D., & Steele, R. G. (2011). An evaluation of a personal electronic device to enhance self-monitoring adherence in a pediatric weight management program using a multiple baseline design. *Journal of Pediatric Psychology, 36*(3), 301–307.

Daniels, S. R. (2009). Complications of obesity in children and adolescents. *International Journal of Obesity, 33*(Suppl. 1), S60–S65. doi:10.1038/ijo.2009.20

Debar, L. L., Wilson, G. T., Yarborough, B. J., Burns, B., Oyler, B., Hildebrandt, T.,…Striegel, R. H. (2013). Cognitive behavioral treatment for recurrent binge eating in adolescent girls: A pilot trial. *Cognitive and Behavioral Practice, 20*(2), 147–161.

Delamater, A. M., Jent, J. F., Moine, C. T., & Rios, J. (2008). Empirically supported treatment of overweight adolescents. In E. J. Jelalian & R. G. Steele (Eds.), *Issues in clinical child psychology: Handbook of childhood and adolescent obesity.* New York, NY: Springer Publishing Company.

Dubois, L., Ohm Kyvik, K., Girard, M., Tatone-Tokuda, F., Pérusse, D., Hjelmborg, J.,…Martin, N. G. (2012). Genetic and environmental contributions to weight, height, and BMI from birth to 19 years of age: An international study of over 12,000 twin pairs. *PloS One, 7*(2), e30153.

Elks, C. E., den Hoed, M., Zhao, J. H., Sharp, S. J., Wareham, N. J., Loos, R. J., & Ong, K. K. (2012). Variability in the heritability of body mass index: A systematic review and meta-regression. *Frontiers in Endocrinology, 3,* 29.

Epstein, L. H., Myers, M. D., Raynor, H. A., & Saelens, B. E. (1998). Treatment of pediatric obesity. *Pediatrics, 101*(3 Pt 2), 554–570.

Epstein, L. H., Valoski, A., Koeske, R., & Wing, R. R. (1986). Family-based behavioral weight control in obese young children. *Journal of the American Dietetic Association, 86*(4), 481–484.

Epstein, L. H., Valoski, A., Wing, R. R., & McCurley, J. (1990). Ten-year follow-up of behavioral, family-based treatment for obese children. *Journal of the American Medical Association, 264*(19), 2519–2523.

Epstein, L. H., Valoski, A., Wing, R. R., & McCurley, J. (1994). Ten-year outcomes of behavioral family-based treatment for childhood obesity. *Health Psychology, 13*(5), 373–383.

Erermis, S., Cetin, N., Tamar, M., Bukusoglu, N., Akdeniz, F., & Goksen, D. (2004). Is obesity a risk factor for psychopathology among adolescents? *Pediatrics International, 46*(3), 296–301.

Farpour-Lambert, N. J., Aggoun, Y., Marchand, L. M., Martin, X. E., Herrmann, F. R., & Beghetti, M. (2009). Physical activity reduces systemic blood pressure and improves early markers of atherosclerosis in pre-pubertal obese children. *Journal of the American College of Cardiology, 54*(25), 2396–2406.

Fisher, J. O., Johnson, R. K., Lindquist, C., Birch, L. L., & Goran, M. I. (2000). Influence of body composition on the accuracy of reported energy intake in children. *Obesity Research, 8*(8), 597–603.

Freedman, D. S., Khan, L. K., Serdula, M. K., Dietz, W. H., Srinivasan, S. R., & Berenson, G. S. (2005). Racial differences in the tracking of childhood BMI to adulthood. *Obesity Research, 13*(5), 928–935.

Glanz, K., Murphy, S., Moylan, J., Evensen, D., & Curb, J. D. (2006). Improving dietary self-monitoring and adherence with hand-held computers: A pilot study. *American Journal of Health Promotion, 20*(3), 165–170.

Golan, M., & Crow, S. (2004). Targeting parents exclusively in the treatment of childhood obesity: Long-term results. *Obesity Research, 12*(2), 357–361.

Golan, M., & Weizman, A. (2001). Familial approach to the treatment of childhood obesity: Conceptual mode. *Journal of Nutrition Education, 33*(2), 102–107.

Golan, M., Weizman, A., Apter, A., & Fainaru, M. (1998). Parents as the exclusive agents of change in the treatment of childhood obesity. *The American Journal of Clinical Nutrition, 67*(6), 1130–1135.

Hebebrand, J., Volckmar, A. L., Knoll, N., & Hinney, A. (2010). Chipping away the "missing heritability": GIANT steps forward in the molecular elucidation of obesity—but still lots to go. *Obesity Facts, 3*(5), 294–303. doi:10.1159/000321537

Herrera, E. A., Johnson, C. A., & Steele, R. G. (2004). A comparison of cognitive and behavioral treatments for pediatric obesity. *Children's Health Care, 33*, 151–167.

Janicke, D. M. (2013). Treatment of pediatric obesity using a parent-only approach: A case example. *Health Psychology, 32*(3), 345–350.

Janicke, D. M., Sallinen, B. J., Perri, M. G., Lutes, L. D., Huerta, M., Silverstein, J. H., & Brumback, B. (2008). Comparison of parent-only vs family-based interventions for overweight children in underserved rural settings: Outcomes from project STORY. *Archives of Pediatrics & Adolescent Medicine, 162*(12), 1119–1125.

Janicke, D. M., Steele, R. G., Gayes, L. A., Lim, C. S., Clifford, L. M., Schneider, E. M., … Westen, S. (2014). Systematic review and meta-analysis of comprehensive behavioral family lifestyle interventions addressing pediatric obesity. *Journal of Pediatric Psychology, 39*(8), 809–825.

Kann, L., Kinchen, S., Shanklin, S. L., Flint, K. H., Kawkins, J., Harris, W. A., … Centers for Disease Control and Prevention (CDC). (2014). Youth risk behavior surveillance—United States, 2013. *Morbidity and Mortality Weekly Report Supplements, 63*(4), 1–168.

Kirschenbaum, D. S., Kelly, K. P., & Germann, J. N. (2009). Efficacy of a screening procedure to identify potentially disruptive participants in an immersion program for the treatment of adolescent obesity. *Obesity Facts, 2*(2), 110–115.

Lazorick, S., Peaker, B., Perrin, E. M., Schmid, D., Pennington, T., Yow, A., & DuBard, C. A. (2011). Prevention and treatment of childhood obesity: Care received by a state medicaid population. *Clinical Pediatrics, 50*(9), 816–826.

Maes, H. H., Neale, M. C., & Eaves, L. J. (1997). Genetic and environmental factors in relative body weight and human adiposity. *Behavior Genetics, 27*(4), 325–351.

Magarey, A. M., Daniels, L. A., Boulton, T. J., & Cockington, R. A. (2003). Predicting obesity in early adulthood from childhood and parental obesity. *International Journal of Obesity and Related Metabolic Disorders, 27*(4), 505–513.

Ogden, C. L., Carroll, M. D., Kit, B. K., & Flegal, K. M. (2014). Prevalence of childhood and adult obesity in the United States, 2011–2012. *Journal of the American Medical Association, 311*(8), 806–814.

Pratt, J. S., Lenders, C. M., Dionne, E. A., Hoppin, A. G., Hsu, G. L., Inge, T. H.,... & Sanchez, V. M. (2009). Best practice updates for pediatric/ adolescent weight loss surgery. *Obesity, 17*(5), 901–910.

Pugliese, J., & Tinsley, B. (2007). Parental socialization of child and adolescent physical activity: A meta-analysis. *Journal of Family Psychology, 21*(3), 331–343.

Pulgarón, E. R. (2013). Childhood obesity: A review of increased risk for physical and psychological comorbidities. *Clinical Therapeutics, 35*(1), A18–A32.

Raynor, H. A. (2008). Evidence-based treatments for childhood obesity. In E. J. Jelalian & R. G. Steele (Eds.), *Issues in clinical child psychology: Handbook of childhood and adolescent obesity.* New York, NY: Springer Publishing Company.

Rhee, K. E., Lumeng, J. C., Appugliese, D. P., Kaciroti, N., & Bradley, R. H. (2006). Parenting styles and overweight status in first grade. *Pediatrics, 117*(6), 2047–2054.

Sanchez, A., Norman, G. J., Sallis, J. F., Calfas, K. J., Cella, J., & Patrick, K. (2007). Patterns and correlates of physical activity and nutrition behaviors in adolescents. *American Journal of Preventive Medicine, 32*(2), 124–130.

Schwimmer, J. B., Burwinkle, T. M., & Varni, J. W. (2003). Health-related quality of life of severely obese children and adolescents. *Journal of the American Medical Association, 289*(14), 1813–1819.

Sleddens, E. F., Gerards, S. M., Thijs, C., de Vries, N. K., & Kremers, S. P. (2011). General parenting, childhood overweight and obesity-inducing behaviors: A review. *International Journal of Pediatric Obesity, 6*(2–2), e12–e27.

Spurrier, N. J., Magarey, A. A., Golley, R., Curnow, F., & Sawyer, M. G. (2008). Relationships between the home environment and physical activity and dietary patterns of preschool children: A cross-sectional study. *The International Journal of Behavioral Nutrition and Physical Activity, 5*, 31.

Stein, R. I., Epstein, L. H., Raynor, H. A., Kilanowski, C. K., & Paluch, R. A. (2005). The influence of parenting change on pediatric weight control. *Obesity Research, 13*(10), 1749–1755.

Tanofsky-Kraff, M., Wilfley, D. E., Young, J. F., Mufson, L., Yanovski, S. Z., Glasofer,... Schvey, N. A. (2010). A pilot study of interpersonal psychotherapy for preventing excess weight gain in adolescent girls at-risk for obesity. *The International Journal of Eating Disorders, 43*(8), 701–706.

Tanofsky-Kraff, M., Yanovski, S. Z., Wilfley, D. E., Marmarosh, C., Morgan, C. M., & Yanovski, J. A. (2004). Eating-disordered behaviors, body fat, and psychopathology in overweight and normal-weight children. *Journal of Consulting and Clinical Psychology, 72*(1), 53–61.

Thakkar, R. K., & Michalsky, M. P. (2015). Update on bariatric surgery in adolescence. *Current Opinion in Pediatrics, 27*(3), 370–376.

U.S. Department of Health and Human Services. (2013). *We can! Energize our families: parent program: A leaders guide.* Retrieved from http:// www.nhlbi.nih.gov/health/educational/wecan/ downloads/leadersguide.pdf

Wardle, J., & Cooke, L. (2005). The impact of obesity on psychological well-being. *Best Practice & Research. Clinical Endocrinology & Metabolism, 19*(3), 421–440.

Whitlock, E. P., O'Connor, E. A., Williams, S. B., Beil, T. L., & Lutz, K. W. (2010). Effectiveness of weight management interventions in children: A targeted systematic review for the USPSTF. *Pediatrics, 125*(2), e396–e418.

Wilfley, D. E., Kolko, R. P., & Kass, A. E. (2011). Cognitive-behavioral therapy for weight management and eating disorders in children and adolescents. *Child and Adolescent Psychiatric Clinics of North America, 20*(2), 271–285.

Wilfley, D. E., Welch, R. R., Stein, R. I., Spurrell, E. B., Cohen, L. R., Saelens, B. E.,... Matt, G. E. (2002). A randomized comparison of group cognitive-behavioral therapy and group interpersonal psychotherapy for the treatment of overweight individuals with binge-eating disorder. *Archives of General Psychiatry, 59*(8), 713–721.

Evidence-Based Interventions for Tourette's and Other Chronic Tic Disorders in Children and Adolescents

Audrey Smerbeck

OVERVIEW

A "tic" is defined as a sudden, rapid, recurrent, nonrhythmic motor movement or vocalization. The *Diagnostic and Statistical Manual of Mental Disorders* (5th ed.; *DSM-5*; American Psychiatric Association [APA], 2013) lists two chronic tic disorder diagnoses. If the individual has only motor tics or vocal tics (but not both), and these tics have continued for a period of more than 1 year, the diagnosis of persistent motor or vocal tic disorder (PMVTD) is applied. If the individual has multiple motor tics and at least one vocal tic for a period of more than 1 year, criteria are met for the diagnosis of Tourette's disorder (TD). Both disorders require symptom onset before age 18 years and require the clinician to rule out alternative causes of tics, including substance abuse and other medical conditions (APA, 2013).

Tics may be categorized as either simple or complex. Simple motor tics are brief and use only one or a few muscle groups. Common examples include eye blinking, grimacing, and shoulder shrugging. In contrast, complex motor tics may take longer to perform or involve multiple muscle groups. Examples include deep knee bends and combinations of simple tics such as simultaneously grimacing and flexing the fingers. Vocal tics produce sound using the vocal

tract and can include simple tics such as grunting, throat clearing, and sniffing, as well as complex tics such as speaking a word or phrase, repeating one's own or another's words ("palilalia" and "echolalia," respectively), or "coprolalia," which is the uttering socially unacceptable words (APA, 2013). Although coprolalia has been portrayed prominently in the media, it in fact occurs in only a very small percentage of individuals with tic disorders (Singer, 1997). A review of 18 published studies found an overall tic disorder prevalence of 0.95% (Robertson, Eapen, & Cavanna, 2009). Furthermore, TD occurs approximately three times more frequently in boys than in girls (Robertson et al., 2009).

Tics are typically experienced as involuntary, although many individuals are capable of reducing or suppressing them for short periods of time (Phelps, 2008). Many individuals report an uncomfortable sensation, known as a "premonitory urge," before performing a tic (Leckman, Walker, & Cohen, 1993). This may be a general feeling of urgency, tension, or unease; or, it may be localized to a specific body part. These sensations are reported to become more intense until the tic is performed, at which point they dissipate.

Tics may in some cases directly cause impairment by interfering with activities or—rarely—by causing physical injury (Lehman, Gilbert, Leach, Wu, & Standridge, 2011). More commonly, tics are associated with negative social consequences, including elevated rates of peer victimization and social isolation (Conelea et al., 2011; Storch, Murphy, et al., 2007). Children with tic disorders may be most impaired by comorbid conditions and associated features, including deficient social skills (McGuire, Hanks, Lewin, Storch, & Murphy, 2013), sleep problems (Storch et al., 2009), anxiety and/or depression (Lewin et al., 2011; Specht et al., 2011), obsessive-compulsive disorder (OCD) symptoms (Fibbe et al., 2012; Robertson et al., 2009; Scharf et al., 2013; Specht et al., 2011), and attention deficit hyperactivity disorder (ADHD) symptoms (Robertson et al., 2009; Scharf et al., 2013; Specht et al., 2011). The latter two conditions are particularly common: 50% to 75% of children with TD also meet criteria for OCD and/or ADHD (Lebowitz et al., 2012; Storch, Merlo, et al., 2007).

Initial diagnosis is typically made based on an interview with the child and his or her caregiver, as well as observation of the tics in conjunction with an evaluation by a pediatric neurologist to rule out alternate causes of tic-like movements, such as seizure disorders or Lesch–Nyhan syndrome (Phelps, 2008). Further rule-outs may need to be investigated based on particular tic topography; for example, visual impairment for a squinting tic or upper respiratory problems for a coughing tic. Formal assessment of tic severity can be completed using the *Yale Global Tic Severity Scale* (Leckman et al., 1989). As tic disorders are associated with a high rate of comorbid conditions (which may be more clinically significant than the tics themselves), assessment with a broad measure of psychopathology such as the *Child Behavior Checklist* (CBCL; Achenbach, 1991) is recommended (Murphy, Lewin, Storch, & Stock, 2013).

Diagnostically, complex tics may be difficult to differentiate from compulsions (Neal & Cavanna, 2013; Worbe et al., 2010). When assessing a child or adolescent, it may be helpful to consider the course of the disorder. Chronic tic disorders most commonly have an onset between 5 and 7 years of age, beginning with simple tics that gradually increase in frequency and complexity until reaching peak severity between 10 and 12 years of age (Specht et al., 2011). Even without treatment, tics commonly decrease during adolescence and early adulthood, although residual symptoms remain in 25% to 50% of patients (Piacentini, Perlman, & Peris, 2007).

ETIOLOGY AND FACTORS CONTRIBUTING TO TD AND OTHER CHRONIC TIC DISORDERS IN CHILDREN AND ADOLESCENTS

Early research into the causes of TD suggest that it is caused by a single autosomal dominant gene (Eapen, Pauls, & Robertson, 1993). Recent investigations, however, have not confirmed the single-gene transmission model, but report very strong evidence of the high heritability of tic disorders, including a 5- to 15-fold increase in the risk of TD among first-degree relatives of individuals with TD (Scharf et al., 2013). Neurologically, tic disorders are associated with abnormalities of the basal ganglia, including decreased volume of the caudate nucleus, specifically in GABAergic and cholinergic neurons, and increases in the innervation of dopaminergic neurons (Bronfeld & Bar-Gad, 2013). The overall effect is disinhibition of the movement systems of the brain.

Sudden onset of TD, OCD, and other conditions has sometimes been reported following a Group A streptococcal infection, a syndrome commonly referred to as PANDAS (pediatric autoimmune neuropsychiatric disorders associated with streptococcus). The existence of PANDAS remains controversial, with some research finding a link between the presence of ongoing neuropsychiatric impairment and blood serum findings consistent with infection, and other research suggesting that the onset or worsening of symptoms at the time of infection was better understood as the result of the psychosocial stress of illness (Murphy, Kurlan, & Leckman, 2010; Snider & Swedo, 2004). Although psychosocial stress is not theorized to cause tic disorders, existing tics may worsen under stressful conditions (Phelps, 2008).

EVIDENCE-BASED INTERVENTIONS AND EMPIRICAL SUPPORT FOR TD AND OTHER CHRONIC TIC DISORDERS IN CHILDREN AND ADOLESCENTS

Unlike the vast majority of disorders listed in the *DSM-5*, chronic tic disorders do not require distress or impairment to be diagnosed (APA, 2013). Accordingly, the first step in planning an intervention is determining whether treatment is necessary, and if so, whether the intervention should target the tics, the youth's social environment, or comorbid conditions. In the case of mild, unobtrusive tics, the sole or primary source of distress may simply be the need for an explanation. For example, a child with a chronic cough is seen by a number of respiratory and allergy specialists who find nothing wrong. Once the cough is determined to be a tic and a diagnosis of PMVTD is made, the patient and family are satisfied that the cough is explained. In such cases, brief education as to the nature of the tic disorder, as well as its course and prognosis, may be sufficient (Sandor & Carroll, 2012).

For many individuals with chronic tic disorders, the source of greatest distress is not the tics themselves but rather others' reactions to them (Conelea et al., 2011; Storch, Merlo, et al., 2007). Psychoeducational interventions are recommended to explain the nature of tic disorders to the child's peers, teachers, and family. Rather than try to reduce or redirect tics, this approach teaches others in the child's environment about tic disorders, the involuntary nature of tics, and—if necessary—debunks common myths about tic disorders. A meta-analysis suggests that this approach can be effective in improving others' attitudes toward people with tic disorders (Nussey, Pistrang, & Murphy, 2013). This method may reduce the likelihood that the youth with TD will be the target of teasing or bullying. Parent and teacher education may also be necessary to explain that neither the normal "waxing and waning" appearance of tics nor the capacity of some individuals to suppress tics for a short period of time should be taken as evidence that the tics are really voluntary (Kepley & Conners, 2007). As children and adolescents get older, social skills training may also be employed to teach them to explain their tic disorder symptoms and any related needs.

School-based accommodations may be necessary to ensure that the child has appropriate access to education. Although mild cases may not need official documentation for academic services, the majority of children with chronic tic disorders in the United States have either a 504 disability accommodation plan or an individualized education plan (IEP), typically directing teachers to ignore, rather than punish, tics and allowing the child to leave the classroom to perform tics in private (Murphy et al., 2013). Other helpful accommodations include preferential seating toward the back or side of the room (so the child's tics are less visible to peers), extended time on tests if the child's tics prevent him or her from working steadily, and alternatives to assignments that would cause unnecessary embarrassment or distress (Kepley & Conners, 2007).

In many cases, children and adolescents with a tic disorder function adequately following psychoeducation, social support, and accommodation. However, some youths require direct intervention to reduce their tics. The European Society for the Study of Tourette Syndrome suggests that clinicians consider treatment when the tics cause pain or injury, the tics have caused social impairment, the tics have caused the patient to develop dysphoric mood, or when either the tics or the effort expended in suppressing them are interfering with meaningful functional activities such as communication, sleep, or schoolwork (Roessner et al., 2011). Of note, tics naturally wax and wane regardless of treatment. Thus, it is possible for a child to have a severe tic, begin an intervention, and see the tic recede *regardless of whether the treatment was effective*. As all treatments have costs, in the form of time, money, effort, and side effects, this phenomenon puts youth at risk of suffering the costs of a treatment that actually offers no benefit. Mental health professionals are advised to reevaluate the necessity and efficacy of treatment repeatedly over long periods of time to control for this phenomenon as much as possible (Roessner et al., 2011).

If the tics themselves are severe enough to merit treatment, there are two types of therapies available: biomedical and behavioral. Biomedical treatments include psychoactive medication, deep brain stimulation, transcranial magnetic stimulation, and injections of botulinum toxin. Medication may be considered when the youth's tics are severe enough to merit treatment on their own, or when the child has a comorbid problem which could be treated with a medication that also reduces tics (Eddy, Rickards, & Cavanna, 2011; Murphy et al., 2013). Pharmacological treatments for chronic tic disorders include a very wide range of therapeutic options, often with a fairly limited evidence base. The most common classes of medication studied are dopamine agonists, including neuroleptics, atypical antipsychotics, and benzamides, as well as alpha-2 adrenergic agonists (Murphy et al., 2013). Other agents that have been investigated include anticonvulsants, the antispasmodic drug baclofen, cannabinoids, tetrabenazine, dopamine agonists, anticholinergics, and benzodiazepines (Eddy et al., 2011; Roessner et al., 2011).

Although the evidence is somewhat limited, formal comparisons of pharmacological treatments of tic disorders have been completed; two major reviews are presented in Table 35.1.

The Canadian Practice Parameters (CPP) "weak recommendation" designation indicates that, although there is some evidence of benefit, any positive effect is closely balanced with risks; particular caution is urged in the case of weak recommendation

combined with low or very low evidence strength. In contrast, a "strong recommendation" indicates that the treatment benefits have been clearly shown to outweigh risks (Pringsheim et al., 2012). The European guidelines rated available medications on the strength of the available evidence, such that a rating of "A" corresponds to greater than or equal to two randomized controlled trials, a rating of "B" corresponds to one randomized controlled trial, and a rating of "C" indicates open-label trials, case studies, and the like, only (Roessner et al., 2011). This ratings distinction is notable in the cases

TABLE 35.1

EVIDENCE STRENGTH AND RECOMMENDATION FOR DRUGS COMMONLY USED IN TIC SUPPRESSION			
Drug Name	Class	Canadian Practice Parameters (CPP)—Recommendation/ Evidence Strength	European Practice Parameters—Evidence Strength
Pimozide	Neuroleptic	Weak recommendation/high	A
Haloperidol	Neuroleptic	Weak recommendation/high	A
Fluphenazine	Neuroleptic	Weak recommendation/low	—
Metoclopramide	Antiemetic	Weak recommendation[a]/low	—
Risperidone	Atypical antipsychotic	Weak recommendation/high	A
Aripiprazole	Atypical antipsychotic	Weak recommendation/low	C
Olanzipine	Atypical antipsychotic	Weak recommendation/low	B
Quetiapine	Atypical antipsychotic	Weak recommendation/very low	C
Ziprasadone	Atypical antipsychotic	Weak recommendation[a]/low	A
Clonidine	Alpha-2 adrenergic agonist	Strong recommendation/moderate	A
Guanfacine	Alpha-2 adrenergic agonist	Strong recommendation[a]/moderate	A
Topiramate	Anticonvulsant	Weak recommendation/low	—
Baclofen	GABA-derivative, commonly used to treat spasticity	Weak recommendation/very low	—
Tetrabenazine	Vesicular monoamine transporter-inhibitor	Weak recommendation/very low	—
Cannabinoids		Not recommended[b]	—
Sulpiride	Benzamides	—	B
Tiapride	Benzamides	—	B

[a]Listed recommendation is for children only; no recommendation could be made for medication use in adults.

[b]Cannabinoids were not recommended for use in children. Use in adults was rated as weak recommendation/low-quality evidence.

GABA, gamma-aminobutyric acid; VMAT, vesicular monoamine transporter.

of neuroleptics pimozide and haloperidol as well as atypical antipsychotics risperidone and ziprasadone. All four drugs received an "A" rating from the European commission, and three out of the four received a rating of "High" for evidence strength from the Canadian group. However, these four drugs are only weakly recommended by the CPP because the risk/benefit ratio is poor. In contrast, the two alpha-2 adrenergic agonist drugs reviewed by both panels (clonidine and guanfacine) were agreed to have moderate to strong evidence supporting their use and were judged by the CPP to have a more favorable balance of risk and benefit.

Comorbid ADHD can be particularly difficult to treat as stimulant medications used to treat the disorder have been reported in some cases to induce or aggravate tics. However, a meta-analysis of pharmaceutical treatment trials examining children with TD and ADHD found that methylphenidate, desipramine, atomoxetine, and alpha-2 agonists all achieved some reduction in ADHD symptoms without exacerbating tics over short-term administration. In addition, the latter two agents (atomoxetine and alpha-2 agonists) were found to reduce tics as well (Bloch, Panza, Landeros-Weisenberger, & Leckman, 2009). Thus, if sufficient ADHD symptom control cannot be achieved with behavioral therapy alone, pharmacological intervention may be considered.

More invasive medical treatments include the use of botulinum toxin, deep brain stimulation, and transcranial magnetic stimulation. Botulinum toxin is considered only when the tics affect a single muscle group and appears most effective with motor tics. A randomized controlled trial found the treatment effective in reducing both tics and premonitory urges, but ineffective in improving quality of life (Marras, Andrews, Sime, & Lang, 2001). Deep brain stimulation has been attempted in a small number of severe, treatment-refractory cases. Implanted electrodes are used to alter brain activity, most commonly in the thalamus or globus pallidus. Small-scale studies have shown promising results but with substantial harmful side effects, including apathy, parathesia, and diminished attentional control (Eddy et al., 2011; Steeves et al., 2012). Transcranial magnetic stimulation appears considerably safer than deep brain stimulation, but evidence of efficacy is limited (Eddy et al., 2011; Steeves et al., 2012).

Psychotherapeutic approaches to treating tics are generally behavioral in nature. A review conducted in 2007 found that only two approaches—habit reversal therapy (HRT) and exposure and response prevention (ERP)—have adequate evidence to treat tic disorders and TD. The four remaining psychotherapeutic treatments—cognitive behavioral therapy, self-monitoring, massed negative practice, and contingency management—have not been studied thoroughly enough to meet evidence-based criteria (Cook & Blacher, 2007). Despite worries that suppressing tics will worsen attention, anxiety, or behavior, evidence suggests a positive or neutral effect on other elements of psychosocial functioning (Rowe, Yuen, & Dure, 2013; Woods et al., 2011). In the same vein, evidence suggests that worries about a "rebound effect" following tic suppression are similarly unfounded (Specht et al., 2013).

The most long-standing approach, HRT has been found effective in the treatment of a wide variety of unwanted repetitive behaviors with both children and adults (Bate, Malouff, Thorsteinsson, & Bhullar, 2011; Cook & Blacher, 2007; Dutta & Cavanna, 2013). HRT teaches individuals to be aware of their tics and to perform an incompatible competing response (CR) when they feel the urge to do a tic (see the following discussion). HRT requires considerable effort to complete and it appears broadly effective in achieving tic reduction, though generally not elimination. HRT is considered "well established" (Cook & Blacher, 2007) with a recent meta-analysis finding significant reduction in tic severity, with a decrease in scores ranging from 18.3% to 37.5% (Dutta & Cavanna, 2013). As HRT relies on some degree of self-awareness, it may be less appropriate for young children, though it has been successfully used with children as young as age 6 years with some modification (Feldman, Storch, & Murphy, 2011).

HRT is the core component of the Comprehensive Behavioral Intervention for Tics (CBIT), which adds relaxation training and parent training components (Piacentini et al., 2010). The parent training approach is a functional one, examining common antecedents and consequences of tics. Although tics are essentially involuntary, the functional approach notes that they can be strengthened or weakened by environmental stimuli presented before or after the behavior occurs (Capriotti, Brandt, Rickftts, Espii, & Woods,

2012; Woods et al., 2008). Although the functional approach has been used as a component of an evidence-based therapy, alone it lacks sufficient data for its efficacy to be judged (Cook & Blacher, 2007).

ERP is based on the underlying idea that tics are negatively reinforced by a reduction in unpleasant premonitory urges (van de Griendt, Verdellen, van Dijk, & Verbraak, 2013). ERP was originally created for use with OCD patients, who are thought to perform compulsions to reduce unpleasant obsessions. As TD has high comorbidity with OCD, many patients may benefit from the use of similar techniques to address both conditions (Woods, Hook, Spellman, & Friman, 2000). In ERP sessions, the child is encouraged to suppress all tics simultaneously for as long as possible while focusing on or eliciting premonitory urges. Thus, ERP treats all tics simultaneously, whereas HRT focuses on one tic at a time. However, ERP places a very high demand on focus and concentration, which may prove unmanageable for younger children and those who have comorbid ADHD. In addition, ERP focuses on premonitory urges and thus may be inappropriate for children who deny having premonitory urges or lack the self-awareness to identify them (van de Griendt et al., 2013). A randomized controlled trial found that ERP was as effective as HRT, though it should be noted that the ERP group received twelve 2-hour sessions while the HRT group received only ten 1-hour sessions (Verdellen, Keijsers, Cath, & Hoogduin, 2004).

HOW TO: A GUIDE TO THE IMPLEMENTATION OF INTERVENTIONS FOR TD AND OTHER CHRONIC TIC DISORDERS IN CHILDREN AND ADOLESCENTS

Habit Reversal Training

Habit reversal training (HRT) is a straightforward and effective behavioral intervention for tics and other unwanted repetitive behaviors, such as nail-biting and stuttering. The major components of the intervention are listed in what follows (Bate et al., 2011; Woods et al., 2008), along with examples explaining how these principles could be applied to a hypothetical 10-year-old TD patient Juanita, seeking treatment for a tongue-thrust tic.

Component I: Awareness Training. Response description develops a child-friendly operational definition of the target behavior. Juanita and her therapist defined her tic as "anytime Juanita sticks her tongue out past her lips." *Response detection* helps the child or adolescent learn to notice each time the target behavior occurs. To increase motivation for this step, Juanita's mother was asked to count her daughter's tics over certain intervals; if Juanita counted the same number of tics as her mother, she was given a small reward (extra computer time).

Early warning premonitory urges are not a prerequisite for the successful application of HRT (Ganos et al., 2012), but if possible, children should be taught to recognize the sensations which precede their tics. Juanita identified a "hot, twitchy" feeling at the tip of her tongue. *Situation awareness* assists children and adolescents identify circumstances that are associated with high rates of tics. Juanita was unaware that her tongue-thrust tic increased while playing video games until her mother mentioned it. Following a week of self-observation, she concurred with her conclusion. If tics appear to be associated with stress, a relaxation-training component may be added as well.

Component II: CR Training. In this phase, the clinician works with the child to select a behavior that will serve as the CR to the tic. A CR is a behavior that is physically incompatible with the tic. Most common CRs act in opposition to the target tic, often by isometrically tensing muscles. For example, a shoulder-shrugging tic might be opposed by pulling the shoulders downward. The CR should be socially inconspicuous and easy to perform without interrupting normal activity. Consideration should also be given to the practical and physical consequences of maintaining the CR position for several minutes multiple times per day. If the child has a physical disability, the therapist may wish to collaborate with a physical therapist and/or physician to ensure that an appropriate CR can be identified. A list of commonly used CRs is available in Woods and colleagues' *Managing Tourette Syndrome: A Behavioral Intervention for Children and Adults.* Once the clinician and child agree on the CR, it is repeatedly practiced in the therapy setting and the youth is coached to initiate the CR whenever the tic behavior begins or a premonitory urge is noted. The CR should be maintained for approximately 1 minute or until the urge goes away. This is practiced and reinforced in the therapy setting before being attempted in everyday life.

Juanita and her therapist selected the following CR for her tongue-thrust tic: Press the tongue to the roof of the mouth and clench the teeth together. This was practiced in the therapy session. Once Juanita could successfully perform the CR, she practiced performing it when she felt the urge to do her tic. She initially held the CR position for only a few seconds, but with coaching from the therapist, she began maintaining it for a full minute. She agreed to try applying the CR in her everyday life.

Component III: Motivation Training. HRT requires children and adolescents to suppress a strong urge in favor of an alternative behavior. Motivation training is used to ensure that the child remains willing to put forth the effort necessary to be successful. *Habit Inconvenience Review* encourages youths to make a list of all the ways in which the tic has caused problems, frustration, or difficulty. The child/adolescent reviews this list periodically to remind himself or herself why HRT is worthwhile. Juanita's list included teasing from peers, feeling self-conscious when others looked at her, and occasionally biting her tongue, among others. *Social Support Training* enlists individuals in the child's life to provide encouragement and prompting. Parents are often enlisted to support child patients by providing reminders to do the CR should the tic behavior occur and praise when the child performs the CR. Juanita's parents were both trained in the social support role.

Component IV: Generalization Training. The final component focuses on helping the child to use HRT across all settings, using a variety of techniques. Symbolic rehearsal is often applied, asking the child to imagine himself or herself in an everyday setting, feeling the urge to perform a tic, and performing the CR behavior instead. To enhance motivation, the youth may be guided to imagine a positive outcome to CR use (e.g., "Now, I feel confident enough to volunteer to write on the chalkboard."). If children and adolescents do not have or recognize premonitory urges, they may be coached to imagine initiating the tic, but performing the CR instead of completing it.

Other generalization techniques may be applied as necessary. For example, a child may be given a small reinforcer if he or she requires X or fewer reminders to perform the CR instead of the tic over a given time interval. Discreet visual cues can be placed in the child's environment. Motivating operations can be adjusted to increasing the desirability of performing the CR instead of the tic. In Jaunita's case, she previously had never worn lipstick because it would be smeared by her tongue-thrust tic. Once she was confidently performing the CR behavior, her mother allowed her to purchase and wear lipstick. The presence of lipstick acted as a reminder to perform the CR instead of the tic and helped Juanita generalize to new situations.

Exposure and Response Prevention

The central premise of ERP is exposure to the premonitory urge (the feeling of physical or mental discomfort that often precedes a tic) without responding by performing a tic. The child/adolescent gradually habituates to the premonitory urge sensation and no longer feels compelled to perform a tic when the premonitory urge is present. ERP generally targets all tics at once, so although Juanita (the mock patient described earlier) was most concerned about her tongue-thrust tic, ERP would address her eye-blinking and throat-clearing tics as well (van de Griendt et al., 2013; Verdellen et al., 2008).

Component I: Response Prevention. ERP for tic disorders begins with two 2-hour sessions during which the child is taught to suppress all tics for longer and longer periods of time. The therapist times the child during these suppression periods and encourages him or her to "beat" the previous time. If the same tic repeatedly occurs, the child is told to focus solely on suppressing that tic for a brief period of time, after which the therapist directs the child to resume suppressing all tics. During these initial sessions, there is no emphasis on premonitory urges.

Component II: ERP. Beginning with the third session, ERP participants are instructed to focus on and strengthen their premonitory urges while continuing to suppress their tics. The urges are maximized using a variety of techniques, including discussion of the premonitory urges themselves, discussion of the tics, guided imagery of situations that frequently elicit tics, and in vivo contact with objects, activities, or situations that frequently elicit tics. If a tic occurs during these sessions, it is noted and the child is encouraged to return to suppressing tics. Unlike HRT, ERP does not teach children to perform an alternative behavior (CR), but to simply refrain from performing the tic. Regular ratings of premonitory urge severity may be taken using subjective units of distress scale (SUDS).

Functional Approach

A functional approach presumes that even seemingly involuntary behaviors like tics can be moderated by environmental variables. In this approach, common antecedents and consequences of tics are identified and then systematically adjusted (Rowe et al., 2013; Woods et al., 2008). One advantage of this approach is that it can be conducted by working solely with the adults in the child's environment, rather than the child himself or herself; because of age or disability, some tic disorder patients lack the cognitive, language, attention, or self-regulation skills to meaningfully participate in direct treatment such as HRT or ERP.

Component I: Function-Based Assessment. The most common antecedents and consequences of the tics are identified. This step can be done by a young child's caretaker or, in the case of older adolescents, self-report. There are a number of ways to conduct a functional assessment, including direct observation, functional analysis, and completion of an observation checklist or form. If using a checklist, the observer is asked to check off how many times each tic occurs in a variety of situations (antecedents). Antecedents typically refer to observable phenomena, such as "watching television," "doing homework," or "playing with peers." If an internal state, such as stress or anxiety, is a suspected antecedent, the clinician should help the observer decide on a list of objective criteria that can be used to determine whether the internal state is present. This helps avoid circular reasoning (i.e., "He does his tics when he's anxious. I know he's anxious because he's doing tics."). The observer should also make note of the specific consequences

that follow each tic or bout of tics. Common consequences that can reinforce tics include social attention and escape from unpleasant circumstances or activities.

Component II: Function-Based Interventions. Once the antecedents and consequences of the child's or adolescent's tics have been established, the therapist should work with the youth and his or her family to determine which environmental factors can be changed and what the most appropriate changes would be.

Example Antecedent-Based Interventions

- Reduce or eliminate time spent in the antecedent condition.
- If the functional approach is being used concurrently with HRT or ERP, a cue can be provided to remind the patient to suppress tics before entering the antecedent situation or activity.
- Take steps to accommodate tics and reduce psychosocial impairment when entering a situation in which they are likely to occur.

Example Consequence-Based Interventions

- Ignore, rather than reprimand, tics to avoid providing social attention.
- Provide psychoeducation to the child's peers to normalize the tic behaviors and reduce the likelihood they will react.
- Consider preventing the child from escaping or avoiding a developmentally appropriate unpleasant situation despite the presence of tics (e.g., remain in bed after bedtime).
- If it is necessary to allow the child to leave a setting because of tics, maintain as many core features of the setting as possible. For example, if a child is excused from the classroom during seatwork because of tics, the child should take the seatwork along and complete it in the alternate setting.

In all cases, the total frequency and severity of tics should be assessed before and after the implementation of the intervention to aid in determining whether the treatment was effective. If the intervention is costly in time, resources, or effort, a more elaborate experimental model (e.g., ABAB reversal, multiple baseline) should be considered.

CONCLUSION

Tourette's disorder and other chronic tic disorders are childhood-onset conditions characterized by sudden, involuntary movements or vocalizations. If the tics do not cause any distress or impairment, there may be no need for intervention beyond brief psychoeducation for family and/or peers to explain the condition and reduce stigma. In other cases, simple accommodations such as occasional "tic breaks" may be sufficient. However, if there is a need to reduce the frequency or intensity of tics, a variety of biomedical and behavioral therapies are available. Among biomedical interventions, alpha-2 agonists were the most strongly recommended medications across two meta-analyses (Pringsheim et al., 2012; Roessner et al., 2011), showing not only efficacy in treating tics, but also in treating the ADHD symptoms that are commonly comorbid with Tourette's disorder (Bloch, Panza, Landeros-Weisenberger, & Leckman, 2009). Effective behavior therapies for tic disorders include exposure and response prevention (van de Griendt et al., 2013; Verdellen et al., 2008), which teaches the child to resist the urge to perform tics, and habit reversal therapy, which focuses on replacing the tic with an incompatible competing response (Bate et al., 2011; Woods et al., 2008). Because tics naturally wax and wane over time, it is possible for an intervention to appear effective when in fact the improvement was coincidental. Similarly, an efficacious intervention to suppress a tic may become unnecessary as the underlying urge to perform the tic fades. As such, practitioners should be especially careful to regularly assess the relative costs, risks, and benefits associated with any intervention for TD or other chronic tic disorders.

SELECT BIBLIOGRAPHY

Bloch, M. H., Panza, K. E., Landeros-Weisenberger, A., & Leckman, J. F. (2009). Meta-analysis: Treatment of attention deficit/hyperactivity disorder in children with comorbid tic disorders. *Journal of the American Academy of Child & Adolescent Psychiatry, 48*(9), 884–893. doi:10.1097/ CHI.0b013c3181b26e9f
This article provides a detailed, empirical analysis of the risks and benefits of pharmacological treatment in children who have both ADHD and tic disorders.

Cook, C. R., & Blacher, J. (2007). Evidence-based psychosocial treatments for tic disorders. *Clinical Psychology: Science and Practice, 14*(3), 252–267. doi:10.1111/j.1468-2850.2007.00085.x
This article reviews the variety and quality of evidence supporting various nonpharmacological tic disorder therapies.

Woods, D. W., Piacentini, J. C., Chang, S., Deckersbach, T., Ginsburg, G. S., Peterson, A. L.,... Wilhelm, S. (2008). *Managing Tourette syndrome: A behavioral intervention guide for children and adults.* New York, NY: Oxford University Press.
This treatment manual guides the therapist in the provision of comprehensive behavior intervention for tics (CBIT), a combination of habit reversal and functional approaches. There are also two companion workbooks available, one for parents who are learning to manage their children's tics, and a second for older adolescents and adults who are learning to manage their own tics.

REFERENCES

Achenbach, T. M. (1991). *Child behavior checklist.* Burlington, VT: University of Vermont, Department of Psychiatry.

American Psychiatric Association (APA). (2013). *Diagnostic and Statistical Manual of Mental Disorders.* Arlington, VA: American Psychiatric Publishing, Inc.

Bate, K. S., Malouff, J. M., Thorsteinsson, E. T., & Bhullar, N. (2011). The efficacy of habit reversal therapy for tics, habit disorders, and stuttering: A meta-analytic review. *Clinical Psychology Review, 31*(5), 865–871. doi:10.1016/j. cpr.2011.03.013

Bloch, M. H., Panza, K. E., Landeros-Weisenberger, A., & Leckman, J. F. (2009). Meta-analysis: Treatment of attention-deficit/hyperactivity disorder in children with comorbid tic disorders. *Journal of the American Academy of Child & Adolescent Psychiatry, 48*(9), 884–893. doi:10.1097/ CHI.0b013e3181b26e9f

Bronfeld, M., & Bar-Gad, I. (2013). Tic disorders: What happens in the basal ganglia? *Neuroscientist, 19*(1), 101–108. doi:10.1177/1073858412444466

Capriotti, M. R., Brandt, B. C., Rickftts, E. J., Espii, F. M., & Woods, D. W. (2012). Comparing the effects of differential reinforcement of other behavior and response-cost contingencies on tics in youth with Tourette syndrome. *Journal of Applied Behavior*

Analysis, 45(2), 251–263. doi:10.1901/jaba.2012.45-251

Conelea, C. A., Woods, D. W., Zinner, S. H., Budman, C., Murphy, T., Scahill, L. D.,…Walkup, J. (2011). Exploring the impact of chronic tic disorders on youth: Results from the Tourette Syndrome Impact Survey. *Child Psychiatry and Human Development, 42*(2), 219–242. doi:10.1007/s10578-010-0211-4

Cook, C. R., & Blacher, J. (2007). Evidence-based psychosocial treatments for tic disorders. *Clinical Psychology: Science and Practice, 14*(3), 252–267. doi:10.1111/j.1468-2850.2007.00085.x

Dutta, N., & Cavanna, A. E. (2013). The effectiveness of habit reversal therapy in the treatment of Tourette syndrome and other chronic tic disorders: A systematic review. *Functional Neurology, 28*(1), 7–12.

Eapen, V., Pauls, D. L., & Robertson, M. M. (1993). Evidence for autosomal dominant transmission in Tourette's syndrome: United Kingdom cohort study. *The British Journal of Psychiatry, 162,* 593–596.

Eddy, C. M., Rickards, H. E., & Cavanna, A. E. (2011). Treatment strategies for tics in Tourette syndrome. *Therapeutic Advances in Neurological Disorders, 4*(1), 25–45. doi:10.1177/1756285610390261

Feldman, M. A., Storch, E. A., & Murphy, T. K. (2011). Application of habit reversal training for the treatment of tics in early childhood. *Clinical Case Studies, 10*(2), 173–183. doi:10.1177/1534650111400728

Fibbe, L. A., Cath, D. C., van den Heuvel, O. A., Veltman, D. J., Tijssen, M. A., & van Balkom, A. J. (2012). Relationship between movement disorders and obsessive-compulsive disorder: Beyond the obsessive-compulsive-tic phenotype. A systematic review. *Journal of Neurology, Neurosurgery, and Psychiatry, 83*(6), 646–654. doi:10.1136/jnnp-2011-301752

Ganos, C., Kahl, U., Schunke, O., Kühn, S., Haggard, P., Gerloff, C.,…Münchau, A. (2012). Are premonitory urges a prerequisite of tic inhibition in Gilles de la Tourette syndrome? *Journal of Neurology, Neurosurgery, and Psychiatry, 83*(10), 975–978.

Kepley, H., & Conners, S. (2007). Management of learning and school difficulties in children with Tourette syndrome. In D. W. Woods, J. C. Piacenti, & J. Walkup (Eds.), *Treating Tourette syndrome and tic disorders: A guide for practitioners* (pp. 242–264). New York, NY: Guilford Press.

Lebowitz, E. R., Motlagh, M. G., Katsovich, L., King, R. A., Lombroso, P. J., Grantz, H.,…Leckman, J. F. (2012). Tourette syndrome in youth with and without obsessive compulsive disorder and attention deficit hyperactivity disorder. *European Child & Adolescent Psychiatry, 21*(8), 451–457. doi:10.1007/s00787-012-0278-5

Leckman, J. F., Riddle, M. A., Hardin, M. T., Ort, S. I., Swartz, K. L., Stevenson, J., & Cohen, D. J. (1989). The Yale Global Tic Severity Scale: Initial testing of a clinician-rated scale of tic severity. *Journal of the American Academy of Child & Adolescent Psychiatry, 28*(4), 566–573. doi:10.1097/00004583-198907000-00015

Leckman, J. F., Walker, D. E., & Cohen, D. J. (1993). Premonitory urges in Tourette's syndrome. *The American Journal of Psychiatry, 150*(1), 98–102.

Lehman, L. L., Gilbert, D. L., Leach, J. L., Wu, S. W., & Standridge, S. M. (2011). Vertebral artery dissection leading to stroke caused by violent neck tics of Tourette syndrome. *Neurology, 77*(18), 1706–1708. doi:10.1212/WNL.0b013e318238253c

Lewin, A. B., Storch, E. A., Conelea, C. A., Woods, D. W., Zinner, S. H., Budman, C. L.,…Murphy, T. K. (2011). The roles of anxiety and depression in connecting tic severity and functional impairment. *Journal of Anxiety Disorders, 25*(2), 164–168. doi:10.1016/j.janxdis.2010.08.016

Marras, C., Andrews, D., Sime, E., & Lang, A. E. (2001). Botulinum toxin for simple motor tics: A randomized, double-blind, controlled clinical trial. *Neurology, 56*(5), 605–610.

McGuire, J. F., Hanks, C., Lewin, A. B., Storch, E. A., & Murphy, T. K. (2013). Social deficits in children with chronic tic disorders: Phenomenology, clinical correlates and quality of life. *Comprehensive Psychiatry, 54*(7), 1023–1031. doi:10.1016/j.comppsych.2013.04.009

Murphy, T. K., Kurlan, R., & Leckman, J. (2010). The immunobiology of Tourette's disorder, pediatric autoimmune neuropsychiatric disorders associated with Streptococcus, and related disorders: A way forward. *Journal of Child and Adolescent Psychopharmacology, 20*(4), 317–331. doi:10.1089/cap.2010.0043

Murphy, T. K., Lewin, A. B., Storch, E. A., & Stock, S. (2013). Practice parameter for the assessment and treatment of children and adolescents with tic disorders. *Journal of the American Academy of*

Child & Adolescent Psychiatry, 52(12), 1341–1359. doi:10.1016/j.jaac.2013.09.015

Neal, M., & Cavanna, A. E. (2013). "Not just right experiences" in patients with Tourette syndrome: Complex motor tics or compulsions? Psychiatry Research, 210(2), 559–563. doi:10.1016/j.psychres.2013.06.033

Nussey, C., Pistrang, N., & Murphy, T. (2013). How does psychoeducation help? A review of the effects of providing information about Tourette syndrome and attention-deficit/hyperactivity disorder. Child: Care, Health, & Development, 39(5), 617–627. doi:10.1111/cch.12039

Phelps, L. (2008). Tourette's disorder: Genetic update, neurological correlates, and evidence-based interventions. School Psychology Quarterly, 23(2), 282–289. doi:10.1037/1045–3830.23.2.282

Piacentini, J., Perlman, A. J., & Peris, T. S. (2007). Characteristics of Tourette syndrome. In D. W. Woods, J. C. Piacentini, & J. T. Walkup (Eds.), Treating Tourette syndrome and tic disorders: A guide for practitioners (pp. 9–21). New York, NY: Guilford Press.

Piacentini, J., Woods, D. W., Scahill, L., Wilhelm, S., Peterson, A. L., Chang, S.,...Walkup, J. T. (2010). Behavior therapy for children with Tourette disorder: A randomized controlled trial. Journal of the American Medical Association, 303(19), 1929–1937. doi:10.1001/jama.2010.607

Pringsheim, T., Doja, A., Gorman, D., McKinlay, D., Day, L., Billinghurst, L.,...Sandor, P. (2012). Canadian guidelines for the evidence-based treatment of tic disorders: Pharmacotherapy. The Canadian Journal of Psychiatry/La Revue canadienne de psychiatrie, 57(3), 133–143.

Robertson, M. M., Eapen, V., & Cavanna, A. E. (2009). The international prevalence, epidemiology, and clinical phenomenology of Tourette syndrome: A cross-cultural perspective. Journal of Psychosomatic Research, 67(6), 475–483.

Roessner, V., Plessen, K. J., Rothenberger, A., Ludolph, A. G., Rizzo, R., Skov, L.,...Group, E. G. (2011). European clinical guidelines for Tourette syndrome and other tic disorders. Part II: pharmacological treatment. European Child and Adolescent Psychiatry, 20(4), 173–196. doi:10.1007/s00787-011-0163-7

Rowe, J., Yuen, H. K., & Dure, L. S. (2013). Comprehensive behavioral intervention to improve occupational performance in children with Tourette disorder. American Journal of Occupational Therapy, 67(2), 194–200. doi:10.5014/ajot.2013.007062

Sandor, P., & Carroll, A. (2012). Canadian guidelines for the evidence-based treatment of tic disorders. The Canadian Journal of Psychiatry/La Revue canadienne de psychiatrie, 57(3), 131–132.

Scharf, J. M., Yu, D., Mathews, C. A., Neale, B. M., Stewart, S. E., Fagerness, J. A.,...Pauls, D. L. (2013). Genome-wide association study of Tourette's syndrome. Molecular Psychiatry, 18(6), 721–728. doi:10.1038/mp.2012.69

Singer, C. (1997). Coprolalia and other coprophenomena. Neurologic Clinics, 15(2), 299–308.

Snider, L. A., & Swedo, S. E. (2004). PANDAS: Current status and directions for research. Molecular Psychiatry, 9(10), 900–907. doi:10.1038/sj.mp.4001542

Specht, M. W., Woods, D. W., Nicotra, C. M., Kelly, L. M., Ricketts, E. J., Conelea, C. A.,...Walkup, J. T. (2013). Effects of tic suppression: Ability to suppress, rebound, negative reinforcement, and habituation to the premonitory urge. Behaviour Research and Therapy, 51(1), 24–30. doi:10.1016/j.brat.2012.09.009

Specht, M. W., Woods, D. W., Piacentini, J., Scahill, L., Wilhelm, S., Peterson, A. L.,...Walkup, J. T. (2011). Clinical characteristics of children and adolescents with a primary tic disorder. Journal of Developmental and Physical Disabilities, 23(1), 15–31. doi:10.1007/s10882-010-9223-z

Steeves, T., McKinlay, B. D., Gorman, D., Billinghurst, L., Day, L., Carroll, A.,...Pringsheim, T. (2012). Canadian guidelines for the evidence-based treatment of tic disorders: Behavioural therapy, deep brain stimulation, and transcranial magnetic stimulation. The Canadian Journal of Psychiatry/La Revue canadienne de psychiatrie, 57(3), 144–151.

Storch, E. A., Merlo, L. J., Lack, C., Milsom, V. A., Geffken, G. R., Goodman, W. K., & Murphy, T. K. (2007). Quality of life in youth with Tourette's syndrome and chronic tic disorder. Journal of Clinical Child and Adolescent Psychology, 36(2), 217–227. doi:10.1080/15374410701279545

Storch, E. A., Milsom, V., Lack, C. W., Pence, S. L., Jr., Geffken, G. R., Jacob, M. L.,...Murphy, T. K. (2009). Sleep-related problems in youth with Tourette's syndrome and chronic tic disorder. *Child and Adolescent Mental Health, 14*(2), 97–103.

Storch, E. A., Murphy, T. K., Chase, R. M., Keeley, M., Goodman, W. K., Murray, M., & Geffken, G. R. (2007). Peer victimization in youth with Tourette's syndrome and chronic tic disorder: Relations with tic severity and internalizing symptoms. *Journal of Psychopathology and Behavioral Assessment, 29*(4), 211–219. doi:10.1007/s10862-007-9050-4

van de Griendt, J. M. T. M., Verdellen, C. W. J., van Dijk, M. K., & Verbraak, M. J. P. M. (2013). Behavioural treatment of tics: Habit reversal and exposure with response prevention. *Neuroscience and Biobehavioral Reviews, 37*(6), 1172–1177. doi:10.1016/j.neubiorev.2012.10.007

Verdellen, C. W., Hoogduin, C. A., Kato, B. S., Keijsers, G. P., Cath, D. C., & Hoijtink, H. B. (2008). Habituation of premonitory sensations during exposure and response prevention treatment in Tourette's syndrome. *Behavior Modification, 32*(2), 215–227. doi:10.1177/0145445507309020

Verdellen, C. W., Keijsers, G. P., Cath, D. C., & Hoogduin, C. A. (2004). Exposure with response prevention versus habit reversal in Tourettes's syndrome: A controlled study. *Behaviour Research and Therapy, 42*(5), 501–511. doi:10.1016/S0005-7967(03)00154-2

Woods, D. W., Hook, S. S., Spellman, D. F., & Friman, P. C. (2000). Case study: Exposure and response prevention for an adolescent with Tourette's syndrome and OCD. *Journal of the American Academy of Child & Adolescent Psychiatry, 39*(7), 904–907. doi:10.1097/00004583-200007000-00020

Woods, D. W., Piacentini, J. C., Chang, S., Deckersbach, T., Ginsburg, G. S., Peterson, A. L.,…Wilhelm, S. (2008). *Managing Tourette syndrome: A behavioral intervention guide for children and adults*. New York, NY: Oxford University Press.

Woods, D. W., Piacentini, J. C., Scahill, L., Peterson, A. L., Wilhelm, S., Chang, S.,…Walkup, J. T. (2011). Behavior therapy for tics in children: Acute and long-term effects on psychiatric and psychosocial functioning. *Journal of Child Neurology, 26*(7), 858–865. doi:10.1177/0883073810397046

Worbe, Y., Mallet, L., Golmard, J.-L., Béhar, C., Durif, F., Jalenques, I.,…Hartmann, A. (2010). Repetitive behaviours in patients with Gilles de la Tourette syndrome: Tics, compulsions, or both? *PLoS ONE, 5*(9). doi:10.1371/journal.pone.0012959

Evidence-Based Interventions for Elimination Disorders in Children and Adolescents: Enuresis and Encopresis

Gretchen Gimpel Peacock, Trisha Chase, and Kerry K. Prout

Elimination disorders in children, including encopresis as well as nocturnal and diurnal enuresis, are common causes of concern for parents. Although these toileting problems are often grouped together when discussing child and adolescent behavioral and health interventions, their etiology, associated complications, and recommended interventions are diverse enough that for the purposes of adequately describing intervention programs for each, this chapter is divided into three subsections with each subsection addressing one of the three elimination disorders.

DIURNAL ENURESIS

Overview

Diurnal enuresis, also referred to as "daytime enuresis" or "daytime urinary incontinence," is characterized by typically involuntary daytime wetting. According to the *Diagnostic and Statistical Manual of Mental Disorders* (5th ed.; *DSM-5*; American Psychiatric Association [APA], 2013), the criteria for enuresis include: repeated voiding of urine into one's bed or clothes for a child at least 5 years old that causes clinically significant distress/impairment or occurs at least twice a week for at least

3 consecutive months (APA, 2013). The wetting cannot be the result of a medical condition or the physiological effect of a substance. Although the *DSM-5* has only one enuresis category, subtypes include nocturnal only, diurnal only, and a combination of the two.

In the United States, toilet training occurs for most children by 48 months of age and commonly occurs between 24 and 36 months of age (Campbell, Cox, & Borowitz, 2009; Schroeder & Gordon, 2002), with urinary continence expected around the age of 5 years (Campbell et al., 2009). Much of the research on prevalence of enuresis in children has focused on both nocturnal and diurnal enuresis—often mixing the two together; however, there are some prevalence data specific to daytime wetting. In a review of the prevalence research (Buckley & Lapitan, 2010), daytime wetting was estimated to occur in 3.2% to 9% of 7-year-old children, dropping to 1.1% to 4.2% in children aged 11 to 13 years, and 1.2% to 3% in children aged 15 to 17 years. It is interesting to note that the authors of this review observed higher prevalence figures in studies conducted more recently, attributing this to greater awareness of daytime wetting as a problem. Rates will often differ depending on how enuresis is defined. For example, in one large longitudinal study (von

Gontard, Heron, & Joinson, 2011), the prevalence estimate of daytime incontinence in 7-year-olds was 7.8%; however, only 1% of children were considered to have "severe" incontinence (defined as wetting two or more times per week).

Etiology and Factors Contributing to Diurnal Enuresis in Children and Adolescents

Influences contributing to daytime wetting include a variety of possible biological and psychosocial factors. One of the more common biological causes is detrusor overactivity, or an overactive bladder in which children have muscle spasms of the bladder wall leading to a sudden urge to urinate and an inability to delay voiding (Campbell et al., 2009; Nevéus & Sillén, 2013). In addition to detrusor overactivity, increased urgency and frequency may result from small bladder capacity, urinary tract infections, or even constipation (Campbell et al., 2009). Dysfunctional voiding, in which the child contracts his or her urinary sphincter when voiding, may occur in some cases of urinary incontinence. Additional biological contributions include various chronic diseases (e.g., diabetes, sickle cell disease); however, it is estimated that such causes are implicated in only 1% to 3% of cases (Schroeder & Gordon, 2002).

Psychosocial factors may also be associated with daytime wetting. Inadequate learning experiences related to toilet training, inappropriate reinforcement, or the stress surrounding toilet training may contribute to incomplete toilet training and ultimately failure to control urination (Schroeder & Gordon, 2002). Delays in other areas of development may also contribute to wetting problems. In one longitudinal study (Joinson et al., 2008), it was found that children who had delays in motor, communication, and social skills were more likely to have daytime wetting. In addition, a difficult child temperament as well as maternal depression and anxiety were associated with increased daytime wetting. Some research has posited that, when children with reduced bladder control engage in intense play, the result is daytime enuresis symptoms (Schulz-Juergensen, Bolte, Gebhardt, & Eggert, 2013). In this context, the child might ignore (or not attend to and recognize)

the body's signal to urinate and ultimately result in urinary incontinence. In addition, it is important to examine any comorbid conditions (e.g., attention deficit hyperactivity disorder [ADHD]), which might contribute to daytime wetting. For example, a child with severe attention difficulties may not attend to physical cues that he or she needs to urinate (Campbell et al., 2009).

Evidence-Based Interventions and Empirical Support for Diurnal Enuresis in Children and Adolescents

Treatment of children with diurnal enuresis should begin with a referral to the child's pediatrician to evaluate and rule out any organic causes of incontinence as well as discuss any appropriate medical treatments. As noted earlier, children who are constipated may have a higher rate of urinary incontinence and treating the constipation may resolve the incontinence. Therefore, it is important for the medical evaluation to include not just an evaluation of urinary systems but all potential bladder and/or bowel issues as well.

Once organic causes have been ruled out, evidence-based practice indicates that behavioral interventions are appropriate. Although evidence-based interventions specifically for diurnal enuresis are limited, research on daytime wetting has stressed the importance of establishing good toileting habits. Thus, looking at toilet-training programs can provide helpful information on effective treatment components for ongoing difficulties with urinary incontinence. One of the first empirically supported toilet-training programs was created by Foxx and Azrin (1973). This program included a number of important characteristics such as distraction-free environment, increased fluid intake (approximately two cups per hour), continuous practice and reinforcement in approaching the toilet, and immediate reinforcement for correct toileting. In their study, Foxx and Azrin (1973b) reported that all children in the sample were trained as a result of the intervention and that toilet training was accomplished in an average time of 4 hours. During the week following training, toileting accidents decreased to near zero and remained at this level throughout a 4-month follow-up. Although this program may be effective, as initially conceptualized and evaluated, it may be more intense than many parents would like.

One of the other main approaches to toilet training is the child-oriented approach initially described by Brazelton (1962). In this approach, toilet training is taught over time as children become increasingly "ready" including being physically ready (e.g., ability to dress/undress), being instructionally ready (e.g., ability to follow directions), and internally ready (e.g., being motivated on own to achieve tasks). As outlined by Brazelton (1962), toilet training begins around 18 months of age, with gradual exposure to a potty chair (e.g., first sitting on the chair with clothes on). As the child begins to use and show interest in the potty chair, the child is encouraged to use it by himself or herself. This method resulted in approximately 80% of children completing daytime toilet training between ages 2 and 2.5 years, with the average age being 28.5 months (Brazelton, 1962).

Although there is much written about how to toilet train, the outcome data on this topic are scarce, especially for typically developing children. Outcome studies on the treatment of enuresis tend to focus much more on nocturnal enuresis, and when studies do focus on toilet training and/or daytime wetting, it is often with a focus on children with developmental delays. In a 2006 review of the literature on toilet training (Klassen et al., 2006), 35 studies that examined some aspect of toilet training were included; however, only a small number examined toilet-training outcomes in children without delays and there were only three randomized trials with children without delays, none of which directly compared the Foxx and Azrin method with the child-oriented method. In reference to the lack of research on approaches to use, the authors noted that "toilet training for healthy children is not a subject that invokes passion among researchers" (Klassen et al., 2006, p. 41). The authors concluded that the lack of research makes it difficult to provide definitive answers but that both of these common methods can produce positive results.

Research on daytime wetting aside from toilet training is limited. In some studies, behavioral components (including timed toileting and use of positive reinforcement for successful toileting) have been found to be effective (e.g., Wiener et al., 2000). Incorporation of Kegel exercises and/ or pelvic floor training are also commonly used in treating diurnal enuresis (e.g., Bachmann et al., 2008; Wiener et al., 2000). Medications, such as oxybutynin and tolterodine, have also been used with some success; however, there are a limited number of randomized controlled trials evaluating medications (Humphreys & Reinberg, 2005). In addition, use of a urine alarm (see the following section on nocturnal enuresis) has been reported in some studies for daytime wetting (e.g., Van Laecke et al., 2006). Given the absence of specific evidence-based guidelines for addressing diurnal enuresis, the following section incorporates recommendations across studies addressing both toilet training and interventions for enuresis.

How to: A Guide to the Implementation of Interventions for Diurnal Enuresis in Children and Adolescents

Behavioral interventions focusing on establishing good toileting habits are important to have in place for children experiencing diurnal enuresis. The recommendations in this section pull from a variety of sources cited earlier including Brazelton (1962), Foxx and Azrin (1973b), and Schroeder and Gordon (2002). If a child is not yet toilet trained, determining readiness and/or interest in toilet training may be important. Understanding when a child is most likely to wet can also be important; thus parents are encouraged to track times of day that the child is currently wetting. Following this, implementing regular toilet sits is important. Parents should use the data from their tracking and have the child sit on the toilet for at least 5 minutes (or until the child urinates) at times he or she is most likely to urinate (Schroeder & Gordon, 2002). Toilet sits may occur on a child "potty chair" or on a regular toilet with a "potty seat" placed on it. Different children (and different parents) have different preferences and as long as the child is comfortable, there is no one "correct" type of toilet to use. It is recommended that parents set a timer so that the child remains seated for the full 5 minutes and to signal to the child when the toilet sit is over. Timed timers, on which the time to go is shown in red and the red gets smaller as the time counts down, may be helpful for children who cannot tell time to better understand that time is getting shorter. Once the child begins to do regular toilet sits, it is recommended that parents cease using diapers, pull-ups, and so forth, so that the child can tell when he or she has wet and so the child has a clear cue that the toilet is to be used (Schroeder & Gordon, 2002).

Some parents who want to train their child more quickly may opt to add some of the components that Foxx and Azrin (1973b) recommend such as increased fluid intake to prompt more frequent practice using the toilet. Parents are instructed to provide their child with an increased amount of liquid in order to promote the need to urinate (although parents should be cautious to not push excessive amounts as too much liquid intake can result in hyponatremia or water intoxication). As an example, Foxx and Azrin (1973b) increased fluid intake by having children drink fluids about every 5 minutes and estimated that about two cups were consumed per hour. If parents use this method, having the child sit on the toilet more frequently (e.g., perhaps as often as every 10 minutes as Foxx and Azrin did) would be appropriate.

As part of the intervention program, parents should provide positive reinforcement (e.g., praise, reward) for each appropriate toileting behavior. Initially, parents should provide immediate praise (e.g., verbal praise, applause, or smile) and/or an immediate reward (e.g., a piece of candy, a sticker on a reward chart) for each toilet sit (both scheduled and child initiated), whether the child urinates or not as well as providing immediate praise for any instance in which the child notices physical cues that he or she might need to urinate and expresses this to parents. In addition, parents might want to provide the child with a special toy during toilet-sit times so that the child receives access to something exciting and special and so that toilet sits do not feel negative to the child. Reinforcers should be changed frequently so that they do not lose their potency and effectiveness. Then when the child successfully urinates on the toilet, more praise or a special reward should be given to the child.

Reinforcement for toileting may be decreased once a child has established toileting habits. Foxx and Azrin (1973b) faded prompts and reinforcers by reducing practice trials after the child successfully completed various toilet-training components without instruction. Practice toilet sits were omitted once children initiated and carried out practice trials without any prompts. At this time, reinforcers

were given intermittently and then eventually discontinued entirely. Parents may opt to phase out toilet sits and reinforcement for using the toilet in a variety of ways but should ensure that the toileting behavior is definitely established (e.g., child is going on his or her own) before ending the reinforcement. In addition to reinforcement for using the toilet, parents may want to implement regular "pants checks" to determine if a child is dry. If the child is dry, he or she may earn a small reinforcer. If the child is wet (or when the child has an accident), this should be treated matter-of-factly. The child should assist with the clean up and clothes changing to the extent possible for his or her developmental level.

As noted earlier, additional elements that may be added to the toileting program to address potential biological causes of enuresis in the child include medications to reduce bladder spasms and biofeedback and/or pelvic floor exercises to help the child learn to control the urinary sphincter muscles. Effectiveness of medications is unclear and some researchers have suggested that medications not be used without first using behavioral techniques. Similarly, evidence for the effectiveness of biofeedback is limited with a recent review suggesting a lack of evidence for its effectiveness (Fazeli et al., 2015). There are studies that do provide some support for this intervention method (e.g., Yagci et al., 2005) but its effectiveness may depend on whether the child presents with dysfunctional voiding.

NOCTURNAL ENURESIS

Overview

As previously mentioned, the *DSM-5* classifies both diurnal and nocturnal enuresis under the same category. Children with nocturnal enuresis have wetting accidents solely at night (or while otherwise sleeping). The prevalence of nocturnal enuresis in children decreases as children grow older. The estimated prevalence rate for children at 4.5 years of age is 8.5% and drops to 1.5% at 9.5 years of age (Butler & Heron, 2008). The prevalence rate varies depending on the definition of enuresis used. The rate increases to 30% at 4.5 years and 9.5% at 9.5 years when children who are wetting the bed less than twice a week are included (Butler &

Heron, 2008). Nocturnal enuresis is uncommon in adolescents; only 1% of individuals who are 15 years or older experience it (APA, 2013). Nocturnal enuresis is more prevalent in boys than in girls, with some studies showing that boys are more than two times as likely as girls to have nocturnal enuresis (Butler & Heron, 2008; Shreeram, He, Kalaydjian, Brothers, & Merikangas, 2009).

There are two types of nocturnal enuresis: primary and secondary. Primary nocturnal enuresis occurs in children who have never been continuously dry for at least 6 months while sleeping. Secondary nocturnal enuresis occurs when a child who has not wet the bed over 6 months begins wetting again. The secondary type is more often associated with psychological or organic problems (Harari, 2013). Nocturnal enuresis is also characterized by whether it occurs alone or in combination with other symptoms. Monosymptomatic refers to nocturnal enuresis without any daytime symptoms. Nonmonosymptomatic nocturnal enuresis refers to nighttime wetting that is accompanied by daytime symptoms such as voiding frequency, voiding urgency, and protective postures with the goal of holding in urine (Harari, 2013).

Most children with nocturnal enuresis do not have a comorbid disorder. However, there are symptom clusters that are more common in children with enuresis including externalizing behavior, sleep problems, developmental delays, and fecal incontinence (APA, 2013). ADHD is the disorder that seems to have the strongest link to enuresis. One study found that children with enuresis were three times more likely to have ADHD than children without enuresis (Shreeram et al., 2009).

Etiology and Factors Contributing to Nocturnal Enuresis in Children and Adolescents

Nocturnal enuresis is considered a biobehavioral disorder with variable causes. However, there seems to be a strong genetic component to nocturnal enuresis. Forty-three percent of children who have one parent who had nocturnal enuresis and 77% of children who have two parents who experienced nocturnal enuresis will develop it as well (Harari, 2013).

Some research has indicated that children with nocturnal enuresis have a higher arousal threshold, which means that it is more difficult to awaken children when they are sleeping (Jenkins, Lambert, Nielsen, McPherson, & Wells, 1996). Specifically, in a study conducted by Jenkins et al. (1996), boys with nocturnal enuresis required a louder noise to awaken them than did boys without nocturnal enuresis. It has been posited that nocturnal enuresis is associated with disruptions in sleep that cause sleep deprivation, resulting in higher arousal thresholds. One study found that 50% of all nighttime awakenings in children with nocturnal enuresis were related to bedwetting. Children whose sleep is disrupted by bedwetting incidents or their caregivers' attempts to prevent bedwetting may have greater difficulty awakening to full-bladder signals (Cohen-Zrubavel, Kushnir, Kushnir, & Sadeh, 2011).

Other hypothesized etiologies for nocturnal enuresis include psychological causes, small functional bladder capacity, and reduced levels of antidiuretic hormones (ADH). There is no solid evidence that psychological factors contribute to the development of nocturnal enuresis but there are psychosocial variables that have been associated with nocturnal enuresis in some studies including stressful and/or traumatic events (Butler, 2004). Small functional bladder capacity has also been hypothesized to lead to nocturnal enuresis. Although there is evidence that children with enuresis have smaller bladder capacity while sleeping than during the day, it is unclear whether this is a result of the child's voiding behavior or a cause of it (Houts, 1991; Kawauchi et al., 2003). Although there is some disagreement between the psychological literature and the medical literature regarding the etiological role of ADH (Houts, 1991), the medical literature includes many studies that have found that reduced levels of nocturnal ADH are associated with nocturnal enuresis (Chang, Yang, Chin, & Tsai, 2012; Fatouh et al., 2013).

Evidence-Based Interventions and Empirical Support for Nocturnal Enuresis in Children and Adolescents

Regardless of the cause, urine alarms have been shown to be the most effective intervention for nocturnal enuresis (Brown, Pope, & Brown,

2011; Friman, 2008; Shapira & Dahlen, 2010). Medications may also be effective in the short term for management of nocturnal enuresis, with imipramine (an antidepressant) and desmopressin (an antidiuretic) being the most commonly prescribed medications. Although desmopressin has been shown to effectively reduce nighttime accidents, it is not viewed as a "cure" because of high relapse rates for children when the medication is discontinued (Brown et al., 2011).

How to: A Guide to the Implementation of Interventions for Nocturnal Enuresis in Children and Adolescents

Urine Alarm Implementation. Urine alarms consist of a sensor that detects moisture and an alarm that is activated by moisture that is placed in the child's bed or attached to the child's undergarments via snaps or clips. Originally, it was thought that the alarm worked through the process of classical conditioning. The alarm served as the unconditioned stimulus (US) and waking up when the alarm went off was the unconditioned response (UR). As the child began to associate the feeling of bladder distension with the alarm going off, the full bladder becomes the conditioned stimulus (CS) and waking up was the conditioned response (CR). More recent theories posit that the alarm works through a process of aversive conditioning or negative reinforcement in which the child learns to wake up before wetting to avoid the loud alarm (Brown et al., 2011).

During the active treatment phase, the child should use the alarm every night. When the alarm sounds, the child should get out of bed and attempt to finish urinating in the toilet. Then the child should change into clean clothing and put clean bedding on the bed. The alarm should be reset before the child falls asleep again. Family preference and child age should determine whether the parent directs the child in the postalarm procedure or whether the child is responsible to follow the steps. However, often the parent will need to be involved and assist the child with following the steps (Friman, 2008). The child should use the alarm until he or she is dry for 14 consecutive nights. Treatment with the urine alarm is effective in 65% to 75% of cases but it can take several weeks for the nocturnal

enuresis to subside and there is a moderate possibility that the child might relapse after use of the alarm is discontinued (Butler 2004). If a relapse occurs, the alarm should be used again until the child is dry for a sustained period of time (e.g., 2 full weeks).

Before beginning treatment, the family will need to determine which type of alarm will work best for them and then to purchase the alarm. Urine alarms are sold at warehouse stores, medical supply stores, pharmacies, and on the Internet (Brown et al., 2011). There are several options from which to choose, including wired and wireless alarms, alarms that wake the parent and alarms that wake the child, and alarms that attach to a pad on the bed or alarms that attach to the child's underwear (Friman, 2008; Shapira & Dahlen, 2010). Wired alarms are easier to set up and reset but the wires may become cumbersome for the child. The wireless alarms are more compact but can be more difficult to use. In addition, alarms come with options to either vibrate, make a sound, or both. Finally, a choice must be made between alarms that wake the parent first or alarms that wake the child and may or may not be loud enough to wake the parents. Although there is not empirical evidence to suggest which type is more effective, it seems that the shortest duration between the child voiding and the child waking up would be most consistent with the theoretical conceptualization of urine alarm treatment (Friman, 2008).

An important component of urine alarm treatment is tracking, which allows the family to determine if improvements are being made in the child's wetting. The parents and child should consider tracking how many wetting episodes occur, how severe the wetting was (e.g., large wet area or smaller wet area), whether the child awoke to the alarm, and whether the child voided more in the toilet after waking. This will allow both the family and the clinician to track progress and determine if changes in the treatment protocol need to be made (Shapira & Dahlen, 2010).

Although the alarm is the central component of treatment, it may be beneficial to add behavioral strategies in conjunction with the alarm (Friman, 2008). For example, if the child lacks motivation to use the alarm properly, then parents might consider using reinforcement strategies such as a token economy or praise each time the child uses the alarm and follows the appropriate procedures when a wetting incident occurs. The focus of the parents' attention should not be on whether the child wets, but on whether the child is using the alarm correctly (Shapira & Dahlen, 2010). If the child is scolded when the parent finds out that the child wet the bed, then the child may become less likely to use the alarm. In addition, having the child assist with cleaning up after an incident may help the child to understand the inconvenience associated with wetting the bed. Finally, it may be useful for children to practice delaying urination and using Kegel exercises to terminate urination (Friman, 2008).

ENCOPRESIS

Overview

Encopresis is a condition in which youths have "repeated passage of feces into inappropriate places" (APA, 2013, p. 357). Children must be at least 4 years of age to receive this diagnosis and the soiling must occur at least once a month for at least 3 months. There are two subtypes of encopresis as defined in the *DSM-5*—a subtype with constipation and overflow and a subtype without this. The subtype with constipation and overflow, often referred to as "functional constipation," is more common and is not considered to be intentional on the part of the child. It is estimated that approximately 80% of children with encopresis have constipation (van Dijk, Benninga, Grootenhuis, Nieuwenhuizen, & Last, 2007). The *DSM-5* further differentiates between encopresis that is "primary," meaning the child has never had bowel control, or "secondary," in which the child was accident-free for a period of time before remitting.

Up-to-date prevalence estimates of encopresis are difficult to locate but in one population-based study (van der Wal, Benninga, & Hirasing, 2005) in the Netherlands, the prevalence of encopresis was 4.1% among 5- to 6-year-old children and 1.6% among 11- to 12-year-old children. Encopresis was more common in boys (3.7%) than girls (2.4%) in this sample. In a sample of 4-year-old children from Norway (Wichstrøm, et al., 2012), the estimated prevalence of encopresis was 6.4%

with almost identical rates in boys (6.5%) and girls (6.3%). Encopresis has been associated with other childhood disorders, with children diagnosed with ADHD being more likely to exhibit encopresis (and enuresis) than children without ADHD (Mellon et al., 2013). Children with encopresis may also be at elevated risk for a variety of social/emotional/behavioral problems including attention problems, anxiety/depression, disruptive and oppositional behaviors, and social difficulties (Joinson, Heron, Butler, & von Gontard, 2006). It is important to note that, although children with encopresis are at greater risk for these problems, it is not clear if these problems are causally related and if so, the direction of the relationship (Mellon, 2012).

Etiology and Factors Contributing to Encopresis in Children and Adolescents

Given that most children with encopresis have constipation, this is the most proximate cause of encopresis in the majority of cases. Thus, when looking for treatment guidelines, programs that target constipation generally as well as encopresis specifically will be helpful to practitioners. Understanding that encopresis often has a biological route may be helpful to children and their families in terms of better understanding this disorder. In one study, it was noted that painful bowel movements was the most commonly reported precipitant of constipation in the early childhood years (Borowitz et al., 2003). Parents in this study also reported that their children with constipation had more painful bowel movements and were more likely to worry about future painful experiences related to bowel movements than were parents of children without encopresis. In discussing potential causes of encopresis, Christophersen and Mortweet VanScoyoc (2013) noted that children with encopresis may be less sensitive to physiological signs indicating the need to have a bowel movement and may retain more stool in their rectum compared with children without encopresis. Given the link to constipation, treatment programs for encopresis often include providing parents (and children) with information on the functioning of the bowels and how constipation can lead to encopresis.

Evidence-Based Interventions and Empirical Support for Encopresis in Children and Adolescents

Effective treatments for encopresis with consti-pation generally incorporate a combination of behavioral techniques (e.g., regular toilet sits with reinforcement) and medical interventions (e.g., prescription of laxatives; use of enemas to ini-tially clear out impacted fecal material) as well as diet recommendations (e.g., avoiding foods that promote constipation). The medical intervention aspect of treatment will be handled by a medi-cal provider (e.g., child's pediatrician, a pediatric gastroenterologist) so it is important for psychol-ogists and other nonmedical providers working with children with encopresis to work closely with the child's medical provider—especially during the initial stages of treatment for a child who has significant constipation. The Constipation Guideline Committee of the North American Society for Pediatric Gastroenterology, Hepatology, and Nutrition (2006) has published clinical practice guidelines for the treatment of constipation in chil-dren. For children with fecal impaction, the first step of treatment is disimpaction. This is typically accomplished with an enema or oral medications including mineral oil and polyethylene glycol elec-trolyte solutions. Following this initial disimpac-tion, maintenance therapy is important to ensure the child does not become constipated again. The medical component of maintenance therapy typi-cally includes use of oral laxatives. Dietary changes may also be important, especially an increased intake of fluid. Although the 2006 practice guide-lines note that a balanced diet (including whole grains, fruits, and vegetables) is recommended, the guidelines also note that there was not enough evi-dence to indicate whether a specific fiber supple-ment was beneficial.

Based on reviews of these treatment recom-mendations (e.g., Brooks et al., 2000) as well as original articles evaluating treatment protocols, the combination of behavioral and medical interven-tions appears to result in the best outcomes in most children. Cox and colleagues have conducted sev-eral studies that suggest "enhanced toilet training" (ETT) may be an effective treatment protocol for children with encopresis. In this treatment method, children are provided with laxative and enema

therapies and parents and children are given edu-cational information on relaxation methods while toileting as well as regularly scheduled toilet sits. In one of the first evaluations of this method (Cox, Sutphen, Ling, Quillian, & Borowitz, 1996), laxa-tives (along with initial enemas) were compared with ETT and with anal sphincter biofeedback. There were significant differences between groups, with 19% of children in the laxative group show-ing improvement, 64% in the biofeedback group, and 71% in the ETT group. In another evaluation of these three treatments (Cox, Sutphen, Borowitz, Kovatchev, & Ling, 1998), ETT was found to have better outcomes for children than the other treat-ment methods alone with an 85% response rate for ETT compared with a 45% response rate for the medical intervention alone and a 61% response rate for biofeedback. In a later randomized controlled trial comparing these three treatments (Borowitz, Cox, Sutphen, & Kovatchev, 2002), children in all three groups experienced a significant reduction in soiling episodes and there were not significant differ-ences among the three groups. A greater percentage of children in the ETT group evidenced significant decreases in soiling at 3, 6, and 12 months post-treatment (e.g., 78% at 12 months for ETT, 61% for biofeedback, and 41% for medication manage-ment alone). However, in terms of being "cured" at 12 months (defined as no soiling for 2 weeks), only 38% of children met this criteria and there were not significant differences among the three treat-ment groups. Studies have also supported the effi-cacy of delivering ETT via the Internet (Ritterband et al., 2013) suggesting that this intervention may be effectively delivered without the need for regular face-to-face meetings with medical/mental health providers.

Another randomized controlled trial using sim-ilar methods compared the use of behavioral ther-apy for constipation in children (van Dijk et al., 2008) to a "standard intervention" that included the use of enemas (if necessary) and laxatives. Children and their parents also received educa-tion regarding constipation as well as praise and "small gifts" from their medical providers. The behavioral therapy component was not speci-fied in detail but consisted of "teaching parents behavioral procedures" and conducting "behav-ioral play therapy with the child in presence of his or her parents" (van Dijk et al., 2008, p. e1335).

Although the behavioral therapy group did not evidence a better treatment outcome than the conventional treatment group, it is important to recognize that the conventional treatment contained behavioral aspects to it and thus children in both groups received some behavioral interventions, which may account for the lack of significant differences between groups. Children in both groups showed a decrease in soiling incidents and an increase in appropriate defecation frequency. Children in the behavioral therapy group did show a greater decline in behavioral problems (present in about one third of the sample at pretreatment) than children in the conventional treatment group.

It is important to note that, in all of these treatment studies, there was a medical component. Thus, although a treatment package including other interventions often produced the most beneficial outcomes, the initial medical intervention is likely an important part of the treatment process. Unfortunately, even with multicomponent packages, initial response rates are often reported to be lower posttreatment, with a persistence of soiling occurring in a higher percentage of children. In a 10-year follow-up study of children treated for encopresis (Michaud, Lamblin, Mairesse, Turck, & Gottrand, 2009) approximately half of these children continued to be constipated and about a quarter of all children continued to struggle with encopresis. The results of this study are consistent with other studies that indicate many children will continue to have difficulties with constipation over time. Given this finding, continued monitoring of children with reimplementation of treatment protocols if there is a relapse is likely important.

How to: A Guide to the Implementation of Interventions for Encopresis

An evidence-based intervention for encopresis should include a multicomponent program. The first step for a clinician is to refer the child to his or her pediatrician (if this has not already occurred). The medical provider would evaluate the presence and severity of constipation and instruct the parents on use of enemas and/or laxatives.

Following the medical consultation, psychoeducation, where the clinician explains to the parents the connection between constipation and encopresis, occurs. Various diagrams of the intestinal system and the impact that constipation has on the colon (e.g., see Christophersen & Mortweet VanScoyoc, 2013) may be helpful for illustrative purposes. Dietary changes may also be discussed with parents including ways to increase fiber and decrease foods that may promote constipation. Following this, parents should be instructed to have their child engage in regular toilet sits. One suggestion (e.g., Schroeder & Gordon, 2002) is to have the child sit on the toilet about 20 minutes after each meal for at least 5 to 10 minutes. Although, if parents are tracking when a child is most likely to have a bowel movement, toilet sits should be scheduled at these times to maximize the likelihood of success. Children should receive a reinforcer for sitting on the toilet with an extra reinforcer for defecating in the toilet. Some programs have also recommended that, while sitting on the toilet, children practice tensing and releasing their anal sphincter muscle for part of the time to learn to use this muscle more effectively and to not tense the muscle while trying to defecate (e.g., Cox et al., 1996). In addition to scheduled toilet sits, parents can conduct regular pants checks and, if the child's pants or underwear are clean, the child can earn a reinforcer. If not, the child should assist in the cleaning process but should not be punished for the soiling incident (Schroeder & Gordon, 2002).

The steps to this program sound fairly simple—and they are. The key, as with many behavioral interventions, is *consistency* in using these procedures and ensuring that reinforcers are truly that—items or activities that the child wants to gain or have access to. In addition, because of the high relapse rate, parents should be encouraged to be vigilant for signs of relapse and reimplement procedures if needed.

CONCLUSION

Toileting difficulties are common concerns of parents of young children. It is fortunate that there are intervention programs based largely on behavioral principles that can be implemented by parents—either alone or with guidance from a clinician. As clinicians work with parents on these issues, they should attend closely to adherence to treatment procedures. Although ongoing work with a clinician may not be needed for all families, initial work on ensuring programs are set up in a manner to maximize the chances that parents and children will follow through is important in helping establish and maintain positive outcomes.

SELECT BIBLIOGRAPHY

Christophersen, E. R., & Mortweet VanScoyoc, S. (2013). Diagnosis and management of encopresis. In *Treatments that work with children: Empirically supported strategies for managing childhood problems* (2nd ed., pp. 109–128). Washington, DC: American Psychological Association.
This chapter provides detailed information on encopresis with a focus on intervention. It also provides in-depth discussion of medical treatments as well as medical-behavioral treatment and includes tracking sheet and diagram that can be used in treatment.

Foxx, R. M., & Azrin, N. H. (1973). Dry pants: A rapid method of toilet training children. *Behaviour Research and Therapy, 11*(4), 435–442.
This article describes an investigation of an intensive and rapid toilet-training program with 34 children between the ages 20 and 36 months. The program components and steps are outlined and findings for the study are reported, including follow-up data.

Friman, P. (2008). Evidence-based therapies for enuresis and encopresis. In R. G. Steele, T. D. Elkin, & M. C. Roberts (Eds.), *Handbook of evidence-based therapies for children and adolescents* (pp. 311–333). Springer ebook. doi:10.1007/978-0-387-73691-4_18
This chapter describes urine alarms in detail. This chapter also discusses adjunctive treatments and elucidates the empirical support for them. Treatment options for encopresis are also presented.

Schroeder, C. S., & Gordon, B. N. (2002). Toileting: Training, enuresis, and encopresis. In *Assessment and treatment of childhood problems: A clinician's guide* (pp. 115–158). New York, NY: Guilford Press.
This chapter provides comprehensive overview of treatment programs for toilet training, nocturnal enuresis, and encopresis. It also includes charts and diagrams.

Shapira, B. E., & Dahlen, P. (2010). Therapeutic treatment protocol for enuresis using an enuresis alarm. *Journal of Counseling & Development, 88*(2), 246–252. doi:10.1002/j.1556–6678.2010.tb00017.x
This is a review article that discusses the etiologies of enuresis and various treatment options for enuresis. A treatment protocol using the urine alarm is described.

REFERENCES

American Psychiatric Association (APA). (2013). *Diagnostic and statistical manual of mental disorders* (5th ed.). Arlington, VA: American Psychiatric Publishing.

Bachmann, C. J., Heilenkötter, K., Janhsen, E., Ackmann, C., Thomä, M., Lax, H., & Bachmann, H. (2008). Long-term effects of a urotherapy training program in children with functional urinary incontinence: A 2-year follow-up. *Scandinavian Journal of Urology and Nephrology, 42*(4), 337–343.

Borowitz, S. M., Cox, D. J., Sutphen, J. L., & Kovatchev, B. (2002). Treatment of childhood encopresis: A randomized trial comparing three treatment protocols. *Journal of Pediatric Gastroenterology and Nutrition, 34*(4), 378–384.

Borowitz, S. M., Cox, D. J., Tam, A., Ritterband, L. M., Sutphen, J. L., & Penberthy, J. K. (2003). Precipitants of constipation during early childhood. *The Journal of the American Board of Family Practice/American Board of Family Practice, 16*(3), 213–218.

Brazelton, T. B. (1962). A child-oriented approach to toilet training. *Pediatrics, 29*, 121–128.

Brooks, R. C., Copen, R. M., Cox, D. J., Morris, J., Borowitz, S., & Sutphen, J. (2000). Review of the treatment literature for encopresis, functional constipation, and stool-toileting refusal. *Annals of Behavioral Medicine: A Publication of the Society of Behavioral Medicine, 22*(3), 260–267.

Brown, M. L., Pope, A. W., & Brown, E. J. (2011). Treatment of primary nocturnal enuresis in children: A review. *Child: Care, Health and Development, 37*(2), 153–160.

Buckley, B. S., & Lapitan, M. C.; Epidemiology Committee of the Fourth International Consultation on Incontinence, Paris, 2008. (2010). Prevalence of urinary incontinence in men, women, and children–current evidence: Findings of the Fourth International Consultation on Incontinence. *Urology, 76*(2), 265–270.

Butler, R. J. (2004). Childhood nocturnal enuresis: Developing a conceptual framework. *Clinical Psychology Review, 24*(8), 909–931.

Butler, R. J., & Heron, J. (2008). The prevalence of infrequent bedwetting and nocturnal enuresis in childhood. A large British cohort. *Scandinavian Journal of Urology and Nephrology, 42*(3), 257–264.

Campbell, L. K., Cox, D. J., & Borowitz, S. M. (2009). Elimination disorders: Enuresis and encopresis. In M. C. Roberts & R. G. Steele (Eds.), *Handbook of pediatric psychology* (4th ed., pp. 287–302). New York, NY: Guilford Press.

Chang, J. W., Yang, L. W., Chin, T. W., & Tsai, H. L. (2012). Clinical characteristics, nocturnal antidiuretic hormone levels, and responsiveness to DDAVP of school children with primary nocturnal enuresis. *World Journal of Urology, 30,* 567–571. doi:10.1007/s00345-011-0753-5

Christophersen, E. R., & Mortweet VanScoyoc, S. (2013). Diagnosis and management of encopresis. In *Treatments that work with children: Empirically supported strategies for managing childhood problems* (2nd ed., pp. 109–128). Washington, DC: American Psychological Association. doi:10.1037/10405-005

Cohen-Zrubavel, V., Kushnir, B., Kushnir, J., & Sadeh, A. (2011). Sleep and sleepiness in children with nocturnal enuresis. *Sleep, 34*(2), 191–194.

Cox, D. J., Sutphen, J., Borowitz, S., Kovatchev, B., & Ling, W. (1998). Contribution of behavior therapy and biofeedback to laxative therapy in the treatment of pediatric encopresis. *Annals of Behavioral Medicine: A Publication of the Society of Behavioral Medicine, 20*(2), 70–76.

Cox, D. J., Sutphen, J., Ling, W., Quillian, W., & Borowitz, S. (1996). Additive benefits of laxative, toilet training, and biofeedback therapies in the treatment of pediatric encopresis. *Journal of Pediatric Psychology, 21*(5), 659–670.

Fatouh, A. A., Motawie, A. A., Abd Al-Aziz, A. M., Hamed, H. M., Awad, M. A., El-Ghany, A. A., ... Eid, M. M. (2013). Anti-diuretic hormone and genetic study in primary nocturnal enuresis. *Journal of Pediatric Urology, 9*(6 Pt A), 831–837.

Fazeli, M. S., Lin, Y., Nikoo, N., Jaggumantri, S., Collet, J. P., & Afshar, K. (2015). Biofeedback for nonneuropathic daytime voiding disorders in children: A systematic review and meta-analysis of randomized controlled trials. *The Journal of Urology, 193*(1), 274–279.

Foxx, R. M., & Azrin, N. H. (1973). Dry pants: A rapid method of toilet training children. *Behaviour Research and Therapy, 11*(4), 435–442.

Friman, P. (2008). Evidence-based therapies for enuresis and encopresis. In R. G. Steele, T. D. Elkin, & M. C. Roberts (Eds.), *Handbook of evidence-based therapies for children and adolescents* (pp. 311–333). Springer ebook.

Harari, M. D. (2013). Nocturnal enuresis. *Journal of Paediatrics and Child Health, 49*(4), 264–271. doi:10.1111/j.1440-1754.2012.02506.x

Houts, A. C. (1991). Nocturnal enuresis as a biobehavioral problem. *Behavior Therapy, 22*(2), 133–151. doi:10.1016/S0005-7894(05)80173-X

Humphreys, M. R., & Reinberg, Y. E. (2005). Contemporary and emerging drug treatments for urinary incontinence in children. *Paediatric Drugs, 7*(3), 151–162.

Jenkins, P. H., Lambert, M. J., Nielsen, S. L., McPherson, D. L., & Wells, M. G. (1996). Nocturnal task responsiveness of primary nocturnal enuretic boys: A behavioral approach to enuresis. *Children's Health Care, 25*(2), 143–156. doi:10.1207/s15326888chc2502_6

Joinson, C., Heron, J., Butler, U., & von Gontard, A. (2006). Psychological differences between children with and without soiling problems. *Pediatrics, 117*(5), 1575–1584.

Joinson, C., Heron, J., von Gontard, A., Butler, U., Golding, J., & Emond, A. (2008). Early childhood risk factors associated with daytime wetting and soiling in school-age children. *Journal of Pediatric Psychology, 33*(7), 739–750.

Kawauchi, A., Tanaka, Y., Naito, Y., Yamao, Y., Ukimura, O., Yoneda, K., ... Miki, T. (2003). Bladder capacity at the time of enuresis. *Urology, 61*(5), 1016–1018.

Klassen, T. O., Kiddoo, D., Lang, M., Friesen, C., Russell, K., Spooner, C., & Vandermeer, B. (2006). *The effectiveness of different methods of toilet training for bowel and bladder control.* Rockville, MD: Agency for Healthcare Research and Quality.

Mellon, M. W. (2012). Encopresis. In P. Sturmey & M. Hersen (Eds.), *Handbook of evidence-based practice in clinical psychology, Vol. 1: Child and adolescent disorders* (pp. 361–387). Hoboken, NJ: John Wiley.

Mellon, M. W., Natchev, B. E., Katusic, S. K., Colligan, R. C., Weaver, A. L., Voigt, R. G., & Barbaresi, W. J. (2013). Incidence of enuresis and encopresis among children with attention-deficit/hyperactivity disorder in a population-based birth cohort. *Academic Pediatrics, 13*(4), 322–327.

Michaud, L., Lamblin, M., Mairesse, S., Turck, D., & Gottrand, F. (2009). Outcome of functional constipation in childhood: A 10-year follow-up study. *Clinical Pediatrics, 48*(1), 26–31. doi:10.1177/0009922808320599

Nevéus, T., & Sillén, U. (2013). Lower urinary tract function in childhood: Normal development and common functional disturbances. *Acta Physiologica, 207*(1), 85–92.

North American Society for Pediatric Gastroenterology, Hepatology, and Nutrition. (2006). Evaluation and treatment of constipation in infants and children: Recommendations of the North American Society for Pediatric Gastroenterology, Hepatology, and Nutrition. *Journal of Pediatric Gastroenterology and Nutrition, 43*, e1–e13. doi:10.1097/01.mpg.0000233159.97667.c3

Ritterband, L. M., Thorndike, F. P., Lord, H. R., Borowitz, S., Walker, L. S., Ingersoll, K. S.,...Cox, D. J. (2013). An RCT of an Internet intervention for pediatric encopresis with one year follow-up. *Clinical Practice in Pediatric Psychology, 1*(1), 68–80.

Schroeder, C. S., & Gordon, B. N. (2002). *Assessment and treatment of childhood problems: A clinician's guide* (2nd ed.). New York, NY: Guilford Press.

Schulz-Juergensen, S., Bolte, L., Gebhardt, J., & Eggert, P. (2013). Intensive playing leads to non-monosymptomatic enuresis in children with low prepulse inhibition. *Acta Paediatrica, 102*(2), e79–e83.

Shapira, B. E., & Dahlen, P. (2010). Therapeutic treatment protocol for enuresis using an enuresis alarm. *Journal of Counseling & Development, 88*(2), 246–252. doi:10.1002/j.1556–6678.2010.tb00017.x

Shreeram, S., He, J. P., Kalaydjian, A., Brothers, S., & Merikangas, K. R. (2009). Prevalence of enuresis and its association with attention-deficit/hyperactivity disorder among U.S. children: Results from a nationally representative study. *Journal of the American Academy of Child and Adolescent Psychiatry, 48*(1), 35–41.

van der Wal, M. F., Benninga, M. A., & Hirasing, R. A. (2005). The prevalence of encopresis in a multicultural population. *Journal of Pediatric Gastroenterology and Nutrition, 40*(3), 345–348.

van Dijk, M., Benninga, M. A., Grootenhuis, M. A., Nieuwenhuizen, A. M., & Last, B. F. (2007). Chronic childhood constipation: A review of the literature and the introduction of a protocolized behavioral intervention program. *Patient Education and Counseling, 67*(1–2), 63–77.

van Dijk, M., Bongers, M. E., de Vries, G. J., Grootenhuis, M. A., Last, B. F., & Benninga, M. A. (2008). Behavioral therapy for childhood constipation: A randomized, controlled trial. *Pediatrics, 121*(5), e1334–e1341.

Van Laecke, E., Wille, S., Vande Walle, J., Raes, A., Renson, C., Peeren, F., & Hoebeke, P. (2006). The daytime alarm: A useful device for the treatment of children with daytime incontinence. *The Journal of Urology, 176*(1), 325–327.

von Gontard, A., Heron, J., & Joinson, C. (2011). Family history of nocturnal enuresis and urinary incontinence: Results from a large epidemiological study. *The Journal of Urology, 185*(6), 2303–2306.

Wichstrøm, L., Berg-Nielsen, T. S., Angold, A., Egger, H. L., Solheim, E., & Sveen, T. H. (2012). Prevalence of psychiatric disorders in preschoolers. *Journal of Child Psychology and Psychiatry, and Allied Disciplines, 53*(6), 695–705.

Wiener, J. S., Scales, M. T., Hampton, J., King, L. R., Surwit, R., & Edwards, C. L. (2000). Long-term efficacy of simple behavioral therapy for daytime wetting in children. *The Journal of Urology, 164*(3 Pt 1), 786–790.

Yagci, S., Kibar, Y., Akay, O., Kilic, S., Erdemir, F., Gok, F., & Dayanc, M. (2005). The effect of biofeedback treatment on voiding and urodynamic parameters in children with voiding dysfunction. *The Journal of Urology, 174*(5), 1994–1997; discussion 1997.

Evidence-Based Interventions for Asthma in Children and Adolescents

Melissa A. Bray, Thomas J. Kehle, Melissa M. Root, Kari A. Sassu, Lea A. Theodore, and Bruce A. Bracken

OVERVIEW

Asthma, a pulmonary condition, is a chronic respiratory disorder typified by persistent underlying inflammation of tissues, airway obstruction (bronchoconstriction), congestion, hyperresponsive airways, and the narrowing of smooth airway muscle (Bray et al., 2005). Asthma causes normal airway functioning to overreact, resulting in coughing, wheezing, chest tightness, shortness of breath, mucous membrane swelling, and extreme difficulty in breathing (Slavich & Irwin, 2014). Significantly, some children with asthma may have severe reactions, such as becoming languid, having difficulty walking and talking, and may develop cyanosis, a condition where a youth's lips and extremities turn blue because of lack of oxygen. It is critical to diagnose appropriately and treat asthma in children because, if left untreated, the disorder will result in long-term lung damage (Bray, Kehle, Peck, Theodore, & Zhou, 2004).

The prevalence rates for asthma increase with age, from 3.2% in children 3 years of age to 15.4% in children aged 15 years, and prevalence rates steadily increase with age (Hammer-Helmich, Linneberg, Thomsen, & Glümer, 2014). Notably, most children are diagnosed with asthma by 5 years of age. An accurate diagnosis requires the child's pediatrician to acquire information regarding a family history of asthma, the child's current condition (i.e., coughing or wheezing when not ill; appearing to have allergies), changes in behavior, such as not playing with other children or refraining from sports-related activities, avoiding certain foods, and experiencing breathing difficulties. Conclusive identification of asthma requires lung function tests, often using a spirometer, which measures the air capacity of the lungs. Specifically, the spirometer will evaluate a child's lungs by determining how much air is inhaled and exhaled, as well as how long the exhalation process takes to complete. Although there is no cure for asthma, once properly diagnosed and an appropriate treatment plan has been implemented, children will feel much better and their quality of life will improve. Clinically, the triggers and symptomatology evidenced by children and adolescents with asthma differ for each individual. However, mental health professionals need to be cognizant of the fluctuating developmental changes that occur as children grow and how the presentation of their asthmatic symptoms may change as children develop. That is, the presentation of asthma symptoms may vary based on the level of development, changes in weather, variation/changes in triggers, the child's overall immune response, and reaction to medication(s).

Asthma is one of the most common chronic medical conditions in children and is the leading cause of school absenteeism (Bray et al., 2005). Research has demonstrated that asthma compromises a child's sleep and ability to concentrate in school, resulting in impaired academic and cognitive functioning. Moreover, children and adolescents with asthma also evidence poor self-esteem and impaired peer relationships, behavioral problems (i.e., impulsivity, hyperactivity, and aggression), restrictions from many physical activities in which their peers engage, both at school and recreationally, and overall, diminished quality of life (Bray et al., 2004, 2005; Dobson, Bray, Kehle, Theodore, & Peck, 2005).

In light of the myriad deleterious medical, academic, behavioral, and social-emotional effects stemming from asthma, it is imperative to properly diagnose, identify the signs of an impending attack, and treat children with this disorder. The ramifications of not doing so are potentially lethal. The intent of this chapter is to describe childhood asthma, including its causes and triggers. Moreover, the chapter elucidates the extant research supporting treatment of the disorder and provides step-by-step empirically based interventions to ameliorate asthmatic symptomatology in children.

ETIOLOGY AND FACTORS CONTRIBUTING TO ASTHMA IN CHILDREN AND ADOLESCENTS

It has been well established that asthma has both physiological and psychological causes. Physiologically, asthma may be caused by genetic predispositions, viral infections, allergens (i.e., pets, dust, pollen, and mold), airborne stimulants (i.e., second-hand smoke and perfume), exercise, air pollution, weather conditions, and respiratory infections (Arashima et al., 2013). These causes restrict activities for children with asthma, limiting their joining in such activities as going on field trips, participating in athletics, and being allowed to eat certain foods. Another biological contributor is gene-to-gene, and gene-to-environment interactions (Bitsch & Stemerding, 2013). In addition to environmental and physical causes, emotions or psychological triggers have also been shown to affect asthma. In particular, stress, embarrassment,

anxiety, and depression have been shown to trigger and exacerbate asthmatic symptoms (Bhattacharya, Chan, & Sambamoorthi, 2014; Bray et al., 2004, 2005; Dobson et al., 2005). The genetic underpinnings and environmental conditions related to stress and anxiety are particularly deleterious to healthy lung functioning (Bhattacharya et al., 2014), and the adverse implications stemming from asthma are unique for every child.

The psychological underpinnings of asthma have been investigated in the field of psychoneuroimmunology (PNI), which examines the interplay of the central nervous system, neuroendocrine, and immune system with psychological variables and their relation to physical health (Bray et al., 2004). Simply stated, this relationship is known as the "mind–body connection," and it has been hypothesized that psychological factors affect both the sympathetic and parasympathetic branches of the autonomic nervous system (ANS), which ultimately reduce lung functioning in asthmatic youths when they are exposed to negative emotions (Bray et al., 2004). Moreover, emerging evidence indicates that central cognitive processes may influence asthmatic symptoms as well as the presentation of immune and physiological markers (Van Lieshout & MacQueen, 2008). In light of these findings, anxiety and/or stress may serve as a precursor for the development and intensification of the disease, as well as contribute to both internalizing disorders and physiological changes in the body. To address the detrimental effects of asthma, researchers have investigated methods of ameliorating the disease. Most notably, psychologically based mind–body interventions focused on improving lung functioning have been studied a great deal (Archibald, Caine, Ali, Hartling, & Scott, 2015).

In addition to physical, environmental, and psychological causes of asthma in children and adolescents, there are correlates of this chronic medical disorder such as living within an inner city, being exposed to or living in high-poverty areas, not having health insurance, being male, being a youth of minority descent, and living in impoverished residential conditions. The greatest number of hospitalizations for asthma attacks occurs in urban areas, with the factors associated with an asthma diagnosis typically identified by 5 years of age.

EVIDENCE-BASED INTERVENTIONS AND EMPIRICAL SUPPORT FOR ASTHMA IN CHILDREN AND ADOLESCENTS

Historically, the traditional treatment for asthma has been the use of medication for both short- and long-term symptom control as well as the avoidance of triggers. However, psychologically based interventions have been used more recently to treat individuals with asthma. Researchers have shown that relaxation and guided imagery (RGI), written emotional expression, yoga, and mindfulness therapy improve pulmonary lung functioning, decrease rates of absenteeism, and improve overall quality of life.

RGI are designed to promote relaxation and reduce negative emotional states. Relaxation appears to be most effective for individuals whose asthma is caused or exacerbated by psychological stressors. When used in conjunction with guided imagery, RGI promotes physical change by decreasing somatic and asthma symptoms (Bray et al., 2004). This method of intervention is effective for children likely because of the mind–body connection; that is, children unconsciously have negative thoughts that rouse their asthmatic symptoms. By replacing these negative thoughts with positive, adaptive thoughts, physiological functioning in the body is affected in an affirmative manner (Peck, Bray, & Kehle, 2003).

Written emotional expression requires individuals to write about stressful life experiences for periods of 10 minutes, 3 to 5 days per week. Researchers do not fully understand the mechanisms that underpin this intervention or serve to improve asthma symptoms. Writing about traumatic events, however, modifies individuals' perception and interpretation of traumatic incidents and facilitates psychological healing and coping, which ultimately enhances lung functioning (Bray et al., 2003). By capitalizing on positive coping strategies, written emotional expression diminishes adverse and negative psychological and emotional responses that trigger asthma symptomatology.

Yoga and mindfulness meditation have also been successfully employed to mitigate the asthmatic symptomatology in children and adolescents. Using the philosophy of Eastern medicine, yoga and mindfulness reduce stress, dissipate excess energy, sharpen concentration, increase mental clarity, and improve overall health (Kabat-Zinn, 1994). By decreasing children's activity levels and simultaneously allowing them to attend to tasks, yoga and mindfulness have a calming effect on the body while also cultivating self-control. These relaxation techniques bring the body back into balance. The rationale for the success of both interventions is that they teach youths to listen to what their bodies are telling them. The human body sometimes is viewed as a repository where emotions are deposited. When children are taught to take quiet time to stop, think, and develop a level of awareness regarding their asthma symptoms, they are better able to note triggers to asthma attacks and be in tune with their disorder.

HOW TO: A GUIDE TO THE IMPLEMENTATION OF INTERVENTIONS FOR CHILDREN AND ADOLESCENTS WITH ASTHMA

Relaxation and Guided Imagery

RGI is a scripted psychological intervention that guides the child through standard muscle relaxation and imagination of either optimal health functioning or a pleasant and relaxing scene. In addition to asthma, RGI has been successfully used for anxiety and depression as well as physical conditions such as breast cancer and postsurgical wound healing (Dobson et al., 2005).

Step 1. The child/adolescent should lie down on an exercise mat or comfortable surface. RGI may be delivered by a mental health professional or using an MP3 or compact disc recording. The service provider may design the script or it can be based on established scripts previously used in research. The RGI script (e.g., Peck et al., 2003) is played or spoken to the child.

RGI can be implemented across different timeframes and with different foci. For instance, in Dobson and colleagues' (2005) study, the relaxation portion of the script instructs the child to release the tension in each separate body part. This progression starts with the toes and moves up the body, ending at the head. The guided imagery component has the person imagining a calm place where he or she can heal the specific part of the body that is being targeted. For children with asthma, they are instructed to imagine healing the bronchial tubes and lungs and think of themselves engaging in an activity where they have no symptoms of asthma. Each intervention session lasts approximately 20 minutes and is conducted three times a week for 6 weeks.

A second example of an effective RGI protocol and timeframe is from Menzies, Lyon, Elswick, McCain, and Gray (2014). They designed a three-part RGI protocol to be used daily for 10 weeks. This protocol involves listening to three different MP3 recordings, each less than 20 minutes. The first track, which is listened to daily for the first 2 weeks, guides the listener through progressive relaxation thoughts and steps. The second track, which is listened to daily for weeks 3 and 4 of the intervention, contains information from the first track and leads the child through imagining him- or herself in a relaxing environment. The third track, listened to daily during weeks 5 and 6 of the intervention, consists of imagining the components of the immune system functioning optimally. During weeks 7 through 10, participants may select any of the three recordings to listen to daily (Menzies et al., 2014). On completion of each track, participants are told to notice that they feel better and are instructed to sense their feelings of relaxation.

The following is an example of an RGI script that has been used by researchers and adopted for use by mental health professionals (Dobson et al., 2005). This script is adapted from work by Achterberg (1985); Achterberg, Dossey, and Kolkmeier (1994); Brigham (1994); and M. Castes (personal communication, February 27, 2000).

General Relaxation:

Please start by making yourself comfortable, shifting your weight so you can feel fully supported, checking to see that your head, neck, and spine are straight. And letting your eyes softly close if that is comfortable for you. And begin by taking a deep breath in, and as you exhale, let all tension flow out from your body. If distracting thoughts come to your attention while we are going through this relaxation procedure, simply put them in a bubble and let them float away. Also, let any outside noises drift away.

Now, concentrating only on the sound of my voice, allowing yourself a few minutes for total relaxation, as I count down from 10 to 1, think of yourself getting more and more relaxed, letting all of the tension and stress flow out. Relax to deeper levels than you can remember: 10, 9, 8…feeling deeply relaxed…7, 6…going deeper…5, 4…deeper and deeper…3, 2, 1. Very good.

Now, let's take a mental trip through your body so that we can identify any remaining tension or anxiety. Begin with your feet. Think of them getting very heavy, relaxing, warming, sinking down. First, your right foot. Then, your left foot. Simply imagine all of the tension flowing out of your feet, allowing the muscles to become very loose and very smooth, tingling, warm. Now, think for a moment about your legs, your calves. Particularly your right calf. Imagine any muscles that are knotted becoming smooth, warm. Now your left calf. Relaxing all the muscles. Your thighs…your right thigh, your left thigh…muscles unknotting, lengthening, warming, all the tension leaving them.

Focus now on your hips, letting any tension resolve, and on your abdomen. Many of us hold a lot of stress and tightness in our abdomens. Let it free. Think for a moment about your back, all the muscles, many, many muscles up and down your back. Let them go, warming, comforting. Your shoulders, let them drop slightly, letting go of any burdens. You are feeling very comfortable now. I want you to think about your right arm, the upper part of your arm, the lower part, and of your right hand, letting go, relaxing. Your left arm, first the upper part and then the lower part, then your hand. Turn them loose for a moment of any responsibilities.

Now in your mind's eye, travel up to the muscles of your neck. Mentally circle your neck, letting all of the tension flow out. Concentrate for a moment on your jaw. Let it drop slightly. Let it become as relaxed as possible. Focus on all the muscles around your eyes, relax. Focus on your forehead, relaxing, warming, smoothing. All around your head, the top part of your head, the back part of your head. See the knots unwinding, all worries and concerns and tension flowing out.

Now, give yourself a few seconds to take another mental trip through your body, identifying any tension remaining. Let it flow out. Allow yourself to achieve new levels of relaxation, of comfort. Remember that when you relax like this, your body begins to heal itself, and you become energized for any activities you have ahead of you. (Achterberg, 1985)

And now that your body is relaxed, we can begin to let your mind relax. Begin daydreaming about a favorite place that is all your own. This is a pleasant and peaceful place where you have no worries, concerns, or fears. It can be somewhere you've been before or in some place that exists only in your imagination. Perhaps you are doing something fun in this favorite place or just relaxing. Allow yourself to be in that special place, and spend some time exploring it…its colors and shapes…textures…sounds…smells…its feeling. And spend a moment now imagining this scene and letting your mind relax totally (pause for 1 minute). (Brigham, 1994)

Healthy Airways and Lungs Imagery:

Step 1. Now that your body and mind are relaxed, you can prepare to travel into your respiratory system and breathe easily. Take some time now to focus in on your lungs…Imagine being able to look into your chest and see the large trachea dividing into smaller airways. These airways disappear deep into the lung tissue, much as the branches of a tree disappear into the leaves.

Notice the bands of muscle tissue wrapping around the outside of the bronchial tubes…As this muscle tissue releases and relaxes, it opens the passageways for breathing. Feel the air moving in and out more easily (pause). (Achterberg et al., 1994)

Perhaps you can imagine focusing in even more closely now and seeing into the inside of the airways…Watch the tiny hairlike cilia that line the inside of the airway walls…working like miniature brooms to sweep mucus upward…and out of the airways, where the body then clears it away.

Feel the air again moving more easily in and out of your lungs (pause).

As you continue your journey through the respiratory system, notice the inner walls of the airways…See their color, and imagine being able to reach out and run your fingers along the surfaces…The lining of the airways is smooth and silky, and a healthy pink in color, much like the inner surface of your mouth…This smooth and silky surface allows the air to pass freely…Hear the sound of the air as it moves freely and clearly in and out of your lungs (pause). (Achterberg et al., 1994)

Now imagine maintaining this healthy state. Your airways respond to any harmless allergens or irritants with calmness. And understand that it is not just your airways that are being shown this…but that you, too, are developing a sense of calmness…less reactive to the environment…more safe and sure, balanced, and stronger than you have ever been. (Naparstek, 1994)

Take a few moments now to notice the changes you have helped create in your breathing system and yourself…relaxed muscles…slow, easy breathing…clear, open, relaxed airways…feeling peaceful and calm…You have restored the natural balance in your body and created healthy lungs going about the work of absorbing oxygen in an easy, relaxed manner. You are in a perfect state of health. And now you are going to spend a moment imagining yourself doing a favorite activity in which you have no problems with your asthma. Imagine all of the sights, sounds, and positive feelings as you breathe easily and comfortably during this activity (pause for 1 minute). (Achterberg et al., 1994; Naparstek, 1994)

To be sure that your breathing system is perfectly healthy, you are now going to visualize a special kind of air that acts to open your airways. Imagine that the air surrounding you has a special color of your choosing. Pick whatever color seems right for you. Breathe in this colored air and imagine that it completely clears your airways. It relaxes the muscles around the outside of your bronchial tubes and clears the inside of the airways for free and easy breathing. This special colored air creates healthy lungs functioning effectively and easily. And know that whenever you feel your asthma coming on, you can close your eyes and breathe in this special air to clear your airways and lungs and help yourself to feel better. (M. Castes, personal communication, February 27, 2000)

In a moment, I am going to count from 1 to 5, and you will come back to full awareness of the room, bringing these healthy images, feelings, and sensations with you. You will feel refreshed and much better than before. 1, 2…slowly becoming aware of the room…3…at the count of 5 you'll open your eyes and be wide awake, feeling relaxed and healthy…4, 5. Eyes open. Re-energized. Feeling much better than before. (Naparstek, 1994; Peck et al., 2003, pp. 111–115)

Step 2. Before treatment, ask the participant the medications he or she uses, especially rescue medication. A daily asthma diary works well for the purpose of charting medicine usage across the treatment timeframe.

Step 3. Spirometry readings can be used to determine if the treatment is affecting lung functioning. A nurse, trained psychologist, or physician can conduct the readings. However, readings can be completed on an infrequent basis and, if unfeasible, the psychologist can rely on asthma symptom reporting. The State-Trait Anxiety Inventory (STAI) State-Anxiety Scale (Spielberger, 1983) is used to obtain a subjective reading of anxiety. Stress can be measured frequently and simply using a 100 mm Visual Analog Scale (Davey, Barratt, Butow, & Deeks, 2007). If depression co-occurs with anxiety and stress, it should be measured as well.

Written Emotional Expression

There are several types of Written Emotional Expression: trauma experiences, stressful experiences, positive experiences, and plans. With trauma and stressful experiences, the child is instructed to write in a journal about issues and events, past and/or present that either cause him or her stress or were traumatic. The second two types use positive psychological strategies that ask the youth to write about positive experiences or plans. This approach can involve having the child write about three things for which he or she is thankful in a letter format or write about plans for the future. Regardless of the type of writing, the activity is typically completed every other day for about 20 to 30 minutes and should be done over the course of about 1 month (Bray et al., 2003).

Step 1. Ask the student to sit down either in the classroom or a separate office. Give the student a prompt that is based on one of the aforementioned types of writing. The writing should be completed in approximately 20 minutes, and the child should be told that his or her writing will be confidential. The child may take the writing with him or her or dispose of it on completion of the writing task.

One example of a script for writing about a traumatic event that can be adapted for use by a psychologist is as follows (D'Souza, Lumley, Kraft, & Dooley, 2008):

Participants are given the standard instructions [Pennebaker & Beall, 1986; Smyth, Stone, Hurewitz, & Kaell, 1999] to write about "a trauma or upheaval or stressful experience that you may be experiencing right now or that you experienced at some other time in your life," particularly "the most stressful that you have experienced and is the most significant to you," and "ideally one that you have not talked about in detail with others." Participants were encouraged to write about the facts, as well as their deepest feelings, and to try to write about the same event for all four writing days. Finally, they were encouraged to "tell a story" and consider writing about how the event has affected their relationships, health, or headaches. Writings were left with the research team at the end of each session. (D'Souza et al., 2008, p. 24)

An example of a writing prompt based on positive psychology techniques is to ask the child to draft a letter to a person who did a good thing for them. They can also be asked to write about three good things that happened to them that week (McCabe-Fitch, Bray, Kehle, Theodore, & Gelbar, 2011).

Step 2. Monitor medication intake. As with the RGI intervention, ask participants for information about what, if any, medications they are currently using. Using a daily asthma diary assists well with capturing medicine usage during the intervention.

Step 3. The same assessment of effectiveness used with RGI should be used with this intervention: spirometry readings, STAI State-Anxiety Scale (Spielberger, 1983), and a 100 mm Visual Analog Scale (Davey et al., 2007). Depression should additionally be measured if it co-occurs with anxiety and stress.

Yoga

Yoga is an ancient discipline that involves breathing techniques and physical exercises. It incorporates a multitude of approaches that include relaxation, meditation, stretching, and physical posturing, all of which augment mental and physical well-being and establish harmony between the mind and body (Bray et al., 2012; Granath, Ingvarsson, von Thiele, & Lundberg, 2006; Khalsa, 2004). In the treatment of physiological and psychological disorders, it is hypothesized that this integration of psychological and physical elements is central to the effectiveness of yoga in mediating symptoms of illness (Jain et al., 1991; Vijaylakshmi, Satyanarayan, & Krishna Rao, 1988). Several studies have found that the techniques associated with yoga may improve the pulmonary function of adults and children with asthma (e.g., Bray et al., 2012; Jain et al., 1991; Vijaykalakshmi et al., 1988). One example of how yoga may be used in the mediation of asthma symptoms follows:

Step 1. Monitor the use of medication and asthmatic symptoms. Monitoring may be done through the use of a daily asthma diary wherein the asthmatic (or a designee) systematically records the amount and type of medications used as well as asthma-related symptoms experienced on a daily basis.

Step 2. Children with asthma are taught basic yoga poses through direct instruction or video instruction. Some companies offer yoga DVDs and online videos appropriate for use with adults and children. Some videos engage children through a more game-like approach to yoga, which may be more appropriate for younger children. The children with asthma should engage in yoga at least three times per week.

Step 3. Spirometry readings and the STAI State-Anxiety Scale (Spielberger, 1983) or the State Anxiety Inventory for Children (STAIC; Spielberger, 1983) are used to assess treatment effectiveness. These assessments should be administered before the yoga intervention is introduced, during each yoga session, and after the treatment has concluded.

Mindfulness

Mindfulness-based stress reduction (MBSR) has been used to effectively improve quality of life for participants with asthma (Pbert et al., 2012) by decreasing panic symptoms and anxiety sensitivity (Kraemer, McLeish, & Johnson, 2015). Specifically, the use of the mindfulness skills, including "observe," "describe," "acting with awareness," "nonjudgmental," and "nonreactivity," have been shown to reduce anxiety-related symptoms, both psychologically and physiologically in participants with asthma (Kraemer et al., 2015). Reducing asthmatics' anxiety improves their quality of life perceptions.

Step 1. Following the protocol used by Pbert and colleagues (2012), the participant should be instructed to complete a body scan, where attention and focus progresses sequentially through the body to increase awareness of sensations; a sitting meditation, where the focus is placed on methodic breathing and awareness of feelings and thoughts; and stretching exercises that are gentle to enhance movement awareness. The instruction should include guidance on using mindfulness daily to assist with symptoms of stress. These techniques can be taught in person or via a CD to allow for daily 30-minute practice 6 days per week.

Step 2. Monitor the participant's anxiety before, during, and after the intervention using the STAI State-Anxiety Scale (Spielberger, 1983).

Step 3. Monitor the participant's quality of life before and after the intervention. An adequate measure of quality of life is the Asthma Quality of Life

Questionnaire (AQOL) which assesses quality of life over the past 2 weeks and produces appropriately reliable and valid scores across domains (Leidy & Coughlin, 1998).

CONCLUSION

Asthma is a chronic inflammatory respiratory disease that is characterized by coughing, wheezing, chest tightness, shortness of breath, and difficulty breathing. Asthma is typically diagnosed in children by 5 years of age and is the leading cause of school absenteeism, as well as producing deleterious academic, behavioral, and social-emotional consequences. If left untreated, asthma may result in long-term lung damage. It has been well established that asthma has both physiological and psychological causes. Medication management for short- and long-term symptom control, as well as the identification and avoidance of triggers, are particularly helpful for children with asthma. In addition, psychologically based interventions based on the mind–body connection, including RGI, yoga, mindfulness, and written emotional expression, have been shown to enhance lung functioning in youths with asthma and improve overall quality of life.

SELECT BIBLIOGRAPHY

Asthma—American Lung Association. Retrieved from http://www.lung.org/lung-disease/asthma
This website provides information about understanding asthma, how to provide an asthma-friendly environment, managing asthma symptoms and reducing triggers. It also provides health education information and an online community for individuals with asthma.

Asthma and Asthma Attack Center. Retrieved from http://www.webmd.com/asthma
This comprehensive website makes available the latest research on asthma as well as an overview of the disease, symptomatology, and treatment.

Gosselin, K., & Ravanelli, T. (1998). *The ABCs of asthma: An asthma alphabet book for kids of all ages.* New York, NY: JayJo Books.
This book is designed for children 4 years of age and older. It is an entertaining and educational book that teaches children, in child-friendly

language, about asthma and how they can live a normal life despite their medical diagnosis. Moreover, the book facilitates explaining triggers of asthma attacks and how to manage the disorder.

Kabat-Zinn, J. (2012). *Mindfulness for beginners.* Boulder, CO: Sounds True.
This book provides step-by-step instructions on how to change thoughts, feelings, and behavior, thereby awakening individuals to their authentic selves. Furthermore, it proffers answers and insights regarding developing a mindful mindset. Finally, it comes with five guided mindfulness meditations on a CD.

REFERENCES

Achterberg, J. (1985). *Imagery in healing: Shamanism and modern medicine.* Boston, MA: Shambhala.

Achterberg, J., Dossey, B., & Kolkmeier, L. (1994). *Rituals of healing: Using imagery for health and wellness.* New York, NY: Bantam

Arashima, Y., Yakubo, S., Ueda, Y., Munemura, T., Komiya, T., Isa, H., & Nakayama, T. (2013). A first case of asthma thought to be caused by Coxiella burnetii infection. *International Medical Journal, 20*(6), 699–700.

Archibald, M. M., Caine, V., Ali, S., Hartling, L., & Scott, S. D. (2015). What is left unsaid: An interpretive description of the information needs of parents of children with asthma. *Research in Nursing & Health, 38*(1), 19–28. doi:10.1002/nur.21635

Bhattacharya, R., Chan, S., & Sambamoorthi, U. (2014). Excess risk of chronic physical conditions associated with depression and anxiety. *BMC Psychiatry, 14*(1), 1–19. doi:10.1186/1471–244X-14–10.

Bitsch, L., & Stemerding, D. (2013). The innovation journey of genomics and asthma research. *Sociology of Health and Illness, 35*(8), 1164–1180. doi:10.1111/1467–9566.12028

Bray, M. A., Kehle, T. J., Peck, H. L., Margiano, S. G., Dobson, R., Peczynski, K.,...Alric, J. M. (2005). Written emotional expression as an intervention asthma: A replication. *Journal of Applied School Psychology, 22,* 141–165.

Bray, M. A., Kehle, T. J., Peck, H. L., Theodore, L. A., & Zhou, Z. (2004). Enhancing subjective well-being in individuals with asthma. *Psychology in the Schools, 40,* 95–100. doi:10.1002/pits.10141.

Bray, M. A., Sassu, K. A., Kehle, T. J., Kapoor, V., Margiano, S., Peck, H. L., & Bertuglia, R. (2012). Yoga as an intervention for asthma. *School Psychology Forum, 6*, 1–11.

Bray, M. A., Theodore, L. A., Patwa, S., Margiano, S., Alric, J., & Peck, H. (2003). Written emotional expression as an intervention for asthma. *Psychology in the Schools, 40*, 193–207.

Brigham, D. D. (1994). *Imagery for getting well: Clinical applications of behavioral medicine.* New York, NY: W. W. Norton & Company, Inc.

Davey, H. M., Barratt, A. L., Butow, P. N., & Deeks, J. J. (2007). A one-item question with a likert or visual analog scale adequately measured current anxiety. *Journal of Clinical Epidemiology, 60*(4), 356–360. doi:10.1016/j.jclinepi.2006.07.015

Dobson, R. L., Bray, M. A., Kehle, T. J., Theodore, L. A., & Peck, H. L. (2005). Relaxation and guided imagery as an intervention for children with asthma: A replication. *Psychology in the Schools, 42*(7), 707–720. doi:10.1002/pits.20119

D'Souza, P. J., Lumley, M. A., Kraft, C. A., & Dooley, J. A. (2008). Relaxation training and written emotional disclosure for tension or migraine headaches: A randomized, controlled trial. *Annals of Behavioral Medicine, 36*(1), 21–32. doi:10.1007/s12160–008-9046–7

Granath, J., Ingvarsson, S., von Thiele, U., & Lundberg, U. (2006). Stress management: A randomized study of cognitive behavioural therapy and yoga. *Cognitive Behaviour Therapy, 35*, 3–10.

Hammer-Helmich, L., Linneberg, A., Thomsen, S., & Glümer, C. (2014). Association between parental socioeconomic position and prevalence of asthma, atopic eczema and hay fever in children. *Scandinavian Journal of Public Health, 42*(2), 120–127. doi:10.1177/1403494813505727

Jain, S. C., Rai, L., Valecha, A., Jha, U. K., Bhatnagar, S. O., & Ram, K. (1991). Effect of yoga training on exercise tolerance in adolescents with childhood asthma. *Journal of Asthma, 28*, 437–442.

Kabat-Zinn, J. (1994). *Wherever you go, there you are: Mindfulness meditation in everyday life.* New York, NY: Hyperion.

Khalsa, S. B. S. (2004). Yoga as a therapeutic intervention: A bibliometric analysis of published research studies. *Indian Journal of Physiology and Pharmacology, 48*, 269–285.

Kraemer, K. M., McLeish, A. C. & Johnson, A. L. (2015). Associations between mindfulness and panic symptoms among young adults with asthma. *Psychology, Health & Medicine, 20*(3), 322–331. doi:10.1080/13548506.2014.936888

Leidy, N. K., & Coughlin, C. (1998). Psychometric performance of the asthma quality of life questionnaire in a US sample. *Quality of Life Research, 7*(2), 127–134. doi:10.1023/A:1008853325724

McCabe-Fitch, K., Bray, M. A., Kehle, T. J., Theodore, L. A., & Gelbar, N. (2011). The promotion of happiness and life satisfaction in children. *Canadian Journal of School Psychology, 26*, 177–192.

Menzies, V., Lyon, D. E., Elswick, R. K., McCain, N. L., & Gray, D. P. (2014). Effects of guided imagery on biobehavioral factors in women with fibromyalgia. *Journal of Behavioral Medicine, 37*, 70–80.

Naparstek, B. (1994). *Staying well with guided imagery.* New York, NY: Warner Books.

Pbert, L., Madison, J. M., Druker, S., Olendzki, N., Magner, R., Reed, G.,...Carmody, J. (2012). Effect of mindfulness training on asthma quality of life and lung function: A randomised controlled trial. *Thorax, 67*(9), 769–776. doi:10.1136/thoraxjnl-2011–200253

Peck, H. L., Bray, M. A., & Kehle, T. J. (2003). Relaxation and guided imagery: A school-based intervention for children with asthma. *Psychology in the Schools, 40*, 657–675.

Pennebaker, J. W., & Beall, S. K. (1986). Confronting a traumatic event: Toward an understanding of inhibition and disease. *Journal of Abnormal Psychology, 95*, 274–281.

Slavich, G. M., & Irwin, M. R. (2014). From stress to inflammation and major depressive disorder: A social signal transduction theory of depression. *Psychological Bulletin, 140*(3), 774–815. doi:10.1037/a0035302.

Smyth, J. M., Stone, A. A., Hurewitz, A., & Kaell, A. (1999). Effects of writing about stressful experiences on symptom reduction in patients with asthma or rheumatoid arthritis: A randomized trial. *Journal of the American Medical Association, 281*, 1304–1309.

Spielberger, C. D. (1983). *State-trait anxiety inventory for children.* Redwood City, CA: Mind Garden.

Van Lieshout, R. J., & MacQueen, G. (2008). Psychological factors in Asthma. *Allergy Asthma Clinical Immunology, 4,* 12–28. doi:10.1186/1710-1492-4-1-12.

Vijaylakshmi, S., Satyanarayan, M., & Krishna Rao, P. V. (1988). Combined effect of yoga and psychotherapy on management of asthma: A preliminary study. *Journal of Indian Psychology, 7,* 32–39.

Neuropsychological Disorders

Neuropsychological Development and Considerations for Prevention

Andrew S. Davis and Adele A. Larsson

OVERVIEW

The hierarchical nature of neurodevelopment, along with the myriad factors that contribute to an observable problem in children, strongly argues for a comprehensive approach when considering prevention and intervention programs for children, or when conducting an assessment. Pediatric neuropsychology adopts such a comprehensive approach because behavior is analyzed through the lens of the child's developing nervous system, along with consideration of constructs that have a reciprocal relationship with neurodevelopment, including genetic, psychosocial, academic, intellectual, and medical factors. This approach is underpinned by having sound knowledge of neurodevelopment. This chapter reviews the empirical support for such a multifaceted approach by considering selected neurodevelopmental concerns and medical variables that present as obstacles to healthy neurodevelopment. Readers interested in additional resources on neurodevelopment might access texts such as Davis (2010); Yeates, Ris, Taylor, and Pennington (2009); and Baron (2004).

ETIOLOGY AND FACTORS CONTRIBUTING TO NEUROLOGICAL DEVELOPMENT IN CHILDREN AND ADOLESCENTS

Prenatal Development

It is virtually impossible to fully consider all facets of prenatal development and the potential difficulties the developing fetus might encounter in a single chapter. Prenatal complications have the potential to result in serious problems for the mother and fetus, ranging from mild developmental delays to maternal death and/or termination of the fetus. When mortality does not occur, prenatal complications may result in increased morbidity with pervasive lifelong effects. This section of the chapter reviews select neurodevelopmental prenatal complications that can be, at least partially, prevented or ameliorated through behavioral interventions with the pregnant mother. Although mental health professionals may not be the primary specialists treating the presenting problem (e.g., gestational diabetes), they are often well suited to provide adjunctive treatment for managing behavioral and psychological interventions. The following section addresses the deleterious effects of *legal* substances on the developing fetus, but professionals should be vigilant about preventing or reducing intrauterine exposure to illicit substances as well.

Intrauterine Toxin Exposure. Substances ingested during pregnancy can affect the developing fetus; intrauterine toxic exposure represents one of the most common, and perhaps the most avoidable, barriers to healthy prenatal development. Toxic exposure can involve the pregnant mother taking illicit drugs, but many ingested toxins are legal substances. Common legal substances ingested or inhaled during pregnancy include alcohol, tobacco, common household products, and heavy metals. Although it is certain that intrauterine exposure to toxins can be potentially hazardous, the pattern of subsequent impairment as well as the interplay between environmental and biological factors are equivocal. Indeed, complicating the idiosyncratic effects of toxic substances are the mitigating risk and resiliency factors that serve to either exacerbate or protect the developing central nervous system (CNS) from intrauterine exposure. For example, a comprehensive review of prenatal toxicity conducted by Williams and Ross (2007), addressed neurodevelopment and prenatal exposure to lead, polychlorinated biphenyls (PCBs), mercury, cocaine, alcohol, marijuana, cigarettes, and antidepressants. Although results were variable, it was found that many common patterns were present: brain development was adversely affected by lead and PCBs; infants exposed to alcohol and marijuana in utero showed long-term attention issues; neonatal cocaine exposure and its negative effects were largely mediated by psychosocial factors; and genetically inherited factors mediated the relationship between maternal smoking and the child's later delinquency. This review reveals that the relationship between intrauterine toxicity and later neurodevelopment is complex and continued research is needed.

Alcohol. Intrauterine exposure to alcohol is especially concerning because it is a powerful neurotoxin that is legal for individuals over a certain age, including pregnant women. As such, there are not the same proscribed consequences for or barriers to obtaining alcohol as there are with illicit substances. Health care workers must contend with

the fact that "preventing fetal alcohol syndrome (FAS) by encouraging pregnant women to abstain from drinking alcohol competes with commercial alcohol marketing" (Glik, Prelip, Myerson, & Eilers, 2008, p. 93). In addition, there is some conflicting information available about the health benefits and dangers of alcohol that are somewhat confusing. Governmental recommendations suggest that alcohol should be consumed in moderation, which is defined as one alcohol drink per day for women and two drinks for men (U.S. Department of Agriculture and U.S. Department of Health and Human Services, 2010). However, although potential benefits of moderate alcohol use have been identified, such as lowering the risk of cardiovascular disease, it is not recommended that anyone start drinking nor increase the amount they drink in an effort to achieve these potential benefits. The document also states that pregnant women should not drink at all because there is no safe level of alcohol use identified for pregnant women. Fetal alcohol spectrum disorder (FASD) is a term that encapsulates a range of conditions resulting from intrauterine exposure to alcohol. Intrauterine alcohol exposure is related to a broad array of deficits, including diminished executive functioning (Rasmussen, 2005) and a decrease in general intellectual abilities (Mattson & Riley, 1998). Such cognitive deficiencies in turn can adversely affect the child's academic, social, emotional, and behavioral development. Indeed, children with FASD are at an increased risk for mental health problems, school dropout, teenage pregnancy, homelessness, abuse and neglect, employment problems, and substance abuse (Brintnell, Bailey, Sawhney, & Kreftin, 2010).

A compelling rationale for FASD prevention programs, rather than a post-hoc intervention, is incredible monetary savings to society, with an estimated lifetime savings of approximately $2 million for an individual with fetal alcohol syndrome (Lupton, Burd, & Harwood, 2004). With respect to FASD, Hankin (2002) divided preventative approaches into three types: universal prevention of maternal alcohol abuse (e.g., directed to the general public but targeted toward pregnant women or women likely to become pregnant), selective prevention of maternal alcohol abuse (e.g., women who may become pregnant who consume alcohol), and indicated prevention (e.g., women at a high risk of having a child with FASD). In a review of prevention programs, Hankin (2002) noted that targeted efforts (selective prevention and indicated prevention) and related "brief interventions for pregnant women can successfully reduce alcohol intake during pregnancy" (p. 64).

Changing High-Risk Alcohol Use and Increasing Contraception Effectiveness (CHOICES; Hutton et al., 2014) is a program developed by the Centers for Disease Control and Prevention (CDC) using behavioral interventions for high-risk women in 1997. Floyd and colleagues (2007) conducted a study as part of the CHOICES project using motivational interviewing delivered during four manualized treatment sessions, as well as one counseling session focusing on contraception use. Female high-risk participants were identified—56% met criteria for alcohol dependence, more than 90% reported illicit drug use, and in excess of 70% reported that they smoked cigarettes. An average of 3.2 counseling sessions were attended by the participants, and the outcomes of the study included reduced drinking during pregnancy as well as ameliorating additional variables under investigation. In essence, women in the intervention group were approximately twice as likely to be at reduced risk for an alcohol-exposed pregnancy at 3-, 6-, and 9-month follow-up sessions. The authors of this study concluded that their brief intervention significantly reduced the risk of an alcohol-exposed pregnancy.

The first session in project CHOICES involves relationship building, a review of fact sheets on alcohol use and contraceptive methods, and advice to schedule a contraceptive counseling and prescribing visit. Instruction is provided in keeping a daily journal for drinking, sexual activity, and contraception. Decision-making processes are reviewed, and access to community resources is made explicit. Participants are also given a gift pack, containing transportation tokens, condoms, and information about follow-up appointments.

In the second session, the content of the client's daily journal is reviewed and discussed, with personalized feedback provided. A contraception-counseling visit is also arranged during this session, along with the development of initial goal statements, change plans, and self-evaluation methods. Exercises in decision making are practiced,

including a discussion of issues related to temptation and confidence.

The third session involves discussion of material from the daily journal, review of decision-making and self-evaluation exercises, completion of goal statements and change plans, and a discussion about contraception counseling. In the fourth session, all previous sessions are reviewed, and goals and change plans are finalized. Follow-up is discussed, and motivational reinforcement and problem-solving support is provided. Readers interested in learning more about project CHOICES could visit the following website: http://www.cdc.gov/ncbddd/fasd/choices-importance-preventing-alcohol-exposed-pregnancies.html.

Tobacco. Similar to alcohol, tobacco is a legal substance that, when used during pregnancy, has the potential to harm both the mother and fetus. Despite declining use (CDC, 2014a), tobacco is widely available and frequently used. Based on data from 2010 collected from 27 sites for the Pregnancy Risk Assessment Monitoring System (PRAMS) 10.7% of women smoked during the last three months of pregnancy (Tong et al., 2013). Of particular concern with tobacco use are the detrimental health risks, such as hypertension and diabetes, which adversely affect the cerebrovascular functioning of pregnant women. Herrmann, King, and Weitzman (2008) found consistent results suggesting prenatal and postnatal exposure to tobacco smoke is associated with higher levels of behavioral problems in children, including higher rates of attention deficit hyperactivity disorder (ADHD), conduct disorder, oppositional defiant behaviors, and irritability, as well as some evidence suggesting lower overall intelligence. These findings are particularly concerning because children with these behavioral problems also tend to experience academic difficulties and are at increased risk of other negative outcomes, such as increased dropout rate, teenage pregnancy, and incarceration (Woodward, Fergusson, & Horwood, 2001).

Many others studies have found a strong association between pre- and postnatal exposure to tobacco and cognitive deficits. Researchers have found a pattern of lower overall cognitive abilities among children born to a mother who reported smoking at least one cigarette per day while pregnant (Julvez et al., 2007). Specifically, these children exhibited lower verbal, quantitative, executive functioning, and working memory abilities. Yolton, Dietrich, Auinger, Lanphear, and Hornung (2005) used the biomarker cotinine as a measure of environmental tobacco smoke (ETS) of 4,399 children and adolescents aged 6 to 16 years with measured cotinine levels equal to or greater than 15 ng/mL signaling ETS exposure. The reading and math subtests of the *Wide Range Achievement Test-Revised* (WRAT-R; Jastak & Wilkinson, 1984) were administered, as well as the Block Design and Digit Span subtests of the *Wechsler Intelligence Scale of Children, Third Edition* (WISC-III; Wechsler, 1991). Results showed significantly poorer reading among children with higher cotinine levels as well as poorer nonverbal reasoning. Yolton and colleagues (2005) also reported that exposure of children and adolescents to nearly any amount of ETS may negatively impact healthy cognitive development.

Lead. Lead is not a substance that is consumed intentionally; however, it still remains a concern for prenatal development because of indirect absorption or ingestion. Although there have been attempts to limit the possibility of lead exposure, lead can still be found in older paint, in some toys, in the air as by-products of industry, and in contaminated water and soil (Gardella, 2001; Hepp, 2011). The most common source of lead exposure in the United States is from lead in homes constructed before 1978 (Blando, Antoine, & Lefkowitz, 2013). Lead exposure can be a concern both during pregnancy as well as after the child is born, and it has been associated with decreased gestation and increased risk of preterm birth and being born small for gestational age (Jelliffe-Pawlowski, Miles, Courtney, Materna, & Charlton, 2006).

Jedrychowski and colleagues (2008) examined the relationship between low levels of neonatal lead exposure on developmental delay. Umbilical cord blood samples taken from 452 infants born at 33 to 42 weeks of gestation were measured for lead levels. The children's mothers were participating in the Krakow Prospective Birth Cohort Study; infants' cognitive development was assessed with the *Fagan Test of Infant Intelligence* (FTII; Fagan, 1991), using the Visual Recognition Memory (VRM) measure. After adjusting for gestational age, child's gender, and maternal education, the likelihood of infants with high exposure to lead having a developmental delay was twofold, meaning about 50% of these infants would be found to have a developmental delay. For each unit of lead concentration measured, infants scored 1.5 points lower on the VRM, with a statistically significant 2.5-point difference between infants of low- and high-lead exposure. These results are consistent with the findings of Jedrychowski et al. (2009) who studied 444 children, comparing their umbilical cord blood lead levels with the Mental Development Index (MDI) of the *Bayley Scales of Infant Development, Second Edition* (BSID-II; Bayley, 1993) administered at 12, 24, and 36 months. They found that significant deficits in cognitive functioning attributable to "very-low" neonatal lead exposure persisted at 24 months and 36 months.

Gestational Diabetes. Gestational diabetes occurs in women without a history of diabetes who develop diabetes while they are pregnant. The prevalence of gestational diabetes in the United States has been estimated to be between 4.6% and 9.2% (DeSisto, Kim, & Sharma, 2014) and "the incidence of gestational diabetes mellitus (GDM) is increasing in the context of the pandemic in obesity and type 2 diabetes (T2D) in both high-income and emerging countries" (Mitanchcz, Burguet, & Simeoni, 2014, p. 445). These women also have an increased risk of developing T2D after their pregnancy (Bellamy, Casas, Hingorani, & Williams, 2009). Other concerns about gestational diabetes include a risk in the offspring for increased weight gain (Crume et al., 2011), which carries with it additional health risks. The research on gestational diabetes is equivocal, with some researchers failing to show a direct link between problems in children related to gestational diabetes separate from problems associated with obesity in pregnant women (Beyerlein, Nehring, Rosario, & von Kries, 2012).

Although the research is still emerging, gestational diabetes should be of concern to mental health professionals because of its increasing prevalence (Ferrara, 2007) and its possible pervasive effect on the developing fetus. In addition, factors such as cesarean delivery and gestational weight gain have been associated with postpartum depression in women with gestational diabetes (Nicklas et al., 2013), which in itself is a risk factor for offspring, including internalizing problems (Verbeek et al., 2012). As such, women with gestational diabetes represent an important population where professionals may help the mother following pregnancy as well as prevent and/or ameliorate the effects of maternal gestational diabetes on the developing child. For example, Pirkola et al. (2010) found that maternal gestational diabetes combined with maternal pregnancy overweight represented a risk factor for the child later becoming overweight at 16 years of age. Moreover, infants born to women of normal weight with gestational diabetes were not at an increased risk of being overweight later in life, suggesting a multifactorial relationship in regard to gestational diabetes.

Prevention and treatment programs for gestational diabetes have a behavioral component. Multiple factors may facilitate changes in eating and physical activity behaviors, including social support from family, health professionals, and peers. To increase physical activity in women who were inactive, Kolu, Raitanen, Rissanen, and Luoto (2013) suggested the following: engage in 150 minutes or more of moderate or vigorous leisure-time activity 3 days a week; participate in five sessions of physiotherapist-guided instruction in various forms of physical activity; track physical activity in an activity diary; report the type, intensity, and duration of sport/activity; and report any adverse events related to physical activity. These findings suggest that health care providers, including psychologists, play an important potential role in preventing the negative outcomes associated with gestational diabetes.

PREVENTION/AMELIORATION OF CHILDHOOD HEALTH PROBLEMS WITH NEUROCOGNITIVE IMPLICATIONS

Mental health professionals are important in the behavioral management of some pediatric health conditions, especially given the link between health status and neurocognitive functioning. Some of these health problems serve as risk factors for each other, and thus addressing one health problem may reduce the risk of others.

Childhood Diabetes

Diabetes represents a particularly insidious disease process with a substantial increase over the decades, with many children having yet to be diagnosed. The increasing incidence is a concern for practitioners for many reasons, including the linkages between pediatric diabetes and cognitive dysfunction. However, it is important to note that the literature is still emerging in this area. For example, research has demonstrated deficits in executive functioning, cognitive flexibility, and concept formation (Ohmann et al., 2010), and depression and anxiety (Reynolds & Helgeson, 2011). In essence, there have been concerns raised about neuropsychological functioning among children with diabetes, although additional research is needed to identify associated risk factors that might confound or explain the findings further.

Although there is a salient genetic component to diabetes, particularly type 1 diabetes (Baker & Steck, 2011; Polychronakos & Li, 2011), there are also environmental factors that contribute to the development and management of the condition. Medication compliance and glycemic control are particularly important for children with diabetes. CDC reported that approximately 151,000 people in the United States under the age of 20 years have been diagnosed with diabetes (CDC, 2014b). Helping children learn how to manage type 1 diabetes can be challenging; "children with diabetes must learn how to test their blood sugar regularly, administer insulin properly, monitor their dietary intake and physical activity, and adjust insulin dosages based on current blood sugar, diet, and exercise. Failure to properly engage in all of these activities could lead to acute episodes of low blood sugar (i.e., hypoglycemia) or high blood sugar (i.e., hyperglycemia)—each of which is associated with hazardous implications for health" (Reynolds & Helgeson, 2011, p. 29). These self-maintenance tasks may feel overwhelming for children and their families, but children must eventually learn how to manage these activities on their own. Behavioral interventions and/or assistance from mental health professionals may be helpful in this process.

Neuropsychological assessments can also help parents and the medical treatment team to determine the extent to which adolescents may contribute to self-care and identify barriers to and opportunities for intervention. For example, executive functioning is often a mediating factor in treatment adherence for children with type 1 diabetes (McNally, Rohan, Pendley, Delamater, & Drotar, 2010). As such, children with executive dysfunction may need assistance with treatment adherence (e.g., planning, organization of insulin as well as meals) as they transition into becoming responsible for their glycemic control.

The American Diabetes Association (2014) noted that even minor weight loss can delay T2D onset and provided suggestions about weight loss. Practitioners should review the American Diabetes Association website and discuss these recommendations with patients and medical treatment teams. CDC also offers an evidence-based national diabetes prevention program in the following website that would be useful to review: http://www.cdc.gov/diabetes/prevention/index.html. The program is intended for prediabetic individuals and those at risk for T2D, and involves lifestyle changes in diet and exercise, with the help of a coach and similar people. The intervention spans a year, with weekly sessions for the first 6 months and monthly meetings for the last 6 months.

School-based interventions for preventing diabetes have appeal, given the inherent structure of the school day as well as support staff who are in place to implement interventions. Grey and colleagues (2004) introduced a school-based program for children with a body mass index (BMI) equal to or greater than the 95th percentile, and a family history of diabetes. In this study an experimental group received coping skill training (CST) in addition to the nutrition education and exercise training also received by the control group. Results showed that the children in the experimental group demonstrated improvement in nutrition knowledge and health behaviors, as well as in glucose and insulin levels when compared with the control group. The authors noted that "CST adds an important component to traditional nutrition education and physical activity for adolescents attempting to decrease their risk of T2DM" (Grey et al., 2004, p. 14), which should be of interest to mental health professionals as coping skills training rests within their sphere of competence.

McGavock, Sellers, and Dean (2007) completed a review of interventions intended to reduce the risk of T2D by focusing on cardiovascular health.

Physical activity has been shown to prevent and manage T2D and cardiovascular disease in adults. Researchers suggested that decreasing the risk of developing T2D or managing T2D in youth should include a minimum of 60 to 90 minutes of physical activity per day of moderate to vigorous intensity and time spent watching television, being on the computer, or playing video games should be limited to less than 60 minutes per day.

Hypertension

The American Heart Association (2014) notes that determining hypertension (high blood pressure) in children is complicated because what is considered healthy is based on gender, age, and height. The organization encourages caregivers to work with doctors to determine what constitutes "normal" blood pressure for individual children. Hypertension is a salient concern for children in the United States as it represents risk factors for other health conditions associated with cognitive problems. For example, hypertension has been associated with memory deficits as assessed on the Digit Span subtest of the *Wechsler Intelligence Scale for Children—Revised* (WISC-R; Lande, Kaczorowski, Auinger, Schwartz, & Weitzman, 2003; Wechsler, 1974), and other physical health complaints including headache, insomnia, and fatigue (Croix & Feig, 2006), which negatively affect academic performance and standardized neuropsychological testing. Children with hypertension also are at an increased risk of having a learning disability (Adams, Szilagyi, Gebhardt, & Lande, 2010).

Early intervention is needed to prevent and/or ameliorate early onset effects of hypertension. Falkner, Gidding, Portman, & Rosner (2008) examined longitudinal outcomes for adolescents with prehypertension and hypertension using data from the National Childhood Blood Pressure database. Multivariate regression analysis related change in blood pressure (BP) with changes in BMI over a 2-year period, with a significant number of boys and girls initially defined as prehypertensive converted into hypertensive at the follow-up (i.e., 14% of boys and 12% of girls became hypertensive after 2 years). In addition, a significant relationship between BMI and systolic blood pressure was found for both boys and girls; the greater the increase in BMI over 2 years, the higher the systolic

BP. Falkner et al. (2008) concluded that adolescents with prehypertension, who were at a risk of developing hypertension, should consider lifestyle changes to control their weight and increase their physical activity, with continued BP monitoring. Basically, risk factors of prehypertension and increased BMI need to be taken seriously by all health professionals. Mental health professionals are encouraged to work with patients and medical providers to monitor risk factors and educate patients and caregivers about hypertension risks.

EVIDENCE-BASED INTERVENTIONS AND EMPIRICAL SUPPORT FOR NEUROLOGICAL DEVELOPMENT IN CHILDREN AND ADOLESCENTS

Mental health professionals are encouraged to help parents and guardians recognize that safe, clean houses minimize environmental toxins. Roberts and colleagues (2009) discussed the risks and prevention of infant exposure to allergens, lead, polybrominated diphenyl ethers (PBDEs), pesticides, endocrine-disrupting compounds, arsenic, cadmium, chromium, mold, and bacteria because of animal feces, saliva, and hair, which are sources of dust-borne viruses and bacteria. To reduce dust and help prevent infant exposure to these dangerous compounds, Roberts and colleagues (2009) recommended performing simple cleaning procedures, providing alternative floor coverings, and using safer cleaning products. Keeping a clean house can start with removing shoes at the entrance as most pollutants found in dust are brought into the house from outside. Also, wiping shoes two times on a doormat "may be 95% as effective as shoe removal" (p. 20). To prevent exposure to toxic compounds, Roberts et al. (2009) suggested installing slat and level-loop carpets or maintaining a noncarpet flooring, such as hardwood, laminate, or tile. Finally, Roberts and colleagues (2009) recommended using safer cleaning products that do not contain the words "Danger," "Caution," or "Poison" for cleaning and keeping pest control products out of children's reach. These simple actions may be the most effective methods to reduce infant or child exposure to compounds harmful to health and cognitive development.

The 2009 report by the CDC (2009) delineated prevention guidelines to manage toxin exposure for children of all ages across a wide variety of environments. The report discusses toxin exposure and its prevention in the home by exploring the toxins found in common personal hygiene products, medications, cleaning supplies, gardening materials, and pest control products. To prevent exposure, the CDC suggested managing control of these substances in the home. For example, the report explained that the use of child-resistant closures (difficult for children under the age of 5 years to open) easily limits access to potentially toxic materials. In addition, caregivers should ensure labels and information about hazardous materials are visible to identify the substance, instructions in case of exposure, storage and use, and cautions for users and children. Research suggests consumers are more likely to notice and follow safety guidelines if they believe the item has "the potential to cause severe injury" (Croft & Harris, 1998).

HOW TO: A GUIDE TO THE IMPLEMENTATION OF INTERVENTIONS FOR NEUROPSYCHOLOGICAL DISORDERS

Pediatric neuropsychologists typically work with children with neurodevelopmental disorders or acquired conditions that impact neurological functioning. As such, it is common for pediatric neuropsychologists to have a high level of interaction with various health care providers in the medical field, such as pediatricians, child psychiatrists, psychologists, and other mental health professionals. These providers often seek a pediatric neuropsychological evaluation in the hope of finding strategies and accommodations to help children and their families, as well as to provide an accurate diagnosis that will improve overall treatment and facilitate medication management if needed. A pediatric neuropsychologist will complete a comprehensive report providing recommendations of evidence-based interventions for children with neurological difficulties. These interventions are often not provided by the neuropsychologist, but rather other professionals in allied health professions who work with the child on a regular basis and are able to monitor the child's progress, including speech-language pathologists, occupational and physical therapists, nutritionists, and nurses (e.g., diabetic management).

With respect to intervention, the allied health professionals who work with youths with neurological deficits have valuable information and insight in treating children and adolescents with CNS trauma. For example, a child diagnosed with developmental dyspraxia may benefit from physical therapy, whereas a child diagnosed with a disorder of written expression may benefit from occupational therapy. Children with a traumatic brain injury (TBI) may have damage to the motor tracts that affect articulation, which would be best served by a speech-language therapist. It is very common for pediatric neuropsychologists to refer their patients to other mental health practitioners to conduct therapeutic interventions and perhaps become the point-persons in working with other health care providers to keep the family informed. Thus, neuropsychological information is frequently used by other health care providers who provide the requisite services, whereas the neuropsychologist works closely with these professionals to ensure that treatment implementation is employed with fidelity and to monitor patient progress.

Another group of professionals with whom pediatric neuropsychologists frequently interact are educational personnel. This includes school psychologists, who are often the best individuals in the school milieu to understand the information contained in the neuropsychological report. School psychologists are typically in a unique position of translating the findings from the neuropsychological evaluation into language appropriate under that state's special education law to ensure that the child receives the proper services. Furthermore, schools often represent the most consistent environment for a child in which reliable service provision may be employed. As such, neuropsychologists often work with school psychologists and other school personnel, such as school counselors, to implement evidence-based interventions to enhance academic, behavioral, and social and/or emotional functioning of youths with neurodevelopmental disorders.

CONCLUSION

The process of neurodevelopment is complex and represents a dynamic interplay among genetics, behavior, demographics, the environment, psychosocial factors, and myriad physiological factors. Each of these elements represents not only a potential barrier to healthy neurodevelopment, but also an opportunity for intervention. Mental health professionals are well suited to provide preventative approaches for reducing risk factors and increasing resiliency in developing children from before birth through adolescence. Many of the prevention strategies discussed in this chapter are considered "common sense" to some (e.g., not drinking alcohol while pregnant or reducing exposure to secondhand smoke), although given the prevalence at which these behaviors occur, the topic still warrants being addressed. In some cases, practitioners may facilitate intervention strategies for children.

In addition to the conditions discussed in this chapter, there are myriad neurological, psychiatric, and other medical problems necessitating hospitalization that have profound cognitive effects on a child's functioning. For many of these conditions, children will continue to exhibit cognitive dysfunction after they become medically stable and leave the hospital. At some point, these children will return to school and psychologists can provide valuable assistance to facilitate the home-to-school transition. In sum, there are a number of health conditions that may potentially have deleterious and pervasive effects on neurodevelopment. This chapter discusses many of these conditions and the behavioral components that provide a direct linkage for prevention and/or intervention.

SELECT BIBLIOGRAPHY

Centers of Disease Control and Prevention (CDC). Retrieved from http://www.cdc.gov/pregnancy/during .html
CDC provides detailed information, common risk factors, the most recent statistics, and related resources regarding the prevention of many of the most serious problems that occur during pregnancy. Links are provided to other topics of interest.

Copeland, K. C., Silverstein, J., Moore, K. R., Prazar, G. E., Raymer, T., Shiffman, R. N.,...Flinn, S. K.; American Academy of Pediatrics. (2013). Management of newly diagnosed type 2 diabetes mellitus (T2DM) in children and adolescents. *Pediatrics, 131*(2), 364–382.
A group including the American Academy of Pediatrics, American Diabetes Association, the Pediatric Endocrine Society, the American Academy of Family Physicians, and the Academy of Nutrition

and Dietetics (formerly the American Dietetic Association) present an evidence-based report outlining practice guidelines and recommendations for the treatment of childhood and adolescent type 2 diabetes.

Davis, A. S. (Ed.). (2010). *Handbook of pediatric neuropsychology.* New York, NY: Springer Publishing Company.
This comprehensive text contains a broad array of topics relevant to the practice of pediatric neuropsychology, including chapters on perinatal complications, fetal alcohol spectrum disorder, development, and toxic exposure.

REFERENCES

Adams, H. R., Szilagyi, P. G., Gebhardt, L., & Lande, M. B. (2010). Learning and attention problems among children with pediatric primary hypertension. *Pediatrics, 126*(6), e1425–e1429.

American Diabetes Association. (2014). Retrieved from http://www.diabetes.org/living-with-diabetes/parents-and-kids/children-and-type-2/preventing-type-2-in-children.html

American Heart Association. (2014). *High blood pressure in children.* Retrieved from http://www.heart.org/HEARTORG/Conditions/HighBloodPressure/UnderstandYourRiskforHighBloodPressure/High-Blood-Pressure-in-Children_UCM_301868_Article.jsp

Baker, P. R., & Steck, A. K. (2011). The past, present, and future of genetic associations in type 1 diabetes. *Current Diabetes Reports, 11*(5), 445–453.

Baron, I. S. (2004). *Neuropsychological evaluation of the child.* New York, NY: Oxford University Press.

Bayley, N. (1993). *Bayley scales of infant development* (2nd ed.). San Antonio, TX: Harcourt Brace.

Bellamy, L., Casas, J. P., Hingorani, A. D., & Williams, D. (2009). Type 2 diabetes mellitus after gestational diabetes: A systematic review and meta-analysis. *Lancet, 373*(9677), 1773–1779.

Beyerlein, A., Nehring, I., Rosario, A. S., & von Kries, R. (2012). Gestational diabetes and cardiovascular risk factors in the offspring: Results from a cross-sectional study. *Diabetic Medicine: A Journal of the British Diabetic Association, 29*(3), 378–384.

Blando, J. D., Antoine, N., & Lefkowitz, D. (2013). Lead-based paint awareness, work practices, and compliance during residential construction and renovation. *Journal of Environmental Health, 75*(9), 20–7; quiz 51.

Brintnell, E. S., Bailey, P. G., Sawhney, A., & Kreftin, L. (2010). Understanding FASD: Disability and social supports for adult offenders. *Fetal Alcohol Spectrum Disorder—Management and Policy Perspectives of FASD,* 399–409.

Centers for Disease Control and Prevention (CDC). (2009). *Fourth report on human exposure to environmental chemicals.* Atlanta, GA: U.S. Department of Health and Human Services, Centers for Disease Control and Prevention.

Centers for Disease Control and Prevention (CDC). (2014a). Current cigarette smoking among adults: United States, 2005–2012. *Morbidity and Mortality Weekly Report, 63,* 29–34.

Centers for Disease Control and Prevention (CDC). (2014b). *Diabetes public health resources.* Retrieved from http://www.cdc.gov/diabetes/projects/cda2.htm

Croft, J., & Harris, F. (1998). *Writing safety instructions for consumer products.* London, UK: Department of Trade and Industry.

Croix, B., & Feig, D. I. (2006). Childhood hypertension is not a silent disease. *Pediatric Nephrology, 21*(4), 527–532.

Crume, T. L., Ogden, L., West, N. A., Vehik, K. S., Scherzinger, A., Daniels, S.,…Dabelea, D. (2011). Association of exposure to diabetes in utero with adiposity and fat distribution in a multiethnic population of youth: The Exploring Perinatal Outcomes among Children (EPOCH) Study. *Diabetologia, 54*(1), 87–92.

Davis, A. S. (Ed.). (2010). *Handbook of pediatric neuropsychology.* New York, NY: Springer Publishing Company.

DeSisto C. L., Kim S. Y., & Sharma A. J. (2014) Prevalence estimates of gestational diabetes mellitus in the United States, pregnancy risk assessment monitoring system (PRAMS), 2007–2010. *Preventing Chronic Disease, 11.* Retrieved from http://dx.doi.org/10.5888/pcd11.130415

Fagan III, J. F. (1991). *The Fagan test of infant intelligence* (2nd ed.). Cleveland, OH: Infantest Cooperation.

Falkner, B., Gidding, S. S., Portman, R., & Rosner, B. (2008). Blood pressure variability and classification of prehypertension and hypertension in adolescence. *Pediatrics, 122*(2), 238–242.

Ferrara, A. (2007). Increasing prevalence of gestational diabetes mellitus: A public health perspective. *Diabetes Care, 30* (Suppl 2), S141–S146.

Floyd, R. L., Sobell, M., Velasquez, M. M., Ingersoll, K., Nettleman, M., Sobell, L.,…Project CHOICES Efficacy Study Group. (2007). Preventing alcohol-exposed pregnancies: A randomized controlled trial. *American Journal of Preventive Medicine, 32*(1), 1–10.

Gardella, C. (2001). Lead exposure in pregnancy: A review of the literature and argument for routine prenatal screening. *Obstetrical & Gynecological Survey, 56*(4), 231–238.

Glik, D., Prelip, M., Myerson, A., & Eilers, K. (2008). Fetal alcohol syndrome prevention using community-based narrowcasting campaigns. *Health Promotion Practice, 9*(1), 93–103.

Grey, M., Berry, D., Davidson, M., Galasso, P., Gustafson, E., & Melkus, G. (2004). Preliminary testing of a program to prevent type 2 diabetes among high-risk youth. *The Journal of School Health, 74*(1), 10–15.

Hankin, J. R. (2002). Fetal alcohol syndrome prevention research. *Alcohol Research & Health: The Journal of the National Institute on Alcohol Abuse and Alcoholism, 26*(1), 58–65.

Hepp, N. (2011). Protecting children from toxicants. *The ASHA Leader, 16,* 12–15.

Herrmann, M., King, K., & Weitzman, M. (2008). Prenatal tobacco smoke and postnatal secondhand smoke exposure and child neurodevelopment. *Current Opinion in Pediatrics, 20*(2), 184–190.

Hutton, H. E., Chander, G., Green, P. P., Hutsell, C. A., Weingarten, K., & Peterson, K. L. (2014). A novel integration effort to reduce the risk for alcohol-exposed pregnancy among women attending urban STD clinics. *Public Health Reports, 129* (Suppl 1), 56–62.

Jastak, S., & Wilkinson, G. S. (1984). *The wide range achievement test, revised.* Wilmington, DE: Jastak Associates.

Jedrychowski, W., Perera, F. P., Jankowski, J., Mrozek-Budzyn, D., Mroz, E., Flak, E.,…Lisowska-Miszczyk, I. (2009). Very low prenatal exposure to lead and mental development of children in infancy and early childhood: Krakow prospective cohort study. *Neuroepidemiology, 32*(4), 270–278.

Jedrychowski, W., Perera, F., Jankowski, J., Rauh, V., Flak, E., Caldwell, K. L.,…Lisowska-Miszczyk,

I. (2008). Prenatal low-level lead exposure and developmental delay of infants at age 6 months (Krakow inner city study). *International Journal of Hygiene and Environmental Health, 211*(3–4), 345–351.

Jelliffe-Pawlowski, L. L., Miles, S. Q., Courtney, J. G., Materna, B., & Charlton, V. (2006). Effect of magnitude and timing of maternal pregnancy blood lead (Pb) levels on birth outcomes. *Journal of Perinatology, 26*(3), 154–162.

Julvez, J., Ribas-Fitó, N., Torrent, M., Forns, M., Garcia-Esteban, R., & Sunyer, J. (2007). Maternal smoking habits and cognitive development of children at age 4 years in a population-based birth cohort. *International Journal of Epidemiology, 36*(4), 825–832.

Kolu, P., Raitanen, J., Rissanen, P., & Luoto, R. (2013). Cost-effectiveness of lifestyle counselling as primary prevention of gestational diabetes mellitus: Findings from a cluster-randomised trial. *PloS One, 8*(2), e56392.

Lande, M. B., Kaczorowski, J. M., Auinger, P., Schwartz, G. J., & Weitzman, M. (2003). Elevated blood pressure and decreased cognitive function among school-age children and adolescents in the United States. *The Journal of Pediatrics, 143*(6), 720–724.

Lupton, C., Burd, L., & Harwood, R. (2004). Cost of fetal alcohol spectrum disorders. *American Journal of Medical Genetics. Part C, Seminars in Medical Genetics, 127C*(1), 42–50.

Mattson, S. N., & Riley, E. P. (1998). A review of the neurobehavioral deficits in children with fetal alcohol syndrome or prenatal exposure to alcohol. *Alcoholism, Clinical and Experimental Research, 22*(2), 279–294.

McGavock, J., Sellers, E., & Dean, H. (2007). Physical activity for the prevention and management of youth-onset type 2 diabetes mellitus: Focus on cardiovascular complications. *Diabetes & Vascular Disease Research, 4*(4), 305–310.

McNally, K., Rohan, J., Pendley, J. S., Delamater, A., & Drotar, D. (2010). Executive functioning, treatment adherence, and glycemic control in children with type 1 diabetes. *Diabetes Care, 33*(6), 1159–1162.

Mitanchez, D., Burguet, A., & Simeoni, U. (2014). Infants born to mothers with gestational diabetes mellitus: Mild neonatal effects, a long-term threat to global health. *The Journal of Pediatrics, 164*(3), 445–450.

Nicklas, J. M., Miller, L. J., Zera, C. A., Davis, R. B., Levkoff, S. E., & Seely, E. W. (2013). Factors associated with depressive symptoms in the early postpartum period among women with recent gestational diabetes mellitus. *Maternal and Child Health Journal, 17*(9), 1665–1672.

Ohmann, S., Popow, C., Rami, B., König, M., Blaas, S., Fliri, C., & Schober, E. (2010). Cognitive functions and glycemic control in children and adolescents with type 1 diabetes. *Psychological Medicine, 40*(1), 95–103.

Pirkola, J., Pouta, A., Bloigu, A., Hartikainen, A. L., Laitinen, J., Järvelin, M. R., & Vääräsmäki, M. (2010). Risks of overweight and abdominal obesity at age 16 years associated with prenatal exposures to maternal prepregnancy overweight and gestational diabetes mellitus. *Diabetes Care, 33*(5), 1115–1121.

Polychronakos, C., & Li, Q. (2011). Understanding type 1 diabetes through genetics: Advances and prospects. *Nature Reviews. Genetics, 12*(11), 781–792.

Rasmussen, C. (2005). Executive functioning and working memory in fetal alcohol spectrum disorder. *Alcoholism, Clinical and Experimental Research, 29*(8), 1359–1367.

Reynolds, K. A., & Helgeson, V. S. (2011). Children with diabetes compared to peers: Depressed? Distressed? A meta-analytic review. *Annals of Behavioral Medicine: A Publication of the Society of Behavioral Medicine, 42*(1), 29–41.

Roberts, J. W., Wallace, L. A., Camann, D. E., Dickey, P., Gilbert, S. G., Lewis, R. G., & Takaro, T. K. (2009). Monitoring and reducing exposure of infants to pollutants in house dust. *Reviews of Environmental Contamination and Toxicology, 201*, 1–39.

Tong, V. T., Dietz, P. M., Morrow, B., D'Angelo, D. V., Farr, S. L., Rockhill, K. M., & England, L. J. (2013). Trends in smoking before, during, and after pregnancy–Pregnancy Risk Assessment Monitoring System (PRAMS), United States, 40 sites, 2000–2010. *Morbidity and Mortality Weekly Report, 62*, 1–19.

U.S. Department of Agriculture and U.S. Department of Health and Human Services (2010). Foods and food components to reduce. *Dietary Guidelines for Americans*, Chapter 3 (7th ed., pp. 30–32). Washington, DC: U.S. Government Printing Office.

Verbeek, T., Bockting, C. L., van Pampus, M. G., Ormel, J., Meijer, J. L., Hartman, C. A., & Burger, H. (2012). Postpartum depression predicts offspring mental health problems in adolescence independently of parental lifetime psychopathology. *Journal of Affective Disorders, 136*(3), 948–954.

Wechsler, D. (1974). *The Wechsler intelligence scale for children, revised*. New York, NY: Psychological Corporation.

Wechsler, D. (1991). *Wechsler intelligence scale for children* (3rd ed.). San Antonio, TX: The Psychological Corporation.

Williams, J. H., & Ross, L. (2007). Consequences of prenatal toxin exposure for mental health in children and adolescents: A systematic review. *European Child & Adolescent Psychiatry, 16*(4), 243–253.

Woodward, L., Fergusson, D. M., & Horwood, L. J. (2001). Risk factors and life processes associated with teenage pregnancy: Results of a prospective study from birth to 20 years. *Journal of Marriage and Family, 63*, 1170–1184.

Yeates, K. O., Ris, M. D., Taylor, H. G., & Pennington, B. F. (Eds.). (2009). *Pediatric neuropsychology: Research, theory, and practice*. New York, NY: Guilford Press.

Yolton, K., Dietrich, K., Auinger, P., Lanphear, B. P., & Hornung, R. (2005). Exposure to environmental tobacco smoke and cognitive abilities among U.S. children and adolescents. *Environmental Health Perspectives, 113*(1), 98–103.

Evidence-Based Interventions for Autism Spectrum Disorders in Children and Adolescents

Frank J. Sansosti and Mary Lynn Doolan

OVERVIEW

Autism spectrum disorder (ASD) is a range of complex neurodevelopmental disorders characterized by deficits in social development, communication, repetitive behaviors and/or interests, and, in some cases, cognitive delays (American Psychiatric Association [APA], 2013). The latest release of the *Diagnostic and Statistical Manual of Mental Disorders* (5th ed.; *DSM-5*; APA, 2013) represents ASD as a single diagnostic category that is differentiated by clinical indicators (e.g., severity of social communication symptoms) and associated features (e.g., known genetic disorders). Across the spectrum, characteristics of ASD manifest uniquely as a collection of symptoms that rarely are the same from one individual to another. At one end of this spectrum are individuals characterized by severe deficits "requiring very substantial support" (Level 3; APA, 2013). Such individuals typically display severe deficits in social communication and/or interactions, extremely limited or intelligible speech, and inflexible behaviors that interfere with functioning. At the other end of the spectrum are those children with difficulties in social communication and restricted behaviors/interests "requiring support" (Level 1; APA 2013). Children at this level often demonstrate an ability to speak in full sentences and engage in conversation, but display odd or atypical attempts/responses to social interactions, difficulty switching between activities, and problems with planning and organization.

Increasing Prevalence. The Centers for Disease Control and Prevention (CDC) recently released prevalence rates from data collected by the Autism and Developmental Disabilities Monitoring (ADDM) Network, indicating that 1 in 68 children met criteria for an ASD (CDC, 2014). This new estimate represents a nearly 30% increase from the 1 in 88 reported in 2008 and continues to reinforce the notion that ASD is the fastest growing developmental disability in the United States. Although it remains unclear as to the exact understanding of such dramatic increases in the number of individuals with ASD, it is likely that some of the increase may be because of increased awareness, improved assessment tools, differences in access to services, and inclusion of a broader spectrum of symptomatology (Mahjouri & Lord, 2012). ASD is reported to occur in all racial, ethnic, and socioeconomic groups (Durkin et al., 2010). However, ASD, on average, is five times more likely to occur in males (1 in 42) than in females (1 in 89) (CDC, 2014), which has been suggested to be caused by a specific gene (PTCHD1) mutation on the X-chromosome (Noor et al., 2010).

Special Educational Service Delivery. Given the increasing prevalence of ASD nationally, it logically follows that state departments of education have also reported significant increases in the number of students with ASD as mandated by the *Individuals With Disabilities Education Improvement Act* (IDEIA, 2004). During the 5-year period from 2007 to 2012, the number of students receiving special education services under the Autism category increased from a total of 256,757 students to 440,592 students, an increase of 72% (IDEA Data Center, 2014). Although such statistics are startling, it is possible that the number of students served under the Autism category is a gross underestimate of the actual frequency of students who need supportive education. This is because of the fact that some children with ASD may receive special education and related services under a different IDEA category. In a prevalence study that employed active case finding among children receiving special education services, Bertrand et al. (2001) found that 66% of students with severe ASD and only 50% of children with higher functioning ASD received services under the Autism classification. In a similar study of children with ASD, only 41% were receiving services under the Autism category of IDEA (Yeargin-Allsop et al., 2003). In both of these studies, data revealed that children with ASD frequently were served under special education designations, such as language/communication impairment, emotional disturbance, specific learning disability, multiple disabilities, and other health impaired. Regardless of which category is chosen, the potential exists that children with ASD represent a large underserved student population.

Inclusion Practices. The increasing numbers of students with ASD within school-based settings occur within the context of a growing emphasis on inclusive education. Federal laws such as IDEIA (2004) and the No Child Left Behind Act (2001) have placed a growing emphasis on the need for students with disabilities, including those with ASD, to be taught alongside their typical peers in a general education curriculum to the greatest extent possible. Furthermore, contemporary reports on the nature of best practice education for students

with ASD have asserted the need for more inclusive programming (e.g., Lord & Bishop, 2010). As a result, the reported number of students with ASD who receive instruction within general education classrooms has grown substantially. Examination of IDEA data pertaining to educational environment demonstrates that students with ASD increasingly have been placed inside the regular education class (more than 80% of the day). Specifically, from 2007 to 2012, the number of students with ASD served in general education contexts increased from 88,688 to 173,879 (IDEA Data Center, 2014), an increase of 96%. In 2012 alone, nearly 40% of children receiving special education services for autism were instructed inside a regular education class for 80% or more of the day. As the number of students with ASD served within general education contexts grows, so do the demands placed on educators.

ETIOLOGY AND FACTORS CONTRIBUTING TO ASDS IN CHILDREN AND ADOLESCENTS

Currently, there is no known single etiology of ASD. Rather, research has posited myriad causes for ASD including genetic, biological, and environmental factors (Huquet, Ey, & Bourgeron, 2013). Significantly, the scientific community has largely concurred with the notion that genes are a considerable risk factor and increase the likelihood that a child will develop ASD. This is supported by several facts including: children who have a sibling with a diagnosis of ASD have a greater propensity to also have the disorder; ASD tends to occur in individuals with certain genetic or chromosomal conditions (e.g., fragile X, Rett syndrome); prescription drugs taken during pregnancy have been associated with the development of ASD in children; and parents who have children later in life are at greater risk for having a child with ASD (Christensen et al., 2013, Hallmayer et al., 2011; Rosenberg et al., 2009). Notably, abnormalities in the structure and shape of the brains of children with ASD, as demonstrated via brain scans, provide some evidence regarding the interplay of how genes may affect brain development or the manner in which brain cells communicate. Moreover, environmental exposure to toxins, such as heavy metals (e.g., mercury), may trigger ASD in children who may already have a predisposition to the disorder because their ability to metabolize and detoxify these pollutants may be compromised. Finally, there has been considerable controversy and debate in the literature regarding the relationship between vaccinations and the development of ASD. Despite extensive research, there has yet to be a study that confirms a link between ASD and the measles, mumps, and rubella (MMR) vaccine.

EVIDENCE-BASED INTERVENTIONS AND EMPIRICAL SUPPORT FOR ASDS IN CHILDREN AND ADOLESCENTS

Today, educators are faced with ever-increasing demands to identify and use evidence-based intervention practices for students with ASD (Sansosti & Sansosti, 2013). In an effort to assist educators, the National Standards Project (National Autism Center [NAC], 2009) conducted an extensive review of the extant literature to rate the strength of evidence supporting a wide variety of interventions targeting the core characteristics of students with ASD. Specifically, this project categorized intervention strategies for students with ASD as "established," "emerging," or "unestablished" (go to www.nationalautismcenter.org for a complete list of interventions and the respective ranking). The nature of this review provides clear guidelines for best practice interventions for students with ASD, and functions as a model of the type of interventions schools should attempt to provide to the greatest extent possible. Although it is likely that many educators, as well as caregivers, will continue to seek alternative, and even unproven, interventions and/or treatments within schools, failure to align school-based practices for students with ASD that have demonstrable support will lead to inappropriate educational programming at least, and, due process hearings at most (Sansosti & Sansosti, 2013).

HOW TO: A GUIDE TO THE IMPLEMENTATION OF INTERVENTIONS FOR ASDS IN CHILDREN AND ADOLESCENTS

Given the increased number of students with ASD who are increasingly served within inclusive contexts, both general and special educators share equal responsibility in developing effective educational strategies. It is unfortunate that research has yet to identify a sole intervention that is appropriate and effective for all individuals with ASD across various educational contexts (Crosland & Dunlap, 2012). Rather, examination of the extant literature has outlined various tools within a toolbox of evidence-based approaches that are necessary for effective educational programming for students with ASD (e.g., Crosland & Dunlap, 2012; Iovannone, Dunlap, Huber, & Kincaid, 2003; Lee & Carter, 2012). This chapter posits that educators should build an approach that uses a combination of evidence-based practices when designing and implementing interventions for students with ASD. Specifically, it is important to note that interventions for students with ASD include each of the following strategies: (a) individualized instruction that incorporates choice and preference; (b) functional programming (i.e., viewing challenging behavior(s) as instructional needs; developing instructional priorities that emanate from the environment); (c) systemic instruction provided within a structured environment; and (d) collaboration with families. Such programming should steadily expose students with ASD to cues, prompts, and interesting and motivating stimuli, as well as employ consistent feedback and repeated exposure in order to be most effective. The incorporation of these characteristics in academic, behavioral, and social skill interventions not only will permit educational teams to support the needs of students with ASD, but also promote positive outcomes.

Individualized Supports That Incorporate Choice and Preference

Because of the heterogeneity of students diagnosed with ASD, it is important that educational programming and interventions take an individualized instructional approach. Because no two individuals with ASD will display the same characteristics or level of impairment to an equal degree, it is important that educators recognize each student as a unique individual by examining the student's strengths and interests when planning classroom interventions (whether instruction is provided within inclusive contexts or specialized settings). When designing/implementing individualized supports and services for students with ASD, educators and mental health professionals should strive to allow the child the ability to exert greater control through *choice making*—the process of allowing a student to select an activity among several alternatives. For example, a child with ASD may be permitted the choice of whether to complete math or reading work first during independent seatwork time. The expectation remains that the student will complete both activities, but the order regarding which to do first is student directed. Related to allowing students to make choices, educators may wish to incorporate the student's *preference*—those objects, tasks, and/or activities a student finds most appealing and naturally rewarding. When choice making and preference can be incorporated into educational programming, students with ASD may exert more control over their lives, thereby decreasing problematic behaviors and increasing time engaged in academic and/or social contexts (Powell-Smith & Vaughn, 2006).

Research endorses the idea that interventions for students with ASD should include individualized elements in order to increase the student's motivation and engagement when learning new skill sets (e.g., Lanou, Hough, & Powell, 2012). The incorporation of individualized supports that align with the interests and strengths of the student promotes higher levels of engagement, which may be a predictor of positive student outcomes during, and in some cases, after an intervention. Evidence-based practices can include individualized elements such as specific hand gestures as a response cue that the child finds engaging (i.e., high-five), using the child's favorite character to teach a skill, or even incorporating a child's strength in mathematics within the language content area. Interventions should take the role of being custom designed for the child in order to cater to individual needs and skill level (Iovannone et al., 2003).

In order to create individualized supports that incorporate choice and preference for the student with ASD, educators and mental health professionals should:

- Identify individualized intervention components that will increase student engagement and motivation to succeed

- Identify individualized goals that prioritize the most prominent student needs
- Provide opportunities for the student (or caregivers) to advocate for choice and preference into any part of the intervention (when applicable)

A specific example of this process is detailed in the following case example.

INDIVIDUALIZED SUPPORTS CASE EXAMPLE: DANTE

Background

Dante is a 12-year-old student who demonstrates a variety of behavioral and social skill concerns. A review of Dante's records reveals a history of language, social, and behavioral difficulties from an early age. At age 3 years, a private neurologist evaluated Dante and diagnosed him with ASD because of continued language delays, poor socialization, aggression, temper tantrums, and an aversion to being touched. Despite these impairments, Dante demonstrates average intellectual abilities and performs well academically (receives As and Bs across all academic content). As a result, he has received the majority of his education within regular education. Despite positive academic competency, Dante has continued to demonstrate difficulty with social skills and emotion regulation (he, at times, can become violent) and has been referred for a reevaluation. Results of Dante's reevaluation indicated that he possessed emotion regulation and social skill difficulties despite having above-average intellectual and academic abilities. Specifically, concerns with regards to anxiety, temper tantrums, feelings of being overwhelmed, inflexibility, and restricted interests were identified. As a result, an individualized intervention was created to reduce the frequency of problem behaviors exhibited in the classroom, and, simultaneously, increase the amount of his academic engaged time.

Intervention Development and Implementation

- *Stress Cards*. Dante assisted in developing a portable visual support to use during stressful situations. Each card was 3.5 × 2 inches and contained three short statements and small pictures to prompt and guide Dante's behavior when he felt overwhelmed/anxious. Dante was taught to use the stress cards—allowing him the choice to remove himself from the class. Using the cards correctly earned Dante points, as this prompt allowed him to keep his emotions under control without threatening or becoming aggressive.
- *Point Store*. By engaging in appropriate behaviors to handle stress, Dante was able to receive points as a motivational and reward tool. Specifically, Dante earned one point for handing the card to his teacher and exiting the classroom. However, Dante earned 15 points for returning to class the same period, 10 points for returning the following period, and 5 points for returning the third period. These points could be exchanged each day for rewards that were chosen by Dante (e.g., free homework passes, computer time during study hall, and a favorite magazine).
- *Social Skills Instruction*. Dante was engaged in both individual and group social skills lessons led by the school psychologist, behavioral specialist, and guidance counselor. These sessions focused on teaching Dante how to recognize, quantify, and express levels of emotions/frustrations, as well as strategies for emotion regulation (e.g., stress reduction, using his stress card).

Outcomes

Dante demonstrated a significant decrease in problem behaviors exhibited in the classroom, allowing him to be more successful within the general education environment. The intervention components were highly individualized to align with Dante's behavioral needs and interests.

Adapted from Sansosti (2012).

Functional Programming

Students with ASD often exhibit problem behavior(s) that can be stereotypical and regimented in nature while also being disruptive to teachers and other students in the classroom. To address such behavioral difficulties, it is essential that educators use an approach to address problem behaviors in a way that not only reduces problem behaviors, but also develops prosocial skills through nonaversive procedures. One approach is positive behavioral support (PBS; Carr et al., 1999). PBS is the process of systematically identifying problem behaviors and their antecedents, developing and understanding the function of a student's behavior, developing hypotheses, and teaching new, functional skills to achieve socially important behavior change. Primarily, interventions under the components of PBS will focus on preventing problem behaviors from occurring and teaching replacement behaviors (e.g., teaching a student to request help instead of turning over desks when frustrated). The educative approach of PBS encourages positive interactions rather than simply decreasing or eliminating problem behaviors.

A very useful hands-on approach of incorporating PBS practices when working with students with ASD is the adoption of the Prevent–Teach–Reinforce model (PTR; Dunlap et al., 2010). PTR is a model of PBS that aligns closely with the principles and procedures of applied behavior analysis (ABA). Specifically, the PTR model is a structured process for supporting students with persistent challenging behavior(s) in kindergarten to eighth grade. There are five main steps in the PTR process: teaming, goal setting, assessment, intervention, and evaluation (see Dunlap et al. [2010] for a complete understanding of the PTR process and procedures). Most germane to this chapter are the three components of the PTR intervention phase. Specifically, educators should use the following criteria when developing and implementing effective behavioral interventions for students with ASD:

- *Prevent Problem Behaviors From Occurring.* A key element of any functional programming for students with ASD is the prevention of problem behavior(s). During this stage, educators should examine the environmental events and/or circumstances that can contribute to the occurrence or maintenance of inappropriate behavior(s). Specifically, educational teams should examine what may be causing a behavior by gathering data on the *antecedents* (What happens immediately before the behavior occurs?) and *consequences* (What happens immediately after the behavior occurs?) of behavior. After these data are gathered, educational teams can make predictions of when a problem behavior will or will not occur and make appropriate changes to the student's activities, settings, or social circumstances to decrease the likelihood of the behavior occurring.
- *Teach Replacement Behaviors.* A critical step for promoting the academic, behavioral, or social outcomes of students with ASD is teaching replacement behaviors. Persistent problem behaviors displayed by students with ASD often are the result of a skill deficit (i.e., the student lacks the skills necessary to regulate emotions and control behavior). As such, building basic skills and competencies through direct teaching is critical for producing long-lasting and durable behavioral change (Sansosti, Powell-Smith, & Cowan, 2010). Replacement behaviors are new skills that provide access to a desirable outcome through the use of socially appropriate and functional alternatives rather than engaging in some form of the inappropriate behavior. For example, a student with ASD may desire access to a ball during recess. His current method for getting the ball is to run up to any student who is playing with the ball, yell "mine," and run away with the ball. A more socially appropriate replacement behavior that is functionally equivalent (i.e., the student gets the same outcome—the ball) is to ask for the ball or to create a sharing plan with another student. To teach targeted replacement behaviors, instruction

must occur systematically by (a) using effective instructional cues (e.g., using gestural, verbal, or, most often, visual prompts to redirect a student's attention to relevant materials), (b) breaking skills down into their component parts and teaching discretely, (c) employing appropriate teaching methods (e.g., prompting, shaping), and (d) rewarding appropriate behaviors consistently.

- *Provide Contingent Positive Reinforcement.* At the core of functional programming is the inclusion of positive reinforcement (e.g., attention, access to desirable items/activities). When it is used *immediately* following the desired behavior and when it is *contingent* on the emission of that behavior, reinforcement can be a powerful tool (Sansosti et al., 2010). To maximize the efficacy of using positive reinforcement, educational teams should select rewards/motivators that are deemed desirable by the student with ASD. As such, parents, educators, and other community partners are encouraged to take time to assess possible rewards by (a) observing the student to determine what he or she finds motivating, (b) asking the student verbally to identify potential rewards, or (c) using a reinforce survey/checklist with the student/family (interested readers can use the Jackpot Online Reinforcement Survey tool; http://jimwrightonline.com/php/jackpot/jackpot.php to create an individualized reinforcement survey for any student).

Systematic Instruction Provided Within a Structured Environment

Perhaps the most important feature of interventions for students with ASD is the provision of systematic instruction occurring within a structured environment. Systematic instruction involves the process of carefully planning for all aspects of a given intervention. When an intervention is designed systematically it will (a) identify the overall educational goals for a given intervention (e.g., increase the number of social initiations); (b) detail the instructional procedures (e.g., use a combination of teacher-led and computer-assisted social skills lessons); (c) outline the implementation procedures (e.g., deliver teacher-led lessons three times per week, supplemented by computer-assisted Social Stories™ three times per week for a period of 8 weeks); (d) identify activities to ensure skill maintenance and generalization; and (e) specify the procedures for data collection and evaluation (e.g., student behavior will be rated each day; student data will be reviewed each week). In essence, interventions that are systematic are those that have a clear, purposeful plan that focuses on detailed aspects of the intervention and uses meaningful data to monitor student outcomes (Sansosti, 2010). It is important that educators and mental health professionals use, to the maximum extent possible, carefully planned interventions that can be evaluated through data-driven practices (e.g., progress monitoring) to determine if the student evidences gains in various domains of functioning (Sansosti & Powell-Smith, 2006; Sansosti et al., 2010). By carefully targeting essential skills to be taught, planning specifically when and how the skills will be taught, and determining data collection methods, educators and mental health professional will have effective programs that engage students with ASD (Iovannone et al., 2003) and that are legally defensible.

In addition to being systematic, an intervention for a student with ASD should be employed in a highly structured environment. An organized teaching environment is imperative for teaching skills to learners with ASD because of difficulties they likely have restricting attention to relevant stimuli and engaging in learning new tasks and skills. As such, any intervention should be delivered in a manner that elicits, facilitates, enhances, and/or supports the acquisition of specific skills. By creating a highly predictable environment, students with ASD will demonstrate improved ability to attend to important stimuli in the environment, thereby promoting learning and decreasing the amount of time engaging in nonfunctional stereotypical behavior (Barton & Harn, 2014). One method for ensuring a structured environment for students with ASD is the use of visual supports/media. In fact, strategies that incorporate visual presentation are considered to be one of the most effective methods for educating individuals with ASD (NAC, 2009; Nikopoulos & Nikopoulou-Smyrni, 2008). The use of visual supports includes pictures, photographs, lists, or other visual material (e.g., computers, mobile technologies) that prompt the child with ASD to engage in a particular behavior or prepare him or her to engage in a particular activity or task (Sansosti & Powell-Smith, 2006). Through the use of visuals, students with ASD require less verbal reminders by teachers and they increase their level of independence (Moore, 2002). Without visual aids, some students with ASD may engage in stereotypical and/or inappropriate behavior(s), while others may sit at their desks doing nothing or spend their time focusing on details of a task making them forget the task entirely. For a comprehensive list and examples of different visual support strategies, see Sansosti et al. (2010).

A specific example of using systematic teaching within a structured environment is detailed in the following case example.

SYSTEMATIC INSTRUCTION WITHIN A STRUCTURED ENVIRONMENT CASE EXAMPLE: ANGELO

Background

Angelo is a 9-year-old boy who attends the fourth grade in an integrated classroom. Both his family and teachers describe Angelo as a child very much interested in science who enjoys experimenting. In particular, Angelo spends a great deal of time developing a juice modeled after ancient Egyptians. Other interests include soccer, video games, and various cartoon characters (e.g., Spider Man and Sponge Bob Square Pants). Main areas of difficulty for Angelo appear to be spontaneously joining in activities. His parents state that it takes a great deal of effort to get Angelo to join in any activity with other children and they often resort to making deals with him (to get him to join in). Angelo's teachers verified this information, stating that Angelo spends most of his time during recess alone. However, when Angelo is interacting with peers, he can become frustrated easily. Often his frustration leads to inappropriate and/or aggressive behaviors. He often says rude and offensive comments to others, chases after those who ridicule him, and throws stones at those with whom he is angry.

Intervention Development and Implementation

- *Social Skills Instruction.* It was recommended that Angelo take part in some form of social skills instruction. Before teaching, the educational team considered additional plans for instruction. These included:
  - Identifying and selecting appropriate instructional materials
  - Providing training to facilitators and others involved in the implementation of the social skills lessons and/or follow-up activities (i.e., lesson components, implementation strategies, use of prompts/reinforcement)
  - Determining whether instruction should be individualized or part of a social skills group (If part of a group, what students should be included or not included, as well as strategies to manage behavior of the group?)
  - Identifying when the lessons will be taught, how long lessons will last, and where the teaching will take place
  - Determining methods of data collection to demonstrate skill improvement

Once the educational team identified its systematic approach (a social skills group), efforts to structure the sequence of lessons were made. These included:

  - Discussing new skills (or reviewing previous skills) in a large group and indicating the importance of such skills
  - Teaching new skills using a series of visual prompts and video-based models (one showing the appropriate behavior, one depicting inappropriate behavior) and simple question–answer commentary
  - Modeling the appropriate behavior by having the students observe the facilitator and other students perform the skill
  - Role-playing the skill with real-life examples provided by other students in the group or by the facilitator
  - Incorporating feedback of role-play performance by peers/facilitators

Outcomes

Angelo demonstrated a significant increase in appropriately joining-in during recess activities. The social skills lessons were taught in a consistent systematized manner and provided within a structured environment that used visual supports to the greatest extent possible.

Family Collaboration

The family members of a student diagnosed with ASD most often has the most insight into their child's needs, styles, strengths, and interests. As such, families should be included as active partners in the intervention process—from development to implementation—to the highest degree possible. Parental input offers a unique and critical viewpoint that can provide the multidisciplinary team insight into the child's developmental history and interpretation of abilities, along with educational services and interventions provided to the student in the past (Sansosti et al., 2010). Family and parental engagement increases the frequency of learning opportunities for the student and can help to maintain and generalize skill sets learned in the classroom across settings (e.g., home, school, and community) throughout the child's entire day, rather than only while in school (Barton & Harn, 2014). Research has also shown that challenging behaviors may be decreased while engagement with academic tasks can increase when parents are included in the execution of interventions (Lequia, Machalicek, & Lyons, 2013). As such, it is beneficial for educational teams to view families as essential partners in educational planning and delivery of supports and services.

Before engaging families, educational teams should consider several aspects. First, a partnership is a reciprocal relationship that involves listening and sharing; *not* telling a family what to do. Educators and teams should continue to offer expertise, but encourage members of the family (as well as the child, when appropriate) to offer their expertise—knowledge of their child! Second, it is important that educational teams recognize that family members may not know how to participate in their child's education. They may be hindered by their own negative experiences within schools, or, more likely, feel ineffective and/or alienated (especially those from different cultural or linguistic backgrounds). Third, educational teams should make a concerted effort to understand the particular family dynamics that may influence availability and/or involvement. Issues such as work schedules, transportation issues, family characteristics, and/or other stressors influence the ability for families to have time to be involved consistently (Crosland & Dunlap, 2012; Iovannone et al., 2003). Educators should account for such dynamics in a nonjudgmental manner, and make appropriate accommodations to account for each family's unique constraints. Fourth, educational teams and mental health professionals should be aware that parental involvement tends to decrease in the higher grades, but the need for parental involvement for students with ASD likely increases. As such, educators should do their best to consider methods for offering families assistance during the complex time of adolescent development. Once such considerations are accounted for, efforts to create a more collaborative partnership between home and school should be of primary focus. Such efforts can incorporate either passive or active approaches, both of which aim to increase the capacity of families and schools to engage in transformational projects that have the power to influence change and enhance programming. The following are seven approaches for forming good partnerships with families of children with ASD:

- *Let Go of Preconceptions*. Make efforts for all educational staff to include families as allies during all aspects of their son's or daughter's educational process (i.e., intervention development and implementation; creating goals for the Individualized Education Plan [IEP]). Do not permit an overly negative attitude to reign supreme during planning discussions. Expect to disagree once in a while, but embrace the opportunity to see things from a different point of view.
- *Set an Inviting Tone*. At the beginning of the school year, share how important the families' contributions are and your desire to partner with them over the course of the next academic year. The focus should be on building good rapport—the most ineffective way to collaborate with families is to meet for the first time only to share negative news about their children's performance.
- *Host a Parent of ASD Support Group*. Provide an ongoing (i.e., once per month) support network whereby families of children with ASD are able to showcase their children, voice their experiences, hear the experiences of others, and/or hear from experts within the community. These events are an excellent opportunity for building rapport because they enable parents to share information about their children's talents and needs, as well as offer occasions for families to collaborate with other families.
- *Organize an ASD Resource Library*. Very often, families of students with ASD are seeking information about all sorts of issues/concerns. Educators can create a resource library for families to access. This library can be organized within the school or hosted on the school website. Either way, the idea is to provide parents access to the most contemporary resources (e.g., books, videos, community pamphlets).
- *Offer Parent Trainings/Workshops*. Perhaps the greatest way to improve family partnerships is to provide opportunities for training and/or workshops. In particular, such trainings should correspond with those interventions that are coordinated within the school and help students learn. For example, if educators are using a series of video-models for a student (or students) with ASD, provide several workshops on how to create effective video-models within the home and or larger community. Other topics may focus on social-emotional regulation, dating, transition planning, and the like.
- *Provide Frequent Opportunities for Ongoing Communication*. Frequent communication that permits parents to voice questions or concerns about interventions and/or student progress should be prioritized with all educational team members. Partnerships are more likely to work when they are sustained. As such, it will be important to increase opportunities to communicate with families of students with ASD. The frequency of communication should depend on the individualized needs of students, but it is ideal

to make personal contact with all families of students with ASD. Newsletters, e-mails, phone calls, and other meetings are all effective ways to check in. Another very effective approach is the use of a daily journal in which educators and parents notify each other of any concerns or accomplishments. Educators and mental health professionals also should create a change in routine notification system such as a card that goes home to parents the day before a change is to take place.

- *Prepare Staff to Work With Families*. It is important to help those who work with families take a different perspective on situations that, at times, can become difficult or emotional. As such, efforts by the school or multidisciplinary team that better prepare staff are fundamental to ensuring long-term, positive student outcomes. Methods to prepare staff can include, but are not limited to: (a) asking staff to evaluate their own assumptions and beliefs and provide appropriate training; (b) using time within teams and/or professional learning committees to discuss hypothetical cases; and (c) providing staff time to process with others difficult conversations or situations.

CONCLUSION

Students with ASD display a variety of academic, behavioral, and social-communication difficulties. Over the past decade, rates in the frequency of students served with ASD within inclusive school-based contexts have increased substantially. With such an increase, it is important for educators and mental health professionals to understand how to effectively build interventions that promote positive student growth. Although a variety of effective, evidence-based interventions for students with ASD exist, no one intervention is appropriate and effective for all individuals with various educational contexts. Rather, it is best to support students with ASD and develop an approach that integrates a number of prevention and intervention strategies from a toolbox of empirically supported concepts. Specifically, it is important to underscore the need for (a) individualized instruction, (b) functional programming, (c) systemic and structured instruction, and (d) family collaboration as vital components

necessary to ensure that the needs of students with ASD within school-based contexts are met.

SELECT BIBLIOGRAPHY

Boardmaker Achieve. Retrieved from https://www.boardmakeronline.com
This website allows practitioners to create individualized visual supports based on students' interests in order to increase their engagement in the intervention.

Dunlap, G., Iovannone, R., Kincaid, D., Wilson, K., Christiansen, K., Strain, P., & English, C. (2010). *Prevent–teach–reinforce: The school-based model of individualized positive behavior support.* Baltimore, MD: Paul H. Brookes Publishing Co., Inc.
This book provides practitioners with PTR approach outlined in an easy-to-use format. Practitioners can print out digitized planning forms and worksheets that can assist in the development of the PTR system within their own schools.

Florida's Positive Behavior Support Project: A Multi-Tiered Support System. Retrieved from http://flpbs.fmhi.usf.edu/index.cfm
This website provides practitioners with online resources for designing and implementing PBS systems within a school setting. It provides school districts with resources to design and implement a PBS system within their own district.

Positive Behavior Intervention & Supports (PBIS). Retrieved from https://www.pbis.org
The National PBIS website provides practitioners with resources that focus on the family, school, community, evaluation of PBIS programs, research on PBIS systems, and training for new teams and other individuals associated with the school.

Sansosti, F. J., Powell-Smith, K. A., & Cowan, R. J. (2010). *High functioning autism/Asperger syndrome in schools: Assessment and intervention.* New York, NY: Guilford Press.
This book provides vital tools for improving the academic, behavioral, and social outcomes of students with higher functioning ASD. Research-based best practices are presented along with reproducibles for educators to use.

REFERENCES

American Psychiatric Association (APA). (2013). *Diagnostic and statistical manual of mental* disorders (5th ed.). Arlington, VA: American Psychiatric Publishing.

Barton, E. E., & Harn, B. (2014). *Educating young children with autism spectrum disorders: A guide for teachers, counselors, and psychologists.* Thousand Oaks, CA: Corwin.

Bertrand, J., Mars, A., Boyle, C., Bove, F., Yeargin-Allsopp, M., & Decoufle, P. (2001). Prevalence of autism in the United States population: The Brick Township, New Jersey, investigation. *Pediatrics, 108,* 1155–1161. doi:10.1542/peds.108.5.1155

Carr, J. E., Horner, R. H., Turnbull, A. P., Marquis, J. G., McLaughlin, D. M., McAtee, M. L., …Braddock, D. (1999). *Positive behavior support for people with developmental disabilities: A research synthesis.* Washington, DC: American Association on Mental Retardation.

Centers for Disease Control and Prevention (CDC). (2014). *Prevalence of autism spectrum disorder among children aged 8 years—Autism and developmental disabilities monitoring network.* Retrieved from http://www.cdc.gov/ncbddd/autism/data.html

Christensen, J., Grønborg, T. K., Sørensen, M. J., Schendel, D., Parner, E. T., Pedersen, L. H., & Vestergaard, M. (2013). Prenatal valproate exposure and risk of autism spectrum disorders and childhood autism. *Journal of the American Medical Association, 309,* 1696–1703.

Crosland, K., & Dunlap, G. (2012). Effective strategies for the inclusion of children with autism in general education classrooms. *Behavior Modification, 36(3),* 251–269. doi:10.1177/0145445512442682

Dunlap, G., Iovannone, R., Kincaid, D., Wilson, K., Christiansen, K., Strain, P., & English, C. (2010). *Prevent–teach–reinforce: The school-based model of individualized positive behavior support.* Baltimore, MD: Paul H. Brookes Publishing Co., Inc.

Durkin, M. S., Maenner, M. J., Meaney, F. J., Levy, S. E., DiGuiseppi, C., Nicholas, J. S.,…Schieve, L. A. (2010). Socioeconomic inequity in the prevalence of autism spectrum disorder: Evidence from a U.S. cross-sectional study. *PLoS One, 5:e11551,* 1–8.

Hallmayer, J., Cleveland, S., Torres, A., Phillips, J., Cohen, B., Torigoe, T.,…Risch, N. (2011). Genetic heritability and shared environmental factors among twin pairs with autism. *Archives of General Psychiatry, 68,* 1095–1102.

Huquet, G., Ey, E., & Bourgeron, T. (2013). The genetic landscapes of autism spectrum disorders.

Annual Review of Genomics Human Genetics, 14, 191–213.

IDEA Data Center. (2014). *Public data and resources.* Retrieved from http://www.ideadata.org/tools-and-products

Individuals with Disabilities Education Improvement Act of 2004 (IDEIA). (2004). 20 U.S.C.§ 614 et seq.

Iovannone, R., Dunlap, G., Huber, H., & Kincaid, D. (2003). Effective educational practices for students with autism spectrum disorders. *Focus on Autism and Other Developmental Disabilities, 18(3),* 150–165. doi:10.1177/10883576030180030301

Lanou, A., Hough, L., & Powell, E. (2012). Case studies on using strengths and interests to address the needs of students with autism spectrum disorders. *Intervention in School & Clinic, 47(3),* 175–182. doi:10.1177/1053451211423819

Lee, G. K., & Carter, E. W. (2012). Preparing transition-age students with high-functioning autism spectrum disorders for meaningful work. *Psychology in the Schools, 49(10),* 988–1000. doi:10.1002/pits.21651

Lequia, J., Machalicek, W., & Lyons, G. (2013). Parent education intervention results in decreased challenging behavior and improved task engagement for students with disabilities during academic tasks. *Behavioral Interventions, 28(4),* 322–343. doi:10.1002/bin.1369

Lord, C. L., & Bishop, S. L. (2010). Autism spectrum disorders: Diagnosis, prevalence, and services for children and families. *Social Policy Report, 24,* 1–21.

Mahjouri, S., & Lord, C. E. (2012). What the *DSM-5* portends for research, diagnosis, and treatment of autism spectrum disorders. *Current Psychiatric Reports, 14,* 739–747. doi:10.1007/s11920–012–0327–2

Moore, S. T. (2002). *Asperger syndrome and the elementary school experience: Practical solutions for academic and social difficulties.* Shawnee Mission, KS: Autism Asperger Publishing.

National Autism Center (NAC). (2009). *Findings and conclusions of the National Standards Project: Addressing the need for evidence-based practice guidelines for autism spectrum disorders.* Randolph, MA: Author

Nikopoulos, C. K., & Nikopoulou-Smyrni, P. (2008). Teaching complex social skills to children with autism: Advances in video modeling. *Journal of*

Early and Intensive Behavior Intervention, 5, 30–43. doi:10.1037/h0100417

No Child Left Behind Act of 2001. (2001). Pub. L. No. 107–110, 115 stat. 1425.

Noor, A., Whibley, A., Marshall, C. R., Gianakopoulos, P. J., Piton, A., Carson, A. R.,...Vincent, J. B. (2010). Disruption at the PTCHD1 Locus on Xp22.11 in autism spectrum disorder and intellectual disability. *Science Translational Medicine, 2*(49), 49–68. doi:10.1126/scitranslmed.3001267

Powell-Smith, K. A., & Vaughn, B. J. (2006). Families of children with disabilities. In G. G. Bear & K. M. Minke (Eds.), *Children's needs III: Development, prevention, and intervention* (pp. 689–704). Bethesda, MD: National Association of School Psychologists.

Rosenberg, R. E., Law, J. K., Yenokyan, G., McGready, J., Kaufmann, W. E., & Law, P. A. (2009). Characteristics and concordance of autism spectrum disorders among 277 twin pairs. *Archives of Pediatric Adolescent Medicine, 163*, 907–914.

Sansosti, F. J. (2010). Teaching social skills to children with autism spectrum disorders using tiers of support: A guide for school-based professionals.

Psychology in the Schools, 47(3), 257–281. doi:10.1002/pits.20469

Sansosti, F. J. (2012). Reducing the threatening and aggressive behavior of a middle school student with Asperger's syndrome. *Preventing School Failure, 56*, 8–18. doi:10.1080/1045988X.2010.548418

Sansosti, F. J., & Powell-Smith, K. A. (2006). High-functioning autism and Asperger's syndrome. In G. G. Bear & K. M. Minke (Eds.), *Children's needs III: Development, prevention, and intervention* (pp. 949–963). Bethesda, MD: National Association of School Psychologists.

Sansosti, F. J., Powell-Smith, K. A., & Cowan, R. J. (2010). *High functioning autism/Asperger syndrome in schools: Assessment and intervention*. New York, NY: Guilford Press.

Sansosti, F. J., & Sansosti, J. M. (2013). Effective school-based service delivery for students with autism spectrum disorders: Where we are and where we need to go. *Psychology in the Schools, 50*, 229–244. doi:10.1002/pits.21669

Yeargin-Allsopp, M., Rice, C., Karapurkan, T., Doernberg, N., Boyle, C., & Murphy, C. (2003). Prevalence of autism in a U.S. metropolitan area. *Journal of the American Medical Association, 289*, 49–55. doi:10.1001/jama.289.1.49

Evidence-Based Interventions for Traumatic Brain Injuries and Concussions in Children and Adolescents

Margaret Semrud-Clikeman, Theresa L. LaFavor, and Amy C. Gross

OVERVIEW

Traumatic brain injuries (TBIs) are insults that occur from an event external to the individual (Semrud-Clikeman & Bledsoe, 2011). These can include open or closed head injuries and are often classified as mild, moderate, or severe. Open head injuries involve an outside material (e.g., bullet or object) that penetrates the skull. With open head injuries, areas of functioning affected by the lesion are strongly related to the region of the brain that is impacted. The majority of TBIs in childhood are closed head injuries and involve rapid acceleration, deceleration, and/or rotation of the head in space without impact with the skull. In acceleration injuries, a moving object makes contact with the head (e.g., a baseball bat). Bruising or contusions in the brain stem, cerebellum, under the corpus callosum, and in the occipital lobes are common in acceleration injuries. Deceleration occurs when the head is moving faster than a stationary object (e.g., head hitting the dashboard of a car); contusions at the site of the injury are common as well as on the opposite side of the impact area, which is referred to as "Contre' coup." Rotations of the head and

neck can occur with both acceleration and deceleration and result in shearing as brain tissue slide over other tissue. In general, the skull is less rigid in children, but damage may still occur.

Damage in a closed head injury can be either widespread or localized. Widespread injury typically involves damage to neurons, which are responsible for the transmission of information through impulses from the front to the back and right and left of the brain. Car accidents and falls are more likely to be associated with widespread damage in the brain as well as child abuse. The frontal lobe and parts of the temporal lobe are most susceptible to injury, especially in mild to moderate TBIs, as they are closest to the skull.

Many different types of accidents and events can result in TBI, including hitting one's head on the corner of a table, falling from a considerable height, being struck by an object such as a baseball bat, whiplash from a car accident, or being tackled during a sporting event. The level of severity depends on the physical and cognitive deficits associated with the injury. Although more severe impact results in greater impairment, it is not possible to predict the level of injury from the nature of the accident alone. The Glasgow Coma Scale (GCS) is a commonly used scoring system used to assess the severity of acute brain injury. The GCS assesses nonverbal responsiveness, motor responses, and verbal responses. Ratings are provided in each area with a maximum total of 15; higher scores indicate better prognosis. Mild TBIs are those that result in less than an hour of loss of consciousness or posttraumatic amnesia (PTA) and a GCS of 13 to 15. Approximately 90% of head injuries are mild (McKinlay et al., 2008). TBIs that are considered to be mild may result in symptoms of headache, fatigue, nausea, dizziness, and mood lability (Semrud-Clikeman & Bledsoe, 2011). Mild head injuries, including blows to the head, may be somewhat common during development and most do not result in permanent damage or alterations in functioning. Head injuries that are accompanied with any loss of consciousness or with confusion should be evaluated if these difficulties continue for more than 10 to 14 days.

Moderate TBIs are those that result in loss of consciousness or PTA for 1 to 24 hours and a GCS of 9 to 12. Persistent difficulties with memory, behavioral regulation, and physical symptoms, such as headaches, are common in moderate TBIs. Secondary symptoms are more common among moderate TBIs and include hematoma and edemas (brain swelling). Severe TBIs are those that result in more than 24 hours of loss of consciousness, or a PTA and GCS of 3 to 8. Most children with severe TBIs are treated emergently and approximately half will die.

CONCUSSIONS

A subset of mild TBI that has recently received increased attention is concussions, in particular, sports- and recreation-related concussions. Concussions are sometimes considered a unique form of mild TBI. A concussion is a blow to the head that results in a disruption of normal brain cellular activity (also called a "neurometabolic cascade"; McCrea, Prichep, Powell, Chabot, & Barr, 2010). They do not consistently result in neuropathological changes or abnormalities on structural neuroimaging studies. Concussions, however, do cause functional impairment (McCrory et al., 2013). Similar to other mild TBIs, functional changes may include loss of consciousness, headache, fatigue, slowed processing speed, and mood changes. Most

concussion symptoms are relatively short-lived, lasting weeks to months, yet some concussions result in lasting functional changes. Although some of the behavioral symptoms may improve quickly, the brain may take more time to recover with neural connectivity, showing full recovery within 7 weeks (McCrea et al., 2013). Furthermore, experiencing multiple concussions increases the likelihood for problematic and possibly continuing symptoms (Karlin, 2011). Postconcussion syndrome (PCS) is a condition when postconcussion symptoms persist for longer than expected, generally 2 months, though there is debate on how many symptoms are needed and the length of symptom presentation required for a diagnosis (Jotwani & Harmon, 2010). Most concussions resolve within the first 2 weeks; however, some individuals continue to show deficits within the first 2 years following injury.

DEVELOPMENT AND TBIs

The effect of TBI on brain development and functioning depends on a number of factors including age, nature, type, and severity of injury, as well as treatment protocol following the TBI (Semrud-Clikeman, 2010). The length of coma has been associated with persistent difficulties and longer comas have been associated with poorer outcomes, overall. In general, younger children show greater and more persistent difficulties following TBIs, likely because of incomplete development of key brain structures (Semrud-Clikeman & Bledsoe, 2011). In addition, difficulties may not be evident until later in development, when affected structures and networks are expected to come online; this is called "growing into the deficit." For example, executive functioning, which refers to higher order cognitive skills that allow for purposeful and controlled problem-solving activity directed toward achieving a long-term goal, begins to develop in late elementary school and continues through young adulthood and is particularly sensitive to injury. Children are generally most susceptible to expressive language difficulties following injury; however, receptive language abilities remain more stable. Compared with adults, children take longer to recover from severe TBI. Although adults generally recover typical functioning within 6 to 9 months after the injury, children take 5 to 6 years to recover, with the most significant recovery occurring 2 to 3 years after injury. The difference in recovery rate is related to the fact that an adult's brain is generally fully formed whereas a child's brain is still developing and some skills may not be seen as deficient until the child "grows into the deficit." For example, many executive function skills are often not expected until the child is older and so deficits will not be seen in younger children but may appear at older ages.

ETIOLOGY AND FACTORS CONTRIBUTING TO TBIs AND CONCUSSIONS IN CHILDREN AND ADOLESCENTS

More than 500,000 children, ages 0 to 14 years, are affected by TBIs each year. In addition, approximately 180,000 children aged 15 to 19 years sustain a TBI (Faul, Xu, Wald, & Coronado, 2010). Males disproportionately sustain TBIs compared with females (McKinlay et al., 2008). Some reports suggest that males and females experience similar rates of TBI under the age of 5 years, but that females are less likely to sustain TBI later in childhood and adolescence. Males experience a significant increase in TBI between 15 and 25 years of age. Child abuse and car accidents account for the majority of TBIs in children from birth through age 4 years; bicycle and pedestrian accidents are the most common causes of TBI in children 4 through 11 years of age. In adolescents ages 15 through 19 years, the leading cause of head injuries are motor-vehicle accidents (Faul et al., 2010), with the teen who is driving sustaining the most injury. TBIs account for the most frequent visit to the emergency room (ER) for children and adolescents.

The following sections review interventions that are frequently recommended for children recovering from TBIs and concussions. One of the issues for TBIs and concussion is the difficulty with validation of many recommendations. Although this is a concern, empirically supported interventions for which there is research support are discussed.

EVIDENCE-BASED INTERVENTIONS AND EMPIRICAL SUPPORT FOR TBIs AND CONCUSSIONS IN CHILDREN AND ADOLESCENTS

Areas of Deficit

Cognitive and Academic Functioning. Mild to moderate TBIs have been associated with greater recovery in functioning, particularly with respect to intellectual abilities (Semrud-Clikeman & Bledsoe, 2011). Although significant academic difficulties are observed in most children with mild to moderate TBIs, full recovery is typically seen within 6 months following the injury. Memory deficits typically show full recovery with 2 to 3 months. TBIs are most commonly associated with difficulty with verbal learning and memory, and working memory. Early symptoms in moderate TBIs including memory problems, attention and concentration, and problem solving typically improve over time.

In contrast, severe TBIs are associated with persistent cognitive deficits and co-occurring psychiatric and physical impairments (Braga, Da Paz, & Ylvisaker, 2005). Performance-based abilities, including visual reasoning and processing speed, appear to be more impacted than verbal abilities (Semrud-Clikeman & Bledsoe, 2011). Complex auditory-verbal learning, such as word lists, is particularly difficult for children following a TBI. Children and adolescents with severe TBIs are more likely to require some type of educational support 2 years postinjury. School achievement has been shown to be problematic for these children; specifically, naming objects, verbal fluency, writing skills, mathematics, memory, attention, and organization have consistently been shown to be affected. As discussed earlier, executive functions are particularly influenced, especially in severe cases of TBIs. These individuals display increased difficulty with inhibitory control and impulsivity and research suggests that new learning and memory difficulties may underlie persistent problems and widening skill gaps in the long term following a TBI (Braga et al., 2005). In addition, physical impairments including slowed gait and motor control likely contribute to ongoing difficulties (e.g., personal care and adaptive functioning), and are more common in severe TBIs compared with mild and moderate injury.

Emotional and Behavioral Issues. Many behavioral and emotional concerns are present following TBIs regardless of severity of injury. Internalizing concerns, such as depression and anxiety, are observed in children shortly after injury and persist over time. The persistence, and sometimes worsening, of these symptoms can occur much longer than other physical symptoms of the injury. Externalizing behaviors are also quite common. Youths often experience irritability, aggression, impulsivity, and inattention following TBIs (Noggle & Pierson, 2010). Because of the increased inattention and impulsivity following injury, children are frequently diagnosed with acquired attention deficit hyperactivity disorder (ADHD), especially those with severe TBIs. Notably, preexisting ADHD places individuals at higher risk of sustaining a TBI, and if they do experience such an injury, they are likely to have increased challenges with attention (Semrud-Clikeman & Bledsoe, 2011). Finally, there is evidence to suggest that social skills and social problem solving are more severely impacted following TBIs, independent of the decreased social skills that might be expected with the aforementioned emotional concerns (Noggle & Pierson, 2010).

Family Systems. Pediatric TBIs involve significant disruption to the entire family system (Braga et al., 2005). Parents often report a lack of medical information, support, and coping strategies following pediatric TBIs. Research has demonstrated that parental stress is reciprocally related to child outcomes following injury. Intervention studies targeting family involvement (e.g., family-focused problem solving, stress-management training) have been shown to reduce internalizing problems in children following TBIs and increase family cohesion among parents and siblings.

Recovery is complicated for many children because there are few outward indicators of injury following the acute phase of recovery (Laatsch et al., 2007). Although physical and motor difficulties are more readily observed, persistent difficulties with cognitive functioning (e.g., verbal and spatial processing, planning, and problem solving) may be more difficult to detect in moderate and severe TBIs. As many neural systems are involved in severe brain injury, a variety of professionals will likely be involved in a child's treatment and follow-up (Braga et al., 2005). These professionals will likely include neurologists, neuropsychologists, social workers, speech and language pathologists, occupational and physical therapists, and care managers. Educators play a vital role in the care of children with moderate and severe TBI; however, they may lack information about the history of the injury and may have limited communication with the professionals involved in working with the family and the child. More empirical research is needed to understand the course and persistent effects of moderate and severe TBIs in children, especially on successful interventions.

Cognitive Rehabilitation

The neurocognitive deficits seen in TBIs and concussions include decreased reaction time and/or speed of information processing, concentration difficulty, short-term and working-memory deficits, problems with new learning and with consolidation of previously learned material, and cognitive fatigue. Research supports two practice guidelines for TBIs including attention remediation and one practice option for behavioral and emotional difficulties (Braga et al., 2005; Laatsch et al., 2007). Attention training has been found to be beneficial in several studies for children with TBIs (Hooft et al., 2005), survivors of cancer (Butler et al., 2008), and children with ADHD (Martinussen, Hayden, Hogg-Johnson, & Tannock, 2005). Given the strong support for attention training, it has been recommended that strategy training for attention problems be a practice standard during the post-acute stage of recovery from TBIs (Cicerone, Faust, Beverly, & Demakis, 2009). Memory interventions, particularly as they relate to explicit instruction of memory strategies as well as employing external aids to prompt memory, have also been shown to be useful (Wilson, 2005).

Speech and language skills have also been studied. Unlike adults, aphasia, a disturbance in the comprehension or expression of language, is not frequently seen in children; rather difficulties with pragmatic or social use of language are affected (Ylvisaker et al., 2007). In addition to these difficulties, children often display problems in their overall ability to formulate sentences, have decreased vocabulary, are less efficient with respect to communication, and demonstrate poorer written language (Coelho, 2007). These additional difficulties are attributed to problems with attention and executive functioning as well as memory rather than language deficits because of the reliance on organization, working memory, and task persistence. Many of the rehabilitation studies for language improvement are quite dated (1990s and before), but suggest that computerized intervention as well as conventional speech and language therapy are empirically supported (Feeney & Ylvisaker, 2003).

A major area of concern is executive functioning for children and adolescents recovering from TBIs. Executive functions are goal-directed behaviors and include organization, planning, and emotional regulation. Although attention and working memory are involved in many of these skills, the difficulty resides in the executive control of these other executive functions (e.g., organization, planning, and emotional regulation). The prevailing view is that the most important rehabilitation technique for executive functions is to systematically teach problem-solving approaches during everyday activities. In order to accomplish this goal, new demands are placed into already well-learned routines and practiced until they become automatic (Slomine & Locascio, 2009). Because of the complex nature of these tasks, these interventions have been shown to be helpful for children and ongoing studies are continuing to establish the ecological validity of these measures (Kennedy, Coelho, & Turkstra, 2008).

There is emerging support for the Direct Instruction teaching technique for remediation of executive functions. This technique is an approach that directly teaches problem-solving strategies coupled with practice, modeling of skills, use of guided practice, and the teaching of generalization (Glang, Ylvisaker, & Stein, 2008). Although there is empirical support for the use of this technique for adults (Cicerone et al., 2005), support for children is generally in the form of case studies rather than large empirical research.

Family-Based Approaches

Although the literature is limited, there is promising evidence that multidisciplinary, family-based approaches, such as the SARAH family-based rehabilitation methodology, are effective in improving the cognitive and physical functioning following moderate and severe TBIs (Braga et al., 2005). Using the method developed by the SARAH network of hospitals, it was found that the longer from the time of injury that rehabilitation is begun, the poorer the outcome. The complete treatment model is available in the book *The Child With Traumatic Brain Injury or Cerebral Palsy: A Context-Sensitive, Family-Based Approach to Development* (Braga & Da Paz, 2006), and addresses multiple areas of development and functioning including motor, cognitive and neuropsychological, speech, language and communication, visual-motor integration and coordination, and activities of daily life. In addition, the book provides recommendations and programmatic activities to address the transition back to school and social, behavioral, and academic issues that arise in the school context.

The SARAH family-based rehabilitation methodology is based on five principles: (a) create an individualized and developmentally appropriate program for the child; (b) create a program that is realistic and viable given the child's injury and prognosis; (c) include the child, parents/caregivers, and family members in the rehabilitation process; (d) conduct the rehabilitation program in the child's natural context to maximize generalization of the skills; and (e) assist the child and family members through support groups and meetings (Braga & Da Paz, 2006). The program includes a preliminary assessment and plan development, assigning two case managers who are members of an interdisciplinary team to work with the family and conduct periodic reassessments over the course of the year.

1. The program begins with a 2-week preintervention assessment.
   a. The parent or caregiver and child visit the rehabilitation center daily for the first 2 weeks and meet with multidisciplinary team members.
   b. Assessments are made by the full team of clinicians including physical, occupational, and speech therapy, neuropsychology, educators, and medical personnel.
   c. Parents and caregivers participate in the assessment by providing their observations, including the child's functioning before the TBI.
   d. Assessments include observations of the child in naturalistic settings.
   e. Additional assessments and exams are conducted by members of the interdisciplinary team.

f. Two case managers are selected from specific disciplines to work with the family based on the child's specific needs

2. The individualized rehabilitation plan is created based on all assessment and observation data.

a. The manual contains a CD-ROM of 185 illustrated activities for the parent and child to complete. The multidisciplinary team selects 8 to 15 activities for each child. Activities are initially printed out and compiled into one manual for the child. As the child progresses, new activities are chosen to replace previous ones.

b. All activities, which were developed by combining the activities from multiple professionals in hands-on and interactive participation, are presented via illustrations and drawings, and include a description of the specific goals for the activity and how to perform it.

i. For example, a physical therapist and a neuropsychologist may have developed an activity together to target trunk strength (physical) and categorization (cognitive). In this example, the illustration depicts a parent or a caregiver helping the child balance while standing at a table sorting objects according to two categories (e.g., size and shape).

c. Case managers conduct occasional school visits and share the activities with educators so that the child may complete them in the school setting as well.

d. Parents and caregivers observe clinicians at first and gradually take over activities and integrate them into daily life. They return to the rehabilitation center once per week to meet with team members.

e. Parents and caregivers participate in support and informational groups.

3. Final assessments are conducted and, if needed, recommendations for continued rehabilitation are made.

HOW TO: A GUIDE TO THE IMPLEMENTATION OF INTERVENTIONS FOR TBIS AND CONCUSSIONS FOR CHILDREN AND ADOLESCENTS

The following section discusses methods, procedures, and interventions that have been successful in working with children and adolescents with TBIs and/or concussions and for which there is empirical and clinical support. This section is by no means exhaustive. Rather, it provides empirically supported treatments that may be implemented in schools and clinics for youths with TBIs.

Following any TBI, a follow-up visit with the referring physician for youths and their families is warranted for continued monitoring of their physical symptoms. For children and adolescents diagnosed with concussions, it is vital that they have ample opportunity to rest and not overstimulate or unnecessarily tax cognitive resources. Consultation with a physician for recommendations regarding exercise and future involvement in athletics is advisable to reduce the likelihood of sustaining another concussion. Youths, parents, and coaches should consider what position the youth will play in organized sports and make every effort to reduce direct hits to the head.

Assessment plays an important role in the management of concussions and TBIs. Evidence-based guidelines for the management of concussion and TBIs include the use of graded symptom checklists, the Standardized Assessment of Concussion, neuropsychological assessments, and the Balance Error Scoring system (Echemendia et al., 2013; Giza et al., 2013). Because of the heterogeneous nature of concussion and TBI, assessments need to include cognitive function, postural stability (balance), neurological status, and medical and/or social history including any comorbid diagnoses that exist (Gioia, Schneider, Vaughan, & Isquith, 2009). Neuropsychological assessments are integral for intervention planning and progress monitoring (Gioia, 2013).

School Reentry Interventions. Empirical studies have indicated that children and adolescents should increase activity, including gradually attending school (Schneider et al., 2013), and should symptoms worsen, pursuits should be reduced and rest be provided. When starting back to an activity (e.g., attending school), the child/adolescent should be able to complete the school day and all related activities including paying attention, taking notes, and transitioning between classes, relatively symptom free for 3 to 4 days before increasing the number of hours or classes he or she attends. If the youth experiences an increase in symptoms, he or she should reduce the amount of activity to the last level where he or she was symptom free. Youths often need help from those around them in adjusting expectations and slowing down. Head injuries, including concussions, often interfere with children's and adolescents' ability to cope with school demands and requirements. The following suggestions are recommended on school reentry:

1. Modify and shorten school expectations as the student recovers, such as homework and assignments to be completed in the classroom.
2. Given the increased need for rest and healing following a head injury, the student should not be required to complete multiple makeup assignments, tests and exams, or attend school for more than a couple of hours when significant physical symptoms (e.g., headaches, nausea, dizziness, and balance disturbances) continue.
3. As symptoms (e.g., headaches, nausea, dizziness, and balance disturbances) decrease and the student increases class attendance, the amount of time spent in school should gradually be increased weekly. It is advisable to alternate attending morning and afternoon classes to maximize student learning.
4. A common difficulty for a child or adolescent postconcussion is to attend to two tasks simultaneously, such as taking notes and listening to the teacher. Therefore, the student would benefit from receiving notes in class ahead of time, having a buddy provide notes for him or her, or recording instruction, particularly if the lesson is didactic in nature.
5. The student may benefit from books and materials on tape given fatigue experienced when reading. Furthermore, when reading is expected, briefer reading passages will minimize lethargy.

Executive Functioning

Interventions for Executive Functioning. Children and adolescents who experience a TBI or a concussion commonly experience difficulty with attention and executive functioning. Given the importance of executive functions to the learning process, it is important to intervene in this area. The following

are empirically supported treatments designed to address executive functions:

1. Encourage the use of a daily calendar to record all school assignments, family activities, as well as personal responsibilities such as cleaning his or her room or completing specific chores. The child or adolescent may require assistance in gauging the amount of time required to complete specific tasks.
2. In using a planner with adolescents, help them be realistic and not overextend themselves. Encourage children and adolescents to thoughtfully examine obligations and responsibilities and select responsibilities that are within the limits of their current level of functioning. As youths gradually improve, responsibilities may be increased.
3. Provide seating near the instructor and preferably away from other potential distractions. Opportunities to work in quiet work areas and small-group or one-on-one instruction may also be beneficial.
4. Adults should secure the youth's attention before giving directions.
5. Keep all oral directions clear and concise. Complex, multistep directions will need to be presented one at a time.
6. Teachers and adults should ask the youth to verbally restate (or paraphrase) the directions to ensure understanding.
7. Clearly label transitions. The student may require more time than peers to gather belongings and initiate and/or end activities.
8. The student should not be asked to complete large amounts of work independently. Instead, use approaches that encourage participation in collaborative activities. When working independently, provide close monitoring and intermittent, discrete prompting to ensure that he or she stays on task, attends to relevant information, and uses appropriate strategies to complete tasks.
9. Allow short breaks to address attentional difficulties may be helpful (e.g., have the student help you collect papers, pass out handouts, drop off or pick up materials at the school office).
10. Assign shorter tasks while increasing the accuracy and quality expectation. The student

should be explicitly shown how to check work for errors and be prompted to check work before turning it in.

11. Break assignments down into small components to make them less overwhelming. After completing a few problems, the student should check in with the teacher and/or parent to receive the next assignment. This allows easy monitoring of pace and accuracy.

12. When the student is capable of taking tests and exams, he or she would benefit from taking them in a quiet area, with directions and/or questions possibly read aloud, given the difficulty with attention and increased headaches while reading and attending to schoolwork.

The Importance of Sleep

Sleep is important for everyone, but especially for those with a history of head injury. It is critical that the child or adolescent sleep a sufficient amount (e.g., 8–10 hours) on a regular basis. Suggestions for improving sleep include the following:

1. Establish a consistent bed time and avoid doing activities other than sleeping in the bedroom. Attempting to stick to the routine, even on weekends, will make it easier to fall asleep readily each night.
2. Avoid taking long naps (no longer than 20–30 minutes) during the day.
3. Avoid eating, drinking, and exercising for 2 hours before going to bed.
4. Develop a nightly, calming ritual to use every night before going to sleep (e.g., take a bath, brush teeth, listen to music).

Behavioral Interventions for TBIs

Externalizing behaviors are common following a TBI in youth and may significantly interfere with daily functioning at home, at school, and in the community. To address these concerns, contingency-management procedures (CMPs), which stem from traditional applied behavioral analysis, and positive behavioral interventions and supports (PBIS) are effective in dealing with behavioral problems. CMPs focus on consequence-based methods whereas PBIS employ antecedent control strategies (Ylvisaker et al., 2007).

When employing a CMP, behaviors are more likely to occur in the future if they have been reinforced and less likely to take place if they have not been reinforced or have been punished in the past. PBIS focus on changing antecedent conditions to promote more adaptive behavior. These antecedents might occur immediately before the behavior, be distally related, or be internal or external to the individual. For example, PBIS procedures might include visual prompts of routines, or incorporate pleasurable activities to improve mood. It is highly unlikely that CMPs occur without antecedent changes or that PBIS happen without the use of consequences. For CMPs and PBIS to work, it is critical to employ both antecedent and consequence methods together, but most importantly, it is imperative to be consistent.

Both CMP and PBIS approaches are evidence-based treatment options (Ylvisaker et al., 2007). The combined use of CMP and PBIS are outlined for two reasons: (a) they are each empirically supported treatments for externalizing behaviors following TBIs in youths; and (b) there is prior research demonstrating effectiveness of using the approaches in combination.

Assessment. Please read the empirically validated steps of interventions that follow.

1. Conduct a functional behavior assessment.
   a. An interview should be conducted with the child and all individuals who work with the child, including primary caregivers, nannies, teachers, grandparents, and so forth.
   b. Include direct observation of the youth in appropriate natural environments as well as various demand-centered contexts within the school setting, that is, different subjects, time of day, and social-related experiences.
   c. When appropriate, conduct functional behavioral analysis. A functional behavioral *analysis* differs from the broader *assessment* in that the functional behavioral analysis is specific to conducting experimentally manipulated observations. The functional behavioral assessment is the overall evaluation, including interviews, naturalistic observations, and/or experimentally manipulated observations.

2. Functional behavioral assessment methods should include data on problematic behaviors, acceptable alternative behaviors, immediate antecedents, distal-setting events, and immediate and delayed consequences, as well as the strengths and weaknesses of the child and/or the adolescent.

3. Additional assessment should include general family, medical, and psychosocial history, as well as neurocognitive strengths and weaknesses. Previous reports and findings should be examined as well as interventions that have been employed to help the child and the success of those interventions.

4. Once the functional behavior assessment is complete, determine behavioral goals. Include appropriate behaviors to increase and undesirable behaviors to decrease.

Antecedent Strategies. Please review the evidence-based interventions for antecedent behavioral strategies designed for TBI and concussions in the following:

1. Consider assessment results to determine how antecedents to promote desirable behavior may be more salient.

2. Determine what skills need to be taught (e.g., communication, daily living).

3. Create a structured daily schedule, including activities that are pleasurable and meaningful.

4. Depending on need, include strategies such as visual schedules, verbal or physical prompting, adjusting task demands to match or be below ability level to promote success, and providing choice.

Consequence Strategies. The following are evidence-based interventions for consequences that may be employed in a behavioral model.

1. Consider assessment results to determine how to use consequences to promote desirable behavior(s).

2. When determining consequences, it may be helpful to assess the value of a variety of reinforcers. If the reward is not reinforcing to the child, the intervention strategy will not work. This can be done by simply asking the child and primary caretakers what the child will work for; that is, what reinforcer(s) is salient enough for him or her to change his or her behavior(s). Alternatively, a reinforcement worksheet may be provided to the student to determine what reinforcers are appealing to him or her.

3. Provide reinforcers for appropriate behaviors, or behaviors that need to increase in frequency, duration, or intensity. It is most helpful to reinforce behaviors that are incompatible with undesirable behaviors. That is, the two behaviors cannot be done at the same time (e.g., keeping hands to oneself is incompatible with hitting a peer).

4. Do not provide the identified reinforcer(s) for problematic behavior. This can be hard because of extinction bursts (i.e., increase in behavior that has previously been reinforced but is no longer reinforced). Extinction bursts may be difficult to completely avoid, but the likelihood or intensity of the extinction burst can be decreased by ensuring the youth has ample opportunity to earn the reinforcer(s) for appropriate behavior.

5. Depending on the need, include strategies such as positive and negative reinforcement, extrinsic rewards until natural reinforcers can take over, time out, and privilege loss.

Generalization and Maintenance. To maintain the gains that children and adolescents develop as well as facilitate generalization, the following evidence-based interventions are recommended:

1. If behaviors are taught in an artificial environment, practice new skills in a natural environment.

2. Teach all caretakers how to implement procedures as needed.

3. Fade interventions gradually, generalize the behaviors, and diminish external support.

CONCLUSION

The literature on TBIs and concussions has burgeoned in recent years as attention to these disorders has increased both in the research literature and in the popular press. A consequence of such coverage has been, at times, misconceptions or ideas about these disorders that may or may not be supported by empirical data. There is also a dearth of empirical studies as to the effectiveness of interventions that are being used. For this reason, it is important that information be carefully appraised and that families and patients be assisted in understanding the difficulties and recovery process that is present for them.

The research and clinical literature has identified a troubling aspect in TBIs and concussions concerning the lack of preparation of school personnel in working with children and adolescents with TBIs and/or concussions (Gioia, 2013). This is an area in which individuals working with school-aged children and adolescents in schools (such as school and clinical psychologists, school counselors, and school social workers) may provide direct assistance to the school system, particularly when reintegrating the children or adolescents back into the school system. It is also important to recognize that many medical personnel do not have the expertise to translate physical issues into language understood by school personnel. The mental health practitioner is in a unique position to provide such support.

SELECT BIBLIOGRAPHY

Centers for Disease Control School Toolkit. Retrieved from http://www.cdc.gov/TraumaticBrainInjury. *This website provides up-to-date scientific information on the assessment, treatment, and prevention of brain injuries, as well as how to find resources in your community.*

National Institute of Neurological Disorders and Stroke (NINDS).
A TBI information page provides information on assessing, treating, preventing TBI across the life span, and development, as well as current scientific trials conducted at the national center. The website can be found at http://www.ninds.nih.gov/disorders/tbi/tbi.htm
This is an online organization dedicated to preventing, treating, and living with TBI. The organization is a service of WETA, Washington, DC's public TV and radio station. This site provides daily news coverage, headlines, and resources for families, professionals, and otherwise interested individuals.

REFERENCES

Braga, L. W., & Da Paz, A. C. J. (2006). *The child with traumatic brain injury or cerebral palsy: A context-sensitive, family-based approach to development.* Oxford, UK: Taylor and Rancis. doi:10.1007/s10072-006-0671-2

Braga, L. W., Da Paz, A. C., & Ylvisaker, M. (2005). Direct clinician-delivered versus indirect family-supported rehabilitation of children with traumatic brain injury: A randomized controlled trial. *Brain Injury, 19*(10), 819–831.

Butler, R. W., Copeland, D. R., Fairclough, D. L., Mulhern, R. K., Katz, E. R., Kazak, A. E.,…Sahler, O. J. (2008). A multicenter, randomized clinical trial of a cognitive remediation program for childhood survivors of a pediatric malignancy. *Journal of Consulting and Clinical Psychology, 76*(3), 367–378.

Cicerone, K. D., Dahlberg, C., Malec, J. F., Langenbahn, D. M., Felicetti, T., Kneipp, S.,…Catanese, J. (2005). Evidence-based cognitive rehabilitation: Updated review of the literature from 1998 through 2002. *Archives of Physical Medicine and Rehabilitation, 86*(8), 1681–1692.

Coelho, C. A. (2007). Management of discourse deficits following traumatic brain injury: Progress, caveats, and needs. *Seminars in Speech and Language, 28*(2), 122–135.

Echemendia, R. J., Iverson, G. L., McCrea, M., Macciocchi, S. N., Gioia, G. A., Putukian, M., & Comper, P. (2013). Advances in neuropsychological assessment of sport-related concussion. *British Journal of Sports Medicine, 47*(5), 294–298.

Faul, M., Xu, L., Wald, M. M., & Coronado, V. G. (2010). *Traumatic brain injury in the United States: Emergency department visits, hospitalizations, and deaths.* Atlanta, GA: Centers for Disease Control and Prevention, National Center for Injury Prevention and Control.

Feeney, T. J., & Ylvisaker, M. (2003). Context-sensitive behavioral supports for young children with TBI: Short-term effects and long-term outcome. *The Journal of Head Trauma Rehabilitation, 18*(1), 33–51.

Gioia, G. A. (2013). *Special considerations in managing concussion in children and adolescents.* Paper presented at the 2013 International Sports Concussion Symposium, Minneapolis, Minnesota.

Gioia, G. A., Schneider, J. C., Vaughan, C. G., & Isquith, P. K. (2009). Which symptom assessments and approaches are uniquely appropriate for paediatric concussion? *British Journal of Sports Medicine, 43 Suppl 1*, i13–i22.

Giza, C. C., Kutcher, J. S., Ashwal, S., Barth, J., Getchius, T. S., Gioia, G. A.,…Zafonte, R. (2013). Summary of evidence-based guideline update: Evaluation and management of concussion in sports: Report of the Guideline Development Subcommittee of the American Academy of Neurology. *Neurology, 80*(24), 2250–2257.

Glang, A., Ylvisaker, M., Stein, M., Ehlhardt, L., Todis, B., & Tyler, J. (2008). Validated instructional practices: Application to students with traumatic brain injury. *Journal of Head Trauma Rehabilitation, 23*, 243–251. doi:10.1097/01.HTR

Hooft, I. V., Andersson, K., Bergman, B., Sejersen, T., Von Wendt, L., & Bartfai, A. (2005). Beneficial effect from a cognitive training programme on children with acquired brain injuries demonstrated in a controlled study. *Brain Injury, 19*(7), 511–518.

Jotwani, V., & Harmon, K. G. (2010). Postconcussion syndrome in athletes. *Current Sports Medicine Reports, 9*(1), 21–26.

Karlin, A. M. (2011). Concussion in the pediatric and adolescent population: "Different population, different concerns". *PM & R: The Journal of Injury, Function, and Rehabilitation, 3*(10 Suppl 2), S369–S379.

Kennedy, M. R. T., Coelho, C. A., & Turkstra, L. (2008). Intervention for executive functions after traumatic brain injury: A systematic review, meta-analysis, and clinical recommendations. *Neuropsychological Rehabilitation, 18*, 257–299. doi:10.1080/09602010701748644

Laatsch, L., Harrington, D., Hotz, G., Marcantuono, J., Mozzoni, M. P., Walsh, V., & Hersey, K. P. (2007). An evidence-based review of cognitive and behavioral rehabilitation treatment studies in children with acquired brain injury. *The Journal of Head Trauma Rehabilitation, 22*(4), 248–256.

Martinussen, R., Hayden, J., Hogg-Johnson, S., & Tannock, R. (2005). A meta-analysis of working memory impairments in children with attention-deficit/hyperactivity disorder. *Journal of the American Academy of Child and Adolescent Psychiatry, 44*(4), 377–384.

McCrea, M. A., Prichep, L. S., Powell, M. R., Chabot, R., & Barr, W. B. (2010). Acute effects and recovery after sports-related concussion: A neurocognitive and quantitative brain electrical activity study. *Journal of Head Trauma Rehabilitation, 25*, 1–10. doi:10.1097/HTR.0b013e3181e67923

McCrea, M., Guskiewicz, K., Randolph, C., Barr, W. B., Hammeke, T. A., Marshall, S. W.,…Kelly, J. P. (2013). Incidence, clinical course, and predictors of prolonged recovery time following sport-related concussion in high school and college athletes. *Journal of the International Neuropsychological Society, 19*(1), 22–33.

McCrory, P., Meeuwisse, W. H., Aubry, M., Cantu, B., Dvoák, J., Echemendia, R. J.,…Turner, M. (2013). Consensus statement on concussion in sport: The 4th International Conference on Concussion in Sport held in Zurich, November 2012. *Journal of Sports Medicine, 47*(5), 250–258. doi:10.1136/bjsports-2013-092313.

McKinlay, A., Grace, R. C., Horwood, L. J., Fergusson, D. M., Ridder, E. M., & MacFarlane, M. R. (2008). Prevalence of traumatic brain injury among children, adolescents and young adults: Prospective evidence from a birth cohort. *Brain Injury, 22*(2), 175–181.

Noggle, C. A., & Pierson, E. E. (2010). Psychosocial and behavioral functioning following pediatric TBI: Presentation, assessment, and intervention. *Applied Neuropsychology, 7*(2), 110–115. doi:10.1080/09084281003708977

Rohling, M. L., Faust, M. E., Beverly, B., & Demakis, G. (2009). Effectiveness of cognitive rehabilitation following acquired brain injury: A meta-analytic re-examination of Cicerone et al.'s (2000, 2005) systematic reviews. *Neuropsychology, 23*, 20–39. doi:10.1037/a0013659

Schneider, K. J., Iverson, G. L., Emery, C. A., McCrory, P., Herring, S. A., & Meeuwisse, W. H. (2013). The effects of rest and treatment following sport-related concussion: A systematic review of the literature. *British Journal of Sports Medicine, 47*(5), 304–307.

Semrud-Clikeman, M. (2010). Pediatric traumatic brain injury: Rehabilitation and transition to home and school. *Applied Neuropsychology, 17*(2), 116–122.

Semrud-Clikeman, M., & Bledsoe, J. C. (2011). Traumatic brain injury in children and adolescents. In A. S. Davis (Ed.), *Handbook of pediatric neuropsychology*. New York, NY: Springer Publishing Company.

Slomine, B., & Locascio, G. (2009). Cognitive rehabilitation for children with acquired brain injury. *Developmental Disabilities Research Reviews, 15*(2), 133–143.

Wilson, B. A. (2005). The effective rehabiliation of memory-related disabilities. In P. W. Halligan & D. T. Wade (Eds.), *Effectiveness of rehabilitation of cognitive deficits* (pp. 143–151). New York, NY:

Oxford University Press. doi:10.1093/acprof: oso/9780198526544.003.0013

Ylvisaker, M., Turkstra, L., Coehlo, C., Yorkston, K., Kennedy, M., Sohlberg, M. M., & Avery, J. (2007). Behavioural interventions for children and adults with behaviour disorders after TBI: A systematic review of the evidence. *Brain Injury, 21*(8), 769–805.

Index